ISBN 0-7730-4314-4

Dedication
To Elvis: Before you, there was nothing. After you, there is no one.

Editing/Pat Swartman
Design/Leslie Smart & Associates Ltd.
Cover Photo/Normunds Berzins
Photo Research/Penny McIlraith
Typesetting/Lithocomp Phototype
Printing and Binding/Bryant Press Ltd.

Canadian Cataloguing in Publication Data

```
Spetz, Steven N., 1940-
   Take notice : an introduction to Canadian law

For use in secondary schools.
Includes index.
ISBN 0-7730-4314-4

1. Law - Canada.  I. Spetz, Glenda S.  II. Title.

KE444.S6 1983      349.71      C83-099335-5
```

Disclaimer
The material contained within this text is believed to be current and
accurate as of the date of publication. However, as changes in the law are
frequent and as laws vary from province to province, the reader should
not rely upon the material within this text to solve actual legal problems.
The reader should obtain competent legal counsel to deal with any
problem that may arise.

Copp Clark Pitman Ltd.
495 Wellington Street West
Toronto, Ontario
M5V 1E9

Take Notice

An Introduction to Canadian Law

Second Edition

Steven N. Spetz
Glenda S. Spetz

Legal Consultant: Alan D. Treleaven, LL.M.
Osgoode Hall Law School, York University

Editorial Development: Marion Elliott

Copp Clark Pitman Ltd.
Toronto

How To Study Law

In a sense, laws are long lists of rules. A few lawyers have devoted a lot of time to learning all these rules. But, with ever-changing laws, this process becomes unending and rather futile, and in fact completely unnecessary for the average citizen. Instead we should realize that *law* is a word that denotes the whole process by which society provides for orderly relations among people within that society. Rather than try to memorize each individual rule, it is far more important to see how the rules are applied and to understand how to solve legal problems as they are actually solved in our legal system.

This is why it is very useful to study actual cases where the law has been applied. It is much easier to understand a law when you see it in action. And at the same time, case law is a cornerstone in our legal system. Cases which have major importance are recorded and referred to by lawyers and judges alike. Every nation has produced its great judges. In the opinions they gave when deciding cases, immense wisdom has been found and adopted by succeeding generations. More important, the case decision makes it clear how the judge interprets the wording of the law in view of the needs of the day. Many laws are not clearly worded, so that in practice considerable interpretation has to be made. When you read a particular law, its meaning may not be very clear. But after you have read a case which illustrates that law, the meaning usually emerges much more clearly.

In reading a case, or attempting to decide one, examine first the facts that are presented. Establish in your mind just who did what, before attempting to apply the law. Next, work out what specific statutes might apply. Perhaps only one will be involved in dealing with the case. Sometimes several statutes or several sections from one statute might possibly apply. Read again the material in this text which you think is relevant to the question. Read the illustrative cases that follow the explanatory material to amplify certain points. What you are trying to do is to find that part of the law which most properly relates to the facts, and to find other cases which are similar and which shed light on possible solutions. Do not make a snap judgment. All cases must have two sides, or there would not be any need for lawyers and judges; the outcome would be automatic. If you are writing out your answer, you might follow a general outline similar to that shown next. This outline is for a criminal case. A civil case would have a similar outline, with *plaintiff* substituted for *the Crown* (prosecution).

General Restatement of the Facts of the Case
Write a short paragraph that repeats the most significant facts of the case. Do not copy the entire case over again, but hit only the highlights.

Arguments Which the Crown (Prosecution) Would Put Forward
Assuming that conviction is the Crown attorney's objective, what are the facts and the pertinent sections of the *Criminal Code* that will be the key to the case?

Preface to the Second Edition

Arguments Which the Defence Would Put Forward

Pinpoint the facts in the case which offer a defence. Are there possible weak points in the Crown's case? Are there facts which under the wording of the *Criminal Code* would make conviction difficult, if not impossible? Assume that you are the accused person—how are you going to try and save yourself?

Final Conclusion

A decision must be reached: Guilty, Not Guilty, or in a few cases no decision because a hung jury found the case impossible to decide. Weighing both sides of the case, give your opinion as to the final outcome, and then support that opinion. Why would the jury reject the Crown's argument? What was it in the defence's case that was convincing? This is where logic comes into play. If there is no precise answer in criminal law because the case appears unique, then derive a decision based upon principles of fairness and common sense. The important thing is not to get the "right" answer, but to demonstrate sound reasoning for the answer you deduced from the facts of the case. Students often worry that they are "wrong" and that they will be writing a conclusion for a guilty verdict when in the actual case the defendant was found not guilty. This is not important, although we all like to be right. Since every case is decided on its merits, there is no such thing as a right or wrong answer, only a good or poor answer.

An Overview

"The history of law has not been logic, it has been experience." These words, spoken by Justice O.W. Holmes of the Supreme Court of the United States, perhaps reflect best the reason most students choose a course in Canadian law. They wish to "experience" the law to the extent possible in the classroom. In attempting to write a textbook for high school students, maximum effort has been made towards trying to assist them in this goal. This text takes the students through the areas of law most likely to be of interest and importance both now, and later in the students' lives. Ours is an adversary system—a process of problem solving by putting the other side's position to the severest test. This experience should not only teach the students some specific facts about the law but also instill a high regard for the complex and demanding tasks which our courts face each day. It should be a great learning experience and a very enjoyable experience. To this end, we have endeavoured to write this text more like a "book" than a text. It is our earnest belief that a text must be enjoyable and interesting to read or it will not be read at all.

Changes from the First Edition

In many ways, this is a new text rather than a revision. Approximately 60 per cent of the text has been rewritten. It is 25 per cent longer than the first edition and new topics have been added. Most prominent of these is a discussion of the *Charter of Rights and Freedoms* and its probable application to many areas of criminal law and civil rights. A substantial section on criminal law evidence has been added along with some important topics of civil law including a discussion of bailments. The question material at the ends of chapters has been increased 300 per cent to afford increased opportunity to put this new-found knowledge to work. The illustration is photographic to provide a more appealing book. The material is up to date as of the autumn of 1983.

Supporting Materials

A complete Student Activity Book has been prepared to accompany the text. The materials in this book are unique in many ways. Of particular popularity is a new style of question entitled "Principles and Cases." Sampling of law classes shows an enthusiastic response to this question format along with its companion "Before the Court."

A Teacher's Manual provides the teacher with helpful materials in presenting and evaluating the students' work. There are numerous charts, reference materials and ideas for examining legal issues which can be used at the teacher's discretion.

Course Organization

The text is sufficiently detailed to support a one-year or two-year program. For a one-year program, it is possible that there is more material than can be covered. Our suggestion is to designate some reading as "core" and some as "for interest only." The arrangement of chapters is by no means unchangeable. Some teachers like to begin with the chapter on police powers while others believe that constitutional law is a priority topic. As well, there is no prohibition upon jumping from chapter to chapter. A discussion of drunkenness as a defence may be best introduced while examining break and enter, for example. Students should be familiar with the text index and should not hesitate to search elsewhere in the text for assistance in answering a question. A two-year program can be organized along many different plans and the text material should more than suffice to meet that need.

Acknowledgements

We wish to express our sincere gratitude to the photo editors of various publications who provided some of the photographic illustrations; to the many people at Copp Clark Pitman who worked long and hard to make the text the very best it could be; and to Michael Parry, Assistant Superintendent of Education, Green Bay Integrated School District, Springdale, Newfoundland, for his incisive comments and recommendations towards improvements in the text.

Steven N. Spetz
Glenda S. Spetz

Contents

Unit

One

Our Legal System

"The Upper House should never set itself against the understood wishes of the people."

Sir John A. Macdonald

Chapter 1

The Foundations of Our Legal System

The Need for Law

If human nature were perfect, there would be no need for laws. But as we know, human nature has its weaknesses, and laws help to prevent these failings from causing problems.

Some people, of course, cause more trouble than others. It must be stressed, however, that the law applies to every member of society, whether someone is a law-abiding citizen or a hardened criminal. There would be no system of law at all if some people were required to accept the discipline of law while others were free from it.

Laws deter people from hurting each other physically. They are designed to reduce property damage. Laws provide us with a reasonable set of rules to guide us through our daily lives. Leaving aside the matter of punishment for breaking a law, let us look at the simple use of laws as rules of conduct. Have you ever watched a group of children playing a simple game? Inevitably, they will discuss the rules. It doesn't matter what the game is, rules are necessary. The basic purpose of the rules is not to get someone in trouble, but rather to ensure that the game can be played at all. If baseball were attempted without any rules, some players would run to third base first, while others would start with first base. There would be no agreement as to what constituted an "out" or how many outs one team could have. The other team would not know when it should have a turn at bat. Eventually, there would be no enjoyment in playing the game at all, and everyone would drift away.

To take another example, the purpose of a *Highway Traffic Act* is primarily to enable us to travel safely and enjoyably. We are told which side of the road to drive upon, how to turn properly, and what speed we should maintain in order not to injure someone else. Without these rules, drivers would travel any portion of the road they liked and at any speed. It would be too dangerous for anyone to take any vehicle onto a highway. So here, too, there is clearly a need for a set of rules.

Laws Reflect Values and Beliefs

The primary problem faced by lawmakers is what laws should be enacted and what should be rejected. We live in a very complex society with people of many different backgrounds.

Generally, laws reflect the values and beliefs that the majority of people hold at the time. Values change and so do laws, but not necessarily at the same time. Often the greatest upheavals in society occur when values change but laws that do not recognize those values stay on the books.

What do we mean by values? Simply put, we mean those things which people value. If we value our lives, we should have laws that provide for protection of life. If we value our property, we should have property laws. If we value our individual rights and freedoms, these values should be contained in our laws.

At the same time, our laws should reflect moral and religious beliefs. This is a difficult requirement to meet since beliefs may vary considerably within a society.

Laws should not specifically impose one religious belief upon all of society. However, lawmakers do have beliefs of their own, and these beliefs at least influence their decisions in passing new laws.

For example, when Parliament abolished the death penalty in 1976, the Members of Parliament expressed a belief that the value of a human life was greater than any possible deterrent factor in executions. Decisions involving values are often a trade-off, meaning that one thing must be given up for another. Our values and beliefs reflect the moral fibre of the nation, and our laws are the outward symbol of those values and beliefs.

Laws Protect Society

No one knows what makes a criminal. Various causes have been suggested, such as heredity or social background, but these theories are unprovable. One parole officer in the United States believes criminals are a product of poor diet. She put a hundred parolees on a special diet, free of junk foods and excess sugar, and found a remarkable improvement in behaviour. Yet, the diet in prisons is well-balanced and healthful and does not seem to have any particular effect upon prisoner rehabilitation.

Since we don't know why we have criminals in our midst, we must deal with them as best we can; so we enact criminal laws. Criminal law should protect society by restraining the deliberate wrongdoer and by providing guidance to a person who might commit a crime out of ignorance.

The protection of the public and the enforcement of the law is placed in the hands of professionally trained police officers. They are paid by society to perform this function. The police stand between citizens and the anarchy of crime. They do not make the laws; they only enforce them. At times, police officers have exceeded their mandate and acted beyond the law, sometimes with brutality, but the citizen who is mistreated by a police officer usually has redress through the courts.

Where there is a lack of confidence and co-operation between citizens and police, crime prospers and flour-

ishes. Realizing this, the police have made their training more intense and specialized, and officers are instructed in the importance of good public relations. Parents who teach their children disrespect for police are doing a disservice to the children, the community, and to the administration of justice. Children who have been taught contempt for police usually have the same contempt for law itself.

Robert Smith wrote in his book, *Where Did You Go?* "The reason kids are getting into trouble with cops is because cops are the first people they meet who say, and mean it, 'You can't do that'."

Laws Provide a Means for Solving Social Problems

Where there is an organized society, there will be social problems. These problems can be dealt with in a variety of ways. One way is to try to solve them by the use of violence; but violence, by its very nature, is destructive, and seldom makes possible any constructive change. A better way to solve social problems is through the enactment of laws that will recognize the problems and provide a rational solution for them.

For example, it was not so long ago that very young children worked in the mines and factories of Britain, Canada, and other industrial nations. Children were well suited to perform certain tasks and they were paid very little. These children suffered grievous harm to their health and often died at an early age. Attempts to persuade mine and factory owners to stop the practice of hiring children were unsuccessful. Each owner said the same thing: "I cannot stop if my competitors won't stop. If they can produce goods more cheaply than I, then they will put me out of business."

Clearly, there was a social problem which would not be solved by voluntary agreement. Legislation had to be enacted to prohibit the employment of children. The law not only benefited the children, but also made the employers stop a practice that they did not particularly like but were unable to stop themselves.

Social problems change as society changes. Therefore, the law cannot be rigid. It must be forward-looking and progressive, just as society is. Some people complain that the law is too slow to act. In some instances, this is true but we must not expect instant solutions to problems that may have developed over a long period of time. Laws that are hastily put together are seldom well written.

The Laws of the Ancients

Laws existed in early civilizations all over the world. These laws were written in many languages on various substances; laws carved into rock survived despite the passage of centuries. Interpreting these laws tells us much about how the people lived in those civilizations. An interesting thing is the similarities among laws enacted in civilizations very much separated by distance. Similarities have been found, for example, in the laws concerning children, property rights, and slaves in areas as far apart as the Middle East and Central America.

While much of this information is available to us, it is difficult to say how much it influences our present-day laws. In the case of Greek and Roman ideas, there is a definite residue which can be found in our present legal system. The laws of the Old Testament express attitudes and concerns which are mirrored in the wording of present-day laws.

Not all the material available can be reproduced here. The following are some examples which will enable the reader to appreciate the importance given to law by early civilizations.

The Code of Hammurabi

Scientists who discovered a diorite column in the city of Susa were delighted when they realized that they had found the only complete pre-Hebraic code of law. It was compiled by the king of Babylon, Hammurabi, around the year 2100 B.C. The code begins with a lengthy tribute to Hammurabi (some historians believe the correct spelling is Hammurapi), then gives tributes to certain gods. Following this are specific passages

dealing with both criminal and civil matters. Property is protected against various trespasses, including theft. Some of the passages can be interpreted as follows:

- If a man has accused a man and has charged him with manslaughter and then has not proved it against him, his accuser shall be put to death.
- If a man kidnaps the son of a free man, he shall be put to death.
- If a man has broken into a house, they shall put him to death and hang him in front of the breach in the house which he has made.

From all appearances, the code was placed in a visible location where all citizens could read it. Historians are not certain whether Hammurabi himself sat as a judge. There is some reason to believe that many citizens could not read, so a scribe stood in front of the column and read the words or answered questions which people might have. It might be an interesting idea which could be used today. A lawyer might stand in front of each courthouse door and answer legal questions for passers-by.

The following may perhaps be the first recorded lawsuit:

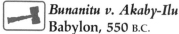

Bunanitu v. Akaby-Ilu
Babylon, 550 B.C.

A widow sued her brother-in-law for the return of some land. The woman and her husband had no children of their own, so they adopted a child. When the husband died, his brother claimed the land which the deceased had owned and seized it, saying that under Babylonian law if a man dies without a male heir, his nearest relative could take his possessions. The widow argued that the adopted child was a male heir. The judges heard the argument and held that the brother-in-law had no right to the land. The land had been partly purchased with the woman's dower when she married her husband. The brother-in-law was also ordered to return a slave he had taken from the woman.

The Greeks

There were numerous Greek schools of thought which followed the teachers who expressed certain ideals. The Sophists were a very influential group during the height of the city-state. They believed in a "natural law" which was superior to any law made by people. One concept was that a human law should only be obeyed if there was a penalty for not obeying it. Natural laws must always be respected.

Socrates, a prominent philosopher, believed a citizen should obey all laws. When Socrates was sentenced to death, he refused to flee into exile to save his life. He felt that he must accept the penalty his state ordered for him as he had enjoyed the benefits the state had given him.

Plato, a pupil of Socrates, argued that law is the rule of reason and must be obeyed to counter human "lower appetites." He was concerned about too much power corrupting leaders and saw law as the only check upon them. He concluded that law was necessary only because perfect leaders could not be found. Plato placed much emphasis upon the preamble, or introductory wording, of a law. The preamble should explain to all citizens the reason for having the law. This would encourage greater compliance with the law because people would support its purpose.

Aristotle, a later Greek philosopher, first described the legal principle of *equity* which means that laws should not be rigidly applied if the laws would cause hardship in special cases. He thought laws were too general and that judges should be free to depart from them where an unfair decision would result.

The Romans

During the centuries of Roman power, a great body of law was brought into existence. We owe the use of Latin in our legal system to the Roman system. Perhaps the most important characteristic of Roman law was the codification of laws. *Codification* is the orderly arrangement of laws into understandable, compact volumes. Laws tend to develop separately over a period of time. The Roman practice was to prepare codes and often revise obsolete laws by preparing new codes.

One of the earliest Roman codes is called the Twelve Tablets. They were prepared by a special committee in 450 B.C. and were published on tablets of bronze or wood. The original tablets were destroyed, but copies survived. The wording of some cannot be understood, but a few of the laws read as follows:

- *Sons shall be under the jurisdiction of the father.* The accepted interpretation of this is that in the Roman state, the *patria potestas* rule gave a father the power of life and death over his children. Daughters were not mentioned because they had no status as persons.
- *Parents shall have the right to sell their children thrice and that is their authority.* The sale of children was sometimes necessary when poverty threatened a family. It is unclear if the law meant the parents could sell only three children or sell one child three times (presumably buying the child back the first two times).
- *If a thief is caught when the theft was committed in the dark, or was caught armed in the daytime, he shall be put to death. If a man commits a theft in the open daylight and is not armed, he shall be sentenced.* The Romans made a distinction between armed and unarmed robbery and theft by day or night. Our present law makes the same distinction between theft and armed robbery.

Canon Law

It would be an error to presume that there is no longer any religious influence evident in Western legal thought. Much of the law that exists today has an origin in the Judaeo-Christian heritage. Ancient Judaism played a distinct role in shaping the origins of our concepts of law. Christians derived a dual obligation from the Bible. On the one hand, the Bible contains God's commandments; on the other hand, it contains warnings not to become enslaved to mere human traditions.

An important feature of the Old Testament is the implication that the laws decreed can be obeyed by anyone of good will. The equality of humanity thus implied is distinctly different from the view of Greek philosophers who thought that there must be a princely, spiritual elite.

Many Christian writers, including St. Augustine, refer to natural law or eternal law. St. Augustine was born in 354 A.D. and was a Roman citizen. He believed that the Church had the duty and the authority to act as a moral veto upon government. "Justice being taken away, what are kingdoms but great robberies?" he asked. He proposed the separation of the Church and the state to ensure the proper role of the Church.

St. Thomas Aquinas was a Dominican friar who taught at the University of Paris during the thirteenth century. Among the commands of natural law he included the care of children by their parents, reverence to God, charity for the poor, and obedience to law. "Only through government can people benefit from the ideas of intelligent and moral leaders," he concluded. He saw the Church as guardian of all spiritual values. "Kings must be subject to priests," he wrote. If a king acted contrary to the good of his subjects, the Church would excommunicate him. Once this was done, all the subjects of that king were freed and absolved from his rule.

The Church developed legal rules to such an extent that in many matters the Church was the court. This was known as *canon law*. In some areas the Church conceded that the king's courts should deal with a matter but declared itself sovereign over anything dealing with the spiritual needs of citizens. This often included a large body of what is now called "family law." Churches conducted trials and gave out sentences. At one time, a male accused was given an interesting choice. If a man could prove that he was able to read, he was held to be a clergyman of the Church, for it was widely believed that only monks and priests knew how to read. This was called "benefit of clergy." A person exercising benefit of clergy could demand to be tried by the Church rather than the king's court or officers. It was hoped, of course, that the Church would go easier upon the accused. Benefit of clergy was abolished in 1827. By then, too many people had learned to read!

Many of the trials conducted by the Church were based upon the intervention of God as final judge. An example would be trial by fire. The accused was required to pick up a white-hot iron bar and walk five paces "with dignity" before putting it down. The burned hands were wrapped with white cloth which was blessed by a priest. In one week, the cloth was removed and if the burns appeared to be healing, the accused was declared innocent as God had intervened to heal the burns. If the burns were festering the accused was declared guilty as God would not help an accused with a guilty conscience. This declaration was likely just a formality because the accused would probably die of gangrene anyway.

Today, canon law plays no direct role in our legal system. What remains is the heritage and effect upon our laws of basic religious beliefs.

The Origins of Canadian Law

Canada has derived its legal system from the two European nations which had the greatest influence upon its early settlement; namely, Great Britain and France. The systems in the two countries were very different. The system of law used in France was based on the earlier Roman law. Under this system of law, it was held that all law proceeded from the emperor—it was made by him. Under the British system, the law existed independently of the monarch. The British king was the fountain of justice, but he was not the fountain of law.

Perhaps the most eloquent champion of this rule was Sir Edward Coke (1552-1634). He was the Lord Chief Justice and often turned kings into raging enemies. In 1616 he had a face-to-face argument with King James I about the position of the king. Coke said, "The law protects the king." James retorted, "That is a traitorous speech! The king protects the law. The king makes judges and bishops." Coke replied, "The king has only the prerogative which the law grants him." Sir Coke lost his job, but amazingly kept his head.

The French system relied heavily upon the codification of law. Codification is a system of organizing all laws into numbered volumes according to the topic, being careful to eliminate duplication. The British system was, for the most part, unwritten. Customs and practices covered most aspects of the law, and written statutes were enacted only when absolutely necessary. They remained separate statutes and were not codified together in any way.

In most of Canada, the British system prevails, while in Quebec the French *Civil Code* is the basic foundation of law.

British Common Law

The British common law is sometimes called the "unwritten system of law." It has as its basis the established customs which have been enforced and enhanced by centuries of legal decisions. It is a system that has developed gradually and that continues to grow in a sensible and effective manner.

The system of common law revolves around what is called the *rule of precedent*, or *stare decisis* — a Latin phrase which translated loosely means, "to stand by what has been decided." The rule of precedent, sometimes called "the sacred principle," requires that like cases be decided alike. A judge attempting to reach a decision in one case relies upon previous cases involving the same kind of circumstances. If the judge can find such a case, the decision made in it will be followed provided the two cases are on "all fours" with each other. This expression means that the legal issues are very similar.

A precedent is established when a judge gives legal force to what had previously been only a custom or tradition, or when a judge makes a new interpretation of an already existing law. Once established, a precedent remains in force until overturned by a higher court or changed by the passage of a new statute. A precedent set by the Supreme Court of Canada (the highest court) can only be changed by the same court's reversing itself in a later decision, or by the passage of a new law that overrules the court's decision. The Supreme Court of Canada has held that there are no *binding* precedents upon itself, but only persuasive precedents. The lower courts must regularly narrow or restrict the scope of a precedent set by the Supreme

Court of Canada by tailoring the principles of law to the facts of a particular case.

A system relying so much on previous decisions naturally requires that cases be recorded in some way for future reference. The practice of recording (or reporting) cases was begun centuries ago, by King Henry I, and there now exists such a vast collection of cases for reference that the practice has earned the name of *case law*.

Precedent provides many benefits to our legal system, including:

- *Uniformity:* Without precedent, similar cases could result in unlike decisions. This would be unfair to those people who did not receive such favourable decisions as others.
- *Predictability:* A lawyer can advise a client as to the probable outcome of a case based on the way similar cases were decided in the past.
- *Impartiality:* The judge cannot show favouritism when guided by accepted principles of law established over a long period of legal history.

At one time, the common law became very rigid. There developed a total unwillingness of any court to overturn a previous ruling. Judges tended to treat all previous rulings as final and were unwilling to question the decisions of their predecessors whom they respected. The courts lost sight of the fact that society was constantly changing and that the law should reflect such changes. This led disgruntled people to petition the king personally to intervene. The king usually referred such matters to an official, the chancellor, who was asked to determine what fairness or *equity* would require. As the number of petitions grew, a separate court, the Court of Chancery, was established to deal with all appeals based upon equity. For several hundred years, there existed in England a double system of courts, with common law in one, and equity in the other. Today, the double system of courts is gone. The appeal courts of Canada administer both common law and equity. In effect, equity has become a part of the common law system, providing relief from an over-rigorous application of the law.

Perhaps the overriding concern of judges is that the

common law can become rigid and work absurdities and injustice. In *Cartledge v. Jopling & Sons* (1963), the British House of Lords said:

> **"**The common law ought never to produce a wholly unreasonable result; nor ought existing authorities to be read so literally as to produce such a result never contemplated when they were decided.**"**

Whenever a judge concludes that a precedent cannot be applied fairly to the case at hand, there is ample support in equity for reaching a totally new decision. The present should not be strangled by the dead hand of the past.

The *Civil Code*

The Province of Quebec does not use common law as the basis for its civil law. Quebec civil law is based upon the *Civil Code* which is modelled after the earlier codes developed by the Romans, later adopted by the French. The retention of the *Civil Code* was a result of the *Quebec Act* of 1774 which provided that:

(1) The size of the province be expanded to restore part of the Labrador coast to Quebec;
(2) Roman Catholics have freedom of worship;
(3) The *Civil Code* be retained for civil law which allowed no trial by jury;
(4) The criminal law remain that of England.

The *Quebec Act* does not mention the subject of language.

The circumstances in which the *Quebec Act* was passed altered drastically after the American Revolution when large numbers of United Empire Loyalists entered Quebec. The English-speaking, mainly Protestant Loyalists had no desire to live under French customs and laws. They soon began to agitate for the establishment of British laws and the maintaining of British traditions. It was to meet their demands that Quebec was divided into Upper and Lower Canada by the *Constitutional Act* of 1791. Upper Canada would be governed by British law, while Lower Canada would retain the *Civil Code* which it still does today.

In Quebec, there is no rule of precedent, but cases are recorded for reference to assist the court in interpreting and applying the *Civil Code*.

The House of Commons adjourns after a lengthy debate over an energy bill.

Our Parliamentary Heritage

The Canadian Parliament has inherited much from the British Parliament. It follows the same traditions, and possesses the same rights and privileges. Without attempting to trace the very long and detailed historical development of the British Parliament, we should examine some of the principles developed which today are the foundation of our own system.

The Privilege of Parliament

The privilege of Parliament means that Members may act in the manner which they consider will best serve the interests of the nation. They may speak openly within the legislature and criticize the government for its shortcomings. Any attempt to curtail this privilege by either the head of state or the courts will be resisted.

When the first English Parliaments were called, the purpose was simply for the king to tell the representatives what he wanted them to do. He usually wanted money and directed them to return to their home counties and raise it. Gradually, the Members began to make demands in return. They brought petitions of grievances and complaints. The king was usually irritated by this behaviour and often told the Members bluntly, "You are here to hear my demands, not present yours." However, this approach would not work. If the king dissolved Parliament without hearing the Members' grievances, the taxes the king demanded were not raised. Throughout this long period of conflict, the tradition developed that the king could not arrest or intimidate Members of Parliament for something they said or did while carrying out the work of the House. When Charles I broke this tradition and stormed into Parliament to arrest some Members who opposed him, he was greeted with cries of "Privilege! Privilege!" Civil war broke out soon afterwards.

The Supremacy of Parliament

> 66 The legislature, within its jurisdiction, can do everything that is not naturally impossible, and it is restrained by no rule human or divine.... The prohibition, 'Thou shalt not steal,' has no force upon the sovereign body. 99

These words, coming from the judge deciding the case of the *Florence Mining Co. v. Cobalt Lake Mining Co.* (1909), express very well the meaning of the rule of law that Parliament is supreme.

The Parliament of Canada and the provincial legislatures may enact any legislation — without regard for property, human rights, or tradition — if they act within their constitutional power. For example, if the federal Parliament, which has power over the penitentiary system, chose to transform every penitentiary into a pitiless dungeon, it could do so. One might say, "But, the *Charter of Rights and Freedoms* would prohibit that." This is a false hope. A government can pass any law that overrides fundamental freedoms by including a "notwithstanding clause," which means that the government can act without complying with the *Charter*. The law would stand as written for only five years, but it could be renewed.

Parliament is supreme. This doctrine means that while the courts are the watchdogs of freedom, the courts do not have the power to prohibit Parliament from enacting certain types of laws.

No Parliament is irrevocably bound by the acts of its predecessors. However, by tradition, each Parliament has honoured the foreign treaties made by previous Parliaments.

Independence of the Judiciary

Another great tradition inherited from Britain is the independence of the judiciary. Judges are free to decide cases as they see fit, according to their interpretation of the applicable statutes and case law. Even though judges may be appointed by the government, once appointed they obey no ruler in making legal decisions.

On numerous occasions, British monarchs tried to order judges to make certain decisions. It is perhaps the greatest achievement of the common law that the judges nearly always refused, even at the risk of dismissal. Queen Elizabeth I tried to influence judges by sending them letters telling them how she wanted cases decided. The letters were ignored. James II dismissed thirteen judges during his reign, but in every case the replacement judge adopted the same attitude of independence.

The independence of the judiciary remains one of our most valued traditions today. For a government official to contact a judge and suggest how a case should be decided would be an act so unacceptable that the official would have to resign. However, this independence works both ways. Judges are expected to make no comments on political matters and are not permitted to vote in elections.

Due Process of Law

To understand the principle of *due process*, let us assume that the police chief of a Canadian city publishes an order in the local newspaper that every person who owns a shotgun must bring it to the police station to have it destroyed. The police chief has decided that shotguns are dangerous and people should no longer be permitted to own them. Most people will ask, "Where does the police chief get the authority to issue such an order?" Since the citizens believe the chief is acting without proper authority, they will ignore the order. They will have correctly realized that there has been no due process of law. Laws are not made at the whim of one official.

At one time, rulers acted in just this manner. By arbitrary decree, they confiscated property and conscripted people's labour. As an example, when the king of England needed sailors for a war, he would authorize the navy to use "press gangs" to raid seaside towns and force any male person they could find to serve in the navy. These "impressed" sailors served for an indefinite period of time and often without pay. They were little more than slaves.

Today, a citizen is entitled not only to the protection of the law, but also to due process of law. The law must be brought into existence publicly, not secretly. If the citizen runs afoul of the law, he or she must be tried before a competent court. At every step, freedoms and due process must be observed.

Due process is specifically guaranteed in s. 1(a) of the *Canadian Bill of Rights*. Sections 7-14 of the *Charter of Rights and Freedoms* deal with the subject of "legal rights" and are directly concerned with due process.

Form in Our Legal System

We sometimes read that a certain accused person was found not guilty of an offence because of a "legal technicality." We may be tempted to find fault with a system that seems to show so much concern for legal procedure or "form." Yet, form is one of the greatest safeguards in our legal system.

Without form, there can be little discipline or order, and this can be a threat to liberty itself. Our system of law therefore prescribes a proper way in which something should be done. This may concern the way in which a police officer arrests an offender, or the manner in which incriminating evidence is obtained. If the proper way is not followed, this may be sufficient reason for the legal proceedings themselves to be stopped. Form is a means of ensuring that law

enforcement officers do not exceed their lawful authority. An officer acting without proper form becomes a trespasser. The importance of form in this respect has long been recognized. Where a British sheriff, in 1338, seized cattle for non-payment of taxes, he was fined for not obtaining a warrant.

The Right To Dissent

The right to dissent means the right to oppose passage of a law or to petition for its repeal or amendment. To some people, dissent goes further. They believe they should refuse to obey a law that they feel violates basic human rights or democratic principles. Numerous writers have discussed this point. Perhaps the best known is Henry David Thoreau. Thoreau was once jailed in Boston for refusing to pay his taxes because he considered the U.S.-Mexican War to be immoral. When a friend came to visit him in jail, the friend said, "Henry, I am surprised to see you in there." To this Thoreau replied, "I am surprised to see you out there." Thoreau later wrote a treatise in which he discussed the problem of what citizens should do when confronted with a law they regarded as unjust. He wrote:

> I hold that government best which governs least. It is the individual's obligation to resist any government action that he cannot morally support. Must the citizen resign his conscience to the legislator? Why has every man a conscience then? We should be men first, and subjects afterwards.... Unjust laws exist. Shall we be content to obey them? Shall we endeavor to amend them and obey them until we have succeeded, or shall we transgress them at once?

Thoreau was not the first person who discussed dissent. St. Augustine said, "An unjust law is no law at all." St. Paul said, "Obey God rather than men." These men believed that there are other values in the world besides legality.

Recalling his experience with the Nazi regime in his country, Reverend Martin Neimoller, a German Protestant clergyman, made the following statement:

> First they arrested the Communists. I was not a Communist, so I did nothing. Then they came for the Social

Democrats. I was not a Social Democrat, so I did nothing. Then they arrested the trade unionists, but I said nothing. Then they arrested the Catholics and the Jews, but I was neither one. At last they arrested me, and there was no one left to do anything about it.

Reverend Niemoller had abandoned his right to dissent hoping that he would be left alone. It did not happen that way.

Whether or not one believes that there is a right to dissent is a matter of personal conviction. However, if the method of dissent is contrary to law, the individual is subject to prosecution and punishment. The right to dissent has generally been described by writers as a non-violent right.

Classifications of Law

There are many ways to classify law according to its particular purpose or form. These classifications do not fit easily into some overall plan or chart; they only suggest various terms which are understood to refer to a particular, specialized area of law.

Criminal Law

Criminal law covers that area of law which specifically prohibits certain acts and provides penalties for those persons committing such acts. Our criminal laws are codified into the *Criminal Code of Canada* which is uniform throughout all of Canada. As well, certain other federal laws contain penalties for violators, and must be considered as being part of our criminal law. An example would be the *Combines Investigation Act.*

Civil Law

Civil law generally refers to all areas of law other than criminal. A civil case involves litigation (a lawsuit) between citizens or groups rather than a trial of a citizen by the authorities. Civil law includes such areas as contracts, property, torts, and many others. The civil law is not uniform across Canada; there are some variations from one province to another.

Constitutional Law

A constitution is a body of basic principles stating the powers and limitations of a government and the way those powers are to be exercised. In Canada, when legal questions arise as to the power of government to enact certain laws, the case is determined by whether or not such power is granted under the *B.N.A. Act* (now the *Constitution Act, 1867*). The Canadian constitution is both written and unwritten. The written section is found in the *Constitution Act* and other constitutional documents. There are also many customs, usages, and conventions which make up the unwritten section of our constitution.

Statute Law

Many of our laws are enacted by our elected legislative bodies. The laws passed by the federal and provincial legislatures are called statutes or Acts. Statutes can be amended or repealed by the same legislature that originally passed them. Municipalities can enact ordinances and by-laws under power granted to them by the provincial legislatures.

Military Law

Members of the armed forces are required to obey laws which are specifically enacted for the proper operation of the military. By its very nature, the military requires a high degree of discipline. Therefore, certain actions constitute offences for military personnel which are not offences if committed by civilians. The military also maintains its own court system, bringing offenders to trial before a court-martial. A military person is still subject to all the laws of Canada as are other Canadians.

Martial Law

Martial law involves a suspension of civil government and an assumption of control by the military authorities until order is restored. Under martial law, civil rights may be suspended. The military authorities may publish harsh regulations about such things as curfews, and take strong action against citizens who disobey these regulations. There is no provision for the declaration of martial law in Canada, but similar powers are covered by the *War Measures Act*.

Under martial law, the armed forces assume direct responsibility for order.

International Law

Numerous treaties, signed by many of the nations of the world, have such universal acceptance that they comprise a body of law viewed as binding upon all nations. The centre of international law is the World Court, located at den Hague, Holland. As an example of international law, if a captain and crew abandon a ship on the high seas, any person who can get aboard the ship and keep it seaworthy, may claim ownership of the ship and all its cargo.

Administrative Law

One of the most difficult things for Parliament and the provincial legislatures to do is to enact legislation that completely governs or regulates a particular subject. The complexity of our society, particularly with regard to rapid scientific advancements, puts a great burden upon Parliament to legislate about matters which Members of Parliament often find difficult to under-stand. As well, new bills cannot be of such enormous length that Members cannot find the time to read them. Finally, in a field where there is ever-present change, Parliament cannot take the time to amend Acts every time a small technical change is required. To dispose of these problems, Parliament is likely to enact a basic Act governing a subject, and then provide authority within the Act for a Cabinet Minister to establish further regulations under the Act. These regulations have the same force of law as the basic Act itself. Parliament also creates semi-autonomous or completely independent boards or commissions to reg-ulate certain industries or carry out specialized work. The Unemployment Insurance Commission and Atomic Energy, Canada are examples of such bodies.

These regulations are known as *subsidiary legislation*. To the average citizen, it is difficult to understand the difference between a statute and the regulations issued under it. For example, a farmer knows milk must be placed in a certain type of container. This is a regula-tion, not a statute. A pilot must obey the regulations of an airport or lose the licence to fly. There are labour regulations, teaching regulations, meat inspection regulations, trucking regulations, stock market regulations, and so on.

Sometimes these regulatory bodies take on what amounts to judicial power in the sense that they can order persons to appear and explain their actions to determine whether they were contrary to regulations. Fines can be meted out. There are appeal boards set up by statutes which hear cases involving citizens who believe they were unjustly treated by regulations. More and more these appeal boards resemble courts. Some statutes contain specific clauses stating that the decision of an appeal board is final and that no appeal may be made to any court.

How much administrative law is there? One study lists 14 855 discretionary powers conferred upon public bodies by federal statutes alone. In Ontario, there are more than 150 agencies that can produce regulations.

When a government agency has a decision to make, the requirements are that it:

(1) Make only decisions which are within its jurisdiction;

(2) Make a decision on the basis of the evidence before it;

(3) Make a decision fairly and not on the basis of bias or prejudice;

(4) Grant a hearing to the people whose interests will be most affected by a decision and give fair notice to those persons.

Even where the law does not require a hearing, the courts will insist upon one if the citizen's rights are seriously affected. Thus prison officials, who have the right to discipline an inmate, have been held by the courts to have an obligation to give a fair hearing and to offer the individual an opportunity to present his or her side of the issue.

The volume of administrative law is impressive. Its importance is equally impressive. In 1981, an order was issued cutting rail service to 21 parts of the country, affecting 1 200 000 passengers and cutting off the economic lifeline of many communities. It was passed with the stroke of a pen, with no public debate, no referral to the Canadian Transport Commission, and no discussion in Parliament. In the same week that this order was signed, the Governor General signed 164 other orders.

On some occasions, the very existence of a board may be a legal question mark. In 1981, the Supreme Court of Canada reviewed a system of boards/tribunals set up to handle most landlord and tenant matters in Ontario (*Re Residential Tenancies Act of Ontario*). The court found that the officials of these boards would have powers so great that they would equal the powers of superior court judges. Constitutionally, a province can create a board and confer upon it some judicial functions, but the province cannot appoint superior court judges nor can it appoint officials with the powers of superior court judges. Only the Governor General can appoint judges of a superior court and the federal government must pay their salaries. The court held that the Act was beyond the legal power of the province of Ontario.

Common Law and Statute Law

Common law is the system upon which our present-day law is founded. Common law consists more of principles and traditions than of specific rules. Statute law is in written form and quite specific in its intent.

Where there is no statute to govern a matter, the court will look to the common law to try to determine what has been customary in such cases. The common law may have no specific remedy for such a situation, but general guidelines or principles may exist which allow the judge to make a ruling. If there is a statute to govern a matter, the statute takes priority over the common law. However, it may be that the statute is not clear and requires some interpretation. In such a case, the interpretation given would probably be that which the common law has always afforded. Thus, even when there is a statute, common law may be called upon to help interpret or give clear meaning to the statute.

Interpreting Statutes

A statute is carefully examined by committees before final wording is chosen. Every effort is made to prevent any confusion about the meaning of words.

However, despite these best efforts, it is often necessary to "interpret" the statute. The following principles are then followed:

- Meanings involved must be taken from the wording of the statute and not from outside sources.
- Words are usually interpreted according to literal meanings unless this leads to some absurdity.
- Words are interpreted in context and not in isolation.
- Where words are ambiguous the statute is considered as a whole in an attempt to discover the intent of the legislature.
- The presumption of the courts is against the alteration of the common law.

It should also be noted that the provisions of all statutes are usually expressed in the masculine gender. However, as s. 26(6) of the *Interpretation Act* points out:

(6) Words importing male persons include female persons and corporations.

The following case involved the interpretation of a provincial statute:

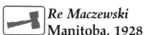 **Re Maczewski**
Manitoba, 1928

According to the *Public Schools Act* of Manitoba, a trustee, to qualify for election, had to be able "to read and write." Maczewski was elected as a trustee. He could read and write Polish and Ukrainian but could not read or write English. The school inspector disqualified him as a trustee and Maczewski took the matter to court. The court held that the words of a statute must be followed if they are specific and clear. The court cannot undertake to assume that the legislature meant something other than what it said. Other statutes required that persons "read and write English." If, in the instance of the *Public Schools Act* the wording only said a trustee must be able to "read and write," then it would be improper for a court to presume that this was just an oversight on the part of the legislature. Maczewski assumed his post as a trustee.

Reviewing Important Points

1. Law can be classified into two main divisions: criminal law and civil law. Criminal laws are codified in the *Criminal Code* and are very uniform throughout Canada. Civil law refers to non-criminal matters and differs somewhat from province to province.
2. Our system of law is based on the British common law in all provinces except Quebec. The civil law of Quebec is an adaptation of the French *Civil Code*.
3. Laws passed by the federal and provincial governments are called statutes, or Acts.
4. Many so-called laws are in fact regulations created by boards and commissions; however, they carry the force of law.
5. One contribution of the Romans to our legal system was the practice of codification — compiling laws in compact, orderly volumes.
6. At one time in history, a person who could read and write could request a Church trial rather than a trial by government authorities.
7. Our legal system includes an independent judiciary, free from any political influence or interference.

Checking Your Understanding

1. What is the danger of the rule of precedent? How can this danger be averted?
2. Common law is sometimes called "unwritten law." How did it derive this name?
3. What advantages does the rule of precedent offer in our legal system?
4. Lawyers sometimes say a case is on "all fours" with a previous case. What do you think this would mean?
5. Explain what is meant by "subsidiary legislation." Why is such legislation necessary?
6. What is the preamble of a law? Why did Plato believe that every law should have a preamble?
7. The common law operates upon the rule that a

lower court must follow the decisions of higher courts. What would happen if lower courts did not do so?

8. Early trials were often "ordeals" such as trial by fire. What was the "logic" or belief behind the idea that such trials were just?

Legal Briefs

1. B is charged with an offence and consults a lawyer. After hearing the facts, the lawyer says, "You stand a very high chance of being convicted." B, not happy at the prospect, asks, "How do you know?" How does the lawyer know? Upon what is the opinion based?

2. Members of Parliament can never be sued for anything said within the House of Commons. Why not?

3. "Parliament can legislate anything it wants." Is this a true statement? Why or why not?

4. When a British Columbia judge made a public criticism about something in the *Constitution Act, 1982,* there was a commotion within legal circles. Why?

5. One of the duties of a defence lawyer is to challenge the legality of any proceeding against a client if the proceeding is not in the proper form. Is this just a way of trying to find "loopholes"? Give a reason for your answer.

6. One of the heritages of the Judaeo-Christian tradition is that laws should be obeyed, but not obeyed blindly. How is the distinction to be made as to which laws should be obeyed?

7. Witness this argument which took place at a trial in 1346:

> Judge: "No precedent is of such force as justice or that which is right."
>
> Lawyer: "I think you should do as other judges have done in the same case, for otherwise we do not know what the law is."

What legal principle(s) are they debating? With which statement do you agree most? Give a reason for your answer.

8. An American judge, Oliver Wendell Holmes, Jr., wrote: "The life of the law has not been logic; it has been experience." What do you think he meant by that statement?

Chapter 2
The Canadian Government

Prelude to Confederation

Prior to Confederation, the provinces of British North America—Upper and Lower Canada, New Brunswick, Nova Scotia, and Prince Edward Island—were governed by provincial assemblies with executive power resting in a governor who was appointed by the Crown. Real authority rested in Great Britain, where little was really known about Canada.

This situation was far from acceptable to the assemblies. In particular, they wanted control over provincial revenue and expenditures, which would give them greater power vis-à-vis the governor. Demands for reform were made with increasing persistence, and numerous confrontations between assemblies and their governors occurred. Finally, in 1837, rebellions broke out in both Upper and Lower Canada. Although these rebellions were short-lived, the British government was forced to reconsider the situation in the Canadian colonies.

In 1838, Lord Durham was dispatched as Governor-in-Chief of all five provinces and Newfoundland, with authority to restore order and make recommendations for their future form of government. The *Durham Report* was one of the greatest contributions ever made in English colonial history. One of its major recommendations was that Upper and Lower Canada (and possibly the other provinces) be united under one legislative body. Dependent on such a union was another significant proposal—responsible government. This would mean a division of power to be shared by the British and colonial governments.

The *Act of Union*, uniting Upper and Lower Canada came into effect in 1841. Responsible government was granted to all the Canadian colonies, including Newfoundland, by 1855.

The question of a union of all the provinces took longer to resolve. Several conferences were held in Canada to discuss a possible union. The most important conference was held in Charlottetown, Prince Edward Island, in 1864. Numerous difficulties became apparent at this conference. The primary problems included:

(1) A desire by the Maritime Provinces to form a union without the rest of Canada;
(2) Disagreement over the form of government;
(3) Jealousy over where the new capital city would be located.

In trying to determine what form of government would be best, the delegates studied numerous constitutions, including that of the United States. Lord Durham had recommended one government for all of Canada, thus abolishing the provincial assemblies. This was unacceptable to most delegates who preferred a *federal* system of government. A federal system is one in which the sovereign powers are divided between a central government and local governments. It is the essence of federal government that each level of government is the sole authority in its field and cannot be interfered with by the other.

The move towards federalism was not without opposition. At the time when Canadian delegates were meeting in Charlottetown, P.E.I. to discuss the possibility of a Canadian union, the U.S. Civil War was raging.

Delegates questioned whether the U.S. constitution, which was also based on federalism, was going to be ripped apart. Some delegates believed that the U.S. constitution contained a fatal flaw regarding residual power. Under the U.S. system of government every power not specifically delegated to one branch of government or the other, rested with the separate states, not with the federal government. The Canadian delegates believed that residual power must rest with the federal government.

Although none of the constitutional conferences held in Canada produced any unanimous agreement, sufficient consensus was reached to officially petition the British government and request that a Confederation be formed of all the provinces.

The *British North America Act* of 1867

The Dominion of Canada was the legal creation of the *British North America Act* which became effective July 1, 1867. The bill was introduced into the House of Lords by the Colonial Secretary and passed both houses without arousing much debate.

This written document is of great importance to Canada and Canadians. It created the Dominion of Canada by uniting the four original provinces and is the common tie uniting the present ten provinces. The Act outlines the powers of the federal and provincial governments and establishes Canada as officially bilingual. Unfortunately for historians, there is no mention anywhere of who wrote it.

The preamble states that the *B.N.A. Act* is to create a constitution "similar in Principle to that of the United Kingdom." This requires some explanation since the United Kingdom does not have a single document referred to as a constitution. We must distinguish between a constitutional "principle" and a constitutional "form." The *B.N.A. Act* is not a duplicate of a law of the United Kingdom. Rather, it is intended to incorporate the same principles of freedom and rights as exist under the constitutional law developed in the United Kingdom over many years.

The *B.N.A. Act* is unlike constitutions found in many countries of the world which are very explicit as to every duty of government. There are many important things about the government of Canada which are not stated, or even suggested, in the Act. For example, there is no mention of any person or office known as the Prime Minister. Yet, it was agreed at the Charlottetown Conference that there would be a Prime Minister who would exercise a great deal of

ANNO TRICESIMO

VICTORIÆ REGINÆ.

●●

C A P. III.

An Act for the Union of *Canada, Nova Scotia,* and *New Brunswick,* and the Government thereof; and for Purposes connected therewith.

WHEREAS the Provinces of *Canada, Nova Scotia,* and *New Brunswick* have expressed their Desire to be federally united into One Dominion under the Crown of the United Kingdom of *Great Britain* and *Ireland,* with a Constitution similar in Principle to that of the United Kingdom:

And whereas such a Union would conduce to the Welfare of the Provinces and promote the Interests of the *British* Empire:

And whereas on the Establishment of the Union by Authority of Parliament it is expedient, not only that the Constitution of the Legislative Authority in the Dominion be provided for, but also that the Nature of the Executive Government therein be declared:

And whereas it is expedient that Provision be made for the eventual Admission into the Union of other Parts of *British North America*:

Be it therefore enacted and declared by the Queen's most Excellent Majesty, by and with the Advice and Consent of the Lords Spiritual

The Dominion of Canada was the legal creation of the British North America Act, 1867.

power. The Act does not mention a Cabinet, yet the concept of a Cabinet was inherent in our government from the very first day of operation.

Perhaps the most extraordinary omission was that the *B.N.A. Act* did not contain an "amending clause"—in other words there was no clause granting the Canadian Parliament the power to make amendments or changes to the Act. Consequently, for nearly 115 years, every time the Government of Canada wanted to make changes to certain parts of the constitution, the British Parliament had to be asked to pass an amendment to the *B.N.A. Act*. For example, in 1940, when the federal government wanted to enact the *Unemployment Insurance Act*, the British Parliament amended the *B.N.A. Act* to recognize such legislation.

Another question was whether the federal government could make a request to the British Parliament to change the *B.N.A. Act* without first getting the consent of the provincial legislatures. On September 28, 1981, the Supreme Court of Canada, in its first televised decision, held that while the federal Parliament was within its legal rights to proceed alone, the federal action was not in accordance with a "convention" (custom) in Canada to first acquire a substantial measure of provincial consent. Following that ruling, the federal government and nine provinces (excluding Quebec) reached an agreement and asked the British Parliament to pass the *Canada Act*. On March 29, 1982 it received royal assent. It was proclaimed by Queen Elizabeth II in Ottawa on April 17, 1982.

One feature of the new Act was to proclaim the *Constitution Act, 1982* and more will be said about that in this unit. The *B.N.A. Act* was renamed the *Constitution Act, 1867*.

The *Constitution Act, 1867* contained no Bill of Rights and few prohibitions upon the powers of government. There were guarantees designed to protect the minority rights of the French and Catholic minorities in Canada overall, and the English-speaking minority in Quebec.

As each province sought to join the Canadian Dominion an amendment to the constitution was required. The following table indicates the year in which each province or territory became a member of Confederation.

---

*Ontario/1867	British Columbia/1871
*Quebec/1867	Prince Edward Island/1873
*Nova Scotia/1867	Yukon Territory/1898
*New Brunswick/1867	Alberta/1905
Northwest Territories/1867	Saskatchewan/1905
Manitoba/1870	Newfoundland/1949

*Original members

Powers under the *Constitution Act, 1867*

Since it was based upon a system of federal government, the *Constitution Act, 1867* identified certain specific powers of the federal government and the provincial legislatures. One of the main purposes of the Act was to separate clearly the powers of the two levels of government. This separation must remain intact and several court rulings have held that it is unconstitutional for either government to try to "delegate" its powers to the other. Some of the more important powers are listed in the following tables; however, it is not a complete list.

Powers of the Federal Parliament: Section 91	
public debt	patents and copyrights
trade and commerce	banks
postal services	bills of exchange
penitentiaries	citizenship
defence	criminal law
navigation and shipping	taxation
currency	Indian affairs
marriage and divorce	old age pensions
unemployment insurance	foreign affairs

(Some of these powers were added by later amendments.)

Powers of the Provincial Legislatures: Section 92	
direct taxation within the province	hospitals and asylums
municipal institutions	solemnization of marriage
property and civil rights	provincial courts and laws
education	natural resources
labour and trade unions	compensation to injured workers

(Some of these powers were added by later amendments.)

Immigration and agriculture are within the powers of both the federal government and the provinces. If a conflict arises, the federal law prevails. Some of the specific powers shown in the two tables were acquired after decisions of the Judicial Committee of the Privy Council in England which had to rule as to which level of government should hold such powers.

Conflict of Power

One must assume that Canada's founders anticipated some conflicts would occur between the federal government and the provinces. It was their intention that where a matter produced conflict between the two, it would first be examined in the light of the specific powers granted under the *Constitution Act, 1867*. If no solution was visible, in all probability they felt that the matter would be resolved in favour of the federal government. There are numerous reasons to make this assumption.

Under the *Constitution Act, 1867*, the federal government, acting through the Governor General, was given the power to disallow any provincial law within one year of its passage. Since Confederation, 112 provincial laws have been disallowed. The last time the power was exercised was in 1943.

Another check on the provinces is the requirement that the Lieutenant-Governors of the provinces be appointed by the Governor General. In selecting a person to fill such a post, the Governor General would select someone with similar views regarding the nature of Canadian federalism. As well, the

Lieutenant-Governors' salaries are paid by the federal Parliament. This suggests that the intent was to make them federal officers.

The retention of residual power in the federal government gives Ottawa the best opportunity to fill any political vacuum. This general power to legislate is expressed in the *Constitution Act, 1867* as follows:

91. It shall be lawful for the Queen, by and with the advice and consent of the Senate and House of Commons, to make laws for the Peace, Order, and Good Government of Canada.

This catch-all phrase, "Peace, Order, and Good Government" has been used by the federal government on numerous occasions as the justification for the passage of laws not specifically covered by the *Constitution Act, 1867*. In most cases, the Privy Council (until 1949) and the Supreme Court of Canada have accepted the legitimacy of statutes passed under the general power of s. 91, particularly in an emergency. An example would be the following case:

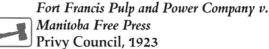

Fort Francis Pulp and Power Company v. Manitoba Free Press
Privy Council, 1923

The newspaper publisher sued to recover money paid to the manufacturers of newsprint. The prices paid had been set by the Federal Paper Control Board. The suit challenged the power of the federal government to impose price controls. The Judicial Committee of the Privy Council held that while it would appear that the price of newsprint would generally come under the provincial power related to property and civil rights, in this case a national emergency existed and the federal Parliament must have the power to pass laws under the Peace, Order, and Good Government clause to deal with national emergencies. The national emergency was the demands of World War I upon Canada's ability to produce sufficient paper, and the concern that after the war there would be speculation that would drive up prices to a very high level.

This does not mean the federal government can pass any law it likes. As was mentioned earlier, it required an amendment to the *Constitution Act, 1867* to allow the federal government to pass the *Unemployment Insurance Act.*

Canada's Unwritten Constitution

The *Constitution Act, 1867* is the basic document which is correctly referred to as the Canadian constitution. However, there are other statutes which, because of their importance, form a second or "unwritten" constitution. This situation exists primarily because Canada inherited the system of British common law. The British constitution is a collection of many Acts rather than a single document. By their very nature, these Acts are interpreted as being "constitutional" laws rather than ordinary laws. In its preamble, the *Constitution Act, 1867* is said to include the principles established in those British statutes. Thus, if Canada passes an Act which resembles a British Act holding constitutional status, the Canadian Act could also assume constitutional status or meaning. As well, the *Dominion Act* of 1875, which created the Supreme Court of Canada, is of such importance that it holds (unofficial) constitutional status. Similarly, the Acts that admitted new provinces are understood to be part of Canada's constitution.

Before the passage of the *Statute of Westminster* in 1931, numerous British Acts applied directly to Canada and affected Canadian constitutional law. Today, no British statutes have any direct application to Canadian law.

The *Statute of Westminster*, 1931

The *Constitution Act, 1867* left Canada in a position that was somewhat less than independent. The British government and the Crown exercised a great deal of control over what took place in Canada and even more control over Canada's external affairs. It was unclear whether Canada was to have any direct role in foreign affairs, for the *Constitution Act, 1867* did not expressly grant to Canada the right to make treaties with foreign nations

On August 4, 1914, Canada went to war with Germany through the unilateral action of the British Parliament. There was no consultation and Canada made no declaration of war. The end of World War I brought from many members of the British Empire a growing demand for full independence. They felt their contribution to the war had been great and they now wanted full recognition as sovereign states. The Imperial Conference of 1926 was devoted almost entirely to this subject. In 1931, the British Parliament passed the *Statute of Westminster* which states in part:

(1) No Act of the Parliament of the United Kingdom would extend to any Dominion unless that Dominion requested and consented to its enactment; and

(2) No Dominion statute was to be declared void because it contradicted a statute of the United Kingdom.

The effect of the *Statute of Westminster* was most evident at the outbreak of World War II in 1939. Canada declared war seven days after the United Kingdom. The war itself, and the formation of organizations such as NATO after the war, have all furnished evidence that Canada is an independent nation in the fullest sense of the word.

One thing which was not affected by the *Statute of Westminster* was the right to appeal cases to the Privy Council. Appeals could still be made to the Judicial Committee of the Privy Council in London until this practice was ended by a Canadian statute enacted in 1949.

The *Constitution Act, 1982*

The Canadian Parliament passed a short statute in 1981 called the *Canada Act*. This statute was a request to the British Parliament to terminate all power to legislate for Canada and to enact the *Constitution Act, 1981*. When it was proclaimed, the Act would change its name slightly from 1981 to 1982.

The *Constitution Act, 1982* has seven parts:

I.   Canadian *Charter of Rights and Freedoms*
II.   Rights of the Aboriginal Peoples of Canada
III. Equalization and Regional Disparities
IV.   Constitutional Conference
V.   Procedure for Amending Constitution of Canada
VI.   Amendment to the *Constitution Act, 1867*
VII. General Provisions

These seven parts will be discussed throughout the text. For example, the *Charter of Rights and Freedoms* will be discussed in detail in Unit Four   Human Rights in Canada.

Amending the Constitution of Canada

Canada now has an amending formula that will permit changes to be made within Canada to the Canadian constitution. The formula requires that changes to the constitution must have the agreement of the federal Parliament and two-thirds of the provinces (seven provinces), representing 50 per cent of the population of all the provinces.

A province whose legislature has not approved an amendment that diminishes that province's legislative powers or rights will be permitted to "opt out." That is, the change will have no effect in that province. However, only up to three provinces may opt out or the entire amendment becomes void.

In the case of an amendment transferring jurisdiction over education or other cultural matters from the provinces to the federal government, fiscal compensation will be given to any province that opts out of the amendment.

For some matters, including the monarchy, certain language rights, and the composition of the Supreme Court of Canada, the unanimous consent of all the provinces and approval by the federal Parliament will be required.

Our Government Today

The Governor General

The chief executive of Canada is the Sovereign (British king or queen), represented by the Governor General. The *Constitution Act, 1867* further mentions that the Governor General is to be advised by a Council, but gives no information how this Council should be chosen.

Most Canadians know little about the powers and functions of the Governor General. The primary reason is that they are seldom exercised. Most of these powers have been assumed by the Prime Minister and Cabinet. Nonetheless, a quick reading of the *Constitution Act, 1867* would cause the reader to assume that Canada is ruled by a person with almost unlimited powers! The Governor General is specifically granted these powers by the Act:

(1) To give assent to or reject, in the name of the Sovereign, all bills passed by the Canadian Parliament, or to refer to the Sovereign any bills for consideration;
(2) To appoint and dismiss the Lieutenant-Governors for all the provinces;
(3) To appoint and dismiss all superior court judges;
(4) To exercise the prerogative of mercy or pardons for criminals;
(5) To appoint and dismiss Ministers;
(6) To dissolve Parliament and call general elections;
(7) To disallow provincial legislation within one ye? its passage.

One must necessarily ask, how did a person i. with such power lose it all? The answer is not si. but as a general statement one could say that it occurred through a gradual process of erosion. On numerous occasions, the Canadian Prime Minister and the Governor General strongly disagreed. The usual result was that at the next Imperial Conference, Canada would complain about the interference by the Crown in Canada's affairs. The British Colonial Secretary would issue a memorandum to the Governor General requesting a more co-operative attitude, and the end result would be a further reduction in the Governor General's powers. Since the Imperial Conference of 1926, the Governor General has seldom made a decision that opposed the will of the Canadian Parliament.

Another explanation of the decline of the power of the Governor General rests in the decline of the power of the Sovereign. Today, the British king or queen is able to do almost nothing without the authorization of the British Cabinet. A similar loss of power by the Governor General is only natural, for surely the Governor General cannot do something which the Sovereign personally cannot do.

The Governor General's term is legally for six years, but is customarily for five years. The Sovereign may remove a Governor General at the request of the Canadian Cabinet. Thus, the Governor General could be fired at the request of his or her own Council!

Initially, the persons appointed as Governor General were British, often either relatives of the Sovereign or military leaders. Vincent Massey became the first Canadian Governor General in 1952. All subsequent appointments have been to Canadians. If the Governor General falls ill and cannot carry out the required legal duties, the Chief Justice of the Supreme Court of Canada temporarily assumes signing authority.

Governor General Jeanne Sauvée takes the oath of office. The Governor General represents the Sovereign as Canada's Chief Executive.

The Senate

The Senate—the Upper House of the legislature—was created as a result of a compromise reached at the Charlottetown Conference of 1864. The smaller provinces, knowing that representation in the Lower House (House of Commons) would be based upon population, were concerned that there would be too few voices in Parliament to speak about their needs and concerns. They urged the creation of a second house. All provinces and all political parties were to be fairly represented. Members would be appointed rather than elected.

The Senate is an independent legislative body, although it seldom tries to oppose a decision of the Lower House except where it feels it can count on popular support. Sir John A. Macdonald held that since only the Lower House is elected, only the Lower House has a clear mandate from the people to enact certain legislation. The Upper House should not try to block that legislation.

Senators are appointed by the Governor General in Council and hold office for life. All Senators must be residents of the provinces they represent.

The House of Commons

The House of Commons, sometimes referred to as the Lower House, is the real workhorse of the Canadian government. The unique character of the House of Commons is that it can speak, as no other body in Canada can speak, for the people. It is not intended to be a committee of the most brilliant minds in Canada. Rather, it is a sampling of diverse interests, races, religions, classes, occupations, and national origins. It is through the election of Members of Parliament that Canadians are allowed to participate in the decision-making process of their government.

Yet, many Canadians misunderstand the basic nature of Parliament. The primary obligation of Members is to Canada, not merely to their own constituency. This isn't to say that Members must ignore the opinions of people who elected them. It is to emphasize that Members must use their own judgment and decide what is best for Canada and not blindly obey the majority opinion of voters. In 1974, John Diefenbaker was very critical of Members who polled their constituents about their opinions regarding capital punishment. This appeared to the former Prime Minister as a way of avoiding responsibility out of fear of making an unpopular decision. Diefenbaker went on to say:

> These Members do not understand the very basic workings of the Parliament in which they sit. The House is not a mouthpiece just to repeat the views of the constituencies. The House must investigate, oppose, debate, and possibly postpone action. In doing these things it must create a more enlightened opinion throughout the nation.

This does not suggest that a Member should be an arrogant, aloof person totally disinterested in the concerns of the people. It suggests that in the final showdown, the vote must be according to that which is deemed best, not necessarily that which is most popular.

The House of Commons will normally give its consent to all bills that the Cabinet submits, but, in so doing, it exercises the vital function of criticism. The attacks made by opposition parties upon proposed legislation often play an important role in determining the final form of a new statute. If consent is not given by the House of Commons, convention requires that the government resign and that elections be held.

The House of Commons is presided over by the Speaker of the House who is elected by the Members. A mace sits on the table before the Speaker as a symbol of his or her authority. Regardless of what party the Speaker represents, he or she must be completely

The House of Commons is presided over by the Speaker of the House who is elected by the Members.

hon-partisan while carrying out the duties of the position. The Speaker must protect the Members from insult and maintain order, decorum, and the rules of the House. It is a very demanding position.

Seats in the House of Commons are apportioned to the provinces by a formula based upon population. The formula ensures that Quebec will receive four additional seats after every ten-year census, even if the population of Quebec declines. This means the number of Commons Members from all the other provinces must be adjusted accordingly. It would appear that, unless the formula is changed, the House of Commons will keep growing in number even if the overall population of Canada remains the same or declines.

The Cabinet

The *Constitution Act, 1867* mentions a "Council" which is to advise the Governor General. There is no mention in the Act as to how this Council is to be chosen. The Act also refers to a "Privy Council" which does exist in Canada, but almost never meets. Some historians believe that the last time the Governor General actually had a meeting with the Privy Council was a meeting attended by the Duke of Connaught during World War I. The federal Cabinet is comprised of Members of the House of Commons who are chosen by the Prime Minister and appointed as Ministers to head the various departments. It is neither the "Council" nor the "Privy Council" mentioned in the Act. Yet, by custom, the federal Cabinet fulfills all the functions of these two bodies, and has assumed great powers in addition.

The Cabinet is to all intents and purposes the real executive authority in Canada. It formulates policies, prepares legislation, is responsible for the administration of the departments of government, and has assumed control over all financial matters.

Under the supervision of Cabinet Ministers, appointed by the Prime Minister, the vital day-to-day activities of government are carried out by a staff of professional civil servants. The mail is delivered, the military is trained, prosecutions are made, appointments are given, and thousands of other government duties are carried out without any direct interference or guidance from Parliament. This is not to suggest that Parliament is not involved in the operation of the government. Members of Parliament are, of course, involved in the pressing matters of the day, particularly new legislation.

Canadian tradition requires that Cabinet Ministers also be members of the House of Commons so that they may be accountable to the House for their actions. Occasionally, a Cabinet Minister may be chosen from the Senate to represent a province or part of Canada that has not elected Members of Parliament belonging to the majority party. This procedure tries to guarantee that all parts of Canada have some Cabinet representation. The Prime Minister generally picks Cabinet Ministers in such a way as to ensure that every province is represented by at least one Minister.

Cabinet Ministers must defend the actions of civil servants working in their departments, or else remove civil servants who are censured. It is also traditional that all Cabinet Ministers publicly support each other's programs, although they may disagree privately, for the defeat of any major program represents a defeat for the Prime Minister. In such an event, the entire Cabinet may have to resign, thus precipitating an election.

Theoretically, Cabinet Ministers are responsible to the Prime Minister, the House of Commons, the Crown, and their electorate. The only body to which Cabinet Ministers are not responsible is the Senate.

The Judiciary

The *Constitution Act, 1867* created no courts, but it empowered the federal government to "create a general court of appeal and any additional courts for the better administration of the laws of Canada." The provincial legislatures may establish whatever courts are desired for the "administration of justice within the province."

By separate statute, the Canadian Parliament established the Supreme Court of Canada in 1875, to exercise appellate civil and criminal jurisdiction for Canada. The court was originally composed of a Chief Justice and five judges. Today the court has a Chief Justice and eight judges. By law, at least three of the judges must be from Quebec. This is to ensure that there are judges on the court familiar with the Quebec *Civil Code*. In 1982, Madam Justice Bertha Wilson became the first woman ever appointed to the Supreme Court of Canada.

In 1982, Madam Justice Bertha Wilson became the first woman ever appointed to the Supreme Court of Canada.

It was initially intended that the Supreme Court of Canada would be the highest appeal court for Canada. However, a strict interpretation of the law created one other possibility; namely, that cases could still be appealed in England to the Judicial Committee of the Privy Council. In fact, some cases could go directly to the Judicial Committee without having first been heard by the Supreme Court of Canada. This situation existed until 1949 when a special statute was passed declaring the Supreme Court of Canada as the final appeal authority.

The primary function of the judiciary is to settle the disputes that come before it. However, the judiciary has other inherent duties as well, including:

- To interpret the laws and give them fuller meaning;
- To protect the people from arbitrary, unauthorized acts of government;
- To ensure the rule of law is maintained.

As the interpreter of the written laws, the courts will set aside as *ultra vires* any laws which are beyond the powers of the legislative body to pass. This is a vital role of the Supreme Court of Canada and fits into that area of law referred to as constitutional law. First, let us define more fully the meaning of the term we have just used. If an Act is *ultra vires* ("beyond the power") it is in excess of the authority conferred by the law, and therefore invalid. For example, a government's powers are limited to carrying out the functions of government specifically granted to it in the constitution.

Because of the nature of the *Constitution Act, 1867* both the provinces and the federal government have sometimes passed laws which appeared necessary to them, but which in fact intruded upon the powers granted in the Act to the other level of government. Some areas are quite distinct and there has never been any confusion about them. For example, the provinces have never raised armies or printed stamps. Concern has arisen primarily over new developments that did not exist when the *Constitution Act, 1867* was passed. For example, which level of government should control aviation? Who should have the power to control atomic energy? Here is an example involving a provincial statute:

Morgan and Jacobson v. A.G. for P.E.I.
Prince Edward Island, 1975

Prince Edward Island passed a law requiring non-resident persons, whether Canadian citizens or not, to obtain permission from the province to purchase either land exceeding 10 acres (4 ha) or land with shore frontage of 5 chains (approximately 100 m). The Supreme Court of Canada held unanimously that the legislation was not ultra vires the province. It was not legislation dealing specifically with aliens; instead, it came under the powers of the province under the *Constitution Act, 1867* to deal with "property and civil rights." The Supreme Court also ruled that the law was not contrary to the federal *Citizenship Act* as it did not prohibit any Canadian from taking up permanent residence in Prince Edward Island and then buying land.

The next case deals with the *Criminal Code,* a federal statute:

R. v. Boggs
Supreme Court of Canada, 1981

Boggs was convicted, under s. 238(3) of the *Criminal Code of Canada*, of driving while disqualified. The section reads:

(3) Everyone who drives a motor vehicle in Canada while he is disqualified or prohibited from driving a motor vehicle by reason of the legal suspension or cancellation, in any province, of his permit or licence or of his right to secure a permit or licence to drive a motor vehicle in that province is guilty of
(a) an indictable offence and is liable to imprisonment for five years; or
(b) an offence punishable on summary conviction.

The Supreme Court of Canada held that s. 238(3) is ultra vires the Parliament of Canada. The issue was whether Parliament can exercise its criminal power under s. 91 of the *Constitution Act, 1867* by providing a criminal penalty for breach of an order made under a provincial statute. The court held that Parliament cannot do so. Violation of a provincial law or regulation cannot be a crime.

Elections in Canada

Under the *Constitution Act, 1867*, the House of Commons may sit uninterrupted for a maximum period of five years. A Canadian government has no predetermined life span. In the normal course of events, a federal election is called a year or so before the five-year period expires. An election is often necessitated because of some major issue on which the government feels it must obtain the support of the people through their ballots. One Parliament, that of 1957-1958, was technically less than six months in duration.

The Prime Minister requests the Governor General to call an election. The Governor General will comply with this request and dissolve Parliament. There was only one occasion in Canadian history when the Governor General refused to call an election. In 1926, Governor General Lord Byng refused to dissolve Parliament when requested by Prime Minister MacKenzie King. Instead, he asked Arthur Meighen, the Leader of the Opposition, to form a government, which he did. The new government had little success, and a general election was called anyway. An election need not be called every time the government is defeated upon one of its proposed bills, but it is traditional for an election to be called any time the government is defeated on a proposal to expend public funds (a "money bill").

Elections are supervised by an independent official called the Chief Electoral Officer, under the requirements of the *Canada Elections Act*. If a candidate is nominated in a riding by one of the recognized political parties, that candidate may run for office. Independent candidates must be nominated on a petition signed by twenty-five qualified voters in the riding. The candidate's consent to run must be indicated in writing and a cash deposit must be made. If the candidate is elected, or wins at least one-half as many votes as the successful candidate, the deposit is refunded. If there is only one candidate, that person is elected by acclamation. The candidate getting the most votes is elected. It is not necessary to receive a majority of the votes cast.

The *Constitution Act, 1867* does not state qualifications for Members of the House of Commons. A separate statute requires that a Member be a Canadian citizen, twenty-one years of age or over. There is no residency requirement. It is not uncommon in Canadian politics for someone to seek a seat in a riding where that person has never lived or even visited. Sir John A. Macdonald once lost his own seat in the riding of Kingston and the Islands, but shortly afterwards won a by-election in British Columbia.

By virtue of British custom, the House of Commons may refuse, by simple vote, to allow an "undesirable" Member to take a seat. Louis Riel was denied his seat by resolution on two separate occasions.

The *Constitution Act, 1867* does not require a secret ballot. The secret ballot was introduced in Canada in 1874. Prior to that, voting was done by open declaration which naturally allowed intimidation and bribery.

The party holding the most seats is asked by the Governor General to form a government. The party leader is appointed Prime Minister, provided that individual won a seat. Strangely enough, the *Constitution Act, 1867* makes no specific mention of any such person as the "Prime Minister" although the framers of the Act certainly knew that such a person would come into existence immediately. The party having the second largest number of seats is declared the Opposition, and its party leader is declared to be the Leader of the Opposition. Parliament is opened again by the Governor General who addresses both Houses together, reading what is called a "Speech from the Throne" outlining the government's proposals for the next Parliament.

How a Bill Becomes Law

A proposed law, called a *bill*, is classed as either a *private bill*, a *private Member's bill*, or a *public bill*. Private bills deal with the needs of a few select persons, or perhaps one individual. They can be introduced in either House, but are normally introduced in the Senate. The object

of a private bill is to amend the law pertaining to some particular community, or to confer a right upon a certain person or body of persons. A private bill requires the payment of a fee to ensure that only serious bills are introduced.

The next type of bill is the private Member's bill. Any Member of the House of Commons may introduce a bill, but unless the Member is a Cabinet Minister, there is little chance it will become law. Most private Members' bills die on the Order Paper without being debated. The Order Paper is the list of proposed new legislation and indicates the order in which the proposals are to be dealt with. The underlying purpose of a private Member's bill is to provide an excellent way for an ordinary Member of the House to criticize the government, or try to influence its decisions. If the suggestion is a good one, and the government chooses to ignore it, then the Member can put the blame on the government for its inaction. If the government adopts the idea and includes it in one of its own bills, the Member can take the credit for the good effect it produces.

The bills that do become law are usually introduced by a Cabinet Minister as part of a continuous policy of carrying out the government's programs. These are referred to as public bills. Many such bills represent attempts to fulfill election promises. Any bill involving the spending of public money must be recommended by the Governor General. The Cabinet usually carries out this function on the Governor General's behalf.

The general procedure in the passage of bills is that they receive three readings in the House of Commons, three in the Senate, and then go to the Governor General to be formally signed and receive royal assent. A bill can originate in either the Commons or the Senate, but if either House makes an amendment to the version which the other House has passed, it must be returned to that House and given one more final reading in the revised form.

The term *reading* means to read, consider, and perhaps debate the contents of a bill. The introduction of a bill must be preceded by forty-eight hours' notice. After that, the Member asks permission of the

Speaker of the House to introduce the bill. Permission is almost always granted, and the Member gives the name of the bill and its general contents. It is seldom debated or voted upon. This is all that comprises first reading.

The second reading is normally the most important one, and usually involves the most prolonged debate. Second reading is devoted to attacking or defending the overall concept of the bill rather than picking upon small details. Amendments can be proposed, or the bill may be referred to a Standing Committee of the House or to a Special Committee for further work. In reporting back to the House, the Committee will recommend either that the wording of the bill be changed, that debate on the bill be postponed, or that the bill be allowed to die on the Order Paper without further debate. If the bill passes the second reading by a majority vote of the Members present, it is then worked on by a Cabinet Minister and staff to smooth out any objectionable or confusing wording. The bill is then given a third reading and, if passed by a majority of Members present, goes to the other House for similar consideration.

Once a bill has been passed by both Houses, it goes to the Governor General, who has three alternatives:

(1) Assent to the bill in the Sovereign's name and sign it, thereby making it law upon the day it is declared to be in force.

(2) Withhold assent (refuse to sign), thereby preventing the bill from becoming law. (This has never been done.)

(3) Reserve the bill for the signification of the Sovereign's pleasure; in other words, let the Sovereign decide whether it should become law. The bill cannot become law unless the Sovereign assents to it within two years.

Even if the Governor General's assent has been given to a bill, the Sovereign may still overrule the Governor General and withdraw assent if this is done within two years. This has never happened in Canadian history.

On a few occasions, the Governor General has signed a bill but delayed declaring it in force, or

declared only part of the bill in force as law. For example, when the amendment was passed to the *Criminal Code of Canada* requiring the mandatory breathalyzer test, part of the bill required the police to give the driver a personal sample of tested breath in a "suitable container." At the time, no suitable container was known to exist, and this portion of the bill was never declared in force. The legality of declaring only part of a bill as law was challenged in the courts, and the Supreme Court of Canada ruled it was within the Governor General's powers to do so. The withheld portion is still not in force, but the rest of the bill is enforceable law.

Once a bill becomes law, it is referred to as an *Act*. It is identified by name and the year of passage. Every ten years, all Acts are bound into a set and are then referred to as *The Revised Statutes of Canada, 1970*, 1980, etc. An Act can be amended or completely repealed in the same manner as it became law in the first place.

Provincial laws are passed in the same manner, except that the provinces have only one house in the legislature. A bill becomes law after being signed by the Lieutenant-Governor of the province. The Lieutenant-Governor has the same three alternatives as the Governor General regarding what action to take on the bill.

Our Court System

The *Constitution Act, 1867* did not create any courts, but provided a plan for Canada to establish federal and provincial courts as needed. Parliament was empowered to establish a court of appeal and any additional courts for the "better administration of the laws of Canada." The provincial legislatures were given jurisdiction over the administration of justice within the province, including the creation and maintenance of provincial courts to enforce both civil and criminal laws. Under this system, the provincial courts have the power to enforce both provincial and federal statutes. This is rather unusual, for in most countries a court could not enforce a law passed by a different level of government. For example, in the United States, a state court could not enforce a federal law. The case would have to be heard in a federal court. In Canada, it is possible for a provincial court to enforce a federal law. An example would be the enforcement of provisions of the *Criminal Code of Canada.* This is a federal law, but provincial courts have the power to try cases under the provisions of the *Criminal Code.*

All superior court judges are appointed by the Parliament of Canada, acting through the Governor General, to hold office during good behaviour. Provincial court judges are appointed by the provincial legislatures. Judges have no responsibility to Parliament; this fact puts the judiciary above the level of political involvement. Judges must retire at the age of seventy-five. A judge can only be removed from the bench for deliberate wrongdoing. Removal requires a joint address of both Houses of Parliament, followed by an order for removal by the Governor General.

All but one of the provinces have essentially similar court systems, based on three main levels: the Supreme Court, which is the highest provincial court; the County or District Court; and the Magistrate's and Small Claims Courts. Each province also has a Court of Appeal which hears appeals from the other provincial courts. Since the names of the courts and some details of court jurisdiction vary among the provinces, it will be convenient to outline the system in Ontario as a representative province.

Ontario Provincial Courts

Small Claims Court
This is a civil court, established to hear claims up to $1000. It is intended to be an informal court where citizens may present claims without hiring a lawyer. No jury trials are permitted.

Provincial Court, Criminal Division
Called Magistrate's Court in some provinces, this is a criminal court which hears offences under the *Criminal Code* and certain other federal statutes, and violations of provincial laws. Presided over by a provincial court judge, the court does not hear jury cases.

Provincial Court, Family Division
This division of the Provincial Court hears all domestic matters under provincial laws dealing with the family, including separation, maintenance, etc. The court can hear certain matters under federal laws such as the *Juvenile Delinquents Act*. Sometimes referred to as Family Court, the court is presided over by a provincial court judge. There are no jury trials in this court.

County Court
This court hears civil cases where the sum does not exceed $15 000. It is also the appeal court from the Provincial Court, Criminal Division by way of *trial de novo,* meaning an appeal for a new trial before a judge of a higher court. Cases before this court may involve a jury. The court can hear criminal cases where the accused has elected to be tried before a judge or a judge and jury.

The High Court of Justice for Ontario (Ontario Supreme Court, Trials Division)
The Trials Division of the Supreme Court hears civil matters as well as serious criminal cases. Cases before this court may involve a jury. There is no maximum ceiling on the sum involved in a case before the court.

The Court of Appeal for Ontario (Ontario Supreme Court, Appeals Division)
This branch of the Supreme Court hears appeals from the Trials Division of the same court and from lower courts. The Chief Justice assigns judges to hear cases, normally sitting as a panel of three judges. Major cases are heard by the entire court of eight judges and the Chief Justice.

Divisional Court
The full name of this court is The Divisional Court of the High Court of Justice for Ontario. It consists of the Chief Justice of the High Court, who is president of the court, and such other judges of the High Court as the Chief Justice may designate. The court hears special appeals, including appeals by way of stated case under any Act other than the *Summary Convictions Act*, appeals from many administrative tribunals, and appeals involving practice and procedure.

Federal Courts

Federal Court of Canada

The Federal Court hears claims directly against the federal government or any of its departments. It also has jurisdiction over appeals against rulings by federal regulatory agencies such as the Canadian Radio and Television Commission. Like the provincial Supreme Court, it has a trials division and an appeals division. There are no jury trials.

Supreme Court of Canada

The Supreme Court of Canada is the highest appellate court in Canada for both civil and criminal cases. It hears appeals against decisions of the provincial Courts of Appeal. The court hears appeals where the validity of federal and provincial statutes is in dispute, hears appeals from the Federal Court, and also gives advisory opinions to the federal government on the interpretation of the *Constitution Act, 1867* and the constitutionality of other laws.

Citizenship Court

A court established for the purpose of bestowing the legal status of Canadian citizenship upon qualified immigrants.

Special Courts

There are some special courts which exist to carry out a single function. Following are two such courts:

Surrogate Court

Probate of wills (proving their authenticity) and administration of estates of persons who died without a will come under the jurisdiction of this court.

Court of Revision

A court where taxpayers may dispute their property tax assessments for local tax purposes. The court does not sit all the year round, but is usually called into session once a year and presided over by a county court or provincial court judge.

Reviewing Important Points

1. The Canadian form of government is a federal union, with power divided between the federal government and the provinces. Residual power rests with the federal government.
2. The basic legal authority for statute law in Canada is the *Constitution Act, 1867.*
3. To change the constitution, an amendment must be passed by the federal Parliament, and then by two-thirds of the provinces, representing 50 per cent of the total Canadian population.
4. Canada's chief executive is the Sovereign, represented by the Governor General.
5. Both the federal and provincial governments have the power to establish courts. The *Constitution Act, 1867* created no courts.
6. To become law in Canada, a bill must be passed by the House of Commons and the Senate. It must then receive royal assent from the Governor General.
7. Provincial courts can enforce both provincial and federal laws.
8. All superior court judges are appointed by Parliament, but are not responsible to Parliament.
9. Judges can be removed from the bench for improper behaviour; they must retire at age seventy-five.

Checking Your Understanding

1. What significant provision was omitted from the original *B.N.A. Act*?
2. Describe two ways in which the federal government may exercise a check upon the power of the provincial governments.
3. A law may be challenged in court as ultra vires. What does this mean?
4. What was the importance of the *Statute of Westminster*?
5. The Governor General may issue "Orders in Council." To what "Council" does this refer?

6. What is the maximum time a Canadian Parliament may sit before an election is called?

7. What is a private Member's bill? Do such bills have a good chance of becoming law? Why or why not?

8. For each of the following situations, determine in what court the case would first appear. Answers will differ by province.

a. A civil lawsuit arises from a motor vehicle accident; the plaintiff claims $7000 in damages.

b. A store wants to sue a customer whose charge account has an unpaid balance of $345.

c. A woman is run over by a truck belonging to the Postal Corporation. She sues for damages.

d. A civil lawsuit for $2 000 000 is filed.

e. A wife complains that the husband is not making the payments promised in a separation agreement.

Legal Briefs

1. On paper, the Governor General is a very powerful official. In reality, does the Governor General have much power? Why or why not?

2. Whom does a Member of Parliament "represent"? If a large majority of people in the riding from which the Member was elected are opposed to a bill, must the MP vote against it?

3. What is "Cabinet solidarity"? Why must Cabinet Ministers all "hang together"?

4. K, a popular member of the Conservative party, has lived all her life in Ontario. She decides to run for election to the federal Parliament from a riding in Alberta. Lawful?

5. The salaries of all Lieutenant-Governors are paid by the federal government. Does this mean the Lieutenant-Governors are federal officers?

6. In some countries of the world, if a citizen does not vote, the citizen is punished by the state. Is this a good policy for Canada to adopt? Why or why not?

7. The *Constitution Act, 1867* (formerly the *B.N.A. Act,*) is the second-oldest, written constitution in the world. Which is the oldest?

8. The king or queen of England is also the king or queen of Canada. True statement?

9. The *Constitution Act, 1982* reads in part:

> **6. (1) Every citizen of Canada has the right to enter, remain in and leave Canada.**

R, a Canadian citizen who is an inmate in a federal penitentiary, desires to leave Canada. Must the prison officials release R?

10. There is no "second-in-command" to the Governor General. What would happen if the Governor General became ill and could not give royal assent to some urgent legislation?

Unit
Two

Criminal Law

Audi alteram partem
("Hear the other side")

Chapter 3

The Nature of Crime

The Purposes of Criminal Law

People sometimes assume that criminal laws have always existed and must exist. This is incorrect, since there were few criminal laws in the British tradition before the Norman invasion of England in 1066 A.D. Prior to the Norman presence, most matters were handled personally. If A killed B, then B's relatives would try to kill A in retaliation. The criminal law had as one of its earliest purposes the elimination of feuds and reprisals.

Criminal law is intended to distinguish between behaviour that is permitted and that which is not. It distinguishes between forbidden behaviour that is seriously wrong and that which is mildly at fault. It provides a means for controlling those persons who would violate the criminal laws. However, there is a constant tendency to make more and more things criminal. Whenever the majority in a society takes a dislike to the behaviour of a minority, the easy solution is to declare that behaviour "criminal" and to use the force of authority to eliminate it.

There are guidelines which can help legislators to decide if an activity should be criminal. The American Law Institute's *Model Penal Code* can be taken as a sample of the purposes of criminal law. The purposes identified are:

(1) To forbid and prevent conduct that unjustifiably and inexcusably inflicts or threatens substantial harm to individual and public interest.
(2) To subject to public control persons whose conduct indicates that they are disposed to commit a crime.
(3) To safeguard from condemnation as criminal, conduct that is without fault.
(4) To give fair warning of the nature of the conduct declared to be an offence.
(5) To differentiate on reasonable grounds between serious and minor offences.

Crimes are not just prohibited; they seem to society to be "wrong" in some manner. If they are wrong, they cannot go unchallenged. If society did not respond to a crime, two problems would be created: (1) Society would condone the act by its inaction; and (2) society would encourage the commission of further crimes. It is also important that criminals not enjoy the fruits of crime. As Justice Davies said in sentencing a participant in England's Great Train Robbery:

> **"**It would be an affront if you were to be at liberty in the near future, to enjoy these ill-gotten gains. I propose to ensure that such opportunity will be denied to you for a very long time.**"**

If one of the purposes of criminal law is to identify actions which are prohibited, then perhaps we have been too successful. There are over 700 sections in the *Criminal Code*. There are nearly 20 000 federal offences; about 20 000 provincial offences in most provinces; and a nearly uncountable number of offences under the regulations created by boards, commissions, and the by-laws of municipal governments. "Ignorance of the law is no excuse" is a very old rule of the common law and is also stated in s. 19 of the *Criminal Code*. Yet it can be said, with reasonable certainty, that no one in

Canada knows all the laws and most Canadians know less than 1 per cent of the laws.

There are certain legal terms that frequently recur throughout this text. An offence punishable on *summary conviction* is a less serious offence which can be dealt with quickly in the courts. An *indictable offence* is a more serious offence. The Crown is the plaintiff in nearly all Canadian criminal cases. The case is brought to court by the *Crown Attorney* as prosecutor. The case is identified by a "name" such as *R. v. Doe*. "R" stands for Rex if a king was on the throne or Regina if a queen was on the throne at the time of the trial. The "v" means "versus" and the name of the accused person follows. If an appeal is made by a convicted person to a higher court, the names are reversed and might read, *Doe v. The Queen*. This is always done upon appeal to the Supreme Court of Canada.

Law reports identify the publisher of the report, the volume, the year, and the page number in the report. For lawyers, this is very necessary in order to locate the specific case. In this text, the heading is much more simplified and will indicate the year and the jurisdiction where the case was heard—either the province, the Supreme Court of Canada, or the Federal Court. For example: *R. v. Binalki*, Ontario, 1973 indicates that someone named Binalki was the accused in a 1973 Ontario case.

An accused person is called the *accused* or the *defendant*. (At one time, the person was called the *prisoner* at the bar.) A person who appeals the case is called the *appellant* and the other person is called the *respondent*. In effect, one party is appealing (appellant) and the other party is responding (respondent) to the appeal. The terms apply equally to the accused or the Crown, depending upon which has brought the appeal.

Other legal terms will be explained as they occur.

Defining Crime

Attempts to give a precise definition of a "crime" often run into trouble. It would be simplest to say that a certain act becomes a crime when Parliament makes it a crime. This does not, of course, change the essential nature of the act itself, but only whether it is legal or illegal. For example, suicide was once a crime in Canada. Today, it is not, but certainly the nature of suicide has not changed. Many legal texts contain definitions of a crime. None of them are perfect, and the definition put forward in this unit could also be criticized as being rather general. Nonetheless, some definition of a crime is essential if one is to have a starting point for the topic being discussed. Thus, a crime could be defined as a wrongdoing or omission that poses a serious danger to the security and well-being of society and that cannot be left unchallenged.

Most of the criminal laws of Canada are contained in one statute, the *Criminal Code of Canada*. However, some other separate statutes, such as the *Combines Investigation Act*, also deal with criminal matters. The codification of criminal laws was first adopted in Canada in 1892. The draft copy was actually a code prepared in Great Britain for use in India but the Indian Parliament rejected it as unworkable for that country. The code sections were numbered in 1906 and a major revision was completed in 1955. Codification is unusual for a nation whose legal system is based on common law. It is more characteristic of French law than English law. In England, offences are set down in separate statutes such as the *Homicide Act*, *Offences against the Person Act*, etc.

The *Constitution Act, 1867* prescribes that the criminal law will be uniform throughout Canada. Therefore, what is an offence in Ontario will also be an offence in Newfoundland. This is not true in the United States where each state has its own criminal laws, although there are federal crimes as well.

It should be noted that, when reading a federal or provincial statute, the various *Interpretation Acts* require that wherever the words "he," "him," or "his" are used, the words "she," "her," or "hers" should also be read into the statute.

Elements of a Crime

A crime is generally comprised of two parts, or elements. The first is the illegal act itself and the second is the mental state of the accused wrongdoer.

Actus Reus

Before an accused person can be convicted of a crime, also called an *offence*, it is necessary for the Crown to prove that the accused committed a certain *actus reus*, which, loosely translated, means "prohibited act." An actus reus can also exist where an accused failed to act where the law required that some action be taken. Criminal negligence and failure to provide necessaries of life to a child are examples of such offences.

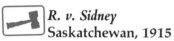

R. v. Sidney
Saskatchewan, 1915

The accused man was charged with manslaughter after the death of his wife and son. Following an argument in their home, the wife took the son and started walking to the house of her parents. She and the boy left at night in a severe snowstorm. They never arrived at her parents' house; they froze to death before reaching their destination. The charge against the husband was based primarily upon his permitting them to leave and not following them or taking any action to protect their safety. He was found not guilty of failing to supply "necessaries." The court felt that the husband was not criminally liable where the wife exercised her free will and chose to leave the shelter provided for her. With respect to the child, because the wife had control of him and there was nothing to show that the wife would get lost or deliberately expose the child to danger, there was no duty upon the husband to intervene.

It must be proven that an act or event prohibited by law occurred; that the accused committed that act or caused that event; and that the accused had a willing mind capable of making a choice. Certain defences can be raised by the accused to demonstrate that the forbidden action was not voluntary. These defences will be discussed later in the text.

There are no common law offences; offences must be clearly stated in a criminal law statute. Nor can the wording of offences be altered to suit the situation.

Thus, in the case of a hunter chased by a farmer's dog, the court was presented with a charge under s. 228 of the *Criminal Code* which makes it an offence to discharge a firearm with intent to wound a *person*. The complaint was worded "with intent to wound a *dog*." (The hunter had shot the dog in self-defence.) The provincial court judge dismissed the complaint as not stating an offence; there was no actus reus known in law (*R. v. Weaver*, Ontario, 1981).

Mens Rea

The second element of a crime is the *mens rea*, meaning "mental capacity." It can also be translated to mean "guilty mind" or "criminal intent" but none of these translations is totally accurate since the meaning of mens rea is complex. Three general areas of mental capacity have been recognized to satisfy the requirement of mens rea:

• *Intent:* The accused intended to commit the crime. When a person does an act, desiring that certain consequences should happen, it is said that those consequences were intended. The person may not know that the consequences will definitely result, but he or she knows that they are substantially certain.
• *Recklessness:* The accused may behave in a manner which indicates awareness that the actions may cause harm, but recklessness as to whether or not harm ensues. Recklessness is the deliberate taking of an unjustifiable risk knowing that an event may result from that risk.
• *Negligence:* In criminal law, negligence is held to be a failure to comply with an objective standard of responsibility. A person acts negligently by doing something which a reasonable person, in the same circumstances, would have refrained from doing.

The actus reus and the mens rea must co-exist at some time during the crime. If a person killed another person by accident, but later admitted to being glad that the victim was dead, the killing remains an accident, not murder. Exact knowledge is not the meaning of mens rea. This is illustrated by the case of a woman who was paid to smuggle jewels into Canada. When caught, she was surprised to learn that she was actually smuggling narcotics; but the offence was not excused by the accused's absence of knowledge as to the exact nature of what she was smuggling.

Some unusual cases do exist, however, where the coincidence of actus reus and mens rea is not exact.

Thabo Meli v. The Queen
England, 1954

The appellants were convicted of murder. The evidence was that in accordance with a pre-arranged plan, they took a man to a hut, got him drunk, then struck him over the head. Believing him to be dead, they took his body and rolled it over a cliff, trying to make it appear that it was an accidental fall. In fact the man was not dead when rolled over the cliff, but died of exposure while unconscious at the foot of the cliff. On appeal, it was argued that there were two separate acts: (1) the act of assault; and (2) the act of putting the body outside exposed to the elements. In the first act — the assault — both actus reus and mens rea were present; but the deceased was not killed in the first act. In the second act, there was no intent to kill the victim because the appellants believed he was already dead. Counsel for the appellants suggested that conviction on a lesser charge of manslaughter would be correct, but not conviction for murder. The Privy Council dismissed the appeal:

> 66It appears to their Lordships impossible to divide up the plan this way. There was one, continuous series of acts. Their crime is not reduced from murder to a lesser crime merely because of the fact that there was a misapprehension for a time during the completion of their crime.99

In *Fagan v. Commissioner of Metropolitan Police* (England, 1969), the accused accidentally drove his car onto a police officer's foot. The officer ordered him to move his car off but the accused left the car where it was for some time. It was not clear whether the accused deliberately turned off the ignition after realizing that the

wheel was on the officer's foot. In any case, he was very slow about starting the ignition and backing off. He was convicted of assaulting the officer even though there was no intent to assault when he drove onto the officer's foot. The mens rea came into being by his failure to get off.

In *Commonwealth v. Cali* (Massachusetts, 1923), a man accidentally started a fire in his place of business. He then did nothing to put out the fire because he wanted to collect the fire insurance. He was convicted of arson. The court concluded that if a person starts a fire accidentally and then purposely refuses to extinguish it, a conviction for arson is possible since the intent could be formed after, as well as before, the fire started.

Transferred Malice

If an accused, with the mens rea of a particular crime, does an act which causes the actus reus of the same crime, the accused is guilty even if the result was unintended. For example, if A, with the intent to kill B, shoots and kills C, thinking that C is B, then A has murdered C, even though A had no intention to kill C. Or, if A, intending to commit burglary, breaks into the wrong house, thinking it belongs to B, A is still guilty of burglary even though the house does not really belong to B.

The requirement is that the actus reus and the mens rea must be of the same crime. For example, if A is annoyed by crows in the garden and blasts at them with a shotgun, it would not be murder if A's neighbour happened to be in the garden at the time and was killed. A could be convicted of manslaughter, however, since this crime requires a different intention.

Motive

Intent is often thought to mean the same thing as motive, but they are very distinct from each other. If the accused commits the actus reus and has the mens rea of a crime, it is entirely irrelevant whether the accused had a good or a bad motive. Assume that

A kills an elderly relative B. A would be just as guilty of killing B, whether the motive was to spare B suffering from a painful illness or to inherit B's money.

This does not mean that motive is not "evidence." Motive is a question of fact which a jury may consider. Proved absence of motive is an important fact in favour of the accused and worthy of note in a charge to a jury. Conversely, proved presence of motive may be an important part of the Crown's case and the jury may hear it, notably on the issues of identity and intention.

Lewis v. The Queen
Supreme Court of Canada, 1979

The appellants Lewis and Santa Singh Tatlay were jointly charged with the murder of P. Sidhu, Tatlay's daughter, and her husband. The instrument which caused the deaths was an electric kettle rigged with dynamite in such a manner as to explode when plugged into an electric outlet. The kettle was sent to the couple by mail. It exploded with fatal results. The accused were found guilty and Lewis' appeal eventually reached the Supreme Court of Canada. It was based upon the sole question of whether the trial judge erred in failing to define "motive" and failing to direct the jury as to the concept of motive. The case was totally devoid of evidence of motive.

The Supreme Court held that motive was not proven as part of the Crown's case but neither was absence of motive proven by the defence. There was no clear obligation in law to charge the jury on motive. Lewis admitted mailing the package but denied making the bomb. He had never met the deceased and had no reason to get involved in a family dispute. Lewis was a miner with the skill and experience with dynamite needed to make the bomb. He could not explain why he drove to another community to mail the package. He also commented to another man to listen to the radio news for "something interesting."

The Supreme Court of Canada upheld the conviction of the two accused men.

Those Incapable of Crime

Some persons are held to be *doli incapax* — incapable of committing a crime. Examples of such persons include children, the insane, spouses in some instances, and the Crown. Insanity as a defence is discussed in more detail later in this unit.

With regard to children, the *Criminal Code* states:

12. No person shall be convicted of an offence in respect of an act or omission on his part while he was under the age of seven* years.

13. No person shall be convicted of an offence in respect of an act or omission on his part while he was seven years of age or more, but under the age of fourteen years, unless he was competent to know the nature and consequences of his conduct and to appreciate that it was wrong.

The law rejects completely any suggestion that children under the age of seven years have the ability to appreciate the nature of their actions so as to be criminally responsible. The law further expresses grave doubts that a person under the age of fourteen years could have such a criminal intent. The Crown may, however, introduce evidence to prove that a person under the age of fourteen was capable of knowing the nature and consequences of conduct engaged in, and knew that the conduct was wrong. There is considerable disagreement among jurists as to whether "wrong" means "legally wrong" or "morally wrong." Children of tender years might know the difference between right and wrong in a moral sense; but it seems unlikely that children would think in terms of "contrary to law" since they probably would have no idea of what the law was.

Husband and wife cannot be convicted of certain offences because of the special position of married persons. A husband and wife cannot conspire together. A married person cannot be an accessory for assisting his or her spouse to escape. Spouses cannot be charged with theft from each other while living together.

---

*Note that in 1984, the minimum age will be increased from seven years to twelve years.

Spouses cannot be convicted of certain sex offences if they take place in private between consenting persons.

In the Canadian system, the person of the Sovereign is exempt from prosecutions for the simple reason that since the courts are His or Her Majesty's courts, there is no court capable of exercising jurisdiction. This immunity can extend to Crown corporations. Although Atomic Energy Canada took an active part in an international, unlawful cartel which manipulated the price of uranium, the corporation and its officers were immune from prosecution. It was held in the case of the *CBC v. A.G. for Ontario* (Supreme Court of Canada, 1959) that the CBC could not be prosecuted for violating the *Lord's Day Act* by broadcasting on a Sunday. However, in *CBC v. The Queen* (1983), the Supreme Court of Canada unanimously held that the CBC was not immune from prosecution for publishing an obscene film. The court held that the CBC was not acting as an "agent of the Crown" at the time, but as an ordinary broadcaster.

Parties to an Offence: Counselling an Offence

The criminal law does not limit responsibility to the person who physically commits a criminal act. If such a limited view were accepted, then certain individuals could, with legal immunity, plan crimes for others to commit. The *Criminal Code* states:

21. (1) Every one is a party to an offence who
(a) actually commits it,
(b) does or omits to do anything for the purpose of aiding any person to commit it, or
(c) abets any person in committing it.
(2) Where two or more persons form an intention in common to carry out an unlawful purpose and to assist each other therein and any one of them, in carrying out the common purpose, commits an offence, each of them who knew or ought to have known that the commission of the offence would be a probable consequence of carrying out the common purpose is a party to that offence.

22. (1) Where a person counsels or procures another person to be a party to an offence and that other person is afterwards a party to that offence, the person who counselled or procured is a party to that offence, notwithstanding that the offence was committed in a way different from that which was counselled or procured.
(2) Every one who counsels or procures another person to be a party to an offence is a party to every offence that the other commits in consequence of the counselling or procuring that the person who counselled or procured knew or ought to have known was likely to be committed in consequence of the counselling or procuring.

The persons who are involved in an offence are generally classed into one of the following groups:

- *Principal offender:* The person having the most active role, usually the person who commits the actus reus.
- *Abettor:* A person who is present assisting or encouraging the principal offender at the time of the commission of the crime.
- *Counsellor:* One who advises the principal offender as to how to commit the crime.
- *Procurer:* A person who solicits the aid of others in taking part in the crime.

The attempt to commit a crime is punishable, although the punishment is normally less than if the crime was fully carried out.

An offence may be committed by any number of persons in these groups.

Mere presence at the scene of a crime is not sufficient to make a person party to it. Some specific act is needed: (1) an act which encourages the principal offender; (2) an act which facilitates the commission of the offence, such as keeping watch or enticing the victim away; or (3) an act which prevents or hinders interference with accomplishment of the criminal act, such as preventing the intended victim from escaping, or being ready to assist the principal offender. If B handed a gun to C, knowing that C had thoughts about shooting D, B would be a party to the offence if C shot D. It would be no defence if B genuinely hoped C would not do it.

Section 21 (2) makes each and every party guilty of every offence any party commits while carrying out the common purpose if the offence was a *probable consequence* of their common purpose. If three persons plan an armed robbery, and one of them commits murder during the robbery, all three are guilty of murder. The act of murder is a probable consequence to a serious offence such as armed robbery.

R. v. De Tonnancourt
Manitoba, 1956

Three men were hitch-hiking west from Winnipeg when they were offered a ride by Father Alfred Quirion. It was their intent to rob whoever picked them up. After a while, the men asked Father Quirion to stop and let them relieve themselves. De Tonnancourt claimed he told one of his companions, Paquin, that he did not want to go through with the robbery as Father Quirion was a nice person and had given them a ride on such a cold day. De Tonnancourt and Paquin testified that they agreed not to carry out the robbery, but the third man, Ferragne, did not. Ferragne said something to the effect, "We are going to do it," then shot and killed Father Quirion. All three men shared $90 taken from the deceased man's wallet. All were convicted of non-capital murder.

They appealed to the Manitoba Court of Appeal. De Tonnancourt and Paquin both appealed on the same grounds, that Ferragne had acted alone. In the summation to the jury, the trial judge had stressed that the jury should consider two points: (1) Whether there had been a common plan; and if so, (2) whether Paquin and De Tonnancourt had clearly indicated to Ferragne that they were dissociating themselves from the plan. The Court of Appeal held that the judge's charge was correct and that if the jury had found them all Guilty, the jury must have concluded that insufficient notice was given to Ferragne to call off the plan. A "mere mental change" or last minute hesitation was not enough.

Section 22 makes anyone who counsels or procures another person to commit an offence a party to the offence, even if the offence was committed in a way different from what was intended. The *Code* also makes a counsellor guilty of any offence counselled regardless of whether the offence was carried out according to instructions or not. If Jones counsels Smith how to carry out an armed robbery, and specifically warns Smith not to get nervous and shoot anyone, Jones is guilty of murder if Smith ignores the advice and kills someone during the robbery.

It is possible for the counsellor or abettor to be found Guilty, while the principal offender is found Not Guilty. This is particularly true where the principal offender lacked mental responsibility. Thus, where an adult sent a child into a building for the purpose of unlocking the door to admit the adult, the adult was convicted while the child was not.

A person who is an *innocent agent* cannot be convicted as a party to an offence. If Brown gives a medicine bottle to Smith and gives instructions to administer the medicine to Jones, Smith is innocent of any wrongdoing if it turns out the bottle contained poison. Smith was the means by which Brown committed the offence. An innocent agent must be truly unaware of any wrongdoing. The agent cannot escape liability by merely closing one eye and deliberately avoiding details of the offence in order to plead ignorance later.

Accessory after the Fact

A person may not be a party to an offence at the time it was committed, but may become involved in the offence later. Anyone who knows that a person has committed an offence must refrain from rendering any help whatsoever that might enable the offender to escape. This includes such things as providing food, shelter, money, transportation, or refusing to tell the police the whereabouts of the offender. Friendship or family ties do not excuse someone for aiding an offender. There is one exception, and this pertains to married persons. The *Criminal Code* states:

> **23. (1) An accessory after the fact to an offence is one who, knowing that a person has been a party to the offence, receives, comforts or assists him for the purpose of enabling him to escape.**
>
> **(2) No married person whose spouse has been a party to an offence is an accessory after the fact to that offence by receiving, comforting or assisting the spouse for the purpose of enabling the spouse to escape.**

A married person may assist his or her spouse after the commission of an offence. The law recognizes that a married person has a duty to remain loyal to his or her spouse regardless of the circumstances since married persons are considered in law as one person, united by marriage. It is significant to note that the law does not permit parents to assist their child to escape criminal liability. It may be hard for some parents to accept that they cannot protect their child from the law, no matter how devoted they might be to that child.

The question then arises whether it is an offence for a person who knows that a crime has occurred not to report that crime. Does a person become an accessory to a crime by remaining silent? The answer is no. At one time the common law made it an offence known as *misprision* for any person not to report a felony to a justice of the peace. Presently, there is no legal duty upon a person to report that an offence has taken place or may take place. The exception to this rule is the act of treason. Any person knowing that a person is about to commit treason must inform a justice of

the peace or other peace officer immediately to prevent that treason from taking place. Failure to report is an offence. However, there is no duty to report if the treason has already taken place. Some laws require that a report be made, but these are reports of occurrences rather than of offences. For example, in the situation of a traffic accident or a child in need of protection, a report from a person having the facts may be required.

It is an offence to falsely report a crime, e.g., to report that a crime has taken place, knowing that it has not.

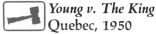 **Young v. The King**
Quebec, 1950

A police constable was murdered in the City of Montreal and the police were looking for Donald and Douglas Perreault in connection with the offence. The defendant, Young, met the Perreault brothers while driving outside Montreal and told them the police were looking for them. Then, according to the evidence, Young offered to hide them at a hunting camp in the woods. The Perreault brothers refused this offer. Young then advised them to avoid Montreal and get rid of their car or change the licence plates as the police had a complete description of the men and the car. The Perreault brothers did so and this made it more difficult for the police to apprehend them.

Young was charged as an accessory after the fact. He was convicted and appealed to the Quebec Court of Appeal which upheld the conviction saying:

> 66There can be no doubt the accused intended to assist the Perreaults to avoid apprehension. His offer to hide them was not accepted, but the information that their names were already known to the police constitutes assistance that would make more difficult their apprehension.99

The court held that any assistance given to a person known to be wanted by the police to hinder that person's capture was sufficient grounds for conviction as an accessory.

Attempts

The fact that a person was unable to carry out a crime because the law intervened or something went wrong does not mean that a crime has not taken place. It is unlawful to attempt a crime. The *Criminal Code* states:

> **23. (1) Every one who, having an intent to commit an offence, does or omits to do anything for the purpose of carrying out his intention is guilty of an attempt to commit the offence whether or not it was possible under the circumstances to commit the offence.**
>
> **(2) The question whether an act or omission by a person who has an intent to commit an offence is or is not mere preparation to commit the offence, and too remote to constitute an attempt to commit the offence, is a question of law.**

The penalty for attempts differs with the nature of the offence, but can result in imprisonment for up to fourteen years.

An attempt must be distinguished from mere preparation for a crime. The intent to commit the crime is not punishable by law, even if preparations have been made. Preparation consists of planning the crime and collecting the materials to use in the commission of the crime. The attempt comes into existence when the first step is taken to put the plan into effect.

Henderson v. The King
Supreme Court of Canada, 1948

Henderson was one of three armed men who drove towards a branch of the Royal Bank of Canada in Vancouver. Upon seeing a police car, the men drove away. They were under police observation and the police pursued them. In the ensuing gun battle, two police officers and one robber were killed. Henderson did not fire his gun, but was charged with murder resulting during an attempted armed robbery. In order for Henderson to be convicted, it was essential that the Crown prove there was an attempted robbery. Otherwise, Henderson would be exonerated from the shooting as it would be legally viewed as an independent act by the other two robbers. Henderson was convicted and his appeal eventually reached the Supreme Court of Canada which upheld the conviction. The court found that the three men had gone beyond the preparation stage and had proceeded with their plan. This constituted attempted armed robbery.

A difficult area of law is found in s. 24(1) of the *Code* which reads, "whether or not it was possible under the circumstances to commit the offence."

Suppose, for example, that an accused tried to pick an empty pocket. The intended objective of theft could not be achieved because of factual circumstances unknown to the accused—the fact that the pocket was empty. Should the accused be convicted?

There are three categories into which cases involving impossibility may fall:

(1) The accused attempts something knowing that it is impossible.

(2) The accused attempts something thinking that it is possible, but it turns out to be impossible because of facts unknown to the accused.

(3) The accused attempts something thinking it is unlawful but it turns out to be lawful. Although the accused had a criminal intent, no illegal act was committed.

In trying to reach fair and just decisions the courts have adopted a rather general rule. The court will ask: Did the accused's actions bring the accused any closer to success? If so, a conviction for the attempt will result. If not, an acquittal may result. In the example of the pickpocket, a conviction would be handed down because getting a hand into the victim's pocket, as opposed to merely standing beside the victim, brought the accused that much closer to success. However, to use another example, if an accused tried to open the combination of a bank safe but had no idea of what the combination was, a conviction would not result because the accused's turning of the dial was not bringing the accused any closer to success. In the third situation where someone commits an act thinking it is unlawful but it turns out to be lawful, that person cannot be convicted. For example, if G bought goods from D under the belief that they were stolen goods, G could not be convicted if it turned out that the goods were not stolen. Criminal intent alone could not convict G.

Haughton v. Smith
England, 1973

The accused was charged with attempting to receive and handle stolen goods. In fact, the goods had been recovered by the police earlier. The police then impersonated thieves, went through the act of delivering the goods to Smith, and then arrested him. The House of Lords held that the accused could not be convicted of the crime as it was a legal impossibility. The accused thought he was committing a crime at the time since he did not know he was dealing with police officers. The accused believed he was committing an offence, but the court must look at what the accused did, not what he thought he was doing. A person cannot be convicted of receiving stolen goods if the goods are not stolen:

66Where the accused has meticulously and in detail followed every step of his intended course, believing throughout that he was committing a criminal offence, [his own belief is not relevant] when in the end it is found that he has not committed a criminal offence because in law that which he planned and carried out does not amount to a criminal offence at all.99

Conspiracy

A *conspiracy* consists of an agreement between two or more persons to effect some unlawful purpose. The crime of conspiracy is complete as soon as the parties agree to commit the offence. It is immaterial that they never had the opportunity to put their plan into effect. The actus reus of conspiracy is the agreement, not the carrying out of the offence. A discussion is not sufficient to prove conspiracy. There must be an agreement and a serious intention to carry out the offence. Conspiracy is an offence even if the parties did not

know that what they agreed to was illegal. A husband and wife cannot conspire together.

Where two persons are tried for conspiracy, one cannot be convicted and the other acquitted. Almost always, conspirators are tried together, but it is permissible to try only one person for having conspired with "persons unknown" who may never be found or brought to trial.

With regard to conspiracy in general, the *Criminal Code* states:

> 423. (2) Every one who conspires with any one
> (a) to effect an unlawful purpose, or
> (b) to effect a lawful purpose by unlawful means, is guilty of an indictable offence and is liable to imprisonment for two years.

As well, the Criminal Code provides the following maximum possible penalties for some specific conspiracies.

Conspiracy	Maximum Possible Penalty
To commit murder	fourteen years
To bring false prosecution	ten years
To induce a woman to adultery	two years
To commit high treason	life imprisonment
To commit sedition	fourteen years
Against a trade union	summary conviction

It is unlawful to conspire in Canada to commit an offence outside of Canada. If two or more persons conspire outside of Canada to commit an offence within Canada, they will be prosecuted as if they had conspired in Canada.

R. v. O'Brien
Supreme Court of Canada, 1954

The accused, O'Brien, was convicted of conspiring to kidnap a woman named Joan Pritchard. He discussed the kidnapping with a man named Walter Tulley. Unknown to O'Brien, Tulley was never serious about the matter and when he realized O'Brien was serious, he informed the police. Tulley was not prosecuted. O'Brien was convicted on the basis of the charge which the trial judge gave to the jury in which the judge stated:

66Counsel for the accused has suggested that the offence is not complete, because Tulley, in his own evidence, said that he had at no time any intention of carrying out the agreement. I tell you as a matter of law, that the offence was complete if, in point of fact, the accused and Tulley did make the agreement which is charged against him, even though Tulley did make the agreement with no intention of carrying the agreement into effect.99

The British Columbia Court of Appeal held that this was misdirection and ordered a new trial. The Crown appealed to the Supreme Court of Canada which agreed with the Court of Appeal that the jury had been misdirected. The Supreme Court held that:

66There can be no conspiracy when one person wants to do a thing and the other does not want to do it.99

There must also be an intention to put the agreement into effect. Since Tulley had neither wanted nor ever intended to carry out the kidnapping, there had been no conspiracy.

The O'Brien case illustrates that a person cannot conspire with himself or herself. There must be at least one other, serious conspirator. In a case where an undercover police agent planned a crime with another person, it was held there was no conspiracy because the police agent had no intention of going through with the crime.

Strict and Absolute Liability

Ignorance of the law is no defence, for if it were it would be a perfect defence. Ignorance of the facts can be a defence in most instances and some criminal laws are worded in such a way as to specifically allow igno-

rance of the facts to be a defence. If a statute provides a penalty for a person "knowingly" or "wilfully" committing a prohibited act, then it can be a defence that the person did not know the prohibited act was being committed—that is, the person was ignorant of the facts. As an example, the Criminal Code makes it an offence to have possession of property knowing it was obtained by the commission of an offence. Thus, a person who buys stolen goods without knowing they are stolen, has a good defence to the charge.

However, most statutes are worded in such a way as to either rule out ignorance of the facts as a defence or are silent on the issue. If the law prohibits selling ground pork as ground beef, should it be a defence for the seller to claim lack of knowledge that the meat was pork? There would be a valid concern that "convenient ignorance" would become rampant in our society. Some laws appear to say bluntly: "Don't do X"! Anyone who does X can expect a penalty without being given a chance to explain why the act was committed. This type of law has been referred to for many years as strict liability and can work hardship at times—convicting people of wrongdoing where there is no sense of guilt. For example, in R. v. Pierce Fisheries (1971) the company was convicted of having a few undersized lobsters among thousands of kilograms of lobsters. The company was very diligent and tried not to let undersized lobsters go through its packing plant, but a few small ones inevitably slipped through. The company appealed to the Supreme Court of Canada which upheld the conviction on the basis that knowledge of the presence of the small lobsters was not required for a conviction. The only proof the Crown needed was that the lobsters were there.

In 1978 a major decision affecting hundreds of thousands of Canadians faced with possible conviction for strict liability offences arose out of a garbage dump.

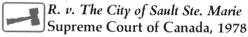

R. v. The City of Sault Ste. Marie
Supreme Court of Canada, 1978

The city and a commercial company were charged under the Ontario Water Resources Commission Act for polluting a creek. The city had caused a dump to be built from which waste found its way to the creek.

The city appealed the conviction on the basis that there was no intention to pollute and that it had not actually built the dump; the company had built it. The Supreme Court of Canada surprised the legal community by creating a third class of offences. Prior to this case it was generally understood that offences either required mens rea or were strict liability. The court decided that there were three classes:

- *Mens rea:* Offences consisting of some positive state of mind such as intent, knowledge, or recklessness. The use of words such as "knowingly" or "wilfully" helped identify such offences, but other offences could require mens rea in the absence of specific wording.

- *Strict liability:* Offences where the Crown does not have to prove the existence of mens rea, but the defence will be available that the accused reasonably believed in a mistaken set of facts which, if true, would render the act innocent. The accused may show that all reasonable steps were taken to avoid the particular event. The accused may demonstrate the existence of due diligence and reasonable care to establish freedom from fault. Public welfare offences would usually fall into this category.

- *Absolute liability:* Offences where it is not open to the accused to escape liability by showing freedom from fault. Such offences must contain specific wording by which the legislature has made it clear that a conviction required only proof of the prohibited act.

The court ordered a new trial so the city could have a chance to offer evidence of due diligence.

The court's decision in *Sault Ste. Marie* did not instantly produce a list of offences in each category. That is a task which will be left to the courts to interpret as cases come before them. As well, the legislatures may alter the wording of statutes if necessary to establish the desired effect of the law.

R. v. Chapin
Supreme Court of Canada, 1979

Chapin was duck hunting from a duck blind. A conservation officer found illegal bait (soy beans and wheat) near the blind and charged her under the *Migratory Birds Regulations.* The *Regulations* make it an offence to hunt birds within 400 m of any bait. It was agreed that Chapin did not put the bait there and did not know it was there. The Supreme Court of Canada held that it was an offence of strict liability and that Chapin could raise the defence of due diligence and ignorance of the facts. It would be impossible for a hunter to search the area around a duck blind in a circle with a radius of 400 m every time he or she wanted to hunt. The offence was not an offence of absolute liability and the accused had established the absence of fault and was acquitted.

Reviewing Important Points

1. The criminal laws of Canada are contained in the *Criminal Code* and other statutes and apply uniformly throughout Canada.
2. The criminal law does not limit responsibility for a criminal act to the person who physically commits it. Every one who counsels, plans, or aids someone else in committing a crime is a party to the offence.
3. The crime of conspiracy is complete as soon as the parties agree to commit the offence. Whether they actually commit it is immaterial.
4. A crime contains two basic elements: the actus reus and the mens rea. These generally translate to mean the prohibited act and the guilty mind.
5. An attempt to commit a crime occurs the moment the first step of a plan is put into effect.
6. A person cannot conspire alone. For a conspiracy to exist there must be two or more persons.
7. Offences are classed as mens rea, strict liability, or absolute liability. If an offence is strict liability the accused may raise the defences of due diligence, reasonable care, and ignorance of the facts.

Checking Your Understanding

1. Give two examples of persons who cannot be convicted of an offence.

2. Must the actus reus and the mens rea of a crime co-exist in time? Explain your answer.

3. What is "transferred malice"? Give an example of such an offence.

4. Does motive or lack of motive prove a person guilty or innocent? Explain your answer.

5. Must every party to an offence physically take part in the commission of the offence? Why or why not?

6. What is an "innocent agent"? Give an example of how someone might be an innocent agent.

7. What is an offence of absolute liability? How might such an offence be worded?

Legal Briefs

1. While walking in the park, B observes C beating and kicking D. B stops, watches a while, then walks on. B makes no effort to assist D and does not report the incident. Is B guilty of an offence?

2. G, while hunting bear, is attacked by a bull moose and shoots it. Provincial law makes it an offence to shoot a moose at any time or season. An offence?

3. H sets a leg-hold trap to catch a wolf, but unintentionally catches a dog. Instead of freeing the dog immediately, H asks around to find out who owns the dog. The owner is located four hours later; meanwhile, the dog has been suffering pain for an extra four hours. Cruelty to an animal?

4. R went with H to the home of J. R knew that H intended to assault J. While H assaulted J, R prevented a friend of J from assisting J and prevented the friend from calling the police. Is R guilty of an offence?

5. T wanted to sell narcotics to M. K acted as a "negotiator" between T and M as to price. K never handled any narcotics. The sale was made and T was arrested for trafficking in narcotics. What is K's position?

6. F went through a marriage ceremony with S. F was already married to C and believed the marriage to S was bigamy. He intended to desert S after getting her money. S learns about F's previous marriage and has him arrested. Unknown to F, C had died the previous year. An offence?

7. P wants to poison B and purchases a substance from H, an underworld figure. P administers the substance to B who suffers no harm. The substance is harmless. Has P committed an offence?

8. G buys a gun, purchases bullets, finds out when P will be home, calls a taxi, drives to the street where P lives, rings the doorbell, is allowed into the house by P's spouse, enters P's living room, takes out the gun, aims it at P, and pulls the trigger. The gun misfires because it has a defective firing pin. At what point, if any, did G attempt to kill P?

9. D and B plan to rob a store. They carry an air pistol that looks like a firearm but it is defective and cannot fire anything. They enter the store and threaten V, the owner. V pulls a gun from beneath a counter and fires at D but misses and kills a customer in the store. Are D and B guilty of homicide?

Applying the Law

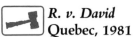

R. v. David
Quebec, 1981

The accused published and sold 4000 copies of a book called *The Cultivator's Handbook of Marijuana*. The early chapters contained information on the nature of the cannabis plant which would be useful to anyone who wanted to grow it. Later chapters contained suggestions about how the plant could be disguised not to look like marijuana. There was also an appendix telling the reader how to tell if marijuana had been treated with some other substance. The accused was charged with counselling an offence. The offence was the cultivating of marijuana contrary to the *Narcotic Control Act*. The Act only prohibits *unlicensed* cultivation of marijuana and the book could be helpful to persons legally growing the plant for medical research. All of the information in the book could be obtained from other sources.

The Quebec Court of Appeal agreed that the growing of marijuana by a person was unlawful only if the person did not have a licence. The court pointed out that under s. 7 of the Act the burden of proof was upon the accused to show that the book was intended for legitimate growers. It was doubtful that there were 4000 such licensed growers. Much of the book was also devoted to purchasing marijuana, not growing it. The preface of the book said: "Cannabis sativa is as old as the world. The era of dishonest business must pass away, and we think that this book is the best way of making this happen." The court took notice of the description on how to hide the plant and finally concluded that the author was recommending disobedience of the law as a way to force the law to be changed. In doing so, the accused was counselling and was therefore convicted.

Questions

1. Can all books about crime be viewed as counselling offences if the books describe how a crime can be committed?
2. Can a person counsel an offence by writing something as impersonal as a book? If a book tells how to make an atomic bomb, would this be counselling? (Such a booklet was published.)
3. The *Charter of Rights and Freedoms* affords everyone "freedom of the press." Do you think the accused would be protected by this if the case was heard today? Why or why not?
4. As the book did not contain any words specifically urging readers to start growing the plant, why did the court conclude that the author was counselling?

R. v. Joyce
British Columbia, 1978

At the accused's trial on a charge of murder, evidence was led that the accused, along with three others, had planned to rob two stores simultaneously to confuse the police. The accused supplied the guns. X, who did the killing, stated during the planning that if he was cornered he was going to use his gun and shoot it out. He said he would not be captured. The accused had anticipated and subsequently shared in the proceeds of the robbery.

The two groups of two men each started out for their designated targets, but when the accused and his partner arrived at their designated spot, they saw a police car parked nearby. For this reason, they could not go through with their robbery and just drove away. Across town, X and his partner carried out their robbery on schedule. During the robbery, a person was shot to death. On the following day, all four were arrested. The accused was convicted at trial of murder and appealed. The appeal was dismissed. The accused did not "withdraw" from the overall scheme. He did not communicate any intention to withdraw to the other members of the gang and shared in the proceeds from the other robbery. The fact that an unforeseen circumstance prevented him from carrying out "his" robbery did not break his connection with the robbery across town because both robberies were part of a common plan. The accidental killing was not outside the scope of the common purpose of the entire group.

Questions

1. Why was the accused "party" to murder?
2. As he did not take part in the robbery that involved the shooting, would this not suffice to say he had withdrawn from the plan? Why or why not?
3. What significance is there in the fact that the accused took a share of the proceeds of the other robbery? Would the case have had a different conclusion if the accused had not shared in the money?

You Be the Judge

1. The accused, a jeweller, faked a robbery; then, after tying himself up, he called for help. The police did not believe the story the accused told and searched the shop where they found money and jewels hidden. The accused then admitted that he faked the robbery because he was later going to make a claim to his insurance company. He was charged with attempted fraud.

However, he had not yet, at the time of arrest, submitted a claim to the insurance company. Would the accused be convicted?

2. Two men and a woman planned an armed robbery. One man waited in a car outside a convenience store. The woman entered the store to look around and gave a signal that no other customers appeared to be present. The second man entered the store and robbed the attendant. For reasons unknown, this man shot and killed the attendant; it was not part of the plan. All three accused escaped together in the car and divided the money. One man was later arrested and revealed the identity of his accomplices. All three were charged with the death of the attendant. Would all three be convicted?

3. The accused was charged with being an accessory after the fact. She assisted another woman, whom she knew was wanted by the police, to avoid capture for several weeks. The accused hid the fugitive and provided her with food. The woman was eventually captured while in the company of the accused who was driving her to another town. The woman was tried on the charge for which she had been wanted and was found Not Guilty. The Crown then proceeded to trial against the accused for being an accessory. The defence counsel asked that the charge be dismissed, arguing that if the wanted woman was not guilty of anything then the accused could not be an accessory. The Crown argued that they were separate matters and not tied in any way. Should the accused be tried?

4. A woman was to be a witness in a case against the accused's friend. The accused was present with the friend when the friend threatened the witness with harm if she testified. The accused said nothing during the entire course of the conversation which took place in the accused's car. Later, the woman asked the accused if the friend was the sort of person who would really carry out the threat that had been made. The accused said yes. Both the accused and the friend were charged with intimidating a witness. Should the accused be convicted?

5. A man held a grudge against another man and told the accused that he wanted to do something to annoy the other person or cause him financial loss. He said he was going to smash the other man's car windows or possibly spill a caustic chemical all over the seats of the car. The accused said he thought these were very crude ideas and that a more subtle approach would be to pour varnish into the gas tank of the other man's car. His friend was not aware of the effect of such a thing so the accused went on to explain that the varnish would mix with the gasoline and cause the total destruction of the car's engine. The man was caught putting a floor varnish into the car and revealed the source of the idea. The accused denied ever suggesting that the man actually use the varnish. He had just discussed the technical aspects of what the substance would do to a car engine. The accused was charged with counselling an offence. Should he be convicted?

6. The accused drove his car negligently and struck a pedestrian walking along the side of a road. The accused had no valid licence and panicked. He drove off, leaving the pedestrian lying partly on the paved surface of the road and partly off the road. Moments later another car came along and the driver did not see the body lying on the road until it was too late; the wheels of his car passed over the victim. Medical evidence supported the theory that the accused did not kill the victim but only injured him. The victim died when the second car passed over him. The accused was charged with causing the death of the victim. Should the accused be convicted?

7. The accused was present, in the apartment of the man with whom she lived, when another man entered brandishing a rifle. The intruder asked her where her boy friend was and the accused gave no answer. The man appeared very angry and intense and waved the gun around in front of her face. He again asked where her boy friend was and the accused pointed towards a bedroom and said, "He's in there." The man rushed into the bedroom and fired two shots, killing the boy friend instantly. He said to the accused as he left, "You saw nothing." The accused later left the apartment and did not go to the police; however, they learned from other persons in the building that she had probably been in the apartment at the time. When questioned, she told the whole story. She was charged with aiding and abetting the offence. Should she be convicted?

Chapter 4

Specific Offences

The specific offences discussed in this chapter are arranged alphabetically. This is not the way the *Criminal Code* is organized, but an alphabetical arrangement permits the reader to locate an offence more quickly.

Usually, each section includes the appropriate parts of the *Criminal Code* and cases which illustrate how they are applied. Don't let the wording of the laws put you off. Laws look confusing because they must try to be as accurate as possible and leave nothing open to question. This need for accuracy often results in lengthy and repetitive wording—there are a great many details that must be included. If you can't understand all the provisions of a law when you've read it, try looking at the cases that follow and then coming back to the law. Often this will clear up the problem.

Abortion

In 1938, a British doctor named Aleck Bourne had a pregnant fourteen-year-old girl brought to him. She had been raped and was in severe shock. He performed an abortion and then gave himself up to the police. He was tried and finally acquitted on the grounds that he had performed the operation in order to save the girl's sanity. It was on the findings of this trial that British law was based until all abortion was legalized in Britain in 1967. For Bourne, the result was unwanted, and he became a founding member of the Society for the Protection of Unborn Children in 1967. To some, the *Bourne* case marks the beginning of "abortion upon demand."

We are uncertain as to the first recorded abortions in history, but there is evidence that the Persian Empire had laws against abortion. We are also told that it was practised in Greece as well as in Rome and that it was resorted to without legal hindrance. Greek and Roman law provided that the unborn were the property of the father.

The common law for centuries permitted abortion prior to a certain time period, called the "quickening" which was the moment the fetus could be recognized as capable of some movement. Christian theology came to fix the point at forty days for a male and eighty days for a female. At the point of quickening the fetus obtained a soul and could no longer be aborted. This view persisted until the nineteenth century and the expression "quick with child" meant the woman was now beyond the point of quickening (or animation) and could not be aborted.

The *Criminal Code of Canada* specifies that it is not homicide to kill a child while still in the mother's womb. The *Code* accomplishes this by declaring that a child still in the womb is not a legal human being.

> **206. (1) A child becomes a human being within the meaning of this Act when it has completely proceeded, in a living state, from the body of its mother whether or not**
> **(a) it has breathed,**
> **(b) it has an independent circulation, or**
> **(c) the navel string is severed.**
> **(2) A person commits homicide when he causes injury to a child before or during its birth as a result of which the child dies after becoming a human being.**

The *Code* clarifies this definition by stating that injury to a child in the womb is still homicide if the child is alive when born, but subsequently dies. If the injury killed the child while still inside the mother, it is not homicide since the child must be in a living state when it proceeds from its mother.

Dehler v. Ottawa Civic Hospital
Ontario, 1979

Dehler brought an application to be appointed as representative of those unborn persons, or that class of unborn persons, whose lives might be terminated by abortion in the defendant hospital. He also asked for further relief that would effectively prohibit further abortions. The question before the court was whether Dehler, or anyone else, could represent the unborn. The High Court of Justice for Ontario held that he could not represent the unborn:

66What then is the legal position of an unborn child? Is it regarded in the eyes of the law as a person in the full legal sense? . . . The short answer to the question is no. While there can be no doubt that the law has long recognized fetal life and has accorded the fetus various rights, those rights have always been held contingent upon a legal personality being acquired by the fetus upon its subsequent birth alive and, until then, a fetus is not recognized as included within the legal concept of persons. **99**

Procuring a miscarriage, commonly referred to as abortion, is an offence distinguished from homicide. Laws against administering poisons to cause miscarriage can be traced back to as early as 1803 in England. The *Criminal Code* states:

251. (1) Every one who, with intent to procure the miscarriage of a female person, whether or not she is pregnant, uses any means for the purpose of carrying out his intention is guilty of an offence and is liable to imprisonment for life.

(2) Every female person who, being pregnant, with intent to procure her own miscarriage, uses any means or permits any means to be used for the purpose of carrying out her intention is guilty of an indictable offence and is liable to imprisonment for two years.

The means to procure the miscarriage can include a drug or other "noxious thing," an instrument of any kind, or manipulation of any kind. It should be noted that s. 251 (1) makes it an offence to use any means to carry out an abortion whether the female is pregnant or not. Therefore, if a person was charged with procuring the miscarriage of a female, it would be no defence to argue that she turned out not to be pregnant after all. Under s. 251 (2) a female can be convicted for procuring her own abortion.

Therapeutic Abortions

Abortion is a very sensitive subject, which involves social, moral, and religious values. Some groups want abortion on demand, while others want it prohibited except in cases where the mother's life is clearly in danger. Canadian law allows abortions under special circumstances. These are called "therapeutic abortions" and may be performed in an accredited hospital. The woman's doctor must make application to a hospital committee for therapeutic abortion. A majority of the members must agree that an abortion is necessary "because in their opinion the continuation of the pregnancy of the female person would, or would be likely to, endanger her life, or health and have so stated in a certificate given to the medical practitioner who will perform the abortion." The doctor who performs the abortion must not be a member of the committee. By a strict application of the law, the committee should deny an application from a woman who wants an abortion simply because she is unmarried or because she does not want any more children. Nor does it assist a woman who fears that the *child* will be unhealthy. The law considers only the woman's health.

This is the wording of the law, but critics complain that the law is applied unequally as some abortion committees are very easy about approving applications while others interpret the law very rigidly. Some hospitals have refused to have an abortion committee at all which means that a patient must go to another hospital, possibly in another city. The committee can consider both the mental and physical health of the mother and many abortions are approved under the mental health aspect which is very difficult for anyone to contradict.

Without a doubt, the most famous case in Canada pertaining to abortion is the following:

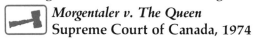

Morgentaler v. The Queen
Supreme Court of Canada, 1974

Henry Morgentaler, a Montreal doctor, was charged with performing an illegal abortion. He was acquitted by a jury, but the Quebec Court of Appeal reversed the decision and substituted a conviction. Morgentaler's appeal was dismissed by the Supreme Court of Canada. The defence relied upon s. 45 of the *Criminal Code* which reads:

> **45. Every one is protected from criminal responsibility for performing a surgical operation upon any person for the benefit of that person if**
> **(a) the operation is performed with reasonable care and skill, and**
> **(b) it is reasonable to perform the operation, having regard to the state of health of the person at the time the operation is performed and to all the circumstances of the case.**

The Supreme Court of Canada held that s. 251 was itself quite specific as to what constitutes a legal, therapeutic abortion, and that the defence of medical necessity was inapplicable. The court concluded that the Quebec Court of Appeal was quite correct in substituting a conviction for an acquittal.

Morgentaler went to prison but the case raised much controversy in Canada. One concern was over the fact that the Court of Appeal overruled a decision by a jury and, instead of ordering a new trial, entered a verdict of Guilty. The *Criminal Code* permitted a Court of Appeal to do this at that time. The *Code* has since been amended to deny a court the power to do this. It was felt that the jury system was too important to our legal system to permit the verdict of a panel of jurors to be replaced by the verdict of a panel of judges.

The controversy did not end since there was pressure upon the Attorney General to do justice to some-

one who had been found Not Guilty by a jury of peers. In 1976 the government set aside Morgentaler's conviction on the original charge and ordered a new trial. The second trial took place in 1976 and this time the defence was changed to that of "necessity" which was used in the *Bourne* case. A jury found Morgentaler Not Guilty and the Crown appealed to the Quebec Court of Appeal which upheld the acquittal. The court held that necessity was a defence to the charge if there was evidence to show that the operation was truly necessary to protect the life and health of the woman. The Crown applied for permission to appeal the case to the Supreme Court of Canada but that court denied permission and the case ended with Morgentaler's acquittal.

Summary of Canadian Abortion Law

In Canada, the present law regarding abortion could be summarized in this manner:

- A legal abortion must be carried out with the consent of an abortion committee in a registered hospital or clinic.
- A physician could perform an abortion without the consent of a committee·if the physician could prove "necessity" in so doing. There is no hard and fast rule as to what constitutes necessity. However, it could include being in a locality that has no committee, lack of time to obtain approval, or possibly psychiatric evidence that a committee's refusal to approve an application was clearly wrong.

Assault or Uttering Threats

At common law, assault and battery were once treated as two separate offences. Thus, assault was the application of force to a person, and battery was the inflicting of harm on the person. In tort law, this distinction is still maintained, but in criminal law the distinction has disappeared and the offences are combined under the single classification of assault. The *Criminal Code* defines assault as follows:

244. (1) A person commits an assault when
(a) without the consent of another person, he applies force intentionally to that other person, directly or indirectly;
(b) he attempts or threatens, by an act or gesture, to apply force to another person, if he has, or causes that other person to believe upon reasonable grounds that he has, present ability to effect his purpose; or
(c) while openly wearing or carrying a weapon or an imitation thereof, he accosts or impedes another person or begs.
(2) This section applies to all forms of assault, including sexual assault, sexual assault with a weapon, threats to a third party or causing bodily harm and aggravated sexual assault.
(3) For the purposes of this section, no consent is obtained where the complainant submits or does not resist by reason of
(a) the application of force to the complainant or to a person other than the complainant;
(b) threats or fear of the application of force to the complainant or to a person other than the complainant;
(c) fraud; or
(d) the exercise of authority.
(4) Where an accused alleges that he believed that the complainant consented to the conduct that is the subject-matter of the charge, a judge, if satisfied that there is sufficient evidence and that, if believed by the jury, the evidence would constitute a defence, shall instruct the jury, when reviewing all the evidence relating to the determination of the honesty of the accused's belief, to consider the presence or absence of reasonable grounds for that belief.

Common assault can be an offence punishable on summary conviction or by indictment. The maximum possible penalty is imprisonment for five years. The maximum possible penalty for assault with a weapon, or assault causing bodily harm is imprisonment for ten years. In this sense, "bodily harm" is hurt or injury to the victim that is more than a trifling injury in nature. It must be an injury that interferes with the victim's health or comfort.

Another form of assault is aggravated assault which can be punished by imprisonment for up to fourteen years. The term "aggravated" is not defined in the *Code*

but would suggest a very vicious form of assault. Assaulting a peace officer in the execution of the officer's duty can bring a prison sentence of five years. Sexual assault is a new offence added to the *Criminal Code* in 1982 and will be dealt with later in this chapter.

Particular attention should be given to s. 244(b) which states that the mere threat, by act or gesture, of doing bodily harm is grounds for conviction provided there are reasonable grounds to believe the assault could be carried out. However, assault does require an act or gesture. Thus, words alone cannot constitute assault. Uttering threats is a separate offence under the *Code*. If Smith threatens, by act or gesture, to thrash Brown, who is twice Smith's size, it is probably not assault since Smith has no apparent ability to carry out the threat. However, should Smith actually launch the assault against Brown, Smith is guilty of assault even if Brown promptly wins the fight.

A situation may arise where a person feels threatened by someone else, anticipating that an assault will be carried out in the near future. What should the intended victim do? Just wait until the assault takes place, or go and have it out with the other person first? A little-known section of the *Criminal Code* provides protection in such a case. Anyone who fears either personal injury to self, spouse, or child, or damage to property from some other person may lay an information before a justice. The justice may order that the defendant (suspected attacker) keep the peace and be of good behaviour for a period not exceeding twelve months. If the defendant will not agree to do so, imprisonment, for a term not exceeding twelve months, may result. If the defendant agrees to do so, but does not keep this agreement, the defendant is guilty of a summary conviction offence.

R. v. Byrne
British Columbia, 1968

The accused went to the box-office window of a theatre and said to the cashier, "I have a gun. Give me all the money or I'll shoot." The cashier did not hand over any money, and it was discovered that the accused did not have a gun. The cashier's evidence was that the accused had his coat over his arm so she could not see his hand. The accused was charged with assault, as well as other offences, but the British Columbia Court of Appeal held that this did not constitute assault. The court held:

> **"**Mere words, unaccompanied by any gesture do not constitute the act of assault.**"**

Had the accused pointed a finger or some imitation of a gun at the cashier, this would have been assault.

One defence to a charge of assault is consent. If the victim gave permission for the accused to touch him or her, then there is generally no assault. By the very nature of the activity, the players of certain sports give consent to other players to make physical contact during the game. This consent does not extend to fights between players which are outside the rules and the give-and-take of the game. Legal authorities have indicated in recent years that there is a lessened willingness to tolerate violence in sports.

Another defence is lawful correction. Certain persons have statutory authority to use force by way of correction. The *Code* states:

> **43. Every schoolteacher, parent or person standing in the place of a parent is justified in using force by way of correction toward a pupil or child, as the case may be, who is under his care, if the force does not exceed what is reasonable under the circumstances.**

Force cannot be used upon a pupil or child out of revenge or cruelty, but only "by way of correction."

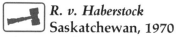 **R. v. Haberstock**
Saskatchewan, 1970

Three pupils on a bus on their way home from school on a Friday afternoon shouted names at the vice-principal who was in the school yard supervising activities. On Monday morning, the boys returned to school and the accused vice-principal saw them, walked up to them, and slapped each of them on the side of the face. The trial judge convicted the accused of assault, finding that one of the boys had not called him names at all and that the

assault was not for the purpose of correction but for retribution. The accused appealed and the Court of Appeal allowed the appeal. The court held that there were reasonable and probable grounds upon which the accused could have concluded that the innocent boy had engaged in conduct deserving of punishment and, in punishing him, the accused did so in the honest belief that he had participated in the name-calling. The accused was entitled to use force by way of correction. The force was reasonable under the circumstances and took place at the first reasonable opportunity. The court recognized that slapping on the face is not a customary manner of exercising discipline, but concluded that under such circumstances a parent would be excused and a teacher is entitled to the same protection.

The making of threats can also be a criminal offence. The *Code* states:

> **331. (1) Every one commits an offence who by letter, telegram, telephone, cable, radio, or otherwise, knowingly utters, conveys or causes any person to receive a threat**
> **(a) to cause death or injury to any person, or**
> **(b) to burn, destroy or damage real or personal property, or**
> **(c) to kill, maim, wound, poison or injure an animal or bird that is the property of any person.**
> **(2) Every one who commits an offence under paragraph (1) (a) is guilty of an indictable offence and is liable to imprisonment for ten years.**
> **(3) Every one who commits an offence under paragraph (1) (b) or (c) is guilty of**
> **(a) an indictable offence and is liable for imprisonment for two years, or**
> **(b) an offence punishable on summary conviction.**

In *R. v. Nabis* (1974), the Supreme Court of Canada held that s. 331(1) (a) does not apply to threats made face to face. The threat must be conveyed by some other means. In *R. v. Carons* (1978), the Alberta Supreme Court held that it was irrelevant if the victim did not realize that a threat had been made. In that case a police officer overheard the threat while listening on an extension phone. The victim said she did not take it to be a threat but the court accepted the police officer's version of what was said. In *R. v. Henry* (1981), a prisoner at a correctional centre said to several persons that he would "kill a policeman" but did not identify any particular officer. The Ontario Court of Appeal held that the threat was not specific, and that it was made face to face with no suggestion that a message be carried to some victim.

An "idle" threat is not a threat. If B says to C, "One of these days I'm going to settle this with you," it is an expression of hostility more than a threat.

An offence similar to assault is *intimidation*. It is an offence for someone to try to compel another person either to abstain from doing anything which that person has a lawful right to do, or to do anything which that person has a lawful right to abstain from doing. Prohibited tactics include: using violence or threats to the person, or to the person's spouse or children; injuring the person's property; threatening the person's relatives in Canada or elsewhere; persistently following the person from place to place; besetting or watching the person's house; and using other similar tactics. The intimidation section of the *Code* can be applied to many situations including labour disputes. This section also prohibits blocking a place of work or a highway.

Automobile Offences

If you were to line up a knife, gun, bottle of poison, and an automobile and ask, "Which weapon is most often used to commit a crime?" the automobile would be the correct answer. Driven by a careful driver, the automobile is a useful tool. Driven by anyone less than that, it kills, maims, destroys and threatens thousands of people every year, and drivers are sent to jail by the hundreds.

The conduct of motor vehicles on the highway is governed by each province. Speed limits, driver testing, licence plates for the car, mechanical safety requirements, insurance—these matters come under provincial, not federal laws. In Ontario, the most sig-

nificant items are covered by the *Motor Vehicle Act* and the *Highway Traffic Act*.

The federal law comes into the picture when the automobile is misused.

Criminal Negligence and Dangerous Driving

The offence of criminal negligence or dangerous driving can be severely punished. The *Criminal Code* states:

233. (1) Every one who is criminally negligent in the operation of a motor vehicle is guilty of
    (a) an indictable offence and is liable to imprisonment for five years, or
    (b) an offence punishable on summary conviction.
    (2) Every one who, having the care, charge or control of a vehicle that is involved in an accident with a person, vehicle or cattle in the charge of a person, with intent to escape civil or criminal liability fails to stop his vehicle, give his name and address and, where any person has been injured, offer assistance, is guilty of
    (a) an indictable offence and is liable to imprisonment for two years, or
    (b) an offence punishable on summary conviction.
    (3) In proceedings under subsection (2), evidence that an accused failed to stop his vehicle, offer assistance where any person has been injured and give his name and address is, in the absence of any evidence to the contrary, proof of an intent to escape civil and criminal liability.
    (4) Every one who drives a motor vehicle on a street, road, highway or other public place in a manner that is dangerous to the public, having regard to all the circumstances including the nature, condition and use of such place and the amount of traffic that at the time is or might reasonably be expected to be on such place, is guilty of
    (a) an indictable offence and is liable to imprisonment for two years, or
    (b) an offence punishable on summary conviction.

Note that subsection (2) concerns the offence which most people refer to as "hit and run." This is certainly a foolish act. Leaving the scene of an accident is, practically speaking, an admission of guilt, even though the driver may not necessarily be at fault.

If we look again at the wording of subsections (1) and (4), we shall see that in spite of similarities, there is an important difference between them. The first mentions criminal negligence. Section 202 of the *Code* states:

> **Everyone is criminally negligent who in doing anything, or in omitting to do anything, that it is his duty to do, shows wanton or reckless disregard for the lives or safety of other persons.**

Duty here means a duty imposed by law, not a moral duty.

The heart of this definition is "wanton or reckless disregard for the lives and safety of others." Although this sounds simple enough, it is not an easy matter to prove. Speeding, racing, and showing off—while being poor driving habits and illegal—do not necessarily constitute criminal negligence. Poor driving habits or bad judgment may cause a serious accident, yet criminal negligence still may not be proven. To prove criminal negligence, the Crown must show that the driver was aware that the lives and safety of others were being risked and was completely unconcerned about the other people. The driver taking a risk may perhaps be quite worried about what might happen if the risk goes wrong, and may be working out mentally how to avert trouble by taking to the ditch, etc. The driver who just plain goofs and pulls out at the wrong time, as the result of lack of attention, cannot be said to be aware that others are in jeopardy and to be wantonly disregarding their safety. One careless act or mistake does not demonstrate criminal negligence. A continuing series of such acts may demonstrate it.

Because criminal negligence is not easy to prove, drivers are more often charged under subsection (4) than subsection (1). This covers "dangerous driving" which is less stringent and easier to prove. Many things a driver does could be called dangerous. Excessive speeding, racing, falling asleep at the wheel, have all been held as sufficient cause for a dangerous driving conviction. In many respects, it is a catch-all. It is worded so generally that any seriously incorrect action behind the wheel could lead to a conviction. It also serves as a lesser included offence for subsection (1). This

means that if the Crown cannot get a conviction under subsection (1), it may still obtain a conviction under subsection (4).

The distinction between criminal negligence and dangerous driving can have important consequences when it comes to the possible punishment. Criminal negligence causing death can result in a maximum sentence of life imprisonment. If injury occurred, the penalty can be up to ten years' imprisonment. Dangerous driving, on the other hand, carries a penalty of only a possible two-year prison term.

Dangerous driving was first made an offence under the *Criminal Code* in 1938. It was dropped in 1954 because it was felt that provincial laws dealing with careless driving were adequate. Certain cases arose which suggested that dangerous driving should be restored as a criminal offence and in 1960 it was restored in the *Criminal Code.* There appears to be no clear distinction between dangerous driving under the *Criminal Code* and careless driving under provincial laws.

For example, the Ontario *Highway Traffic Act* makes it an offence to drive "without due care and attention or without reasonable consideration for other persons using the highway." How does this definition differ from that of dangerous driving? Both require some degree of carelessness, fault, or negligence. This is true even if the driver is doing the best job possible, but is an incompetent driver. It has been suggested that the primary difference is that a person could be charged with careless driving even in a very remote place where it could be shown there was no danger to anyone because no one was around. Dangerous driving, on the other hand, requires evidence that someone was endangered.

Several cases have also raised the question of whether there is a difference between "advertent" and "inadvertent" negligence. These are not easy terms to define, but advertent negligence generally means that the person was aware of what he or she was doing, while inadvertent suggests unawareness. Hence the question, "Was the person aware that he or she was driving negligently or dangerously?" The question can then be extended to ask whether mens rea is an element of the offence of criminal negligence or dangerous driving. Must the Crown prove that the driver knew or intended to drive in such a manner? Generally, the courts have concluded that the nature of criminal negligence is such that advertent negligence is required, but that dangerous driving requires only inadvertent negligence. Careless driving falls below both of them and requires only inadvertent negligence. However, it is wrong to say that *intent* is necessary to prove any of these offences. This is putting too strong a meaning upon mens rea in this area of law.

R. v. Binus
Supreme Court of Canada, 1968

The accused was convicted of dangerous driving and appealed to the Ontario Court of Appeal. He contended that the trial judge erred in instructing the jury on what constituted dangerous driving. The judge had told the jury that mens rea was not involved and they need not consider it. The defence claimed that unless it could be shown that the accused had intended to drive in a dangerous manner, he could not be convicted. The Court of Appeal held that while the trial judge had not fully explained dangerous driving to the jury, there were no grounds for a new trial, and the appeal was dismissed. The court stated:

> **"**In the case at the bar, the trial judge ought to have given the jury clearer direction than he did as to what constitutes dangerous driving, especially in view of its relation to the greater offence of criminally negligent driving and to the lesser offence of careless driving under the provincial law. He ought to have told them that on a charge of dangerous driving it was not necessary for the Crown to establish that the accused intended to jeopardize the lives or safety of others by the way he drove ... but it was incumbent on the Crown to prove beyond a reasonable doubt that (1) the accused did not drive with the care that a prudent person would exercise ... and (2) the accused in failing to exercise such care, in fact, endangered the lives or safety of others whether or not harm resulted.**"**

The Supreme Court of Canada upheld the decision of the Ontario Court of Appeal.

Following a conviction under the *Criminal Code*, the provincial authorities may decide to suspend or cancel the accused's driving permit. As well, the provinces may apply penalties for driving without a licence, but the Supreme Court of Canada held in *R. v. Boggs* (1981) that driving without a licence cannot be a criminal offence.

R. v. Gaudreault
Ontario, 1978

The accused drove a car onto a patio in front of a high school. Another student climbed on the hood of the car and the accused put the car into reverse and gunned the motor. The second student fell from the car and suffered injury. The issue of the case was whether the accused was driving dangerously in a "public place." The Ontario Court of Appeal upheld a conviction saying that the patio was a place to which the public had ready access and was therefore a public place.

The courts have been fairly consistent in holding that a passenger is a member of the public and that the driver carrying passengers can be convicted of dangerous driving even if no other traffic or pedestrians are nearby. Thus, if a driver operates a vehicle in a dangerous manner in a remote area, far removed from other traffic, the driver can still be convicted for endangering any passengers in the car.

Impaired Driving

The Criminal Code also provides penalties for the offence of impaired driving. The drunk driver is a continuing problem in Canada. The *Criminal Code* states:

> **234. (1) Every one who, while his ability to drive a motor vehicle is impaired by alcohol or a drug, drives a motor vehicle or has the care or control of a motor vehicle, whether it is in motion or not, is guilty of an indictable offence or an offence punishable on summary conviction and is liable**
> **(a) for a first offence, to a fine of not more than two thousand dollars and not less than fifty dollars or to imprisonment for six months or to both;**

(b) for a second offence, to imprisonment for not more than one year and not less than fourteen days; and
(c) for each subsequent offence, to imprisonment for not more than two years and not less than three months.

It is not necessary for the accused to be driving the vehicle to be convicted under s. 234. The *Code* requires only that the accused had care or control. An intention to drive or set the vehicle in motion is not something the Crown must prove.

R. v. King
Supreme Court of Canada, 1962

The Crown appealed from a decision of the Ontario Court of Appeal which had overturned the accused's conviction at trial on a charge of impaired driving. The accused had two teeth extracted and was given an injection of sodium pentothal as a pain killer. The dentist stated that the patient signed a form which contained the words, "Patients are cautioned not to drive after anaesthetic until head clears." The accused said he felt perfectly normal when he walked to his car. Later, he drove into another vehicle at an intersection. Police found the accused staggering about, unable to remember anything. The accused's sole defence rested upon his claim that he had no knowledge of the effect of the drug and he was unaware of the fact that he was impaired when he took the responsibility to drive his car. The Supreme Court of Canada found the accused Not Guilty. The court held that there was a reasonable doubt as to whether the accused realized when he got into his car that he was or might become impaired. The existence of mens rea could not be proved, and the Court of Appeal had not erred in holding that mens rea was an essential element of the offence of driving while impaired.

R. v. King is considered an important case in that it determined that mens rea is an element of the offence of impaired driving. However, the case clearly distinguishes between an accused who unknowingly was impaired and an accused who voluntarily consumed alcohol or drugs and must therefore be penalized if he or she later drives.

Breathalyzer Tests

Section 234.1(1) of the *Code* permits an officer to demand a roadside breath test if the officer reasonably suspects a driver of having alcohol in the body. It is an offence to refuse to comply with this demand. The tester does not measure the amount of alcohol in the blood, but has three possible readings: PASS, WARN, FAIL. If the driver fails the test, an offence has not been committed at this point, but the driver will be required to take the complete test at a police station. The Supreme Court of Canada has held that a driver does not have any right to consult a lawyer before taking the roadside test because the driver is in no jeopardy of being convicted of anything at this stage.

The machine used by most police departments to test alcohol levels in the blood is the Borkenstein Breathalyzer. Its use is authorized in the following section of the *Code*:

235. (1) Where a peace officer on reasonable and probable grounds believes that a person is committing, or at any time within the preceding two hours has committed, an offence under section 234 or 236, he may, by demand made to that person forthwith or as soon as practicable, require him to provide then or as soon thereafter as is practicable such samples of his breath as in the opinion of a qualified technician referred to in subsection 237 (6) are necessary to enable a proper analysis to be made in order to determine the proportion, if any, of alcohol in his blood, and to accompany the peace officer for the purpose of enabling such samples to be taken.

Refusal to comply with the demand to take the test, without reasonable excuse, is an offence. The possible penalties are the same as contained in s. 234(1).

Failing the Borkenstein test could result in a conviction. Therefore, the Supreme Court of Canada has held that a driver does have the right to consult a lawyer before taking this test because, at this point, the driver is in possible jeopardy. However, the driver cannot use this right as a means of trying to stall the test and the officer can insist that testing proceed in order to complete the tests within the required two hours.

A key phrase in s. 235 is "reasonable and probable grounds." The officer must have a reason for demanding a breath test. Another important word is "demand." The officer must not merely request that the driver take a test; the officer must demand it.

Two tests must be given with a complete pause of fifteen minutes between tests. Thus, most officers will wait at least sixteen minutes between tests. If it is found that the proportion of alcohol in the driver's blood exceeds 80 mg of alcohol in 100 mL of blood (a 0.08, or higher, reading), the driver is guilty of an indictable offence or an offence punishable upon summary conviction. The possible penalties are the same as contained in s. 234 (1).

No person is required to give the police a sample of blood or urine. However, if a person has been injured in an accident and is bleeding, a test can be made of this blood without the person's permission.

A controversial area is whether police can stop cars just to determine if the driver had been drinking. In

Ontario, police carried out spot checks of drivers under a program called R.I.D.E. —Remove Intoxicated Drivers Early. The Ontario Court of Appeal held in *R. v. Dedman* (1981) that the police could stop cars under their powers under the *Highway Traffic Act*. Once the motorist had stopped (the court said "voluntarily") there was nothing to stop the officer from smelling the driver's breath. The *Dedman* case contrasts with the following case:

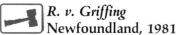

R. v. Griffing
Newfoundland, 1981

When a police officer stopped the accused to check his driver's permit and insurance, the officer noted the smell of alcohol. The officer demanded a breath test, but the accused refused. The officer started to write an appearance notice when the accused suddenly slammed the car door on the officer's knee and struck the officer in the face. The accused was charged with assaulting the officer while in the course of police duties. The court held that the officer had no legal authority to stop the vehicle in the first place and thus was not acting within the course of police duties. The accused was convicted of common assault but not of assaulting an officer.

The Supreme Court of Canada has not ruled on either *Dedman* or *Griffing*. It is possible that when it does so the court may also take into consideration the wording of s. 8 of the *Charter of Rights and Freedoms* which states that "Everyone has the right to be secure against unreasonable search or seizure."

A difficult question is whether an accused should be charged with impaired driving (s. 234) *and* driving with more than the allowable amount of alcohol in the blood (s. 236), arising from the same incident. Both the British Columbia and Quebec Courts of Appeal have held that the accused may be convicted of both offences. However, the practice of many Crown Attorneys is to charge an accused with both offences because, too often, accused persons find legal defences to the breathalyzer test. If the accused is convicted of one charge,

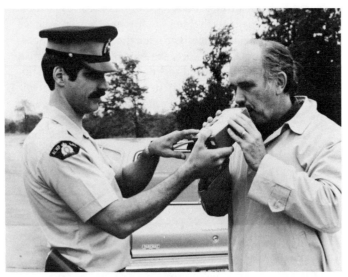

A police officer may demand that a driver take a roadside breath test if the officer has reason to believe the motorist is impaired.

the Crown will usually withdraw the other. Most courts accept the possibility that an accused could be convicted of both impaired driving and refusal to take a breathalyzer test.

Defences to charges under s. 236 include errors in administering the tests, consumption of the alcohol after the time of driving, or failure of the police to serve the accused with copies of the test certificates. A more important defence is found in the wording of s. 237 (1) (a) which states:

> **(1) In any proceedings under section 234 or 236,**
> **(a) where it is proved that the accused occupied the seat ordinarily occupied by the driver of a motor vehicle, he shall be deemed to have had the care or control of the vehicle unless he establishes that he did not enter or mount the vehicle for the purpose of setting it in motion;**

To expand upon this point, if the accused was behind the wheel when the officer approached the car, there is a presumption that the accused had care and control. The accused is permitted to introduce evidence to try to show that he or she was there for some reason other than putting the vehicle in motion (e.g., running the heater to stay warm). This is a matter of credibility, of course. If the judge does not believe what the accused says, a conviction will most likely follow. However, if the judge does believe the accused's explanation of why he or she was behind the wheel, does that mean the accused *must* be acquitted? In *Ford v. The Queen* (1982), the Supreme Court of Canada said "No." The court held that if the accused successfully rebuts the presumption in s. 237 (1), the Crown may still introduce other evidence to show care or control. Ford had been in and out of several cars during a drinking party and when apprehended was running his motor and sitting behind the wheel. He argued that he was just running the heater and that someone else would drive his car home later. The P.E.I. Court of Appeal, supported by the Supreme Court of Canada, held that even though the Crown could not rely upon s. 237 (1) it could introduce other evidence and obtain a conviction.

Temporary Suspension

Alberta and Ontario have enacted provincial laws that permit a police officer to temporarily suspend the driver's permit of a driver under the influence of alcohol. The Ontario law provides that if a roadside test activates the "Warn" light on the tester, the officer may suspend the permit for twelve hours and compel the driver to have the vehicle towed to a storage area. The "Warn" light normally activates around the 0.05 reading on a breathalyzer. The Act has been criticized as broadening police powers and effectively lowering the federal limit of 0.08 to 0.05. While there is no fine involved, the cost of towing the car can be viewed as a penalty. Supporters of the Act are pleased with a process that takes impaired drivers off the road even though they may be just below the legal limit. It is very likely that the Alberta or Ontario law will be tested in the courts as an infringement of the *Charter of Rights and Freedoms* which states that every person has the right not to be arbitrarily detained.

Break and Enter

In most cases there is no confusion about whether or not the accused broke and entered a building. This is referred to as "burglary" in everyday language. In certain situations, however, the matter may not be so simple. What is the exact meaning of break? What constitutes entry? If a person fraudulently obtains a key to enter a place to steal things, did the person break in? The *Criminal Code* defines "break" as breaking any part or opening any thing that is used or intended to be used to close or to cover an internal or external opening. The *Code* further defines "entry" as insertion of any part of the body inside the building. Entry also includes shoving any instrument inside, such as a hook. With regards to break and enter, the *Code* states:

> **306. (1) Every one who**
> **(a) breaks and enters a place with intent to commit an indictable offence therein,**
> **(b) breaks and enters a place and commits an indictable offence therein, or**

(c) breaks out of a place after
   (i) committing an indictable offence therein, or
   (ii) entering the place with intent to commit an indictable offence therein,
is guilty of an indictable offence and is liable
   (d) to imprisonment for life, if the offence is committed in relation to a dwelling-house, or
   (e) to imprisonment for fourteen years, if the offence is committed in relation to a place other than a dwelling-house.
   (2) For the purposes of proceedings under this section, evidence that an accused
   (a) broke and entered a place is, in the absence of any evidence to the contrary, proof that he broke and entered with intent to commit an indictable offence therein; or
   (b) broke out of a place is, in the absence of any evidence to the contrary, proof that he broke out after
      (i) committing an indictable offence therein, or
      (ii) entering with intent to commit an indictable offence therein.

For the purposes of s. 306 "place" means a dwelling-house, a building or any part of it, a railway vehicle, vessel, aircraft, or trailer, or a pen or enclosure where animals are kept for breeding or commercial purposes.

Note that breaking *out* of a place is deemed to be break and enter. This would include the actions of a person who entered a place lawfully, hid until the building was locked, then stole something and broke out to escape. If a person obtains entrance by such means as a stolen key, or collusion with another person who purposely left a door open, this would be break and enter. Generally, if a person entered without lawful justification or excuse, by a permanent or temporary opening, the burden of proof lies upon the accused to show that break and enter was not committed.

An essential ingredient of the offence of break and enter is the intent of the wrongdoer. It must be shown that the accused entered for the purpose of committing an indictable offence. The difficulty of proving such an intent caused Parliament to enact s. 306(2) which states that evidence that the accused broke and entered is, in the absence of any evidence to the contrary, proof that the accused intended to commit an

The offence of breaking and entering a dwelling house is punishable by imprisonment for ten years.

indictable offence. This is an example of a reverse onus clause casting a burden upon the accused to explain intent. Failure to do so will probably result in conviction.

 ### R. v. Proudlock
Supreme Court of Canada, 1978

The accused boarded with Mark Shields, above the restaurant owned by Shields' mother. One night the accused entered the restaurant by putting a ladder against an outside wall and breaking a window. He was seen by a maintenance worker. Upon arrest, he told the police he had no reason for entering. He repeated this at trial, saying "I don't know why I did it." He added that he would not steal anything. The trial judge did not find Proudlock's testimony to be in the least bit believable. The defence counsel argued that Proudlock had offered "evidence to the contrary" as required in s. 306(2) (a). The issue which the Supreme Court had to decide was whether evidence that was not believable was evidence to the contrary. The court held that evidence to the contrary was believable evidence only. If the trial judge did not believe the evidence given, it was viewed the same as no evidence at all, and the statutory presumption operated to convict the accused.

Dwelling-Houses

The *Code* makes it a separate offence for a person to enter a dwelling-house for the purpose of committing an indictable offence. This could be stretched to include gaining admittance to a house under false pretences. It could include walking into a house through an unlocked door. The *Code* reads:

> **307. (1) Every one who without lawful excuse, the proof of which lies upon him, enters or is in a dwelling-house with intent to commit an indictable offence therein is guilty of an indictable offence and is liable to imprisonment for ten years.**
> **[Section 307 (2) contains a reverse onus clause similar to that of section 306 (2).]**

As mentioned, s. 307 also contains a reverse onus clause putting the burden of proof upon the accused to explain his or her presence within that dwelling-house. Thus, where an accused gained admission to a house by fraudulently pretending to be a government inspector searching for the source of a transmission that was interfering with radio reception in the area, the court held that unless proven otherwise the accused entered that house for the purpose of committing an indictable offence.

Lesser Offences

Entering a building without lawful authority is not always break and enter. The accused could be charged merely with trespass. This is due to the wording of s. 306 which indicates that the purpose of entering must be to commit an indictable offence within. Assume that Brown and Smith are evicted from a night club for unruly behaviour. Since they cannot get past the person at the door, they go round to the rear of the club and break in through a window to join their friends inside. They would not be convicted of break and enter because their purpose for entering was not to commit an indictable offence. A drunk found sleeping in the basement of a church was deemed not to have entered for the purpose of committing an indictable offence and was acquitted on a charge of break and enter.

A person charged with break and enter could be found guilty of a lesser included offence, that of possession of housebreaking tools. There is no precise list of what tools could be used for such a purpose — screwdrivers, iron bars, glass cutters, and many other devices could be used. This does not mean possession of a screwdriver is illegal. However, the *Criminal Code* places the burden on the accused to prove that housebreaking was not intended. A person found at the rear of a store with a large screwdriver at about 2:00 a.m. was convicted of possession of housebreaking tools.

Where the Crown is unsure of a conviction for break and enter, it may prefer a lesser charge such as trespass or theft. The accused may try to avoid conviction for break and enter by pleading Guilty to one of the lesser offences.

R. v. Dobson
British Columbia, 1962

The accused, who was an employee of a clothing store, wanted to steal some valuable items of clothing. He placed a piece of plastic between a rear door and the door jam so that while the door appeared to be closed (and locked) it could be opened from the outside. He returned at night and entered the store through the rear door, but was arrested before he could carry off the items of clothing. The charge against the accused was break and enter, but the accused entered a plea of attempted theft. The court convicted the accused of break and enter, holding that the piece of plastic used to make it possible to open the door would fit within the meaning of "instrument" and that he had entered without lawful justification.

Criminal Negligence

Carelessness or indifference towards the lives and safety of other persons is not permissible. It may lead to a charge of *criminal negligence*. The *Criminal Code* makes it an offence to behave in a manner that shows this carelessness or indifference.

> 202. (1) Every one is criminally negligent who
> (a) in doing anything, or
> (b) in omitting to do anything that it is his duty to do, shows wanton or reckless disregard for the lives or safety of other persons.
> (2) For the purposes of this section, "duty" means a duty imposed by law.
> 203. Every one who by criminal negligence causes death to another person is guilty of an indictable offence and is liable to imprisonment for life.
> 204. Every one who by criminal negligence causes bodily harm to another person is guilty of an indictable offence and is liable to imprisonment for ten years.

We have already encountered criminal negligence in our discussion on automobile offences and probably most cases of criminal negligence involve motor vehicles. However, criminal negligence can occur in many other situations.

In a charge of criminal negligence, it is not necessary to prove that what the accused did was in itself unlawful. The two main elements of proof are that (1) the accused had a legal duty to perform, which was not done, and (2) by a wrongful act or omission the accused showed a wanton or reckless disregard for others. One problem with criminal negligence cases is that negligence is also a tort and the general elements of proof bear some similarity. However, it is a well-accepted fact that the proof required is not the same. Negligence sufficient to create civil liability is not necessarily sufficient to convict a person of criminal negligence.

A charge of criminal negligence does not require that someone was hurt or killed. It requires only that the accused was wanton or reckless towards others. Since this involves basically an attitude towards others as much as a behavioural pattern, it

has been held that mens rea is an essential element of the charge. This does not suggest that the accused knew or intended to harm someone, but only that the accused knew what was being done at the time the act was committed, and showed no regard for the possibility that other persons were being gravely endangered.

 ## R. v. Coyne
New Brunswick, 1958

The accused was convicted of criminal negligence and appealed to the New Brunswick Court of Appeal. The facts of the case are that he was walking along a road in a wooded area carrying a rifle when he met a woman named Devers who told him she had been looking for some boys. Later, the accused said he saw three objects he believed to be deer and shot at them. The moving objects were the boys and a bullet from Coyne's rifle grievously wounded one of them. At the time, the wounded boy was wearing a red-checkered shirt, and another boy was wearing a red hunting jacket. The distance between the accused and the boys was estimated to be 200 feet (60 m). The trial judge stated:

66In my opinion an ordinary prudent man would have made sure he was firing at a deer.... I cannot but hold the accused, before firing his rifle, omitted to take the necessary precaution required by law.**99**

The Court of Appeal upheld the conviction. It was not enough that the accused believed he was shooting at a deer. The fact remained that the firing of the rifle was intentional, not accidental. The court emphasized that *honest negligence is not a defence.* The court concluded that the accused man's conduct showed a reckless disregard for the lives and safety of others.

In the case of *R. v. Coyne*, the defence was using the argument that the accused had "honestly" believed he saw deer. There was no intent on his part to endanger or harm a human being. Thus, the defence contended, without intent there is no mens rea and the accused should not be convicted. The court rejected this defence, holding that mens rea existed in the intentional act of shooting, and that was enough. It was not necessary to prove that Coyne intended to shoot at someone, but only that he was reckless as to the object at which he was shooting.

Another section of the *Criminal Code* deals with negligence by medical practitioners, or persons who hold themselves out to have medical skills. While doctors can be sued in tort for negligence (malpractice), they can also be charged criminally.

> **198. Every one who undertakes to administer surgical or medical treatment to another person or to do any other lawful act that may endanger the life of another person is, except in cases of necessity, under a legal duty to have and to use reasonable knowledge, skill and care in so doing.**

It is a doctor's duty to have the degree of knowledge, skill, and care possessed and exercised by other members of the profession under similar circumstances. The doctor must use generally accepted medical techniques. The law does not demand perfection and there is no liability upon a doctor if another doctor claims he or she would have demonstrated greater skill and knowledge. It is no defence that the accused sincerely wanted to help someone. If the accused lacked the skill, then the accused endangered the patient's life by giving the false impression of possessing medical skill. Also, the patient might have been prevented from seeking proper medical help by confining the treatment to the accused.

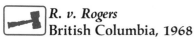
R. v. Rogers
British Columbia, 1968

Rogers had a medical degree but was struck from the rolls of the College of Physicians and Surgeons of B.C. in 1960. He established a practice calling himself a "naturopath" and inscribed on his door "E.E. Rogers, M.D., C.M." He treated a one-year-old child who had chicken pox followed by skin eczema. The child was in a hospital, under the care of specialists, and began to improve and gain weight. The child was released from hospital, and his parents began taking him to Rogers who prescribed a special diet to improve the skin problem. Under this diet the child worsened, and eventually died. The cause of death was malnutrition. Other doctors criticized the diet as totally inadequate and lacking in protein.

Rogers was charged under the *Criminal Code*, and during his trial the judge charged the jury as follows:

> **❝**I want to make it clear to you that the standard of professional skill, knowledge, and care required of a physician and the standard of knowledge, skill, and care required of any person whatever his qualifications, who undertakes to administer medical treatment, is an objective standard. In other words, in a particular case it is entirely irrelevant what the particular practitioner or person *thinks* is the level of skill, knowledge, and care with which he gave treatment. The only test is whether in fact and regardless of what he may think about it, he did act with the competence the law requires of him. Failure to act with that degree of competence is negligence.**❞**

Rogers was convicted and the conviction was upheld by the Court of Appeal.

The *R. v. Rogers* case further emphasizes that honest negligence is no defence. It is no defence for a doctor, or any other person, to say, "I thought I was giving the patient the proper treatment. I thought I was helping the patient." The law would reply, "It is not a question of whether the doctor thought proper treatment was being administered but whether or not this was actually the case."

Drug Offences

When discussing drug offences, there are two federal statutes that must be considered: the *Narcotic Control Act* and the *Food and Drugs Act*. The *Criminal Code* contains no specific provisions regarding drugs as it is felt that this subject requires special legislation.

Narcotics

The present *Narcotic Control Act* was passed in 1961. This Act sets up a schedule of substances, both natural and artificial, which are declared narcotics. (The word narcotic comes from the Greek word narkotikos, meaning "numbing.") Possession of or trafficking in these narcotics without lawful authority, such as a medical prescription, or lawful purpose is illegal. The schedule of narcotics is quite long, but the general narcotic groups are as follows:

(1) Opium poppy, its preparations, derivatives, and salts, including opium, codeine, morphine, and thebaine
(2) Coca, including coca leaves, cocaine
(3) Cannabis Sativa, including cannabis resin, marijuana (marihuana)
(4) Phenylpiperidines
(5) Phenazepines
(6) Amidones
(7) Methoadols
(8) Phenalkoxams
(9) Thiambutenes
(10) Moramides
(11) Morphinians
(12) Benzazocines
(13) Ampromides
(14) Benzimidazoles

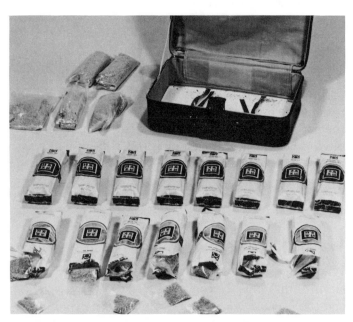

The unlawful importation of narcotics into Canada is punishable by a mandatory sentence of imprisonment for not less than seven years.

The maximum possible penalty for possession of a narcotic on summary conviction, for a first offence, is a fine of up to $1000 or imprisonment for six months, or both. For a subsequent offence, the maximum possible penalty is a fine of up to $2000 or imprisonment for one year, or both. Should the Crown proceed against the accused by way of indictment, the conviction could result in a sentence of up to seven years in prison.

Possession of Narcotics

In cases dealing with possession of a narcotic, one thing the Crown must prove is that the accused had possession. The *Narcotic Control Act* states that possession is the same as defined in the *Criminal Code*, which reads:

> **3. (4) For the purposes of this Act,**
> **(a) a person has anything in possession when he has it in his personal possession or knowingly**
> **(i) has it in the actual possession or custody of another person, or**
> **(ii) has it in any place, whether or not that place belongs to or is occupied by him, for the use or benefit of himself or of another person; and**
> **(b) where one of two or more persons, with the knowledge and consent of the rest, has anything in his custody or possession, it shall be deemed to be in the custody and possession of each and all of them.**

It is clearly stated that possession is not limited to having personal possession at the time of arrest. A group of persons can all be charged with possession even if only one person physically possessed a narcotic at the time, as long as the other members of the group knew of the possession and consented to it. Thus, where three persons were sharing a single marijuana cigarette, all were deemed to have possession.

Another point the Crown must prove is that the substance seized was a narcotic. For this purpose, the Crown may use as evidence a certificate by an analyst stating that the analyst has analysed or examined the substance and stating the results of this analysis. A copy of the certificate and a notice that the Crown intends to introduce the certificate as evidence must be provided to the accused, or to the accused's defence counsel, a reasonable amount of time prior to trial. If the defence counsel wishes to cross-examine the analyst, the analyst may be required to attend at the trial for this purpose.

A third point which the Crown must establish is that the accused knew he or she was in possession of a narcotic. That is, mens rea is an essential element of the offence. While the *Narcotic Control Act* does not state that a person must "knowingly" or "wilfully" have possession, a decision by the Supreme Court of Canada concluded that knowledge was an essential element of the offence. This important rule was established in the following case.

Beaver v. The Queen
Supreme Court of Canada, 1957

The appellant, Louis Beaver, and his brother, Max Beaver, were convicted of possession of a narcotic and declared to be habitual criminals. From their conviction, Louis Beaver appealed to the Supreme Court of Canada. The facts of the case are as follows: An RCMP undercover agent, using the false name of Al Demeter contacted Louis Beaver through a drug addict named Montroy. Demeter posed as a man who wanted to buy heroin and Louis Beaver agreed to sell it to him. Unknown to Demeter, Montroy and Beaver schemed to cheat Demeter and sell him sugar of milk instead of drugs. On the appointed day, the Beaver brothers and Demeter conducted the sale. Unknown to the Beaver brothers, the drug package they picked up at a secret drop point actually contained a narcotic, diacetylmorphine, instead of sugar of milk as they had intended. It is unknown how this situation arose. The appellant's defence was that he never intended to deal in drugs and never knew the parcel contained a drug. The trial judge instructed the jury that whether the appellant had mistakenly believed the package contained a harmless substance was irrelevant and must not be considered. The trial judge also said that as long as the package contained the narcotic and the accused had possession of it, the offence was complete.

The Supreme Court of Canada compared the present case with one where a person might go to a druggist and request a harmless substance and be mistakenly sold a narcotic, without being aware of the fact. The court further concluded that:

66To constitute possession, where there is a manual handling of a thing it must be co-existent with knowledge of what the thing is, and both these elements must co-exist with some act of control. When these three elements exist together, it must be conceded then that it does not matter if the thing is retained for an innocent purpose.99

The conviction was quashed.

In *Beaver v. The Queen* the Supreme Court recognized the possibility that a person could innocently or mistakenly come into possession of a narcotic. It could even be planted on the person. The court concluded that the risk of an unjust conviction was sufficiently great that Parliament must have intended that knowledge be an essential element of the offence.

If the Crown succeeds in establishing these three points, practically the only defence left open to the accused is that he or she had lawful possession of the narcotic, such as through a medical prescription.

Trafficking in Narcotics

If an accused has been convicted of possession of a narcotic, the accused is then given an opportunity to show that he or she was not in possession for the purpose of trafficking. The *Narcotic Control Act* defines trafficking as follows:

2. Definitions. In this Act ...
"traffic" means
(a) to manufacture, sell, give, administer, transport, send, deliver or distribute, or
(b) to offer to do anything mentioned in paragraph (a) otherwise than under the authority of this Act or the regulations.

(Strictly speaking, the *purchase* of a narcotic is not an offence.) Note, in particular, that trafficking can include giving a narcotic to someone. We usually think of trafficking as an illegal *business*, but this is not always the case. The maximum possible penalty for trafficking in narcotics is life imprisonment.

In a case of trafficking, the burden of proof is upon the accused to show, on a balance of probabilities, that he or she was not in possession for the purpose of trafficking. The accused must adduce evidence to show this or be convicted without further evidence from the Crown. The accused does not have to prove this point beyond a reasonable doubt, but need only raise enough of a defence so as to show, on a balance of probabilities, that he or she was not going to traffic in the narcotic. If the accused presents evidence on this point, the Crown may introduce evidence by way of rebuttal. The primary defence the accused may raise against the charge of trafficking is that the narcotic was solely intended for personal use. The quantity of narcotics involved is not necessarily proof of this, as many narcotic traffickers move only a small amount of drugs at one time. It is not a defence to the charge that the accused only intended to give or share some of the narcotic with family or friends. While the accused might feel that this is not trafficking in the true sense, since the drugs are not being sold for profit, the offence is complete if any of the narcotic is given to another person, regardless of who that person may be.

R. v. Whalen
Newfoundland, 1974

The accused was acquitted on a charge of possession of cannabis resin for the purposes of trafficking. The Crown appealed to the Court of Appeal. The facts are that the accused admitted buying the drug for his own use, but then admitted sharing it with his friends. The magistrate held that the Crown had not been able to show that the accused's purpose in buying the drug was for "giving mainly." The Court of Appeal held that the accused's intention when he bought the drug was unimportant. On the accused's own admission, he was guilty of

the offence as charged. The *Narcotic Control Act* shifts the burden of proof in criminal proceedings to an accused and requires an accused to prove on a "balance of probabilities" that possession is not for the purpose of trafficking. If an accused admits to having shared the drugs with others, the court must conclude that this was one of the purposes in possessing the drug, regardless of whether this was the purpose in originally buying it.

In *R. v. Oakes* (1983), the Ontario Court of Appeal held that the procedure in s. 8 of the *Narcotic Control Act*, which requires the accused to give evidence to show that he or she was not in possession for the purposes of trafficking, is ultra vires on the grounds that it is contrary to the Canadian *Charter of Rights and Freedoms*. The court held that the section was unconstitutional because it violates a person's right to be presumed innocent until proven guilty. The case will most likely be appealed to the Supreme Court of Canada for final disposition.

Smuggling narcotics into Canada is punishable by imprisonment for not less than seven years and a possible maximum sentence of imprisonment for life. (The judge *must* sentence the convicted person to at least seven years in prison.) Cultivating opium poppy or marijuana in Canada is punishable by imprisonment for seven years.

In *R. v. Blondin* (1970), the Supreme Court of Canada held that a person charged with importing a narcotic may be convicted whether that person either knew the substance was a narcotic (not necessarily the particular narcotic) or was "wilfully blind" to the fact.

In 1978, British Columbia passed the *Heroin Treatment Act* which provides for compulsory treatment for a period of three years including possible detention for six months. The legislation was challenged as being an unlawful intrusion by the province into an area of federal jurisdiction. However, in 1982, the Supreme Court of Canada held that the Act was intra vires the province and therefore legal. The court held that the legislation relates to health and is within provincial jurisdiction. The Act is not meant to be punitive but to end a patient's dependence on heroin. (Part 2 of the *Narcotic Control Act* contains a provision for custody and treatment of addicts, but the part has never been declared in force.)

In *R. v. Hauser* (1979), the Supreme Court of Canada held that the *Narcotic Control Act* is not a criminal law statute but comes under the general jurisdiction of Parliament to legislate for the "Peace, Order and Good Government" of Canada. The court then concluded that the Attorney General of Canada has power to prosecute offences under the Act.

Controlled and Restricted Drugs

The second federal statute pertaining to drugs is the *Food and Drugs Act*. The Act does not declare drugs to be narcotics, but only recognizes that certain substances should not be available to the public without medical reason. The Act establishes two classes of drugs, *controlled drugs* and *restricted drugs*.

Controlled drugs are listed on Schedule G of the Act and include such groups as amphetamines and barbiturates. These are generally referred to as the "uppers" and "downers" of the drug scene—drugs that provide rapid change in mood. Probably the most commonly abused drug is benzedrine, known for its ability to pep up persons, keep them awake, and provide a strong muscle stimulant. "Bennies" are well known to truck drivers trying to stay awake on long hauls, students cramming for exams, and some professional athletes who want to be "up" for a big game. Barbiturates are depressants, which include sleeping pills and tranquillizers. It is not an offence to be in possession of amphetamines or barbiturates. It is only an offence to be in possession for the purpose of trafficking, or to actually traffic in the drugs. A person charged with trafficking in a controlled drug, or with possession for the purpose of trafficking is liable on summary conviction to imprisonment for eighteen months, or on conviction by indictment to imprisonment for ten years. Under the *Food and Drugs Act*, trafficking is defined as "to manufacture, sell, export, import, transport, or deliver." The Act does not prohibit giving as the *Narcotic Control Act* does.

Restricted drugs are listed on Schedule H of the Act and include all hallucinogenic drugs except alcohol and tobacco. There are many such drugs, and more are being invented all the time. They are usually referred to by their initials rather than their long medical names. Included in this group are LSD, MDA, DET, MMDA, and DMT. These drugs cannot legally be in a person's possession without a doctor's prescription. Therefore, as is not the case with controlled drugs, mere possession is an offence. Unlawful possession is punishable upon summary conviction by a maximum possible fine of $1000 or six months' imprisonment, or both. Conviction by indictment may result in a maximum possible fine of $5000 or imprisonment for three years, or both. Trafficking, or possession for the purpose of trafficking may result in a sentence of eighteen months upon summary conviction or imprisonment for ten years by way of indictment.

R. v. Johnston
Alberta, 1980

The accused was charged with possession of LSD, a restricted drug, for the purpose of trafficking. At trial the accused admitted possession but denied he was trafficking. The evidence was that the accused and three of his friends entered into a joint venture to buy 405 "hits" of LSD. The *Food and Drugs Act* defines "traffic" to include "manufacture, sell, export from or import into Canada, transport or deliver." The accused was to buy the drugs, bring them to the other participants, and deliver their share. The Crown argued that this would fall within the meaning of "deliver." The Court of Queen's Bench held that a joint venture was not an arrangement that included delivery and the accused was found guilty of possession but not of trafficking.

Firearms and Offensive Weapons

The control of guns and other weapons is a major problem for law enforcement agencies all over the world. Nor is it a recent problem. During the seventeenth century, King Charles II published an edict that no person who had an income of less than £100 per year could own a gun.

The law regarding weapons is not limited to guns. The term "weapon" can include various devices dangerous to the public. Section 2 of the *Criminal Code* provides a definition:

> "offensive weapon" or "weapon" means
> (a) anything that is designed to be used as a weapon, or
> (b) anything that a person uses or intends to use as a weapon, whether or not it is designed to be used as a weapon, and, without restricting the generality of the foregoing, includes any firearm as defined in section 82.

Certain types of weapons are classified as "prohibited" and may not be lawfully possessed by private citizens.

Possession of a weapon can be an offence under the following section:

> 85. Every one who carries or has in his possession a weapon or imitation thereof, for a purpose dangerous to the public peace or for the purpose of committing an offence, is guilty of an indictable offence and is liable to imprisonment for ten years.

Carrying a concealed weapon is contrary to s. 87 of the *Code* and can bring a five-year sentence.

Whether or not something is a weapon may depend upon its inherent character. A sword or bayonet is designed to be used as a weapon. A pocket knife or butcher knife is not so designed. If we start with the premise that a knife is a tool used for peaceful purposes, then it becomes a weapon only if the circumstances show that it has been converted from a tool to a weapon by something the accused has done. In *R. v. Halvorsen* (1979), the British Columbia Court of Appeal acquitted the accused who had been found in a bar in possession of a jack-knife with a blade 4 inches (10 cm) long. There was no disturbance in the bar and there was no inference that the knife was possessed for a purpose dangerous to the public. In *R. v. Graham* (1977), the accused entered a high school dance with a butcher knife hidden in a bag. The accused said the knife was for peeling oranges but there were no oranges in the bag. The Ontario Court of Appeal upheld the accused's conviction for carrying a concealed weapon.

Prohibited Weapons

Certain objects are called prohibited weapons. It is an offence to possess, import, buy, sell, give, lend, or deliver such a weapon. It is an offence to be an occupant of a motor vehicle in which a prohibited weapon is *known* to be located.

Section 82 (1) of the *Code* identifies prohibited weapons as follows:

> (a) any device or contrivance designed or intended to muffle or stop the sound or report of a firearm,
> (b) any knife that has a blade that opens automatically by gravity or centrifugal force or by hand pressure

applied to a button, spring, or other device in or attached to the handle of the knife,

(c) any firearm, not being a restricted weapon described in paragraph (c) of the definition of that expression in this section, that is capable of firing bullets in rapid succession during one pressure of the trigger,

(d) any firearm adapted from a rifle or shotgun, whether by sawing, cutting or other alteration or modification, that, as so adapted, has a barrel that is less than eighteen inches [forty-five centimetres] in length or that is less than twenty-six inches [sixty-five centimetres] in overall length, or

(e) a weapon of any kind, not being an antique firearm or a firearm of a kind commonly used in Canada for hunting or sporting purposes, that is declared by order of the Governor in Council to be a prohibited weapon.

The maximum possible penalty for possession of a prohibited weapon is imprisonment for five years.

The *Criminal Code* authorizes the Governor General to declare weapons to be prohibited by administrative order, correctly referred to as an Order in Council. Weapons declared to be prohibited include tear gas, Mace, kung fu sticks, shuriken throwing devices, the Taser Public Defender electrical gun, the Constant Companion belt knife, the Spiked Wristband, and many others.

Restricted Weapons

Other weapons are not illegal but controls are exercised over them. The *Code* defines a restricted weapon as any of the following:

(a) any firearm, not being a prohibited weapon, designed, altered or intended to be aimed and fired by the action of one hand,

(b) any firearm that
  (i) is not a prohibited weapon, has a barrel that is less than eighteen and one-half inches [roughly forty-five centimetres] in length and is capable of discharging centre-fire ammunition in a semi-automatic manner, or
  (ii) is designed or adapted to be fired when reduced

to a length of less than twenty-six inches, [sixty-five centimetres] by folding, telescoping or otherwise, or

(c) any firearm that is designed, altered or intended to fire bullets in rapid succession during one pressure of the trigger and that, on the day on which this paragraph comes into force, was registered as a restricted weapon and formed part of a gun collection in Canada of a bona fide gun collector, or

(d) a weapon of any kind, not being a prohibited weapon or a shotgun or rifle of a kind that, in the opinion of the Governor in Council, is reasonable for use in Canada for hunting or sporting purposes, that is declared by order of the Governor in Council to be a restricted weapon.

The *Code* defines a firearm to be a weapon that can propel a projectile at a speed of over 500 feet (150 m) per second.

Everyone who owns a restricted weapon must have a Restricted Weapon Certificate for each such weapon. Application must be made to the local police department. Possession of an unregistered restricted weapon or possession of a registered weapon in a place other than authorized is punishable by five years in prison.

Other Weapons

Hunting rifles, shotguns, and ammunition may be purchased by anyone over the age of sixteen. All persons wishing to purchase firearms must first obtain an Acquisition Certificate. One certificate will allow the holder to acquire any number of firearms. A certificate is not needed if a person over age sixteen borrows a firearm and uses it under the guidance of a person lawfully in possession of the firearm. A certificate will not be granted to a person with a conviction for a firearms offence under the *Criminal Code*, a person with a history of mental disorder treated within the past five years, or a person with a history of violent behaviour.

Miscellaneous Offences

There are numerous offences related to weapons. The following is only a partial list:

• Making false statements to acquire a certificate;

- Pointing a firearm (loaded or unloaded) at another person;
- Carrying a weapon, or an imitation thereof, for a dangerous purpose;
- Giving, lending, transferring, or delivering a firearm to a person under age sixteen who has no certificate;
- Selling, giving, or lending a firearm to a person of unsound mind, impaired by alcohol or drugs;
- Selling or lending a person a weapon if the person has no certificate;
- Failing to report a lost or stolen firearm;
- Using, carrying, transporting, shipping, or handling a firearm in a careless manner;
- Storing or displaying a firearm or ammunition in a careless manner;
- Discharging a firearm with intent to wound, maim, or disfigure any person.

Use of Firearm during Commission of an Offence

A very important section of the *Code* is s. 83 which makes it a separate offence to commit an offence while armed.

> **83. (1) Every one who uses a firearm**
> **(a) while committing or attempting to commit an indictable offence, or**
> **(b) during his flight after committing or attempting to commit an indictable offence,**
> **whether or not he causes or means to cause bodily harm to any person as a result thereof, is guilty of an indictable offence and is liable to imprisonment**
> **(c) in the case of a first offence under this subsection, except as provided in paragraph (d), for not more than fourteen years and not less than one year; and**
> **(d) in the case of a second or subsequent offence under this subsection, or in the case of a first such offence committed by a person who, prior to the coming into force of this subsection, was convicted of an indictable offence or an attempt to commit an indictable offence, in the course of which or during his flight after the commission or attempted commission of which he used a firearm, for not more than fourteen years and not less than three years.**

> **(2) A sentence imposed on a person for an offence under subsection (1) shall be served consecutively to any other punishment imposed on him for an offence arising out of the same event or series of events and to any other sentence to which he is subject at the time the sentence is imposed on him for an offence under subsection (1).**

 Nicholson v. The Queen
Supreme Court of Canada, 1981

The accused was convicted of robbery with use of a firearm and was sentenced to four years in prison for robbery and one year for use of a firearm. The Crown appealed on the ground that the sentence for use of a firearm should have been three years because it was the second such offence committed by the accused. The evidence was that the accused had been a party to an armed robbery prior to this robbery, but the accused did not have a firearm during the first robbery. His accomplice did. The issue was whether s. 83 applied to persons who had been a party to an offence during which another person used a firearm or whether it applied only to the accused using a firearm. The Supreme Court of Canada held that the section applied to persons who are party to an offence during which another person uses a firearm. This was the second offence for the accused and the proper sentence was a minimum of three years.

Seizure of Weapons

Where a justice or judge believes that it is not in the interests of a person, or not in the public interest, that a person should possess a firearm, a warrant may be issued authorizing seizure. An officer can seize a weapon without warrant if the officer believes that an offence is being committed or has been committed against any *Criminal Code* provisions. A dwelling-house can be entered with a warrant to search or an officer may enter without warrant where the officer believes a person's safety is in danger. The owner of any seized weapon may make application to have it returned.

Colet v. The Queen
Supreme Court of Canada, 1981

The appellant was charged with attempted murder and attempted bodily harm all of which arose out of his defence of his property. The city wanted to tear down Colet's shack and he made it known he would resist that by force. Believing he had a firearm, police obtained a warrant to seize any firearms in his possession. When the police arrived with the warrant, Colet threw gasoline at them from a room of the building. He made other threats. The Supreme Court of Canada held that the officers had not acted lawfully because they had no warrant to *search*, only a warrant to *seize*. The warrant to enter a person's property must be subject to a strict construction of its terms since it is a very important common law principle that persons should be secure in their homes against unreasonable intrusions by police.

Homicide

Killing another person is known as homicide, a word derived from *homo* ("human") and *cide* ("killing"). Homicide can be culpable or non-culpable. Non-culpable homicide is that for which no one is accountable or blameworthy. It is not an offence. Culpable homicide is an offence and is classed as either murder, manslaughter, or infanticide. The *Criminal Code* states:

205. (1) A person commits homicide when, directly or indirectly, by any means, he causes the death of a human being.

(2) Homicide is culpable or not culpable.

(3) Homicide that is not culpable is not an offence.

(4) Culpable homicide is murder or manslaughter or infanticide.

(5) A person commits culpable homicide when he causes the death of a human being,

(a) by means of an unlawful act,

(b) by criminal negligence,

(c) by causing that human being, by threats or fear of violence or by deception, to do anything that causes his death, or

(d) by wilfully frightening that human being, in the case of a child or sick person.

(6) Notwithstanding anything in this section, a person does not commit homicide within the meaning of this Act by reason only that he causes the death of a human being by procuring, by false evidence, the conviction and death of that human being by sentence of the law.

Since we must all die sometime, culpable homicide is nothing more than an unlawful acceleration of death. In essence, it is robbing a person of some of the time he or she might have spent in this world. It is no defence that the victim was already suffering from a fatal disease or was under a sentence of death. Even if someone would have lived only a matter of hours, it is culpable homicide to deprive the person of those few hours. The *Criminal Code* places a time limitation upon culpable homicide of one year and one day.

210. No person commits culpable homicide or the offence of causing the death of a human being by criminal negligence unless the death occurs within one year and one day commencing with the time of the occurrence of the last event by means of which he caused or contributed to the cause of death.

Thus, if medical technology can manage to keep the victim alive for a year and a day, then no one can be convicted for causing the person's death. A cutoff point is necessary, otherwise a person could be charged with homicide if the victim died years after being assaulted.

Euthanasia

Our law does not make suicide illegal. It does prohibit one person from carrying out the wishes of another asking to be killed. No person can legally give consent to be killed.

Euthanasia, or mercy killing, is a controversial subject. Those who support euthanasia believe that medical procedures can be extended too long, causing the patient to suffer extended pain and degradation. They argue that where there is no hope of recovery, the patient should be allowed to die and in some situations put to death. Opponents have both religious and medical arguments against euthanasia.

There is no statutory definition of death, and medical practitioners are not unanimous about the moment when death — including the much heralded concept of "brain death" — actually occurs. This creates almost unsurmountable legal problems for a doctor who might consider permitting a patient to die. Section 199 of the *Criminal Code* could be interpreted to make a physician criminally responsible for not taking all possible steps to preserve a life. Shutting off a respirator could be viewed as criminal negligence. Also, s. 212 of the *Code* says that culpable homicide is *murder* when the person who causes the death of a human being *means* to cause that death.

Some people have prepared "living wills" which are documents giving directions in the case of a terminal illness. These living wills usually ask that lifesaving techniques be stopped when the prognosis for recovery is negligible and death is being postponed unduly. No province has legislation giving any legal recognition to such documents and a doctor could only take the existence of a living will into consideration along with all other factors in the situation.

Determining the Cause of Death

A crucial question in many homicide cases is, "What caused death?" No person can be held responsible for an event which would have occurred anyway. It must be proven that the accused *caused* the victim's death. If Brown shoots Smith, and Smith dies immediately, there is no doubt that Brown caused Smith's death. However, suppose Brown shoots Smith, and Smith undergoes surgery; Smith is carelessly given too much anaesthetic, and dies. Can we say Brown caused Smith's death? Possibly, but we are more accurate if we now say that Brown's actions "contributed to" Smith's death.

In order to hold the accused criminally responsible, how much does he or she have to contribute to the victim's death? There is no set rule. Some judges believe the accused must have substantially contributed to the victim's death, while other judges believe that anything greater than a trivial amount is sufficient to convict. On this subject, the *Criminal Code* states:

207. Where a person, by an act or omission, does any thing that results in the death of a human being, he causes the death of that human being notwithstanding that death from that cause might have been prevented by resorting to proper means.

The meaning of s. 207 is that it is no defence to homicide to say that if someone else had acted properly, the death would not have occurred. If Brown stabs Smith, and then calls an ambulance which fails to show up, Brown cannot raise as a defence that Smith would not have died if the ambulance had arrived and taken Smith to a hospital. Or, if Brown stabs Smith and a doctor incorrectly diagnoses the wound as superficial, Brown cannot raise as a defence the doctor's mistake.

The act of the accused need not be the sole cause of death. It may set off another event which results in death. If Brown robs Smith with violence, leaving Smith unconscious on the road to be run over by a truck and killed, then the law would hold that Brown caused Smith's death. The intervening act of Smith's being run over by a truck was foreseeable, and Brown must accept the blame. However, suppose Brown robbed Smith and gave Smith a fractured skull requiring hospital treatment. If, during hospitalization, Smith accidentally contracted scarlet fever and died, can we say that Brown caused Smith's death? Probably not, for scarlet fever was not a foreseeable consequence of robbery with violence.

There are numerous interesting cases dealing with medical treatment following injury in which the defence counsel raised the issue of whether death was caused by the injury itself or by the medical treatment. The law would generally hold that if the medical treatment was given in good faith by bona fide medical personnel, it is no defence to the charge for the assailant to claim that the treatment was unnecessary or unskilful. This would not apply to a case where the medical treatment given was grossly negligent. One authoritative case on this issue is the following.

R. v. Jordan
England, 1956

The accused stabbed a man who died in hospital. Evidence was given at the trial that the victim was given an antibiotic, terramycin, and an abnormal amount of intravenous liquid. He developed broncho-pneumonia and died. The accused was convicted of murder. He appealed to the Court of Criminal Appeal which established these general rules:

(1) Medical evidence is admissible to show that the medical treatment of a wound was the cause of death and that the wound itself was not.
(2) If the medical treatment killed the victim independently of the wound, the wound is not the cause of death. This presumes the medical treatment was grossly negligent.
(3) If the medical treatment and the wound combined to cause death, and it is impossible to separate the two as to causation, then the accused would be guilty of homicide, provided the medical treatment was not grossly negligent.

The Court of Appeal noted that the stab wound was almost healed when the victim died. The terramycin was given to prevent infection, but the victim was intolerant of it. Additional amounts were given to him despite the fact that he developed definite symptoms of intolerance. The excessive fluid given intravenously filled his lungs with water bringing on pneumonia. The court held that the stab wound was not the cause of death and quashed the conviction.

The *Jordan* case was not without criticism in both legal and medical circles, but it established that there was some defence open to the accused to show that medical treatment was in itself so negligent that death ensued from it, not from the original injury. Another interesting case occurred three years later.

R. v. Smith
England, 1959

The accused stabbed a man twice with a bayonet. Friends of the victim carried him to a medical centre, but tripped over tent poles in the dark and dropped him several times. A medical officer incorrectly diagnosed the wounds as superficial and administered little medical care. The victim died. The defence raised the issue of causation of death emphasizing:

(1) The victim's friends aggravated the wounds by dropping the victim.
(2) With proper medical care, the victim would have had an estimated 75 per cent chance of recovery.

The accused was convicted and appealed, but the Court of Appeal upheld the conviction saying:

  “If at the time of death the original wound is still an operating cause and a substantial cause, then the death can properly be said to be the result of the wound, albeit that some other cause of death is also operating.**”**

The court mentioned the *Jordan* case and emphasized that it was a particular case depending upon its exact facts.

Murder

Perhaps the best-known classification of homicide is murder. At one time, murder required what was called "malice aforethought." This meant, in effect, that it had to be premeditated. Our present law requires neither malice aforethought nor premeditation to constitute murder. The common law has generally held that murder can arise in any one of the following ways:

- *An intention to kill any person*: It is not necessary that the killer got the right victim. If Brown intended to kill Smith but unintentionally killed Jones instead, this is still murder.
- *An intention to cause grievous bodily harm to any person*: It is impossible to inflict injury upon a person just short

of death and know exactly how much force can be used. It is enough that the accused intended grievous harm which resulted in death.

- *An intention to do something unlawful, where it is foreseeable that death might result*: A good example is armed robbery. If there is shooting and someone dies, it is no defence to say, "I did not intend any shooting."

The common law definitions have given way to the definitions contained within the *Criminal Code*. The *Code* defines murder as follows:

> **212. Culpable homicide is murder**
> **(a) where the person who causes the death of a human being**
> 　**(i) means to cause his death, or**
> 　**(ii) means to cause him bodily harm that he knows is likely to cause his death, and is reckless whether death ensues or not;**
> **(b) where a person, meaning to cause death to a human being or meaning to cause him bodily harm that he knows is likely to cause his death, and being reckless whether death ensues or not, by accident or mistake causes death to another human being, notwithstanding that he does not mean to cause death or bodily harm to that human being; or**
> **(c) where a person, for an unlawful object, does anything that he knows or ought to know is likely to cause death, and thereby causes death to a human being, notwithstanding that he desires to effect his object without causing death or bodily harm to any human being.**

Culpable homicide is murder when a person causes the death of another person while committing, or attempting to commit treason, sabotage, piracy, hijacking an aircraft, resisting arrest, prison break or escape from custody, assaulting an officer, sexual assault, sexual assault with a weapon, aggravated sexual assault, kidnapping, robbery, break and enter, or arson.

It is no defence that the accused did not mean to cause death as long as the force applied to the victim was done for the purpose of facilitating the offence or the escape after committing the offence. The death may occur from a variety of causes such as using a weapon, administering a drug, or wilfully stopping the breathing of the victim by any means.

Canadian law classifies murder as either first degree murder or second degree murder. All murder that is not first degree murder is second degree murder.

Murder is first degree murder when:

(1) It is planned and deliberate; or
(2) The victim is a police officer, sheriff, or other peace officer, or a jailer or prison employee; or
(3) The victim was killed during the hijacking of an aircraft, sexual assault, sexual assault with a weapon, aggravated sexual assault, or kidnapping or forcible confinement, or the attempt to commit any of these offences.

 R. v. Droste
Ontario, 1981

The accused planned to kill his wife by setting fire to the family car and running it into a bridge abutment. The plan went wrong and by mistake the accused's two children were killed in the fire set for the wife. The accused was convicted of first degree murder. The accused appealed on the grounds that he could not be convicted of first degree murder of his children because he did not plan or intend to kill them. The Court of Appeal upheld the conviction:

"We think that the trial judge correctly instructed the jury that if they were satisfied beyond a reasonable doubt that the appellant's intention to kill his wife was planned and deliberate and that in the course of carrying out that intention he caused the death of the children by accident or mistake, that the resulting murder constituted first degree murder.**"**

The mandatory penalty for first degree murder is imprisonment for life without eligibility for parole for twenty-five years. However, after fifteen years, the inmate may apply for a reduction of the number of years he or she must wait before being eligible for parole. The penalty for second degree murder is imprisonment for life without eligibility for parole for ten years.

R. v. Cote
Supreme Court of Canada, 1964

Two men, Cote and Dumas, acting together, set out to break into the house of Phillipe Raymond by night and steal his money. While the men were in the house, Raymond was awakened and Cote seized him, saying to Dumas, "We'll have to tie him up." Dumas tore up a pillowcase and some clothing worn by the victim and tied and gagged him. When they left, they heard the victim making noises through the gag. Two days later the victim was found dead. An autopsy revealed he had broken bones, internal bleeding, and had suffered asphyxia (lack of air). Cote and Dumas were convicted of murder. The Quebec Court of Appeal ordered a new trial and the Crown appealed to the Supreme Court of Canada. The Supreme Court of Canada held that both men should remain convicted of murder. Cote contended that it was the sole action of Dumas that caused death. The court rejected that argument saying:

> 66Could the jurors reasonably believe that while one of the aggressors was getting materials and using them to gag and bind the victim's hands and feet, the other remained inactive taking no part in the affair?99

It is possible to convict of murder even though the body is never found. Where a man murdered a woman and threw her body over the side of a ship, he was convicted although her body was never recovered. The following case further illustrates this point.

R. v. Chambers
Ontario, 1947

A girl, five years of age, vanished. The accused was the last person seen talking to her. The accused at first denied knowledge of her whereabouts, but later confessed that he had killed her and had thrown her body into a large furnace at the canning factory where he was employed as a security guard. The defence argued that he could not be convicted of murder as he was the only witness against himself and he was unreliable. The defence pointed out that the accused had tried to kill himself and that it would be unsafe to believe his confession since he could be inventing the whole story merely to bring punishment upon himself. The court concluded that the evidence was sufficient to convict the accused even in the absence of any trace of the body.

Manslaughter

The next form of culpable homicide is manslaughter. Manslaughter is a lesser included offence of murder. This means that a person charged with murder might be found not guilty of murder but guilty of manslaughter if the facts supported a conviction for this lesser charge. The term manslaughter generally covers all homicides which are not murder or infanticide. Some nations further classify manslaughter as "voluntary" or "involuntary" but Canada does not make any such distinction. The *Criminal Code* states:

> **215. (1) Culpable homicide that otherwise would be murder may be reduced to manslaughter if the person who committed it did so in the heat of passion caused by sudden provocation.**
>
> **(2) A wrongful act or insult that is of such a nature as to be sufficient to deprive an ordinary person of the power of self-control is provocation for the purposes of this section if the accused acted upon it on the sudden and before there was time for his passion to cool.**
>
> **(3) For the purposes of this section the questions**
> **(a) whether a particular wrongful act or insult amounted to provocation, and**
> **(b) whether the accused was deprived of the power of self-control by the provocation that he alleges he received,**
> **are questions of fact, but no one shall be deemed to have given provocation to another by doing anything that he had a legal right to do, or by anything that the accused incited him to do in order to provide the accused with an excuse for causing death or bodily harm to any human being.**
>
> **217. Culpable homicide that is not murder or infanticide is manslaughter.**
>
> **219. Every one who commits manslaughter is guilty of an indictable offence and is liable to imprisonment for life.**

The question of provocation is an important one in many cases. Manslaughter may result from a sudden loss of self-control brought on by some action or words which caused the slayer to lose self-control. The insult that caused the slayer to lose self-control must be such that an "ordinary person" would be sufficiently provoked to kill the victim. It is unclear as to just what characteristics make up the ordinary person. It is a matter which can be left to the jury to try to understand. In *Beddar v. Director of Public Prosecutions* (England, 1913), the judge included these words in the charge to the jury:

> 66No court has ever given, nor do I think ever can give, a definition of what constitutes a reasonable, ordinary, or average man. That must be left to the collective common sense of the jury.99

Further, the provocation must be such that the slaying takes place almost immediately, before there has been a chance for the temper of the slayer to cool. If the opposite happens — that is if the slayer broods and builds up hatred for the victim — the defence of provocation will not be accepted, for there was time for the slayer's passion to cool.

Provocation does not excuse the slayer, but only shows that murder was not the intention. It can serve to reduce murder to manslaughter. In the United States, the defence of "temporary insanity" is sometimes raised where there has been severe provocation. This defence is not accepted in Canada.

The provocation does not necessarily have to come directly from the victim, but there must be some connection between the insult and the victim. A furious person could not go out and kill just anyone because of being insulted and enraged by someone else.

In the following case, the question of provocation was discussed in some detail, as it involved a victim who was not the one who insulted or aggravated the slayer. Prior to this case it was generally held that the provocation had to come directly from the victim and no one else.

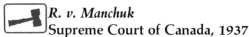

R. v. Manchuk
Supreme Court of Canada, 1937

The accused was having an argument with his neighbour, Seabright, over a property line. He struck Seabright blows from which he died. Seabright's wife was in the doorway of her house a short distance away. Manchuk immediately rushed at her and killed her also. Manchuk was tried for the slaying of the husband and found guilty of manslaughter. The jury concluded that there had been provocation. Manchuk was then charged with the murder of the wife. In this trial the trial judge told the jury they could not accept the defence of provocation because the wife had done nothing to provoke Manchuk. The trial judge included in the charge to the jury the specific words:

> 66Please understand clearly that the provocation justifying such a reduction in the charge must have come from the person who was killed and not from anybody else.99

The Ontario Court of Appeal set aside Manchuk's conviction and ordered a new trial, holding that the judge's charge to the jury was wrong. The Crown appealed to the Supreme Court of Canada which upheld the Court of Appeal. The Supreme Court agreed that provocation could come from someone other than the victim, if the accused was under the belief that the victim was a party to those acts of provocation, even if this belief was wrong. The decision reads in part:

> 66We think the trial judge ought to have asked the jury to consider whether, in the blindness of his passion, aroused by the quarrel with the husband, the accused, suddenly observing the wife [close to] the scene of the quarrel and of his mortal assault on the husband, attacked her on the assumption that she was involved in the acts of the husband.99

Manslaughter is a very diverse crime, taking in many acts which result in death. Some of these acts are legal while others are illegal. An act that is legal but done so carelessly that no regard for others is present can result in a conviction. An act that is illegal but is done with no intention to cause harm to any person can result in manslaughter if a person is killed by that act. For example, in 1975 two men were convicted of manslaughter for burning down a Montreal night club killing thirty-seven persons. The two men stated that they neither intended to harm anyone nor even burn down the building, but only set a fire to annoy the doorman who had ejected them from the club.

Infanticide

The third classification of culpable homicide is infanticide. It is a rare offence which applies only to the mother of the child shortly after birth. If the mother is mentally deranged because of the effects of childbirth, and kills her child deliberately or through gross neglect, then she commits an offence. The maximum possible punishment for infanticide is imprisonment for five years.

Obscene Matter

One of the most difficult areas of our criminal law is that relating to obscene matter. Our society has a strong tradition that the freedom of the press and other forms of communications must be carefully preserved, and that the law should be very reluctant to try to control what people may see or read. Yet, the depravity of some persons in producing films and books depicting the most abnormal and unacceptable human behaviour seems unbounded except by the law. There is particular concern about the relationship between obscene matter and young offenders. The tendency of young persons to emulate what they see or read is not unknown to police officers and the courts. When a movie was shown on television in the United States in which teenage thugs set fire to a person, real episodes occurred in three cities within a month.

There are two words commonly used which are *not* synonymous; namely, obscenity and pornography. Pornography, in the strictest sense, means writing about prostitution. Obscenity generally means matters acceptable in private, but not in public, including foul language, off-colour remarks, and behaviour that is crude or shocking. The term pornography has been extended by common usage to include any publication that is immoral.

The primary justification usually suggested for prohibiting the sale of obscene matter is not that the public will merely have better minds, but rather that a person who is exposed to obscene matter is likely to be pushed to overt behaviour which is either criminal or gravely immoral in its nature. Attempts to regulate public morality on this justification are easily documented in both Canadian and British law. In *R. v. Curl* (England, 1727), Lord Hardwicke declared:

> **❝**Obscenity is an offence at common law, as it tends to corrupt the morals of the King's subjects and is against the peace of the King. Destroying morality is destroying the peace of the government, for government is no more than public order, which is morality.**❞**

Nearly 250 years later, we find a remarkably similar statement by another British judge.

Shaw v. Director of Public Prosecutions
England, 1961

The accused was convicted of an offence under the *Sexual Offences Act* and the *Obscene Publications Act* of England. He appealed to the House of Lords. The facts of the case are that the accused published a directory called "Ladies Directory" which contained the names, addresses, and telephone numbers of prostitutes. The book also contained some nude photographs and descriptions of perverse acts these prostitutes would perform. The court's decision was read by Viscount Simons who stated:

> **❝**There remains in the courts of law a residual power to enforce the supreme and fundamental purpose of the law, to conserve not only the safety and order but also the moral welfare of the state.**❞**

The conviction was upheld.

Legal Definitions of Obscenity

Obscene matter is defined in the *Criminal Code* as follows:

> **159. (8) For the purpose of this Act, any publication, a dominant characteristic of which is the undue exploitation of sex, or of sex and any one of the following subjects, namely crime, horror, cruelty, and violence, shall be deemed to be obscene.**

As used in this section, the word "sex" does not confine itself only to intimate *acts* between two individuals. It can be read in the broad sense that it includes descriptions or pictures of the male or female person in a manner that is obscene.

The word "exploitation" has various meanings but normally means to take advantage of the subject matter in a manner inconsistent with its purpose, merely to excite the reader. However, the *Code* requires more than just exploitation, it requires "*undue* exploitation" which goes beyond that which could be called appropriate or warranted. In trying to determine what is undue exploitation, the courts have adopted the test of "accepted community standards of tolerance." This suggests that what might be obscene in a small town could be acceptable in a large city.

The manner of display is irrelevant. If the material is obscene, then it does not matter if it is openly displayed or hidden on back shelves. The judge must view the publication as a whole and not selective aspects of it. Novels may have to be judged by different standards than magazines. In the case of novels, the literary merits of the work must also be examined. If the sexual passages are not a necessary and integral part of the literary theme, then the work may be obscene.

The basic definition has two parts. The first is the undue exploitation of sex alone. The second is the undue exploitation of sex coupled with other possible themes, including crime, horror, cruelty, or violence. Thus, sex is explicitly a part of both definitions. A publication cannot be obscene merely because it contains too much violence, crime, cruelty, or horror. Somewhere it must also combine sex with one of the other themes.

As a matter of procedure, a judge can issue a warrant to seize material that is alleged to be obscene. The occupier of the premises where the material was seized will receive a summons to show cause why the matter seized should not be forfeited to the Crown. Basically, then, the matter is deemed obscene unless the occupier can give a good argument that it is not and that it should be returned.

Everyone commits an offence who makes, prints, publishes, distributes, circulates, or possesses for the purpose of publication, distribution, or circulation any obscene written matter, picture, model, photograph, or other thing. It is an offence to publicly exhibit a disgusting object or an indecent thing. The maximum possible penalty is imprisonment for two years.

R. v. The Coles Company Limited
Ontario, 1964

Copies of a novel entitled *Fanny Hill* were seized from Coles Book Store. In such cases, the burden is on the seller of the books to convince the court that the books are not obscene. The Crown does not have to prove the books are obscene but need only show that the seizure has been properly authorized by a judge. The Crown does not have to call any witnesses and may cross-examine witnesses called by the bookseller. The trial judge found *Fanny Hill* was obscene and that the book contained material of perversion and gross indecency. The Supreme Court of Ontario reversed the decision of the trial judge by a vote of 3-2. The court declared that while the book showed a seamy side of life, it had literary merit.

Other Offences

It is unlawful to appear nude in public. The question of dancing or performing while not fully dressed has resulted in a variety of decisions that give no clear-cut interpretation of this section of the *Code*.

The *Code* also prohibits immoral or obscene theatre performances, mailing obscene matter, or producing or selling a "crime comic." A crime comic is a publication that exclusively or substantially comprises matter depicting pictorially the commission of crimes real or fictitious.

Customs officers have the authority to refuse entry into Canada of literature which they consider obscene. Film censorship boards may restrict the permissible age of viewers of certain films, delete parts of films, or ban certain films entirely. The Supreme Court of Canda held in the case of *Nova Scotia Board of Censors v. McNeil* (1978) that provincial censorship boards do have the constitutional authority to review, cut, or ban films.

Sexual Offences

In 1983, Canada officially repealed an offence that had existed for thousands of years—the offence of rape. Cases involving rape had become very difficult to prosecute because of the reluctance of the victim to testify and because the rules of evidence had become very complex. Also repealed was the offence of indecent assault.

A new group of offences, generally called sexual assault, have replaced those repealed. The burden of proof and the evidence required are much less complex and it is hoped that trials will devote less time to challenging the character of the accused and the complainant and more time to the facts of the case.

Sexual Assault

There is no specific definition in the *Code* as to what comprises a sexual assault. Section 244(2) states that sexual assault is a form of assault. Thus, it will be left for the courts to decide what is a sexual assault. It is reasonable to assume that sexual assault will require some form of touching of the sexual parts of another person. It may or may not include sexual intercourse. If intercourse is involved, it is possible that this would be interpreted as aggravated sexual assault.

The offence can be committed equally by a male or female upon another male or female. The maximum possible penalty for sexual assault is imprisonment for

ten years. If the assault causes bodily harm or is carried out with a weapon, the maximum possible penalty is fourteen years.

Aggravated sexual assault is defined in the *Code*:

246.3 (1) Every one commits an aggravated sexual assault who, in committing a sexual assault, wounds, maims, disfigures or endangers the life of the complainant.

(2) Every one who commits an aggravated sexual assault is guilty of an indictable offence and is liable to imprisonment for life.

In earlier trials for sexual offences, it was often held that an accused could not be convicted unless there was some corroboration to back up the victim's complaint. Corroboration is not required any longer.

Generally, no evidence may be introduced about the previous character or sexual activity of the complainant (the person assaulted). There are three exceptions to this rule of exclusion:

246.6 (1) In proceedings in respect of an offence under section 246.1, 246.2 or 246.3, no evidence shall be adduced by or on behalf of the accused concerning the sexual activity of the complainant with any person other than the accused unless

(a) it is evidence that rebuts evidence of the complainant's sexual activity or absence thereof that was previously adduced by the prosecution;

(b) it is evidence of specific instances of the complainant's sexual activity tending to establish the identity of the person who had sexual contact with the complainant on the occasion set out in the charge; or

(c) it is evidence of sexual activity that took place on the same occasion as the sexual activity that forms the subject-matter of the charge, where that evidence relates to the consent that the accused alleges he believed was given by the complainant.

Historically, a husband could not be charged with the rape of his wife. Now that the offence of rape has been repealed, the *Code* gives no special protection to married persons. A husband or wife may be charged with sexual assault in respect of his or her spouse, whether or not they were living together at the time of the offence.

It is an offence to administer to a female person any drug, intoxicating liquor, or any other substance with intent to stupefy or overpower her in order to enable any person to have illicit sexual intercourse with her. The maximum penalty for such an offence is imprisonment for ten years.

Age Limitations

The *Criminal Code* establishes minimum age limitations regarding the legal authority of a person to consent to sexual activity.

> 146. (1) Every male person who has sexual intercourse with a female person who
> (a) is not his wife, and
> (b) is under the age of fourteen years,
> whether or not be believes that she is fourteen years of age or more, is guilty of an indictable offence and is liable to imprisonment for life.
> (2) Every male person who has sexual intercourse with a female person who
> (a) is not his wife,
> (b) is of previously chaste character, and
> (c) is fourteen years of age or more and is under the age of sixteen years,
> whether or not he believes that she is sixteen years of age or more, is guilty of an indictable offence and is liable to imprisonment for five years.
> (3) Where an accused is charged with an offence under subsection (2), the court may find the accused not guilty if it is of opinion that the evidence does not show that, as between the accused and the female person, the accused is more to blame than the female person.

The first thing that should be emphasized is that ignorance of the female's true age is not a defence. This is true even if she lied about her age. There are almost no defences to a charge under s. 146(1) pertaining to a female under the age of fourteen years. This is an offence worded in terms of strict prohibition and will not afford the accused the defence of mistake. Nor can the defence raise the matter of whether the female person was the instigator of the sex act, or whether the female person was of previously chaste character. It is not a defence that the female person under age fourteen consented to the act.

There are two possible defences to a charge under s. 146(2). The first defence is that the female was not of previously chaste character. The second defence relates to whether the female was more to "blame" than the male. If the female person was the instigator of the act, the accused cannot be convicted. The first defence, that of the female's character, often makes the trial a very unpleasant proceeding for the complainant. The accused must discredit the moral character of the female —show that she was not of previously chaste character —in order to avoid conviction. Whether or not she was a virgin prior to his knowledge of her is not sufficient evidence of her character. Important points include her reputation in the community, her knowledge of other males (or their knowledge of her), and general descriptions of her moral behaviour. The female complainant would have to undergo cross-examination. This can be a very harsh experience and often leads to the feeling that it is the female who is on trial, not the accused. For this reason, many females refuse to testify.

No male person can be convicted of an offence under s. 146 or s. 150 (incest) if the male person was under the age of fourteen years at the time of the alleged offence.

It is an offence for any person to take, or cause to be taken, an unmarried person under the age of sixteen years out of the possession of, and against the will of, the parent or guardian of that person. It is also an offence to receive, take, entice away, or harbour a child under the age of fourteen years with intent to deprive the parent or guardian of the possession of the child.

Soliciting and Procuring

By definition, a *prostitute* is a person of either sex who engages in prostitution. Prostitution is not a criminal offence. It is the act of soliciting that is unlawful. In *R. v. Hutt* (1978), The Supreme Court of Canada held that soliciting must be more than merely asking someone if that person wanted to purchase sex. It must be done in a "pressing and persistent manner." The court also held that a police car is not a public place. Thus, the definition under the *Criminal Code* of soliciting in a public place for the purpose of prostitution was not met.

Procuring a female person to have sex with another person is an offence. It is also an offence to operate a common bawdy house. A bawdy house means a place that is kept, or occupied, or resorted to by one or more persons for the purpose of prostitution or the practice of acts of indecency. It is also an offence to knowingly take or transport a person to a bawdy house.

The British Columbia Court of Appeal held in *R. v. Dudak* (1978) that a male customer of a prostitute could not be convicted of an offence as only the prostitute "solicits." However, the Ontario Court of Appeal reached the opposite conclusion in *R. v. Palatics* (1978). The Ontario court held that a male person, seeking the services of a prostitute, is "soliciting."

Municipalities that have tried to remove prostitutes from their streets have been hampered very much by the decision in *R. v. Hutt*. It is not unlawful for prostitutes to be on the street and if they do not solicit in a pressing and persistent manner, there are no grounds for arrest. In 1983, a Calgary by-law prohibiting the use of streets for the purpose of soliciting for prostitution was struck down by the Supreme Court of Canada. The city had argued that the law controlled a nuisance on city streets, but the Supreme Court held that the by-law was a hidden attempt to punish prostitutes. The by-law was declared ultra vires on the ground that it was a matter of criminal law and exclusively within the powers of the federal government.

Theft, Robbery, and Related Offences

Theft

Theft requires an intention to deprive another person of property. It can also include an effort to render the property unusable even though the thief does not intend to keep the property. What the thief does with the property after taking it is important in determining the thief's intention. If the thief takes property such as

a car and then abandons it, a conviction for theft is very difficult to obtain because the car can easily be returned to its owner who can be traced through registration. However, if the thief removed things from the car before abandoning it, then theft could be proven. As another example, if a thief took property such as a coat and abandoned it far from the place where it was taken, the thief could be convicted of theft because it would almost certainly be lost to the owner forever. The basic presumption when a person is caught in the act of unlawfully taking property is that it was that person's intention to commit theft. The accused may rebut this by introducing evidence that the intention was other than theft. Therefore, a person caught leaving a store with unpaid for merchandise will be convicted of theft, unless that person can give the court some other, believable explanation.

The *Criminal Code* defines theft as follows:

> **283. Every one commits theft who fraudulently and without colour of right takes, or fraudulently and without colour of right converts to his use or to the use of another person, anything whether animate or inanimate, with intent,**
>
> **(a) to deprive, temporarily or absolutely, the owner of it or a person who has a special property or interest in it, of the thing or of his property or interest in it,**
>
> **(b) to pledge it or deposit it as security,**
>
> **(c) to part with it under a condition with respect to its return that the person who parts with it may be unable to perform, or**
>
> **(d) to deal with it in such a manner that it cannot be restored in the condition in which it was at the time it was taken or converted.**
>
> **(2) A person commits theft when, with intent to steal anything, he moves it or causes it to move or to be moved, or begins to cause it to become movable.**
>
> **(3) A taking or conversion of anything may be fraudulent notwithstanding that it is effected without secrecy or attempt at concealment.**

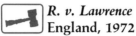

R. v. Lawrence
England, 1972

This case involved a taxi driver who overcharged an Italian visitor to London. The victim did not speak English and did not understand British currency. He went to the taxi driver and showed him an address. The victim did not know the proper fare, so he gave the driver a £1 note. The accused then gestured for the victim to hold his wallet open and removed another £6 which was far in excess of the correct fare which was less than £1. The House of Lords held that this was theft because there had been a dishonest deprivation of funds from the victim. The victim did not complain about the money being taken and had not asked for the return of it. Thus, the accused pleaded the defence that there had been a commercial transaction to which both parties consented. The court did not accept this defence, holding that consent is no answer when one party acts dishonestly. The victim did not protest the theft because he did not know at the time that a theft was taking place.

The criminal law seems to afford no remedy to a property owner whose property is constantly "borrowed" without permission by someone such as a neighbour. If Jones borrows Brown's lawn mower without permission, and contrary to Brown's instructions, there is no apparent criminal offence as long as Jones leaves the mower in the open where Brown can easily recover it. Brown could bring the practice to a halt through a civil action for trespass, but there appears to be no remedy in criminal law. Unauthorized borrowing becomes theft only when the borrower denies the owner the use of the property by locking it up, hiding it, etc. Similarly, the borrowing of the property for an inordinate length of time could constitute theft. If Jones told Brown, "I'll return your mower in twenty years," this would constitute theft, for the owner is deprived of the property for such a long time that the act really constitutes an outright taking.

The penalty for theft differs with the value of the goods taken. If the value of the goods is less than $200, the maximum penalty is imprisonment for two years. If the value is more than $200 or where the property taken is a testamentary instrument, the maximum penalty is ten years' imprisonment. It is unlawful to advertise immunity from prosecution if the thief returns the property.

Certain offences which resemble theft have been set aside and made separate offences. These include such things as defacing a cattle brand, wrongly taking cut or drift timber, and falsifying or destroying documents of title. Significantly "joyriding" is also included. As we have mentioned, it is difficult to prove theft if a person takes property, uses it, and then abandons it in such a way that the owner is able to recover it. Since this provides a defence in many cases where automobiles have been taken without the owner's consent, the *Criminal Code* makes joyriding a separate offence.

295. Every one who, without the consent of the owner, takes a motor vehicle or vessel with intent to drive, use, navigate, or operate it or cause it to be driven, used, navigated, or operated is guilty of an offence punishable on summary conviction.

A very serious offence is mail theft, which is punishable by imprisonment for ten years.

Cattle theft is punishable by imprisonment for ten years. The *Criminal Code* defines cattle to include any horse, mule, ass, pig, sheep, or goat.

Theft of a credit card is a separate offence punishable by imprisonment for ten years.

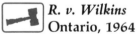

R. v. Wilkins
Ontario, 1964

The accused was apprehended by a police officer while riding on a three-wheeled vehicle called a service-car. The accused had taken the vehicle from a meter-enforcement officer while the officer was writing a parking ticket. He claimed he did it as a joke because the meter officer was giving his friend a ticket. The trial judge convicted the accused of theft, but the Court of Appeal quashed the conviction, saying that theft was not proven, but a charge of joyriding would have been appropriate.

No husband or wife commits theft by taking anything that is, by law, the property of the other if the taking occurs while they are living together. A husband or wife can be guilty of theft if either takes the property of the other while deserting or intending to desert the other. Also, if one spouse takes the property of the other, while they are living apart, this is theft. It is also theft for any other person to assist either a husband or wife to take the property of the other.

Robbery

Robbery is an aggravated form of theft. It requires (1) theft, and (2) force, or the threat of force, applied to the victim. The offence of robbery is complete when the theft is complete.

There must be force directed at some person in order to distinguish robbery from theft. If a purse snatcher easily grabs a purse away from the victim, there is no robbery, but only theft. If the victim refuses to release the purse, and the thief applies force to the victim to get the purse, this constitutes robbery. A weapon is not necessary to carry out a robbery, although if a weapon or even an imitation of a weapon is used, it constitutes armed robbery. The *Criminal Code* defines robbery as follows:

> **302. Every one commits robbery who**
> **(a) steals, and for the purpose of extorting whatever is stolen or to prevent or overcome resistance to the stealing, uses violence or threats of violence to a person or property;**
> **(b) steals from any person and, at the time he steals or immediately before or immediately thereafter, wounds, beats, strikes or uses any personal violence to that person;**
> **(c) assaults any person with intent to steal from him; or**
> **(d) steals from any person while armed with an offensive weapon or imitation thereof.**

Robbery can result from a theft which goes awry, requiring the thief to fight in order to escape. Let us assume that a thief has acquired the desired articles but is immediately detected by the owner who attempts to stop the thief's escape. This causes the thief to strike the owner in order to escape, and the theft becomes robbery (s. 302(b)). However, suppose the thief escapes the owner and runs several steps. Then another person tries to grab the thief, causing the thief to assault that person. Is this theft or robbery? In all likelihood it would be treated as theft from the first person and assault upon the second person who grabbed the thief.

Subsection (c) includes assault *with intent to steal* as robbery. Under the common law, if a thief assaulted a person in order to commit robbery more easily and then found the victim had nothing worth stealing, the matter was treated as assault only. The *Code* specifically defines this as robbery. If Jones hits Smith on the head in order to go through Smith's pockets with ease, only to find that Smith has no money, it would be wrong to claim that Jones had the intention only to assault Smith. Jones intended to rob Smith, and that is the offence of which Jones should be convicted.

The maximum penalty for robbery is life imprisonment. Since theft is punishable by imprisonment for ten years, it is understandable why the accused would prefer to be charged with theft.

R. v. Sloan
British Columbia, 1975

Sloan appealed from his conviction for attempted robbery contrary to s. 302(d) of the *Criminal Code*. The accused had attempted a robbery using his finger to give the appearance of having a gun. The question arose whether the conviction could be upheld as there was no imitation of an offensive weapon. The Court of Appeal allowed the appeal. To be convicted, one must be armed with or in possession of a weapon or an imitation of one. It was held that a finger could not be an "imitation" of a weapon.

Possession of Stolen Goods

Another offence related to theft is the unlawful possession of stolen goods. The *Criminal Code* states:

312. (1) Every one commits an offence who has in his possession any property or thing or any proceeds of any property or thing knowing that all or part of the property or thing or of the proceeds was obtained by or derived directly or indirectly from
   (a) the commission in Canada of an offence punishable by indictment; or
   (b) an act or omission anywhere that, if it had occurred in Canada, would have constituted an offence punishable by indictment.

In s. 312, the word "knowing" is extremely important. Ignorance of the fact that the goods were stolen is a defence to the charge of unlawful possession. In order that the defence of ignorance should not become a perfect defence, the *Criminal Code* allows the Crown to introduce evidence relating to the accused's past experience with regard to stolen goods. The Crown may introduce evidence to show that stolen property, other than the property that is the subject-matter of the present proceedings, was found in the possession of the accused within twelve months before the present proceedings were commenced. The Crown may also introduce evidence to show that the accused has been convicted within the past five years of theft or unlawful possession of stolen goods.

In a case of unlawful possession, the Crown often relies upon what is known as the *doctrine of recent possession*. This means that if the Crown can establish that the accused has come into possession of goods recently stolen, then there is a prima facie case of unlawful possession which the accused must rebut. The accused must give some explanation as to how he or she came by these goods and the jury must decide whether this explanation "could reasonably be true." The accused need not prove the story, but only raise some doubt in the juror's minds. The burden remains on the Crown to prove the offence beyond a reasonable doubt. If the accused refuses to testify, then the Crown may rely upon the doctrine of recent possession to convict the accused.

The penalty for unlawful possession differs with the value of the goods. If the value of the goods exceeds $200, the maximum penalty is imprisonment for ten years. If the value does not exceed $200, the maximum penalty is imprisonment for two years.

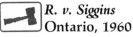
R. v. Siggins
Ontario, 1960

The Crown appealed an acquittal of the accused on the charge of possession of stolen goods. The accused was also charged with theft, and when the jury found him Not Guilty of theft, the trial judge refused to allow the jury to consider the charge of unlawful possession. The Court of Appeal held that the trial judge had erred. If the accused had been convicted of theft, he could not also be convicted of unlawful possession of stolen goods. However, if the jury acquitted of theft, they might convict on the charge of unlawful possession.

Obtaining by False Pretence

Section 320 of the *Code* makes it an offence to obtain by false pretence or false statement the delivery of personal property, the payment of money, the making of a loan, the extension of credit, the making or accepting of a bill of exchange (cheque, draft, or promissory note), or the discount of an account receivable.

This section makes it an offence to write a cheque knowing that it will be dishonoured. If the cheque is dishonoured, the offence of obtaining by false pretence shall be presumed, unless the accused can show that when the cheque was written the accused had reasonable grounds to believe the cheque would be honoured.

A number of cases involving price tag switching have been held by the courts to come under this section. If a person switches price tags on two items and then pays for the item at the lower price, the courts have held that theft is not the proper change since some payment was made. Obtaining by false pretence is the more appropriate charge.

Fraud

Fraud is a massive topic and many sections of the *Code* pertain to special forms of fraud such as mail fraud, keeping false records, bank fraud, manipulating stocks, and many others. A very basic definition is found in the following section:

338. (1) Every one who, by deceit, falsehood or other fraudulent means, whether or not it is a false pretence within the meaning of this Act, defrauds the public or any person, whether ascertained or not, of any property, money or valuable security,

(a) is guilty of an indictable offence and is liable to imprisonment for ten years, where the subject matter of the fraud is a testamentary instrument or where the value thereof exceeds two hundred dollars; or

(b) is guilty

(i) of an indictable offence and is liable to imprisonment for two years, or

(ii) of an offence punishable on summary conviction, where the value of the property of which the public or any person is defrauded does not exceed two hundred dollars.

R. v. Monkman
Manitoba, 1980

The court held in this case that the failure of the accused to notify the government of a change in her income was fraudulent when she kept receiving social assistance payments as a result of her non-disclosure. The court held that while the words "deceit" and "falsehood" in s. 338 may require some false representations as distinct from silence or non-disclosure, the words "other fraudulent means" are not so limited and are to be given the widest possible meaning to include all cases where there is proof of dishonesty.

Reviewing Important Points

1. Offences are classified as summary conviction offences (less serious) and indictable offences (more serious).

2. Some offences are worded in such a way that the burden of proof is shifted onto the accused. Such offences are said to include "reverse onus clauses."

3. It is not homicide to kill a child which is still in the mother's womb. Abortion is an offence distinguished from homicide.

4. The offence of assault does not necessarily involve the actual infliction of bodily harm.

5. Driving while ability is impaired is a criminal offence. A police officer must have a reason for demanding a breath test. Refusing to take a breath test is a summary conviction offence.

6. Theft is the taking of property with the intent to deprive the owner of it. Robbery is theft with violence or threat of violence.

7. In the charge of break and enter, entry includes the insertion of any part of the body inside the building. Breaking *out* of a place can also be held to be break and enter.

8.(a) Possession of narcotics is not limited to having personal possession at the time of arrest.

(b) Trafficking in narcotics can include *giving* a narcotic to someone. It is *not* confined to business deals.

(c) Possession of "controlled drugs" is not an offence; possession of "restricted drugs" is.

9. Prohibited weapons are totally illegal and may not be possessed by anyone; restricted weapons may be possessed only if a police permit is obtained.

10. In a charge of homicide, the accused will be held criminally responsible if the act of the accused contributed substantially to the victim's death. The accused's act need not be the sole cause of death.

11. It can generally be said that murder requires a specific intent, while manslaughter requires only a general intent.

12. All parties to an offence are considered parties to murder if a death ensues while carrying out that offence.

13. Murder can be reduced to manslaughter if it can be proved there was sufficient provocation to cause the slayer to lose self-control.

14. In a charge of criminal negligence, it is not necessary to prove that what the accused did was in itself unlawful.

15. Obscene matter can be generally defined as that which contains an "undue exploitation of sex."

Checking Your Understanding

1. What circumstances are required in order for a woman to have a legal abortion?

2. If a driver receives a demand from a peace officer to take a breathalyzer test, what rights has the driver in regard to first speaking with a lawyer?

3. How soon after the making of the demand must the breathalyzer tests be concluded?

4. How many breathalyzer tests must be taken? What is the "failing" limit?

5. In a charge for possession of narcotics, the Crown must prove three things. What are they?

6. Identify three situations in which a person may use force or physical contact upon another person.

7. What is criminal negligence?

8. What is a lesser included offence in the offence of break and enter?

9. What document must be obtained before a person can lawfully purchase a firearm?

10. What condition or circumstance can reduce a charge of murder to a charge of manslaughter?

11. What is the proper charge if a person takes someone's automobile for an unauthorized ride but then returns the automobile?

12. What is the doctrine of recent possession?

Legal Briefs

1. B owes money to C and refuses to repay it despite repeated requests from C. C, and a large "humungus" companion confront B and threaten instant bodily harm if the money is not paid. B hands over the money. Theft? Robbery? Some other offence?

2. R wants to rob the XYZ Corp. warehouse. R conspires with K, an employee, to leave a door unlocked and the alarm system shut off. That night R enters the warehouse and is arrested while loading stolen goods into a truck. Break and enter? Theft? Some other offence?

3. H and C form a suicide pact. H buys sleeping pills with legal prescriptions acquired over a period of six months by going to different doctors and pharmacies.

H and C take the pills but only C dies. Has H committed an offence?

4. G, a known homosexual, "propositions" C in front of C's friends. G (falsely) suggests that C has accepted such invitations before. C is infuriated by the ridicule heaped on him by his friends and beats G so savagely that G dies. Murder? Manslaughter? Not homicide?

5. T takes a ring from H, believing it to be valuable. A jeweller appraises the ring as "costume jewellery — not worth anything." Disgusted, T returns the ring to the place from which she took it. Theft? Attempted theft? No offence?

6. T and N have a fight. T pulls out a knife and says, "I'll cut you into little pieces." N runs away with T in pursuit. N runs in front of a truck and is killed. Is T guilty of an offence?

7. While R, an Ontario resident, is in a New York motel, S, a drug smuggler, puts a packet of drugs into the hubcap of R's car. R is unaware of this. After R returns to Ontario, S expects to locate R's car and recover the drugs. R's car is checked at the border and the drugs are found. Advise R.

8. Assume in Question 7 that R knows the packet is i the car and has been paid $500 to bring it into Canad; R does not know what is in the packet because S has said, "Don't ask — it's better that you don't know." Advise R.

9. During a protest march, some shop windows are broken by protestors. H, not part of the protest, finds the merchandise in the windows tempting. H reaches through a broken window and takes a tape recorder. Break and enter? Theft? Some other offence?

10. P, a surgeon, performs an abortion upon M, who was six months pregnant. Much to P's surprise, the infant is alive when removed from M's body. P orders that no one give any care to the infant who dies an hour later. Has P committed an offence?

11. G, the director of a hospital, is angry and concerned about overcrowding. Patients are in beds in the hallways and hospital staff are working overtime every day. G makes a statement to the media that the hospital can accept no more patients. An ambulance arrives with K, the victim of a heart attack. G tells the

ambulance driver to take K to another hospital in another city, 30 km away. K dies enroute. Has G committed an offence?

12. D plants a bomb in a building and calls the building supervisor to report the bomb. The supervisor, thinking D is a crank caller, does not believe the story. The building is not evacuated and the bomb explodes killing two people. What offence(s) has D committed? What offence(s) has the building supervisor committed?

13. Police raid M's bookstore and seize a novel which some people think is obscene. The judge concludes that the novel is indeed obscene. M's lawyer tells the court that M stocks more than 2000 different books at one time, receives all the books automatically from a distributor, and has never read any of the books in the store, including the one seized. Will M be convicted?

14. Z removed a wallet from E's purse in a store. E got a glimpse of Z's hand and tells B, the store manager. B confronts Z near the exit and demands that she not leave the store. Z asserts that she is free to leave if she wants and, when B puts a restraining hand upon her, Z hits B. Z is caught in the parking lot by three store employees and is turned over to police who find the wallet. What offence(s) has Z committed?

Applying the Law

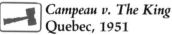

Campeau v. The King
Quebec, 1951

The accused, a teacher, was found guilty of common assault upon three children. The children attended the school in which the accused was teaching. The evidence showed that the accused punished Yvon Vincent, aged eight, by taking his arm by the wrist and striking with the back of the boy's hand across the corner of the teacher's wooden desk several times, causing injury. The same treatment was applied to two girls who were also struck on the arms with a stick. The children had not done their lessons and had made fun of the teacher. Campeau appealed his conviction to the Quebec Court of Appeal. In part, the decision reads:

"The schoolmaster has a right to use force to discipline children. What would be under the law an assault is permitted in the case of school children, provided the offence committed by the child merits punishment and that the punishment is reasonable and appropriate to the offence. That the punishment may cause pain hardly needs to be stated; otherwise its whole purpose is lost. If the pupil suffers bruises it does not necessarily follow that the punishment is unreasonable. However, if the master is careless in the manner of punishment he may, by that fact alone, be held responsible. There will be no disagreement that if the master strikes a pupil on the head, by way of discipline, his act is unjustified; the reason being that there is danger of doing permanent harm by striking a delicate part of the body such as the head. A teacher has a heavy responsibility and in imposing corporal punishment he must be extremely careful. There are a number of parts of the body where the bones are well protected by thick flesh and it is to these parts that force should be applied. The hand is not such a part. It may be that in the early nineteenth century cruelty to school children was permitted in their interests, but in the present century the attitude has changed and the master who strikes a child where permanent damage may occur must take the consequences. I would dismiss the appeal.**"**

Questions

1. According to the Court of Appeal, what are the two basic criteria that must be met to justify punishment of a pupil?
2. Does s. 43 of the *Code* actually authorize "punishment"?
3. Is there any historic accuracy to the judge's statement that at one time "cruelty to children was permitted in their interests"?
4. What parts of the body do you think the judge had in mind when he said there are a "*number of parts* of the body where the bones are well protected by thick flesh and it is to these parts that force should be applied"?
5. Should s. 43 be repealed entirely?

R. v. Woodman
England, 1974

The accused and his son were charged with theft when they took scrap metal away from the premises of a company. The premises were a disused factory belonging to English China Clays Company and the indictment alleged that the metal was the property of that company. In 1970 the company went out of business and signed a contract with the Bird Group of companies to dismantle the building and to remove all scrap metal. The Bird Group did most of the work but did not take all the metal present, finding that some was inaccessible and not worth the time to remove. During the next four years, despite "No Trespassing" signs, numerous persons went onto the property looking for anything of any value that could be carried away. The accused was such a person and believed that no one cared if he or anyone else removed anything from the site because it was abandoned by its owners. The Court of Appeal upheld a conviction of the accused, saying that a mistaken belief that no one would object to the taking of property which was the property of another is no defence.

❝So far as this case is concerned, arising as it does under the *Theft Act*, we are content to say that there was evidence of English China Clays being in control of the site and in control of articles on the site as well. The fact that it could not be shown that they were aware or conscious of the existence of this or any particular scrap iron does not destroy the general principle that control of a site by excluding others from it is prima facie control of articles on the site as well.❞

Questions

1. From all appearances, China Clays did not want anything on the site. Why was the accused convicted?
2. Was the court, in this case, saying that there is no such thing as "lawful garbage picking"?
3. Who owns garbage? No one? Anyone that wants it?
4. Is there property that belongs to no one, or does all property belong to someone?
5. If a property owner does not know that someone is taking the property, does that alter the charge of theft against the person taking it? Does it matter whether the property owner cares if the property is taken?

R. v. Louison
Supreme Court of Canada, 1975

The appellant passenger forced a taxi driver to stop, robbed him of his wallet, and locked him in the trunk. Later when the passenger opened the trunk, the driver struck him on the back with a hammer. The appellant took the hammer from the driver and struck him with it repeatedly over the head, killing him. The appellant appealed his conviction for murder principally on the ground that the trial judge had failed to put to the jury the defence of provocation. Evidence of the alleged provocation was contained in a statement made to the police, and the statement was ruled admissible. The majority held the appeal should be dismissed.

❝Provocation should consist of a wrongful act or insult sufficient to deprive an ordinary person of power of self-control. While the issue of provocation was for the jury, the question of whether or not there was any evidence of a wrongful act was one of law for the presiding judge. In the present case, the trial judge had correctly held that, in view of the treatment to which the appellant had subjected the driver, not only were the driver's actions on being released from his cab not wrongful but they were to be anticipated. The wrongfulness of an act relied upon as being provocation was to be decided on a consideration not merely of the act itself but of all the surrounding circumstances.❞

Questions

1. What is the definition of provocation?
2. Can a person who commits a crime claim that he or she was "provoked" by the victim? Give a reason for your answer.
3. Was it "wrongful" for the taxi driver to hit the accused with a hammer?
4. The court ruled that the actions of the taxi driver were to be "anticipated." Do you agree with that conclusion? Why or why not?

You Be the Judge

1. A juvenile had a small bank account containing less than $10. By error the bank began depositing to this account $3000 per month. The accused saw it as a bonanza and began withdrawing money and spending it for every type of luxury item available. When the bank discovered the error, the accused gave a statement to the police that he knew the money was not his. "I almost flipped out," he said to the investigating officer. The accused was charged with theft. The defence argued that there had been no "taking" as the money had been given to the accused by the bank and the bank even verified the balance when the accused questioned the amount. Should the accused be convicted?

2. The accused owned a chimpanzee that was often on display at carnivals, circuses, and exhibitions. The animal was normally docile but had an unpredictable nature and had bitten and attacked humans on two previous occasions. The chimp was at an exhibition when the accused invited a nine-year-old girl to "shake hands" with the chimp. When the girl went to do so, the animal unexpectedly seized her by the head and threw her a considerable distance. Expert evidence was led that a chimp is three times as strong as a human and if a chimp has ever attacked a human it is very likely to do so again. The accused was charged with criminal negligence. Should the accused be convicted?

3. The accused escaped from prison and during her period of freedom broke and entered a cottage. The accused was charged with break and enter as well as being unlawfully at large (prison break). Referring to the charge of break and enter the accused testified that she broke into the cottage to find a place to sleep. She also looked into a refrigerator to see if she could find anything to eat but there was no food in the cottage. Should the accused be convicted of break and enter?

4. The accused was charged with impaired driving. The accused had been out drinking with another woman who was driving the accused's car. The two women had an argument and the other woman left the car. The accused was sitting on the passenger side of the front seat when the other woman got out and walked away, leaving the motor running. The accused moved over behind the wheel, put the car in gear, and drove into a ditch. The police found her there and charged her with impaired driving. The defence centred around the argument that the accused had not entered the vehicle with the intention of driving. She had entered with the intention and expectation of being a passenger and she had become a temporary driver only because of the actions of the other woman. Should the accused be convicted?

5. The accused man's wife parked their car in a parking lot and met the accused in a restaurant. The accused drank a large quantity of beer in the restaurant. When they left, the accused got into an argument with the parking lot attendant who called the police. When the police arrived they found the accused sitting behind the wheel. The wife was supposed to drive the car home, but she was still in the restaurant. Nonetheless, the police officer demanded that the accused take a breathalyzer test which he refused to do. He was charged with refusal to take the test. Should the accused be convicted?

6. The accused and some friends took a car which belonged to the landlord of the accused. The accused brought the car back and the landlord angrily told her never to take the car again. The accused took the car again four days later. She was by herself at the time. The landlord called the police who went over to the house. While the police were there making a report, the accused drove back into the driveway and was arrested. She was charged with stealing a vehicle. Should the accused be convicted?

7. The accused was dismissed from her job without notice. There was just cause for her dismissal and about that point there was no argument. However, she was ordered from the company premises so quickly that she forgot to take with her certain personal items kept in a locker at the rear of the plant. Two nights later, she went back to the plant and entered through a window which she knew had a defective lock. She collected her personal articles and

was leaving through the same window when the police arrested her. She was charged with break and enter. Should the accused be convicted?

8. The accused, while driving his automobile, struck and injured a pedestrian. There were several witnesses at the scene and they all told the investigating officer that, in their opinion, the pedestrian was completely at fault. The accused had done some drinking that day and was fearful that someone would later raise the issue that he was drunk. This prompted him to ask the officer to give him a breathalyzer test to "prove he was not drunk" at the time. The officer said he did not have to take a test but the accused insisted that he wanted to do so to clear his name. The accused and the officer went to the police station and the accused took two tests. The tests showed respective readings of 120 mg and 125 mg of alcohol in 100 mL of blood; accordingly, the accused was charged with impaired driving. At the trial, the defence lawyer asked that the results of the tests be thrown out because the officer had not demanded that the tests be taken as the *Code* requires. Should the accused be convicted?

Chapter 5

Defences to Criminal Charges

It is an established principle of our law that the court must observe this maxim: *Audi alteram partem* ("hear the other side"). The *Criminal Code* further guarantees every accused person the right to make a full and complete defence to the charge. Some defences are general and may be raised against any charge, including the defence that the accused did not commit the act charged. Other defences are more specific and may be raised against specific charges. The accused has a right to legal counsel, and the duty of that counsel is to put the Crown's case to the fullest test.

The defences discussed in this section have not been arranged in any special order. They are not intended to be all-inclusive, but rather encompass those defences most commonly raised against serious charges.

Some of the defences discussed are specifically defined in the *Criminal Code*. Others are common law defences that were developed in England. When the *Criminal Code* underwent a major revision in 1955, all common law offences (crimes) were abolished, with the exception of contempt of court. However, the *Criminal Code* specifically retained all common law defences to crimes.

The Defence of Insanity

Most crimes require both a prohibited act and a certain mental capacity. The common law has long recognized that certain kinds of insanity could provide a defence against criminal conviction. Originally, an accused would be found "Guilty of the offence as charged, but

not responsible by reason of insanity." He or she was then sent to a mental institution. The practice of convicting the accused even while recognizing insanity gradually gave way to a practice of finding the accused Not Guilty by reason of insanity.

Insanity Defined in the *Criminal Code*

Section 16 of the *Criminal Code* defines the defence of insanity as it applies to Canadian law.

> **16. (1) No person shall be convicted of an offence in respect of an act or omission on his part while he was insane.**
>
> **(2) For the purposes of this section a person is insane when he is in a state of natural imbecility or has disease of the mind to an extent that renders him incapable of appreciating the nature and quality of an act or omission or of knowing that an act or omission is wrong.**
>
> **(3) A person who has specific delusions, but is in other respects sane, shall not be acquitted on the ground of insanity unless the delusions caused him to believe in the existence of a state of things that, if it existed, would have justified or excused his act or omission.**
>
> **(4) Every one shall, until the contrary is proved, be presumed to be and to have been sane.**

The defence of insanity is very complex and it should be kept in mind that our discussion here must necessarily be somewhat short. It is not possible to examine all the pertinent case law on this vast topic.

The *Criminal Code* does not define mental illness as such. It merely defines the kind of mental illness that affords a defence to the criminal charge. In this context the *Code* includes "disease of the mind." We should note that there is a distinction between disease of the mind and disease of the brain. Certain diseases can affect behaviour without directly affecting the brain. To be insane, a person must be either in a state of natural imbecility or suffer from a disease of the mind. Simply being in one of those conditions, however, is not enough. To provide a defence, either condition must exist to the extent that it renders the accused incapable of appreciating the nature and quality of an act or omission *or* incapable of knowing that an act or omission is wrong. In *Schwartz v. The Queen* (1977), the Supreme Court of Canada held that the word "wrong" means "legally wrong." Other words have similarly required extensive definition.

R. v. Barnier
Supreme Court of Canada, 1980

The trial judge in this case told the jury that the word "appreciating" means the same thing as "knowing." The Supreme Court of Canada did not agree with that definition. The court held that the word "know" has a positive connotation requiring a bare awareness, the act of receiving information without more. The act of "appreciating" is a second stage in a mental process requiring the analysis of knowledge or experience in one manner or another. The court concluded that there had been misdirection and a new trial would be required.

In *Cooper v. The Queen* (1979), the Supreme Court of Canada held that, in a legal sense, disease of the mind embraces any illness, disorder, or abnormal condition which impairs the human mind and its functioning, *excluding* self-induced states caused by alcohol or drugs as well as transitory mental states such as hysteria or concussion. The court also stated that whether the accused has a disease of the mind is a *legal* question, not a medical question, and that medical witnesses cannot state whether the accused has a disease of the mind. Medical witnesses can describe the accused's *condition* but must leave the final determination to the jury.

Consequences of the Defence of Insanity

The law makes a basic assumption that every person is sane. The accused may raise the defence of insanity and need not prove it beyond a reasonable doubt, but only upon a balance of probabilities. If the accused does not raise the defence of insanity, the Crown may raise it. This may seem unusual, but there is good reason why the Crown may want to do so. Statistical studies show that, through the parole system, persons convicted of serious offences have a better chance of release than do persons placed in mental institutions. In other words, a plea of Not Guilty by reason of insanity may condemn the accused to a longer period of incarceration than a plea of Guilty. If the Crown believes the accused is dangerous and in need of psychiatric help, then the Crown has a duty to request that the court consider the sanity of the accused.

An accused found Not Guilty by reason of insanity must be placed in an institution. Commitment does not require further certification. The judge completes a Lieutenant-Governor's Warrant which requires the accused to stay in the institution until released by order of the Lieutenant-Governor of the province. In most provinces, the case must be reviewed by a medical panel every six months.

If an accused is found Guilty, the judge must sentence the accused, not send the accused to a mental hospital no matter how much the judge believes the accused needs psychiatric help.

A judge may at any time during proceedings remand the accused to a mental hospital for a period of observation not to exceed thirty days, when, in the judge's opinion, supported by the evidence of at least one qualified medical practitioner, there is reason to believe the accused may be mentally ill. Where a medical practitioner is not available, and compelling circumstances exist, the judge may remand the accused for observation for a period not exceeding thirty days without the evidence of a medical practitioner. The judge may remand the accused for a period of observation not exceeding sixty days with the written opinion of at least one medical practitioner that a longer period is

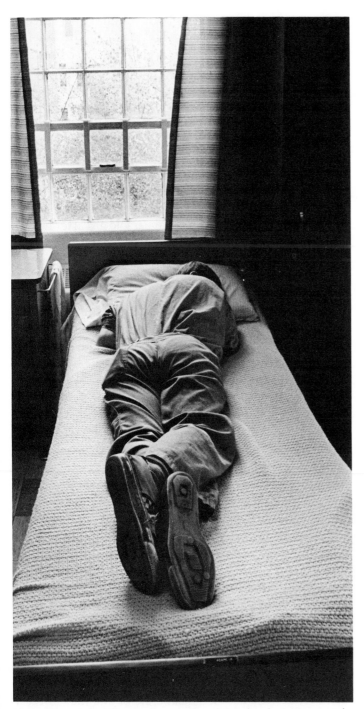

Under our criminal law system, an accused found to be insane must be acquitted as the accused lacked the necessary mental capacity to commit a crime.

necessary. This could lead to a permanent committal upon the certification of two psychiatrists that the accused is insane.

Kjeldsen v. The Queen
Supreme Court of Canada, 1981

The appellant was charged with first degree murder of a woman taxi driver whom he had hired to drive him from Calgary to Banff. His only defence was insanity as there was no question concerning the fact that he had killed the woman. He was convicted at trial. The Court of Appeal dismissed his appeal, but a verdict of guilty of second degree murder was substituted because of the failure of the trial judge to instruct the jury adequately on the difference between first and second degree murder. The appellant's appeal was based on the ground that the court did not properly interpret the law pertaining to insanity in relation to his condition. The appellant had been a mental patient in Alberta. He was given a day pass which permitted him to leave the hospital. The murder occurred shortly afterwards. The defence centred primarily upon the word "appreciating" in s. 16 of the *Code*. The appellant was classed as a psychopath. Medical witnesses for the Crown testified that a psychopath could fully appreciate the nature and quality of personal acts while being indifferent to their consequences. Defence witnesses took the opposite view. The issue, stated in the form of two questions, becomes: Was the appellant at the time of the commission of the act which killed the victim suffering from a disease of the mind within the meaning of that expression in s. 16 of the *Code*? If so, did the disease of the mind have the effect of depriving him of the capacity to appreciate the nature and quality of his acts at the time of his attack upon the deceased?

The trial judge had told the jury that "to appreciate" means to realize what you are doing at the time and to also appreciate all the consequences flowing from your act. This did not require that the accused would feel remorse or guilt for what he had done. It required a knowledge and appreciation of the physical nature of the act.

The Supreme Court of Canada held that there had been no misdirection and dismissed the appeal.

The Defence of Drunkenness

Our law has wrestled with the question of mental impairment caused by alcohol for a long time. There is a general reluctance to excuse the behaviour of any person simply because the person was drunk at the time. This revulsion generates from the belief that drunkenness itself is a moral vice, and that to combine drunkenness with other wrongful behaviour is doubly wrong rather than excusable. Originally, the common law required that drunkenness was never a defence for it

The defence of drunkenness is applicable to crimes requiring specific intent. The accused may show that he was too drunk to form the necessary mens rea of the crime.

was caused by the accused's own voluntary act of getting drunk. One of the earliest texts on criminal law in England stated that, "He who is guilty of any crime whatever through his voluntary drunkenness shall be punished for it as if he had been sober." The law stood this way for many years.

One of the most instructive cases dealing with the defence of drunkenness was *Director of Public Prosecutions v. Beard.*

 Director of Public Prosecutions v. Beard
England, 1920
The accused killed a thirteen-year-old girl after having raped her. His only defence was that because of drunkenness the charge should be manslaughter, not murder. In the ruling against the accused's appeal from conviction, the House of Lords rejected this defence. The judges ruled that all the prosecution had to prove was that the death resulted from the commission of a crime of violence and that the accused had intended to commit that crime. In delivering the decision, Lord Birkenhead emphasized that the accused's drunkenness had only caused him to give way to a violent passion, and that this alone did not rebut the presumption that the accused had intended the natural consequences of his acts.

In the *Beard* case, Lord Birkenhead set down three rules concerning drunkenness as a defence. These rules form the basis of the law on this subject today, and our discussion of drunkenness will follow these rules. (Note that in these three quotations from Lord Birkenhead all references to male persons should be read as applying equally to female persons.)

• *Rule One:* "Insanity, whether produced by drunkenness or otherwise, is a defence to the charge."

If an accused person has consumed so much alcohol as to render the accused insane, he or she may enter a plea of insanity to the charge and be found Not Guilty by reason of insanity. In this case, the accused will be remanded to a mental hospital.

Drunkenness that leads to insanity is a rare occurrence, but disease of the mind which stems from prolonged drinking can cause insanity. If drunkenness produces a state of mind that would otherwise relieve an accused from responsibility, then it provides an adequate defence to the charge. One such disease of the mind is *delirium tremens*, called the "d.t.'s" for short. Delirium tremens is a disorder of the nervous system which may set up an attack of delusional insanity. It is caused by long indulgence in alcohol which affects the entire nervous system and the brain. Delirium tremens may cause either permanent or temporary insanity. In either case, it allows the defence of insanity.

- *Rule Two:* "Evidence of drunkenness which renders the accused incapable of forming the specific intent essential to constitute the crime should be taken into consideration with the other facts provided in order to determine whether or not he had this intent."

If the drunken person is drunk to the point of not knowing what he or she is doing, this is a defence to any charge, such as murder, in which a specific intent is essential; but the accused is still liable to be convicted of manslaughter for which no specific intent is required. In general, drunkenness is a factor to be taken into consideration is deducing intent from the actions of the accused.

If a crime requires intention, drunkenness may help to show that there was no desire for the consequences. If the crime requires recklessness, drunkenness may show that there was no ability to foresee what might occur. Drunkenness is not a blanket defence to everything. It only provides evidence regarding the mental state of the accused and may tend to prove that intent (mens rea) was absent.

Some sections of the *Criminal Code* are very specific on the degree of intent required. Normally, the words "intentionally" or "with intent" are used. Other sections of the *Code* omit any mention of intent, and the courts have had to interpret each section with respect to intent. The effect of drunkenness may be that it affords only a partial defence. The accused may be acquitted of one charge, but found to have had enough mental capacity to commit a lesser included offence. Assault causing bodily harm can be reduced to common assault. Murder can be reduced to manslaughter, and so on. The words "specific intent" are open to interpretation, but generally it can be said that they mean an "intent of a recognized character required by law as an element of a certain offence."

R. v. George
Supreme Court of Canada, 1960

The accused was charged with the robbery of an elderly man. During the course of the robbery, the victim was badly beaten and dumped into a bathtub of water until he agreed to give the accused what money he had — a total of $22. The accused was found Not Guilty of the charge of robbery by reason of his drunkenness, but was convicted of common assault. The accused appealed to the British Columbia Court of Appeal and the conviction was quashed. The Crown then appealed to the Supreme Court of Canada which restored the conviction for common assault. The Supreme Court ruled that the acquittal of the accused on the principal charge of robbery by reason of drunkenness did not mean that he was incapable of forming the general intent to use force which was all that was required under the relevant section of the *Criminal Code*. In its decision, the court held that:

❝Evidence that the accused was in a state of voluntary drunkenness cannot be treated as a defence to a charge of common assault. The accused's own statement indicates that he knew he was applying force to the person of another.**❞**

- *Rule Three:* "Evidence of drunkenness falling short of a proved incapacity in the accused to form the intent necessary to constitute the crime, and merely establishing that his mind was so affected by drink so that he more readily gave way to some violent passion does not rebut the presumption that a man intends the natural consequences of his acts."

It may be said that drink may cause a person to commit an act on a sudden impulse that the person could have resisted if sober. That is no defence. The accused person may say that everything was "hazy," but if the person knows what he or she is doing, even though things are unclear, alcohol affords no defence. The consumption of alcohol is no defence where a person consumed alcohol to get false courage, or to overcome reluctance. Where a person says, "I wouldn't have done it if I had not been drunk," there is no defence.

In some cases of murder, where the defence attempted to have murder reduced to manslaughter on the grounds of provocation, drunkenness was combined with provocation and admitted in evidence as one defence. There is some reason to believe that a drunken person may have a lower "boiling point" than a sober person and be more readily provoked. However, this acceptance of drunkenness and provocation combined as one defence is not widespread. A careful reading of the *Criminal Code* shows that the test of provocation is whether it would "deprive an *ordinary person* of the power of self-control." It would seem incorrect to treat a drunken person as an ordinary person.

Canadian law no longer accepts the principle of "proved incapacity" as suggested by Lord Birkenhead. This principle suggests that the burden is upon the accused to prove he or she did not have the necessary intent. Rather, the judge must stress in the charge to the jury that the burden is upon the Crown to prove that the accused had the necessary intent while the defence need only raise on a balance of probabilities that the accused did not.

Attorney General for Northern Ireland v. Gallagher
England, 1961

The accused man had a grievance against his wife, about which he had brooded for a long time. He bought a knife and a bottle of whisky, either to give himself courage to do the deed or to drown his conscience after having done it. He did, in fact, kill his wife. Concerning the defence of drunkenness, the trial judge directed the jury as follows:

> 66You should direct your attention to the state of his mind before he opened the bottle of whisky. If he was sane at that time, he could not make good the defence of insanity with the aid of that bottle of whisky.99

The defence appealed on the grounds that the jury was wrongly charged. The defendant was a psychopath, and the defence argued that drink brought on an explosive outburst in the course of which he killed his wife. Defence counsel felt this should have been put to the jury as a possible defence. The House of Lords restored the conviction that had been overturned by an appeal court. Lord Denning delivered the court's decision and included these words:

> 66A psychopath who goes out intending to kill, knowing it is wrong, and does kill, cannot escape the consequences by making himself drunk before doing it.99

Canadian courts have altered *Rule Three* somewhat and do not tell a jury that it is a *presumption* that a person intends the natural consequences of personal acts. The words *reasonable inference* are preferred. An important question is whether the judge should instruct the jury regarding the accused's *intent*, or *capacity to form intent*. The Supreme Court of Canada has said that if the accused had the capacity to form the specific intent, then the defence of drunkenness does not succeed.

In *Pappajohn v. The Queen* (1980), the Supreme Court of Canada held that mistake of fact, brought on by drunkenness, may be a defence to a charge of rape where the accused alleged that he mistakenly believed the victim was consenting. Although the crime of rape has been repealed, the issue of consent is a possible issue under the wording of s. 244(4) which pertains to all forms of assault. If the accused's drunkenness caused him to mistakenly believe the victim was consenting, this is a defence which the judge must instruct the jury to consider.

The Defence of Automatism

One of the essential elements of a crime is the actus reus (the prohibited act). If an accused person can establish that he or she did not act, it will be possible to escape criminal responsibility.

It is common knowledge that there are things which can cause a physical movement of the body without a conscious mental effort. The body's system of muscular reflexes is one such example. If someone is suddenly seized upon, that person may instinctively strike out. Later, it may be necessary to say apologetically, "I'm sorry I broke your nose, but you startled me." Yet, there is probably no real reason to apologize, for it was the body that reacted, not the mind. If a person's physical movements are not subject to the control of the mind, the first essential element of criminal liability, namely voluntary conduct, is lacking. This is the basis of the defence of *automatism*.

A good definition of automatism was provided in the case of *Rabey v. The Queen* (Supreme Court of Canada, 1980):

> 66Automatism is a term used to describe unconscious, involuntary behaviour, the state of a person who, though capable of action is not conscious of what he is doing. It means an unconscious involuntary act where the mind does not go with what is being done.99

An important question is, can a state of dissociation between the mind and the body exist for a prolonged period of time? The answer is "Yes." This state of dissociation can last for a lengthy period of time and result in physical activity which the doer may not be able to recall and over which he or she had no control at the time. Memory of details is not necessarily inconsistent with automatism. There are occasions when an accused can remember bits and pieces of what he or she did, particularly if someone tries to help the remembering process.

Insane and Non-Insane Automatism

Some of the causes of automatism are internal, meaning they develop within the person's body. Other causes are external, such as a blow on the head. Our law has generally attempted to distinguish the two types by called them *insane* and *non-insane* automatism. The primary difference between the two types is not so much the effect upon the accused at the time of the alleged offence, but rather what must be done with the accused after the offence. If an accused person is found Not Guilty by reason of insane automatism, the person must be committed to a mental hospital for treatment. If found Not Guilty by reason of non-insane automatism, the accused is set free. As an example, if an accused person had suffered a blow on the head, there would be no reason to confine the person to a mental hospital if he or she had recovered from that blow.

Insane automatism can include such things as hardening of the arteries, tumours, or any brain damage caused by various diseases including venereal disease. The condition that exists is not temporary, and while the person may be rational from time to time, that person is far from being well and may suffer another seizure at any time.

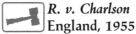 **R. v. Charlson**
England, 1955

A father invited his ten-year-old son to look out of the window at a rat in the river below. When the boy did so, the father struck him on the head with a hammer and threw him out of the window causing bodily harm. There was no evidence as to why the father did this. The father had only a vague recollection of the incident. The father was charged with attempted murder, but was found Not Guilty on the grounds of automatism. The accused was suffering from a cerebral tumour. The court held that:

> 66A man suffering from cerebral tumour is liable to an outburst of impulsive violence over which he has no control.99

There are seven recognized conditions which might give rise to a state of non-insane automatism: (1) sleepwalking, (2) carbon monoxide poisoning, (3) a stroke,

(4) a physical blow, (5) pneumonia, (6) psychological stress, and (7) emotional upset. It should be stressed that these conditions *might* cause a state of automatism, but their existence is not in itself proof of such a condition. The evidence must support a contention that automatism existed and the accused must establish the defence of automatism on a balance of probabilities.

 ### *Bleta v. The Queen*
Supreme Court of Canada, 1964

Bleta was acquitted of the non-capital murder of one Hairedin Gafi. The Crown appealed the decision and the Ontario Court of Appeal ordered a new trial on the grounds that certain psychiatric evidence should not have been admitted. Bleta appealed to the Supreme Court of Canada which restored the acquittal. At the trial, witnesses testified that they saw a fight between the two men. Bleta was knocked down and struck his head on the pavement, and Gafi started to walk away. Bleta regained his feet, followed Gafi, pulled out a knife and stabbed Gafi to death. Two of the witnesses testified that Bleta appeared dazed. The defence rested on a claim that Bleta suffered from automatism caused by the blow on the head. The trial judge said in the charge to the jury:

66The doctor says that the actions of the accused when he stabbed the deceased were purely automatic and without any volition on the part of the accused. He was, in fact, in the condition of a sleepwalker or an epileptic . . . . If you accept that evidence, then as I have told you, the law is that the accused is not guilty of anything.99

The Supreme Court of Canada considered this a proper charge and the jury was correct in returning a verdict of Not Guilty.

The Defence of Double Jeopardy

It is a basic principle of our system of justice that the Crown, with all its financial resources and power, should not be allowed to make repeated attempts to convict an individual for one particular act, thereby subjecting the person to emotional ordeal, anxiety, and financial ruin, as well as increasing the chance that he or she may be eventually convicted of some offence if enough attempts are made. It is also an established rule of law that a person shall not be punished twice for the same offence. To do so is to place the accused into *double jeopardy*, something our law will not permit.

If an accused has been tried previously on the same charge, or on a charge arising from the same act, the accused may enter a plea of *autrefois acquit* or *autrefois convict*. These two terms are defined as follows:

• *Autrefois acquit* (formerly acquitted): A special plea by which the accused alleges to have already been tried for the same offence before a competent tribunal and acquitted.

• *Autrefois convict* (formerly convicted): A special plea by which the accused alleges to have already been tried for the same offence before a competent tribunal and convicted.

A successful plea of autrefois acquit or autrefois convict is a bar to another prosecution for the same offence, the attempt to commit that offence, or for an offence necessarily included in the previous charge. In determining the validity of a plea of autrefois acquit or autrefois convict, the true test is *substantial identity* of the offence of which the accused is now charged with the previous offence for which the accused was acquitted or convicted. As a general rule, a judge should stay an indictment (not proceed) if satisfied that the charges therein are founded on the same facts as the charges in a previous indictment on which the accused has been tried; or that the charges form a part of a series of offences of the same or similar character as in the previous indictment.

The law does not say a person cannot be punished twice for the same *act*, but says that the person cannot be punished twice for the same *offence*. A person can commit more than one offence by the same act. However, the Crown is expected not to attempt to "load" the indictment by including every conceivable offence under the *Criminal Code* with which the accused could possibly be charged. The "shotgun" method of charging a person with many offences relating to one act in the hopes that he or she will be convicted of something is unacceptable in law.

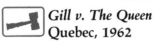

R. v. Kienapple
Supreme Court of Canada, 1974

The accused was convicted during his trial of (1) rape and (2) carnal knowledge of a female under fourteen years of age. Both convictions arose from the same act. The accused appealed his conviction for carnal knowledge on the grounds that having been convicted of rape he could not be convicted of the second offence as this was placing him in double jeopardy for the same offence. The Supreme Court of Canada allowed the appeal and quashed the second conviction. The principle of autrefois convict barred a conviction for carnal knowledge once the conviction for rape had been made. It was proper to charge the accused under both sections of the *Criminal Code*, and if rape had not been proven, a conviction for carnal knowledge would have been proper. However, the accused could not be convicted of both offences.

The preceding case is the origin of what is known as the "Kienapple Principle." Briefly stated, the principle is that if there is a verdict of guilty on a first count in the indictment, and the same or substantially the same elements make up the offence charged in the second count, the accused should not be convicted of the second count since that will produce a multiple conviction for what is basically one criminal offence. The principle applies only if the two counts are of similar gravity.

A dismissal of a charge because of a defect in the proceedings is not an acquittal, and a charge may be laid again. A hung jury is not an acquittal either, and the accused may be re-tried on the same charge.

In some cases, a different plea is entered, that of *res judicata*, which is defined as follows:

- *Res judicata pro veritate accipitur* (a thing adjudicated is received as the truth): Res judicata presupposes that there has been an issue and a competent tribunal to decide that issue, and that the tribunal has so decided. Once a matter between parties has been decided, it cannot be raised again. Res judicata prevents the Crown from questioning the fundamental decision of an earlier proceeding.

Res judicata appears to be very similar to autrefois acquit or autrefois convict, but it is definitely different. While autrefois acquit and autrefois convict are special pleas entered to prevent the proceedings from continuing, res judicata is a plea entered in common law along with a plea of Not Guilty to the offence. It means, in substance, that the court cannot permit the Crown to introduce evidence at the second trial for the purpose of trying to show that the verdict of the first trial was wrong. That is, the second trial cannot be a forum of triumph over the first. The effect of such a plea is to deny the Crown much of the evidence it might hope to introduce.

Gill v. The Queen
Quebec, 1962

Gill caused the death of his wife and son by the discharge of a shotgun which he was cleaning. He was charged with the death of his wife by criminal negligence and found Not Guilty. The Crown then charged him with the death of his son by criminal negligence. The accused invoked autrefois acquit. The trial judge rejected this special plea, so the accused pleaded Not Guilty and further pleaded res judicata. The accused was convicted at his second trial from which he appealed to the Quebec Court of Appeal. The Court of Appeal agreed that the judge had correctly rejected the plea of autrefois acquit but that the plea of res judicata was a proper defence. The court concluded that the Crown was in essence trying to have a second jury consider the question which had already been decided by the first jury. Once the judge had seen the evidence given at the earlier trial, and knew the cause of the wife's death as disclosed at the trial, the judge was in a position to determine whether the same issue was before the court again. The moment the judge became aware that the issues were the same, the defence was entitled to raise the defence of res judicata and object to any evidence tending to establish that the accused was criminally negligent in the doing of a particular thing of which he had already been judged innocent.

The Defence of Drug Impairment

Traditionally, drug impairment caused by voluntary consumption of any drug was treated the same way as impairment by alcohol, for alcohol is itself a drug. The effects upon the mind were thought to be the same.

Recently, however, the increased use or abuse of drugs and the development of new synthetic drugs have caused problems for legal experts. In the first place, some drugs can produce such mind-bending results that the accused may for a time be truly insane. However, such insanity will only be temporary; the effects usually wear off after a few hours, and the person will then return to normal. Nevertheless, the defence of temporary insanity, in itself, has never been accepted in Canadian law. The same applies to the defence of diminished responsibility. The problem seldom occurs in relation to alcohol, since drunkenness rarely causes what could be called true temporary madness.

In the second place, drunkenness may affect the mind enough to relieve the accused of a specific intent, but as often as not, the alcohol still leaves the accused capable of forming a general intent. Furthermore, it is often found that the alcohol caused the defendant more readily to lose self-control. The accused may have been unable to resist an impulse to do something

he or she *really wanted to do*. Legally, this does not afford the accused a defence. With other drugs, the problem is that persons may do certain acts that they had no desire to do at all. Their behaviour may become so inexplicable that it cannot be said that the effect of the drug was merely to wear down their ability to resist an impulse. This absence of motive, intent, or even reason has caused concern among lawyers and judges that drug abuse affords a greater defence than drunkenness and that the present wording of the law has no method of dealing with it.

 R. v. Bucci
Nova Scotia, 1974

The accused was acquitted of car theft because he was too high on drugs to be able to form a specific intent required for theft. In acquitting the accused, the judge said:

&&I cannot leave this decision without expressing my feeling of dissatisfaction. The accused has escaped conviction because the Crown has been unable to rely as it normally does upon certain essential facts to each charge. Society cannot protect itself against such anti-social behaviour with its present machinery.&&

It should be mentioned here that while Bucci could not be convicted of car theft, he probably could have been convicted of impaired driving.

It would be incorrect to give the impression that drug abuse is a perfect defence. It is not. Its primary effect is to prove that the accused could not form a specific intent. The accused may still be convicted of another offence that does not require a specific intent.

The Defence of Duress

Regarding duress, the *Criminal Code* states:

17. A person who commits an offence under compulsion by threats of immediate death or grievous bodily harm from a person who is present when the offence is committed is excused for committing the offence if he

believes that the threats will be carried out and if he is not a party to a conspiracy or association whereby he is subject to compulsion, but this section does not apply where the offence that is committed is treason, murder, piracy, attempted murder, sexual assault, sexual assault with a weapon, threats to a third party or causing bodily harm, aggravated sexual assault, forcible abduction, robbery, assault with a weapon or causing bodily harm, aggravated assault, unlawfully causing bodily harm, arson or an offence under ss. 249 to 250.2 (abduction and detention of young persons).

Thus, duress is a defence where threats of immediate death or serious injury to oneself or members of one's family are sufficient to overpower the normal resistance to do something criminal.

R. v. Carker
Supreme Court of Canada, 1967

Carker was in his cell in a British Columbia prison when other prisoners began to riot and smash everything in their cells. Another prisoner told Carker to join in the riot or he would be killed at some later date. Carker believed this threat and smashed up the things in his cell. When charged for his actions, Carker pleaded duress. His counsel argued that in a prison environment, when one inmate tells another that he is going to be killed, there is every reason to believe it can be done. The trial judge rejected the plea of duress and convicted Carker. The British Columbia Court of Appeal quashed the conviction. The Crown appealed to the Supreme Court of Canada which restored the conviction, saying that locked in his cell Carker was in no immediate danger. The court saw no reason for Carker's actions when he could have requested protection from the prison authorities or requested a transfer to another prison if necessary.

A threat against property is not sufficient; there must be a threat against a person. Duress is a defence in all but the most violent crimes.

R. v. Paquette
Supreme Court of Canada, 1976

Paquette had been forced, under threats of death, to drive two other persons to a store in order that those two, to his knowledge, could commit a robbery. After the robbery, he tried to frustrate the escape of those who had forced him to drive the vehicle. A bystander was killed during the robbery and Paquette was charged with murder by virtue of s. 21(2) of the *Code* as a party to the offence. The Supreme Court of Canada held that s. 17 is limited to cases where the person seeking to rely upon it has himself committed an offence and went on to conclude:

    ❝The section uses the specific words 'a person who commits an offence.' It does not use the words 'a person who is a party to an offence.' This is significant in the light of the wording of s. 21(1) which, in para. (a) makes a person party to an offence who actually commits it. Paragraphs (b) and (c) deal with a person who aids or abets a person committing the offence. In my opinion, s. 17 codifies the law as to duress as an excuse for the actual commission of a crime, but it does not, by its terms, go beyond that. *R. v. Carker* ... dealt with a situation in which the accused had actually committed the offence.**❞**

The Defence of Self-Defence

In cases of assault or homicide, any person accused of causing injury or death to another person may raise the defence of self-defence. Self-defence is a complete defence to the charge if it is accepted by the court. That is, it does not merely reduce the charge, but allows that the accused be found Not Guilty of any offence.

There are several sections in the *Criminal Code* dealing with self-defence, but the best general definition is found in the following section:

    34. (1) Every one who is unlawfully assaulted without having provoked the assault is justified in repelling force by force if the force he uses is not intended to cause

death or grievous bodily harm and is no more than is necessary to enable him to defend himself.

(2) Every one who is unlawfully assaulted and who causes death or grievous bodily harm in repelling the assault is justified if

(a) he causes it under reasonable apprehension of death or grievous bodily harm from the violence with which the assault was originally made or with which the assailant pursues his purposes, and

(b) he believes, on reasonable and probable grounds, that he cannot otherwise preserve himself from death or grievous bodily harm.

Perhaps the most important general rule is that the force used in self-defence cannot be greater than that which is "reasonably necessary." Violence may be met with violence, but the threatened person cannot over-react. A person cannot provoke an attack and then strike down the attacker. The *Criminal Code* defines "provocation" as "blows, words, or gestures."

Where someone could have avoided a fight, but sought not to do so, that person may not be able to claim self-defence. If Smith "invites" Brown to step into the alley to settle their differences, and Brown accepts, Brown cannot claim self-defence; Brown voluntarily went into the alley for the purpose of a fight. Dueling is illegal in Canada, and where the two parties agree to a fight of any kind, it may be treated as a form of duel.

A police officer may use reasonable force to maintain order and defend the public. Parents may use force to protect their children. Any person may use force to protect anyone under his or her care or charge. For example, school teachers could use force to protect their pupils. In every case, the amount of force must not exceed that which is necessary.

Someone who owns or who is in the possession of property may use force to prevent a trespasser from removing it. The person cannot assault the trespasser; but if the owner lays hands on the property and the trespasser forcibly removes it, the trespasser commits assault and the owner may use self-defence against this assault.

Every person in possession of a dwelling-house may use reasonable force to prevent any person from forcibly entering the house or trespassing on the property. The *Criminal Code* also permits persons to gather upon that property to defend it, and the police cannot order them to disperse as an unlawful assembly. Hence, the traditional right of friends and neighbours to gather together to provide mutual protection for the property of one person is entrenched in our criminal law. The *Criminal Code* does not specifically say whether those gathered for this purpose may be armed, but as long as other provisions in the *Code* dealing with firearms are met, this would also be lawful.

Whether or not the force used was reasonable is not an objective test applied from outside. The important question is whether the accused believed reasonable force was being used, as the next case will illustrate.

R. v. Cadwallader
Saskatchewan, 1966

The accused, a fourteen-year-old boy, was charged in Juvenile Court with the unlawful killing of his father, thereby being delinquent under the *Juvenile Delinquents Act*. The accused had lived alone with his father after his mother died when the accused was five years old. His father was a brooding man who often threatened the boy. On the day of the slaying, the boy was upstairs when he heard his father coming up the stairs saying he would kill the boy. He saw that his father carried a rifle. The accused loaded his own .22 calibre rifle and fatally shot his father. In all, the father was struck by five bullets, the last one at close range. The trial judge convicted the accused, saying that excessive force was used. The trial judge concluded that when the last shot was fired at close range it was for the purpose of ensuring that the father was dead. The Court of Appeal quashed the conviction, holding that:

66The test as to the extent of justification is whether the accused used more force *than he, on reasonable grounds, believed necessary*. The determination must be made according to the accused's state of mind at the time. It is clear he acted in self-defence. He used only sufficient force as *he* reasonably thought necessary. You cannot put a higher test on a fourteen-year-old boy than that known to our law. **"**

If one person uses excessive force, while allegedly employing self-defence, and the other person dies, the "doctrine of excessive force in self-defence" should apply. The minimum requisites of the doctrine are:

- The accused was justified in using some force to defend against attack, real or reasonably apprehended.
- The accused honestly believed the amount of force used was justified.
- The force used was excessive only because it exceeded what the accused could reasonably have considered necessary.

The Defence of Necessity

Where a person is compelled to act without any other choice, that person can claim that he or she really did not act voluntarily. As an example, let us suppose that a court has revoked Brown's privilege to drive a motor vehicle anywhere in Canada for two years. During this time, Brown's neighbour rushes over saying, "Drive me to the hospital. I've severed an artery and will bleed to death!" Brown drives the neighbour to the hospital and is seen by a police officer who knows Brown has no lawful right to drive. To the charge of driving while the licence to do so is suspended, Brown raises the defence of *necessity*.

There is no iron-clad rule as to what constitutes a valid defence of necessity. Courts are reluctant to hear an accused say, "It was necessary for me to break the law." Necessity must be taken in the strictest sense. It cannot be equated with mere expediency. (Perhaps Brown could have found another way to get the neighbour to the hospital in time.) Hunger has never been accepted as a defence to the charge of stealing food or money. Homelessness is not a defence to trespass.

Several intriguing cases exist involving persons adrift in lifeboats. In one case, two desperate survivors of a sunken ship killed and ate a third survivor. They claimed necessity. In another case, some sailors threw passengers out of an overcrowded lifeboat. They claimed it was necessary to prevent the entire lifeboat from sinking. Legal experts are very much divided as to whether self-survival justifies killing others. It is instinctive in some people, but not all people, for there are many cases of individuals voluntarily dying so others may live, as happened in the sinking of the *Titanic*. The American judge, Justice Cardoza once wrote, "There is no rule of human jettison. There is no right to save the lives of some by killing others."

Henry Morgentaler successfully raised the defence of necessity in his second trial when he was charged with performing an illegal abortion.

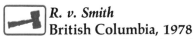

R. v. Smith
British Columbia, 1978

The accused was charged with driving a vehicle while her blood-alcohol level was in excess of the legal limit. She testified that she drove the car because she was fleeing from her husband who would have caused her serious bodily harm if she had not driven away from their house. She raised the defence of necessity and was acquitted.

The Defence of Entrapment

While it is perfectly acceptable for police to sit and wait for persons whom they believe will try to commit an offence and then arrest them, it is not as readily acceptable that police should first encourage or instigate the offence in order to arrest the person who commits it. *Entrapment* basically involves the police first luring, inducing, persuading, harassing, or bribing a person to commit an offence that would otherwise not have been committed; and then arresting the person for that offence.

Entrapment has never been formally recognized as a defence in Canadian or British courts. In a few, rare cases, the accused was found not guilty by some round-about means, but not by a formal recognition of entrapment as a defence. The following is such a case.

Lemieux v. The Queen
Supreme Court of Canada, 1967

The accused was convicted of break and enter. His appeal from conviction was dismissed by the Ontario Court of Appeal and he further appealed to the Supreme Court of Canada. The facts of the case are that police were anxious to catch those responsible for break-ins in the Ottawa area. Police were contacted by one R. Bard who said he could make it possible to catch the gang in the act. A "target" house was selected and, with the owner's consent, the police waited inside. Bard, Lemieux, and a third man drove up to the house. Lemieux waited in the car while Bard and the third man broke in. Police arrested all three. Lemieux's defence centred around his claim that he had never committed such an offence before and that Bard had approached him and solicited his participation in the break-in. On this evidence, the Supreme Court quashed the conviction. The court held that the evidence indicated that the owner of the house had authorized the police officers to take possession of the house and deal with it as they pleased. The police had not merely consented to Bard's breaking into the house with the assistance of others, but had urged him to do so. The court concluded:

❝To break and enter under these circumstances is not an offence.❞

There are indications that entrapment may soon be given full recognition as a defence. Section 24(2) of the *Charter of Rights and Freedoms* states that evidence shall be excluded if its admission would "bring the administration of justice into disrepute."

The following drug case further suggests that entrapment will eventually be given full recognition in our legal system.

R. v. Amato
Supreme Court of Canada, 1982

The accused was arrested in Vancouver in 1977 after selling eighty-five grams of cocaine to an undercover RCMP officer and a heroin importer who was working for the RCMP as an informer. The accused was unable to get the Crown to produce the informer as a witness at his trial. He contended that the informer would support his contention that he had been bullied into making the sale. The court noted that the RCMP officer and the informer had used "persistent solicitation" to persuade Amato to make the sale. However, the majority of the court held that this was not entrapment. It was significant that the decision stated that the facts did not support the defence of entrapment, "assuming it was available." In separate opinions, five of the Justices said that entrapment could be a defence where it brings the system of justice into disrepute and where the police action is "shocking and outrageous." In those instances, it is the judges who must invoke the exclusionary rule and reject evidence illegally obtained because it threatens the integrity of the criminal justice system. The court did not make specific mention of the *Charter of Rights and Freedoms* since the court originally heard the case before the *Charter* was enacted.

The Defence of Mistake

The common law recognizes that an honest and reasonable belief in the existence of circumstances which, if true, would have made the act an innocent one, may be a defence. The maxim is: *ignorantia facti excusat; ignoranti juris non excusat* ("ignorance of the fact excuses; ignorance of the law does not excuse"). It may be helpful to the reader to refer to the earlier discussion in Chapter 3 of "Strict and Absolute Liability" as the discussion there pertains to mistake of fact as well.

In *R. v. Tolson* (England, 1889), the accused woman was told that her husband's ship had been lost at sea with all hands. Believing herself to be a widow, she remarried. When her husband turned up alive and well, she was charged with bigamy but was acquitted as her ignorance was ignorance of the facts, not ignorance of the law. In *R. v. Rees* (1956), the accused was convicted for having intercourse with a female under the age of eighteen. He was charged under the *Juvenile Delinquents Act* which makes it an offence to "knowingly and wilfully" contribute to a child becoming a delinquent. The female was actually just past her sixteenth birthday. The court held that mistake of fact was a defence because the Act specifically required that the accused act "knowingly and wilfully." As was mentioned earlier, certain offences are absolute liability offences and mistake of fact is not a defence.

There is a fine but important distinction between *mistake* of law and *ignorance* of law. It can be argued that ignorance of the existence of a law is not a defence, but a mistake in interpreting the law while trying to obey it could be a defence.

Molis v. The Queen
Supreme Court of Canada, 1980
The accused was charged with possession of MDMA, a substance which he legally manufactured before it was added to the list of restricted drugs by a regulation published in the *Canada Gazette*. The accused was totally unaware that the law had changed and that he could no longer lawfully possess the substance. He was unaware of the existence of the *Canada Gazette*. The Supreme Court of Canada held that the offence was not one of absolute liability and that the defence of due diligence was available to the accused. However, the court clarified this further by saying that "due diligence" means due diligence in trying to obey the law, not "due diligence" in trying to learn of the existence of a law or its interpretation. The conviction of the accused was upheld.

Reviewing Important Points

1. The law makes a basic assumption that every accused person is sane.
2. An accused found Not Guilty by reason of insanity must be placed in an institution.
3. Drunkenness can be a defence to crimes which require the formation of a specific intent.
4. The defence of temporary insanity, in itself, has never been accepted in Canadian law.
5. A defence of automatism cannot be raised where a person is aware of committing an offence and was aware of it at the time.
6. It is a general rule that the force used in self-defence cannot be greater than that which is "reasonably necessary."
7. If the defence of self-defence is accepted by the court, it allows the accused to be found Not Guilty of *any* offence.
8. Mistake is no defence where a law has established absolute liability.
9. Entrapment may eventually become a defence in situations where the police encouraged the commission of an offence that otherwise might not have been committed.
10. It is an established rule of law that a person shall not be punished twice for the same offence.
11. Duress can be a defence to some offences, but not all. Serious offences such as murder or treason cannot be excused by duress.

Checking Your Understanding

1. For what reasons might the Crown raise the issue of the accused's sanity?
2. Can drunkenness be a defence to any charge?
3. What is the Kienapple Principle?
4. What is the difference between res judicata and autrefrois acquit?
5. Which of the following statements is correct?
a. An accused cannot be tried twice for the same act.

b. An accused cannot be tried twice for the same offence.

c. An accused cannot be tried twice for more than one offence arising from the same cause or matter.

6. What is the fundamental difference between insane automatism and non-insane automatism?

7. Does the accused have to prove the lack of criminal intent because of drunkenness, or does the Crown have to prove that the accused had criminal intent despite drunkenness?

8. What do these words mean when used in the context of the defence of insanity?

a. wrong

b. know

c. appreciate

d. disease of the mind

e. specific delusion

Legal Briefs

1. K shot and wounded C, a cashier, during a robbery. K pleaded guilty to robbery and to the commission of an offence while armed. He was sentenced to six years in a penitentiary. After K had served one month, C died from the wound. K was then charged with murder. Double jeopardy?

2. A ship bound for the United States was forced by a severe storm to seek haven in a Canadian port. Canadian customs officers boarded the ship and found narcotics. The five persons aboard were charged with importing a narcotic into Canada. What defence to this charge?

3. B stole some goods and was caught moments later. She was charged with theft and possession of stolen goods. Valid charge?

4. J committed a driving offence and pleaded guilty. The Ministry of Transportation sent J a notice that his driver's permit was suspended for six months. J did not receive the notice and continued to drive. He was charged with driving while under suspension. Mistake of fact?

5. Police set up an undercover operation to "fence" stolen goods. For six months, the two officers bought stolen goods and secretly filmed all transactions. R was one of the persons filmed and was later charged. Entrapment?

6. After E left her brother's home, she felt dizzy and wrecked her car. The police charged her with impaired driving. E's brother, J, testified that he put two depressant pills into E's coffee "as a joke." Should E be convicted of impaired driving? Is J guilty of any offence?

7. M thinks up a complicated scheme to take control of a corporation through a share exchange plan. M consults a law firm to determine if the idea is legal. The firm holds meetings with lawyers from the provincial Securities Commission. M is then advised by the law firm that the idea is legal. M carries out the takeover and is charged with violation of the *Securities Act*. The trial judge convicts M, holding that the law firm and the provincial lawyers misinterpreted the law. M appeals. What should the Appeal Court do?

8. Y murders his brother-in-law for no apparent reason. Y states that God talked to him and told him that he was very wicked and must die. God then told him to do something that would result in his being executed. (Strangely, God did not tell Y that the Canadian Parliament repealed the death penalty.) Y states that he committed murder because he knew murder was legally wrong and that he would be hanged for it. Is Y legally insane?

9. T is a relatively normal person when sober, but when drunk is very violent. He leaves a bar in a highly intoxicated state. S, a friend, thinks T needs help and approaches. T does not recognize S and imagines that S has a knife in his hand. Without warning he fatally stabs S. What defence?

10. D drinks a considerable amount of alcohol at a party. The host tells D that if she drinks a peculiar combination of milk, honey, aspirin, and mashed bananas all the alcohol in her blood will be immediately neutralized. D does so and drives home. Enroute she is stopped by the police and subsequently fails a breathalyzer test. Has D a defence?

Applying the Law

Schwartz v. The Queen
Supreme Court of Canada, 1976

The appellant was charged with two murders. Evidence was heard that the accused was in a violent and frenzied state when arrested. The trial judge told the jury that the word "wrong" in s. 16(2) means "wrong according to law, wrong in the sense the act was forbidden by law." The appeal was based on the contention that this was misdirection and that "wrong" means "wrong contrary to the ordinary standard of reasonable men."

❝The test as to knowledge of 'wrong' which is stated by Dixon C.J. in the *Stapleton* case is as to whether the accused knew that his act was wrong according to the ordinary principles of reasonable men. I find it difficult to see how this test really differs from the test as to whether he knew he was committing a crime. Surely, according to the ordinary principles of reasonable men, it is wrong to commit a crime .... If there is a difference between these tests, and it could be contended that the commission of a particular crime, though known to be illegal, was considered to be morally justifiable in the opinion of ordinary men, I do not see why a person who committed a crime in such circumstances should be protected from conviction if suffering from disease of the mind, and not protected if he committed the crime when sane.**❞**

The minority of Justices thought that if Parliament meant "wrong" to mean "legally wrong" then Parliament would have chosen the word "unlawful" or "illegal."

Questions
1. As used in s. 16(2) what does the word "wrong" mean?
2. Does the majority opinion appear to say that "legally wrong" and "wrong according to the standards of reasonable men" actually have the same meaning? Could an action be illegal but not wrong by the standards of ordinary persons?
3. Would the section be more understandable if the word "wrong" were changed to "unlawful"?
4. Is it not possible for a person to know that an action is illegal and contrary to law and still be insane? For example, in the *Stapleton* case mentioned, a mother killed her child believing that God called upon her to offer a sacrifice and atonement. She knew that to kill was contrary to the law of the land.
5. What do you think the definition of "wrong" should be in this section? Should it be reworded, and if so, how?

Rabey v. The Queen
Supreme Court of Canada, 1981

The accused, a university student, was emotionally attracted to the victim. She did not return that feeling. The day before the offence, he discovered a letter which the victim had written to a friend in which she expressed an interest in another man. The letter also described the accused as a "nothing." On the day of the incident, the accused picked up a rock from the geology laboratory to take home to study and then by chance met the victim. He said he felt "strange" for a while as they walked. He asked her what she thought of a mutual friend, and she replied he was just a friend. The accused then asked what she thought of him, and she replied that he was also just a friend. The accused then struck the victim with the rock and began choking her. Another student who came along described the accused as pale, sweating, glassy-eyed, and as having a frightened expression. A psychiatrist testified that the accused entered into a complete dissociative state. His self-image was shattered by the letter and the conversation the next day triggered the dissociative state into a violent form. The psychiatrist then said that a dissociative state is not a disease of the mind, that there was no evidence of a pathological condition, and there was only a very slight chance that the disorder would occur again. A psychiatrist called by the Crown testified that the accused was not in a dissociative state but in a state of extreme rage or possibly suffering from a disease of the mind called hysterical neurosis. The accused was acquitted at trial on the ground that he suffered from non-insane automatism. The Court of Appeal ordered a new trial saying that if the accused was in a state of automatism it was as a result of a definite disease of the mind and his defence must be insanity. The accused appealed to the Supreme Court of Canada which upheld the Court of Appeal:

❝In general, the distinction to be drawn between insane and non-insane automatism is between a malfunction of the mind arising from some cause that is primarily internal to the accused, having its source in the psychological or emotional makeup or in some organic pathology, and a malfunctioning of the mind which is the transient effect produced by some specific external factor such as concussion.**❞**

Questions

1. The Supreme Court distinguished between insane automatism and non-insane automatism. According to the court, non-insane automatism must have what source?

2. One psychiatrist thought Rabey was simply in a great state of "rage." If the court had accepted this view, what would the verdict have been?

3. Why was the defence pressing for a decision that the accused suffered from non-insane automatism?

You Be the Judge

1. The accused was charged with the theft of logs taken outside a company's logging boom. The logs were clearly marked with the company's identification tag. The accused believed that she had a legal, salvage right to the logs. Her belief was based upon a booklet published by the provincial Ministry of Resources which stated that logs outside a boom were logs that anyone could collect and sell back to the company. The booklet was contrary both to the *Criminal Code* wording on the subject and to established case law. The Crown argued that only the courts could make determinations about such matters, not provincial government departments. Should the accused be convicted?

2. The accused, an alcoholic, decided to leave his common law wife with whom he had argued for months. While drunk, he poured charcoal lighter fluid over much of her furniture and into her deep freezer. His intent, he later stated, was to "ruin" everything but not to cause a fire. He was admittedly so drunk at the time that he was not absolutely certain what he was doing or why. A fire did start and two children died in the blaze. The defence was drunkenness. Of what offence, if any, should the accused be convicted?

3. The accused was charged with the following offences: assaulting a police officer; assaulting a person assisting the officer to arrest the accused's friend; assault causing bodily harm (two counts); obstructing a peace officer in the execution of the officer's duties; and later resisting personal arrest. The defence counsel admitted that the incident had taken place as the police described it, but argued that the indictment was "loaded" and that the accused was facing multiple convictions. Of what offence(s) should the accused be properly convicted?

4. A woman was charged with giving false testimony at a preliminary hearing. The defence raised was duress. The accused had been told by one man, in the company of two other men, that she would be killed if she testified against their friend who was charged with an offence. At the hearing the woman gave false evidence that destroyed the Crown's case. During the hearing, the three men sat in the courtroom and listened to what the woman said. One of them reportedly made a hand motion across the front of his neck as a form of intimidation. Should the accused woman be convicted?

5. The accused was charged with impaired driving. He was a heart patient who felt severe chest pains and decided to go to the hospital. When he realized that he had left his heart medication at his office, he drank 280 mL of brandy to temporarily calm his heart palpitations before driving. When stopped by a police officer, he told the officer he was "in pain" but gave no further details. The defence raised at trial was necessity. Should the accused be convicted?

6. The accused was a heroin user who supported her

habit by buying and reselling stolen goods. The accused did not buy and sell heroin; she only bought it for her own use. An undercover police agent attempted to sell a leather coat to the accused for heroin, but the accused refused. The agent returned again and pretended to be sick and desperately in need of a fix. Feeling sorry for the agent, the accused exchanged two capsules of heroin from her private supply for the coat. She was charged with trafficking. Should the accused be convicted?

7. The accused went to a carnival where he consumed a large amount of alcohol which he carried in a bag. He became very intoxicated and left the carnival at midnight. He walked down a residential street; then broke into a house. In the house, he opened a refrigerator looking for something to eat. He was "discovered" by four small dogs who began to bark. The accused then chased the dogs around the house yelling and waving a small cane he won at the carnival. The homeowner summoned the police who removed the accused and charged him with break and enter. Should the accused be convicted?

Unit
Three

The Criminal Justice System

"The Law of England would be a strange science indeed if it were decided on precedents only. Precedents serve to illustrate principles, and to give them fixed certainty."

Lord Mansfield, 1774

Chapter 6

Criminal Procedure

Initiating a Criminal Prosecution

A criminal prosecution usually begins with the laying of a charge, or more correctly, an *information*, before a justice. The information is usually laid by a police officer, but the *Criminal Code* empowers anyone to lay an information if there are reasonable and probable grounds to believe that an offence has been committed. The justice then commands the person accused to appear at a specified time and place.

If the accused has been arrested, he or she will appear before a magistrate, provincial judge, or justice of the peace within twenty-four hours in most cases. At this first appearance, the accused should try to obtain bail and legal assistance but does not need to plead. The accused's case will then be *remanded* (held over) to a later date, during which time the services of a lawyer must be obtained unless the accused intends to defend the case personally.

It is a saying that "Time does not run against the Crown." This means there is no criminal *Statute of Limitations* in Canada as there is in much of the United States. Under American law, most states require that a person be charged with an offence within a certain number of years after the offence occurred. If this is not done, the accused is beyond the law as it pertains to that offence, even if the accused publicly admits to committing the offence. In Canada, there are very few periods of limitations. The most important one pertains to summary conviction offences. A charge by way of summary conviction must be brought within six months of the offence. Treason charges

must be brought within three years, and certain sex offences within one year.

If the time limitations requirements are met, and they usually are, the accused will be advised prior to a second appearance whether the offence as charged will be by way of summary conviction or indictment. Serious offences are called *indictable offences*, and less serious offences are called *summary conviction offences*. Some offences are considered either summary conviction or indictable offences, and the Crown may choose which procedure it will follow. These are called *hybrid offences*.

Although most prosecutions are conducted by the Crown, the law permits a private citizen to conduct the prosecution of a summary conviction offence personally or through counsel. In order to personally prosecute an indictable offence, the private citizen must obtain the permission of the Attorney General or the court.

The decision to charge any person is based upon an honest belief that there is sufficient evidence of guilt to justify the charge. Although the police may have made the arrest and laid the information initially, continuation of the case is the decision of the prosecutor, usually known as the Crown Attorney. The Crown Attorney has no investigative staff personally and must rely upon the police to gather the necessary evidence. If the charge is a summary conviction offence, or an offence over which the magistrate has absolute authority (see Election of Trial), the charge is read to the accused who is asked to plead Guilty or Not Guilty. Trial by magistrate then takes place without the intervention of a jury. If the accused pleads Guilty, there is no trial; the magistrate only considers sentence.

An accused charged with a summary conviction offence need not appear in person, but may instead be represented by counsel. However, if the magistrate desires, the accused's attendance may be compelled. If the accused does not appear, the magistrate may have the accused arrested. In some provinces, the magistrate is referred to as a provincial court judge.

Election of Trial

The magistrate (or provincial court judge) must place the offence with which the accused is charged into one of three categories:

- Those over which the magistrate has absolute authority; or
- Those over which the magistrate has no authority; or
- Those over which the magistrate has authority with the consent of the accused.

Offences over Which a Magistrate Has Absolute Authority (s. 483)

1. Theft, other than cattle theft*
2. Obtaining by false pretences*
3. Possession of stolen goods*
4. Defrauding the public or a person of property or money*
5. The attempt to commit numbers 1-4 above
6. Keeping a gaming or betting house
7. Bookmaking or placing illegal bets for others
8. Operating an illegal lottery
9. Cheating at a game
10. Keeping a bawdy house
11. Fraud in relation to fares

---

*This only applies where property is not a testamentary instrument and value does not exceed $200. Testamentary instrument includes any will, codicil, or other testamentary writing.

If the accused has been charged with one of these offences, the magistrate *must* hear the case. The accused cannot insist upon a trial by jury in a higher court, simply because the offence does not merit the time and expense of a major trial.

Offences over Which a Magistrate Has No Authority (s. 427)

1. Treason
2. Alarming Her Majesty
3. Intimidating Parliament
4. Inciting to mutiny
5. Sedition (using language to incite rebellion)
6. Piracy
7. Piratical acts
8. First or second degree murder
9. Accessory after the fact to treason or murder
10. Acceptance of a bribe by a judicial officer
11. Attempting to commit any offence mentioned in numbers 1 through 7
12. Conspiring to commit any offence mentioned in numbers 1 through 10

The *Criminal Code* regards the preceding offences as sufficiently serious that they must be tried by judge and jury in a superior court of criminal jurisdiction. In most provinces, this means the Supreme Court of the Province. Some offences, including sexual assault, sexual assault with a weapon, sexual assault causing bodily harm, aggravated sexual assault, attempted murder, bribery, criminal negligence, manslaughter, or the threat to murder someone, require a trial by judge and jury unless the accused specifically elects trial by judge alone. The attempt to commit these offences is included, as is conspiracy to commit them. The exception is the Province of Alberta where the accused may elect to be tried for any indictable offence by a judge of the Supreme Court of Alberta without a jury.

Offences over Which a Magistrate Has Authority with Consent of the Accused

For the remainder of the indictable offences, the accused may elect to be tried in one of three ways. The following words are put to the accused by the magistrate:

> You have the option to elect to be tried by a magistrate without a jury; or you may elect to be tried by a judge without a jury; or you may elect to be tried by a court composed of a judge and jury. How do you elect to be tried?

The Attorney General or Deputy may require a jury trial in any case where the accused is charged with an offence punishable by imprisonment for more than five years.

The chart shown below indicates the various possible avenues of procedure from arrest up to the trial. In Nova Scotia, a grand jury would have to hear the evidence after the preliminary hearing and before the trial itself.

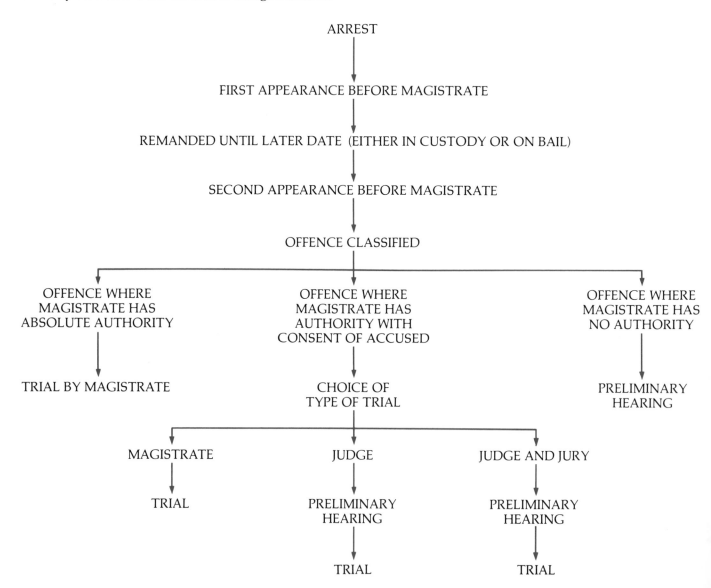

Preliminary Hearing

If the accused elects trial by judge or by judge and jury, or the offence is one over which the magistrate has no authority, the magistrate must conduct a *preliminary hearing*. The charge is read; then witnesses for the prosecution are called, sworn, examined and cross-examined. The accused may call witnesses, or give evidence personally. Surprisingly, the statement of the accused does not have to be made under oath. Before the accused gives evidence, the magistrate must issue a warning that anything the accused says at the preliminary hearing will be recorded and may be introduced as evidence at the trial, whether the accused testifies at the trial or not. Therefore, it is generally wise for the accused not to say anything at the preliminary hearing.

Having heard the evidence at the preliminary hearing, the magistrate will either commit the accused for trial or dismiss the charge. The evidence need not prove that the accused committed the offence; it must only raise a strong likelihood that the accused did so. The preliminary hearing is a screening process to ensure that persons are not held for trial on totally inadequate evidence. One important purpose of the preliminary hearing is to offer the accused information about the Crown's case. The Crown Attorney does not have to call every single witness, but enough material witnesses must be called to establish clearly the case the Crown will pursue against the accused. The defence counsel has an early opportunity to cross-examine these witnesses and test the strength of their testimony. Defence counsel can then properly advise the accused whether a Guilty plea to a lesser offence might be in order.

The *Criminal Code* permits the Attorney General to prefer a *direct indictment* against an accused. This procedure permits the indictment of the accused without a preliminary hearing, or even permits the indictment of an accused after a magistrate dismissed the charge at a preliminary hearing. An accused may request that no publicity be permitted regarding the hearing. If the magistrate agrees, then the media cannot publish the names or events of the hearing.

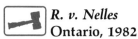

R. v. Nelles
Ontario, 1982

Susan Nelles, a nurse, was charged with four counts of murder in the deaths of babies at the Toronto Hospital for Sick Children. After much publicity and a preliminary hearing lasting forty-five days, the judge found that Nelles could not be prosecuted for the crimes. The judge criticized the police handling of the investigation and chastised the Crown for proceeding with the case on such weak evidence. In addition to the trauma of the hearing, Nelles may never be able to return to nursing because of the publicity. The Nelles family spent $100 000 on legal costs for her defence.

Pleas

The accused must either enter a plea personally or else a plea of Not Guilty will be entered for the accused by the judge. At one time, the law required that the accused enter a plea personally or the trial could not continue. In order to force a plea from the accused, the person would be tortured. The normal method was "pressing" which was to place heavy weights upon the accused, sometimes for many days, until the accused made a plea. Why would an accused not want to plead? The reason was that if the accused was tried and convicted, the accused's estate might be forfeit to the Crown and, in the case of a titled accused, the title might be revoked; this would affect the accused's family and descendants. An accused might prefer to be tortured to death rather than enter a plea.

In 1728 a man named Burnwater was taken to Newgate Prison, pressed under 400 pounds (180 kg) of iron for two hours, and then had his thumbs tied together with whipcord. He eventually pleaded Not Guilty, was convicted and hanged.

The plea is the accused person's answer to the charge made against him or her. It must be made orally and in open court. The judge asks the accused, "How do you plead? Are you Guilty or Not Guilty?" An accused may plead Guilty to some counts in an indictment and Not Guilty to others. The accused may plead Not Guilty as charged, but Guilty to a lesser included offence. However, there is no guarantee that the Crown will agree to a plea to a lesser included offence and the trial may proceed upon the original charge. There are special pleas, such as insanity, double jeopardy, and others which are discussed under the sections dealing with defences.

Plea Bargaining

Prior to the actual trial, an "unofficial" process called *plea bargaining* often takes place. Because the cost and time of a trial, particularly a jury trial, is very great, a bargain can sometimes be reached between the defence counsel and the Crown Attorney.

The defence counsel has a fair idea of how much evidence is stacked against a client and also knows the odds in favour of obtaining a complete acquittal if the Crown tries to get a guilty verdict on the major offence. The defence counsel discusses the case with the Crown Attorney and seeks agreement that if the Crown will not insist upon a conviction for a major offence, the accused will plead Guilty to a minor offence or a lesser included offence. For example, if the Crown will drop a charge of break and enter, the accused will plead Guilty to a charge of possession of burglary tools.

With plea bargaining many cases can be settled quickly and without costly trial. The accused receives some punishment, but not the maximum. The Crown is assured of a conviction for some offence, even though it is not a major offence. If the Crown refuses to bargain, then it is possible that the defence will succeed in a complete Not Guilty decision. The defence counsel cannot engage in plea bargaining without the consent of the accused. No defence counsel should urge a plea of Guilty for a client when the accused insists upon personal innocence.

Critics of plea bargaining say that often an accused is persuaded to plead Guilty to a lesser offence, when there was every reason to believe a complete acquittal might have been obtained. The judge takes no part in plea bargaining, although a judge can plainly guess that some bargaining has taken place. It is improper for anyone to tell the accused that if he or she pleads Guilty to a lesser offence, the judge will "go easy" on the accused. Critics also point out that plea bargaining gives the accused the impression that the legal system is something that can be manipulated—that deals can be made. Supporters of plea bargaining insist that without it courts would be overworked and needless expense would be incurred.

In his book, *Let's Make a Deal*, John Klein discovered that 53 per cent of offenders in prison had been involved in a deal of some kind. Most deals occurred primarily in relationships between the offenders and the police. Only a minority were the outcome of involvement with the Crown Attorney. The bargains struck involved significant benefits to offenders, such as dropping of charges against their accomplices, particularly where the partners happened to be lovers or spouses; the dropping of charges against the offenders themselves; the facilitation of bail; and arrangements for the securing of lenient sentences. In exchange for these benefits, the police allegedly gained by the recovery of such items as illegal explosives, firearms, stolen property, and drugs. Furthermore, the police benefited in a more general sense because they improved their clearance rates and, most importantly, they preserved the flow of that lifeblood of any police department—information.

A proposed amendment to the *Criminal Code* will provide a proper basis for conferences involving the judge, defence lawyer, and Crown Attorney to determine if a bargain can be made. Such conferences have already taken place on a test basis in Ontario. However, in the case of *R. v. Dubien* (Ontario, 1982), the judge told the lawyers the accused would be sentenced to five years no matter which crime was admitted. The Ontario Court of Appeal held that the sentence could not be discussed before a plea was made.

Absconding Accused

If the accused absconds (voluntarily goes away and hides) during any phase of the proceedings, the court may continue the trial, convict the accused "in absentia," and pass sentence. Where an accused has absconded, defence counsel may continue to defend the accused during the trial.

Trial by Jury

A Brief History

To most Canadians, the jury system is unchallengeable. It is viewed as a cornerstone of democracy and the essence of a fair trial for the accused.

The jury system was not planned. It developed through a long and strange history with dramatic turns made at different points in history. The jury was at times the accuser of a person. Juries were sometimes little more than legal lynch mobs, currying the favour of an ill-tempered ruler.

The concept of a group of persons sitting in judgment developed simultaneously in distant parts of the world. It is commonly found in nearly every known civilization, which leads one to think that it may be a social phenomenon to which all human minds turn.

The Egyptians had a jury system hundreds of years before the birth of Christ. Called the *kenbet*, it consisted of eight members, four from each side of the Nile. The Greeks had the largest juries, called *dikasts*. Each year six thousand citizens over thirty years of age were chosen to hear trials. They were arranged into panels of five hundred each, with a thousand in reserve to fill vacancies. Socrates was sentenced to death by a dikast, and said upon his sentence, "If I could only have won over thirty more votes."

The Romans developed the *judex* which required the drawing up of a document outlining the nature of the problem. A magistrate presented the evidence to a jury along with careful instructions about the law and the verdicts that were available.

When the Normans invaded England, they found the Saxons were using a trial by ordeal system which the Normans disliked. They substituted for it a system of "oath-taking" to get at the truth. This oath-taking system became very complex and was called trial by *compurgators*. Each party would bring as many people as possible to swear that their witness was a truthful witness who should be believed. Whoever had the most compurgators won. The Normans retained the right of the nobility to demand trial by combat. The pageantry and excitement of such trials eventually ended when the Pope prohibited them.

There are many jury systems around the world that have twelve jurors. There is no known explanation for choosing the number twelve, although some believe it represents the Twelve Apostles.

The Magna Carta, signed by King John in 1215, promised that every "freeman" would have the "judgment of his peers" before being punished.

Initially, an accused person could not be represented by a lawyer as it was believed that the lawyer would try to confound the issues and confuse the jury. The belief that no accused should have a lawyer stemmed from the unanimous verdict rule. An early law book stated: "The evidence whereby he shall be condemned ought to be so plain and evident, that all the counsel in the world may be presumed able to say nothing against it or in his defence."

Until 1870, it was a strict rule that once the jurors began deliberating, they were not allowed to eat or drink. This was to speed up the verdict. If the jurors were too slow in reaching a verdict, the judge would load them into carts and take them to the next town so that they could continue deliberating while the judge heard the next case. Traditionally, the judge ordered that the jurors should have neither "meat, nor water, nor candle."

For many years, juries decided cases more upon their personal knowledge of the parties and the surrounding facts than upon the evidence presented to them. In 1816, Lord Edenborough stunned the legal world by ruling in *R. v. Sutton* that a judge who tolerated a verdict based on facts not brought out in the evidence, but founded instead on the jurors' personal knowledge of the case, was in error.

Electing Trial by Jury

At this point, it might be well to reflect upon the wisdom of choosing a trial by jury. The accused should not automatically choose trial by jury assuming that the chances of getting off are greater. There are advantages and disadvantages to jury trial.

What Advantages?

- The verdict in criminal cases must be unanimous. If the defence can convince one juror, conviction is barred.
- Jurors may represent the same social level as the accused, which may be lower than that of a judge. Jurors may have more empathy than the judge with the accused.
- The right to challenge jurors should provide for an unbiased jury.
- A good defence lawyer knows how to work on juries. The lawyer's rhetorical abilities will make a greater impression on jurors than on a judge.

What Disadvantages?

- Jurors can be very prejudiced against certain defendants: they can be influenced by the social level, appearance, race, nationality, etc., of the accused. A jury may take one look at a hippie-type, accused of drug possession, and be convinced of the person's guilt before any evidence has been presented.
- Jurors can be swayed by a good Crown Attorney. Just as a defence lawyer can work on a jury, so will a good prosecutor be equally successful.
- Jurors often don't understand the law and may reach a wrong verdict simply because of a misunderstanding, despite what the judge instructs them to do.

Rather than demand trial by jury automatically, the accused should discuss the advantages and disadvantages with a lawyer before deciding how to be tried.

Empanelling the Petit (Petty) Jury

To serve on a petit jury, a person must be a Canadian citizen, must not have been convicted of an offence for which he or she was sentenced to more than twelve months in prison, and must not be employed as a lawyer, law student, member of the clergy, police officer, or doctor. Each province may establish further qualifications for a person to sit on a jury. Ontario accomplishes this under the *Juries Act*. The prospective jurors, chosen from a voters' list, are summoned to court where each name, address, and a number is placed on a card. Then the process of empanelling the jury begins.

The defence attorney and the Crown Attorney may challenge "for cause" any prospective juror because the person is not qualified to be a juror (for such reasons as being physically unfit, not being a citizen, or having a record of conviction). However, the most common cause for challenge is that the juror is not "indifferent" between the Crown and the accused. This could include such things as the juror being prejudiced, having strong feelings about a certain type of case, having prior knowledge of the case, or being related to the accused. If a juror has already decided the guilt or innocence of the accused, that juror is not indifferent and can be challenged for cause. There is no limit as to how many jurors may be challenged for cause. The judge may require a challenge for cause to be made in writing and the other party may contest such a challenge.

In accepting a juror, counsel says, "Content," meaning "I am content to have this juror." In addition to challenging jurors for cause, the defence may remove jurors by "peremptory challenge." A peremptory challenge has no cause; it is just a right given to the defence to remove a person from the prospective list of jurors because counsel believes the person will be unsympathetic. The number of peremptory challenges varies with the offence:

- For the offence of high treason or first degree murder—twenty challenges.

- For an offence, other than high treason or first degree murder, punishable by imprisonment for more than five years—twelve challenges.

- For all other offences—four challenges.

The Crown Attorney also has four peremptory challenges and may also direct up to forty-eight jurors to "stand aside" until other jurors have been examined. A juror who stands aside is not eliminated. That juror merely goes to the end of the line until it is seen if twelve jurors can be found from among the other prospects. If a full jury is not formed, those who stood aside are called again until the jury is filled.

It is the petit jury that will hear the evidence in the case and determine if the accused is Guilty or Not Guilty. In all provinces, a petit jury consists of twelve jurors. Their verdict must be unanimous; that is, all twelve jurors must agree. In the Northwest and Yukon Territories the petit jury consists of six persons. If a juror becomes ill during the trial, the judge may excuse the person and continue the trial with eleven jurors. The judge may do this with two jurors, as long as there are at least ten jurors remaining to reach a verdict. There must be at least five jurors remaining to reach a verdict in the Territories.

The *Charter of Rights and Freedoms* guarantees that a person has the right to use either French or English in any court of law under federal jurisdiction. The *Charter* also recognizes English and French as the official languages of New Brunswick, at the specific request of that province. Residents of Quebec will continue to have the right to use either language before the courts of that province, as will the residents of Manitoba. Ontario has designated eight areas as bilingual for trial purposes. The application of a party who speaks French requires that the judge and jury shall be bilingual. Evidence given in French shall be recorded and transcribed in that language. The jury roll is divided into two parts: those persons who speak English only and those persons who speak both English and French. There is no list of persons speaking only French.

Conduct of the Trial

The events in a criminal trial follow a general sequence which is standard throughout Canada, although some differences may occur in special circumstances. Our system of law is based upon what is called the "adversary system" which means the two parties are pitted against each other in the courtroom. Some countries do not use the adversary system, but rather think of the trial as a fact-finding inquiry. The adversary system places a strenuous demand upon both sides and requires the best possible effort from each. It is intended to bring out all the facts and expose untruths at the same time.

The Indictment

When the trial first begins, a Bill of Indictment is read to the accused. (Usually, it is just called "the indictment.") The accused has the right to know the charge under the right of habeas corpus. An objection to the indictment for a defect apparent on its face may be made by a motion by the defence counsel to quash the indictment. This is within the jurisdiction of the judge. At one time, the wording of the indictment had to be technically very precise or it would be thrown out for any small irregularity. The proper writing of an indictment which would stand up in court became a legal art in itself. Today, the rules are not quite so strict.

INDICTMENT

Canada: Province of British Columbia
The accused, Frederick V. Griffin
of Vancouver, British Columbia
has been charged that on or about
September 5, 19--, he unlawfully did
break and enter a certain place, to wit,
Discount Stores, situate and being at
127 Centre Street, Vancouver, B.C.,
with intent to commit an indictable
offence therein contrary to section
306(1)(a) of the *Criminal Code*.

An accused is entitled to know the exact charge against him or her so that a full answer to the charge can be made.

An indictment may be objected to if it contains *duplicity*. Duplicity can mean several things, including alleging that the accused committed either offence A or offence B, but the Crown is not certain which. If an indictment or count is vague, or brought under the wrong Act or the wrong section of an Act, the judge may quash any count within the indictment or the entire indictment. If the error is slight, the judge has the discretion to "amend" it, meaning to make small corrections.

R. v. Godfrey
Supreme Court of Canada, 1957

The accused was charged with conspiracy to commit robbery. The indictment did not include any particulars about with whom the accused conspired, or when or where. The Supreme Court of Canada held that the indictment was too vague and quashed it. The court concluded:

66Where an alleged offence is stated too generally, and in terms which do not clearly identify the facts that allegedly occurred, the accused is not afforded a proper defence for he does not know what particular allegations he must rebut.99

If an offence as worded in the *Criminal Code* or any other statute uses the words "knowingly" or "wilfully" then the indictment must also contain these words. If they do not appear, the indictment will be quashed.

In early English trials, the first time the accused knew the charge was when it was read in court. Today, the accused is provided full particulars of the alleged offence well in advance of the trial so that a defence may be prepared.

In Canada, the accused is referred to as either the "accused" or the "defendant." In earlier times, the accused was referred to as "the prisoner at the bar." If the accused is convicted and appeals, the accused is usually referred to as the "appellant." If the Crown appeals an acquittal, the accused is known as the "respondent."

Questioning and Cross-Examination

Questioning of a witness must take a particular format. The first questioning of a witness is the direct examination and is conducted by the lawyer representing the party who called the witness. A witness may testify only as to what has been personally seen, heard, smelled, tasted, or touched. A witness may only repeat what others have said for the purpose of showing that the statement was made, but not for the purpose of proving the truth of that statement. This questioning is followed by cross-examination, conducted by the opposing lawyer. This may be followed by redirect questioning and possibly recross-examination, if necessary.

Cross-examination, if done carelessly, can end up by contributing to the opponent's case. The purposes of cross-examination are:

(1) To elicit new information not given;
(2) To obtain a different interpretation of the facts;
(3) To challenge the powers of observation and recall of the witness;
(4) To test the reliability and credibility of the witness.

Cross-examination is a very important part of the trial procedure. It reduces the impact a witness may at first have had on the jury. The questions must generally be confined to the testimony the witness has already given. It cannot be turned into a new direct examination of the witness. Cross-examination can uncover that the witness was exaggerating, guessing, lying, wrongly recollecting the facts, holding back information, or showing bias. The accused does not have to testify; but if the accused wants to do so, he or she must be prepared to undergo cross-examination by the Crown Attorney.

If the accused testifies, it may be asked whether the accused has ever been arrested or convicted of a criminal offence. This is a test of the accused's credibility. If the accused does not testify, no one may mention that the accused has been convicted before. An exception to this rule occurs when an accused has been charged with possession of stolen property; in this case, evidence that the accused was, within five years before the proceedings were commenced, convicted of theft or possession of stolen property is admissible at any stage in the proceedings. The accused must be given three days' notice that the Crown intends to introduce this evidence. A defence counsel knows that cross-examination can be very ruthless and, for this reason, may keep the accused off the stand. The Crown may not suggest to the jury that the accused was afraid to testify and therefore must be guilty. The right not to testify remains the accused's right throughout the proceedings. The accused has the right to be present at all times during the trial unless he or she disrupts the trial, at which time the judge may exclude the accused from the courtroom.

Criminal Court Procedure

Note: The chart asumes the existence of a jury. The chart will also apply to a trial before a judge without a jury.

Opening arguments by the Crown Attorney to the jury, stressing how he or she will establish guilt.

↓

Case for the Crown. Evidence and witnesses are called by the Crown to establish the guilt of the accused. Each witness is cross-examined by the defence counsel after giving direct testimony. The Crown may re-examine a witness if desired.

Defence chooses to call evidence. The defence counsel is permitted to make opening argument to the jury.

↓

The case for the defence. Evidence and witnesses are called by the defence to establish the innocence of the accused and/or suggest the accused would have no motive or opportunity to commit the offence. The accused may testify in his or her own behalf, if desired. There is no rule that the accused must be the first witness for his or her own defence. Each witness is cross-examined by the Crown after giving direct testimony.

↓

Rebuttal of defence evidence by the Crown. The Crown may call witnesses to refute the evidence given by defence witnesses, including evidence given by the accused.

↓

Surrebuttal of the Crown's evidence by the defence. The defence may counter the Crown's rebuttal evidence.

↓

Closing arguments by the defence counsel to the jury.

↓

Closing arguments by the Crown Attorney to the jury.

Defence chooses to call no evidence.

↓

Closing arguments by the Crown Attorney to the jury.

↓

Closing arguments by the defence counsel to the jury.

Note: There is a distinct advantage to being the last to address the jury. The closing arguments are in the form of a summation, each side stressing what it wants the jury to take special note of and keep uppermost in mind.

Voir Dire

If either counsel has doubts about the admissibility of evidence, the judge tells the jury to leave the courtroom so that the evidence may be heard in their absence. This procedure is called *voir dire* (speak the truth). The term strictly means a preliminary hearing of the evidence of a witness to determine if the person is of sound mind or is a reliable witness who should be believed. It has been extended to include a determination by the judge of whether the evidence in question is admissible. The judge listens to the evidence, and either recalls the jury to hear the evidence or refuses to let them hear it. The judge could allow some of the evidence to go to the jury and prohibit the rest.

Erven v. The Queen
Supreme Court of Canada, 1978

The Supreme Court of Canada allowed an appeal by the accused from a conviction in Nova Scotia on a charge of possession of narcotics for the purpose of trafficking. It was held (6-3) that no statement made out of court by an accused to a person in authority can be admitted into evidence against the accused unless the prosecution shows, to the satisfaction of the trial judge, that the statement was made freely and voluntarily. The admissibility of the statement is to be determined on a voir dire even when, from the circumstances under which it was made, the statement appears to be obviously voluntary. The voir dire and the trial have distinct functions: the one, to determine admissibility of evidence; the other, to determine the merits of the case on the basis of admissible evidence. An accused may testify on a voir dire without prejudicing the privilege not to take the stand before the jury. The accused may be examined with respect to the statement allegedly given, but not upon the question of personal innocence or guilt.

Witnesses

In Canadian law, surprise witnesses and surprise evidence are not allowed. The accused is not entitled as a right to have statements of Crown witnesses prior to the trial. However, it is established practice that the prosecution cannot conceal the existence of witnesses merely to catch the defence by surprise. Customarily, the Crown lists all the witnesses it plans to call on the back of the Bill of Indictment and provides this to the defence counsel prior to trial. If the Crown does not call these witnesses, the Crown must make them available to the defence. The Crown also provides the defence with any statements, reports, or other documents it intends to present at the trial, keeping in mind that the Crown must safeguard evidence and not let it be accidentally destroyed. The Crown provides the defence with the arrest and conviction record of the accused. If the indictment is not sufficiently precise in its wording, the defence may make application for "particulars." This means the defence wants more specific information about the alleged offence so that it may prepare its case. If the judge agrees, the Crown will be ordered to provide more specific information.

A witness who has testified during a trial can be recalled for the purpose of testifying about new matter not mentioned in the previous testimony, to correct the previous testimony, or to lay foundation for impeachment of the credibility of other witnesses. The witness cannot be recalled just to repeat the earlier testimony. Nor can the witness by recalled merely because the defence counsel or Crown Attorney forgot to ask a certain question. The trial judge has the discretionary power to decide if a witness may be recalled.

A court may limit the number of witnesses called to testify about a single point in order to save time. Witnesses are often excluded from the courtroom while other witnesses testify. A witness cannot read from any notes he or she has made. A witness may refresh his or her memory from notes made *at the time* of the alleged offence, but not from notes made later. This is particularly important with regard to police officers and their notebooks and reports.

If a witness proves "adverse" (hostile) to the party which called the witness, that party may "impeach" the witness's credibility—assuming the hostility was not expected. The other party may object to this and a witness may be declared hostile only after the judge has heard submissions from both counsel. A party cannot call a witness with the pre-determined intention of discrediting the witness.

Where a witness refuses to testify or refuses to answer a question without reasonable excuse, the *Criminal Code* provides that the judge may order the witness to answer. Refusal can mean being jailed for up to eight days and then being brought back to the court and ordered to answer the question. If the witness still refuses, he or she can be jailed for another eight days. This process can go on indefinitely.

Perjury

Section 120 of the *Criminal Code* states:

> **Every one commits perjury who, being a witness in a judicial proceeding, with intent to mislead gives false evidence, knowing that the evidence is false.**

In *Wolf v. The Queen* (1974), the Supreme Court of Canada held that it is perjury for a person to say it is not possible to remember something when there is strong evidence to suggest that it is possible.

Under s. 124 it is an offence to make contradictory statements. The possible punishment for perjury is imprisonment for fourteen years.

If an acquitted accused gave false evidence at the trial, the accused cannot be retried upon the original charge but can be charged with perjury.

Staying the Proceedings

A rather unusual power rests with the Attorney General of Canada or of a province or counsel whom the Attorney General instructs; namely, the Attorney General may interrupt the proceedings in a criminal case any time after an indictment has been found. The Crown Attorney may direct the clerk of the court to make an entry on the record that the proceedings are "stayed." They may remain stayed for up to one year. This means the proceedings are suspended, but the charge has not been dropped. The Crown might want

to stay proceedings in order to gather more evidence or to submit a detailed legal argument to the court on a particular point. The judge cannot prevent the proceedings from being stayed. In one case, the stay was entered while the jury was deliberating, but the judge allowed the jury to give its verdict anyway, saying that "things have gone too far to stop now." The Court of Appeal overruled the judge and disallowed the verdict, holding that the judge could not stop the proceedings from being stayed right up to the time the verdict was given in open court.

Trial Transcript and Exhibits

A complete transcript is kept of the entire trial. Items introduced as exhibits are kept in the court's possession until the end of the trial, after which a description or photograph is made of them. Some of the exhibits are the property of others and some are so large the court could not possibly keep them.

Instructing the Jury

After the closing arguments, the judge must instruct the jury as to its duty. Since jurors have not been trained in the law and probably have not read the *Criminal Code*, they must take the law as the judge explains it to them. The judge must enlighten the jury as to the verdicts it may consider. The judge's words are the totality of the law that the jury should apply to the facts of the case. The judge will cover such things as reasonable doubt and presumption of innocence, and advise the jury to refuse to consider defences put forward, which, as a matter of law, cannot be accepted. If the judge did not serve this "screening and instructing" role, the jurors would have to consider so many potential defences put upon them that they would not know their proper duty. In this summation, the judge may give an opinion as to the importance of evidence and to the credibility of the witnesses. The judge may not give an opinion as to the guilt or innocence of the accused.

Instructing (or "charging") the jury is a very important part of the trial, for if the judge instructs the jury wrongly, the jury will reach a wrong verdict. Many appeals have stemmed from the manner in which the judge put the charge to the jury.

After the judge instructs the jury, it retires to the deliberation room. Then the judge will ask both the Crown and defence attorneys if they have any complaints about the manner in which the jury was instructed. If they have valid objections, the judge may recall the jury and instruct it again. If the jurors still do not understand the possible verdicts open to them they may ask the judge to give them further explanation as to the law.

The Verdict and the Directed Verdict

After being charged by the judge and instructed in its duty, the jury retires to the jury room to deliberate upon a verdict. Once in the deliberation room, jurors are not allowed to communicate with anyone except other jurors until their verdict is decided. A bailiff is sworn under oath to keep the jury sequestered (isolated) and in the bailiff's charge while it deliberates. The jury may ask to hear testimony read from the court reporter's notes, see exhibits, or ask the judge to clarify a point of law.

The jury must be unanimous in its verdict. Failure to reach a verdict will usually lead to the judge's recalling the jury and instructing it once more in its duty and the law. If no decision is reached, the jury is discharged. This is referred to as a *hung jury*, and the judge may order the entire trial repeated with a new jury.

Determining a verdict is often not simply a question of finding the accused Guilty or Not Guilty. The jury might find the accused Not Guilty of one count and Guilty of another. Or, the jury might find the accused Not Guilty as charged, but perhaps Guilty of an "attempt" to commit the offence. In some cases, the accused might be found Guilty of a lesser included offence. The important point is that the jury must take

the law from the judge and return a verdict which the judge indicated was available to it.

While the judge is the sole judge of the law, the jury is the sole judge of the facts. The judge cannot interfere with the jury's deliberations and interpose a personal opinion.

 R. v. McKenna
England, 1960
In the trial of three men accused of theft, the jury deliberated for over two hours until the judge called the jury back into the courtroom and chastised them as follows:

66I have disorganized my travel arrangements out of consideration for you already. I am not going to disorganize them any further. In ten minutes I shall leave this building and if by that time you have not arrived at a conclusion in this case, you will be kept all night and we will resume this matter at quarter to twelve tomorrow. I don't know why in a case which does not involve any study of figures or documents you should require all this time to talk about the matter. Do not worry yourselves about legal quibbles. Use your common sense; bring in a bit from outside.**99**

The jury brought in a verdict of Guilty in six minutes. The accused appealed the conviction on the grounds that the judge had prejudiced the jury. The Court of Appeal agreed and the conviction was quashed.

However, there are situations which can require that the judge intervene in the process of the jury reaching a verdict. In some cases, it may be a matter of *law* that the accused be found Not Guilty and the judge must direct the jury to find accordingly. Remember, the judge is the sole judge of the law.

At one time in legal history, the defence counsel could raise a question of *demurrer* to the evidence. This meant that the facts alleged were admitted as true, but still did not prove an offence occurred. This was a dangerous thing for the defence to do—admitting the facts! Today, rather than a demurrer, the defence counsel, at the close of the Crown's case, may rise and request a *directed verdict* of Not Guilty, as a matter of law, since the essentials of the crime have not been proven. The judge, if in agreement with the defence counsel, will direct the jury to find the accused Not Guilty. The defence does not have to present any evidence. There is no need, for the Crown has not proven its case. (In England, a different procedure is followed. The judge "takes the case from the jury" and personally finds the accused Not Guilty.) The directed verdict saves time and expense in the trial and prevents a wrongful conviction which the accused could later easily have reversed in an appeal.

 ### R. v. Sandhu and Sandhu
British Columbia, 1975

In this case, there was a motion for a directed verdict of Not Guilty. The two accused had been charged with non-capital murder. There was evidence that they beat the deceased who died a month later after three operations for pancreatitis. The doctor who operated on the deceased testified that there was no evidence of any injury to the abdomen and that if an acceleration of the pancreatitis had been due to an external injury there would have to have been evidence of injury to the pancreas or the organs around the pancreas. The doctor said that there was nothing at all to suggest that this had occurred. At the request of the defence counsel, the judge directed the jury that it might reach a verdict of Not Guilty of non-capital murder, but then advised the jury that the trial would continue on the basis that the indictment would be understood to include a count of *attempted* non-capital murder.

When the jury returns its verdict, the foreman or forewoman announces the decision. Either counsel may ask that the jury be polled individually, in which case each juror must stand and state his or her verdict. The jury is then discharged and the jurors are not sub-ject to jury duty again for three or five years depending upon the province.

One of the great strengths of the jury system is that the jurors do not have to defend or justify their decision to anyone. Jurors are free to talk about the case after it's over. At one time in English legal history, if a jury acquitted in a case where the judge thought a conviction was proper, the judge could fine or imprison the entire jury until they changed their verdict. This was considered a penalty for going against their oath. The last time this was done was when the Chief Justice of the Court of Star Chamber imprisoned a jury in 1602 for acquitting an accused of murder. Thereafter, one of the most valued traditions of the jury system became apparent. When laws were passed that were unpopular with the common people, the people had a solution — they simply would not convict anyone for violating those laws no matter how conclusive the evidence. The only course left was for Parliament to repeal the laws. At one time, for example, there were more than a hundred minor offences for which a person could be hanged. Jurors would not convict their friends and neighbours of any of these offences because they refused to see them hanged for such trifling matters. No amount of blustering or instruction by the judge could get jurors to return a verdict of guilty. Eventually, most of these laws were repealed or the penalty lessened.

To a great extent, this was the reason for the outcry in the first *Morgentaler* trial. A jury found Morgentaler Not Guilty despite instructions from the judge that Morgentaler had raised no valid defence. The Court of Appeal substituted a verdict of Guilty. Legal historians felt that permitting this type of verdict would destroy the jury system, for a panel of judges had substituted their verdict for that of a panel of "peers." The Supreme Court of Canada upheld the decision of the Quebec Court of Appeal but cautioned that the process of replacing a jury acquittal with a verdict of Guilty was "to be used with great circumspection" — meaning done only with much caution. The law was later amended to prohibit a Court of Appeal from substituting a Guilty verdict after a jury had acquitted.

Reviewing Important Points

1. Time does not run against the Crown. While a summary conviction charge must be brought within six months of the date of the offence, there is no time limit for prosecuting an indictable offence.
2. The purpose of a preliminary hearing is to determine if there is sufficient evidence to commit the accused for trial.
3. Some minor offences must be tried by the magistrate alone, without a jury.
4. If an accused will not plead, a plea of Not Guilty is entered for the accused.
5. The process of plea bargaining reduces the court's workload by permitting an accused to plead Guilty to some lesser offence.
6. The jury's verdict must be unanimous in a criminal case.
8. If the defence does not call evidence, the defence has the advantage of addressing the jury last.

Checking Your Understanding

1. For certain offences, the accused is offered three choices of trial. What are they?
2. Name three advantages to electing trial by jury.
3. Explain the circumstances in which a judge might direct the jury to find the accused Not Guilty.
4. What is a voir dire? What is its purpose?
5. The jury is the sole judge of the facts. What does this mean?
6. State three purposes of cross-examination. A noted criminal lawyer once wrote: "Never ask a question during cross-examination to which you do not know the answer yourself." Done carelessly, cross-examination can work against the party doing the questioning. Can you suggest a reason why?
7. What is a peremptory challenge?

Legal Briefs

1. Part way through the trial, a juror dies. Must a new juror be chosen and the trial re-conducted?
2. When charged with unlawfully being in a dwelling-house, the accused was asked what method of trial she wished to elect. She replied, "I elect to be tried in the Supreme Court of Canada." Will she get her wish?
3. Criminal lawyer: "The reason I plea bargain is to get the Crown to bring the charge down to what my client should have been charged with in the first place." Meaning?
4. A man charged with sexual assault is tried by a jury comprised of twelve women. Fair trial?
5. The accused thought his trial would not come up for several hours so he went to the coffee shop in the same building. He was called for trial and when he did not answer the judge issued a bench warrant for his arrest. Did the accused abscond?
6. A woman was charged with the murder of her husband nineteen years after she allegedly killed him. Proper procedure? Can a person get a fair trial after nineteen years have elapsed?

Applying the Law

 R. v. Littlejohn
Ontario, 1978
During the jury's deliberation, a note was sent by the members which read: "The problem is that one of us knows of guilt but cannot bring one's self to say it outright and make it unanimous. Please advise us." The judge brought the jury back in and reminded them of their oath and duty. Two hours later the judge received another note: "We are getting nowhere. Advise." The judge told the jury to have dinner and then to continue. Five hours later another note was sent stating: "Deadlocked." The judge brought the jury back and told them:

❝I have a feeling that someone may be evading his or her duty, not paying attention to the oath that they have taken and that's what is discouraging . . . . So, if during the time that the sheriff is arranging accommodation for you, you are able to come to a verdict that will be fine, but if not, you will have to stay locked up overnight and continue your deliberations in the morning because I don't think it is really a question of being deadlocked. I think someone is not following the oath that was taken. If I thought for one moment that you are really deadlocked, then I would dismiss you, so that's it. **"**

Ten minutes later the jury returned with a verdict. On appeal by the accused, it was held that the appeal should be dismissed. A trial judge should avoid language which is coercive and which constitutes an interference with the right of the jury to deliberate in complete freedom uninfluenced by extra pressures. In deciding whether a judge's words cross the line between exhortation and coercion, the entire sequence of events must be looked at. In the present case, the judge's answers to the two notes were impeccable; the final answer did not, in the unusual circumstances, constitute coercion. The judge's final instruction made it clear that the judge was prepared to accept genuine disagreement but not the arbitrary withholding of a verdict.

Questions
1. What should the judge tell a jury that appears unable to reach a unanimous verdict?
2. In this case, what words spoken by the judge might have appeared coercive or threatening to the jury?
3. What do you think a juror's oath states?
4. Do you think jurors would be intimidated by the words, "you will have to stay *locked up* overnight"? Why or why not?

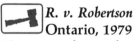 **R. v. Robertson**
Ontario, 1979
The accused was charged with murder. The controversy arose over the jury's deliberations. Court opened at 9:30 a.m. when defence evidence continued. Counsel for the accused and the Crown addressed the jury, and the trial judge delivered the charge to the jury ending at 4:00 p.m. The jury returned at 6:00 with a question, and again at 9:50 with a further question and a request that the

entire cross-examination of a medical witness be read to them. They returned at 10:45 with a question that indicated they had not fully grasped the issue committed to them, and they requested that the cross-examination of another medical witness be read. At 12:55 a.m. they had a further question and the ensuing discussion lasted for fifty-five minutes. They returned at 2:30 to announce that they were deadlocked and could not in good conscience arrive at a verdict. The trial judge exhorted them to continue, indicating that some person or persons must be "holding out." He renewed his instructions and told them that they had a right to disagree. However, he said that if he, as a judge, had said that he could not make up his mind, he would be regarded as a poor judge. He sent the jury back out. They returned at 3:23 with a verdict of Guilty. At no time did the judge suggest to the jury that if they wished to go to a hotel and resume deliberations in the morning, arrangements would be made to that effect. The undesirability of keeping the jury at work far into the night, except in special circumstances, was unfair to the accused and to the Crown. The verdict was set aside and a new trial ordered.

Questions
1. Is there a strategic purpose in keeping a jury deliberating non-stop? For example, many labour negotiators involve the parties in round-the-clock bargaining with good results.
2. Is the expression "holding out" a fair one for the judge to use when discussing the jury's deadlock? Why or why not?
3. Is there some time limit beyond which a jury should not deliberate? What do you think it might be?

You Be the Judge

1. The accused was charged with criminal negligence causing death after being responsible for an automobile collision while impaired. The accused's lawyer and the Crown Attorney did some plea bargaining and the

accused pleaded Guilty to impaired driving only. The trial judge adjourned the trial, saying, "The Crown does not appear to be taking this case seriously. I am going to invite the public to submit recommendations to me as to whether such a plea should be accepted." The defence appealed to the Court of Appeal asking that the trial judge be ordered to proceed with sentencing the accused for impaired driving. Was the trial judge following proper procedure?

2. The defence counsel and the Crown Attorney made a bargain that the accused would plead Guilty to a charge of possession of a narcotic if the Crown would drop the charge of trafficking. The accused then cooperated with the police in breaking up a drug ring. When the trial was held, a new Crown Attorney had taken over the case. This person refused to abide by the bargain on the grounds that agreements made by a previous Crown Attorney were not binding upon the current Crown Attorney. The defence lawyer asked the judge to dismiss the trafficking charge and to accept the plea of possession. Must the judge do so?

Chapter 7

Evidence, Appeals, and Punishment

Some Evidence Rules

The question as to what evidence may be used against an accused is covered by the *Canada Evidence Act* and by a large body of case law that has developed over the years. Since there are few statutes dealing with evidence, judges have formulated the rules on the basis of what they consider proper in keeping with the spirit of equity. It should also be accepted that many of the rules were developed in the belief that jurors were not very intelligent and could be swayed by evidence cleverly presented. In this section we can discuss only some of the evidence rules. The subject is too vast to discuss in complete detail.

As you read the information in each section, keep in mind that there are many exceptions to every rule. There are thousands of rules of evidence and compiling them all would be nearly impossible. In 1979, the Law Reform Commission of Canada published its report on evidence and concluded that the rules of evidence have scarcely changed at all since the turn of the century.

Again, for ease of reference, the rules are arranged in alphabetical order.

Character Evidence and Previous Convictions

The use of evidence of an accused's character during the course of a trial is divided into two categories — good character and bad character — and each category is treated differently.

The Crown cannot initiate any line of questioning to lead the jury to believe that the accused has the disposi-

tion of a criminal. In keeping with the basic human attitude common to most of us, the majority of jurors believe that "bad people" commit crimes. If the Crown can demonstrate that the accused is a "bad person," a conviction will probably follow — even if the evidence does not support it.

The other side of the coin is evidence of good character. Surprisingly, the defence may adduce evidence of good character to show that the accused is unlikely to have committed the offence. In *R. v. Barbour* (1938), the Ontario Court of Appeal held:

> **❝**A much wider latitude is allowed to the accused . . . to show, not only that it was not likely that he committed the crime charged, but that *he was not the kind of person likely to do so.***❞**

However, if the accused puts his or her good character in evidence, the Crown may then introduce contrary evidence of the accused's bad character. With the permission of the court, the accused's previous record may be introduced as evidence.

Under the *Canada Evidence Act*, any witness may be questioned as to whether he or she has been convicted of an offence. If the witness denies having been convicted, the opposite party may prove the fact of a conviction. This rule also applies to the accused. If the accused testifies on his or her own behalf, the accused can be questioned about prior convictions as a test of *credibility*, not of *character*. Credibility is relevant only to determine if the witness's evidence ought to be believed, but does not directly establish guilt or innocence.

Circumstantial Evidence

There are generally two kinds of evidence, direct evidence and circumstantial evidence. Direct evidence can be subject to only one error — human mistake. If J testifies to seeing S shoot B, this is direct evidence. It is possible that J suffers from poor vision and mistakenly identified S as the slayer. However, if J testifies to finding B dead with S standing over B, holding a smoking gun, J cannot say that S shot B. The circumstances indicate that S *might* have shot B, but there is no direct evidence to prove it. S might have found the gun beside B and picked it up.

It is possible, although somewhat dangerous, to convict a person upon circumstantial evidence. How much evidence is required? In *R. v. Cooper* (1978), the Supreme Court of Canada stated:

> **❝**It is enough if it is made plain to the jury that before basing a verdict of guilty on circumstantial evidence, they must be satisfied beyond a reasonable doubt that the guilt of the accused is the *only reasonable inference* to be drawn from the proven facts.**❞**

The following case turned on the question of circumstantial evidence:

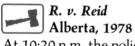

R. v. Reid
Alberta, 1978

At 10:20 p.m. the police checked the service station where the accused was employed. All was in order and the accused was starting to close up, a chore that would take forty-five minutes. At 11:25, the accused and another man were seen leaving the station. Inspection by the police revealed a window broken inwards. Money was missing along with some goods. The accused did not testify at the trial and the case centred around circumstantial evidence. If the accused had left at 11:05, which is when he should have left, he would have no reason to be back in the building with another man at 11:25. If the accused had not left the building prior to 11:25, he would have heard someone break the window. The absence of any explanation from the accused left the court to conclude that the accused left at 11:05 or earlier, returned with his accomplice and broke back into the building. He was convicted upon this circumstantial evidence.

Confessions

The classic statement of the rule of admissibility of statements made by the accused is found in *Ibrahim v. The King* (England, 1914):

> **❝**It has long been established as a positive rule of English criminal law, that no statement by an accused is admissible in evidence against him unless it is shown by the prosecution to have been a voluntary statement in the sense that it has not been obtained from him either by fear of prejudice or hope of advantage exercised or held out by a person in authority. The principle is as old as Lord Hale.**❞**

A statement made by the accused is either inculpatory (self-implicating) or exculpatory (denying guilt or involvement). In *R. v. Piche* (1970), the Supreme Court of Canada held that an involuntary statement is inadmissible even if shown to be true. This decision was reaffirmed in *Horvath v. The Queen* (1979) where an accused made a series of statements while in and out of an hypnotic state. The police examiner was very skillful and while no attempt was made to hypnotize the accused, tapes showed that it had happened. The confessions were all held inadmissible. In *R. v. Romansky* (1981), a polygraph operator talked to the accused in a monologue, often repeating that the accused should "respond." The accused broke down and confessed. The confession was ruled inadmissible.

An important consideration in a case may be the identity of the person to whom a statement is made. If the person is a "person in authority" then the rules of admissibility are stricter, for the accused believes the statement is being made to a person who could get the accused into legal trouble. If the listener is not a person in authority, the rules are less strict.

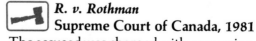

R. v. Rothman
Supreme Court of Canada, 1981

The accused was charged with possession of hashish

and refused to make any statement. He was placed in a cell with an undercover police officer wearing dirty clothes and needing a shave. The accused was initially suspicious and said to the officer, "You look like a narc." However, the accused later confided in the officer his involvement in narcotics. The issue was whether this statement could be admitted in evidence. The Supreme Court of Canada held that it was admissible. The court concluded that the officer was not a person in authority at the time because he was not regarded as such by the accused. There was no evidence that the officer used unfair methods of persuasion to get the accused to discuss his drug dealings.

There are two sections of the *Charter of Rights and Freedoms* which could affect the admissibility of statements in the future. Under s. 10(b) everyone has the right, on arrest, to be informed of the right to counsel. If the police do not inform an accused of this right, any subsequent statement made by the accused may be inadmissible. Under s. 24(2) evidence can be excluded if the admission of it would bring the "administration of justice into disrepute." A confession obtained by trickery or deceit might be excluded under this section.

Corroboration

The classic definition of corroboration is found in *R. v. Baskerville* (England, 1916):

> 66We hold that evidence in corroboration must be independent testimony which affects the accused by connecting or tending to connect him with the crime. In other words, it must be evidence which implicates him; that is, which confirms in some material particular not only the evidence that the crime has been committed, but also that the prisoner committed it. 99

Several sections of the *Code* deal with corroboration. These sections state that no accused shall be convicted of certain offences, including incest, seduction of a female between sixteen and eighteen, forgery, and perjury upon the evidence of only one witness unless the

evidence is corroborated in a material particular by evidence that implicates the accused.

Section 586 of the *Code* requires that no person shall be convicted of an offence on the *unsworn* evidence of a child without corroboration. A child who does not understand the nature of an oath may be permitted to testify without taking an oath, as long as the child understands that he or she is expected to tell the truth. If the child testifies under oath, the rule does not apply. In *R. v. Fletcher* (1982), the Ontario Court of Appeal held that a child's understanding of an oath does not require a belief by the child in a God or Supreme Being. Nor does it require that the child understand that he or she is telling God that what will be said is the truth. The important consideration is whether the child understands the solemnity of the occasion, and the added responsibility to tell the truth which is involved in taking an oath. This is over and above the normal duty to tell the truth which is an ordinary duty of social contact.

The Canada Evidence Act *requires that a child not be permitted to testify under oath unless the child understands the nature of an oath.*

One difficult area of law is that of the evidence of accomplices. Accomplices are very tempted to try to minimize their role in a crime and shift the blame to the other persons involved. Judges have traditionally given juries long instructions warning of the danger of convicting an accused on the uncorroborated testimony of an accomplice. In *Vetrovic and Gaja v. The Queen* (1982), the Supreme Court of Canada expressed the view that such evidence rules had become too complex and technical and that accomplices did not belong in some special "untrustworthy" class. The court said that the *Baskerville* definition was technical to the point of being unsound. The decision reads in part:

> **❝**It would have been sufficient for the trial judge simply to have instructed the jury that they should view the testimony of Langvard (an accomplice) with great caution, and that it would be wise to look for other supporting evidence before convicting the appellants.**❞**

Exclusion of Evidence

Canadian law holds that the illegality of the means of obtaining evidence generally has no bearing on its admissibility. If, for example, D's home is entered and searched without a warrant, the police could be sued in civil court by D, but any evidence found during the search would still be admissible against D. The leading case is the following:

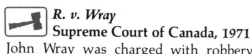

R. v. Wray
Supreme Court of Canada, 1971

John Wray was charged with robbery and the murder of a gas station operator. A confession was obtained by "trickery, duress and improper inducement." Wray told the police where he threw the rifle and the police found the weapon there. The trial judge ruled that Wray's confession was inadmissible. When the Crown Attorney then wanted to adduce evidence as to the part taken by Wray in finding the weapon, the trial judge refused to permit it on the grounds that, since the confession was inadmissible, the evidence stemming from the confession was inadmissible. The Supreme Court of

Canada held that the evidence was admissible since *there was no judicial discretion permitting the exclusion of relevant evidence* on the grounds of unfairness to the accused.

It is possible that courts will begin to apply s. 24(2) of the *Charter of Rights and Freedoms* which pertains to evidence bringing justice into disrepute, and exclude evidence obtained by dubious or unlawful means.

Hearsay

Hearsay is a complex area of law and there are many exceptions to the rule. Basically, a witness can only testify as to what has been personally seen, heard, touched, or smelled. The witness cannot relate what someone else has said about such things because the witness does not know personally whether these are the true facts. Accordingly, because of this lack of personal knowledge, the witness cannot swear to be telling the truth. A witness giving evidence which is hearsay cannot be cross-examined to test the accuracy or truth of the evidence. The rule of hearsay does not apply to words spoken by the accused, since the accused is not a compellable witness. Therefore, a witness may testify as to anything the accused was heard to say. The witness is not swearing that it is true, but only that the accused said it.

In *Phillion v. The Queen* (1977), the Supreme Court of Canada held that a polygraph operator cannot testify about the results of a test taken by the accused. The court rejected such testimony as hearsay. The accused would not have to testify under oath; there would be doubts about the accuracy of the machine; and further doubts about the ability of the operator to properly analyse the results.

There are some notable exceptions to the hearsay rule. The first is dying declarations. A statement is admissible if made by a person, now deceased, who had a settled, hopeless expectation of death almost immediately before that death, *provided* the statement would have been admissible if the person had lived.

For example, if B is dying and C asks, "Who shot you?" and B replies, "I don't know. It was too dark to see, but I think it was D," this would not be an admissible statement since it was not factual evidence.

Another exception to the hearsay rule is a statement against penal interest. A statement which might ordinarily be inadmissible might be admissible if it places the person making it in immediate jeopardy of being personally prosecuted. It is generally believed that people will not lie to implicate themselves.

Incriminating Questions

Canada does not have a Fifth Amendment like the United States. A witness cannot refuse to answer a question on the grounds that it may tend to incriminate him or her. However, under the *Canada Evidence Act*, the witness is protected in that the answer given shall not be used at any trial or civil proceeding against the witness. Although our law requires a witness to answer, it does afford protection by guaranteeing that what the witness says cannot later be used to convict that person. A witness must specifically ask the judge for this protection.

Section 13 of the *Charter of Rights and Freedoms* states that "A witness who testifies in any proceedings has the right not to have any incriminating evidence so given used to incriminate that witness in any other proceedings, except in a prosecution for perjury or for the giving of contradictory evidence." This section may be interpreted to provide protection to the accused even though protection was not specifically requested during the first trial.

Leading Questions

Leading questions can only be asked of a witness during cross-examination. A leading question is one that tends to suggest the answer wanted.

A question is also leading if it assumes a controversial fact which has not yet been proven or testified to, or makes assumptions which are not admitted by the other party.

Similar Fact Evidence

While the Crown cannot try to attack the accused's character by adducing evidence of previous convictions, there are cases where previous convictions are relevant evidence. The primary such occasions occur where the Crown wishes to show whether the acts in the alleged offence were deliberate or accidental; or to rebut a defence—such as involuntary conduct, mistake, or innocent explanation—which would otherwise be open to the accused.

In a few cases, the manner in which a crime has been committed can be important. If a crime is committed in a very peculiar way, and there is evidence that the accused has committed crimes in such a way, it is relevant to bring this out. In some situations, the *modus operandi* ("method of operation") of the accused is like "fingerprints" on the crime scene.

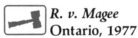

R. v. Magee
Ontario, 1977

The deceased, a fifteen-year-old girl, was picked up while hitch-hiking, raped, strangled, and stabbed in sexual areas. At trial, the Crown attempted to introduce the testimony of a fourteen-year-old female witness that the accused, some seven months earlier, had picked her up while hitch-hiking; had raped and stabbed her; and had tried to strangle her. On the voir dire, the witness's identification of the accused was challenged. It was held that the evidence was admissible. The striking features of the accused's method, taken along with other similar facts, could lead the jury to find an abnormal propensity for a particular kind of violence and to conclude that the offences were committed by the same person. That the identification was challenged did not make the evidence inadmissible where such evidence was capable of being clear and convincing to the jury.

Spouses

Under s. 4 of the *Canada Evidence Act*, a husband and wife are protected in that they are not compellable witnesses against each other; they cannot be compelled to disclose any communications made between them during their marriage. There are exceptions to this rule, including various sex offences, defiling or neglecting a child, bigamy, and theft from the other spouse while separated.

The wife or husband of an accused is a competent and compellable witness against his or her spouse for many offences if the victim was under fourteen years of age. Such offences include criminal negligence, assault, sexual assault, and murder.

It is important to note that, just because a spouse cannot be *compelled* to testify against the other, this does not mean the spouse may not do so voluntarily. The information is not privileged. In *R. v. MacPherson* (1980), the Nova Scotia Court of Appeal held that in a charge of child abuse, a spouse is a competent and compellable witness against the other. The protection of the child takes a higher priority than the marital unity and harmony of the parents.

Wiretap

A communication that has been intercepted is inadmissible as evidence against the originator of the communication or the person intended to receive it, unless the interception was lawfully made; or unless the originator or the person intended to receive it expressly consents to the admission. However, other evidence obtained by interception is not inadmissible. A lawful intercept order must be authorized by a judge of a superior court, the Attorney General of a province or of Canada, or the Solicitor General of Canada.

 R. v. Ashok Dass
Manitoba, 1979
Police entered the home of the accused and installed a "bug" pursuant to a warrant issued under s. 178.13 of the *Code*. The defence argued that the interception was unlawfully made. The Crown argued that the authority to intercept carries with it by implication the authority to enter premises by force or stealth in order to implant the device. The Manitoba Court of Appeal held that the police had unlawfully

trespassed but that this did not invalidate the authorization to intercept. The evidence obtained was held to be admissible, but the court firmly asserted that those who had committed the trespass could be answerable in some other criminal or civil action.

❝The authority to intercept is not an authority to break the laws of the land. If, in effecting an interception, an officer commits a trespass, assaults a person, causes injury to some individual by negligence, or the like, the authorization to intercept gives the officer no protection .... I see nothing in the *Criminal Code* which gives a judge the power to authorize or condone illegal entry.**❞**

The *Ashok Dass* case illustrates a problem the police may have. They have powers to intercept, but they cannot use illegal methods to do so. It would be unlikely that a search warrant could be issued to permit planting a "bug." A search warrant is issued to search for something already on the premises, not to put something there.

Coroner's Jury

No one is exactly certain when the office of coroner first began, but records as far back as the twelfth century mention coroners. The coroner is a medical officer whose basic duty is to inquire into the deaths of all persons within a specific territory, usually a county. Everyone knowing that death has occurred must notify a coroner. With this notification a medical-legal inquiry begins. The coroner has the power to take possession of the body and to make such investigations as are necessary to determine the cause of death. If the death occurred from natural causes, the doctor in charge will issue a death certificate and no further investigation will be held. In other cases the coroner may decide to hold an inquest. In Ontario the inquest will involve the coroner and five jurors chosen by the coroner from the voting list. It will examine evidence and hear witnesses to determine, when, where, how, and by what means the person died. An inquest is nearly always held where the death may have been due to violence, negligence, misconduct, malpractice, a disease or sickness not treated by a doctor, misadventure or dangerous practices, or where the death occurred under suspicious circumstances during pregnancy.

The coroner's jury may make recommendations so that a similar death can be avoided in the future. These recommendations are not binding in nature upon anyone, including the government.

Young Offenders

Since 1892, young offenders have been treated differently than adults under the *Juvenile Delinquents Act*. This Act provided that children should be tried in a separate court, without publicity, and without the formality of a criminal trial. The Act never applied in the Province of Newfoundland.

In *Morris v. The Queen* (1979), the Supreme Court of Canada stunned family law lawyers by holding that a juvenile, convicted of an offence under the Act, had been convicted of a *criminal* offence. This was contrary to what many believed to be the "child-saving" feature of the Act which supposedly protected the juvenile from acquiring the stigma of criminal.

In 1982, Parliament passed the *Young Offenders Act* which will replace the *Juvenile Delinquents Act* in 1984. There are many important provisions of this Act, some of which are as follows:

- The minimum age at which a child can be charged with a criminal offence will be twelve years. Children under twelve will have to be dealt with by provincial legislation.
- The definition of a "young person" in the Act includes a person under eighteen years of age. At the request of a province, the federal Parliament may lower the age in that province to sixteen or seventeen years.
- The Act limits the definition of "offence" to breaches of federal acts, regulations, rules, ordinances, and by-laws. This will exclude some offences formerly

found in the *Juvenile Delinquents Act* such as "sexual immorality" or any provincial offence.
- The maximum possible fine will be increased from $25 to $1000. The young person may be given the opportunity to participate in a work program to discharge the fine.
- A young person has the right to counsel and legal aid.
- The young person may be placed on probation for a period not exceeding two years. There are some mandatory conditions of probation and other conditions may be added by the judge.
- The Act places a high priority upon restitution and compensation to the victim. As well, the offender can be required to repay the innocent purchaser of stolen property which had been sold to the purchaser by the offender and subsequently returned to its owner.
- The Act abolishes parental responsibility for offences committed by a young person. The *Juvenile Delinquents Act* did permit the judge to hold parents liable in some situations.

There are some concerns about the new Act. The first is the increased workload upon Youth Courts due to the probable increase in cases involving persons sixteen and seventeen years of age. In 1979, this age group committed over 12 000 *Criminal Code* offences. Another concern is the absence of any jurisdiction over a child under the age of twelve. In 1979, this group committed over 6000 *Criminal Code* violations. It would appear that persons under age twelve cannot be arrested and cannot be brought into any court for violation of federal law. Thus, the necessary result is that the provinces will have to enact laws dealing with children who get into trouble. A final question mark is whether the age of eighteen was a suitable uniform age to establish. Many lawyers believe that the age level of criminals has been declining, not rising, and that age sixteen would have been a more logical choice. A former Ontario provincial court judge commented, "When I became a judge, I thought I was going into an adult court. Most of the offenders before me were under age eighteen."

There are other concerns about the new statute. Some critics feel that the federal government is trying to pass the total responsibility for dealing with young offenders onto the provinces. The provinces will have to decide whether they will take no action to deal with the new numbers of children under their jurisdiction or spend large amounts of money for new courts and facilities.

The Act contains elaborate provisions designed to safeguard the rights of young offenders. A young offender cannot receive a punishment greater than the maximum that could have been given to an adult for the same offence. On the other hand, the court may impose innovative conditions upon the young offender. The Act allows the court to impose "such other reasonable and ancillary conditions as it deems advisable and in the best interest of the young person and the public." This could include conditions such as attending school regularly and staying out of places where known offenders gather.

The Act permits trials to be held *in camera* ("excluding the members of the public"), if it is in the best interests of the young offender to avoid publicity and embarrassment. A young offender over the age of fourteen years is eligible for transfer to an adult court for a very serious offence.

The relationship of the young offender and the police will be altered somewhat. The Act provides that no statement made by a young offender is admissible unless it is voluntary. The person taking the statement must explain to the young offender that he or she is under no obligation to give a statement and that any statement given may be used in evidence. Before making the statement, the person must be given an opportunity to consult with parents or a lawyer.

Young offenders may not be photographed or fingerprinted except in cases where they would be treated as adults and subject to the *Identification of Criminals Act*. If a young person is not convicted, all photographs and fingerprint cards must be destroyed. All police records on young offenders must be kept in a central file and made available to the defence lawyer for the young

person. As well, all records of offences "alleged to have been committed" must be kept on file and made available. There is no prohibition upon release of these files to other persons, such as parents. It is a matter of police discretion. If the young person is acquitted, all records pertaining to those proceedings must be destroyed. If the young person has been convicted of an offence, but does not get into trouble again, the records will also be destroyed. In the event of a summary conviction offence, the records will be destroyed two years later. For an indictable offence, five years later. If, after becoming an adult, the young person is granted a pardon, the records must be destroyed.

One of the major departures from the old law is that the Youth Court will have virtually no authority over adults. There is no authority to order parents to contribute to the child's support, nor can parents be fined or otherwise held responsible for the acts of their children. There are some provisions in the *Criminal Code* or provincial statutes that may deal with such matters, but they are not within the powers of this court.

The Act continues to protect the privacy of the young offender. It is an offence to publish, by any means, the name of the young person charged or the name of a young person, the victim of an alleged offence, who is appearing as a witness.

If the court believes the young person is mentally or emotionally disturbed, the person may be remanded for examination for eight days. This can be extended to thirty days. The same tests of insanity will now be applied to young offenders as are applied to adults.

There is no longer any procedure for "sealing" the records of a young offender when the person becomes an adult. If the person is later charged in an adult court and adduces evidence of good character, the prosecutor must be allowed to introduce evidence of previous convictions of the accused as a young offender. The court cannot allow the accused to introduce "good" character with immunity. Thus, it is reasonable to suggest that the young offender will have a criminal record until a sufficient number of years have passed for the record to be destroyed.

Appeal Procedures

The right to appeal is vital to our system of criminal law. Without it, wrong decisions would never be corrected. Trial judges themselves feel reassured that should they reach an improper decision there are courts of appeal which will put the matter right. Appeal cases often bring out the most dramatic and important decisions in legal history.

An appeal must be made within thirty days of conviction unless there are extenuating circumstances requiring more time. During this time, the convicted person is kept in a provincial jail rather than being sent to a federal penitentiary.

The appeal must have valid grounds. An appeal cannot be vexatious, frivolous, or made just to delay punishment. Appeals are usually made for one or more of the following reasons:

- The judge erred by admitting evidence that should not have been admitted, or by excluding evidence that should have been admitted.
- The judge either wrongly instructed the jury or misdirected himself or herself on the law.
- The judge or the jury was not impartial and should not have convicted the accused on the evidence presented to it.
- New evidence is now available which was not available at the trial and this evidence is relevant, credible, and nearly conclusive.
- The law contravenes basic rights or conflicts with other laws such as the *Bill of Rights* or the *Charter of Rights and Freedoms*.

Appeal from Conviction by Accused: Indictable Offences

A person convicted of an indictable offence may appeal the conviction or sentence. Appeals do not involve re-trying the case except in a trial de novo which will be explained later. Most appeals involve a study of the transcript of the case by the Court of Appeal along with oral and written arguments by counsel for both sides. A convicted person may always appeal the conviction on a question of law. If the conviction is appealed on a question of fact, or of mixed law and fact, the convicted person must first obtain permission from the Court of Appeal.

Appeal from Acquittal by Crown: Indictable Offences

If the accused has been found Not Guilty, the Crown may appeal on a question of law. The Crown cannot appeal on a question of fact.

Appeal by Way of Stated Case: Summary Convictions

Where a summary conviction case hinges upon a question of law only, either the Crown or the accused may appeal by way of stated case. This requires the magistrate, provincial court judge, or justice of the peace who heard the case to submit in question form the issues in the case to the provincial Court of Appeal. The appeal is studied by one judge, in chambers, who decides the legal issue and advises the magistrate whether the case was decided correctly or not.

 ### R. v. Piggly Wiggly Canadian Ltd. Manitoba, 1933

An employee of the defendant company incorrectly short-weighed bags of sugar. The company was convicted under the *Weights and Measures Act of Canada*. The company directed the magistrate that it wished the question of employer's liability stated to the Court of Appeal. The magistrate postulated these two questions:

"First. Is knowledge, guilty knowledge, an essential element of the offence created by s. 63 of the *Weights and Measures Act*?

Second. Is an employer liable under that section for the acts or omissions of his servant?"**

The Court of Appeal replied "No" to the first question and "Yes" to the second question and included legal arguments to explain each answer.

The decision of an appeal by stated case does not bar a further appeal to the full Court of Appeal, but requires permission from the Court of Appeal.

Appeal by Trial de Novo: Summary Conviction Cases

Trial de novo stands for "new trial" and means just that. The person making the appeal is usually concerned with the fairness of the first trial and may particularly feel that all the facts were not brought out. At a trial de novo, witnesses are again called, exhibits produced, and a full trial conducted over again. Neither side is limited to the same evidence used in the first trial. The Court of Appeal may order a new trial before the same court or a higher court. Usually, a trial de novo is conducted before a county court judge without a jury. In the provinces of Newfoundland and Prince Edward Island, the case is heard before a Judge of the Supreme Court. Either side may further appeal a decision reached at trial de novo. In the case of *R. v. Jordan* (1971), the Supreme Court of Nova Scotia ruled that the right of the Crown to appeal by trial de novo does not put the accused into double jeopardy and is not contrary to the *Bill of Rights*.

Appeal of Sentence

Either the accused or the Crown may appeal on the grounds that the sentence imposed is inappropriate. The accused may appeal on the grounds that the sentence is too harsh in relation to the crime and in relation to sentences received by other offenders convicted of the same offence. The Crown has the right to appeal on the grounds that the sentence is too lenient and does not serve as a deterrent to either the accused or to other persons who might be tempted to commit the same crime.

The Court of Appeal may dismiss the appeal or vary the sentence within the limits prescribed by law for the offence of which the accused was convicted. Where a minimum sentence is prescribed by law, there is no appeal against the minimum sentence being assessed.

The accused and the Crown could both appeal the sentence. Some critics point out that the Crown sometimes appeals only to intimidate the accused into withdrawing an appeal. That is, the Crown won't appeal unless the accused does. This puts the accused in a risky position and pressures the accused to withdraw the appeal rather than risk having the Court of Appeal accept the Crown's arguments and impose a longer sentence.

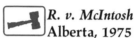

R. v. McIntosh
Alberta, 1975

The respondent, McIntosh, was convicted for trafficking in heroin and the Crown appealed from the lenient sentence imposed on the grounds that the main consideration in sentencing ought to be the deterrent effect on others. The accused claimed that he had had a change of heart. The appeal was allowed and the sentence was increased to three years' imprisonment. The Court of Appeal agreed with the Crown's submission and the practice of all appellate courts in Canada that in sentencing for trafficking in what were called hard drugs, the main consideration had to be the deterrent effect on the offender and, what was probably more important, on others. If there was a true change of heart on the part of the respondent, it was more properly for the Parole Board to consider.

Powers of Provincial Courts of Appeal

Each province has a Court of Appeal, although they are referred to by different names. Cases are heard by a panel of judges. The number is usually determined by the Chief Justice who may appoint three, five, or more judges to hear a case. If the case is of great significance, the entire court may hear the case.

The provincial Courts of Appeal have numerous alternatives open to them in disposing of appeals.

Appeal against Conviction by Accused
The court may:

(1) Dismiss the appeal summarily without reasons;

(2) Dismiss the appeal on the grounds that the verdict was proper, notwithstanding some irregularities, as long as no substantial miscarriage of justice occurred;
(3) Set aside the conviction on the grounds of insanity and remand the accused to the custody of the Lieutenant-Governor of the province for treatment in a mental hospital;
(4) Allow the appeal and order a new trial;
(5) Allow the appeal and enter a verdict of acquittal.

Appeal against Acquittal by the Crown

The court may:

(1) Dismiss the appeal;
(2) Allow the appeal, set aside the acquittal, and order a new trial;
(3) *Except where the verdict is that of a court comprised of a judge and jury*, allow the appeal, enter a verdict of Guilty with respect to the offence of which, in its opinion, the accused should have been found Guilty except for an error in law, and pass a sentence that is warranted in law.

Prior to an amendment in 1976, the Court of Appeal had the power to overturn the acquittal reached by a jury and enter a Guilty verdict in its place. After the *Morgentaler* case (see the section on Abortion in Chapter 4), the *Criminal Code* was amended to remove this power. The Court of Appeal can order a new trial if it feels a jury has wrongly acquitted the accused, but it cannot enter a verdict of Guilty. If the accused was tried by a judge without a jury, the Court of Appeal can still change the verdict to one of Guilty.

Appeals to the Supreme Court of Canada

There is no automatic right to appeal every case to the Supreme Court of Canada.

If either the Crown or the accused wishes to appeal from the decision of the provincial Court of Appeal, the appeal must be based upon a question of law, and there must have been at least one dissenting opinion in the Court of Appeal. That is, at least one judge of the Court of Appeal disagreed with the decision of the

As the highest court in Canada, the Supreme Court of Canada is the final authority upon the criminal law. Appeals sometimes require permission from the court to have the case heard.

majority. If there was no dissenting opinion, an appeal to the Supreme Court of Canada requires prior consent from the court. A person acquitted of an indictable offence at trial, but who had the acquittal set aside by a Court of Appeal, may appeal to the Supreme Court of Canada.

Summary conviction offences always require permission to appeal to the Supreme Court of Canada.

Criminal Procedure and Avenues of Appeal

Criminal procedure and avenues of appeal differ from province to province. The procedure and avenues of appeal in the Province of Ontario are outlined in the following diagram and are typical of most provinces.

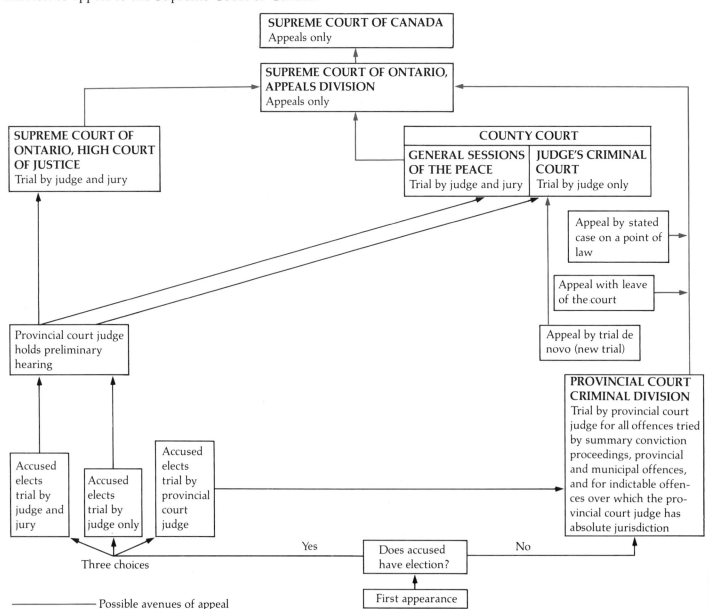

Punishment for Crime

Purposes of Punishment

Our society generally accepts that any wrongdoing of a serious nature must be met with a form of punishment. At the same time, society does not agree upon either the purpose of punishment or, in many cases, the form it should take. To some people, revenge is a primary purpose. This is particularly the attitude of the victim of a crime or the victim's family. To others, a sense of justice or fair play dominates.

The overall purpose running through our concept of punishment is to protect the public. Where it can be established that an offender represents a danger to the public, the offender is jailed to prevent the recurrence of any further offence by the same wrongdoer. Another purpose is to serve as a warning to others who might be thinking of committing an offence. In a very old case, the judge sentenced the accused and then said: "I am sentencing you to hang not so much because you stole a sheep, but so that others will not steal sheep." Another intended purpose is to extract some retribution from the offender. Somehow, there is a feeling that the offender should "pay" for the crime. If the offender is fined, this payment is being made directly. If the offender is jailed, we tend to say that he or she is "serving" a sentence, which suggests that in so doing the offender is serving society and repaying a debt to society. The wrongdoer may also be ordered to compensate the victim. Finally, a more recently stated purpose of punishment is to rehabilitate the offender. The success of this program is open to question. It depends upon whether the attitudes and behaviour of the offender can be altered while in jail—but this cannot be known with any degree of certainty until the offender is eventually released.

Principles of Sentencing

One of the most difficult decisions a judge ever has to make is what sentence to give a convicted person. There are many forces that bear upon the final deci-sion. In some offences, the judge has no choice—a particular sentence is mandatory. The judge must be aware of the community attitudes. A severe sentence often reflects public anger or revulsion over the crime. Another point the judge must consider is the prevalence of a type of crime. If a particular crime is on the upswing, sentences should generally be increased as a deterrent. A judge must be aware of the sentences given to other persons convicted of the same offence. There should be some uniformity in sentencing or it could be argued that equality before the law is not observed by judges passing sentence. A judge may take into account the amount of harm done. Strictly speaking, this is not an element of the offence. An offender might be convicted of assault causing bodily harm which resulted in minor abrasions to the victim. Another offender might be convicted of assault causing bodily harm, which caused the victim to be hospitalized for a month. The sentence might vary with the amount of injury the victim sustained. A very significant factor for the judge to take into account is the character and record of the convicted person. The judge often asks for a pre-sentence report. While there is no precise requirement as to what such a report should contain, it usually contains information about the convicted person's family life, education, employment record, and previous convictions. Reading this information about the person helps the judge to have some idea of what punishment would best serve both society and the convicted person. The pre-sentence report is especially important in the case of first offenders.

 R. v. Demeter and Whitmore
Ontario, 1976

Two youths, aged sixteen and seventeen, were convicted of an armed robbery. The trial judge sentenced them to two years less one day determinate, and two years less one day indeterminate. The Court of Appeal held that the judge was too concerned with general deterrence. The principles for sentencing young offenders must be different from those appropriate for adults:

❝In considering what an appropriate sentence is for the very young, the paramount consideration must be their immediate rehabilitation. Speedy apprehension, arrest, public trial, and a criminal record, with its consequences, should be the best deterrent for those young persons who may be tempted to commit an offence such as this.**❞**

The accused had spent three months in custody and the sentences were reduced to the time already served.

Imprisonment

For many offences, the penalty is imprisonment. Our criminal laws generally set only the maximum sentence a judge may give, though certain offences, including repeated narcotic offences and repeated impaired driving offences, require a minimum sentence. In the United States, laws often set both a minimum and a maximum, legally binding the judge to sentence the accused to prison for at least some period of time. For example, in some states, an offence may require imprisonment for "not less than two, nor more than ten years." Offences in Canada fall within categories allowing a sentence of six months upon summary conviction and two, five, ten, or fourteen years, or life imprisonment for indictable offences. For any conviction of an offence punishable by five years or less, the judge may impose a sentence of imprisonment or a fine, or both. That is, the judge can fine without also giving a jail sentence. If there is a conviction upon indictment of an offence for which the maximum possible penalty is over five years, the judge may jail and fine, but cannot impose only a fine. There must be imprisonment, even if for only one day. There is no limit to the fine that can be set, although it is expected that it will be reasonable. Where a Canadian law does not provide a specific penalty, s. 115 of the *Criminal Code* provides a maximum two-year prison sentence. For example, this would apply in the case of the *Trade Marks Act* which provides no specific penalty for violation.

If several offences are committed and perhaps several *counts* or occurrences are listed under each, the judge may award one sentence for all of them, separate sentences for each to run concurrently (at the same time), or separate sentences to run consecutively (one after the other). If the judge does not specify how the sentences are to be served, it is assumed that they will run concurrently.

If the term of imprisonment is for less than two years, it is served in a provincial jail. If the term is for two years or more, it is served in a federal penitentiary. When a judge wants to make it absolutely clear that the accused should be placed in a provincial jail, the judge will sentence the accused to "two years less one day."

The *Criminal Code* empowers a judge to impose an intermittent sentence of up to ninety days and provide that it be served at the times the judge directs, such as nights, weekends, etc.

Dangerous Offenders

If a person has been convicted of committing a "serious personal injury offence" and the offender constitutes a threat to the life, safety, or physical or mental well-being of other persons on the basis of evidence establishing (1) a pattern of repetitive behaviour showing a failure to exercise personal restraint; (2) a pattern of persistent aggressive behaviour showing indifference as to the consequences to other persons; or (3) behaviour of a brutal nature with likelihood of no restraint in the future, the court may find the accused to be a *dangerous offender* and impose a sentence of detention in a penitentiary for an *indeterminate* period. This means that the accused has no set release date.

A "serious personal injury offence" includes an indictable offence (other than treason, first degree or second degree murder) involving the use or attempted use of violence against another person, or conduct endangering or likely to endanger the life or safety of another person, for which the accused may be sentenced to imprisonment for ten years. Most sexual offences also fall into this category. A person is a dangerous offender if that person's conduct shows an habitual failure to control sexual impulses.

Fines

Many offences prescribe that a fine may be imposed along with a jail sentence or in place of a jail sentence. Often a term of imprisonment is stipulated only if the fine isn't paid. An accused might be sentenced to a fine of "$200 or in default to a term of 30 days." In summary conviction cases, a fine is generally limited to $500 in the case of an individual and $1000 in the case of a corporation. A person is customarily given up to fourteen days to pay the fine. More time may be given when special circumstances are shown.

Suspended Sentence

If the accused has been convicted of an offence for which no minimum penalty is prescribed, the judge may suspend imposing a sentence and release the accused under the conditions of a probation order. The accused still has a record of conviction; it is just that no sentence was passed. The terms of a probation order generally require the accused to maintain the peace, refrain from certain habits such as drinking alcohol, avoid contact with known criminals, and possibly maintain steady employment. The convicted person usually has to report to a probation officer. A probation order can continue in force for not more than three years. After that time, the convicted person cannot be sentenced. Violation of a probation order is an offence punishable on summary conviction. The accused, if convicted of breach of probation, can then be sentenced on the original offence. For example, Jones was convicted of break and enter, received a suspended sentence, and was placed on probation. After two years, Jones violated the terms of the probation order, was convicted and was fined $100 for the violation. Jones was then returned to the court which had convicted Jones of break and enter, and was sentenced to eighteen months in jail for that offence.

Absolute and Conditional Discharge

If the court considers it to be in the best interests of the public not to convict the accused, an order can be issued to direct that the accused be discharged absolutely or on the conditions of a probation order. Absolute discharges are not common in Canadian law. A person receiving an absolute discharge is released without conditions. A conditional discharge applies only to a person who pleads Guilty or is found Guilty of an offence other than an offence for which a minimum punishment is prescribed by law or an offence which, in the proceeding commenced against the accused is punishable by imprisonment for fourteen years or life. A person who pleads Guilty to a lesser offence may not be able to get a discharge because the original proceeding commenced against the accused may have had a penalty of fourteen years, or life imprisonment. A person who receives a conditional discharge and commits another offence may have the discharge set aside. A conviction will then be entered, and the person will be sentenced. A person receiving a discharge has been neither convicted nor acquitted. The matter is still open to have the court convict at any future time. After three years for an indictable offence, and one year for a summary conviction offence, the accused may apply to have a record of the conditional discharge removed from the files.

Indeterminate Imprisonment

In Ontario and British Columbia, if an offender commits an offence which is punishable by three months' imprisonment or more, the court may impose a definite term of imprisonment "in the common jail," then add an indeterminate term of imprisonment. Under the *Prisons and Reformatories Act of Canada* a male offender could receive a definite sentence of two years less one day, plus an indeterminate sentence of two years less one day. Thus, the maximum period of custody under the provisions of the Act is four years less two days. An example might be, "Twelve months definite, and six months indefinite." Exactly when the convicted person is to be released is then determined by the prison or reformatory officials, based upon the progress of the person while incarcerated.

For females, the court may impose only an indefinite sentence no longer than two years less one day. The Act specifically states that it be served in a "reformatory."

Indeterminate term in this context is not to be confused with an indeterminate term given to a person sentenced to a federal penitentiary for an indefinite term of preventive detention.

Restitution

A court that convicts an accused of an indictable offence may order the accused to compensate the person aggrieved by the accused's crime. The accused must pay out an amount of money as satisfaction or compensation for any financial loss or damage to property suffered by the victim. The court may also order property returned to the lawful owner or person to whom it is entitled.

Community Service Orders

In special circumstances, a court may decide that rather than impose a jail sentence or a fine, a better course of action would be to require the convicted person to perform a certain number of hours of community service. For example, in *R. v. Richards* (1979), the trial judge did not pass sentence upon the accused, a musician and leading member of the Rolling Stones band. The judge ordered the accused to give a benefit performance at the auditorium of the Canadian National Institute for the Blind, either personally or with a group of musicians requested by the blind young people associated with the CNIB. The Court of Appeal upheld the sentence. Richards had been convicted of possession of a narcotic. The court held that a custodial sentence would serve little purpose in this case.

Death

In Canada, the death penalty, called "capital punishment," was abolished in 1976. It had been carried out by hanging.

The last two persons hanged in Canada were Arthur Lucas and Ron Turpin. They were executed on December 11, 1962. Between that date and 1976, the federal Cabinet commuted all death sentences to imprisonment for life.

A Criminal Record

There are great disadvantages to having a criminal record. Many jobs require "bonding" which is a term meaning a form of personal insurance on your honesty. An employer may require employees who handle money or valuables to be bonded. A person with a criminal record often cannot obtain bond, and would thereby be denied these employment opportunities. A person may be denied employment opportunities if that employment requires a licence. For example, it is very difficult to become or remain a lawyer if one has a criminal record.

A criminal record will not necessarily deny a Canadian the right to obtain a passport, but other countries have the right to refuse entry into their country to Canadians (and other nationals) who have conviction records.

A person resident in Canada, who is not a Canadian citizen, may be deported after conviction for certain offences. If not deported, the person may still be denied the opportunity to obtain Canadian citizenship.

It is possible to have a criminal record removed from the files. Application must be made to the Solicitor General of Canada two years after a summary conviction sentence has been served, and five years after an indictable offence has been served. The National Parole Board will eventually rule upon the application.

Canada's Prison System

The federal government, through the Canadian Penitentiary Service and the National Parole Board, is responsible for all adults sentenced to federal penitentiaries. Exceptions are persons who are mentally ill or have tuberculosis. They remain the responsibility of the provinces.

Who Goes to a Penitentiary?

Not every lawbreaker ends up in a federal penitentiary. A person convicted and sentenced to two or more years in prison will serve that sentence in a federal penitentiary. A shorter sentence will be served in a provincial jail. The penitentiary system itself is divided into three different kinds of prisons: maximum security, medium security, and minimum security. The chief deciding factors determining where a person will serve a sentence are the danger which that person would represent to the public upon escape, and whether or not the person will attempt to escape. A convict is placed in a penitentiary on the following basis:

- *Maximum security:* The convict is expected to make active attempts to escape; upon escape, the convict would be dangerous to the public.
- *Medium security:* The convict is not expected to make active attempts to escape, but if given the opportunity to escape, would probably do so. Upon escape, the convict would probably not be dangerous to the public.
- *Minimum security:* The convict is not expected to make any attempt to escape; upon escape, the convict would not be dangerous to the public.

Approximately 50 per cent of the prison population is in a medium security prison; 35 per cent is in a maximum security prison; and the remaining 15 per cent in minimum security.

Punishment or Rehabilitation?

There is considerable disagreement as to just why the convict is in the prison. Is the convict there to be punished, or to be rehabilitated? Essentially the idea has been to put people in prison to prevent them from repeating their crimes. The prison system is a comparatively recent development in our legal history. Traditionally, punishments were far more direct —for example, execution or mutilation by cutting off an ear or a hand. When imprisonment was first introduced, it was seen purely in terms of punishment. Prison sentences were frequently for life, and prison conditions were very harsh; it was intended that the prisoner

should *suffer* for the crime. However, when shorter prison sentences became common, the question of rehabilitation was brought to the fore.

Rehabilitation in prison was an idea that was slow to be accepted by society. Yet, imprisonment without rehabilitation is without much purpose. If imprisoned persons are to be returned to society, should not an attempt be made to improve their behaviour before letting them go? Now, most of those imprisoned are eventually released. The purpose of rehabilitation is to improve their attitude and approach to life by finding out what caused them to commit their offences and dealing with this cause. Then, when they are released it is hoped that they will not repeat their previous behaviour. There is one great difficulty in this idea, generally called the "prison dilemma." If a person has not been able to function in a free society, and is put in prison, how can the prison teach that person the way to behave in a free society when the prison itself is anything *but* free? Rehabilitation takes the form of trying to educate and train the person so that the person can become self-supporting and not have to turn to crime for economic reasons. At the same time, psychological studies are made, and individuals are asked to try to understand why and how their former behaviour was unacceptable. No one claims present efforts at rehabilitation are a complete success, but an attempt must be made.

The Incorrigibles

Roughly 80 per cent of the federal inmate population in Canada has previously served time in either a provincial or federal prison. What occurs is a build-up in prisons of the same individuals who repeat offences and return again and again. About 80 per cent of inmates who commit another offence, upon release, do so within eighteen months.

A result of this trend is that the population in federal penitentiaries tends to be much older than that of provincial jails. Only 20 per cent of the persons entering a federal penitentiary are doing so for the first time. There is concern that they will be well schooled in crime by the other 80 per cent.

Overcrowding and other tensions inside federal penitentiaries have sometimes led to destructive riots.

The professional dwellers are referred to as *repeaters* or *recidivists*. Why can't prison reform them? No one has the answer, including the inmates themselves, though many explanations have been suggested by both inmates and penologists, including:

- Alcoholism, leading to criminal acts through diminished mental responsibility;
- Inability to get a job, since an "ex-con" so often finds society will not trust someone who has committed a crime;
- Inability to adjust to the freedom of society after years in a non-free environment;
- Lack of skills which afford opportunity in the job market;
- Absence of any community roots—no family or friends with whom to relate.

There are those who believe that inmates like it in prison and are happy to return there. While this might be true in a few cases, it is generally denied by the majority of inmates who clearly want to get out and stay out of prison. However, they fear they will never be able to do so. Inmates complain that prisons are so big and ugly that their whole sense of self-esteem is destroyed. Society is not only punishing them, but "rubbing it in" in every possible way. They become angry and resentful, and in these circumstances rehabilitation becomes almost impossible.

Privileges

All mail, in and out, is subject to censorship, although not all of it is read. No one has the time to read all that mail. All incoming mail is opened before being given to the inmate, because it is possible to mail small amounts of drugs or even weapons inside an envelope. An inmate may send a sealed letter to an MP, MPP, or the Solicitor General. Inmates must buy their own writing materials and stamps.

Unless they are being punished for something, all inmates have visiting privileges. There is no limit to the number of visits, although visits may be curtailed if they are interrupting the inmate's work or study times. The prison tries to make special consideration for visitors who have travelled long distances to see an inmate.

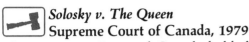 **Solosky v. The Queen**
Supreme Court of Canada, 1979

The Supreme Court of Canada held that prison officials may open mail addressed to an inmate and sent by the inmate's lawyer, and vice versa. While recognizing the historic "privilege" between lawyer and client, the court held that the necessity of maintaining prison security requires that mail be opened to determine if the contents are a bona fide communication between lawyer and client. The contents should be read only where there is reason to believe otherwise and the person reading the letter must maintain the confidentiality of its contents.

Temporary Absences

As part of the attempt to rehabilitate them, inmates are sometimes allowed to leave the prison for a short period, such as a weekend. These inmates are unguarded and are trusted to return on time. This program has caused some concern, because occasionally the inmate does not return. However, there is much to be said for this program.

Of the approximately 9000 persons now in federal penitentiaries, many can be released without endangering public safety. If they are to merge successfully back into society, it is wise to let them do it a little at a time, rather than just open the door and say, "Go—and sin no more." The inmate has nothing to gain and everything to lose by failing to return since this will mean losing the chance for another leave. The inmate may be transferred to a tougher prison and chances of early parole will be reduced. The inmates themselves become very concerned when someone escapes while on a temporary absence, for they fear that a few wrongdoers will ruin the program for everyone else. The absence policy certainly involves risks, but the alternatives involve the greater risk that rehabilitation won't succeed at all. For many inmates the temporary absence program makes all the difference between successful rehabilitation and becoming an incorrigible.

Parole

Parole is an important part of Canada's penal system. An inmate may apply to the National Parole Board in Ottawa after serving one-third of the sentence. Parole is strictly selective and only about one-third of those who apply are granted it. In a parole application, the inmate should state reasons for deserving to be placed on parole and should give details of a proposed parole program and plans for the future. Anyone may apply for parole on behalf of the inmate or help the inmate by arranging a parole program and community support.

The Parole Board takes the following factors into consideration when making its decision:

- The nature and gravity of the offence;
- Past behaviour;
- Total personality of the inmate—whether the inmate can be trusted in society;
- Whether the parolee would be likely to return to crime and the possible effect on society in that event;
- The efforts made by the inmate during imprisonment for self-improvement through better habits, education, and vocational training and how well these demonstrate the inmate's desire to become a good citizen;
- Whether there is anyone in society who would help the inmate on parole;
- The inmate's plans and whether they will aid in rehabilitation;
- What employment the inmate has arranged, or may be able to arrange;
- How well the inmate understands the personal problems underlying the inmate's anti-social behaviour.

Inmates are often puzzled as to why one inmate is granted parole and another refused it. What does an inmate have to do, apart from just "being good"? The acid test is whether the inmate's attitude towards crime has changed. Members of the staff at the inmate's prison are asked for reports on attitude and progress and these reports play an important part in the Board's final decision.

There is an outcry from the general public each time a person on parole commits a crime, and the Board must be careful in its selection process. The success or failure of the parole depends more upon the community than upon the parolee or the Board's selection process. If a parolee can find employment and someone in the community for moral support, the parolee's chances of avoiding trouble are excellent. If the community rejects the parolee outright, the person's chances for success are very small. Despite rare cases such as that of a parolee who robbed the cab driver picking up the parolee at the prison gate, the Board is usually correct in selecting whom it releases. Parole does work; it can work better.

Reviewing Important Points

1. An accused who testifies can be asked about prior convictions as a test of credibility, but not of character, unless the defence counsel has chosen to put the character of the accused in issue.
2. A person can be convicted upon circumstantial evidence if the guilt of the accused is the only reasonable inference that can be reached.
3. A confession must be made voluntarily without fear of prejudice or hope of special advantage being held out to the accused.
4. A person cannot be convicted solely upon the unsworn evidence of a child.
5. Evidence obtained illegally is admissible, nonetheless, if relevant to the case—subject to s. 24(2) of the *Charter*.
6. A person sentenced to more than two years in jail will serve the time in a federal penitentiary.
7. If a person is declared a dangerous offender, that person has no set release date.
8. Someone given a conditional discharge has no criminal record. Such a person will receive no sentence if that person abides by conditions set by the court.

Checking Your Understanding

1. Name three factors which a judge might be expected to consider when determining the sentence of a convicted person.
2. What is the significance of a judge's giving a jail sentence of "two years less one day"?
3. Is there a difference between a suspended sentence and a conditional discharge? If so, what?
4. What is corroboration? Give one example of when it would be required.
5. Canada has no general "Rule of Exclusion" regarding evidence. What does this mean?
6. What is hearsay? Under what conditions might hearsay be admissible?
7. If a witness is asked a question, the answer to which will implicate the witness in a crime, must the witness answer? Explain.

Legal Briefs

1. An accused was charged with a sex offence. There were no witnesses to verify the testimony of the complainant. The Crown sought to call people from the community who would testify that the complainant was an honest person who would not lie about such a thing. Admissible?
2. The accused was charged with possession of stolen goods. He was arrested at the house of a woman with whom he lived. Police told him that unless he confessed, they would arrest the woman, too, and her children would have to be taken into the custody of the Children's Aid Society while she was in jail. The accused confessed. At trial, it was argued that the confession was improperly obtained and inadmissible. Admissible?
3. Accused committed an indecent assault upon a thirteen-year-old girl. Although she was not sworn, she testified without being under oath. There was no other evidence against the accused. Could he be convicted?
4. Referring to evidence, an English court stated: "It

matters not how you get it; if you steal it, it will still be admissible in evidence." True statement?

5. The police have an authorization to intercept communications between Y and G. They want to install a device on G's telephone and plant a "bug" in her home to hear conversations. How can the police get into the home (lawfully) to install this device?

6. The accused was charged with an offence committed in Ontario and was sentenced to a reformatory for twelve months definite and eighteen months indefinite. If the accused had committed the same offence in Alberta, or another province outside Ontario or British Columbia, the most he could have received would have been six months. He appealed on the ground that he did not receive "equality under the law" as guaranteed in the *Charter of Rights and Freedoms*. Is he correct?

7. During a store robbery, two clerks got a good look at the robber. A police detective showed them some photos. One clerk said to the detective: "That is the person." The other clerk said: "That looks like the person." At trial, neither clerk was available since both had moved away. The Crown called the detective as a witness. Can the detective tell the court what the clerks said?

8. During direct examination by the Crown Attorney, the witness was asked: "What was the victim doing when struck by the accused?" Valid question?

9. The accused was charged with selling alcohol to a person under legal age. The minor was called as a witness and the defence lawyer asked her, "How old are you?" The minor replied, "Seventeen." "How do you know?" challenged the lawyer. "I was born on September 10, 19--," she replied. "How do you know?" repeated the lawyer. "My mother told me so," responded the witness. At this, the lawyer shouted, "That's hearsay!" Is it hearsay?

Applying the Law

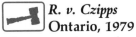

R. v. Czipps
Ontario, 1979

The accused was charged with having in her possession a knife for a purpose dangerous to the public peace. The Crown proposed to call her husband at her trial. The trial judge ruled that as the charge did not allege violence — actual, attempted, or threatened — to the person of the husband, the husband was not a competent witness against her. A "competent" witness is one who is capable and acceptable to both parties. A "compellable" witness is one who can be required to testify in a trial regardless of the person's personal wishes not to do so. As the Crown had no other evidence, the accused was acquitted. The Court of Appeal said:

    "At common law a spouse was generally not a competent witness against the other spouse. An exception was where the charge in a criminal prosecution alleged interference with the person, liberty, or health of the other spouse. In the present case the charge does not so allege but the Crown alleges that the evidence of the husband will disclose such interference. That question has very recently been considered in the British Columbia case of *R. v. Sillars:* 'In this case, of course, we are concerned with the issue of whether a wife should be competent to testify for the prosecution against her husband not only in a case where the charge alleges that the husband has interfered with the person, liberty or health of the wife, but also in the case where the charge does not make such an allegation but the evidence of the wife as to the circumstances surrounding the incident on which the charge is based would reveal that the husband had threatened her person, liberty or health. I cannot see why there should be a distinction between the two cases. If a wife is competent to testify against her husband where the charge against him alleges interference with the wife's person, liberty or health, she should logically, be competent to testify where the evidence of surrounding circumstances discloses a threat to her person, liberty or health, even though the charge does not allege such a threat. Either case should be regarded as an exception to the general rule that a spouse should not be permitted to testify against the other spouse because to permit such testimony would cause dissension in the matrimonial home, or disrupt matrimonial harmony.'"

The court went on to hold that in this case the husband might be a competent witness for the Crown but that he was not compellable and therefore on the new trial the judge should conduct a voir dire to ascertain whether the husband's evidence disclosed a threat to his person and whether he was willing to be a witness.

Questions

1. Why should husbands and wives not be free to testify against each other in any situation?
2. This case illustrates one exception to the normal rule that spouses are not compellable against each other. What is that exception?
3. What did the Court of Appeal conclude was the proper procedure to follow?

R. v. O'Brien
Supreme Court of Canada, 1978

The respondent O'Brien and a man named Jensen were jointly charged with possession of a narcotic for the purpose of trafficking. O'Brien was arrested and convicted. Jensen fled the country. Following the respondent's conviction, Jensen returned to Canada but charges against him were stayed. Later, Jensen went to the office of Simons, the lawyer for O'Brien, and told the lawyer that he, Jensen, had committed the offence alone and that O'Brien was completely innocent of the charge. He agreed to testify to that effect but died before the hearing. The British Columbia Court of Appeal having granted leave to adduce "fresh evidence," Simons repeated Jensen's statement before that court which allowed the appeal and directed an acquittal. Leave to appeal to the Supreme Court of Canada was granted and the court held that Simons' evidence was inadmissible as hearsay.

It is settled law that evidence of a statement made to a witness by a person who is not personally called as a witness is hearsay and inadmissible when the object of the evidence is to establish the truth of what is contained in the statement. The evidence being offered by Simons to prove that Jensen and not O'Brien had committed the act, was a classic example of hearsay and was inadmissible unless it fell within an exception to the rule. The respondent argued that it was a statement against penal interest. However, such a statement must meet certain requirements. These are:

(1) The fact stated must be to the declarant's immediate prejudice;
(2) In making the statement, the declarant must know that the fact stated is against the declarant's own interest;
(3) The declaration must be made to such a person and in such circumstances that the declarant will be vulnerable to penal consequences as a result;
(4) The vulnerability to penal consequences must not be remote.

Jensen did not make his statement of guilt until ten months after O'Brien had been convicted and almost six months after the charges against himself had been stayed. He made his statement in the privacy of Simons' office and refused to swear an affidavit. His obvious desire was not to create damaging evidence, detrimental to his own interest. Looked at from Jensen's viewpoint, the statement could not be used against him and failed to fall within the exception to the hearsay rule. The evidence being inadmissible, the conviction of the accused could not be altered.

Questions

1. What is hearsay? What was the statement alleged to be hearsay in this case?
2. Why was the statement made by Jensen not a confession of the crime?
3. Jensen was very sick when he saw Simons. In fact, he was sick from drug abuse and his death resulted from that condition. The court was aware of this. What effect might this have had upon the final decision?
4. Why did the Supreme Court of Canada finally rule that the statement could not be admitted?

You Be the Judge

1. The accused was charged with the murder of a small girl. He was a member of the search party looking for the girl and he said to another man, "I'm afraid we may find something here." Then the accused found the body. The accused washed his clothes the day after the girl disappeared. According to the uncorroborated evidence of small children, the accused was in the vicinity the day the crime occurred. A safety pin found near the scene of the crime was similar to one in the possession of the accused. Hair and cloth found clutched in the hand of the girl were not the same as that of the accused. The accused cooperated with the police, answered all questions, and never wavered in denying his innocence. Is there sufficient evidence for a conviction?

2. On a charge of second degree murder, the Crown sought to tender evidence in the form of a statement made by the victim to police shortly after the shooting incident. The accused said to the police, "I did not mean to hurt him; it was an accident." To this, the victim replied, "No, it wasn't. She tried to kill me." The police officer gave the accused a formal warning that she would be charged. The accused repeated that it was an accident and the victim again replied, "You did it on purpose." The victim died shortly afterwards. Should the victim's statement be admitted?

3. The accused was charged with an offence involving violence. The Crown offered into evidence a transcript of the accused's interrogation. Because the accused spoke only Greek, the police questioned her through an interpreter who translated the police questions into Greek and the accused's answers into English. A stenographer made a transcript in English of the questions and answers. The defence argued that the entire transcript was inadmissible as hearsay since it was not the direct words of the accused but the words of the interpreter. The interpreter could have changed the meaning of what the accused said, or what was asked of her, making it appear that the accused was admitting to something to which she did not admit at all. Should the transcript be admitted?

4. The accused appealed from a conviction for robbery. The accused made two statements to the police on two different dates. The first was ruled inadmissible because it had been obtained by coercion. The defence argued that the second statement should also be inadmissible. The defence adduced evidence by a psychiatrist to show that the accused had an "extraordinary fear of police." After the frightening experience of the first confession, the accused would make any statement the police wanted. The defence argued that the second confession had been tainted by the first and both must be excluded. Should the second statement be admitted?

5. Under the *Criminal Code*, a private communication that has been intercepted electronically is inadmissible unless it was authorized or consented to by one of the parties. The accused was charged with arson and was in a polygraph room of the RCMP. A hidden camera and microphone recorded everything in the room. While alone in the room, the accused got down on his hands and knees, put his arms into the air and said, "O God, let me get away with it just this once." The Crown argued that it was a soliloquy (a person talking to himself) and admissible. The defence argued that it was an unauthorized interception of a communication between the accused and another person—God. Should the statement be admitted?

Unit
Four

Human Rights in Canada

"*My right to swing my arm ends where my neighbour's nose begins.*"

Lord Atkin

Chapter 8

Understanding Basic Rights

The Concept of Rights

Before we attempt to examine the subject of human rights, it will be useful to attempt a definition of some of the words often used. A *right* may be defined as a claim of an interest possessed by a person which is conferred upon that person and protected by law. A *liberty* is what a person may do without being prevented from doing so by law. A *freedom* is basically synonymous with a liberty. These definitions do not encompass every possible use of these words, but they provide a framework for the use of these words in this unit.

A person's rights must go hand in hand with that person's duties and obligations; for where a person becomes totally involved in only personal rights, he or she generally begins to disregard the rights of others.

Civil Disobedience

During the 1960s, there was widespread unrest on university campuses throughout North America. The Vietnam War was the primary issue in the United States, and to some extent it had repercussions in Canada as well. Other serious problems were racial unrest and a feeling that government was becoming indifferent to people, and basically "unjust." Protest demonstrations of all sorts became a common sight, taking the popular form of a sit-in or perhaps just a massive rally.

On the other hand, advocates of strict law and order reject entirely the concept of disobedience to established law, labelling those who propose such behaviour as radicals and unstable persons. One thing is certain, however; an unjust law will be resisted. People will find ways around it, break it secretly, and connive constantly to escape it. Probably no law was ever more violated than the law regarding Prohibition. People simply refused to accept a law that said they could not drink alcohol. Thus, however laudable were the intentions of Prohibition, it was doomed to failure. John Stuart Mill, in his treatise, *On Liberty*, concluded that laws destined to make someone a good person or a better person are bound to fail. Mill wrote:

> The only purpose for which power can be rightfully exercised over any member of a community against his will is to prevent harm to others. His own good, physical or moral, is not a sufficient warrant. He cannot be compelled to do [something] because in the opinion of others, it would be wise or right.

Mill's conclusion was that laws regulating the morality of the community could not be respected or enforced unless it could be shown that the laws were necessary to prevent harm to other members of the community.

This brings us to a basic question: Does a law command reverence and obedience simply because it is a law? Thoreau rejected such an idea outright with his statement, "Unjust laws exist." To obey an unjust law requires people to set aside their own morality and sense of justice in favour of the expedient.

If we too readily accept the idea that some laws should not be obeyed, we are faced with a dilemma as to which laws should be disregarded. What are the criteria for singling them out? There is no universally accepted solution to this question. Let us suppose that each person was allowed to obey only those laws which he or she liked. This would probably result in the complete absence of any laws at all, since people would not be inclined to obey any laws that others ignored. Such a situation is generally referred to as *anarchy*. Anarchists believe that there should be no government and no laws, because these institutions restrict the freedom of the individual. They consider that repressive governments and laws have been the cause of discontent and strife in society. However, they forget that the freedom of one individual may infringe on that of another, and that one of the basic functions of government and law is to reconcile the interests of the various sections of society. Without government and law, there would be chaos.

Is there an alternative to the extremes of rigid law on the one hand and anarchy on the other? Hopefully, there is, and Canada has attempted throughout its history to maintain such a system. The Canadian legal system attempts to provide representative government to enact laws that will meet the needs of the majority of people, while at the same time maintaining the individual rights and freedoms of all persons and protecting the special rights of minority groups. It is a difficult task, and its success depends upon two major factors: (1) the willing co-operation of the Canadian people to work together; and (2) the responsiveness of the government to make appropriate changes when needed. Canada's record in maintaining this delicate system is not perfect, but it is good. At times, pressures upon the government have caused actions which infringed upon the rights and freedoms of individuals. At times, the courts have had to inject a sobering note into the situation and restore the balance. This is one of the roles for which the courts are well-suited, for the rash and unwise actions taken for the sake of expediency can be compared against the record of several hundreds of years of law—with the hoped for result that unjust laws will not survive. Thomas Jefferson once said, "A government that can do very much for you can also do very much to you."

The Canadian Charter of Rights: An Overview

On April 17, 1982, Queen Elizabeth II signed a proclamation fixing that date as the date on which the *Canada Act* came into force. The *Canada Act* declared into force the *Constitution Act, 1982*. Part I of that Act is the *Canadian Charter of Rights and Freedoms*. Yet, in the minds of many Canadians, the *Charter* has taken on the characteristics of a separate document in itself.

It is true that the *Charter* is a lengthy document, too long to discuss totally in this text. It should also be kept in mind that, at the time of this writing, very few court cases have been decided upon the basis of anything contained within the *Charter*. Thus, there is more speculation than fact as to how the *Charter* will become part of Canadian law.

Throughout the remainder of this chapter, reference will be made to some of the more significant portions of the *Charter* and how they might affect the current state of case law.

It is also important at the outset to keep in mind that the *Charter* does not represent totally new rights and freedoms never before held by Canadians. The *Charter's* predecessor, the Canadian *Bill of Rights*, covered many of the same topics and the *Bill* was not repealed when the *Charter* was enacted. Thus, the *Charter* does make certain rights and freedoms part of the Constitution, but they are not totally unique in their wording. There are also limits to freedoms. This is specifically noted in s. 1 of the *Charter*:

> **1. The *Canadian Charter of Rights and Freedoms* guarantees the rights and freedoms set out in it subject only to such reasonable limits prescribed by law as can be demonstrably justified in a free and democratic society.**

Prosecutors will undoubtedly argue that, even if there may have been a violation of one of the rights guaranteed in the *Charter*, the violation is within such reasonable limits as s. 1 states. It will be the courts who will determine whether a limit is reasonable. The question will be not whether there has been a violation but whether there is a rational basis for it—a basis within the tolerance and acceptance of people in a democratic society. The words "prescribed by law" would appear to include statutes and the common law rules. A mere administrative practice might not meet the requirement of s. 1.

Working in the opposite direction is s. 7 of the *Charter* which provides the greatest scope for challenging legislative and government action:

> **7. Everyone has the right to life, liberty and security of the person and the right not to be deprived thereof except in accordance with the principles of fundamental justice.**

Section 7 is similar to the "due process" clause of the Fifth and Fourteenth Amendments to the U.S. Constitution. It is significant to note that s. 7 does not include the word "property." Thus, the *Charter* does not specifically prevent people from being deprived of their property without adherence to fundamental justice. This is a major difference from the American wording which does protect property rights.

Sections 1 and 7 have opposite effects; s. 1 will be used to uphold government action while s. 7 will be used to try to strike it down. This is likely even though s. 1 is also the provision which guarantees rights and freedoms.

Section 52 of the *Charter* declares that any law that is inconsistent with the *Constitution Act* (and *Charter*) is of no effect. This is called the "primacy clause" but there is an important exception to this. A province can pass legislation that contravenes s. 2 and ss. 7 to 15 of the *Charter* by stating in the legislation that it is to take effect "notwithstanding" the *Charter*. Thus, provinces can partially exempt themselves from the primacy clause. Any federal or provincial law containing a "notwithstanding" clause expires in five years unless specifically renewed. Thus, a government cannot permanently "opt out" of the *Charter of Rights and Freedoms*.

Human Rights under the Criminal Laws

Arrest

The very word *arrest* is difficult to define. A generally accepted definition is: To deprive a person of liberty by some lawful authority for the purpose of compelling the person's appearance to answer to a criminal charge. Arrests can be made with or without a warrant, and can be made by either a peace officer or a citizen under certain conditions.

A proper arrest requires more than the speaking of mere words. An arrest requires that the arresting person also seize or touch the accused. Seizing or touching are not necessary if the officer gives notice of the arrest and the arrested person submits. It would not be an arrest to telephone someone, say there is a warrant outstanding for the person and that he or she is now under arrest. Courts have held that "capture" and "apprehension" are words synonymous with

A police officer may arrest without warrant any person found committing a criminal offence.

arrest. Where a police officer captured an offender at gun point, there was no requirement of the officer to also touch the offender to complete the arrest.

R. v. Whitfield
Supreme Court of Canada, 1970

The accused had been convicted on a charge of escaping from lawful custody. The evidence was that a warrant was out for his arrest when he was seen, driving a car, by a police officer. The car stopped at a red light and the officer went up to the open window and said, "I have a warrant for you. Stop the car and shut off the ignition." The accused tried to drive off but was blocked by traffic. The officer caught up with the car again, reached through the window, and grabbed the accused by the shirt, saying, "You're under arrest." The accused was able to break the officer's hold and drove off. The Ontario Court of Appeal reversed the accused's conviction, saying that he could not be convicted of escaping from custody because he had never been "custodially arrested." The Supreme Court of Canada restored the conviction saying that since the accused had been informed of the warrant, had been told he was under arrest, and had been seized hold of by the officer, the arrest was complete. It was no defence that the accused was able to shake off the arresting officer.

Arrest with a Warrant

An *arrest warrant* is a document signed by a justice directing a police officer to whom the warrant is addressed to arrest the accused. A warrant must name the accused, set out briefly the offence of which the accused is charged, and order that the accused be brought before the justice who issued the warrant. The warrant can be executed by arresting the accused wherever he or she is found within the territorial jurisdiction of the justice by whom the warrant was issued. In the case of a person being pursued by the police for an offence (referred to in the *Criminal Code* as

"fresh pursuit"), the arrest may be made anywhere in Canada.

Arrest without a Warrant

There is not always time to have the formality of an arrest warrant drawn up and presented to a justice. For this reason, the *Criminal Code* allows a peace officer to arrest an accused without a warrant under certain conditions. The *Code* reads as follows:

> **450. (1) A peace officer may arrest without warrant**
> **(a) a person who has committed an indictable offence or who, on reasonable and probable grounds, he believes has committed or is about to commit an indictable offence,**
> **(b) a person whom he finds committing a criminal offence, or**
> **(c) a person for whose arrest he has reasonable and probable grounds to believe that a warrant is in force within the territorial jurisdiction in which the person is found.**

The wording of this section requires further study. In the first place, we should note that whereas subsection (a) refers to "indictable offences," subsection (b) concerns "criminal offences." As we mentioned in a previous unit, indictable offences are the more serious offences. The term "criminal offence" refers to any offence, that is, both indictable and summary conviction offences. Therefore, the peace officer must know the law and know which are indictable offences and which are not. Where an officer believes that a person has committed or is about to commit an offence, the officer can arrest that person only if the offence is an indictable one. On the other hand, the officer knows that he or she can arrest a person found committing any type of criminal offence.

However, there are exceptions to this. The *Code* requires the officer to consider alternatives to arrest, even where the person has been caught red-handed. The officer is not to arrest the accused where it is possible to summons the accused or give an Appearance Notice (similar to a traffic ticket) as a means of getting the accused to court. Some of the offences for which the officer should consider alternatives to arrest are theft under $200, keeping a bawdy house, gambling, etc. Those offences which could be considered less serious, and which do not represent a danger to the public, do not require an arrest. As long as an officer has the correct identity of the accused and is reasonably sure that the public safety is not endangered, the officer is directed by the *Code* not to make an arrest unless there is reason to believe the accused person will not appear for trial.

By virtue of s. 10 of the *Charter of Rights*, an officer is required to give certain information to an arrested person. The section states:

> 10. Everyone has the right on arrest or detention
> (a) to be informed promptly of the reasons therefor;
> (b) to retain and instruct counsel without delay and to be informed of that right; and
> (c) to have the validity of the detention determined by way of habeas corpus and to be released if the detention is not lawful.

The biggest change brought about in the law is contained in s. 10(b) which requires the officer to inform an arrested person of the right to counsel. Prior to the enactment of the *Charter*, the officer did not have to tell an arrested person about the right to counsel. This section could be interpreted in such a way as to make inadmissible any statement or confession made by an arrested person who was not informed of the right to counsel. The leading case at present is *Hogan v. The Queen* (1975) in which the police refused to allow the accused access to his lawyer who was at the police station. The police told the accused that he could not see his lawyer until after he took the breathalyzer test. The Supreme Court of Canada held that while Hogan's rights had been violated, the results of the breathalyzer test were nonetheless admissible. It is possible that future cases will reach an opposite conclusion.

Arrest by Citizens

If the law seems confusing for a peace officer, it is equally confusing for a citizen. The *Criminal Code* provides certain sections under which anyone may make an arrest.

449. (1) Any one may arrest without warrant
(a) a person whom he finds committing an indictable offence, or
(b) a person who, on reasonable and probable grounds, he believes
   (i) has committed a criminal offence, and
   (ii) is escaping from and freshly pursued by persons who have lawful authority to arrest that person.
(2) Any one who is
(a) the owner or a person in lawful possession of property, or
(b) a person authorized by the owner or by a person in lawful possession of property,
may arrest without warrant a person whom he finds committing a criminal offence on or in relation to that property.
(3) Any one other than a peace officer who arrests a person without warrant shall forthwith deliver the person to a peace officer.

If the arrested person was caught in the act of committing an indictable offence, or was caught while freshly pursued after having committed an offence, the arrest by a citizen would be lawful. The obvious problems are (1) How many citizens know what are indictable offences; and (2) if someone is running away, how does the citizen know whether those in pursuit have lawful authority to arrest that person?

For example, under s. 388 of the *Criminal Code*, the wilful damaging of someone's property under the value of $50 is not an indictable offence. A property owner is permitted to arrest someone who is damaging the owner's property under the wording of s. 449(2). However, this authority does not extend to arresting someone who is damaging someone else's property. Assume that Jones parks next to you in a parking lot. If Jones catches a vandal damaging Jones' own car, Jones may arrest the vandal. If Jones catches a vandal damaging your car, the situation becomes confused. If the damage is more than $50, it is an indictable offence and Jones could arrest the vandal. If the damage is less than $50, it is not an indictable offence and Jones could not arrest the vandal. Jones could wait until the damage reaches $50 and then move in on the vandal, but in all probability, any citizen would not stand by and ponder the law. The citizen would take action against the vandal and possibly seize the person on behalf of the property owner. Conceivably, the citizen could be sued for doing this. However, there is a section in the *Criminal Code* which could save our good citizen from such a pitfall. It reads:

> **30. Every one who witnesses a breach of the peace is justified in interfering to prevent the continuance or renewal thereof and may detain any person who commits or is about to join in or to renew the breach of the peace, for the purpose of giving him into the custody of a peace officer, if he uses no more force than is reasonably necessary to prevent the continuance or renewal of the breach of the peace or than is reasonably proportioned to the danger to be apprehended from the continuance or renewal of the breach of the peace.**

The unfortunate feature of this section of the *Criminal Code* is that it does not define what is a "breach of the peace" and it only allows action to prevent a continuance of the breach of the peace. It does not specifically authorize arrest, but only allows that the guilty party be "detained" (without explaining how). It allows no action if the guilty party has stopped what he or she was doing. If Jones came up just as our friendly vandal finished smashing your car, Jones could not detain the vandal since the vandal was not going to continue any further. However, one can see that this section could give a person authority to interrupt someone during the commission of a breach of the peace—whatever that is.

Use of Force

People usually do not want to be arrested. Some may object strenuously—even to the point of resisting with physical violence. The *Criminal Code* recognizes that an arrest may require physical violence in return and establishes the ground rules for the use of force while effecting an arrest.

> **25. (1) Every one who is required or authorized by law to do anything in the administration or enforcement of the law**

> **(a) as a private citizen,**
> **(b) as a peace officer or public officer,**
> **(c) in aid of a peace officer or public officer, or**
> **(d) by virtue of his office,**
> **is, if he acts on reasonable and probable grounds, justified in doing what he is required or authorized to do and in using as much force as is necessary for that purpose.**
>
> **(4) A peace officer who is proceeding lawfully to arrest, with or without warrant, any person for an offence for which that person may be arrested without warrant, and every one lawfully assisting the peace officer, is justified, if the person to be arrested takes flight to avoid arrest, in using as much force as is necessary to prevent the escape by flight, unless the escape can be prevented by reasonable means in a less violent manner.**

When a person runs away, it is difficult for a police officer to weigh the risks of over-reacting to the situation. If the officer takes violent action, there is a possibility that innocent bystanders may be hurt. There is also the possibility that the person running away is acting hastily and actually hasn't done anything. Probably the most difficult decision a police officer ever has to make is whether or not to use a firearm. If the fugitive is dangerous, the public safety may demand that the officer fire shots. On the other hand, the police officer could be making a mistake and end up personally in court to justify the actions taken.

Priestman v. Colangelo and Smythson; Priestman v. Shynall and Smythson
Supreme Court of Canada, 1959

Police officers charged with duties of preserving the peace are not subject to civil liability if, while they are acting reasonably within the course of their duties, injury results to innocent persons. This principle is referred to in law as *damnum sine injuria*, meaning "damages without wrong."

In this case, uniformed police officers pulled alongside a car driven by a seventeen-year-old youth, Smythson. Priestman, one of the police officers ordered Smythson to "pull over." Instead, Smythson sped away, pursued by the police car.

The police officer driving the car attempted to force Smythson to stop, but Smythson continually swerved to prevent this. At one point the police car nearly crashed into a tree. Priestman fired a warning shot in the air with his revolver, but Smythson did not reduce speed. As the two vehicles approached a busy intersection, Priestman became concerned that an horrendous collision might occur at the intersection, so he fired a shot at the left rear tire of the car Smythson was driving. Just as he fired, the police car struck a large bump in the road causing Priestman's shot to go high. The bullet struck and killed Smythson. Smythson lost control of the car which hit a pole and then struck and killed two women, Colangelo and Shynall.

The Ontario Court of Appeal held Priestman liable for negligence. The Supreme Court of Canada overturned this decision, holding that since Smythson had already nearly killed the police officers by running them off the road, and since Smythson was approaching a busy intersection, Priestman had acted reasonably in trying to stop Smythson before he reached that intersection and caused a major collision. For Priestman to have acted otherwise would have involved "ignoring his obligation to endeavour to prevent injury to other members of the public at the intersection which would be reached within a few seconds by the escaping car." Two justices dissented from the majority decision, holding that when the police realized that pursuit would cause Smythson to race through an intersection, their proper action would have been to discontinue the pursuit. The shooting took place on a crowded residential street. The duty to apprehend was not as great as the duty to take care not to injure bystanders.

Under s. 27 of the *Code* every one is justified in using as much force as is reasonably necessary to prevent the commission of an offence if the person committing the act would be subject to arrest and if the act would be likely to cause immediate and serious injury to the person or property of anyone.

Duty of Arresting Person

The *Criminal Code* requires that every one who arrests a person, with or without a warrant, give notice to the arrested person of the process or warrant under which the arrest is made and the reason for the arrest. Police have no authority to take a person into custody for questioning or on the grounds of "suspicion." Either a person is under arrest or not, and, if not, the person is free to proceed without police interference.

Koechlin v. Waugh and Hamilton Ontario, 1957

Koechlin was walking along a road with another youth when Officers Waugh and Hamilton drove up in an unmarked car and stopped. Both officers were wearing plain clothes. They demanded that the two youths identify themselves. The other youth complied with the demand, but Koechlin first asked that the officers identify themselves. Hamilton produced a badge and said he was a police officer, but Koechlin also wanted to know his name and the number on the badge. As Koechlin continued to refuse to co-operate, the officers got out of the car and a fight ensued. Hamilton later testified that Koechlin's suspicious behaviour was the primary reason for suspecting that he was a person police were looking for in connection with burglaries in the area. Koechlin resisted arrest strenuously and another police car was summoned to help subdue him. He was held for one night, incommunicado, then released. He sued for assault and false arrest. The trial judge awarded Koechlin damages, from which the police officers appealed. The appeal court upheld the trial judge's decision saying:

66In this case the police officers exceeded their powers and infringed upon the rights of the plaintiff without justification.**99**

The rights of the individual in this situation are now further supported by s. 9 of the *Charter* which states:

9. Everyone has the right not to be arbitrarily detained or imprisoned.

The word "arbitrarily" as used in this section could have numerous meanings, but it generally means "at the whim of some other person," or "without grounds."

Obstruction; Duty To Assist Officer

The *Criminal Code* allows an officer to call upon a citizen to render assistance when the officer is arresting another person. Section 118 of the *Code* also makes it an offence to obstruct the officer in the conduct of the officer's duties.

> **118. Every one who**
> **(a) resists or wilfully obstructs a public officer or peace officer in the execution of his duty or any person lawfully acting in aid of such an officer,**
> **(b) omits, without reasonable excuse, to assist a public officer or peace officer in the execution of his duty in arresting a person or in preserving the peace, after having reasonable notice that he is required to do so, or**
> **(c) resists or wilfully obstructs any person in the lawful execution of a process against lands or goods or in making a lawful distress or seizure,**
> **is guilty of**
> **(d) an indictable offence and is liable to imprisonment for two years, or**
> **(e) an offence punishable on summary conviction.**

It is not necessary for the officer to formally "deputize" the citizen; the officer need merely call upon the citizen to render assistance and give instructions as to what the citizen is to do. A citizen must comply, insofar as that citizen is reasonably capable of so doing. Failure to assist the officer is punishable by imprisonment for up to two years. The requirement to assist the officer cannot be construed so as to require any citizen to assist a peace officer in that citizen's personal arrest. That is, an officer cannot say, "Help me to arrest you." Neither is there any obligation upon any citizen to help the officer obtain evidence against that citizen. The following is a significant case involving obstruction:

Moore v. The Queen
Supreme Court of Canada, 1979

The accused rode his bicycle through a red light and made it very difficult for a motorcycle police officer to catch him. When stopped, he refused to give the officer his name and address. The officer arrested him and charged him with obstruction. He was convicted of the offence and the Supreme Court of Canada upheld his conviction, despite a general recognition that Canadians have a basic right not to have to give their identification to police officers whenever the officers demand. It was stated:

> **"**I am of the opinion that the officer was under a duty to attempt to identify the wrongdoer and the failure to identify himself by the wrongdoer did constitute an obstruction of the police officer in the performance of his duties .... The refusal of a citizen to identify himself under such circumstances causes a major inconvenience and obstruction to the police in carrying out their proper duties. So that if anyone were engaged in any balancing of interest, there could be no doubt that the conclusion to which I have come would be that supported by the overwhelming public interest.**"**

It is very easy to misinterpret what the court held in *Moore*. The court did not say that in every instance persons must identify themselves to police. Moore was convicted for his *failure to act*, not his failure to speak. Once the officer made it clear that it was the officer's duty to issue a ticket, Moore's refusal to identify himself was a refusal to act that amounted to obstruction. However, if a police officer approaches a person and, without having seen the person committing an offence, demands: "Who are you and what are you doing here?" it is not obstruction for the person to refuse to reply.

Search and Seizure

It is perhaps best to start a discussion of this topic with the basic statement that the police have no authority to search a person or premises except as specifically authorized by statute or where the right to search has long been recognized by the common law. As well, a section of the *Charter of Rights and Freedoms* will weigh heavily upon the cases which will arise in the years ahead:

8. Everyone has the right to be secure against unreasonable search or seizure.

This is very similar wording to the Fourth Amendment of the *U.S. Constitution* which reads:

> The right of the people to be secure in their persons, houses, papers, and effects, against unreasonable searches and seizures, shall not be violated and no Warrants shall issue, but upon probable cause, supported by the Oath or affirmation, and particularly describing the place to be searched and the person or things to be searched.

It is most likely that decisions of the U.S. Supreme Court will be frequently cited in Canadian courts as the U.S. amendment has had more than two hundred years of judicial interpretation.

There are other points of interest which may arise from s. 8. If a search is unreasonable, the person whose body or premises were searched, may obtain, under s. 24 of the *Charter*, "such remedy as the court considers appropriate." The type of remedy not being specified, we can assume that the person could sue for damages. The person could also demand the return of anything seized. If the prosecution wants to hold these things as evidence, the court would be faced with a difficult decision. Having found the search unreasonable, would the court be justified in then saying that the Crown could continue to hold what was seized?

Another question to be decided is whether a search could be "lawful" but still "unreasonable." Police might obtain a proper search warrant but then carry out a search in an unreasonable manner. Or, if the same premises are searched repeatedly, without results, could recurring visits by the police be held to be unreasonable?

Lastly, the courts will have to define what is a search. Is it a search to "inspect" something? Is it a search to have a trained dog smell parcels to detect narcotics? Is it a search to use metal detectors upon people entering a room or airplane? There is much work ahead for the courts in the area of searches.

Under the Common Law

Authority is established in common law for police to search a person *after* the person has been arrested. The police may remove the person's clothing to do so. In the case of a female, only a police matron may conduct a search, unless there is an emergency situation that requires immediate search. Police may take from any arrested person, (1) evidence of a criminal act, (2) weapons of any type, and (3) articles that the accused person could use to inflict personal injury. Police will usually take from an arrested person such items as belts or any article that could be used to commit suicide once the person was locked in a cell. The search of a person may include a search inside the person's body. Certain small items such as drugs can be concealed in the orifices (openings) of the body and these orifices are subject to search. The police do not have the right to make someone vomit something that may have been swallowed, but they do have the right to watch for it should it later pass through the body. Police do not have the right to injure a person in carrying out their search.

 R. v. Brezack
1949

Two RCMP constables were waiting for a known narcotics peddlar. Information told them he was transporting illegal drugs in his mouth in waterproof capsules. When they saw him, they rushed him and knocked him down. One officer clamped a hand tightly around Brezack's throat to prevent him from swallowing the evidence. The other officer put a hand in Brezack's mouth to search for the drug capsules. Brezack bit the officer's hand. No drugs were found in Brezack's mouth, but drugs were later found in his car. He was charged with resisting the search and committing assault by biting the officer. Brezack's defence counsel contended that lawful search did not extend to forcing one's hand into a person's mouth and that the accused was justified in biting anyone who did so. The judge did not agree, holding that since the circumstances were such that the officers believed the drugs to be in the mouth, it was their clear duty to search there.

Under the *Criminal Code*

The *Criminal Code* generally defines lawful search (1) with a warrant and (2) without a warrant. Search warrants are obtainable from a justice before or after the beginning of a prosecution. When applying for a search warrant, the police must clearly state to the justice what they expect to find. A warrant is not a fishing expedition just to see what a person has inside the premises; however, while a warrant is being enforced, if anything is found that is reasonably believed to be held for an illegal purpose, it may be seized.

The important point to stress here is that police are not prohibited from seizing other things illegally possessed, even though these things are not mentioned in the search warrant. For example, if police obtain a search warrant to search for narcotics, and find none, but find illegal weapons instead, they may seize the weapons and arrest the person in whose possession they were found. A search warrant issued under the *Criminal Code* does not automatically extend to a search of persons on the premises, unless the police first arrest these persons. This is not true of all warrants, since, as we shall later see, some warrants issued under other statutes also permit the search of persons. Unless the justice authorizes the search to take place at night, it may only be executed by day. A search in respect of a criminal offence may be made on a Sunday.

Under the *Criminal Code* there are provisions for police to search a premises without a warrant. In some cases, persons in the premises may also be searched. One such provision deals with illegal weapons.

> **103. (1) Whenever a peace officer believes on reasonable grounds that an offence is being committed or has been committed against any of the provisions of this Act relating to prohibited weapons or restricted weapons, he may search without warrant, a person or vehicle or premises other than a dwelling-house, and may seize anything by means of or in relation to which he reasonably believes the offence is being committed or has been committed.**

The power to search without warrant extends to every situation except a dwelling-house. Note that this section authorizes the search of vehicles without a warrant.

The *Criminal Code* also permits a peace officer to search any vehicle or vessel upon which the officer believes animals are being improperly transported. Police have a right to enter any premises, including a dwelling-house, if they believe on reasonable grounds that inside there is a fugitive for whom an outstanding warrant exists. This is a result of a 1975 Supreme Court of Canada decision that police officers have the right to break into a home without a search warrant as long as they identify themselves and have reasonable grounds to believe a wanted person is inside.

Under Other Federal Laws

There are several federal laws that authorize police to conduct searches, including the *Narcotic Control Act*, *Food and Drugs Act*, *Customs Act*, and even the *Temperance Act*.

Narcotic Control Act

> **10. (1) A peace officer may, at any time,**
> **(a) without a warrant enter and search any place other than a dwelling-house, and under the authority of a writ of assistance or a warrant issued under this section, enter and search any dwelling-house in which he reasonably believes there is a narcotic by means of or in respect of which an offence under this Act has been committed;**
> **(b) search any person found in such place; and**
> **(c) seize and take away any narcotic found in such place, any thing in such place in which he reasonably suspects a narcotic is contained or concealed, or any other thing by means of or in respect of which he reasonably believes an offence under this Act has been committed or that may be evidence of the commission of such an offence.**

The "drug raid" has almost no bounds. In one episode, police raided a Fort Erie, Ontario pub and searched forty-three patrons who were inside. Thirty-six of these patrons were females who were required to strip and submit to a complete search by police matrons. No drugs were found. The search was totally lawful under the *Narcotic Control Act*, s. 10(1) (b) which permits the search of persons.

Under the *Food and Drugs Act*, police and inspectors have considerable power to search and also to extract information from persons on the premises. An inspector may at any reasonable time enter any place without warrant where on reasonable grounds the inspector believes any article to which the Act or regulations apply is manufactured, prepared, packaged, or stored. The inspector may examine any article and anything he or she believes is used or is capable of being used to manufacture, prepare, or package food or drugs. An inspector can open containers, examine books, seize articles, and may demand reasonable assistance of persons present. The inspector may ask questions and it is an offence to obstruct or make false statements to an inspector.

Another law containing sweeping powers of search is the *Customs Act*, a federal law covering every aspect of goods entering Canada. The Act empowers a customs officer to board and search vessels, and vehicles, break open containers, buildings, and packages, search any person aboard a vessel or vehicle, and seize any goods which it is believed are subject to forfeiture. The power of a customs officer could not be more thorough. It is important to remember that if a person attempts to bring goods illegally into Canada, the *Customs Act* not only empowers customs officers to search everything and everyone, but also empowers the seizure of the goods and the vehicle in which they were transported. Vehicles used to bring goods illegally into Canada may be forfeited to the Crown.

Under the Provincial Laws

Various provincial statutes authorize peace officers to conduct searches for things not covered by federal statutes. For example, the laws of most provinces empower a game warden to search for game illegally taken or taken using illegal means. Under the Ontario *Game and Fisheries Act*, a constable may stop, search, and seize any vehicle, aircraft, boat, or launch, or any railway car including a caboose. The constable may enter any hunting, mining, lumber, or construction camp and search both the camp and persons in the camp if it is believed on reasonable grounds that game or fish, unlawfully taken, will be found.

One area of continuing controversy is the power of police to stop vehicles. In most provinces, the provincial laws dealing with highway traffic empower police to order a vehicle to stop and make it an offence not to stop. The officer may then demand certain papers such as a driver's permit and proof of insurance. The officer may be empowered to conduct a mechanical inspection of the vehicle. Does this constitute a search of the vehicle? The provincial liquor laws may provide justification to open the trunk or look under the seats. For example, the Ontario *Liquor Control Act* authorizes a police officer to search a vehicle if there are reasonable grounds to believe that liquor is unlawfully within the vehicle. If the officer smells alcohol on the driver's breath, this may lead to a demand for a breathalyzer test. Ontario, British Columbia, and Alberta have provincial laws permitting the officer to temporarily suspend a driver's permit if the driver has been drinking, even if the driver is not legally impaired.

The power of search is quite extensive and there seldom exists a situation in which an officer needs to search someone but cannot find the legal means to do so. The interpretation given to s. 8 of the *Charter* may alter this situation.

Writs of Assistance

There exists in Canada a document known as a *Writ of Assistance*. This is a writ issued to federal officers by the Federal Court of Canada. It permits the officers to enter any place in Canada, at any time, and compel the assistance of any persons to either assist them to enter or to assist them within. No search warrant is necessary. The writ generally remains with the officers as long as they are assigned to a particular type of duty, such as drug enforcement.

Britain no longer authorizes such writs and the Fourth Amendment to the *U.S. Constitution* specifically prohibits them. In fact, the abuse of such writs by British officers prior to the American Revolution is the precise reason the Fourth Amendment contains its requirement that all search warrants state "particulars."

The use of Writs of Assistance is declining in Canada and they are now found primarily in remote areas where it can be very difficult for an officer to locate a judge or justice of the peace to sign a search warrant.

Presumption of Innocence: The Right To Remain Silent

It is an established rule of our common law that an accused person is innocent until proven guilty beyond a reasonable doubt. The accused does not have to introduce any evidence whatsoever to establish innocence. This common law principle is now embodied in the *Charter* which states:

> **11. Any person charged with an offence has the right (d) to be presumed innocent until proven guilty according to law in a fair and public hearing by an independent and impartial tribunal.**

To ensure that the jury applies this principle, the judge, in giving the *charge* (instructions) to the jury, must explain the principle very closely. Following is an example of the words a judge might use in making this explanation:

> I will now deal with what is known in law as the presumption of innocence. Simply put, it means that the accused person is presumed to be innocent until the Crown has satisfied you, beyond a reasonable doubt, of the accused's guilt. It is a presumption which remains with the accused from the beginning of the case until the end. The presumption only ends if you are satisfied that the accused is guilty beyond a reasonable doubt.
>
> If, after hearing my charge, and considering all the evidence and arguments of counsel, you conclude that the Crown has failed to prove to your satisfaction beyond a reasonable doubt, that the accused committed the offence with which the accused is charged, it is your duty to give the accused the benefit of the doubt and to find the accused Not Guilty.

Some judges go on to explain what would constitute a reasonable doubt — an honest doubt rather than one imagined to avoid responsibility in finding a verdict. If the accused did not testify in self-defence, a judge will caution the jury to draw no conclusion from that. The accused has no obligation to assert personal innocence except for the plea of Not Guilty. If a judge improperly charges the jury, it serves as grounds for an appeal. For this reason, judges are very meticulous in their wording to the jury. After the jury retires to consider the verdict, both the Crown and defence counsel have the right to voice objections to the manner in which the judge gave the charge to the jury. If the judge feels these objections have any merit, the judge will recall the jury and charge them again. It may take several attempts to satisfy counsel, or the judge may finally conclude that counsel's objections have no merit.

Woolmington v. Director of Public Prosecution England, 1935

Reginald Woolmington was convicted of the murder of his wife, Violet Woolmington. The two were living apart and Reginald went to see her to ask her to come back to him. He told the jury that he took along a rifle (with the barrel sawed short to conceal it under his coat) in order to frighten her by saying he would kill himself if she did not return to him. When he went to show the rifle to her, it became tangled and went off, killing her instantly. There were no eye witnesses. Woolmington pleaded it was pure accident. In the charge to the jury, the judge included these words:

> **66**All homicide is presumed to be malicious and murder, unless the contrary appears from circumstances of alleviation, excuse, or justification. The Crown has got to satisfy you that this woman, Violet Woolmington, died at the prisoner's hands. They must satisfy you of that beyond any reasonable doubt. If they satisfy you of that, then he has to show that there are circumstances to be found in the evidence which has been given from the witness box in this case which alleviate the crime so that it is only manslaughter or which excuse the homicide altogether by showing that it was pure accident.**99**

The House of Lords quashed the conviction on the grounds that the judge had wrongly charged the jury. The judge had placed a burden upon the accused to prove it was an accident. The decision reads:

66The burden is upon the Crown to prove it was not an accident. The Crown must prove (a) death as a result of a voluntary act of the accused and (b) malice of the accused. If the jury is satisfied with his explanation, or is left with a reasonable doubt, the prisoner is entitled to be acquitted.99

The *Woolmington* case is considered an important decision since it emphasizes that the burden of proof rests upon the Crown and not upon the accused. If the evidence leads the jury to the inescapable conclusion that the accused committed the offence, the accused will be convicted. There is no requirement to switch the burden of proof from the Crown to the accused.

R. v. Appleby
1972

Appleby was convicted under the *Criminal Code* for having care and control of a motor vehicle while his ability to drive was impaired. Appleby did not give evidence in his defence. He was convicted under a section of the *Code* which reads:

237. (1) ...
(a) where it is proved that the accused occupied the seat ordinarily occupied by the driver of a motor vehicle, he shall be deemed to have had the care or control of the vehicle unless he establishes that he did not enter or mount the vehicle for the purpose of setting it in motion.

In his appeal to the Supreme Court of Canada, Appleby argued that his right to a presumption of innocence as guaranteed under the *Bill of Rights* was violated by the *Criminal Code*. The Supreme Court rejected his appeal, holding that:

66The statutory presumption required that an accused do no more than raise a reasonable doubt .... The

burden shifts to the accused to show, on a balance of probabilities, that there was a lawful excuse for his possession. There is nothing in the section that deprives an accused of the right to be presumed innocent until proven guilty. The right to be presumed innocent is a way of expressing the fact that the Crown has the ultimate burden to establish guilt.99

The court concluded that the law could still put a burden on the accused to counter the evidence presented by the Crown.

Since the law makes such a strong case for presumption of innocence, it must seem somewhat peculiar that the criminal law does, in some instances, alter the principle. There are some sections of the *Criminal Code*, and other statutes, which place the accused in the position of having to offer evidence or face an almost certain conviction. Such wording is generally referred to as a *reverse onus clause*. Here are three examples of such clauses, as indicated by the words in italics:

Narcotic Control Act (Trafficking)
8. [first part omitted]
... and *if the accused fails to establish* that he was not in possession of the narcotic for the purpose of trafficking, he shall be convicted of the offence as charged and sentenced accordingly.

Criminal Code of Canada (Break and Enter)
306. [first part omitted]
(2) For the purposes of proceedings under this section, evidence that an accused
(b) broke and entered a place is, *in the absence of any evidence to the contrary*, proof that he broke and entered with intent to commit an indictable offence therein;

Criminal Code of Canada (Prowling at Night)
173. Every one who, without lawful excuse, *the proof of which lies upon him*, loiters or prowls at night upon the property of another person near a dwelling-house situated on that property is guilty of an offence punishable on summary conviction.

What is the effect of a reverse onus clause? It does *not* mean the accused is guilty unless proven innocent. The Crown must still establish the actus reus. The accused is then required to rebut the presumption of having the necessary mens rea. The extent of this burden differs from section to section. Section 306 only requires "evidence to the contrary" while s. 173 requires "proof" which is a more stringent requirement. To what extent must the accused meet this presumption of intent? It is generally held that the accused does not have to prove absence of criminal intent beyond a reasonable doubt, but only upon a *balance of probabilities.*

The right to silence is obviously upset by reverse onus clauses. It is understood by Canadians that, when accused of a crime, they have the right to remain silent. This right extends from the period of police questioning right through the trial. The protection against self-incrimination has a long history. In England it was brought forth as a protest against the inquisitorial methods of the Ecclesiastical Courts. During this time the law permitted any defendant to be questioned, under torture if necessary. After 1660 it became a rule that persons could not be compelled to testify against themselves. If there were no such rule, an accused who was guilty of a crime (or who might be found Guilty) would have only three possible choices (all equally poor): (1) answer truthfully and be convicted; (2) lie and commit perjury; or (3) refuse to testify and be jailed for contempt of court. How much of a burden a reverse onus clause can place upon an accused was dealt with in the following case:

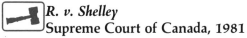

R. v. Shelley
Supreme Court of Canada, 1981

Shelley was a small-time jewel trader who bought gems and jewellery from people and resold these items for a profit. All his purchases were made from individuals and he had no knowledge regarding the origins of the things he bought. He was charged with a violation of the *Customs Act* of Canada which makes it an offence to have possession of goods unlawfully imported into Canada. This Act also contains a reverse onus clause:

248.(1) The *burden of proof lies* upon the owner or claimant of the goods or the person whose duty it was to comply with this Act or in whose possession the goods were found.

The Crown proved that some of the jewellery was manufactured outside of Canada. It then took the position that Shelley either had to prove that the jewellery was lawfully imported into Canada or else be convicted. Shelley had no idea as to how or when the jewellery entered Canada and could not defend himself. The Supreme Court of Canada held that such wording was too harsh and denied the accused his right to be presumed innocent. As the case predated the *Charter* it was decided under the *Bill of Rights*. In the opinion of the court:

66[To apply the *Customs Act* as stated would] leave the accused with the impossible burden of proof and would amount to an irrebuttable presumption of guilty against him, denying him of the right to be presumed innocent. 99

The accused was acquitted.

It is possible that many reverse onus clauses may be eventually challenged under the *Charter of Rights and Freedoms* as a violation of the principle of "presumption of innocence."

Detention and Habeas Corpus

The *Criminal Code* requires that a peace officer who has arrested a person with or without a warrant must cause that person to be taken before a justice to be dealt with according to the law:

- Where a justice is available within twenty-four hours, without unreasonable delay and in any event within twenty-four hours of arrest; or
- Where a justice is not available within twenty-four hours, as soon as possible.

These provisions apply unless the peace officer releases the person under any provision of the *Criminal Code.* The accused person may apply for bail immediately and the onus is upon the Crown to justify why the accused must be kept in custody. More will be discussed on this procedure under the section on "The Right to Bail."

Persons who believe they are unlawfully held in custody may file with the court, either personally or through others acting on their behalf, a *Writ of Habeas Corpus ad Subjiciendum*. The writ is used to test the legality of a person's imprisonment and is directed to the persons detaining the prisoner demanding that they produce the body so the court can then inquire into the detention. The Writ of Habeas Corpus means in English that "you have the body"—so produce it! The *Habeas Corpus Act* was first passed in England in 1679 but its common law origins date back much further than that. England passed a similar statute in 1784 extending the right of habeas corpus to Canada.

Section 10(c) of the *Charter* includes habeas corpus as a legal right. It is possible, however, that this is not an absolute right because s. 33 of the *Charter* permits Parliament or a provincial legislature to remove, for five years at a time, this or other rights. It is also possible that, in an emergency situation, suspension of habeas corpus could fall under the umbrella of s. 1 of the *Charter* as a "reasonable limit" of rights. The *War Measures Act* comes to mind as a statute that would conflict directly with the right of habeas corpus.

Generally, the rights under habeas corpus are of two types: (1) the right to know the reason for being detained; and (2) the right to trial without undue delay.

If a court determines that a Writ of Habeas Corpus is not the appropriate remedy, it will simply deny the writ. Canadian courts consider a Writ of Habeas Corpus to be a serious matter and will not issue a writ if there is a more appropriate remedy available through ordinary criminal proceedings.

The *Criminal Code* requires that where a person has been detained in custody for thirty days on a summary conviction offence, or ninety days on an indictable offence, without trial, then a judge shall conduct a hearing to determine whether or not the accused should be released from custody.

Questioning

When a person is arrested, that person must be advised of the charge and of the right to counsel. The person may also be asked whether he or she wishes to make a statement. The officer will normally caution the person as follows:

> You are charged with _____ contrary to section _____ of the *Criminal Code*. Do you wish to say anything in answer to that charge? You are not obligated to say anything unless you wish to do so, but whatever you say will be taken down in writing and may be given in evidence.

The accused does not have to make any statement and does not have to sign anything. Police have the authority to question the accused as long as the accused is held in legal custody. Where an accused contacted a lawyer and was told to say nothing, it was held that the police were not obligated to stop questioning the accused even though the lawyer did not wish the client questioned in the absence of counsel and told this to the investigating officer. The police continued their questioning and the accused made a voluntary statement which the court held was admissible. The *Charter* does not contain any specific reference to the right of an accused not to answer police questions or to be advised of the right to remain silent.

The Right to Counsel

The *Charter* states that every person arrested or detained has the following right:

> 10 ...
> **(b) to retain and instruct counsel without delay and to be informed of that right.**

The right to counsel is an important but somewhat complex right. Prior to 1836, there was no common law right to counsel. At one time the accused was not even allowed to cross-examine Crown witnesses or present his or her own witnesses. Since 1836, the law has held that an accused is entitled to be represented by counsel. The reason is that the law and court procedure can be very complex and the accused has a right to understand the proceedings. The accused has a right to counsel who will ensure that the accused's legal rights are protected and that the Crown is put to the severest test of its case. However, if an accused does not want counsel, or does not obtain counsel in time for the trial, it does not mean the accused cannot be tried. Neither the *Charter* nor the *Criminal Code* prohibits conviction because a lawyer is not present at the trial.

The word "counsel" means a barrister or solicitor. The *Criminal Code* guarantees the right of the accused to "make full answer and defence personally or by counsel." It should be noted that the *Charter* does not guarantee a person legal assistance at trial. It only affords the right to retain a lawyer. However, it is debatable whether or not a person can get a "fair hearing" without a lawyer.

In *R. v. O'Connor* (Ontario, 1965), it was held that there is no such limit as "one call." The accused was told by police he could only make one telephone call to his lawyer. The court held that the accused must be given "reasonably opportunity" to find a lawyer. It was held in *R. v. Balkan* (Alberta, 1973) that the accused must be allowed to have a private conversation with his lawyer without the police listening in.

In *Hogan v. The Queen* (1972), the accused gave a sample of his breath after being denied counsel. The Supreme Court of Canada held that this did not affect his conviction.

There is no requirement that an accused *must* have a lawyer, since a person may personally conduct the defence in court. However, an accused should not be forced to do this, particularly in a complex matter — as the next case illustrates.

Barrette v. The Queen
Supreme Court of Canada, 1976

When the accused's lawyer failed to appear at trial, the trial judge denied the accused an adjournment, giving as a reason the large number of cases that were being postponed. The court held that on the facts of this case, the accused was deprived of a fair trial. The judge's discretion in denying an adjournment must be based on reasons well founded in law. The court noted:

66When the case against the accused is such that he cannot defend himself without testifying, he certainly is in great need of the assistance of counsel.99

A new trial was ordered.

Most courts maintain a *Duty Counsel* who is a qualified lawyer on duty to assist persons recently arrested. Anyone who does not have a lawyer to contact should ask to see the Duty Counsel; it is advisable to say nothing until talking with this person. Duty Counsel will assist the arrested person in applying for bail and requesting legal aid if needed.

If a person cannot afford a lawyer, that person should seek legal aid. Every province has some form of legal aid plan to assist persons without the financial means to hire a lawyer. In Ontario, an application is made to the Area Director of the Legal Aid Plan. The application is investigated by the Department of Social and Family Services as to the financial ability of the applicant to pay any of the legal costs. If legal aid is authorized, an applicant pays to the plan the part of the costs assigned to the applicant. The applicant may then personally choose a lawyer as long as the lawyer is a member of the Law Society of Upper Canada. Neither the court nor the general public knows that the accused is receiving assistance under the Legal Aid Plan.

R. v. Ewing and Kearney
British Columbia, 1974

The two accused persons brought a motion seeking to prohibit any provincial court judge from proceeding with trial so long as they were unable to obtain counsel. The two were charged with possession of narcotics and contended they were unable to obtain counsel. The application contended that they were unable to make full answer and defence and that to proceed against them before they obtained counsel would be abuse of process. The Supreme Court of British Columbia dismissed the application. The ruling reads:

66Every accused person has the same right to retain

counsel of his choice. However, if an accused, for some reason, has been unable to retain counsel it does not follow that he will not receive a fair trial. A special obligation is cast on the judge to protect the interests of the accused and prevent any abuse of process. There is no legislation which directs that an accused cannot be tried for a criminal offence unless he is represented by counsel. **"**

The above case illustrates that a person cannot hold up criminal proceedings by delaying the act of obtaining counsel. If this were permitted, an accused could drag out a criminal action for years by taking months to obtain counsel, and then just before trial dismissing that counsel and demanding more time to find another counsel. This process could go on indefinitely—except that the courts will not allow it.

If an accused appears for trial without counsel, then the trial judge must take extra precautions to ensure that the accused knows his or her rights and understands each step of the proceedings. The judge remains neutral in this process, as always, but is compelled to provide considerable advice to the accused as to what action may be taken.

The Right to Bail

An arrested person may not have to wait in jail until trial. A justice may grant *bail* by (1) requiring the person to put up a sum of money or pledge property to guarantee he or she will appear for trial; or (2) release the person in his or her own recognizance. If the person does not appear for trial, the bail is forfeited and a bench warrant issued for the person's arrest.

Section 11(e) of the *Charter* states that a person is "not to be denied reasonable bail without just cause."

For many years, a person seeking bail had to give a good argument as to why bail should be received. The present system is that the burden is placed upon the Crown to establish why a person should not be granted bail.

The process of bail actually begins with the first encounter with the police officer. The officer must make a judgment whether or not it is necessary to

arrest the person. (The possible reasons are discussed under the section on "Arrest.") As an alternative to arrest, the officer may, upon obtaining the identification of the person, issue an Appearance Notice not unlike a traffic ticket. Or, the officer could obtain the identity of the accused and request later that a justice issue a summons. Once the accused is taken into custody, every person of authority is responsible for examining the possibility of effecting the person's release when detention is no longer necessary. This includes the desk sergeant, the investigating officer, and eventually the justice.

There is a right to bail, but it is not an automatic right. The Crown may request that the accused be kept in custody until trial on either of two major grounds, namely:

- That detention is necessary to ensure the accused's attendance in court to be dealt with according to law; or
- That detention is necessary for the public interest or for the protection of the public, including a likelihood that the accused will, if released, commit a criminal offence.

The Crown does not have to prove that the accused will either escape the jurisdiction of the court, or commit another offence; it must only introduce evidence that there is a likelihood of this happening. However, the burden remains upon the Crown and, in the absence of a very good argument, the justice would be obligated to grant bail.

Criticism of the laxity of the system resulted in a revision to the *Criminal Code* which made the process more stringent. Under s. 457, a justice is expected to detain in custody any accused charged:

- With an indictable offence, while awaiting trial for another indictable offence;
- With an indictable offence, if the accused is not a resident of Canada;
- With being unlawfully at large while awaiting trial for another offence;
- With an offence under s. 4 (trafficking) or s. 5 (importing) of the *Narcotic Control Act.*

However, the accused must still be given a reasonable opportunity to show cause why detention is not justified or necessary. If a justice releases the accused, the justice must include in the record a statement of reasons for releasing the accused.

An accused charged with treason, sabotage, hijacking, or murder can only be released on bail by a judge of a superior court of criminal jurisdiction.

Identification

In Canada, the RCMP is responsible for maintaining a central record system of persons charged with or convicted of a criminal offence. The earliest system was one of measurements. It involved measuring unchangeable portions of the body such as the forehead, nose, ears, arm between elbow and wrist, etc. While this system was accurate, it was unwieldy because it defied any logical filing system. It quickly gave way to photographs and fingerprints.

Anyone charged with an indictable offence may be fingerprinted and photographed under the *Identification of Criminals Act*. To this extent, the police may use reasonable force should a person resist. If a person was not arrested, the police may request that a justice summons the person to come in for the fingerprinting process. If the person fails to appear, an arrest warrant may be issued. Failure to appear or to comply with a summons is an indictable offence punishable by imprisonment for two years. The police may photograph more than just the face of the accused. "Identification" may include scars and tatoos which can identify a person who may otherwise be disguised.

Unfortunately, there is nothing in the Act which requires the police to destroy a fingerprint and photo-

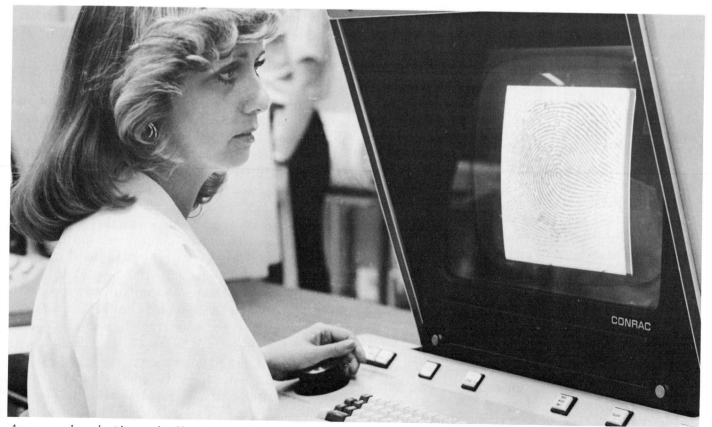

Any person charged with an indictable offence may be fingerprinted. The police may retain this record even if the accused is later acquitted.

graphic card. If a person is arrested, charged with an indictable offence, fingerprinted and photographed, the person does not have a criminal record. However, he or she has an arrest record. Should the charge later be dropped, or should the person be found Not Guilty, no right exists to go back to the police and demand that the arrest record be destroyed.

There is no obligation on the part of any accused to participate in a police line-up. If the accused voluntarily participates in a line-up, the privilege against self-incrimination is not violated. The police, for their part, are allowed under their investigative powers to make every reasonable effort to identify the accused. Therefore, before putting a person in a line-up, there is no obligation upon the police to warn the accused that identification may result and thereby contribute to a conviction. If an accused refuses to participate in a line-up, he or she may still be confronted face to face by any witnesses for the purpose of identifying the accused.

R. v. Marcoux and Solomon
Ontario, 1975

The appellants were convicted on a charge of breaking and entering. The main point at issue in the appeal was the admission of evidence by the trial judge that the appellant Marcoux had declined to participate in a police line-up. The appellant contended that the judge improperly instructed the jury. The Supreme Court of Canada ruled that there was no obligation on the trial judge to tell the jury that Marcoux's refusal should not be held against him. The judge had properly told the jury that the accused did not have to take part in a line-up, and had left it to the jury to draw its own inference from the refusal. The appeal was dismissed. In its decision the court held:

66The invitation to participate in a line-up was extended by the police for no improper purpose. In many cases it might well be considered an advantage to have the benefit of a line-up. In fact, in cases where no line-up

was made available to the prisoner, the failure to follow such a course might well be a matter of adverse comment on the part of counsel for the accused. The evidence in question was not inadmissible on the ground that it offended the maxim that no one was bound to incriminate himself.99

A person charged with an offence may not attempt to alter dramatically his or her appearance before trial. Any attempt to do so could result in a charge of "obstructing justice," or "wearing a disguise with the intent to commit an indictable offence." The latter charge stems from the fact that obstructing justice is an indictable offence. In one case, where an accused, prior to his trial, coloured his hair, grew a beard, and wore glasses which he had not worn before, the court ordered him charged with obstructing justice as the accused was clearly trying to make it impossible for witnesses to identify him. In another case, where a defence counsel advised a client to wear a wig at trial, the court found the lawyer to be in contempt of court.

There are a few statutes that specifically require a person to give identification to a police officer when asked. An example is the *Highway Traffic Act* (in Ontario, and most other provinces) which requires a driver of a motor vehicle to supply personal identification and produce ownership and insurance papers for the vehicle. Failure to do so may result in arrest. However, identification could be required in another manner, somewhat more indirectly. If police officers are attempting to identify persons whom they believe have committed an offence, in order to issue them a summons or a Notice of Appearance rather than arresting them, the accused persons must identify themselves. If they refuse to identify themselves, the *Bail Reform Act* (now incorporated into the *Criminal Code* as well) directs the police to arrest the persons in order to secure their identity. The point is this: identifying yourself may avoid an unnecessary arrest. Police do not have unlimited authority to demand that citizens identify themselves at any time. However, the previously cited case of *Moore v. The Queen* illustrates the potential danger of being convicted of a criminal offence for failure to provide identification when there is a requirement to do so.

Snooping

The development of sensitive electronic devices that can pick up voices and transmit them long distances has become very widespread and a danger to privacy. Because of their small size, these devices are referred to as "bugs" and the practice of using them to intercept communications is called "bugging."

In Canada, the *Criminal Code* places restrictions upon bugging including the following:

- It is unlawful to possess, sell or purchase any device for the purpose of interception of private communications, without a licence.
- It is an offence to use any device to intercept a private communication, unless:
  (a) Consent is given to intercept by one of the parties to that communication;
  (b) A person engaged in telephone work intercepts a communication in the course of that work;
  (c) An authorization has been received by a judge's order to intercept a communication.

The more difficult question is whether police can use any method they please to legally bug people. Police forces must frequently enter private premises to install bugs; later they may have to re-enter those premises to repair or to remove the bugs. Such entries are unlawful trespasses, but not crimes since breaking and entering is not a crime unless the person has the intention of committing an indictable offence within the premises. It is also difficult to say that entering to install a bug is an "unreasonable search or seizure" because the police are neither searching nor seizing.

Police who feel that a wiretap is necessary in order to obtain evidence of a crime can obtain legal permission to intercept. A judge can grant this permission under the *Criminal Code* (s. 178.13) and the Solicitor General can grant a warrant under s. 16 of the *Official Secrets Act*. Once the police are given permission to intercept a communication, the question arises as to whether this permission carries with it the implied authority to enter the premises in order to install a bug. This question was placed before the Manitoba Court of Appeal in the *Ashok Dass* case.

In this case the court warned that an officer could become involved in a serious incident if detected by an occupier while trying to install a bug on the premises. The occupier could react violently and the officer might be civilly and criminally liable.

The *Dass* case was not heard by the Supreme Court of Canada and some lawyers are still of the opinion that there is an implied authority to install a device once authority to intercept has been granted. In other words, the *Dass* case cannot be relied upon as "good" law.

Mental Examinations

Several sections of the *Criminal Code* authorize a justice to order in writing that a person be sent for psychiatric observation for a period not exceeding thirty days, where in the opinion of the justice, supported by the evidence of at least one duly qualified medical practitioner, there is reason to believe that the accused is mentally ill. The period can be as long as sixty days if the justice is satisfied that a longer period is necessary. In cases of emergency, it is possible to dispense with the opinion of the medical practitioner. There is no appeal from such an order but the accused may refuse to be examined by any psychiatrist. Following this examination, the accused is brought back to court and the question of fitness to stand trial is then raised. The hospital may recommend that the accused be returned to the hospital and entered as a certified patient.

It can be very difficult for a person to obtain release from a mental hospital as he or she will be confined there indefinitely until release is ordered by the Lieutenant-Governor of the province. There are recorded cases of Canadians spending their entire adult lives in mental institutions without ever being told the reason, or even being given an opportunity to argue for their release. In recent years, most provinces have adopted a review procedure to ensure that people are not held in mental institutions unnecessarily.

Cruel and Unusual Treatment or Punishment

The *Charter of Rights* states:

12. Everyone has the right not to be subjected to any cruel and unusual treatment or punishment.

As Canada does not have a history of torture chambers or dungeons, it might be easy to overlook the potential applications of this section. It may be used as the basis of attacks upon sentences imposed on the grounds that the severity of the sentence is out of proportion to the seriousness of the offence. Certainly, any gross disproportionment could be attacked. If a person received fourteen years for something which normally brought a much shorter sentence, the section could apply.

The Supreme Court of Canada did consider whether the death penalty constituted cruel and unusual treatment. In *R. v. Miller* (1976), all the members of the court concluded that it did not. The case was brought under the forerunner to the *Charter*, the Canadian *Bill of Rights* (which is still in force).

In *McCann v. The Queen* (1976), the Federal Court of Canada held that it was cruel punishment for penitentiary inmates to be subjected to solitary confinement, for long periods of time, with cells lighted twenty-four hours a day, and minimal opportunity for exercise. However, the court concluded that this was purely an administrative matter which must be left up to penitentiary officials and which was not within the powers of the court to order stopped. It could be expected that under the new *Charter* a court would be more likely to order a practice stopped if it found it to be cruel and unusual. Note that the practice must be cruel *and* unusual, not cruel *or* unusual. In the *McCann* case, there was considerable discussion about the fact that the punishment was usual for those who got into trouble. While it might be cruel, it was not unusual.

A number of specific penalties have been attacked as cruel and unusual, but with no success. Important examples might be the mandatory seven years' imprisonment for importing narcotics and the confinement of an insane person for an unknown period of time at the pleasure of the Lieutenant-Governor. Preventive detention of dangerous offenders has also been upheld as not being cruel and unusual.

Reviewing Important Points

1. If a peace officer believes, on reasonable and probable grounds, that someone has committed or is about to commit an indictable offence, the officer may arrest that person without warrant. For all other offences, the officer must "find" the person "committing" the offence.

2. A peace officer may not have to arrest the accused. Under certain conditions, the officer may summons the accused or issue a Notice of Appearance.

3. The police have no authority to take a person into custody for questioning or on the grounds of suspicion.

4. If a peace officer requests a person to assist in the arrest of someone, it is an offence to refuse.

5. When searching premises with a search warrant, police may seize any articles that are reasonably believed to be held for an illegal purpose.

6. A Supreme Court of Canada decision allows police to search a house without a search warrant if they believe a fugitive is hiding inside.

7. A person charged with an indictable offence must submit to being fingerprinted and photographed.

8. Some statutes contain clauses which put the burden upon the accused to give evidence showing absence of a criminal intent, or establishing a certain fact. Such clauses cannot place the accused in a position which makes it impossible to conduct a defence.

9. Our criminal law system places the burden upon the Crown to show cause why an accused should be kept in jail, pending trial, rather than be released on bail.

10. Police may obtain legal authority to wiretap from a judge or the Solicitor General. It is unclear whether this authorization is also authorization to break and enter in order to install the device.

Checking Your Understanding

1. What must an officer tell a person whom the officer has arrested?
2. How does the law differ regarding a citizen's power of arrest as compared to a police officer's power of arrest?
3. What is the general rule regarding the use of force when making an arrest?
4. Give a brief explanation of the principle of the "presumption of innocence."
5. Explain how a "reverse onus clause" may affect the right to silence of an accused.
6. Describe two situations in which citizens would have the duty to identify themselves.
7. What rights are guaranteed under the principle of habeas corpus?

Legal Briefs

1. A police officer stopped a car with two male occupants. The officer asked the driver for a driver's permit, which was shown. The officer asked the passenger for identification, which the passenger refused to give. The officer stated that police were looking for an escaped prison inmate and that if the passenger did not provide identification he would be charged with obstruction. Lawful demand?
2. A police officer had a conversation with an accused about a theft. Not satisfied with the replies, the officer said, "I will have to arrest you. You'll have to come to the station." The accused fled on foot, but was later arrested. Did the accused unlawfully escape arrest?
3. Two youths were hanging around an arcade which had experienced an increase in drug-related problems. A person approached the youths, showed identification as a city detective, and said, "Empty your pockets." Legal demand?
4. Students in a school classroom were suddenly told to remain in their seats. A team of police and trained dogs entered the room. The dogs were led up and down the aisles smelling for narcotics. None were found. Were the students unlawfully detained?
5. V was charged with the murder of her husband, but did not testify at her trial. The trial judge, in the charge to the jury, told them that while the accused did not have to testify, they could "draw such conclusions as they deemed proper" from her failure to testify on such an important matter. Proper charge?
6. When P was arrested, she was told by the officer that she did not have to make a statement. She was told that she had been arrested under authority of an arrest warrant upon a charge of conspiracy to import narcotics. She was then asked if she wished to try to "contact anyone" by telephone. Have the police met all the legal requirements?
7. When arrested, R called a lawyer who said that R should not make any statement. The lawyer repeated this instruction to the arresting officer, saying, "I do not want my client questioned." Must the police accept this situation?
8. When T was involved in an automobile accident, the original charge against her was "dangerous driving" and the Crown elected to proceed by way of summary conviction. When one of the injured persons died, the Crown changed its election and notified the accused that the trial would be by way of indictment. T was ordered to appear for fingerprinting and photographing. Must T comply?
9. Police obtained a legal authorization to install a listening device upon D's telephone and in his office. D, suspecting this had taken place, hired an expert to "scan" his office. The devices were found and D smashed them. D was charged under s. 387(1) of the *Criminal Code* which states: "Every one commits mischief who wilfully (a) destroys or damages property." Is D guilty of mischief?
10. When officer S was shot by a robber, police were of the opinion that the robber had also been hit by a bullet from S's police revolver. When police questioned a suspect, H, they became aware that he was favouring his right leg. The police sought a search warrant requesting authority to take H to a hospital for an x-ray. If the x-ray showed a bullet in H's leg, the police then wanted a warrant to authorize a "medical search" to remove the bullet. Should such warrants be granted?

Applying the Law

 O'Connor v. The Queen
Supreme Court of Canada, 1966

The accused was driving his car when he was stopped by a police officer at about 1:30 a.m. The officer believed the accused had been drinking and demanded that the accused take a breathalyzer test. At the police station, the accused took two tests and failed both. He was charged with driving with more than 80 mg of alcohol per 100 mL of blood. The accused then asked for permission to call his lawyer and was allowed one telephone call. The accused could not reach his lawyer and the police denied him any more calls and drove him home. The accused was convicted of the charge, but a judge of the Supreme Court of Ontario overturned the conviction on the grounds that the accused had not been warned of the gravity of the offence; had not been told that he was under arrest; and further that the accused had not been allowed to obtain counsel. The Ontario Court of Appeal restored the conviction and the Supreme Court of Canada upheld this decision, leaving the accused convicted of the charge. The Supreme Court of Canada's decision reads in part:

❝The evidence in the present case does not disclose that the circumstances under which the police refused to allow the accused while under arrest to contact a lawyer were such that he was deprived of the right to a fair hearing in accordance with the principles of justice.❞

Questions

1. Why did the judge feel that O'Connor's rights had been violated?
2. Why did the Supreme Court of Canada conclude that the accused's rights had not been violated?
3. Would the final result have been different if O'Connor had asked permission to telephone the lawyer *before* he took the tests and the police had denied this request? Why or why not?
4. Do you think the case would be decided differently if it took place today, after the passage of the *Charter of Rights and Freedoms*? Why or why not?

R. v. Lykkemark and Funk
Alberta, 1982

A confrontation arose between police and persons in attendance at a noisy party. Some beer bottles were thrown causing damage to a police car. The police tried to break up the party by scattering people and telling them to leave the area. The accused F was told to leave two or three times but did not do so. The accused L said he was told to leave but that he was arrested by another officer before he had a chance to comply. Both men were charged with obstruction. The trial judge convicted F but acquitted L. In convicting F, the judge stated that the police have a duty to preserve order and to protect citizens and property from criminal acts. When the demands to the accused were made by police, the police were pursuing a clear and reasonable purpose to break up an unlawful assembly. The decision to remain, in the face of obvious police duty to act, constituted obstruction, frustrating in part the intent of the police demand. Wilfulness was implicit in a refusal made under such conditions.

Questions

1. Since being on a public street is not an offence, why was the accused convicted?
2. Would this case suggest that every time a police officer says to a citizen, "Move along," the refusal to do so would be obstruction? Why or why not?
3. Canada no longer has vagrancy laws. Would an obstruction charge be an effective way of stopping people from "hanging around" a certain place? Why or why not?
4. In Chapter 9, there is a definition of an unlawful assembly. Would a street party be an unlawful assembly? Why or why not?

You Be the Judge

1. Police received a complaint that a man was exposing himself indecently on a certain street corner. They were given a good description of the man and went to the location. There they found a man who matched the description; however, he was doing nothing indecent. They asked him to account for his presence on the corner, but he declined to give any reply. The police arrested the man. He was charged under the following section of the *Criminal Code*.

> **169. Every one who wilfully does an indecent act**
> **(a) in a public place in the presence of one or more persons, or**
> **(b) in any place, with intent thereby to insult or offend any person,**
> **is guilty of an offence punishable on summary conviction.**

Was the arrest lawful?

2. A transit inspector saw the accused and a friend going through a parking lot trying to open car doors. Police were called and the inspector advised the officer where the two youths were. The officer went to a basement apartment. The door was open and the officer asked one of the youths if he lived there but received an abusive reply. The officer told both youths they were under arrest and entered the apartment through the open door. There was a struggle between the officer and one of the youths while the other youth and a third man watched. The officer obtained assistance from other police and the two youths were taken into custody. One of the charges was assaulting the officer. Should the accused youth be convicted of this offence?

3. The accused was detained in the office of a shopping mall by security officers. She was accused of shoplifting. The police arrived and she was charged with theft. She submitted to a search of her shopping bag, but refused to put on a pair of handcuffs. After some further argument about the handcuffs and being allowed to pay for merchandise taken, the accused suddenly ran out of the office and escaped. She was later located, arrested, and charged with theft and escaping arrest. On the charge of escaping arrest, defence counsel extracted from all the witnesses for the Crown that at no time had anyone actually said to the accused, "You are under arrest," and no one had ever touched her in conjunction with these words. Should the accused be convicted of escaping arrest?

4. Police flew a helicopter close to the ground above the back yard of the accused's house. The police were searching for marijuana plants which were not visible from the road. The accused was later arrested on a charge of cultivating marijuana. She argued that she should not be convicted because (1) the police did not have a warrant; (2) they did not have reasonable and probable grounds to believe there was marijuana growing in her yard (they acted on a tip); and (3) she had been subjected to "unreasonable search," contrary to the *Charter of Rights*. Was there an unreasonable search?

5. Police officers suspected the accused of having burglarized a drugstore. They went to the accused's house, rang the doorbell, and asked the whereabouts of the accused during the night in question. While talking to the accused, they saw some cigarette cartons inside the doorway. Among the items stolen were cigarettes. The police then entered the home, without a warrant and without permission, and conducted a search. They found more cigarettes and other items which could have been stolen. At the trial for break and enter and theft, the accused argued that the search had been unlawful and unreasonable and that the goods seized could not be entered in evidence. The Crown acknowledged that the goods represented the only case it had against the accused. Should the evidence be admitted?

Chapter 9

Preserving Our Heritage of Freedom

Human Rights and Historic Freedoms

Jurisdiction over human rights is a divided responsibility between the federal government and the provinces. The federal government has been influential in those areas of rights and freedoms which affect all Canadians. The *Constitution Act, 1867* gives the power of "property and civil rights" to the provinces in s. 92(13). There are specific provisions in the Act dealing with civil rights pertaining to the Roman Catholic religion, English-speaking people in Quebec, and French-speaking people elsewhere.

Many Canadians believe that there has never been serious discrimination of any sort in Canada. To counter this, one must necessarily ask, "Compared with what other country?" Canada has indeed had its blemishes in the field of civil rights. To start with, slavery has existed in Canada. Indians captured other Indians and made them slaves. Early French military incursions often resulted in Indians being sent back to France as slaves. Black slaves were imported into some of the Maritime provinces. Slavery existed in Canada until it was made illegal in England in 1833.

As Canadian historians know very well, much of the great expansion of the railroads across Canada was achieved with Chinese labour. For many decades, these Chinese were not given any status in Canada at all. The federal government refused to deport them, but that did not prevent the provinces from denying them the right to vote and restricting them in many other ways, particularly in employment. For example, British Columbia law denied Chinese the right to work in any underground mines or in logging camps on provincial Crown land. These laws were later extended to Japanese as well.

Canada has paid scant attention to the wishes and rights of its native people. Although there were fewer Indian wars in Canada than in the United States, the rights of Indians were frequently set aside or ignored in favour of the demands of the growing white population. The last major uprising was that of the Métis, led by Louis Riel in 1885.

The harsh treatment of the Japanese-Canadians during World War II and similar mistreatment of Ukrainians, from time to time, demonstrates that national groups were sometimes singled out for persecution. Religion was often the motive behind mistreatment of other groups and individuals. The Jehovah's Witnesses have been hounded in many parts of Canada, particularly in Quebec.

Section 2 of the *Charter of Rights and Freedoms** affirms the historic recognition of certain fundamental freedoms. It states:

> **2. Everyone has the following fundamental freedoms:**
> **(a) freedom of conscience and religion;**
> **(b) freedom of thought, belief, opinion, and expression, including freedom of the press and other media of communication;**
> **(c) freedom of peaceful assembly; and**
> **(d) freedom of association.**

*Note: Section 2 is one of the sections subject to the "override" provision.

The interpretation of these freedoms has been a difficult one. Our discussion in this chapter will try to encompass what the courts have traditionally said about these freedoms and also try to anticipate where changes may be likely in the future.

Freedom of Religion

The student of European history knows well the many wars fought over differences of religion. These conflicts eventually led to a policy that the church and the state must be separate bodies and that no government should order its people to practise one religion. Canada inherited this principle from Britain. However, this separation of church and state does *not* mean that the state cannot give recognition to a God or Deity, to observance of religious holidays, or to school prayers. Perhaps the most common target of court actions is the *Lord's Day Act*, a federal statute with implementing provincial statutes, which prohibits the conduct of business on Sundays. The validity of this statute has been upheld in every single instance in which it was challenged. In *Robertson and Rosetanni v. The Queen* (1963), the issue was the operation of a bowling alley on Sunday. The Supreme Court of Canada held that the *Lord's Day Act* was not in conflict with the *Bill of Rights*.

The following comment was made by Chief Justice Bora Laskin in one of his books on constitutional law:

> Although there is no established religion in Canada today, and although in practice the situation has not been much different from that in the United States, separation of church and state has never been an avowed policy of Canadian legislators, and, in fact, various parts of Canada once had established churches. The fact that the Supreme Court upheld the *Lord's Day Act* leads to the conclusion that freedom of religion in Canada, since the passing of the *Bill of Rights*, is intended to include only a guarantee against infringement of its free exercise, and not a guarantee against the establishment of religion.

In 1958, as a form of protest, a group in British Columbia known as Doukhobors, stopped sending their children to public schools. The Doukhobor children were then made wards of the Crown and sent to school elsewhere in the province. This was contested in the case of *Perepolkin et al. v. Superintendent of Child Welfare* (1958). The Supreme Court of British Columbia rejected that Doukhobor action and gave a definition of freedom of religion:

> 66Freedom of religion is freedom from religious dogma. It is not freedom from law because of religious dogma.99

In these two sentences, the court stated clearly what many Canadians misunderstand. Freedom of religion means that people cannot be forced to accept a religion chosen by the government. They cannot be required to pray, attend a religious service, or adopt beliefs of a religious nature. However, freedom of religion does not mean that people can excuse themselves from obeying the law because the law contradicts their religious beliefs. As the court concluded in the *Perepolkin* case:

> 66This clearly in my mind involves the claim that a religious sect may make rules for the conduct of human behaviour and that these rules become for all the world a part of the sect's religion. This cannot be so.99

It is a criminal offence to disturb religious worship, or assault or arrest one of the clergy performing or about to perform a religious service. In *Chaput v. Romain* (1955), Quebec Provincial Police interrupted a meeting of Jehovah's Witnesses taking place in a private home. The Supreme Court of Canada upheld an award of damages in a civil action. The justices also were of the opinion that the officers had committed a criminal offence.

Perhaps the best-known case involving freedom of religion is the following:

Roncarelli v. Duplessis
1959

Roncarelli was a proprietor of a restaurant in Montreal who, as a Jehovah's Witness himself, often acted as a bondsman for a large number of other Jehovah's Witnesses. In 1956 his licence to sell liquor was cancelled by the Quebec Liquor Commission. Roncarelli brought an action against the Premier of the province arising out of the cancellation of that licence. It was alleged that Premier Duplessis personally ordered the cancellation of the licence both as Premier and Attorney General. The Supreme Court of Canada decided in favour of Roncarelli and awarded damages of $25 000. The majority held that the Premier had acted in a private capacity and not in the lawful exercise of his duties. The court concluded that the Premier had used his personal power to bring economic ruin upon a citizen without trial.

The *Charter of Rights* will most likely be the basis for future cases involving freedom of religion. Most likely the first of these cases will centre around the *Lord's Day Act.* In view of the consistency with which the Supreme Court of Canada has upheld the validity of this statute, it is unlikely that any challenge will be successful. Another possible area of interest is that of narcotics. A number of cases have been brought in the United States in which a religious group argued that it made regular use of narcotics in its religious ceremonies and that the government could not prohibit such use. In 1962, the U.S. Supreme Court held that Navaho Indians had the right to use peyote during religious services as the Indians had used peyote for centuries.

A complicating factor is that religion is not defined in any of the great documents of the world purporting to protect freedom of religion. When people claim that something is part of their religion, there is no specific basis upon which that claim can be proved or disproved.

Political Freedom

Canada has seldom found it necessary or desirable to prohibit a particular brand of political belief from being preached or practised. Notable exceptions might include the FLQ and communism. Communism, or bolshevism as it is sometimes called, has been made illegal during short periods of Canadian history, pri-

marily during World War II, despite the fact that Canada and the Soviet Union were allies during the war.

The dislike of communism was most intense in the Province of Quebec, where there were further attempts to legislate against it. One particularly notorious statute was tested in the following case.

Switzman v. Elbling and Attorney General of Quebec
1957

A Quebec law, the *Communist Propaganda Act*, made it illegal for a person to use a house to "print, publish, or distribute any newspaper or document tending to propagate communism or bolshevism" on pain of imprisonment. Known as the "Padlock Law," this Act allowed the Attorney General of Quebec to order a house closed up for a period of not more than one year. Elbling, a landlord, ordered Switzman, a tenant, to vacate the house he occupied because Switzman was violating the law and Elbling was afraid the authorities would padlock the house. Switzman sued Elbling for breach of contract (their lease) and the Province of Quebec joined the civil action in order to uphold the validity of the law. The Supreme Court of Canada held that the *Communist Propaganda Act* was ultra vires the province because it created a criminal offence — a power belonging only to the federal government. The court said in its decision:

❝While a province may legislate on the civil consequences of a crime created by the Dominion, or on the suppression of conditions leading to a crime, it may not *create* a crime to prevent another that has been validly established (e.g., sedition).**❞**

Before discussing the *Switzman* case, let us look at an earlier case which appears to be similar, but was not quite the same.

Bedard v. Dawson
1923

The Supreme Court of Canada upheld a Quebec statute which provided for the closing of premises known as disorderly houses (i.e., used for gambling and prostitution) upon conviction of the owner or occupier under the *Criminal Code* for running a disorderly house. The law was upheld under s. 92(13) of the *B.N.A. Act* [now the *Constitution Act, 1867*] as dealing with "property and civil rights" and being concerned with the suppression of conditions favouring crime rather than being concerned with criminal legislation in itself.

There is a distinct difference between the *Switzman* and *Bedard* cases. In *Bedard*, the court held that it was within the power of a province to close up a place once the owner or occupier had been convicted of a criminal offence. This was a reasonable action to take in order to prevent a recurrence of the crime by permitting the place to be used again for illegal purposes. The types of crimes that the court had in mind were gambling and prostitution.

In *Switzman*, the province had gone too far. Instead of waiting for the occupier of a property to be convicted of a crime and then padlocking the place, the *Communist Propaganda Act* made it a crime to do something, and then empowered the province to padlock the premises. The court held that the province could not declare anything to be a crime. This is a federal power only.

The *Switzman* decision did not nullify the *Bedard* decision. A province can still padlock premises if they have been used for a criminal purpose.

What effect might the *Charter of Rights* have upon political freedom? The *Charter* guarantees "freedom of thought, belief, opinion, and expression" which would certainly encompass political thought and opinion. However, this is one of the sections that can be set aside under the "notwithstanding" clause. It would be conceivably possible for the Parliament of Canada to once again declare a political party, philosophy, or belief to be unlawful.

Freedom of the Press

Historically, Canada has fared well in maintaining a free and viable press. This is probably true because the freedom of the press is well protected in the United Kingdom and the United States.

We should not, however, pretend that this is a total, unimpeded freedom; it is not and never was. There have always been restrictions upon the press. The press cannot be used to print sedition or libel. During wartime, the press can be censored lest valuable information be given to the enemy. If publications are indecent, they may be seized. There are many other examples of limitations upon the press.

Not everyone agrees as to what freedom of the press means. In 1977, the British Royal Commission on the Press offered this definition: "We define freedom of the press as that degree of freedom from restraint which is essential to enable proprietors, editors, and journalists to advance the public interest by publishing the facts and opinions without which a democratic society cannot make responsible judgments."

Freedom of the press consists, then, of two elements: the freedom to receive information and opinion, and the freedom to disseminate that information and opinion. Freedom of the press has received recognition in the *Bill of Rights*, the *Charter of Rights and Freedoms*, and in provincial statutes in Alberta, Quebec, and Saskatchewan.

The constitutional position of freedom of the press was decided in the following case:

Re An Act To Ensure the Publication of Accurate Laws and Information
Supreme Court of Canada, 1938

The Government of Alberta thought that newspapers were not accurate in their reporting of new social legislation and often failed to explain a proposed law completely. The legislature passed a law requiring every newspaper to register with the government and to publish any statement the government provided relating to any policy or activity of the government within twenty-one days. Any contravention of the Act was punished by prohibition from further publication. The Supreme Court of Canada held the law to be ultra vires the province. The court's decision reads:

66The *Press Bill* is ultra vires the Alberta legislature under s. 129 of the *B.N.A. Act* [now the *Constitution Act, 1867*] to curtail the right of public discussions or to reduce the political rights of its citizens as compared with those of other provinces or to interfere with the workings of Parliamentary institutions. The federal Parliament is the sole authority to curtail, if deemed necessary and in the public interest, the freedom of press and the equal right in that respect of all citizens throughout the Dominion.99

In giving the majority opinion, Justice Cannon concluded:

66The province cannot interfere with [a person's] status as a Canadian citizen and his fundamental right to express freely his untrammelled opinion about government policies and discuss matters of public concern.99

There are several interesting aspects to the *Alberta Press* case. The first is that the Supreme Court established that persons resident in Canada have certain rights all across the country. Whether or not these rights fall directly under the jurisdiction of the federal government according to the *B.N.A. Act (Constitution Act, 1867)* the court took the view that one province cannot substantially lessen the basic rights of citizens within its borders as compared with those enjoyed by other Canadians. Thus, the court indicated that it would take a hard look at laws that substantially reduced the rights of citizens in one province.

Another interesting aspect is that the court did not say that freedom of the press could never be curtailed, but that any curtailment would have to be made by the federal government, not a province. There are a number of provisions in the *Criminal Code* which affect freedom of the press. One prohibition is seditious libel and the leading case is the following.

Boucher v. The King
Supreme Court of Canada, 1950

The accused was prosecuted for distributing a pamphlet entitled *Quebec's Burning Hate for God and Christ and Freedom is the Shame of All Canada*. This pamphlet denounced, in extreme language, the inter-

connections between the Quebec political world and the religious establishment, affirming that the former were at the beck and call of the latter. The Supreme Court of Canada held that the use of strong words is *not* sufficient to lead to a conviction for seditious libel. Even an intention to promote ill-will and hostility among Canadian citizens would not suffice. The court concluded that there would have to be an intention to incite the Canadian people to violence and to create public disorder or disturbance to obtain a conviction under this section of the *Criminal Code*. The court held that this pamphlet did not go that far and that the accused should be acquitted.

One problem that has often come before the courts is the "privilege" of a reporter to protect a news source. Canadian courts have been quite consistent in the view that a reporter enjoys no immunity or privilege. In the absence of any specific "shield" statutes, reporters can have their notes subpoenaed or may themselves be required to give evidence to reveal their sources. In *Belzberg v. B.C. Television Broadcasting* (1980), a television reporter did not want to reveal a source but the B.C. Supreme Court ruled that the overriding public interest required that the name of the informant be revealed so that the person could be subpoenaed.

We might lastly examine freedom of the press and control of the press. Competition laws in Canada have not been particularly effective in preventing most of the newspapers in Canada from falling into the hands of just three large corporations. In most cities there is just one newspaper, and in some provinces one family owns all the newspapers.

Freedom of Assembly and Association

The *Charter of Rights* guarantees freedom of *peaceful* assembly. The word "peaceful" is necessary to distinguish between a lawful assembly and an unlawful assembly or riot. The *Criminal Code* generally defines an *unlawful assembly* as one comprised of three or more persons who have the intent to carry out any common

The Charter of Rights *guarantees freedom of peaceful assembly, thus protecting the right of Canadians to demonstrate their opposition to government action.*

purpose, and who are assembling in such a manner as to cause the fear that they will disturb the peace tumultuously. A *riot* is an unlawful assembly that has *begun* to disturb the peace tumultuously; it requires the participation of twelve or more persons. A riot is deemed to be in progress after the reading of a proclamation by a law officer that a riot is taking place and that everyone present must depart.

Freedom of assembly is a very important part of our political freedom. A totalitarian government prohibits political freedom by prohibiting gatherings of persons to discuss grievances and plan political action. It is important to consider *where* the assembly may take place. There is no freedom of persons to assemble anywhere they want. The "protest demonstration," which became very popular during the 1960s, brought this issue very much into the legal spotlight. The following case examined the question of assemblies taking place on public property.

Attorney General for Canada and Dupond v. Montreal
Supreme Court of Canada, 1978

The City of Montreal passed an ordinance prohibiting the holding of any assembly, parade, or gathering on the public domain of the City of Montreal for a time period of thirty days. Under a by-law, the city could invoke the thirty-day limit any time it thought necessary for public order. The appellant, Claire Dupond, attacked the constitutional validity of the by-law. The Supreme Court of Canada held that the by-law was not ultra vires the city. The court stressed the temporary nature of the ban. The city was not banning all gatherings forever but was dealing with violent demonstrations in a logical manner. The suppression of conditions likely to favour the commission of crimes is within provincial jurisdiction. The court also noted that demonstrations are distinct from freedoms of speech, assembly, and association. Demonstrations are a collective action displaying force rather than appealing to reason. The court also concluded that there is no historic right to hold demonstrations on public property:

❝The right to hold public meetings on a highway or in a park is *unknown* to English law. Far from being the object of a right, the holding of a public meeting on a street or in a park may constitute a trespass against the urban authority in whom the ownership of the street is vested even though no one is obstructed and no injury is done; it may also amount to a nuisance.**❞**

Chief Justice Laskin gave the dissenting opinion in the *Dupond* case. He felt that the by-law went too far and gave the city the power to prohibit legitimate dissent. He referred to the case of *District of Kent v. Storgoff* (1962) in which the Supreme Court of British Columbia struck down a by-law which tried to prohibit members of a Doukhobor sect from entering a city containing a prison where a large number of Doukhobor members were serving sentences. Protesters, about 1000 in number, were intending to march on the prison and had begun to do so from their homes about 400 miles away. The by-law declared an emergency and prohibited the protesters from entering the city. The court held, in that case, that the situation could be dealt with only by the federal government under its criminal law jurisdiction.

There have been few cases involving freedom of association. The Federal Court of Canada has held that an inmate, released on parole, could be ordered as a term of parole, not to associate with other ex-convicts. This has been considered a reasonable limitation which did not violate freedom of association.

The Canadian *Bill of Rights*

The Canadian *Bill of Rights* should be associated with the man who pressed for its passage, former Prime Minister John Diefenbaker. The bill received royal assent in 1960 and is still in force. It was not repealed when the *Charter of Rights and Freedoms* was enacted.

The *Bill of Rights* and the *Charter* cover many of the same topics, but the *Bill of Rights* is only a statute passed by the Parliament of Canada, not a permanent constitution. Further, it has no application to those

areas under provincial jurisdiction. The statute applies only to the federal government.

The *Bill of Rights* has three parts:

- A preamble affirming general principles;
- Part I which recognizes specific rights and freedoms;
- Part II which explains the applications of the Act.

From its inception, the *Bill of Rights* was dogged by one enduring problem. It was recognized that it created no new rights, but only affirmed existing rights. Thus, there was no incentive upon the courts to effect drastic changes in the existing case law. The courts had long been applying principles of basic human rights and would continue to do so in the same general way. If there was any expectation that the Supreme Court of Canada would make a strong shift towards greater recognition of human rights, it occurred in the following case, regarded by lawyers as the "high-water mark" of liberal interpretation of the *Bill of Rights*.

The Canadian **Bill of Rights** *was enacted in 1960 as a result of a determined effort on the part of Prime Minister John Diefenbaker to affirm basic human rights.*

R. v. Drybones
Supreme Court of Canada, 1970

Drybones, a Dogrib Indian, was found drunk in a Yellowknife hotel on Saturday night. He was arrested, fined ten dollars Monday morning, and released. He was fined under a provision of the *Indian Act* which reads:

95. An Indian who
(a) has intoxicants in his possession,
(b) is intoxicated, or
(c) makes or manufactures intoxicants,
off a reserve is guilty of an offence and is liable to a fine of not less than ten dollars and not more than fifty dollars, or to imprisonment for a term not exceeding three months or to both fine and imprisonment.

The magistrate could just as easily have fined Drybones under the *N.W.T. Liquor Ordinance* for being drunk in a public place, but chose instead to levy a fine under the *Indian Act*. Under either statute the actual fine probably would have been the same —although technically the *Indian Act* carries a higher maximum fine than does the *Liquor Ordinance*. The significance of the case became apparent when Drybones appealed his conviction on the following grounds:

(1) Since there are no Indian reservations anywhere in the Northwest Territories, an Indian could not legally consume intoxicants anywhere. There is no similar prohibition placed upon a non-Indian.
(2) The maximum possible fine is greater under the *Indian Act* than the maximum possible fine under the *N.W.T. Liquor Ordinance*. Thus, an Indian faces a potentially greater penalty for doing the same thing as a non-Indian.

The Supreme Court of Canada held that Drybones had been denied "equality before the law" as guaranteed by the *Canadian Bill of Rights,* and that the section in question of the *Indian Act* was inoperative as it contravened the guarantees under the *Bill of Rights*.

Court watchers who thought a new era had arrived were to see their hopes ended when the same Supreme Court made a considerable retreat from the high-water mark of *Drybones* in the next case, which also involved an action commenced by a native person.

Discrimination per se is not prohibited in Canada—a situation that sometimes brings native people into conflict with the government.

Attorney General of Canada v. Lavell
Supreme Court of Canada, 1973

Lavell contested s. 12(1) of the *Indian Act* which states that women who marry non-Indians lose their Indian status. Indian men may marry non-Indian women without losing their status, and they can bring their wives and any children their wives have from a former marriage to live as Indians on a reserve. The Supreme Court of Canada took the interpretation of the *Bill of Rights* rather narrowly on this question, holding that the *Bill of Rights* does not prevent a discriminatory law from being passed in Canada; it can only make sure people are discriminated against equally. Since Lavell had not been treated differently *from other Indian women*, she was not discriminated against unfairly, but rather given special treatment (i.e., the special treatment due to all Indian women).

The *Drybones* and *Lavell* cases appear to be somewhat inconsistent, unless we accept the possibility that there is a different law for Indian men than Indian women. Yet, both cases were decided by the same court. The concept of "equality" remains somewhat elusive, but what is clear is that a law can be targeted at a specific group without creating some form of discrimination. As long as everyone within that group is treated equally, there is no discrimination.

Since the *Bill of Rights* and *Charter of Rights* cover similar topics, there is some question as to why the *Bill of Rights* was not repealed. One likely answer lies in the fact that s. 15 of the *Charter*, which deals with equality rights, does not come into force until 1985. During the period 1982-1985, the *Bill of Rights* will have to continue to provide this protection.

Equality, Discrimination, and the *Charter of Rights*

Under the constitution, all Canadians will be equal before the law and will enjoy equal protection of the law. In using the word "will" it should be noted that

the equality section of the *Charter of Rights* does not take effect until 1985. Until that time, other statutes, including the *Bill of Rights*, will have to afford similar protection. The future section of the *Charter* reads:

> **15. (1) Every individual is equal before and under the law and has the right to the equal protection and equal benefit of the law without discrimination and, in particular, without discrimination based on race, national or ethnic origin, colour, religion, sex, age or mental or physical disability.**
>
> **(2) Subsection (1) does not preclude any law, program or activity that has as its object the amelioration of conditions of disadvantaged individuals or groups including those that are disadvantaged because of race, national or ethnic origin, colour, religion, sex, age or mental or physical disability.**

Subsection (2) means that "affirmative action" programs are not prohibited. An example of an affirmative action program is giving special job preference to native people among whom unemployment is highest. The federal government could also give preference to persons from one nation wishing to emigrate to Canada when political conditions in that nation created large numbers of refugees.

Subsection (1) affords equality rights. It should be noted that these rights extend to every individual and not just to Canadian citizens. They would theoretically extend to persons illegally in Canada as well as legal immigrants.

The word "discrimination" is not easily defined and can be easily misconstrued. The word was discussed by the Supreme Court of Canada in the case of *A.G. of Canada v. Lavell* which was explained previously in this chapter. The court came to the following general conclusions about the meaning and application of discrimination:

- Discrimination, in itself, is not prohibited by the *Bill of Rights*. Where a special law is aimed at a special group, the fact that the group is treated differently than other Canadians is not a form of discrimination prohibited by the *Bill*. Discrimination would be unacceptable where one member of such a group did not receive the same treatment, under the law, as other members of the same group. We have numerous special laws which affect only certain groups of people including juveniles, alcoholics, and insane persons. Special laws to deal with their special needs do not constitute discrimination.

- "Equality before the law" refers to a concept of law which is virtually impossible to realize in practical terms. "Equal administration of the law" probably describes more accurately what the courts set out to achieve — meaning that a law should be applied equally to those affected by it.

- Given the traditional high regard of the courts for the Canadian Parliament, it is very unlikely that the courts will declare any law invalid if the courts can find reasonable grounds for Parliament to have passed such a law. In other words, the courts assume that Parliament never *intends* to discriminate because that would imply that Parliament ignores both the wording of statutes and the basic principle of equality.

When we look at Canadian legal history, in the light of these general conclusions about discrimination, we see a spotted record. At times, Canadian legislators made a very definite attempt to discriminate. Discrimination has existed in Canada against Asians, blacks, Indians, and other minority groups. This discrimination sometimes appeared in the form of legislation enacted to prevent non-whites from establishing a permanent residence in Canada.

The black population of Canada is relatively small. This is in part due to the efforts of immigration officers to prevent blacks from entering Canada. During a period in the early part of this century when farm land was being made available to U.S. residents free of charge, immigration officers used covert methods to learn if an applicant was black and then denied the application.

While no province had specific laws denying blacks access to public facilities, neither did the provinces have laws prohibiting denial of facilities to blacks. In 1924, an Ontario court held that a tavern owner could refuse to sell beer to a black. In 1947 a black woman bought a ticket for a theatre in Nova Scotia and was told she had to sit in a section reserved for blacks. She refused and was thrown out of the theatre and also fined $20. Her appeal to the Nova Scotia Supreme Court was refused.

Discrimination against blacks was common in many parts of Canada until the provinces began to enact legislation such as *Fair Employment Practices Acts, Fair Accommodations Practices Acts, Equal Pay Acts,* etc. The province first to deal with the issue fully was Saskatchewan, which passed its *Bill of Rights* in 1947. The *Bill* prohibits discrimination in employment, business practices, land ownership, trade and professional organizations, and education. The first black Member of Parliament was elected in 1968.

The greatest resentment and racial discrimination was reserved for the Asians. As most Canadians know, Asians were encouraged to come to Canada to provide the vast amount of labour needed to build Canadian railroads. These Asians were expected to make some money and then return home. A great many laws were passed to make it uncomfortable for them to stay. Chinese and Japanese were denied citizenship, voting rights, and working permits. They were not allowed to bring their wives and children with them. Many obstacles were put in their way to ensure that they did not try to establish homesteads here. A head tax was levied upon every Chinese coming into the country. At first this tax was $50, then finally $500 per person. British Columbia enacted twenty-six laws designed to discriminate against Asians. Most of these were ruled ultra vires by the courts or were invalidated by the federal government. One such law required any resident of the province who could not write a European language to pay a fine of $500. The federal government disallowed the law. Another case which tested the legal power of the province to enact such laws was the following:

Union Colliery of British Columbia v. Bryden Privy Council, England, 1899

This case involved a challenge to a law of British Columbia, known as the *Coal Mines Regulation Act* which stated that no Chinese persons were to be employed in any mine working below ground. The Supreme Court of British Columbia upheld the constitutionality of the law, but the Privy Council held that it really dealt with aliens, immigrations, and naturalization which was a federal matter. No discussion of segregation or racial discrimination entered into the case. The law was held to be ultra vires the province on the basis of the *B.N.A. Act* [now the *Constitution Act, 1867*] which granted these powers to the federal government.

The provinces were most insistent in denying Asians the right to vote. The white population envisioned a great "yellow peril" engulfing them if Asians could vote. They were concerned that some political party would capitalize upon the Asian vote and not only give full citizenship to Asians but also open the doors wide to unlimited Asian immigration. In 1900, a Japanese resident of British Columbia tested the validity of such a law.

Homma v. Cunningham
British Columbia, 1900

Under the *Provincial Elections Act* of British Columbia, "No Chinaman, Japanese or Indian shall have his name placed on the Register of Voters for any Electoral District or be entitled to vote at any election." A Japanese, Tomekichi Homma, applied to have his name placed on the list and was refused. He sued the Collector of Voters, Thomas Cunningham. The Supreme Court of British Columbia ordered Homma's name put on the voters' list. The Supreme Court of Canada upheld the British Columbia court's decision. However, upon appeal to the Privy Council, the decision was reversed.

The Privy Council's decision meant that it was not ultra vires for the province to deny the vote in a provincial election to a British subject on the basis of racial origin. It meant that provincial laws could make life very unsatisfactory for aliens, as long as the laws did not deal with them directly on any grounds other than race. Even though a Japanese might acquire Canadian citizenship, the province could still keep a Japanese off the provincial voters' list.

It was during World War II that racial discrimination appeared at its worst with the forced evacuation of Japanese from the west coast. Some 22 000 Japanese, many of them Canadian citizens, were removed from the coast and settled in internment camps, often in ghost towns. They were kept there for the duration of the war. While they were interned, their homes, businesses, fishing boats, automobiles, and every other possession were sold at auction at giveaway prices. After the war, they were given some repayment by the federal government for their losses, but it was very inadequate. In effect, the Japanese had been the victims of legalized theft.

We must look closer at the purpose in selling their property instead of holding it in trust as the Japanese were originally promised. The purpose remained the same as it had always been — to discourage the Japanese from remaining in Canada. When they realized that even if they returned to British Columbia after the war, they would have no homes to go to — no property — the Japanese saw quite well the intention of the British Columbia government. Prime Minister King also said in the House of Commons that it would not be in the best interest of the Japanese, or the Province of British Columbia, to have the Japanese once again congregate in that province. The Prime Minister hoped the Japanese would spread out and seek residence in all the provinces of Canada. To over 3000 Japanese, however, this was not even a possibility. They were stripped of their citizenship or landed immigrant status and deported to Japan.

When the war ended, the Japanese brought a collective lawsuit against the federal government and the Province of British Columbia. The Privy Council saw no merit in their case, holding that despite any sympathy one might feel for a group treated so badly, legally it was quite within the powers of the Canadian government to act in this way.

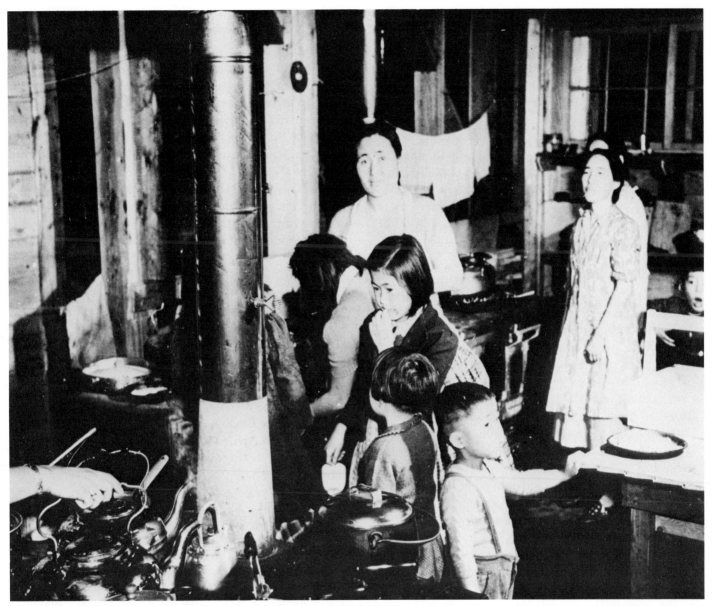

Under the War Measures Act *thousands of Canadians of Japanese descent were placed into detention camps for the duration of World War II.*

Since World War II, the provincial governments and the federal government have moved strongly towards ending discrimination in all forms. Every province now has special legislation in this field and the federal government has made it a part of the constitution.

These provincial laws will be discussed later in this chapter.

One area of lingering discrimination is discrimination by sex. Section 15 includes sex as a prohibited ground of discrimination, but this section is among those that could be by-passed under the "notwithstanding" clause. Because of concern by women that equality of the sexes was not fully protected, the *Charter* contains another section dealing with this matter. It reads:

> **28. Notwithstanding anything in this *Charter*, the rights and freedoms referred to in it are guaranteed equally to male and female persons.**

This special clause was added at the request of women's groups to reassure them that their rights will be protected. This is a guarantee that cannot be over-ridden by a provincial legislature or Parliament.

Another right contained in the *Charter* pertains to language. English and French have equal status as the nation's official languages in all institutions of the Government of Canada. The *Charter* also recognizes that English and French are the official languages of New Brunswick, at the specific request of that province. Education is a somewhat complex field, but basically if the person's mother tongue is French, but the person lives in a mainly English-speaking province, the person has a right to have his or her children educated in French. If the person was educated in English in Canada and lives in Quebec, that person's children can attend an English-speaking school in that province. This provision has not yet been fully adopted in Quebec and will not be until authorized by the Quebec Assembly.

If people believe that their rights and freedoms have been infringed upon, they may "apply to a court of competent jurisdiction to obtain such remedy as the court considers appropriate and just in the circumstances." This rather vague phrase would suggest that a civil action could be brought on the basis that someone's rights had been violated. An injunction might be issued or property ordered returned. It is unclear whether this could translate into a criminal charge against the wrongdoer.

The *War Measures Act*

Canada, like many nations of the world, has gone through very difficult periods when the very continued existence of the nation seemed to be at stake.

The threat of invasion during World War II was seriously discussed in the House of Commons, although history later revealed that neither the Japanese or Germans had any such plans.

Most nations have a law that permits the government to act in time of crisis. For example, a threatened government could declare martial law. There is, however, one unsatisfactory result from declaring martial law — the civil administration is completely set aside by the military which assumes control. There is no provision in Canada for the declaration of martial law. As an alternative, Canada has a law that permits the federal government to take very strong measures to protect the nation's interests. Yet, the results upon the citizen remain very similar.

Passage of the *War Measures Act*

When World War I broke out, Prime Minister Robert Borden committed himself to the awesome task of piloting Canada through a major war. One of his first considerations was what to do about German ships in Canadian waters and German citizens resident in Canada. He asked his advisors to draft a bill that would be very flexible, allowing him to make orders and regulations whenever needed, relating to nearly every topic. On August 20, 1914, the *War Measures Act* received royal assent, with only one Member of Parliament voting against it.

The following sections from the *War Measures Act* will give an indication of its scope.

> **2. The issue of a proclamation by Her Majesty or the Governor in Council shall be conclusive evidence that war, invasion, or insurrection, real or apprehended, exists and has existed for any period of time therein stated, and of its continuance, until by the issue of a further proclamation it is declared that the war, invasion, or insurrection no longer exists.**
>
> **3. (1) The Governor in Council may do and authorize such acts and things and make from time to time such orders and regulations as he may by reason of the existence of real or apprehended war, invasion or insurrection deem necessary or advisable for the security, defence, peace, order and welfare of Canada; and for**

greater certainty, but not so as to restrict the generality of the foregoing terms, it is hereby declared that the powers of the Governor in Council shall extend to all matters coming within the classes of subjects hereinafter enumerated, that is to say:

(a) censorship and the control and suppression of publications, writings, maps, plans, photographs, communications and means of communication;

(b) arrest, detention, exclusion and deportation;

(c) control of the harbours, ports, and territorial waters of Canada and the movements of vessels;

(d) transportation by land, air or water and the control of the transport of persons and things;

(e) trading, exportation, importation, production, and manufacture;

(f) appropriation, control, forfeiture and disposition of property and of the use thereof.

6. (5) Any act or thing done or authorized or any order or regulation made under the authority of this Act shall be deemed not to be an abrogation, abridgement, or infringement of any right or freedom recognized by the Canadian Bill of Rights.

The Act also provides that the Governor in Council may prescribe penalties up to $5000 fines and five years in prison. All orders made under the force of the Act have the force of law. No person arrested upon suspicion of being an enemy alien shall be released without the consent of the Minister of Justice.

The Powers of the *War Measures Act*

The *War Measures Act* lies somewhat inert unless needed. It is similar to a powerful club sitting on a shelf — unused, but within easy reach. As indicated by s. 2, the Governor in Council (in reality the federal Cabinet) may bring the Act into force by issuing a proclamation that war, invasion, or insurrection, real or apprehended, exists and has existed for any period of time stated. It is significant to note that the threat may be only "apprehended."

Having proclaimed the Act to be in force, the federal Cabinet must lay the proclamation before Parliament immediately, or if the House of Commons is not in session, within fifteen days after Parliament recon-

venes. If ten or more Members move that the matter be debated, it requires debate, but the House of Commons has no actual authority to overrule the Governor in Council except by public pressure. The provision to have the proclamation debated at all was not added to the Act until 1960. Having made the proclamation, the federal Cabinet may issue orders pertaining to the emergency situation at hand. All orders issued have the force of law and need not even be made public if the Cabinet wishes. How extensive could these orders be? A review of the powers granted under s. 3(1) will show the conditions which could be brought into existence. Here are but a few possibilities:

- Seizure, censorship, or closure of newspapers, radio and television stations;
- Arrest of anyone without charge being laid, indefinite detention without trial, removal of habeas corpus;
- Establishment of concentration camps for detainees;
- Deportation of persons out of Canada including citizens;
- Search and seizure of private homes;
- Seizure of private property to include all factories, ships, every means of transportation;
- Seizure of all privately owned weapons.

The list could be much longer, but these actions indicate the rather unlimited powers the government assumes under the Act.

The *War Measures Act* returns to its inert status when the Governor in Council issues another proclamation that the threat no longer exists. Any person in detention must then be charged with a specific crime or released.

Application of the *War Measures Act*

The *War Measures Act* was applied during World Wars I and II. During World War II, repressive actions were taken against Japanese-Canadians, Jehovah's Witnesses, communists, and even an obscure organization called "Technocracy, Inc." In 1945, a *secret* order was issued for the arrest, interrogation, and detention of any person who "might be likely to communicate information to an agent of a foreign government or act in a manner prejudicial to the public safety." This ambiguous order resulted in numerous arrests, but few convictions.

On October 5, 1970, the British Trade Commissioner, James Cross, was kidnapped in Montreal by one faction of the FLQ (Front for the Liberation of Quebec). The kidnapping came on the heels of many bombings and other acts of violence in Quebec. Shortly afterwards, the Quebec Labour Minister, Pierre Laporte, was kidnapped. The federal government invoked the *War Measures Act.*

Whether the *War Measures Act* was a necessary response to the FLQ is a matter of controversy. Some unhappy aspects were recorded, only a few of which include the following:

(1) Among those arrested were persons who had been active in politics against the established representatives of the Montreal city council and Quebec legislature.
(2) Persons were arrested upon no more information than their names being found in someone else's telephone address book.
(3) Arrested persons were packed into small jail cells for days and weeks.
(4) The families of arrested persons could not learn where their relatives were being held or why.
(5) The federal government had no list or knowledge of who had been arrested, upon what grounds, or where they were being held.
(6) Membership in the FLQ was made a crime *ex post facto*, meaning if a person had ever belonged to the FLQ that person could be convicted and jailed.
(7) Quebec police departments began acting autonomously, without accepting direction from or reporting to Ottawa.
(8) Police departments complained that they received contradictory orders from the federal government and the provincial government—no one seemed to have overall authority and many orders were unsigned.

Pierre Laporte was murdered; James Cross was freed in a deal; and some FLQ members were allowed to leave Canada. Believing the worst had passed, the government ordered the *War Measures Act* lifted. How

many people had been arrested was never clearly known, but most estimates are in the vicinity of 650.

Canada, like most nations, requires the power to counter any threat from within or outside its borders. The question remains, does this power have to be so efficient that it rivals the power of the worst totalitarian regimes? Adolf Hitler once said, "The real strength of totalitarian governments is that they force the democracies of the world to emulate them."

The *War Measures Act* and Human Rights Legislation

The Canadian *Bill of Rights* had no effect during the imposition of the *War Measures Act*. The *War Measures Act* specifically states that it operates in a manner that is understood not to be an infringement of any right or freedom. This is the closest example of a "legislative lie" that can be found anywhere, for the operation of the Act violates many of the rights supposedly granted by the *Bill of Rights*.

The difficult question is whether the *War Measures Act* could be invoked in the same manner as it was during the 1970s and not be contrary to the provisions of the *Charter of Rights*. In its present form, much of the *War Measures Act* would be inoperative. However, Parliament could amend the Act to say that it shall operate "notwithstanding" a provision included in s. 2 or ss. 7 to 15 of the *Charter*. Thus, the "fundamental freedoms" and "legal rights" sections could be by-passed. The wording of s. 1 could also be applied. A court might hold that the stern measures of the *War Measures Act* are within the "reasonable limits" justified in a "free and democratic society" if the Act was being used to protect society from a serious attack upon it from an enemy determined to destroy democracy in Canada.

Provincial Human Rights Legislation

All the provinces now have human rights statutes on the books. Employment was one of the first areas where provincial laws sought to eliminate discriminatory practices. This is discussed further in Unit Twelve.

The *Charter of Rights and Freedoms* has not made provincial legislation obsolete. It is unlikely that the *Charter* will be construed to apply between individuals. Rather, it is likely to apply between an individual and a branch of government. Thus, there is still need for other legislation protecting the individual from the actions of another individual, such as a landlord.

Provincial laws vary considerably in their scope and wording. To get an exact knowledge of the situation in each province would require that the reader obtain the provincial statutes. Our discussion here will centre upon the statutes of three provinces, which are typical in their wording of legislation found across Canada.

The Ontario *Human Rights Code*

Revised in 1981, the *Code* establishes certain prohibited grounds of discrimination. Included are: race, colour, ancestry, place of origin, citizenship, ethnic origin, creed, family status, sex, marital status, age, receipt of public aid, handicap, and record of offences. Not all of these grounds apply to every form of activity. For example, a record of offence applies only to employment and harassment in the workplace. In short, a person cannot be denied a job because of a criminal record; however, that person could be denied accommodation.

The activities covered by the *Code* include access to services, access to goods, access to facilities, occupancy of accommodation, harassment by a landlord, employment, harassment in the workplace, and membership in a trade union.

A person who feels that discrimination has occurred may file a complaint with the Human Rights Commission which may investigate the complaint, hold hearings, and award fines up to $25 000.

Re Toronto General Hospital
Ontario Human Rights Commission, 1978
Two women doctors filed a complaint with the Commission when they were fired from the hospital and three male doctors hired in their place. The Commission found that the marital status of the women was the prime factor in their dismissal. The hospital considered it was justified in letting the women go because they were not "principal breadwinners." The investigator found that one of the doctors was earning more than her husband. In any case, the Commission held that:

> **❝**Making hiring decisions on the basis of the breadwinner concept, while neutral in form, is nevertheless discriminatory in operation and in violation of human rights.**❞**

The complainants were also subjected to other forms of petty discrimination such as being referred to as "the girls" rather than as "doctors," being denied the opportunity to examine patients, and having to share one locker while each of the male doctors had his own. The doctors received $6000 in compensation for lost income. The hospital agreed to improve its facilities for women doctors and, in future, to judge applicants only on their professional abilities, not on their marital or family status.

In an interesting discrimination case, the Supreme Court of Canada had to decide whether discrimination is also a tort which would permit a private lawsuit as well as a complaint through the Commission.

Bhadauria v. Board of Governors of Seneca College
Supreme Court of Canada, 1981
The plaintiff applied for a teaching position at the defendant college and although very qualified was not granted so much as an interview. Not satisfied with the actions of the Human Rights Commission of Ontario she brought an action in tort against Seneca College. The Ontario Court of Appeal held that discrimination is a tort and is actionable notwithstanding any action taken by a Human Rights Commission. The Supreme Court of Canada overturned this decision and held that a tort cannot exist where there is an alternative statutory method of dealing with the problem. The court found that the Ontario legislation is an exhaustive and all-inclusive document that provides for procedures and reme-

dies when a person believes he or she has been the target of discrimination. To also establish the tort of discrimination would be confusing, for it would give the plaintiff two chances to succeed. If an action by way of complaint to the Commission was not successful, the defendant could be forced to defend the action again in civil court. The court concluded that the intent of the Ontario legislature was that procedures under the *Code* were to be the only procedures available to a person who alleged discrimination.

The Alberta *Individual's Rights Protection Act*

The Act prohibits discrimination by reason of race, religious beliefs, colour, sex, physical characteristics, age, ancestry, or place of origin. The Act applies to renting accommodation, advertisements, services, employment, trade unions, and public services.

It is illegal for any person to display any notice or sign for the purpose of discrimination. Job application forms cannot request information concerning the subjects of prohibited discrimination and employers cannot ask applicants to include photographs.

Employers must pay males and females equal pay for work of similar nature.

Sexual harassment is prohibited. This is defined as unwanted sexual solicitation made by a person in a position of authority. An employer who knows that one employee is harassing other employees, yet takes no corrective action, may be liable.

The Newfoundland *Human Rights Code*

The Act generally establishes as prohibited grounds of discrimination race, religion, religious creed, political opinion, colour, or ethnic, national or social origin. Areas covered under the Act include public accommodation, commercial and dwelling units, employment, trade unions, job applications, advertisements concerning employment, and publications.

The Act requires that male and female workers be paid the same under the following conditions. The workers are employed in the same establishment;

working under the same conditions; doing the same or similar work; doing jobs requiring the same or similar skill, effort, and responsibility.

Exclusions

In nearly all provinces, the human rights statutes do not apply to private organizations, religious orders, or charitable institutions. There are various other exclusions including certain occupations which are very personal in nature such as a "live-in" companion or homemaker. Organizations such as the Girl Scouts have not been required to accept male applicants; and, in Ontario, the Court of Appeal held that a boys' hockey league did not have to allow a girl to play on a team (*Re Cummings*, 1979).

Reviewing Important Points

1. Section 2 of the *Charter of Rights and Freedoms* affirms that everyone has the fundamental freedoms of religion, expression, press, and assembly.
2. None of the great documents in the world purporting to protect freedom of religion defines "religion."
3. Only the federal government would have the power to place direct limitations upon freedom of the press.
4. In Canada, newspaper reporters have no "privilege" to protect their news sources.
5. An unlawful assembly is generally defined as a gathering of three or more persons who are disturbing the peace tumultuously.
6. There is no common law or historic right of persons to hold protest demonstrations upon public property.
7. The Canadian *Bill of Rights* was not repealed when the *Charter of Rights and Freedoms* was enacted.
8. Section 15 of the *Charter of Rights and Freedoms*, which prohibits discrimination, does not take effect until 1985.

Checking Your Understanding

1. What is the accepted interpretation of "freedom of religion"?

2. What was Quebec's "Padlock Law"? Against whom was it directed? What did the Supreme Court of Canada decide about this law?

3. What was the Alberta *Press Bill*? Why was it passed? What did the Supreme Court of Canada decide about it?

4. Freedom of the press has never been an absolute freedom. State two examples where the press could be prohibited from publishing something.

5. Why does the *Charter of Rights and Freedoms* protect freedom of *peaceful* assembly rather than just freedom of assembly?

6. What is meant by saying that "discrimination per se" is not unconstitutional or illegal in Canada?

7. Did the *Charter of Rights* create any new rights or freedoms for Canadians? If so, name as many as you can.

Legal Briefs

1. H was charged with indecent assault upon a male person and was sentenced to seven years in prison. Indecent assault upon a female person carried a maximum penalty of only five years in prison. H appealed on the ground that the law was discriminatory and that the sentence should be reduced. Valid ground of appeal?

2. S, an inmate in a federal penitentiary, refused to shave. He was forcibly shaved by four guards and suffered injury. He argued that his right of "security of the person," as guaranteed by the *Charter of Rights*, was violated. Is S correct?

3. D was arrested on a drug charge and held in custody. She brought an action requesting that the court order her release under s. 6(1) of the *Charter* which states that "Every citizen of Canada has the right to enter, remain in, and leave Canada." D proved that she is a Canadian citizen and expressed a wish to leave Canada. Should she be released?

4. J, a naturalized Canadian citizen, entered Canada in 1947. In 1982, a West German court indicted him for war crimes committed in 1942-1943 and sought his return to Germany to stand trial. J argued that under s. 6(1) of the *Charter* he could not be extradited against his wishes. Can J remain in Canada?

5. R was arrested for unlawful possession of marijuana. At his trial R asserted that marijuana was an important element in his religion. It helped him to communicate with God and to better perceive good and evil in the world. Will freedom of religion excuse R?

6. Q refused to rent an apartment to a couple of Asian origin. When questioned by an investigator from the Human Rights Commission, Q replied that she had nothing against Asians but that she "preferred" white tenants. "Given four applicants," she said, "cannot a person choose the one she likes most? Must I take the first person who applies?" How would you respond to Q's question?

7. B was charged with break and enter. As she had a very long criminal record, her lawyer advised B not to take the witness stand because the Crown could ask her about her record. B sought to have the trial judge permit her to testify without being asked about her record. Her motion was based upon the claim that, if the Crown could ask about her record, then her right "to be presumed innocent until proven guilty" would be denied. Do you agree with B?

8. G brought an action against the federal government alleging that the *Indian Act* discriminated against her. Under the *Indian Act*, the Crown is the administrator of the estate of every male Indian who dies while living on a reserve. An Indian man cannot name his wife as the administratrix of his estate, but a white man can do so. Discrimination?

9. L, a Jewish storekeeper, wanted to operate her business on Sunday. The Jewish Sabbath is Saturday, not Sunday. L argued that because Sunday is the Christian Sabbath she was being denied freedom of religion by not being permitted to operate her business on Sunday. Is L correct?

10. M, a Moslem, applied to enter Canada as an immigrant. On his application M stated that he had three

wives to whom he was lawfully married under the laws of his native land. Would M be permitted to bring his three wives with him?

Applying the Law

Saumur v. City of Quebec and A.G. for Quebec
Supreme Court of Canada, 1953

A by-law for the City of Quebec provided penalties to any person who distributed in the streets of the city any book, pamphlet, tract, circular, or other publication without the written permission of the Chief of Police. Members of the Jehovah's Witnesses distributed their literature contrary to the by-law. Saumur was among those charged with violation of the law. The case was appealed to the Supreme Court of Canada which held that the by-law was ultra vires the City of Quebec. The decision includes this wording:

> **"**From 1760 onward, religious freedom has been recognized as a fundamental principle in the Canadian legal system, and the statutory history of the expression 'property and civil rights' shows tha matters of religious belief were never intended to be within s. 92(13) of the B.N.A. Act [now the *Constitution Act, 1867*]. The conclusion is that freedom of religion is outside of provincial legislation, and neither a newspaper or a religious tract can be placed under the uncontrolled discretion of a municipal officer in respect of its sales or distribution through use of streets.**"**

Questions

1. According to the Supreme Court, which level of government does *not* have jurisdiction over freedom of religion and its exercise? Did the court specifically say that any level of government could restrict freedom of religion?
2. Some religious groups are very aggressive in trying to sell literature. There have been complaints of people blocking escalators, entrances to buildings, and church property. Should a city not be able to prohibit such activity? Does the *Saumur* decision suggest that a city could never interfere with this activity? Why or why not?
3. Compare *Saumur* (1953) with the case of *Dupond* (1978). Does the court appear to be saying that the streets are available, without limitation, for distributing or selling religious ideas, but not available for political ideas? Why or why not? Has the decision in *Dupond* made the earlier decision of *Saumur* ineffective? Why or why not?

Cronan v. Minister of Manpower and Immigration
Immigration Appeal Board, 1973

Cronan was denied admission to Canada on the ground that he had been a past member of the Communist Party. He had been unable to obtain from the Department any indication as to how he could satisfy the Minister that he had ceased all association with the Communist Party or any subversive organization. He brought an action on the ground that he was denied a fair hearing as required under the *Bill of Rights* and that his freedom of association and expression was being used unlawfully as a reason to deny him admission to Canada. The appeal board ruled that as entry into Canada is a privilege, not a right, the appellant could not claim the protection of the *Bill of Rights*. The board stated:

> **"**Would ... Cronan have acquired the right to enter Canada? The answer is 'No,' because all immigrants or non-immigrants, who are admitted, enter Canada not by right but as a privilege.**"**

Questions

1. Does the *Bill of Rights* extend only to persons resident in Canada?
2. Would the case be decided differently under the new *Charter of Rights and Freedoms*? Why or why not?
3. What is the distinction between a right and a privilege? Would the *Charter* extend to privileges as well as rights? For example, if driving an automobile is a privilege, would there be any legal recourse for a person whose driver's licence was revoked without any reason? Why or why not?

You Be the Judge

1. H, a landed immigrant in Canada, committed a serious offence and was ordered deported back to her country of origin. H had a child who was born in Canada. The father of the child was not married to H, but the father was a Canadian citizen. H's counsel argued that if H was deported she would have to take her child with her and that this would be a violation of the child's constitutional rights. The Crown argued that the child would have the right to later return to Canada and assert her citizenship. There was no right of the mother to remain in Canada simply because she had a child who was a citizen of Canada. Who would succeed?

2. L, an Indian, was charged with murder and elected trial by judge and jury. Counsel for L made a request that all members of the jury should be Indians. The motion was based upon the contention that the accused had the right to be tried by his peers in an impartial tribunal. The argument continued by alleging that an Indian could only get a fair trial if judged by other Indians. The Crown contested this claim and stated that jurors should be selected by the usual procedure. Who would succeed?

3. The complainant alleged that he had been fired from his job because the employer had discriminated against him by reason of his religion. The complainant was a Sikh and his religion required that he wear a turban and beard. The job he held was that of a security guard. The company had a policy that all guards must wear a uniform, which included a cap and badge, and that all guards must be clean shaven. The company fired the complainant when he would not shave and could not wear the hat. Who would succeed?

4. A woman complained of sex discrimination, alleging that a slogan in a local restaurant was offensive and promoted a negative image of women. The sign read: "If your wife can't cook, don't divorce her. Keep her as a pet and eat at this restaurant." Under the provincial law, it is illegal for any person to publish or display any notice, sign, symbol, or emblem for the purpose of discrimination because of sex. The restaurant explained that its sign was meant only to be humorous and was not to be taken seriously. It refused to remove the sign. Who would succeed?

5. A female teacher married a divorced man. The marriage took place outside the church and she was fired from her teaching job by the Catholic School Board that employed her. The Board felt that it had the right to insist upon minimal codes of conduct and moral example from its teachers. The teacher complained to the Human Rights Commission that she had been unjustly dismissed for reasons which were religious in nature and that this violated her freedom of religion. Who would succeed?

Unit
Five

The Law
of Torts

"The rule that you are to love your neighbour becomes, in law, you must not injure your neighbour."

*Lord Atkin, in
Donoghue v. Stevenson*

Chapter 10

Intentional Torts

What Is a Tort?

From 1066 A.D. until the end of the Middle Ages, French was the official language of British courts. While only a handful of French legal terms remain in usage in our common law, one survivor is the word "tort." The root word is *torquere* which is Latin for "to twist." It is very difficult to construct a single definition that encompasses every possible aspect of a tort, but generally a tort can be defined as wrongful or injurious misconduct committed by the defendant outside of a contractual obligation, redressible by some appropriate legal action brought by the plaintiff.

It could be said that there are an "infinite" number of torts because there are an "infinite" number of ways to wrong another person. Despite centuries of slow development, the process of creating new torts is not concluded. The law is capable of establishing new torts as new circumstances arise.

A tort must have several basic characteristics. First, it must cause harm. The person alleging harm and starting a lawsuit is called the *plaintiff*. The plaintiff files a *writ*, alleging injury by the *defendant* and asking the court to award some form of remedy for this injury.

Second, a tort must be recognized by the law as coming within a broad area of actions for which the injured person should be compensated. For example, at one time the law did not recognize nervous suffering as an injury for which a person could be compensated. Today, nervous suffering is so recognized.

Third, to constitute a tort the actions of the defendant must violate a duty or responsibility owing to the injured person. It must be shown that the defendant did not have a right to do what was done and that the plaintiff has a right to redress.

Fourth, in order for the plaintiff to commence an action in tort, there must be no specific remedy provided by statute. If there is an established system to deal with the plaintiff's problem, no action lies in tort. Thus, in 1981, the Supreme Court of Canada held in *Bhadauria v. Seneca College* that "discrimination" is not a tort since there were specific provincial laws to deal with allegations of discrimination.

Some torts are intentional, others unintentional. The circumstances may vary enough that it is sometimes difficult to separate the two. It is generally thought that tort law is not concerned with the state of mind of the defendant (also called the *tortfeasor*), but only with the defendant's actions. This is true for some torts, but not all. Some torts contain an element of *malice* or deliberate intent to injure the plaintiff. For example, if a political candidate decides to injure an opponent's reputation by forging a letter, allegedly written by the opponent, in which disparaging remarks are made about certain minority groups, this would be an intentional tort. There is nothing accidental about it and the *malice* shown would be of great importance to the court.

A different example would be a careless driver who runs a red light and smashes into another vehicle. The court would not be concerned with any discussion about whether the negligent driver intended to hit the other vehicle, but only about the manner of the person's driving.

Intentional torts generally include interference with another individual's person, land, goods, or reputation. Other torts are normally thought of as unintentional.

Certain torts have developed in such a way that specific defences have been recognized by the courts. Where these defences have become very refined, they will be discussed in a separate section. Other torts do not have defences quite so refined and the primary task of the defence is only to refute the claims made by the plaintiff.

It can be said that tort law serves four purposes: justice, compensation, appeasement, and deterrence. The plaintiff wants justice done, compensation for a loss, a soothing of hurt feelings, and a warning to the defendant and others not to do the same thing again. To a certain extent, tort law is a giant ombudsman, since every court in Canada is potentially available to every citizen who feels wronged. Tort law encompasses the doctrine, *ubi jus ibi remedium* which means "Where there is a right, there is a remedy."

Certain types of statutes have reduced, to some extent, the importance of tort law. For example, in all the provinces there is legislation to provide a universal coverage for injured workers, thus prohibiting any private lawsuit.

Who Can Commit Torts?

Tort law does not apply the same rules of mental capacity as do criminal law or contract law. Tort law is concerned more with action than intent. A bad intention does not necessarily make damages actionable, and a good intention is not necessarily a defence. Children may commit torts under many circumstances and a section of this unit will deal with children's torts. Persons of unsound mind can commit unintentional torts unless they are so mentally disturbed as to be incapable of voluntary action.

A husband and wife are not responsible for the torts committed by the other just because of the marital relationship. In most provinces, a husband and wife cannot sue each other in tort as they are deemed to be one legal person. There is a gradual movement away from this historic prohibition. Ontario law now permits husbands and wives to sue each other for injuries to person or property.

A corporation may sue and be sued in its own name. Principals are liable for the torts committed by their agents in the course of their duties, and employers are liable for torts committed by their employees within the scope of their employment. In such situations, the injured party would sue both the employer and the employee. Partners are liable for torts committed by other partners within the scope of the business partnership. The Crown is liable in tort for actions committed by employees of the Crown, provided the employees would be found liable if they were sued directly.

Intentional Interference with Another Person

The common law has long held that individuals should be free to conduct their daily affairs free from threats, injury, or confinement by others. It is a tort for anyone, without lawful excuse, to do any of these things.

Assault and Battery

Although the words *assault* and *battery* are often used interchangeably, they are two distinct torts. The confusion in usage arises from the circumstance that the two often occur together, or in rapid succession.

Assault represents the threat by one person to commit bodily harm to another person, with the reasonable belief by the other person that the wrongdoer has the present ability to carry out the threat. It is said that, "Assault takes place in the mind of the victim." This means that if the victim feels real mental apprehension it is assault, even if the attacker had no real intention to carry out the threat.

Battery involves the actual application of violence against the victim by the defendant. Such violence need not be major or substantial. The least touching of a person can be battery. It is essential that the defendant do something which *directly* affects the victim. Thus, if the defendant threw a rock at the victim, it is battery. If the defendant digs a pit so that the victim will fall into it, it is not battery.

Assault and battery are intentional torts. The accidental touching of another person is not a tort.

Assault can be verbal. It can be a gesture such as picking up a weapon and waving it menacingly. Bat-tery does not have to cause serious harm. It could include actions such as striking, shoving, pouring water upon the person, spitting, kissing, clipping hair, and many other actions. It does not have to be an action with malice. A practical joke could be battery. This happened in a case where the defendant deliberately pulled a chair away from the plaintiff who was about to sit down.

Battery is the unauthorized touching of another person. Brawls and other violence in sports have led to an increased number of civil actions by injured players.

Bruce v. Dyer
Ontario, 1966

The defendant, attempting to pass a line of cars, was unable to do so because of an oncoming vehicle and attempted to pull into the space between the first and second cars. The plaintiff in the second car, accelerated and closed the gap so that the defendant was forced to fall back and enter the space between the second and third cars. Thereafter, the plaintiff claimed that the defendant drove with his high beams on in retaliation. The defendant admitted this but said it was a passing signal and that on each occasion the plaintiff accelerated to prevent him from passing. After the defendant had followed the plaintiff for about ten miles (sixteen kilometres), the plaintiff stopped his car on the paved portion of the highway, gesturing with his fist. The defendant was forced to stop behind the plaintiff. The plaintiff got out of his car and came towards the defendant, still gesturing with his fist. The two met, and the defendant struck the plaintiff. The plaintiff's jaw had been weakened by bone disease and he suffered a serious fracture. In an action for damages for assault and battery, it was held that the plaintiff had committed an assault upon the defendant when he stopped his car in such a way that the defendant could not drive around him. Refusal to let a person pass, when he had a right to do so, was an assault. The plaintiff continued that assault by gesturing at the defendant. The defendant was justified in defending himself. He used no more force than was reasonably necessary. The plaintiff had endangered the life of the defendant and his family and invited the treatment he received. The plaintiff's case was dismissed.

Medical Assault and Battery

A physician who treats a patient or performs an operation must first obtain the consent of the patient. Consent requires that the patient be fully informed of the nature of the medical procedure, the risks, and the alternatives; and that the patient voluntarily give consent. Often a form is signed for this purpose. If anything is done beyond what the patient consented to, the form is of little significance. The consent form only gives permission to perform the operation. The form does not excuse negligence, no matter how it is worded. If the patient is unconscious, the doctor may apply procedures necessary to protect life and safety, but no more. Any further treatment must be postponed until the patient can give consent. In a surgical assault and battery case, the patient is not complaining about the adequacy of treatment, but about the fact that the treatment was done at all.

Mulloy v. Hop Sang
Alberta, 1935

The plaintiff doctor sued for professional fees for an operation involving the amputation of the defendant's hand which was badly injured in an automobile accident. The defendant would not pay the fees and counterclaimed for battery. The doctor was called to the hospital and examined the patient's hand which was covered by a piece of dirty cloth. The patient said he wanted the doctor to "fix" his hand but not to amputate it. He said he would prefer to have it looked after in his home town of Lethbridge. The doctor replied that he would be governed by the conditions which he found when anaesthetic had been administered. The patient did not reply to these words by the doctor. On examination, the doctor found the hand could not be saved and amputated it. Given that the patient understood little English and had given explicit instructions not to amputate, the trial judge found that the doctor was not justified in taking the patient's failure to respond to the doctor's last words as some form of consent. The amputation was necessary. It was done in a professional manner, but it was done without the patient's consent and could have been done in Lethbridge as the patient preferred. The trial judge held:

"It might have been different if the defendant had submitted himself generally to the doctor and had pleaded with him not to perform an operation and the doctor had found it necessary to do so afterwards. The defendant's instructions were precedent and went to the root of the employment. The plaintiff did not do the work he was hired to do, and must, in my opinion, fail in his action. **"**

The judge then concluded that the defendant was entitled to damages of $50 for the shock of having his hand amputated despite his instructions to the contrary.

The key to cases of surgical assault is whether the operation was immediately necessary or whether it could wait. In *Marshall v. Curry* (Nova Scotia, 1933), a doctor performing a hernia operation also removed a diseased testicle. The judge held that a surgeon acting in order to save the life of the patient is not exposed to liability.

Surgical assault may arise as an issue if a member of a religious denomination is given a medical treatment which is prohibited by that person's religion. In most provinces the consent of a parent is required if a patient is under the age of sixteen. If consent is withheld, a guardian may be appointed by the court; consent may then be given to apply medical treatment.

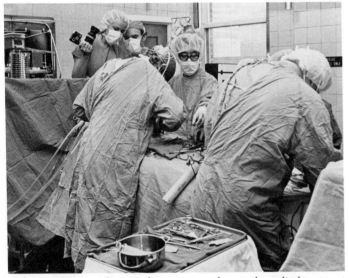

A patient who sues a doctor for battery sues not because the medical treatment was inadequate, but because the treatment was done without consent.

False Imprisonment

Historically, people have struggled against all comers for the right to remain at liberty. "Liberty" in its purest sense means freedom to move at will. False imprisonment violates people's liberty as well as their dignity. To give a formal definition: False imprisonment is the unlawful restraint or coercion of persons against their will and without justification, subjecting them to a total restraint of movement by causing their confinement or preventing them from leaving the place where they are.

If someone has voluntarily consented to be restrained, that person cannot later sue. The emphasis is upon the impression created in the victim's mind, which is very similar to the feeling of apprehension felt when assault is committed. A partial restraint does not constitute imprisonment. For example, if there are two doors leading out of a room, and a person blocks one of them, the alleged victim cannot claim to have been imprisoned when it is obvious he or she could have gone out the other door. Unintentionally confining a person does not constitute false imprisonment; but if the person suffers harm it is still possible to sue for negligence. For example, if a person carelessly locked someone inside a deep freeze locker, not knowing the person was inside, the suit would allege negligence, not false imprisonment. To deprive a person of freedom for even a short period of time is usually considered to be imprisonment. If the driver of a car proceeds at such a speed as to prevent a passenger from getting out, or if a person is set adrift in a boat, or if submission is obtained by misusing authority such as the power of arrest, these would all constitute false imprisonment.

Chaytor et al. v. London, New York and Paris Association of Fashion Ltd. and Price Newfoundland, 1961

The plaintiffs, Vera Chaytor and John Delgado, were employees of Bowring Brothers, Ltd., a department store in St. John's, Newfoundland. On the day in question they went across the street and entered the department store of the defendant, a competitor, in order to do some "comparison shopping." In other words, they wished to look over their competitor's goods and prices. They were stopped by Price, the manager of the defendant store, who called them "spies," asked his store detectives to watch them, and called the police to arrest them as "suspicious characters." The plaintiffs accompanied the police in order to avoid embarrassment and because they felt compelled to do so. They were detained for about fifteen minutes at the police station and were then released without any charges being laid. They sued Price and his employer for false imprisonment. The court held that although they were not physically mishandled, they were "psychologically imprisoned" because of the threat implied in having store detectives standing over them. They felt that they were not free to leave and that to try to do so would only bring more public humiliation. The situation amounted to false imprisonment and the plaintiffs were awarded damages.

Defences to Assault, Battery, and False Imprisonment

There are several defences which the defendant could raise if sued for assault, battery, or false imprisonment. One defence is consent. If the plaintiff consented to the action, then there can be no liability upon the defendant. The consent must have been a truly "informed consent" which means that the plaintiff fully understood what was going to take place.

Another defence is self-defence. It may be raised as a defence whenever the defendant used force to ward off an attack or to protect other persons. A person in control of land is entitled to use reasonable force to remove a trespasser, provided the removal would not put the trespasser into a position of danger.

A parent or teacher is authorized by the criminal law to use force upon a child or pupil by way of correction, as long as the force is not excessive.

It is also a defence to show that the touching was not intentional, since assault and battery are intentional

torts. If a person is bumped in a crowded elevator, it is not actionable. Being indecently touched in a crowded elevator would be actionable.

Provocation is not a defence. However, if the court finds that there is provocation, it is likely the damages will be reduced.

Inflicting Nervous Suffering

Injury can take the form of an illness resulting from nervous shock. It must, however, be an actual illness; mere anguish or fright is not enough. Courts are willing to recognize that injury can be inflicted upon the nervous system of a person and that this can cause other complications, even death. The injury may or may not have been intentional. Intentional injury is more likely to be actionable in court.

 Wilkinson v. Downton
England, 1897
Downton told the plaintiff that her husband had suffered two broken legs. He said the husband had sent him to tell her to bring two pillows and fetch him home. The story was false, a prank invented by Downton. The plaintiff suffered mental and emotional shock and was ill for several weeks after. The court awarded her damages for her injury.

This early case was significant because it was one of the first that recognized such a thing as emotional illness.

The law does not require each person to have the same amount of intestinal fortitude, only a *reasonable* amount. That is, ignorance of the fact that the victim was already nervous or squeamish does not excuse the injury, but the excessively timid soul who faints at any unpleasantness cannot claim damages.

The source of the shock cannot be too remote. This means the relationship between the accident and the resulting injury must be close enough for it to be said that the defendant could reasonably have foreseen that what was being done was going to cause someone nervous shock.

Hay v. Young
England, 1943

Hay, who was pregnant at the time, was getting off a bus when she nearly witnessed a motorcycle collide with a car only a short distance away. She did not see the actual impact, but was jolted by the noise of the collision. The motorcycle operator was killed, and Hay saw the body. Later, when the body was removed, the large amount of blood still on the street caused her to experience "instant nervous jangling." She did not improve and was hospitalized. Later, her child was stillborn. She sued the estate of the dead cyclist for nervous shock. The court rejected her suit contending it was too remote to say that the cyclist could have foreseen causing her or anyone nervous shock.

Trespass

Trespass to Land

Originally, trespass meant only that a person entered someone else's property for the purpose of trying to deprive the owner of it. This action frequently led to violence—even to death. Therefore, the king's agents were called to remove the trespasser before someone was killed. Later, as boundaries became more fixed and the problem of encroachments and squatters became more widespread, the meaning of trespass expanded to include any illegal entry of property regardless of purpose. A present-day definition of trespass would be the act of entering someone's land without invitation and without the knowledge or consent of the owner.

Trespass may be intentional or unintentional. An intentional trespass can result in damages being awarded to the owner regardless of whether or not any damage was done to the property. The trespasser's reasons for entering do not excuse the trespass, nor does the fact that the trespasser is unaware that entry is forbidden. If no property damage is done, the amount the court would award would be relatively small in most cases. If damage did occur, the court

would normally award a sum equal to the property damage done, and often an additional sum as a deterrent or punishment for unruly behaviour.

An authorized or accidental entry of land may be permissible when it starts, but become trespass later. If a person refuses to leave when ordered to do so by the owner, that person becomes a trespasser regardless of the manner of entry. The owner has a right to use reasonable force to evict the trespasser. Therefore, a homeowner has a right to forcibly evict an unwanted person from the house. However, a criminal charge against the property owner may result unless the trespasser is allowed to leave of his or her own accord. Only reasonable force may be used to remove a trespasser who will not go. If a trespasser strikes a person who is lawfully removing him or her from the property, the trespasser commits assault and battery.

A property owner cannot set traps or arrange dangerous configurations to injure trespassers. To do so is a criminal offence.

All provinces have a statute similar to Ontario's *Trespass Act* which makes trespassing an offence punishable by a fine. The property owner or peace officer may make an arrest under the Act; this should be sufficient to discourage repeated trespassing.

Trespass to Chattel Property

Not all property is land. Much of it is movable property such as cars, furniture, jewellery, clothing, etc. This type of property is known as *chattels*.

The common law provides for actions against persons who interfere with chattels belonging to others. Stealing is the most obvious example, for thieves intend to remove the stolen chattels permanently from their owners and deprive them of ownership. But stealing and taking are not necessarily the same thing. For example, the law distinctly separates car theft from joy-riding. Car theft implies an intention to keep the car or parts of it. Joy-riding involves only illegal use of the car which will eventually be returned to the owner.

There are various ways that a person may commit trespass to chattel property. They are generally grouped into one of these two categories:

Conversion: This is a tort involving interference with the goods of another which denies that other's right or title to the goods. Refusing to let the owner have goods which have been sold to him or her; disposing of goods which belong to someone else; delivering or selling goods to a third party; and destroying goods to prevent the owner from having them are all examples of conversion.

Detinue: An action for detinue alleges that the defendant is wrongfully withholding chattels from the owner. The defendant does not deny title and does not intend to convert the chattels, but he or she will not return them. Such a situation normally arises when the defendant believes a valid counterclaim against the owner exists and is holding the goods as security against that claim.

While trespass to chattels is usually done intentionally, it may be done accidentally. Yet, the wrongdoer remains liable. For example, even if a defendant believes, although mistakenly, that the chattel is his or hers, or that the owner consented to the taking of it, the defendant is still liable.

Consolidated Company v. Curtis
England, 1892

Curtis was an auctioneer who sold chattels entrusted to him by a client. The chattels were not the property of the client; they belonged to Consolidated. After he was paid, the client disappeared and Consolidated sued Curtis for conversion. Curtis pleaded ignorance in the matter, contending he was only an agent for someone else. The court held him liable, even though he was ignorant of the true facts, since it was he who had deprived the owner of the use of the chattels and transferred them to someone else.

Refusing To Return Property

Merely having possession of another's property is not necessarily wrong. If you find a wallet on the street, it would be reasonable to pick it up and retain it for the owner. A person who rents goods and does not return them on time may be guilty of breach of contract, but not conversion. Nor does the finder of goods have to hand them over if the alleged owner cannot establish to the finder's satisfaction that he or she really is the lawful owner. A person who advertises finding a large sum of money will be pursued by many false claimants. It is reasonable that the person invent some test to identify the true owner. In fact, if a finder carelessly surrendered chattels to a false claimant, the true owner might hold the finder liable for conversion for delivering up chattels to the wrong person.

Finders Keepers

Ordinarily, the person who finds a chattel acquires a good title of ownership to it against all others, except the true owner.

The question of where the chattel was found may have a great deal to do with the case. Courts have generally held that the land owner has the better claim to anything found on his or her land, regardless of who found it. If something is found on public property, it comes under the possessory title of the person who finds it.

In most cases, after a reasonable effort has been made to locate the true owner, the chattel reverts to the finder.

Defences to Trespass

There are three defences most commonly raised by the defendant against an action for trespass. The first is consent. The giving of consent could be written, oral, or implied by the plaintiff's actions. For example, if a contract authorizes a person making repairs to hold goods until paid, there is no trespass. The second defence is legal authority. If a statute authorizes a certain action, no action lies against the defendant who acts within the confines of this authority. If a statute authorizes an inspector to enter premises without notice or warrant, the inspector does not trespass in making such an entry. The third defence is necessity. If a passerby enters private property to put out a fire or effect a rescue, it is not trespass.

Defamation

An action for defamation offers the injured person legal remedies for injury to reputation. The word "fame" suggests a status of recognition and honour. To defame a person is to remove this status and injure the esteem that other people hold for the person. Therefore, defamation is not a tort because it hurts a person's pride or self-respect, but rather because the person's good name and status in the community have been hurt.

Defamation can be committed by various methods. Generally, tort law attempts to divide defamation into two categories, *libel* and *slander*. Libel includes those statements which are printed, written, filmed, or recorded in a permanent manner. Slander includes oral statements only.

Our civil courts now hold that libel is far more serious than slander, and the amounts of money awarded in libel cases are far greater than in slander cases. The general reason is that libel endures longer than slander. Slander is usually a one-time thing. The only audience to hear it are the immediate listeners. Slander is usually something said on the spur of the moment, in an instant of anger or carelessness, and often regretted. Libel, on the other hand, may have a greater audience. If it is printed in newspapers, magazines, or handbills, the readers may number in the millions. If printed in books, the libel occurs over and over again as long as future generations read that particular book.

Slander

To sue a person for slander successfully is not necessarily easy. A case for slander must establish the following:

The Statements Were Made Public
As mentioned, defamation is not injury to self-pride or personal esteem, but loss of public esteem. If a nasty comment is made only to the person involved and no third party hears it, then it cannot be said to have caused a loss of public esteem for the simple reason that the public did not hear it. The legal requirement is that the slander has escaped the privacy of the speaker and the listener and has reached a third party. Whether this was intentional or accidental does not matter. One case concerned remarks made by someone to a colleague when they were alone in an office. The remarks were meant to be made in private, but they were overheard by a secretary in the next room because the office walls were thin. The court consequently found them to be slanderous. It is not slander if the injured party repeats what was said to third persons. Therefore, if a person went about asking, "Did you hear what Smith said to me?" and then repeated their conversation, the person would merely be slandering his or her own self.

The Statements Must Cause Actual Harm to Reputation
A person cannot succeed in a slander suit because he or she is touchy and sensitive to criticism. The injury must be determinable in some form of financial loss or lowering of community status. The court holds that slander must be such that "right-thinking" persons in the community might be led to believe it. The loss of friends is not grounds for suit, for as the court held in one case, "They were not true friends who would believe slander and desert the plaintiff." The plaintiff must be prepared to show how the damage arose and what value could be placed upon it. The plaintiff must also show that damages suffered were a direct result of the slander and not too remote. A suit for slander will fail if it can be shown that no one believed what was said. In this situation there would be no loss of prestige in the community.

Mere name-calling does not necessarily qualify as slander, although it may constitute assault. Name-calling is essentially abuse aimed at a person's pride, not his or her community standing. Much also depends on the tone of voice, the manner of the conversation, and the purpose that the speaker had in mind. It is not actionable slander to make derogatory remarks about a group so large that it is impossible to say that the comment was aimed at one individual.

Slander may be made by innuendo, or by a remark that is an attempt to hide who it is aimed at but permits anyone to recognize the subject simply by reading between the lines.

Albrecht v. Burkholder
Ontario, 1889

The plaintiff was one of a family of four unmarried daughters. The defendant said to another man that he heard Charlie Brayley had gotten "one of the Albrecht girls in trouble." The plaintiff sued for slander when this statement was reported to her. The defendant based his defence upon the fact that he said "one of the Albrecht girls" but did not say which one, and that the word "trouble" is a harmless word that can mean many things, not necessarily pregnancy as the plaintiff assumed. It was easy for the counsel for the plaintiff to establish that of the four daughters, two were very young and that only the plaintiff and her other sister could have been the one. Since the plaintiff was the only sister to have been in the company of Charlie Brayley, the innuendo was sufficient to point directly to the plaintiff and no one else. The counsel introduced evidence to show that right-thinking persons in the community would have understood the word "trouble" to mean pregnancy when used in this context. The trial judge reluctantly dismissed the case on the grounds that the plaintiff could not definitely establish that the remarks were made about her and not one of her sisters. The judge did agree that "trouble" meant pregnancy in the sense it was used, and pointed out that the defendant had won his case only on the technicality that he did not mention any woman by name. The judge would not allow the defendant to recover his court costs because he was wrong in speaking innuendoes about the character of young women and to date had never attempted to apologize.

Slander Per Se

In certain cases, the plaintiff may succeed without proving actual loss from slander. In such cases, the nature of the slander is so vile *per se* ("in itself") that it is assumed that some loss must have occurred. For example, if the plaintiff is accused by the defendant of taking part in a crime, of having a criminal record, of having some loathsome disease, of being unfit or dishonest in his or her business or profession, or of having been immoral or unchaste, then the plaintiff may succeed without having to prove either loss of status in the community or financial loss. The only element of proof that need be shown in these special cases is that the defendant did in fact make the statement publicly.

Libel

The tort of libel lies in the publication of the defamation in a permanent form, e.g., in writing, printing, carving, drawing, film, photograph, record, or sound tape. Since the damages for libel are usually greater than for slander, and the proof required less stringent since permanent evidence exists, it is advantageous to the plaintiff to show that a statement is libel, not slander.

Through a variety of cases, it has been held that any public broadcast of defamatory words or images is libel. Public broadcast includes radio, television, and film presentations. Ontario and British Columbia have specific statutes designating such broadcasts to be libel.

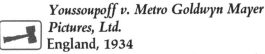

Youssoupoff v. Metro Goldwyn Mayer Pictures, Ltd.
England, 1934

Metro Goldwyn Mayer produced a movie about the Russian monk, Rasputin, and his influence over the Czar and Czarina. The film also showed the murder of Rasputin. In the film, a woman named Natasha was shown to have relations with Rasputin which involved either seduction or rape (the viewer cannot be certain). The plaintiff was a member of the Czar's household, Princess Irina Alexandrovna, who was married to Prince Youssoupoff. The prince is depicted in the film as being one of the assassins of Rasputin. The plaintiff sued the film company because it was obvious that people would believe she was the same person as Natasha and because her husband was defamed and the family name discredited. She was successful in her suit and was awarded £25 000 damages.

The film company appealed. The appeal court had to deal with several questions, the first being whether it was libel or slander. The elements of proof would be different accordingly. It was held to be libel. The second question was whether or not right-thinking people would believe that Natasha was Irina. The court held that they would. Lastly, was the fim defamatory? The court held that to suggest that a woman had relations with another man, whether she was seduced or ravished, still held her up to ridicule or contempt. The appeal was dismissed and damages were not reduced.

Libel does not have to be intentional. That is, if a person intentionally publishes what he or she believes to be harmless material and it turns out to be libel, that person is responsible even though no harm was meant. At the same time, if a person writes something that is defamatory but does not intend any publication whatever, and the words are accidentally published or viewed by a third party, the person is responsible. For example, if a writer sends a nasty letter addressed to a person and that person's private secretary opens the letter along with the other mail, then the letter has been published in the true meaning of the word and constitutes libel.

It is important to note that there is a time limitation in defamation cases. In most provinces a notice in writing, complaining of the objectionable material, must be served on the defendant within six weeks to two months after the plaintiff first becomes aware of the defamation. The lawsuit must be commenced within three to six months later, differing from province to province. The defendant may wish to print a correction or a complete retraction in order to apologize and to minimize possible damages. However, this does not excuse the matter completely.

Generally, the law does not recognize defamation of a deceased person as actionable. Unfortunate as this

may be for the reputation of a deceased person, the basic obstacle is that a deceased person has no legal standing and family members can only bring an action if their personal reputations also suffered.

10 The Toronto Sun, Tuesday June 9, 1981

Toronto's Other Voice
DOUGLAS CREIGHTON, Publisher
DONALD HUNT, General Manager
PETER WORTHINGTON, Editor in Chief
ED MONTEITH, Managing Editor
THOMAS PEDDIE, Treasurer
J.D. MacFARLANE, Editorial Director
Proprietor — The Toronto Sun Publishing Corporation
333 King St. E Toronto M5A 3X5, 947 2222

EDWARD DUNLOP, President 1971-1981

We were wrong

When this newspaper was formed almost 10 years ago, our first editorial promised we would be outspoken, independent and masters of our own newsroom.

We said we would depend on readers, and readers could depend on us. We were sensitive to the fact that starting a tabloid could result in odious comparisons with other tabloids. And we tried to ensure that our news coverage was good, honest, fair.

The success of our efforts is obvious from the public acceptance of the paper.

Nor have we stopped being contentious, opinionated, provocative. None of which is incompatible with fair and honest coverage.

Last week the *Sun* ran a story linking the Honorable John Munro, Minister of Indian and Northern Affairs, to the purchase and sale of Petrofina shares, prior to that company's takeover, through a company in which we said he was a director.

The story also linked Jack Pelech, Mr. Munro's former law partner, to the same transaction. It also linked Maurice Strong with the purchase and sale of Petrofina shares through a Swiss company.

The reporters who uncovered this story assured their editors of factual, documented back-up for it. The editors accepted this without examining the documents in detail.

In fact the newspaper has no such documented information as it relates to Messrs Munro, Pelech or Strong, and the allegations are unfounded.

The story also indicated that Wallace McCain of Florenceville, N.B., purchased 8,000 Petrofina shares. The suggestion that Wallace McCain had, or made use of any inside information in the acquisition of 8,000 shares of Petrofina Canada Ltd. in October, 1980, is unfounded in fact.

To be unable to substantiate a story which received widespread distribution requires, of course, that we not only apologize unequivocally to Messrs Munro, Pelech, Strong and McCain, but also to admit to our readers that the credibility we have taken pride in since we began, is now in question and, human nature being what it is, may remain in doubt for some time.

Internal changes are being made to ensure, as best we can, that this will not happen again.

We hope that, editorially, the readers of the *Sun* are well served and will continue to be.

Regrettably, however, when the Prime Minister described the *Sun*'s Petrofina story as "garbage", it appears on this particular story that he was not far from the truth.

We are very sorry.

In a libel action, the defendant may try to reduce his or her liability by publishing a retraction and apology. This does not eliminate liability completely, however.

Defences against Libel and Slander Actions

Under our common law system, there are a variety of defences which can be raised against a libel or slander action. These include truth, privilege, and fair comment.

Truth

The chief ingredient of a suit for defamation is that the plaintiff has been injured by false statements. If the defendant can prove that the statement is true, then the plaintiff's case will fail since the court will not award damages to uphold the quality of character that the plaintiff does not have. The court will not defend the honour of a thief or the virtue of a person of ill repute. The criminal law does not hold exactly the same viewpoint. Truth is not a valid defence when it can be shown that the matter was printed only for the purpose of ruining the defamed person and not for the public good. It is possible to be convicted of criminal libel even if the facts were true, where the motive for printing them was vicious and without any value to the public.

Proving the truthfulness of a statement is not always easy. When a person's character is attacked, it is necessary to bring witnesses and evidence to substantiate that attack. The only proof that a person is a thief is that he or she stole something. To prove a person is a liar requires evidence that the person makes false statements. If a series of nasty names are used, then each and every one must be proven. If the defendant called the plaintiff a "thief, swindler, dope-pusher, liar, and blackmailer" and could prove every accusation except the allegation of blackmail, then the plaintiff would win the suit, despite a terrible showing in all the other categories.

Absolute Privilege

Another valid defence against libel is to claim absolute privilege. There are situations which allow a person to speak without fear of civil action; the person is granted immunity for what was said.

Examples of absolute privilege include what is said inside the Parliament and legislature buildings during Parliamentary proceedings. It is felt that the free functioning of government must not be limited in any way. However, a Member of Parliament does not have the same privilege outside the House. Outside on the steps, if Members repeat for reporters what they said inside, they may be sued.

The record of judicial proceedings cannot be actionable in a tort suit. All members of the court and all witnesses are free to speak openly. To proceed otherwise would injure justice since persons would not be certain whether it was safe to offer evidence in open court for fear of a suit later. Similarly, a lawyer enjoys complete privilege with a client and cannot be made to divulge any conversation with the client, even if called to do so as a witness. Conversations between husband and wife are also privileged. This immunity is felt to be necessary to avoid unfortunate social problems.

Qualified Privilege

Certain persons are immune from libel suits because they enjoy a qualified privilege. Qualified privilege means that persons who, because of the nature of their duties, are required to comment about others may do so without action being brought against them as long as their comments are fair, and not vicious.

Newspapers enjoy some degree of qualified privilege. By revealing certain matters, a newspaper runs the risk of a libel suit. The newspaper relies upon its duty to inform the public as its protection, claiming qualified privilege. The newspaper must be fair in its presentation of the facts and avoid taking a personal vendetta against the person named.

Fair Comment

To make a comment about public figures and matters is the right of everyone, including publishers. Our political system encourages citizens to criticize, believing that open discussion is a healthy part of democracy.

The same attitude extends towards art, literature, drama, and sports. Nothing requires that all comments be favourable. If you don't like a stage play, you may say so. If a critic doesn't like the art on display at the local studio, he or she may print a critical opinion of it. If a hockey player plays poorly, the sports editor may say so. The only requirement is that the comments be fair and not a predetermined effort to injure the person rather than criticize the person's work. The comment must confine itself to the subject at hand and not stray into personalities.

Simma Holt v. Sun
British Columbia, 1977

As a Member of Parliament, Holt went to California to study that state's penal system. She and another MP had an interview with an inmate named Lynnette (Squeakie) Fromme. Fromme was asked by Holt if she knew whether or not Charles Manson, the convicted mass-killer, had been in Vancouver in 1968. The Vancouver *Sun* ran an editorial about Holt's activities in California and suggested that she was more interested in getting a good "story" than she was in carrying out her duties. Holt sued on the basis that her reputation had been lowered, that she had been subjected to contempt and ridicule, and that the article had suggested she had misused public funds. The court held that Holt had been libelled:

❝The defence of fair comment depends upon the comment having been made upon a matter of public interest, made upon true facts. . . . I find that there is no basis upon which it can reasonably be said that interviewing Fromme or any prison inmate was beyond the scope of what the plaintiff was paid to do. . . . Nor is there any basis for saying that she failed or neglected her duty to concentrate on finding ways to improve Canada's prison system.**❞**

The following case also involves fair comment and illustrates the potential hazards of publishing "letters to the editor."

Cherneskey v. Armadale Publishers
Supreme Court of Canada, 1978

Two law students wrote a letter to the editor of the Saskatoon *Star-Phoenix*. The letter criticized Alderman Morris Cherneskey for his opposition to an Indian alcoholic rehabilitation centre in a predominantly non-Indian neighbourhood. Cherneskey had warned that the area would turn into a "ghetto." The letter was published under the headline, "Racist Attitude." Cherneskey sued the newspaper. The issue concerned the defence of fair comment. Unfortunately for the newspaper, the two students who wrote the letter had left Saskatoon and were not available at the trial. This proved to be fatal for the defence because it could not prove that the opinions stated in the letter were an honest expression of the real view of the persons making the comment. The newspaper editor could only testify to assuming that the letter did contain a true opinion by the writers. The editor also testified that the letter did not represent the views of the newspaper. The Supreme Court of Canada upheld the trial judge's decision not to put the defence of fair comment to the jury:

❝There was no evidence to show that the material published, which the jury found to be defamatory, represented the honest opinion of the writers of the letter, or that of the officers of the newspaper which published it.**❞**

Concern over the *Cherneskey* case caused the Ontario legislature to amend its *Libel and Slander Act* extending the defence of fair comment to all matters about which a person *could honestly hold the opinion*. Other provinces have not followed suit, but the effect in Ontario is that, now, the same facts as in the *Cherneskey* case could not render a newspaper liable as long as the views are views which any person might reasonably and honestly hold.

Invasion of Privacy

Historically, invasion of privacy has had almost no recognition in Canadian courts. The courts have often stated that if there is to be some specific protection of a person's privacy, then the legislative branch of government should pass a statute providing such protection. Manitoba, British Columbia, and Newfoundland have such statutes. The Newfoundland *Privacy Act* states in s. 3(1) "It is a tort, actionable without proof of damage, for a person, wilfully and without a claim of right, to violate the privacy of an individual." The Act then defines the degree of privacy a person can reasonably expect and lists the types of interference that could be considered invasion of privacy.

There is evidence that the courts are becoming willing to recognize invasion of privacy as a tort without specific legislation. In *Saccone v. Orr* (1981), an Ontario court awarded damages to the plaintiff when the defendant tape-recorded a conversation between the two men without the plaintiff's knowing it. The tape recording was played at a city council meeting and was reported in the newspaper. It was agreed that there was no libel involved, as the tape recording was authentic. However, the trial judge held that it was invasion of privacy.

 Athans v. Canadian Adventure Camps Ltd.
Ontario, 1977

The plaintiff was a professional water-skier. He used a photograph of himself to promote personal appearances and to enhance his reputation. The defendants used a line drawing of the same photograph to advertise their summer camp. The court held that Athans had a proprietory right in the exclusive marketing of his image and name and that the defendants had invaded his privacy and person by using his image without his consent.

Reviewing Important Points

1. A tort is wrongful or injurious conduct, committed by the defendant outside of a contractual obligation, redressible by some appropriate legal action brought by the plaintiff.
2. Some torts, such as assault, battery, and defamation, are intentional torts.
3. Children and insane persons can commit certain torts.
4. Assault permits the plaintiff to recover damages even if the plaintiff felt no fear or suffered no injury.
5. A person cannot sue for false imprisonment if he or she voluntarily consented to be restrained.
6. Nervous suffering is a recognized injury for which an injured person may sue.
7. Trespass to land is any entering of land without invitation and without the consent of the owner.
8. The person who finds lost chattel property acquires a good title to it against all others, except the true owner.
9. Slander is defamation in oral form. Libel is defamation in written, printed, or recorded form. Libel is more serious than slander.
10. The primary defence against an action for defamation is to prove that the statement was true.

Checking Your Understanding

1. Assault and battery usually occur together, but this is not always the case. Give an example to show how assault and battery could occur separately.
2. It has been said that the number of torts is "infinite." What does this statement mean?
3. What is the purpose of a hospital's requiring a patient to sign a consent form prior to an operation?
4. Can a property owner use force to evict a trespasser? If so, to what extent?
5. What is the difference between conversion and detinue?
6. What two things must the plaintiff prove in an action for slander?

7. What is slander per se? Give an example.

8. Slander can be committed by innuendo. What does this mean? Give an example of innuendo.

9. Some persons may speak about important issues with complete immunity. This is called absolute privilege. Give two examples of persons enjoying absolute privilege.

10. Newspapers rely upon the defence of fair comment. What is fair comment? Give an example of something a newspaper might print that goes beyond fair comment.

Legal Briefs

1. The defendant B, shoots W's dog, believing the dog was a wild dog that had been bothering B's cows. Did B *intend* to kill the dog? Liability?

2. Y enters the hospital for a series of tests. She signs a consent form. During the tests she has a heart attack and heart surgery is done without negligence. Can Y sue the hospital and doctor for battery?

3. While she is getting off a bus, G's "trick knee" fails her and she grabs B's arm to try to regain her balance. They both fall and both are injured. Is this battery against B?

4. While standing near the edge of a stairwell, H sees a group of ill-behaved young persons coming towards her. They are shoving and pushing each other and paying no attention to other people. H backs up to get out of their way and falls down the stairs. Liability?

5. A and B argue. A waves a fist at B and shouts, "If I was not a religious, peaceful person, I'd beat you to a pulp!" Assault?

6. R, a fire fighter, is part of a rescue team that removes injured people from a train wreck. He later suffers nervous shock from the experience. Could he bring an action against the railroad?

7. As a practical joke, D takes L's canoe and sinks it in five metres of water. The canoe is not damaged. L learns who took the canoe. What possible tort has been committed? Liability?

8. J is angry with K, his former employer, who just fired J. J makes a record at a studio and mails it to K. K plays it and hears J identify himself and then say many uncomplimentary things about K. Slander? Libel?

9. To continue the preceding question, assume that K then tells his wife about the record and she asks to hear it. K plays the record for her. Would this alter J's potential liability?

10. A newspaper erroneously reports that C was killed in a traffic accident. B, a friend of the family, clips the article from the newspaper and mails it to C's mother along with a letter of condolence. C's mother has a heart attack. The newspaper later prints a correction. Discuss the possible liability of the newspaper and B.

Applying the Law

Halushka v. University of Saskatchewan
Saskatchewan, 1965

In order to earn $50, Halushka consented to serve as a "guinea pig" in an experimental test of a new anaesthetic. He was told that it was a safe test and that there was nothing to worry about. He was told that an incision would be made in his left arm and that a catheter tube would be inserted into his vein. He then signed a consent form which released the doctors and everyone else from liability for "untoward effects or accidents" due to the tests. When the plaintiff asked the meaning of this latter phrase, he was told it covered an accident such as falling down the stairs at home after the tests.

The test followed the procedure described except that the catheter, after being inserted in the vein in the patient's arm, was advanced towards his heart. As the tube neared his heart, the anaesthetic agent was administered. The catheter tip was advanced through the heart chambers into the pulmonary artery. A few minutes later the patient suffered a complete cardiac arrest.

The physicans administering the test took immediate steps to resuscitate the heart by manual massage. This required an incision in the chest and spreading the ribs. After one minute and thirty seconds, the patient's heart began to beat again. He was unconscious for four days. He remained in the hospital for ten more days. He was paid the $50 and was told he could receive more if he signed a complete release. Halushka sued for negligence and trespass, seeking damages of $22 500. The hospital raised the defence of consent, relying upon the consent form. The court awarded damages to Halushka:

> **"**In ordinary medical practice, the consent given by the patient to a physician or surgeon, to be effective, must be an informed consent freely given. It is the duty of the physician to give a fair and reasonable explanation of the proposed treatment including the probable effect and any special risks. Although the appellant ... informed the respondent that a new drug was to be tried out, he did not inform him that the new drug was in fact an anaesthetic of which he had no previous knowledge, nor that there was risk involved with the use of an anaesthetic. ... The respondent was not informed that the catheter would be advanced to and through his heart but was given to understand that it would be merely inserted in the vein of his arm. While it may be correct to say that the advancement of the catheter to the heart was not in itself dangerous and did not cause the cardiac arrest, it was a circumstance which, if known, might very well have prompted the respondent to withhold consent.**"**

Questions
1. Why was the consent form signed by Halushka not a defence for the hospital?
2. Halushka knew that he was being used for an experiment. Did he know there was a risk?
3. Why did the court place emphasis upon the fact that the doctors did not tell Halushka that they would push the catheter through his heart?
4. Did Halushka have to prove that the experiment caused his heart attack? Give a reason for your answer.
5. Suppose Halushka had signed the complete release without any legal advice. Do you think he would have lost all his rights by so doing? Why or why not?

 ### *Marathon Music v. Morrisey*
Newfoundland, 1973

A young recording artist had contracted with a record company for the production by the company of phonographic recordings of her voice in song. In the contract were terms which provided for repayment by the artist of all costs in recording her performances by means of charges against her future royalties from the sale of records. An error in the calculation of these royalties, subsequently corrected, prompted the young woman to beat an immediate path to the door of the local representative of a newspaper. A story appeared in daily circulation print shortly thereafter wherein the singer was quoted as requesting that the story be told of the carryings on of her recording company so that other young performers would not be "taken for a ride." In the article the name of her recording company had wrongly been referred to by the name of a subsidiary distributing company. This second company brought an action against the singer and the newspaper for libel.

In dismissing the action, the Supreme Court of Newfoundland found that the article had not been published either about or concerning the plaintiff. The words used were true and constituted fair comment when referred to the recording company. In the circumstances the phrase "taken for a ride" was assumed to mean "an artist being placed in a position where more is expected of the artist than will be received" and this was found to be fair comment in light of the actions of the recording company.

Questions
1. Did the court appear to place much emphasis upon the error made in the names of the companies? Why or why not?
2. If the mistake in calculating the royalties was corrected, what grievance did the singer have against her company?
3. The court held that "taken for a ride" was a fair comment in this situation. Do you agree? Why or why not?

Dwyer v. Staunton
Alberta, 1947

The plaintiff was a rancher residing near Lundbreck, Alberta. The defendant was also a rancher living to the north of the plaintiff. One winter, the highway running past the farm of the plaintiff was so blocked with snow drifts as to be impassable. On the day in question, employees of an oil company had bulldozed a way to Lundbreck from a point some distance north of the plaintiff's farm following the highway where possible and at other times going through the fields. The bulldozer was not able to follow the highway alongside the ranch of the plaintiff and opened a way for about a quarter of a mile through the plaintiff's gates and fences and over his land. The following morning, the defendant in his car, with four or five other cars, started for Lundbreck. They were stopped by the plaintiff who maintained that no one had any right to cross his land. He said he would allow them to cross this one time but not to do it again.

In town, the parties discovered that the bulldozer was broken and the highway could not be opened that evening. They attempted to return home over the plaintiff's land. There was an argument and the defendant drove his car through the two-strand barbed wire gate and was followed by other cars and trucks. The plaintiff sued the defendant for trespass.

The court held for the defendant, citing the rule that "regard for the public welfare is the highest law." A private mischief must be endured if the alternative is that others must suffer a public inconvenience. Hence, if a highway is out of repair and impassable, a person may lawfully proceed over adjoining land since it is for the common good that there should be free passage for the public. There are private rights and public rights and the rights that are higher are the public rights. The defendant caused no unnecessary damage.

Questions

1. Why did the court conclude that the defendant was justified in crossing the plaintiff's land even after being told not to do so?
2. Was the conduct of the defendant reasonable in the circumstances? Give a reason for your answer.
3. Can you think of a situation where private rights would take greater priority over public rights?
4. Assume that after a natural disaster, public authorities demand that you take ten disaster victims into your home. Do you think you would have the right to refuse this order?

You Be the Judge

1. The plaintiff, who had been shopping in the self-service department of the defendant's department store, was tapped on the shoulder by a house detective, accused of stealing a cake of soap, and requested by her to go upstairs to one of the offices. The plaintiff had not committed any theft, but still she thought it advisable, in view of the crowded state of the store, to go to the office without making a scene. She went upstairs accompanied by the detective and her assistants and, upon being searched, satisfied them that a mistake had been made. The detective stated that she did not think she had arrested the plaintiff; she had only wanted to question her and she had had every intention of letting the plaintiff out of the room once satisfied that she did not have the soap. The detective said it was her duty to protect her employer's goods. The plaintiff said she did not know if the woman could have actually prevented her from leaving, but she felt she was not free to do so. Who would succeed?
2. The plaintiff sued the defendant for damages arising from emotional upset. The defendant regularly drove the plaintiff's children to a nearby Sunday School every Sunday morning. On the day in question, the defendant drove negligently and his car was struck by a train. One of the children was killed outright and the other critically injured. The plaintiff did not go to church that day, but his wife did. She took the same route as the defendant and arrived at the train crossing forty minutes after the accident. She was told by a police officer that one of her

children was dead and that the other had been taken to a hospital along with the defendant. The wife went home and told her husband of the accident; then the two of them went to the hospital. Against the advice of a doctor, the plaintiff insisted on seeing his son while the child was "still alive." He spent ten minutes with him. The child recovered from his injuries, but the plaintiff began to suffer nervous disorders within days of the accident. He could not sleep and was unable to carry out the simplest of chores. His wife persuaded him to enter a mental hospital and after six months he improved slightly. In the situation, it was necessary to hire help to fulfill the tasks the plaintiff had previously done. The plaintiff sued the defendant for "nervous suffering." Who would succeed?

3. The plaintiff brought an action against a hospital and its resident anaesthetist. The anaesthetist was responsible for the administration of an anaesthetic to the plaintiff during an operation. The defendant saw the plaintiff for the first time just prior to the commencement of the operation and just after she had been sedated. She said, "Please don't touch my left arm. You'll have nothing but trouble there." Apparently, she had previously had difficulty with attempts to find a vein in her left arm. The defendant's response was, "We know what we are doing." To commence the operation, the defendant administered the anaesthetic in the plaintiff's left arm. During the operation, the needle slipped out of the arm causing some of the anaesthetic solution to leak into the tissue of the arm. Normally this only results in the patient's having a sore arm for a day, but the plaintiff suffered a very severe and unexpected reaction to the solution in her arm. She brought an action for battery. Who would succeed?

4. The plaintiff, an elderly doctor, became too ill to practise for several months as a result of emotional distress. The plaintiff had written a critical letter to a television program, *Tabloid*. His letter was read on the air, following which the master of ceremonies invited viewers to write "and cheer up Mr. Robbins." The plaintiff's name and address were then flashed on the screen several times. The plaintiff was beseiged with letters, telephone calls, and pranks. He sued the CBC for holding him up to ridicule and causing an invasion of his privacy. The CBC raised the defence of fair comment. Who would succeed?

5. The accused woman was charged with trespass, under the *Petty Trespass Act*, for picketing during the course of a labour dispute with one of the tenants of a shopping centre. She, and other employees who were on strike, were parading up and down in front of one shop when the manager of the shopping centre ordered them to leave. The pickets contended that they had a public right to picket. The manager pointed out to them that the shopping centre was private property, owned by a private corporation which rented store space to the stores in the centre. The manager insisted that they get off the shopping centre property and picket on the highway outside the entrance to the centre. When the accused would not leave, she was arrested and charged. Who would succeed?

6. The plaintiff was employed as a coal miner. On the occasion in question, a dispute over working conditions arose and the plaintiff and thirty-one other men refused to work. They also sought to leave the mine shaft, but the manager refused to send the elevator cage down for them. This situation continued for about twenty minutes before the plaintiff was allowed to leave. He brought an action for false imprisonment, saying that once he had made it clear to his employer that he wanted to leave his work place, the employer had to accommodate that wish. The defendant company argued that the worker had entered the mine on the understanding that he would be brought up at the end of his shift and that the company had no obligation to bring him up earlier. Who would succeed?

Chapter 11

Negligence: The Giant of Torts

Negligence

Negligence is difficult to define and difficult to understand if looked at as just one tort. There are many kinds of negligence and each has relatively different rules governing it. As a general definition, we could say that negligence consists of doing or omitting to do something which a reasonable person would do or not do under the circumstances; and failing to exercise a duty of care towards others where a reasonable person could foresee that the neighbour would be injured. This definition differs from the definition of criminal negligence which holds that criminal negligence is a wanton and reckless disregard for the lives and safety of others. Civil cases do not require such a strong element of proof that the defendant behaved "wantonly."

The "Reasonable Person"

Perhaps the most interesting part of our definition is the term "reasonable person." Who is a reasonable person? Probably the reasonable person is given to thoughtfulness, never making snap judgments. The reasonable person acts upon careful consideration, not upon emotional impulses. With each action he or she carefully considers the probable results and avoids any behaviour that might present a danger to others. The reasonable person is never careless, never leaves things lying around where they might injure someone. Is this a reasonable person, or a perfect person—and does he or she really exist?

It still remains important to accept the rule of the reasonable person because the rule is firmly accepted in tort law and will be at the heart of many cases. The law does not expect perfection, but it looks for behaviour that would be called reasonable.

Essentials of Proof

The handling of a tort case requires a certain order of presentation of evidence. There are several elements that must be proven, including duty of care, required standard of care, proximate cause, and foreseeability. The lawyer for the injured party tries to organize the case to satisfy these elements of proof. Not every case contains all such elements, but in any given case most of them will be found. It should not be assumed that any one carries more significance than another.

Duty of Care

The plaintiff must show that there existed a duty of care, recognized by law, governing the conduct of everyone for the protection of all others. The duty of care implies that the defendant is in control of his or her own actions; or that the defendant has assumed control of an article which, from his or her actions or failure to act, could cause injury to someone else. A person who drives a car has a duty of care to other motorists, pedestrians, passengers, and property. The person who digs a pit has a duty of care not to let others fall into it. If it can be shown that the defendant did not have a duty of care to anyone, including the plaintiff, the defendant is not liable for negligence.

The earliest cases held that a duty of care could exist only if there was a contract between the two parties. In *Winterbottom v. Wright* (England, 1842), the driver of a stagecoach was injured when a wheel collapsed. He sued the man who had a contract with the coach company to maintain their coaches. The defendant had obviously been derelict in his maintenance duties but the court denied the plaintiff's claim because there was *no contract* between the coach driver and the mechanic.

The separation of duty of care from contract was bound to happen, since otherwise the most severe injustices could be worked upon the public. A dramatic reversal of the earlier principle occurred in the following case:

Donoghue v. Stevenson
England, 1932

The plaintiff, Donoghue, brought an action against Stevenson who was the manufacturer of bottled ginger beer. Donoghue became ill after finding the remains of a decomposed dead snail in the bottom of a bottle she had just consumed. The plaintiff contended there was negligence on the part of Stevenson for not having a system of proper inspection of his bottles. The defendant argued that Donoghue had no cause of action against him because there was no contract between them. The bottle was actually purchased by a friend who gave it to Donoghue. The defendant relied upon the principle established in *Winterbottom v. Wright* that there is no duty of care except that arising out of contract. The trial judge decided in favour of Stevenson and Donoghue appealed. The House of Lords reversed the judgment and awarded damages to Donoghue. The court's decision was delivered by Lord Atkin who wrote:

❝A person who engages in the manufacture of articles of food and drink intended for consumption by the public has a duty of care to those whom he intends to consume his products .... The rule that you are to love your neighbour becomes, in law, you must not injure your neighbour, and the lawyer's question, 'Who is my neighbour?' receives a restricted reply. You must take reasonable care to avoid acts or omissions which you can reasonably foresee would be likely to injure your neighbour. Who, then, in law, is my neighbour? The answer seems to be — persons who are so closely and directly affected by my act that I ought reasonably to have them in contemplation as being so affected when I am directing my mind to the acts or omissions which are called in question.**❞**

The events of this case might seem trivial but the legal issue was of great importance. The "neighbour principle" would henceforth dominate negligence law and extend everyone's potential liability to previously unknown levels.

Required Standard of Care

Having established that the defendant did owe the plaintiff a duty of care, the court must then examine whether or not the amount of care required was met. Negligence can be construed as conduct falling below the standard or amount of care a reasonable person would provide under the circumstances.

Precise rules cannot be set down about the amount of care required because far too many possibilities exist. One of the characteristics of tort law is that it has never tried to establish hard-fixed rules. Rather, it follows general guidelines, and each case is ensured of a full hearing on its merits. Legal standards of care and moral standards do not necessarily coincide in every case. Therefore, it is possible to have sympathy for a plaintiff and still not afford any remedy because there was no legal obligation imposed upon the defendant. At the same time, failure of a person to obey every provision of a statute does not necessarily render that person liable in tort to someone injured. If your car was struck by a driver who had no driver's licence, you must still prove who was at fault. The fact that the driver doesn't have a licence, as required by law, may help your case in proving that the person wasn't a skilful driver; but it won't automatically win it.

Medical cases often afford a good basis for the examination of the rule of standard of care. Patients who have had ill effects from treatment are inclined to sue the doctor for malpractice. Such suits raise the question as to whether or not the treatment was approved medical practice or was below the quality of treatment the patient had a right to expect.

MacDonald v. York County Hospital et al. Ontario, 1974

David MacDonald fractured his left ankle in a motorcycle accident. He was treated by the defendant, a senior staff surgeon at the York County Hospital. The doctor was qualified as a general surgeon but did not claim to be a specialist in the area of cardiovascular surgery. The doctor placed the plaintiff's leg in a cast from his toes to his groin. Because of vascular deficiency caused by excessive compression from the cast, gangrene developed necessitating the amputation of the plaintiff's toes and, later, part of the leg below the knee.

The patient had complained of pain continually, but the doctor failed to check on him for eighteen hours, despite nurses' reports on the change in condition. The court cited a definition of standard of care from *R. v. Bateman* (1925):

"If a person holds himself out as possessing special skill and knowledge and he is consulted, as possessing such skill and knowledge, he owes a duty to the patient to use due caution in undertaking the treatment. If he accepts the responsibility and undertakes the treatment and the patient submits to his direction and treatment accordingly, he owes a duty to the patient to use diligence, care, knowledge, skill, and caution in administering the treatment . . . . The law requires a fair and reasonable standard of care and competence.**"**

The defendant admitted that he had made an error in judgment but argued that he was not negligent. The court disagreed and held that he had breached his duty as a physician toward the plaintiff as his patient. The trial judge also held that the hospital was jointly liable, but the Court of Appeal reversed the decision against the hospital.

In *Reibl v. Hughes* (1980), the Supreme Court of Canada held that it is negligence for a surgeon not to explain fully the scope of an operation, the inherent risks, and possible alternatives. The surgeon need not discuss every minute detail, but the patient cannot be said to have given an "informed consent" if important information was withheld—information that might have caused the patient not to have the surgery.

It is important to note that the initiation of malpractice suits against doctors in Canada is limited in most provinces to a period of one year. In most cases the one-year period is considered to extend one year after the last date the patient was treated by the doctor for a particular ailment or injury. If the patient doesn't discover the malpractice until more than a year later, the right to sue will probably be barred. There is a discretion in the court to extend the time for commencing an action when the victim could not reasonably have been aware that such negligence had occurred.

Proximate Cause and Remoteness

There must be a reasonable relationship between the defendant's conduct and the injury. This relationship is called the *proximate cause*. If there is no relationship, the case is dismissed on the grounds of remoteness. Students of science are familiar with the cause-effect approach of investigation. In some cases, whether or not the defendant committed a certain act is not in dispute. The legal argument centres on whether or not this act caused the bad effect upon the plaintiff. In cases involving direct cause and effect, most arguments are easily settled. The cases that come before the courts are usually a result of indirect causation or a string of events.

If the court finds a chain of events is unbroken and not freakish, liability rests upon the person who started the chain. On the other hand, it would be a valid defence to show that another act, separate and distinct, entered the chain at some stage and created a new situation. This is called *novus actus interveniens* ("an intervening act") which breaks the chain of events so that the cause is too remote from the effect to be considered negligence by the person who started the chain.

Chapman v. Hearse
Australia, 1961

Chapman drove his car negligently and collided with a car in front of his. That car turned over and the occupants were trapped inside. Chapman lay unconscious on the highway. Another car stopped and the driver Cherry, a physician, got out and went to attend to Chapman. Hearse came driving along, also negligently, and killed Cherry. Hearse was sued by Cherry's estate and had large damages levied against him. Hearse in turn sued Chapman for starting the entire accident which got him into so much trouble. (In law, Hearse alleged that Chapman was a joint tortfeasor and liable for some of the damages.) The trial judge held that Chapman should pay one-fourth of the damages Hearse was ordered to pay to Cherry's estate. Chapman appealed.

Chapman's case centred on the question of novus actus interveniens. The death of Cherry, in Chapman's view, was caused by an intervening act; it was not a result of his hitting the car in front of him. Chapman admitted his liability to the man he hit, but no further. Hearse argued that it was not too remote to foresee that one's negligence could cause an accident which might also involve injury to those who came to render aid. Chapman's counsel argued that Hearse's negligent driving was an intervening act that severed the chain of liability between Chapman's driving and the death of the doctor. The appeal court upheld the decision against Chapman and required him to pay one-fourth of the costs. In its viewpoint the two accidents were not separate accidents, but a part of a chain of events which Chapman started.

Persons are only obliged to exercise care towards those whom they can reasonably foresee might be injured by their acts or omissions. This means that everyone should be aware of what is likely to happen to other ordinary persons. This does not mean that the defendant must be able to predict exactly who would be injured and how, but only that the defendant must have been able to have foreseen that the plaintiff belonged to a class of persons whose existence and likelihood of injury was reasonably capable of being contemplated.

Hughes v. Lord Advocate
England, 1963

Post office employees were working on a hole into a sewer. They went for a tea break, leaving the hole open, with a shelter tent over it guarded by kerosene lamps. While they were gone, two young boys entered the tent, taking one of the kerosene lamps. One boy tripped over the lamp which then fell into the hole, causing an explosion. The boy was thrown into the hole where he was severely burned. The workers were found negligent in leaving the hole uncovered and unattended. The defence was based upon the argument that the accident was unforeseeable, particularly when considering the peculiar events involved. The workers did not foresee the boys entering the tent, breaking a lamp, and igniting sewer gas. The House of Lords, however, disagreed:

❝The accident was but a variant of the foreseeable, clearly within the risk created by the negligence, especially having regard to the fact that its cause was a known source of danger (the lamp) even if it behaved in an unpredictable way.❞

Res Ipsa Loquitur ("The Act Speaks for Itself")

The burden of proof in a civil case is normally on the person who initiates an action or alleges that some wrongdoing has been done. In a negligence suit, the plaintiff must prove that the defendant was negligent. However it is conceivable that the plaintiff would not be able to determine exactly how the defendant caused the injury. The accident may be completely without explanation. In such a case, all the plaintiff can introduce is circumstantial evidence and let the absence of an explanation lead the jury to conclude that the defendant was negligent even though it cannot be proven how.

When an accident lacks a logical explanation the act speaks for itself. If the act speaks for itself, the burden is now on the defendant to show that the accident might have happened without negligence on his or her part. The defendant may, for instance, try to show how the accident actually did happen or show, through affirmative evidence, that he or she was not negligent.

 Byrne v. Boadle
England, 1863

The plaintiff was walking past a shop owned by Boadle. A barrel of flour fell from a second floor loft and struck Byrne. He suffered serious injury and sued. The defence based its argument on the lack of any evidence that the workers in the shop had been negligent. The court awarded damages to Byrne, holding that:

> **"**A barrel could not get out of the loft without some negligence. To say that the plaintiff must prove how it happened is preposterous. The accident alone is prima facie evidence of negligence. The act speaks for itself.**"**

This case shows the helplessness of an injured party, in certain situations, when trying to establish how he or she was injured. Struck without warning, seeing nothing, helped by no witnesses — such a person would be totally without protection unless the rule of law put the burden of proof on the defendant in such cases.

This principle does not apply to every case. In order for a plaintiff to rely upon the doctrine of *res ipsa loquitur* ("the act speaks for itself"), the following requirements must be met: (1) The accident must have been of a kind which does not ordinarily happen unless there has been negligence; (2) the defendant must have been in control of the overall situation or in control of the instrument which caused harm; and (3) the exact cause of the injury must be unexplained, for once the specific act or omission has been established, there is no longer need for an inference of causal responsibility.

What must the defendant do to shift the burden of proof back to the plaintiff? Modern thinking holds that it is enough to show that the injury might reasonably have been caused without negligence on the defendant's part. If the defendant provides reasonable alternative explanations or shows that the instrument causing injury was no longer under his or her control, the burden of proof returns to the plaintiff and the case is treated as an ordinary case of negligence.

 Wylie v. R.C.A.
Newfoundland, 1973

One month after purchase, the plaintiff's new television set caught fire. The set was destroyed and the house damaged. The manufacturer suggested various possible causes not related to the set, but the court held that these were very improbable explanations. The court agreed that it was very difficult for the defendant to defend itself against the action when the set was destroyed, but that this did not totally prejudice the case against either the plaintiff or the defendant. The cause of the fire was unexplained and the principle of res ipsa loquitur put the burden upon the defendant to provide a strong, plausible explanation that would free it from liability.

Contrast this case with *MacLachlan & Mitchell Homes Ltd. v. Frank's Rental* (Alberta, 1981) in which a rental set also caught fire and damaged a home. The Alberta Court of Appeal held that there was no duty upon Frank's Rental to open and inspect sets unless there was evidence of malfunction. In fact, constantly opening them would increase the likelihood of malfunction. The court heard evidence from the manufacturer that 150 000 sets of this model had been sold and no fires had ever been reported. The case against Frank's Rental was dismissed. In *Phillips v. Chrysler of Canada* (Ontario, 1962), the plaintiff had an accident because of a defect in a used car. The court held that the plaintiff failed to prove negligence and, due to the lapse of time, res ipsa loquitur could not assist the plaintiff. This was because there was too long a time since the car had left the factory. The plaintiff was the fifth owner and the manufacturer could not be liable, indefinitely, for mechanical defects.

Volenti Non Fit Injuria ("Voluntary Assumption of Risk")

Voluntary assumption of risk bases its legal holding upon the thinking that a person cannot sue for damages in tort when that person consented to what happened. The Latin expression, *volenti non fit injuria*, means, "no wrong is done to one who consents." It also means that the plaintiff, having freely entered into a relationship with the defendant, and knowing that there might be some risk involved, has agreed not to blame the defendant if he or she suffers from that risk. The plaintiff has personally assumed the risk and has absolved the defendant.

The courts have held that the risk must have been recognizable. A person cannot be said to have consented to a risk when that person did not know the risk was there. Or, if a person accepts one risk but is injured by another, unexpected risk, he or she cannot be said to have consented to it. Thus, in an Ontario case, a man was warned not to walk out on a dock during the winter because the dock was icy and he might fall. He went anyway, but didn't fall—the entire dock collapsed! The court awarded damages to him because the risk he accepted was the risk of falling, not the risk of having the dock fall down with him on it.

McCarthy v. Royal American Shows Inc.
Manitoba, 1967

The plaintiff, a girl of sixteen who weighed 180 pounds [81.65 kg], broke her ankle after sliding down a 39 foot long [11.89 m] steel slide at a fun house. She followed the instructions given to her and stopped herself at the bottom by hitting a rubber pad feet first. Her ankle broke upon impact. The defendants contended that, the slide was safe and had been used by nearly 70 000 persons without incident. Engineers who testified for the plaintiff demonstrated that the rubber pad at the bottom was too tightly compacted and, having no room to expand, was quite rigid and hard. The court held that there was an implied promise, by the defendant, that the slide was safe. The defendant did not live up to that promise. The defendant's argument that the plaintiff used the slide at her own risk was rejected by the court. In rejecting the argument of "volenti non fit injuria" the judge concluded that, where a person is led to believe that an amusement is safe, that person cannot be said to have consented to a risk which she knew nothing about. The plaintiff was awarded $3500 in general damages and $1674.32 in special damages.

A worker who is employed in a dangerous job must accept the risks of the job; those hazards are accepted when that particular job is taken. The worker cannot blame anyone for ordinary accidents.

However, in *Hambley v. Shepley* (Ontario, 1967), the Ontario Court of Appeal held that a police officer could recover personal damages from the defendant who smashed into the officer's car at a roadblock. (The officer could not get out of the car in time to avoid being hit.) While the police officer had voluntarily placed the car at the roadblock the court held that the officer had not absolved the defendant of liability and had not forfeited personal rights against the defendant.

Contributory Negligence

A plaintiff who fails to act carefully and neglects his or her own safety or interest is guilty of *contributory negligence*. At one time under the common law, if the plaintiff were guilty of even the slightest contributory negligence, he or she would receive no damages from the defendant. The harshness of this rule has been reduced by statute laws which permit the court to *reduce* the damages, if the plaintiff contributed to the injury, but not eliminate the damages entirely.

In some cases contributory negligence embraces the rule of "last opportunity" which holds that blame rests chiefly with the person who had the last opportunity to avoid the accident, even if that person did not create the dangerous situation. The court may, in some situations, also consider the age, intelligence, experience, and other personal characteristics of the plaintiff to determine if the plaintiff should have acted differently.

Thornton v. Board of School Trustees
British Columbia, 1975

Gary Thornton was fifteen years of age and nearing completion of a course in gymnastics in his high school. On the day in question Gary and some other students went into an equipment room and obtained a springboard and some foam chunks. The foam chunks were placed around a wrestling mat as a landing area and the boys began doing somersaults. Not satisfied with this activity, the boys then took a box-horse and placed it at the end of the board. They jumped from the box-horse onto the springboard and were attempting complete somersaults onto the mat. The teacher was not observing this activity as he was filling out report cards elsewhere in the gym. Some of the boys started trying "circus tricks" including double somersaults off the board. They were very unsuccessful at these tricks and landed very hard. One boy went to the teacher and reported that he had hurt his arm. The teacher told him to run cold water on it. It turned out that the arm was broken. The teacher then went to look at the landing area and concluded that it was too small. He told the boys to put more mats around the area. He saw, but did not question, the configuration of a springboard and box-horse. He did not ask any of the boys what they had been doing, including the boy who hurt his arm.

Shortly afterwards, Gary Thornton broke his neck when he landed on the mat; he suffered total paralysis of his four limbs. The court held that the configuration was "an attractive trap" and that the teacher and the school board were both liable. The court then dealt with the issue of contributory negligence. The decision was that Gary had not contributed to his own injury despite the fact that he obviously had been taking part in dangerous stunts. It was held that Gary did not have the same experience as his instructor and that he could not have recognized the fact that his actions were a grave danger to himself. It followed that he did not realize that he should have asked the teacher for guidance or instructions. Had he been an experienced gymnast, the conclusion might have been different, but he had had less than twenty hours of experience in gymnastics.

Conversely, some degree of contributory negligence was found in the following case:

Greisman v. Gillingham
Supreme Court of Canada, 1934

The plaintiff fell into an open elevator shaft; the door was left open by the defendant. The court found the defendant negligent for leaving the door open, but also held that the defendant was not completely at fault because the plaintiff should have looked where he was going. The fault was apportioned at 90 per cent by the defendant, and 10 per cent by the plaintiff.

The Thin Skull Rule

If the defendant causes injury to the plaintiff — an injury for which the defendant would be liable in any circumstance — should the defendant be partially excused because the *extent* of the injury was not foreseeable?

To illustrate this problem, let us assume that the plaintiff was struck by the defendant's car. The bump was very slight and a healthy person would have received very little injury. It turns out that this defendant had the misfortune of striking a person suffering from advanced arthritis and degenerative back discs. Rather than suffering scant bruises, the plaintiff was crippled to the point of being unable to work and sued for a large sum. Should the plaintiff receive damages based upon the actual injuries or upon the injuries that a reasonably healthy person would have received in the same situation? The basic rule is that you must take the victim as you find him or her. If a person is negligently injured, it is no defence to the claim for damages that that person would have suffered less injury, or no injury at all, if he or she had not had an unusually thin skull, weak heart, or some other abnormality.

Strict Liability

Strict liability is one of the more difficult aspects of law to understand. It deals with instances of liability in which the defendant is held liable even though he or she did not intend to cause harm and did not act negligently. There are numerous areas of law where it can apply. The keeper of a wild animal may be liable if the animal escapes and does harm — even if the keeper did everything reasonable to ensure that the animal would not escape. The person who publishes a defamatory statement may be liable for the published libel — even if he or she did not know it was false.

More frequently, strict liability pertains to land and the use of land. The most famous case is the following one.

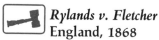

Rylands v. Fletcher
England, 1868

Fletcher brought an action against Rylands and Horrocks to recover damages for injury to his mines caused by water flowing into them from a reservoir built on the defendants' land. The declaration alleged negligence on the part of the defendants. Fletcher, with the permission of the landowners and tenant, had a working coal mine on certain property. Rylands and Horrocks owned a mill near the land. With the same landowner's permission, they built a reservoir in order to supply water to their mill. They hired competent engineers and contractors to construct the reservoir and they did not know that coal had ever been worked under or near the site. When the reservoir was completed and was partially filled with water, one of the old mine shafts gave way and water

flowed into Ryland's mine and flooded it. The question was whether the defendants were liable for damages even though there appeared to be no negligence in the manner in which the reservoir was built. The court found the defendants liable:

> **❝**We think that the true rule of law is that the person who, for his own purposes, brings on his lands and collects there and keeps there anything likely to do mischief if it escapes, must keep it in at his peril, and, if he does not do so, is prima facie answerable for all the damage which is the natural consequence of its escape.... The person whose grass or corn is eaten down by the escaping cattle of his neighbour, or whose mine is flooded by the water from his neighbour's reservoir, or whose cellar is invaded by the filth of his neighbour's privy, or whose habitation is made unhealthy by the fumes and noisome vapours of his neighbour's alkali works, is damnified without fault of his own; and it seems but reasonable and just that the neighour, who has brought something on his property which was not naturally there, harmless to others so long as it was confined to his own property, but which he knows to be mischievous if it gets on his neighbour's, should be obliged to make good the damage which ensues if he does not succeed in confining it to his own property. **❞**

The defendants appealed to the House of Lords, but the decision in favour of the plaintiff was upheld.

Rylands v. Fletcher is a unique case because it does not fit easily into the rules of tort law. It is not trespass, negligence, or nuisance in the true sense, but tends to combine a bit of each. It could be said to have created a new tort — the requirement to carefully control inherently dangerous things. A narrow interpretation would include these principles: (1) The substance causing harm must be inherently "mischievous" or dangerous; (2) the defendant must have brought it onto his or her land — it was not there naturally; (3) the defendant must have failed to control it by allowing it to escape and cause damage to the plaintiff on his or her land.

Schunicht v. Tiede
Alberta, 1980

Tiede, an experienced aerial crop duster, was spraying a herbicide from his aeroplane over crops on his lands in order to kill weeds. A light wind was blowing and some of the herbicide spray drifted on to 40 acres (16 ha) of Schunicht's adjacent lands. Schunicht's alfalfa crop was damaged by the chemical and he sued Tiede. The court held that herbicide spray was not naturally on the defendant's lands but was brought there by him. It was a substance that could do damage to others if it was not handled with care and was allowed to escape. Thus the court concluded that the rule of *Rylands v. Fletcher* should be applied and the defendant held liable for the crop damage.

Automobile Negligence

Automobile negligence covers all the elements of any negligence case, but is also subject to special rules created by statutes in addition to the rules of common law.

Owner's Liability

The owner of a motor vehicle, as well as the driver, is liable for loss suffered by any person by reason of negligence in the operation of the motor vehicle. When ownership of the vehicle is established, the burden then passes to the owner to prove that the vehicle was being used by some other person without the owner's consent. The owner would have a good defence if he or she could show that the vehicle was stolen. The owner is not liable if the vehicle is misused by a person who had no right to have it. The owner cannot escape liability just because a person who had permission to drive the vehicle did not obey the owner's instructions.

For example, B lends a car to C, with instructions that no one else is to be allowed to drive it. C allows D to drive the car and an accident results. B, as owner of the car, is liable for the accident even though C disobeyed B's instructions by allowing D to drive. This kind of liability is called *vicarious liability* which means that the law holds one person liable for the misconduct of another person.

Payne v. Donner et al.
Saskatchewan, 1981

The defendant, Eugene Foy, permitted his daughter to drive his truck, but instructed her never to let anyone else drive it. One day his daughter picked up her boyfriend, John Donner, and disobeyed her father's instructions by letting Donner drive the truck. Donner struck and injured Payne who sued Foy as the owner of the vehicle. Foy denied liability. He testified that he was very fond of his new truck, did not allow anyone but members of his family to drive it, and had always told them never to permit any non-family member to drive it. Thus, he argued, Donner had his vehicle without his permission. The *Vehicles Act* of Saskatchewan relieves the owner of liability if the vehicle is taken out of the person's possession "wrongfully." The court held Foy to be liable. There was no evidence that Donner "wrongfully" *took* the vehicle from the daughter's possession. The oral instructions given to the daughter were not sufficient to show wrongful taking. The burden was upon the defendant to prove wrongful taking, which he did not do.

Liability to Passengers

A passenger who rides for free assumes a foreseeable risk in accepting the ride. This risk is the normal hazard of highway driving and the possible miscalculation by the driver. Under the principle of voluntary assumption of risk, no claim can be made by a passenger against the driver unless the passenger can show that what happened was beyond the ordinary risk of driving. In most provinces, a statute requires that the plaintiff prove that the driver was guilty of *gross negligence*. There is no exact definition of what gross negligence is. We can only assume that the phrase means "a very great negligence." In Ontario,

Quebec, and British Columbia the law does not require gross negligence, but just ordinary negligence.

A passenger who paid a fare for a ride in a bus or a taxi can sue the owner or driver for ordinary negligence. Cases where people have formed "car pools" and chipped in money to pay for the driver's gasoline have generally not been held to be fare-paying situations.

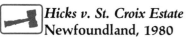 **Hicks v. St. Croix Estate**
Newfoundland, 1980

The plaintiff was a gratuitous passenger in a car owned and driven by St. Croix. St. Croix, Hicks, and Moriarity were the three men in the car at the time of the accident. All had been doing some heavy drinking, but Moriarity did not drink as much as the other two and did all the driving until just before the accident. They drove from drinking spot to drinking spot and eventually stopped at the home of Moriarity's girl friend. He got out, left the motor running, and said he would be back very shortly. Shortly afterwards, St. Croix slid behind the wheel and said to Hicks, "We're not waiting for him" and backed on to the highway. Moriarity, thinking he was going to be stranded, ran down the driveway and just managed to get into the car as it started off. St. Croix soon began driving at very high speed and ignored words from the other two men to slow down. He rolled the car attempting a curve at 75 m.p.h. (120 km/h). St. Croix was killed and Hicks seriously injured. The court found that St. Croix had driven in a manner that was grossly negligent. It also found that Hicks had not voluntarily accepted the risk of riding with the deceased:

66Once the car started to move it would have been the height of folly for the plaintiff to try and get out of the car. From that moment on the plaintiff, through no conscious or deliberate act of his own, was at the mercy of a reckless driver in the person of the defendant.99

Burden of Proof

When a motor vehicle strikes a pedestrian or some property other than a moving vehicle, provincial law places the burden of proof upon the driver to show absence of fault. Without such proof, the court will presume that the driver was not driving carefully.

Contributory Negligence and Motor Vehicles

A person guilty of contributory negligence may receive reduced compensation depending upon the extent to which he or she contributed to the injuries sustained. He may receive nothing at all, although this is rare.

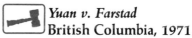 **Yuan v. Farstad**
British Columbia, 1971

Farstad was the sole cause of an accident to the Yuans which killed the husband and injured the wife. The wife sued Farstad for damages on behalf of herself and her deceased husband. The husband was not wearing his seatbelt and was thrown out of the car and fatally injured. The wife was wearing a seatbelt. The court allowed the wife 100 per cent for her damages but only 75 per cent on behalf of her deceased husband. The defence introduced substantial evidence to show that had the husband been wearing his seatbelt he would likely not have been killed. His failure to do so was interpreted by the court to be contributory negligence. That is, he had the means to reduce his own injuries but did not resort to those means.

The plaintiff will not automatically have damages reduced for not wearing a seat belt. The defendant must show, through expert opinion, that the plaintiff suffered a type of injury that a seat belt would have prevented or lessened.

Assumption of Risk and Motor Vehicles

Where it can be shown that the plaintiff assumed the risk of accident, no action can be supported. In those provinces which do not permit a passenger to sue the driver unless there was gross negligence, the law presumes that the act of accepting a ride involved the assumption of risk by the passenger.

Where there is evidence of gross negligence, the driver may still use the principle of volenti non fit injuria as a defence against a suit brought by a passenger. However, the burden lies upon the driver to prove that the passenger agreed, either by actions or expressly in words, to exempt the driver from liability. There must be some bargain that demonstrates the passenger had agreed to take risks and give up any right of later action.

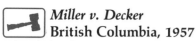 *Miller v. Decker*
British Columbia, 1957

The defendant Decker and some friends went to a beer hall and became very intoxicated. Later, they drove to a dance. After the dance, Decker rolled his car and injured Miller who had been with him all night. Decker was found to have been guilty of gross negligence in his driving, but since Miller knew Decker was intoxicated he accepted the risks. No damages were allowed, and the plaintiff's appeal was dismissed.

Inevitable Accident

An inevitable accident is one which the party accused of causing the accident could not have prevented by reasonable care and skill. For this defence to succeed, it must be proved that the defendant did not "cause" the accident at all; or that since there were only a certain number of causes possible, the defendant did not create any of them. There are two general categories into which this defence can be divided, that of machine failure and driver failure.

Machine failure means that a driver loses control of a vehicle because of a mechanical malfunction over which the driver has no control. The malfunction must be one that the driver had no warning about or one that could not be detected by ordinary mechanical inspection. Thus, driving a vehicle known to be in poor mechanical condition rules out the defence of machine failure when an accident finally occurs.

Driver failure means that an accident occurs because of a physical problem which suddenly seizes the driver. For example, if a driver has a sudden heart attack while driving, with no previous history of such attacks, the driver would not be liable for the resulting acci-

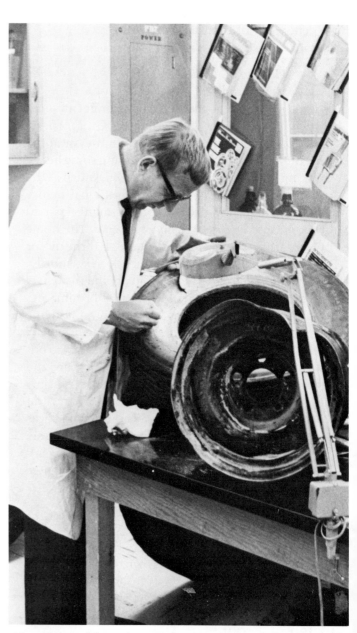

After an automobile accident, experts are sometimes asked to examine the wreckage to determine the cause of the accident.

dent. However, a driver who suffered repeated black-outs would be liable if he or she had one while driving.

Inevitable accident is an uphill fight against the great volume of evidence against the defendant. Considerable effort must be made by the defendant to show that nothing he or she could have done would have prevented the accident.

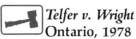

Telfer v. Wright
Ontario, 1978

Telfer suffered injury when her car was involved in a head-on collision with Wright's car which had suddenly crossed into her lane. Telfer brought an action in negligence against Wright.

At trial, the judge was asked to consider the defence of unavoidable accident. The defendant gave evidence that immediately prior to the accident he blacked out. The plaintiff verified this by testifying that the defendant appeared to be slumped over the steering wheel immediately prior to the accident. Further evidence was introduced by Telfer's counsel about previous dizzy spells and blackouts on the part of the defendant. In particular, Wright had felt dizzy earlier that day, but he claimed that the feeling had passed allowing him to drive. Wright denied the assertion that he had blacked out once before while driving. The trial judge accepted the defence of unavoidable accident holding that the defendant could not have foreseen that he would black out on the day in question and cause an accident. The Court of Appeal overturned this decision, holding that the defendant knew he had a medical problem and a history of blackouts and that he knew he had been dizzy approximately twenty minutes before the collision. As he was on the wrong side of the road it was his burden to explain how the accident could have happened without negligence and to show that he could not have prevented it. He should have anticipated that it was dangerous for him to drive and taken the precautions necessary to avoid harm to the plaintiff.

Reviewing Important Points

1. In most instances, the law does not require perfect behaviour, but it does require reasonable behaviour.
2. The plaintiff must prove that the defendant had a duty of care and that the injury was foreseeable.
3. Professional people must provide their clients or patients with a reasonable standard of care.
4. If a separate, intervening act breaks the chain of causation, the defendant will not be liable.
5. When an injury lacks a logical explanation, the act may speak for itself and the burden of proof shifts to the defendant.
6. A plaintiff who voluntarily accepts a risk cannot complain of the injury.
7. A plaintiff who contributes to the injury will have the damage award reduced.
8. A person who brings onto his or her land an inherently dangerous thing will be strictly liable if it is allowed to escape from control.
9. The owner of a motor vehicle is liable if another person drives the vehicle and causes injury. The owner can escape liability by showing that the driver had the vehicle without the owner's consent.
10. In most provinces, a passenger who rides for free can sue the driver if the driver was guilty of gross negligence. This does not apply in Ontario, Quebec, and British Columbia.

Checking Your Understanding

1. What four elements must normally be proven in a negligence case?
2. What circumstances must be present for the rule of res ipsa loquitur to apply?
3. What must the defendant do to counter the application of res ipsa loquitur to a case against him or her?
4. What two things must exist to say that a plaintiff voluntarily accepted a risk?
5. What is the basic law of liability if a motor vehicle strikes a pedestrian?

6. What is an inevitable accident? What two possible explanations might a defendant try to establish?

7. What is a novus actus interveniens?

Legal Briefs

1. A negligently drives into a hydro pole. The pole is old and rotten and falls over even though A was going only 10 km/h. It falls across the highway in the path of B. B swerves to avoid the pole and hits C who was jaywalking and standing in the street. D sees the accident and is so emotionally upset that she later suffers a miscarriage. Discuss the liability of A to C and D.

2. If there is a standard of "the reasonable person" how can stupid people ever be expected to meet what the law expects of them? Should tort law have a special set of rules for people of very low intelligence? Should there be special rules for people who are accident prone?

3. An airplane goes down somewhere over the mid-Atlantic and no trace of it is ever found. No reason for the disappearance is ever determined. Can the families of the lost passengers sue the airline?

4. A chef accidentally starts a fire in the kitchen of a restaurant. A customer sitting near the kitchen door sees the flames and panics, shouting, "Fire! Run for your lives!" Even though the kitchen staff has the fire under control, people rush for the door and some are injured in the crush. Liability of the restaurant?

5. Workers for a city dig up a large section of a sidewalk to repair a broken water pipe. They leave the hole open when they go home that evening. As a warning to pedestrians, they place wooden horses, equipped with small lamps, around the pole. There is enough of a gap between the horses to allow a person to walk through. D, a blind person, comes along using a white cane, passes between the horses without realizing there is a hole ahead, and falls into the excavation. Discuss the liability of the city to D.

6. B suffered a knee injury in an accident three years ago. Inside the door of the ABC store, B slips on snow and water (tracked in by shoppers and not cleaned up), and the fall aggravates B's previous injury. B's leg is amputated. Liability of ABC store?

7. V is working in his garden when he hears a loud noise. He goes to investigate the cause and finds bits of wood, cloth, and a dead body in his garden. He suffers nervous injury. Investigation shows that a coffin and corpse was placed on board an airplane which had a flight route that would place the airplane over V's property at exactly the time of the noise. Further investigation shows that the airplane cargo door was carefully closed when the plane left and was still closed when it arrived. No crew member was in the cargo hold during flight. Experts testify that it is impossible for the door to open itself and close itself during flight. Liability of the airline company?

8. Two train guards, in assisting a late passenger, jump onto a moving train, carelessly knocking a parcel out of the passenger's arms. The parcel falls under the train causing its contents—fireworks—to explode. The explosion causes scales, some distance away, to fall over on G. Liability of the railroad company to G?

9. A ship enters a harbour to escape a storm and ties up at a dock belonging to the XYZ Co. The waves repeatedly toss the ship against the dock until the dock collapses. Liability of the ship's owner to the XYZ Co.?

10. A woman signs a consent form to have a sterilization operation. She is told that a very tiny scar will result. Because of their religious views, she does not want other family members to know that she had the operation. She is not told that there is a very small chance of bowel perforation. During the operation her bowel is perforated and a second operation is necessary to save her life. The second operation leaves a very large, visible scar. Liability of the surgeon who performed the first operation?

Applying the Law

Horsley et al. v. MacLaren et al.
Supreme Court of Canada, 1972

The defendant, MacLaren, owned a cabin cruiser named *The Ogopogo*. On May 7, 1961, he invited some friends for a cruise on Lake Ontario. The water was choppy and most of the passengers went below. A passenger named Matthews went topside and for no apparent reason fell overboard. MacLaren stopped the cruiser about 50 feet (15 m) away, put it into reverse, and backed towards Matthews in the water. When close to the body, MacLaren cut the motor but the rough water immediately separated the boat from the motionless body. Another passenger tried to hook onto Matthews' clothing with a pike but could not do so. MacLaren started the motor again and again tried to back the boat close enough to Matthews so that he could be reached. Much evidence was given at the trial about this method which was criticized as the improper way to try to approach a person in the water. It was contended that the proper method was to swing the boat in a circle and come back at the body bow first or "head-on" and pull alongside. MacLaren acknowledged that this might have been a better method, but said he thought the manoevre could also be done stern first. A passenger, Horsley, removed some of his clothing and jumped into the lake. He did not tell anyone of his intention before doing so. Another passenger, named Jones, also jumped into the lake. She was later rescued. Matthews' body sank and was never found. Horsley was pulled from the lake but was dead from exposure to the cold water.

Matthews' family sued MacLaren but did not succeed. There was no negligence on the part of MacLaren in causing Matthews to fall overboard; and while MacLaren's method of rescue was not very good, there was also reason to believe that Matthews was dead very shortly after hitting the water. He was motionless all the time he was seen in the lake. Horsley's family also sued MacLaren, alleging that because of MacLaren's inept attempts to rescue Matthews, Horsley was "forced" to attempt a rescue by entering the water. The defendant argued that Horsley voluntarily exposed himself to a risk by entering the water as he did. Horsley did not tell anyone what he was going to

do. In particular, he did not tell MacLaren, who as Master of the ship, would have ordered Horsley not to jump into the lake. The defendant pointed out that Horsley did not wear a life jacket and that he added to the problem that already existed by entering the water and necessitating the rescue of two persons instead of one.

The trial judge awarded damages to the plaintiff. He held that it was MacLaren's inept rescue attempt that compelled Horsley to jump into the water and that such negligence was the cause of Horsley's death. The Ontario Court of Appeal reversed this decision and the case was appealed to the Supreme Court of Canada which upheld the Ontario Court of Appeal:

    “In the present case a situation of peril was created when Matthews fell overboard, but it was not created by any fault on the part of MacLaren; and before MacLaren can be found to have been in any way responsible for Horsley's death, it must be found that there was such negligence in his method of rescue as to place Matthews in an apparent position of increased danger subsequent to and distinct from the danger to which he had been initially exposed by his accidental fall. In other words, any duty owing to Horsley must stem from the fact that a new situation of peril was created by MacLaren's negligence which induced Horsley to act as he did . . . . I do not think that the evidence justifies the finding that any fault of his induced Horsley to risk his life by diving in as he did.**”**

Two justices dissented and thought that MacLaren was negligent and that Horsley felt he had to take matters into his own hands because Matthews was not going to be rescued unless something more positive was done.

Questions
1. Since MacLaren did not cause Matthews to fall overboard, what duty did MacLaren owe to Matthews?
2. Knowing that lake water in May can be so cold that it can kill a human in minutes, did Horsley act reasonably?

3. What led the Court of Appeal to conclude that MacLaren was not liable for Horsley's death?

4. Do you think the case was rightly decided? Why or why not?

Haines v. Bellissimo
Ontario, 1977

From 1971 to the date of his death, the late Robert Haines was under the care of the defendant doctor, as an outpatient of the Department of Psychiatry at a university medical centre. The widow of the deceased alleged negligence on the part of the defendant doctor in failing to take steps to prevent the suicide of her husband. Robert Haines had a history of mental illness that dated back to the 1950s. He had secured employment as a high school teacher and was head of the science department of his school. However, he encountered great tension and stress in teaching and had to resign. He was erratic in behaviour and incoherent at times. He tried to study accounting but could not cope with the course. He suffered manic-depressive moods and would not take the pills prescribed by Bellissimo to deal with depression. He had no family life and talked of suicide. He held a job as a zoo grounds-keeper for a while. When the plaintiff learned that he had bought a gun, she became alarmed and called Bellissimo who came to the house. He argued with Robert who finally surrendered the gun. The next day he spoke with the doctor on the telephone and apologized about the gun incident. Two days later he shot himself to death with another gun. The suit alleged that the doctor was negligent in not recognizing in Robert Haines a state of depression that was suicidal and in not committing him to a hospital for intensive care. Admission would have presented no difficulty. In the alternative, the plaintiff alleged that the doctor should have given her and her family special instructions about what to watch for in the continued care of her husband. The trial judge rejected the action:

66While there was an element of paranoia in the reaction of Haines to the threat of calling the police, I am not satisfied that the reaction of this man was totally disproportionate to the facts. He was in no way delusional. He had no previous experience with guns and when he first arrived home on the evening of June 28 he reprimanded his wife for disclosing that he had a loaded gun on the premises. It may be that he was concerned that it was illegal to have a loaded gun in the house . . . . I accept the evidence that Bellissimo acted reasonably in the belief that his therapeutic relationship, so important to the continued treatment of Haines, was intact. I do not consider that Bellissimo was negligent in failing to give [the plaintiff] more instructions than he did; namely, to call him or the resident psychiatrist should any problem arise.**99**

Questions

1. What duty of care does a psychiatrist have towards a patient?

2. Should the psychiatrist have had Robert Haines *involuntarily* committed, even if it meant destroying the doctor-patient relationship?

3. Was Haines clearly dangerous to himself? Why or why not?

4. What brought the judge to hold that it was not a mistake to simply take the gun away from Haines?

Smith v. Leech Brain & Co.
England, 1962

The defendant's negligence resulted in a piece of molten metal's striking and burning the lip of the plaintiff's husband. At the time, the burn was treated as a normal burn. Ultimately, the place where the burn had been began to ulcerate and cancer was diagnosed. After radium treatments and several operations, the man died. In an action for damages by the widow it was proved that the burn was a cause of the cancer and death:

66In those circumstances, it seems to me that this is plainly a case which comes within the old principle. The test is not whether these employers could reasonably have foreseen that a burn would cause cancer and that he would die. The question is whether these employers could reasonably foresee the type of injury he suffered; namely, the burn. What, in the particular case, is the amount of damage which he suffers as a result of that burn, depends upon the characteristics and constitution of the victim. Accordingly, I find that the damages which the widow claims are damages for which the defendants are liable. **"**

Questions

1. Since the defendants could not foresee that an injury would cause cancer, what was the basis for finding them liable?
2. The victim either had a high susceptibility to cancer or it was already present in his body. Should this not have been taken into consideration? Why or why not?
3. If very large damage awards can be obtained for very small injuries, what message is there for all of us?

You Be the Judge

1. The plaintiff's well was polluted by gasoline. Approximately two hundred metres away was a gas station. The plaintiff complained and the oil company tested the storage tanks and found no sign of a leak. The problem persisted and the plaintiff had to have a new well dug. She sued the oil company for the cost. The company defended the action on the grounds that there was no evidence before the court to show that their tanks were the source of the problem. Their tests continually indicated no leakage. Who would succeed?

2. A went to B, a tire manufacturer, and bought retread tires. A wanted them installed on the front of his truck, contrary to warnings from the manufacturer. When A insisted, B (reluctantly) installed the tires on the front of the truck. The truck was involved in an accident caused by the improper use of retread tires. The injured party sued both A and B. Who is liable?

3. J a high school student, was carrying out a chemistry experiment, the purpose of which was to determine the atomic weight of tin. She commenced the experiment in accordance with a Department of Education lab manual, verbal instructions received on the previous day, and instructions written on the chalkboard. J oxidized some tin with nitric acid and then heated the residue over a burner in order to obtain a dry residue. J was unclear as to what was to be done next, but the instructor was not available for consultation. J raised the heat and the mixture blew up in her face causing damage to tear ducts and scarring. The court heard that while goggles were readily available the students were not required to wear them at all times. The lab manual recommended goggles but did not emphatically require them. It was concluded that J had first underheated, then superheated, the mixture and that this had caused the explosion. J sued the instructor and the school board. The defence centred around J's failure to follow the instructions and her failure to wear the goggles that were readily available. Who would succeed?

4. The plaintiff's husband was injured in a car-pedestrian accident. The defendant admitted negligence for the accident. Fourteen months later the plaintiff's husband committed suicide as a result of pain and depression arising from his injuries. The plaintiff brought an action for damages under the provincial law permitting dependants to sue after a family member has a "fatal accident." The defendant argued that the husband's suicide was not actionable against him as he did not cause his death. Prior to the accident the deceased man had no visible emotional abnormalities. The accident changed his outlook on life completely. Who would succeed?

5. Pellets of phostoxin, a poisonous fumigant used for killing insects, were stored on the defendant grain company's property. The storage shed was not locked at all times and some young boys stole some pellets. Because of the pellets' strong odour, the boys put one pellet in the plaintiff's car as a practical joke. The plaintiff noticed the odour but did not conduct a search until alerted by the police. While searching his car for the pellet, he got a strong exposure to fumes and became ill. Afterwards, he suffered chronic depression and physical illness. He was convinced he was "poisoned" and could not work. He sued the defendant grain company for negligence. The defendant argued

that the plaintiff's illness was more psychological than real, that some of his problems came from another medication which he was taking, and that this constituted a novus actus interveniens. Who would succeed?

6. G, a locksmith, installed deadbolt locks on the doors of M's home because M was very concerned about burglary. While M was away, the home was entered and valuables stolen. A consultant studied the locks and found that one had been improperly installed. A gap had been left in the frame which made the lock almost useless. Counsel for G argued that there were no grounds for liability. G had not "guaranteed" that the locks would keep out thieves. G had only installed the locks as requested and would have to correct any improper installation. To hold G liable, the lawyer continued, would be tantamount to saying that every locksmith was an "insurer" of every house upon which locks were installed. This was too great a burden to place on the defendant. Who would succeed?

Chapter 12

Torts and Property

Nuisance

Nuisance can be divided into two categories, public nuisance and private nuisance. A public nuisance is one that annoys the general public and as such must be dealt with by government authorities. Only Parliament can prohibit a criminal public nuisance. Section 176 of the *Criminal Code* makes it an offence to commit a "common nuisance" and thereby endanger the "lives, safety or health of the public." The provincial legislatures are limited to prohibiting a non-criminal public nuisance. It is important to recognize that if a nuisance is a public nuisance, no private lawsuit by a plaintiff is permissible. A citizen can initiate an action only if it can be demonstrated that the citizen suffered a separate and special damage, distinct from what the general public suffered.

 Hickey v. Electric Reduction Co.
Newfoundland, 1972
A group of fishermen sued the defendant company for polluting Placentia Bay, and thereby destroying their livelihood. The case was dismissed because the plaintiffs' damage was not unique from that of other persons using the bay. The court held that the matter was a public nuisance, not a private nuisance.

An individual who is affected by a nuisance retains the common law right of action. A private nuisance may be committed in one of two ways. The first is conduct by the defendant which results in physical damage to the land of the plaintiff as an indirect consequence of what is done on the land of the defendant. The second is conduct which causes inconvenience to the plaintiff making it impossible for the plaintiff to enjoy his or her land. The forms of nuisance are infinitely various and include an assortment of activities and substances including noise, smell, smoke, water, dirt, dust, chemicals, vibrations, radio transmissions, and so on.

Nuisance centres around land. The plaintiff is entitled to the "quiet enjoyment" of his or her land and the defendant is entitled to the "reasonable use" of his or her land. The court tries to mediate between the two. It is important to realize that it is not correct for a defendant to say, "It's my land, I can do anything I want on it." The common law has long held that every occupier of land must make reasonable use of the land. There is no right to do anything one's heart desires to the annoyance of others.

 Hollywood Silver Fox Farm Ltd. v. Emmett
England, 1936
On his property, the plaintiff raised silver foxes for their pelts. The animals would only breed for a brief time period each year and it was important that nothing should disturb them during those few days. The plaintiff and his neighbour, Emmett, did not get along. During the foxes' breeding season, Emmett sent his son, with a large-bore gun and black powder, to shoot rabbits as close as possible to the fox farm. This shooting lasted several days and

upset the foxes so much that none of them mated. The plaintiff sued for damages amounting to the loss of a year's pelts. The defendant argued that it was his right to hunt when he pleased on his land. The court awarded damages to the plaintiff:

> **❝**No one has an absolute right to create noise on his own land.**❞**

In a nuisance action, the plaintiff does not have to prove negligence or illegality on the part of the defendant. The defendant may be doing what he or she is doing very carefully and it may be quite legal. However, it may still be a nuisance.

There are a number of defences which the court may consider. First, the defendant may show that the land is being used reasonably and that the plaintiff is over-sensitive. Second, the activity may have been going on for a very long time. If an activity has been conducted for many years without any complaints, it is unlikely that the court will order it stopped unless changed circumstances can be shown. Third, an action specifically sanctioned by law and contributing to the public good can seldom be stopped by a nuisance action. A person who lives next to a train track could not bring an action demanding that no trains run at night.

The plaintiff in a nuisance case may request a variety of remedies. The first is an *injunction* which is a court order directing the defendant to cease and desist from creating the nuisance. The plaintiff may also be awarded monetary damages. If the nuisance continues, the plaintiff can sue again. The payment of damages once is not licence to continue the nuisance.

Occupier's Liability

The common law originally held that a person entered another person's land at his or her own risk. Gradually, it developed that the occupier of land (not necessarily the owner) did owe a duty of care to persons who entered. The duty was based primarily upon negligence in not keeping the premises in a proper state of repair.

In 1866, in the case of *Indermaur v. Dames,* a British court held that a person who enters property by permission has a right of action if injured by a hidden danger.

> **❝**And with respect to such a visitor at least, we consider it settled law, that he, using reasonable care on his part for his own safety, is entitled to expect that the occupier should on his part use reasonable care to prevent damage from unusual dangers which he knows or ought to know.**❞**

Having established that a duty could be owed, the courts then developed rules which tried to classify persons into categories, according to their purpose and their lawful right to be on the property. This process of classification has been criticized and has been discontinued in some provinces.

The occupier of property may be liable if persons are injured by risks which the occupier ought to have reasonably foreseen and removed.

Persons Entering by Right

Some persons, including the owner, acquire a right to enter property. The public has a right to enter places that are open to the public. Some public servants enter property in the performance of their duties. Many people enter property by right of contract. A person who buys a ticket to a hockey game enters the arena under this contractual right, and has a right not to be injured by hidden dangers. Often such tickets contain words which try to limit the liability of the occupier. Such words, called *disclaimer clauses,* are often rejected by the courts as having no legal recognition.

 Wilson v. Blue Mountain Resorts
Ontario, 1974

The plaintiff was hurt while skiing in an unmarked, dangerous gully. The defendant relied upon the printing on the admission ticket which stated: "The holder of this ticket, as a condition of being permitted to use the facilities of the area, agrees: (1) To assume all risk of personal injury or loss of or damage to property." The court held that the plaintiff did not know there was such printing on the ticket and that he had not read any such limitation clauses on tickets issued by other ski resorts. The words on the ticket had not been brought to his attention. In such circumstances, the defendant had not contracted out of liability.

Persons Who Enter To Conduct Business: Invitees

An *invitee* is a person who enters property for the purpose of conducting business in which the invitee and the occupier have a mutual interest. This category can include a very large number of persons such as patients, clients, customers, delivery and service personnel, and many others. The invitee must use the main entrance and has no permission to wander all over the property.

The occupier must use reasonable care to prevent injury from unusual dangers about which he or she knows or ought to know. Ignorance is no defence. The occupier should inspect the property regularly in order to find dangers before invitees get hurt.

 Norman v. Les Galeries St. Laurent
Newfoundland, 1981

The plaintiff suffered injury when he fell down an interior staircase in a shopping mall owned by the defendant. His fall had been caused by the slippery condition of the stairs, the result of melting ice and snow which had not been removed by mall employees. The defence contended that such tracking in is a normal winter occurrence and that the plaintiff should have been more alert and careful. The court disagreed and held that an invitee has the right to expect stairs to be safe, dry, and properly maintained by maintenance personnel. Therefore, the snow and ice constituted an unusual danger for which the defendant was liable.

Persons Entering by Invitation as Guests: Licencees

The next group may be thought of as social guests or *licencees*. A licencee has entered as the guest of the occupier, or a member of the occupier's family, for a purpose in which the occupier has no financial interest. Whatever transpires during the visit, it is still assumed that it was intended as a social visit. The duty of the occupier towards a guest is to warn of *unusual dangers of which he or she is aware*. The obligation goes no further. Since this obligation is less stringent than that towards invitees, many cases hinge on the question of the category to which the injured person belongs. It is easier to sue the occupier successfully if the plaintiff can show that he or she was an invitee. The defendant would like to show that the injured person was a licencee because then it would be a valid defence to show that the occupier did not know of the dangerous condition.

Weigall v. Westminister
England, 1936

The mother of a patient in a hospital fell on a loose mat on a waxed floor and suffered injury. The hospital contended that since the plaintiff was visiting a patient, she was a licencee or guest of the hospital, and that the hospital was not liable since it did not know of the dangerous condition. The court held that the plaintiff was an invitee since her purpose for being in the hospital was not a social one, but the business-like purpose of inquiring into the condition of a member of her family. The plaintiff was awarded damages against the hospital. The court placed much importance on the fact that the plaintiff was paying the hospital bill. A guest is seldom called upon to pay for a social visit.

There is a growing tendency in the common law to treat the invitee and the licencee very much the same. The distinction still exists, but is diminishing in significance.

Persons Entering Without Authority: Trespassers

A trespasser is a person who enters land without the occupier's consent and without "colour of right" to be there. A person may intentionally or unintentionally trespass. Once the occupier knows a trespasser is on the property, he or she may take action to remove the trespasser. If the occupier does not act, the trespasser may become a licencee since he or she has the tacit permission of the occupier to remain.

The occupier has no duty to warn unseen trespassers about dangerous conditions on the property. However, once the owner knows the trespasser is there, the trespasser must be warned of dangers. The occupier must not, without giving warning, suddenly change the condition of the land so as to create a danger which could cause injury to a trespasser who enters unaware of the danger. The occupier cannot set traps for trespassers either. In Canada, setting traps for people is a criminal offence.

A trespasser has no right of action against the occupier, regardless of how the injury occurred, unless the occupier attacked the trespasser or set a trap. This rule applies to children as well. No greater duty is owed by the occupier to a child trespasser than to an adult trespasser, except that where there is a duty to warn of danger, the duty may be greater towards children.

Alberta law requires that if the occupier knows or has reason to know that a child is trespassing and that there is a danger to that child, the occupier has a duty to see that the child is reasonably safe from that danger.

Statutes Regarding Occupier's Liability

Alberta, British Columbia, and Ontario have adopted the same basic wording as a British statute to eliminate the classification differences between invitee and licencee. The statutes are not identical but all require the occupier to take such care as is reasonable to see that persons entering property are reasonably safe while on the premises. There are some exclusions such as trespassers, persons who enter to commit crimes, and those who voluntarily accept the risk.

Special Status of Children

The problem of trespass by children is a very real one. Children do not appreciate dangers, property rights, or fine points of law as well as adults do. They are curious, adventurous, and even brazen at times. They will climb over or squeeze under the most formidable obstacles to reach what they want.

The freedom that children take for granted and their natural curiosity about things they don't understand, has brought about some special requirements for their protection. The law still maintains that, where children enter property as trespassers, they have no right of action against the occupier. But children are not always trespassers: they may be licencees under a rule of law called *allurement*.

Allurement works the same for children as for animals. In a very old case, the court ordered a person to stop luring grouse from a neighbour's game preserve by scattering corn kernels. A person who lures a child onto property cannot complain that the child trespasses. This is true even if the allurement was unintentional, which it usually is. A child cannot be expected to resist temptation, at least not to the same extent as would an adult. Property owners and occupiers must take every precaution to anticipate the lure their property presents to children.

Glasgow Corporation v. Taylor
Scotland, 1922

A child of seven was poisoned from eating berries in a botanical garden. The garden authorities knew that the berries were poisonous but they never thought that anyone would eat them; they took no measures to fence them off or to post signs. The corporation was held liable.

Nevertheless, in the following case, the trespassing child was not awarded damages for injuries suffered:

Wade v. CNR
Supreme Court of Canada, 1977

The plaintiff, eight years of age, was severely injured when he fell while attempting to jump onto the ladder of a moving boxcar. The infant had been playing in a sand pile belonging to the defendant corporation some 50 feet (15 m) from the track. The accident occurred at a private right of way belonging to the CNR and not at a public crossing. It was submitted by counsel for the plaintiff that the sand pile was an allurement because the neighbourhood children often played there. This brought them into close proximity with moving trains and they were tempted to try to ride them. There was no fence to keep children out of the sand pile. The Supreme Court of Canada held that the CNR was not liable. The driver had no warning of the child's action. The absence of fencing was not a causative factor. The corporation had a right to keep a sand pile on its property for its uses and did not have to fence it as the sand pile itself was not a hazard.

Damage by Animals

Society is much less agrarian today than it was, say, fifty years ago; the large majority of persons live in industrial centres, not on farms. Therefore, the number of court cases arising involving damage caused by horses and cattle is decreasing. At the same time, the number of cases involving pets owned by city dwellers is increasing. The favourite pet continues to be the dog, with cats running a close second. While many of these animals are timid and stay close to home, others are aggressive and wander about, often at night. Many communities have by-laws restricting the freedom of animals to wander, and requiring licensing and immunization against disease.

Damage by Wild Animals

The law divides animals into one of two categories: wild by nature (*ferae naturae*) or domesticated by nature (*mansuetae naturae*). If a person owns or keeps a wild animal with a dangerous, wild nature, that person must control the animal to a very high degree and will be held strictly liable if it injures someone. Such animals include lions, tigers, bears, elephants, large monkeys, and many others. It is the duty of the owner to prevent any kind of injury from the animal even if the owner believes that the animal is harmless. The injury could include attacking a person, frightening a person, or causing a person to fall while fleeing from the animal. Thus, the owner of a pet leopard must keep it where children will not try to pet it; otherwise, the owner will be strictly liable if the leopard bites or claws a child.

When a domestic animal shows a vicious streak, it must be treated the same as a wild animal. It must be assumed that it has lost its domestic nature and has reverted to being a dangerous, wild animal. The owner of a bull that gores must be careful to fence the animal away from persons and other animals. The owner of a horse that throws riders cannot continue to use that horse in a riding stable. A vicious dog must be chained or kept behind a chain wire fence.

The keeper of a naturally wild animal is under a strict liability not to let the animal harm any person.

The owner of a wild animal could escape liability by showing any of the following: (1) consent of the victim—an employee entering an animal's cage to clean it; (2) contributory negligence—someone trying to pet a dog after being clearly warned not to touch the animal; (3) an act over which the owner has no control—a vandal opening a cage door; or (4) an act of God—a landslide which derails a circus train and releases the animals. In each instance the owner must show that he or she was very diligent. In the third example, the court might question why the cage had no lock.

Damage by Domesticated Animals

What is the liability of the owner of a dog that bites someone? Many people think they have the answer because they have heard the old adage, "The dog is entitled to the first bite." The rule doesn't work that simply and perhaps it would be better forgotten altogether. Dog owners are successfully sued the *first* time their dog bites someone or even claws or knocks them down. The true interpretation of the rule of liability is known as the "scienter" which means the owner is liable if he or she even suspected the dangerous disposition of the animal. If the owner knows that the dog jumps on people, the owner is liable the first time the dog knocks someone down. If the dog has snarled and snapped at people before, the owner cannot act surprised because the dog actually took a chunk out of an unsuspecting victim. The dog had clearly given signs that it was "wont" to bite. The owner's knowledge of the animal's tendency must be related to the injury.

Manitoba, Ontario, and Newfoundland do not require proof that the dog had a tendency to bite. Rather, the owner is held strictly liable unless it can be shown that the victim caused or contributed to the injury. The Newfoundland law states that "It shall not be necessary for the person seeking damages to show a previous mischievous propensity or to show that the injury was attributable to neglect on the part of the owner."

Most provincial laws permit a court to order the destruction of a vicious dog.

Porter v. Joe
Nova Scotia, 1980

Porter was operating his motorcycle in a city park when a black Labrador retriever collided with his machine, causing him personal injury and damage to his motorcycle. Evidence was that two dogs belonging to Joe were playing on the grass in the company of the daughter of the defendant. Joe encouraged members of his family to take the dogs to the park for exercise. They were violating a by-law which prohibited the presence of dogs in the park unless the dogs were on a leash. However, the judge did not give this by-law any emphasis in trying to determine fault in this case. The dog did not attack the motorcycle but rather just ran into it while romping with the other dog. The defendant agreed that when the dogs started playing actively they became heedless of voice commands and unaware of other persons. The plaintiff was awarded damages and costs, but these were reduced 35 per cent for contributory negligence. The plaintiff might have avoided the collision if he had been more alert.

Animal Trespass

If an owner of cattle, sheep, horses, or other farm animals does not keep proper fences, the owner can be liable for "cattle trespass" if the animals go onto the property of others. No actual damages need be proven.

Cattle trespass does not extend to dogs and cats. Such straying animals are normally dealt with under municipal by-laws, although a property owner might bring an action in nuisance against the owner of an animal constantly allowed to run at large and cause damage. Most provincial laws make a dog owner liable if the dog trespasses and injures or frightens cattle. Farmers may shoot such dogs if they are on the farmer's land.

Animals that escape control and go onto highways may cause accidents when struck by motor vehicles. This is a difficult area of law, but generally the owner is expected to keep fences in good repair and not to let animals enter highways. If it can be shown that the animal managed to escape by some peculiar means, the owner is not liable. If a horse that has never jumped a fence suddenly does so when frightened by lightning, the owner is not liable for not building a higher fence.

Reviewing Important Points

1. A private lawsuit cannot be brought to stop a public nuisance. Only public authorities can deal with a public nuisance.
2. No one has an absolute right to create noise on his or her own land.
3. The occupier of land owes a duty of care to keep persons who enter the land reasonably safe from injury.
4. An invitee is a person who enters property for the purpose of conducting business in which the invitee and the occupier have a mutual interest.
5. A licencee is a person who enters property as a social guest.
6. Special care must be taken towards children who enter property. Dangerous objects that attract children are called allurements.
7. The owner of a naturally wild animal is under a strict liability if that animal injures someone.
8. Dog owners are liable for injuries caused by the dog if the dog has shown a previous tendency to cause injury. In some provinces the rule has been changed to strict liability.

Checking Your Understanding

1. State and briefly explain three defences to private nuisance.
2. What duty of care does a property occupier owe to an invitee? To a licencee? To a trespasser?
3. What basic reasons require that children who enter property be safeguarded differently than adults?
4. What is the liability of a person who keeps a naturally wild animal? What if the animal is normally very docile?
5. What is the "scienter" in regard to animals?

Legal Briefs

1. The plaintiff lived next door to a golf course. At times, while working in her garden she had to duck golf balls struck by less-than-gifted golfers. She sought a court order requiring the golf club to build a high fence. Evidence showed that golf balls came onto her property at the rate of three per week. Should the order be granted?
2. Whenever C played the piano and sang, her downstairs neighbour D howled and beat on the water pipes with pans. D contended that his racket was no worse than hers. What action should the court take?
3. On his property, R collected a large pile of manure which he used in his garden. He extolled the virtues of organic gardening. When the wind blew in a certain direction, his neighbour, T, became painfully aware of the existence of the organic matter. The manure also attracted flies. R argues that flies were a natural occurrence in the world. T brought an action against R for nuisance. What decision should the court reach?
4. S was annoyed that an iron company was polluting a stream that ran through her property. While S had several other sources of good water, she deliberately permitted her animals to drink from the bad water. Liability of the iron company?
5. G enjoyed flower gardening but his neighbour, Y, was allergic to many pollens from flowers. Y tried to enjoin G from carrying on his hobby. Must G comply?
6. W entered a store to get change for a parking

meter. W did not intend to buy anything in the store. She fell over an obstacle and was hurt. Liability of the store?
7. H fed a stray dog which then hung around her house for two weeks. When the dog bit a delivery boy, H contended that the dog was not hers. Liability?
8. B owned an animal that was half-wolf and half-dog. Should it be classed as *ferae naturae* or *mansuetae naturae*?
9. An old, toothless lion escaped from a circus. H woke up in a campground and found the lion sleeping inside his tent. H had a heart attack. The circus insisted that the lion would not and could not harm anyone. Liability of the circus?

Applying the Law

Lock v. Bouffioux
British Columbia, 1978

The plaintiff was a six-year-old child who was burned while visiting the farm of her uncle, the defendant. The plaintiff was observing the defendant's daughter, aged twelve, painting a portion of the defendant's barn. Since wasps were interfering with the painting job, the defendant took some gasoline, poured it on the wasp nest, and ignited it. After the fire died down, the daughter asked the defendant if she was to pour more gasoline on the nest. The defendant said, "No, the wasps will go away." The defendant then left the area. Shortly after, the daughter obtained some more gasoline with the intention of pouring it on the wasp nest. Some of the gasoline spilled onto the ground where a flame from the earlier fire ignited it and caused the burns to the plaintiff. The gasoline was kept in a large tank which was not locked and which was readily available to anyone, including the children. This was not an unusual practice on a farm. The court held the defendant liable. The defendant was under a duty to take reasonable care to see that the plaintiff was safe in using the premises. The defendant knew that his daughter was at least contemplating using more gasoline. He knew, or ought to have known, that there was still flame from the earlier fire. He did nothing to make the gasoline unavailable. He did not clearly forbid the children to touch the gasoline nor did he instruct them as to the grave risk in its use. He did nothing to reduce or eliminate the risk which he could have foreseen.

Questions

1. What duty of care did the defendant owe to the plaintiff?
2. Was the act of the daughter not an "intervening act" that would excuse the defendant from liability? Why or why not?
3. Was gasoline an allurement in this case? Why or why not?
4. Do you agree with the decision in this case? Give a reason for your answer.

Schenck v. The Queen
Ontario, 1981

The plaintiffs, Schenck and Rokeby, brought an action for damage done to peach and apple orchards. The orchards adjoined highways designated by the Minister of Transport as "bare pavement." These highways were given the highest level of winter maintenance including application of large quantities of salt. The plaintiffs proved that the salt killed their trees. The action alleged three possible grounds: negligence, the rule in *Rylands*, or nuisance. The court awarded damages only upon the ground of nuisance.

In a nuisance case the court must balance the substantial harm to the plaintiff against the social utility of safe highway travel. Fruit farming is also socially desirable and not an unusually sensitive use of land. The court found that the Crown was not immune from such an action. Although the Crown would not be liable in nuisance if the nuisance was the *inevitable* result of doing what the statute had authorized, the defendant had not satisfied the onus of proving that this damage was inevitable.

66Nor has the government satisfied the onus of proving that this nuisance constitutes an inevitable result of the statutory duty; to the contrary, as I view the evidence the nuisance cannot be considered an unavoidable consequence of a winter highway maintenance operation. The method by which the program is to be effected and its details are not specified by the legislation and, as I indicated earlier, substances other than salt can be used for de-icing and if used in the vicinity of the orchard would cure the interference.**99**

Questions

1. Did the court conclude that putting salt on a highway is a necessary action to make the road safe?
2. Why would salting a highway not be a public nuisance?
3. What significance did the court place upon the word "unavoidable" in this case?
4. Could car owners whose cars rust because of road salt bring an action against the government for this nuisance? Why or why not?

Martin v. Lowe
British Columbia, 1980

The plaintiff, aged seventy-nine, was walking with her husband along a street in Victoria on an autumn afternoon. She noticed two young people and a large dog nearby. The dog was "smelling around" the grass near the fence beside her as she went by and seemed to pay no attention to her. The young people walked past the plaintiff quickly and then, noticing that the dog was lagging behind, one of them gave a sharp whistle. The dog ran towards the young people but was not immediately able to get by the plaintiff and her husband. Therefore, it took the shortest available route and charged between the plaintiff's legs. The plaintiff was carried a short distance on the dog's back and then she fell to the pavement, suffering injury. She sued Lowe, the young man with the dog, and also Lowe's parents since the dog lived at their house. The court was told that Lowe lived in an apartment where he was not permitted to have a dog, and therefore his dog lived with his parents. Lowe produced a receipt given when he bought the dog, a St. Bernard. The case against the parents was dismissed since the court concluded that the dog did not belong to them. While a city by-law prohibited dogs from being off a leash, the trial judge did not consider that relevant in determining liability. He found Lowe was negligent in not controlling his dog and awarded the plaintiff damages against him.

Questions

1. In nearly every case, violation of a municipal by-law regarding dogs running loose is not considered relevant to a case alleging negligence. Why do you think this is so?
2. Since the dog lived with Lowe's parents, presumably they fed it, etc. Why would they not be the owners of the dog?
3. The dog's actions were not totally abnormal for a dog trying to get past a human. Why was it not a valid defence that the dog intended no harm to the plaintiff?
4. Were the plaintiff and her husband not partly at fault for blocking the sidewalk?

You Be the Judge

1. The defendant company constructed a nine-storey building immediately adjacent to and flush with the west wall of the plaintiff's two-storey building. The projection of the roof of the defendant's building resulted in an increased snow-load on the plaintiff's roof. The defendant was aware, before construction, of the inevitable damage to the plaintiff's building but argued that it was something it could not prevent by changing its construction plans in any way. The defence was centred around reasonable use of land. Who would succeed?
2. The plaintiff's source of water was a well, fed by percolating water from a nearby stream. The defendant commenced logging operations on property upstream from the plaintiff and built a road over the stream to facilitate the removal of logs. As a result, the plaintiff's water supply became saturated with mud and was made unfit for human consumption. The plaintiff argued unreasonable use of land. Who would succeed?
3. The plaintiff, who was eighteen years old at the time, rented a boat from the defendant. At the time he was required to pay the hourly rate, produce a driver's licence, and sign a form which said in part, "I understand that the owners take no responsibility for the safety of any occupant of the boat." The plaintiff went boating with three younger friends. During the ride the plaintiff sat upon the bow of the boat and was consequently thrown into the water. He came into contact with the motor's propeller and suffered serious injury. He sued the owner of the boat, alleging that the owner should have taken extra precautions in view of the youth of the persons renting the boat. The defendant ought to have inquired of the plaintiff's experience and to have warned of the danger of being seated elsewhere than in one of the seats. The defendant relied upon the exclusion or disclaimer clause of the contract. Who would succeed?
4. Although warned not to do so, children consistently played in two adjacent parking lots of a church. The church installed a chain across the entrance to one lot and painted the chain a fluorescent red. The infant plaintiff was injured when she rode her bicycle off the street into the entrance and struck the chain. The infant sued. The plaintiff had not been in the neighbourhood recently. She had approached the entrance very rapidly, without knowing that something "new" had taken place; namely, that a chain had been erected. She was going too fast to be able to stop in time. Who would succeed?
5. An action was brought by a mother on behalf of her two infant children who were burned in an accident. Randy was nine and Robin eight years of age. The boys went searching for an escaped rabbit and arrived at the defendant's property, the gates to which were always open. The defendant received chemicals in large drums which were transferred into cans for the wholesale and retail market. Empty drums were

stored outside of the buildings. The drums could not be emptied completely and contained a small amount of fluid. Randy had a tendency to play with matches. He dropped a lighted match into a pool of liquid near the barrels. The liquid caught fire and spread to a pile of barrels. One barrel caught fire and exploded. Both boys were burned and injured by flying metal. The action alleged negligence on the part of the defendant in storing flammables so carelessly. The defendant argued that the boys were trespassers and that Randy's propensity to play with matches was an intervening act which relieved the defendant of liability. Who would succeed?

6. The plaintiff was riding a horse along a rural road. The defendant's dog ran onto the road and barked at the horse. The horse threw the plaintiff off, causing injury. The horse then ran down the road and was struck by a car at an intersection. The horse had to be shot. The plaintiff sued for injury and for the value of the animal. The defence was based upon the "natural tendency" of dogs to bark at other animals and the fact that the owners were not required to keep the animal on a leash on their own property. They had no warning that the dog would suddenly rush out onto the rural road and chase the horse. Who would succeed?

Chapter 13

Torts: Further Aspects of Liability

Employer's Liability

Many workers are covered by workers' compensation which provides monetary compensation for injuries suffered on the job. Compensation is awarded to the worker by the Workmen's Compensation Board whether or not the injury was caused by the worker's carelessness. Thus, when a worker is covered adequately by workers' compensation the case will probably not come before a civil court.

Some workers, however, are not protected by workers' compensation. Examples are some white collar workers, casual or part-time workers, domestic servants, and independent parties who are performing a short service for the employer. The following discussion is based upon the common law principles that would apply assuming the worker was not covered by workers' compensation.

The Employer's Liability to Employees

Under English common law, the terms used to denote employer and employee are "master" and "servant." We have gotten away from using these terms in everyday life, because they imply a type of relationship that is no longer acceptable to most people.

Towards the middle of the nineteenth century unions began to acquire some legal recognition. Laws were passed to limit child and female labour in factories, although these laws were often not well enforced. Courts began to question seriously the assumption that employers owed their employees nothing in the way of safety. In the next half-century, cases estab-

An employer has a duty to provide his or her employees with a safe system of work and to ensure that safety regulations are followed.

lished that by common law employers had certain duties toward employees. These duties generally fell into four categories. Employers had to hire competent fellow workers so injury would not result because of a careless or untrained co-worker. Employers had to provide a safe place to work and a safe system of work. Lastly, employers had the duty either to provide proper safety equipment or else to ensure that workers provided their own and used it.

The Employer's Liability to Third Parties

An employer also has a responsibility to third parties for the actions of employees. This situation may include one employee injuring another employee. In some cases the employer is liable even though not personally guilty of wrongdoing. This is referred to as vicarious liability which, as we have seen, means to be responsible for the misconduct of another person. The employer-employee relationship is only one of many ways vicarious liability comes into existence.

An important question regarding vicarious liability is whether or not the employer should be responsible for everything the employees do. If a person works for a company and during lunch break goes across the street and hits someone else, should the company be liable? Certainly not. But, if a person is employed to collect bills and, while doing so, hits the debtor, would the company be liable? Probably so, because this incident occurred while the employee was carrying out the employer's business. However, an employer does not have an automatic, around-the-clock responsibility for everyone on the payroll.

 *Jennings v. CNR*
Ontario, 1925

A CNR ticket collector got into an argument with a passenger and hit him. The trial judge did not hold the employer responsible, but the appeal court did. It was held that since the assault arose while the collector was collecting a ticket from the injured party, it was an act of employment and required the CNR to be responsible for the tort of its employee.

Product Liability

The supplier of a product, whether manufacturer, wholesaler, or retailer, is liable for personal injuries and damage to property caused by a defect in the product if the defect arises from the supplier's failure to exercise reasonable care in the manufacture, preparation, labelling, or inspection of the product.

General Basis of Liability

The test of liability is reasonable care, but in many cases the courts have held that if the injured person proves the existence of a defect at the time the product left a manufacturer's hands, and proves that the injury was caused by the product's defect, negligence will be inferred. In these circumstances it is very difficult, in real practice, for a manufacturer to escape liability.

Where a buyer of goods is injured by defects in them, the buyer may also have recourse against the person who sold the product. Because the implied obligations in the sale contract have been breached, the seller will be liable for the buyer's loss, even though the seller had no means of discovering or avoiding the defect. This is a form of strict liability based on the contract between the parties, but it is limited in its application since it applies only in favour of a buyer and only against a seller.

In certain cases, an injured person will fail to recover damages because it is not possible to prove negligence. If, for example, the manufacturer has obtained a defective part from another supplier, the manufacturer may not be liable.

A basic problem exists if it is not the buyer of the product who is injured by the product but, instead, a member of the buyer's family. The injured person had no contract of sale with the supplier and the absence of this contract makes it difficult to sue. This is called *privity of contract* and, in the case of *Greenwood Shopping Plaza Ltd. v. Beattie* (1981), the Supreme Court of Canada gave new strength to the privity of contract rule. In that case the court held that, in a suit by a third party, employees were not protected by a contract negotiated between an employer and that third party. The court said that the employees were not in privity of contract with the third party and therefore could not claim the protection of their employer's contract. In a Quebec case, *Kravitz v. General Motors* (1980), the Supreme Court of Canada allowed contract action by a consumer directly against a manufacturer although no contract link existed. As the case was based upon the Quebec *Civil Code*, it has doubtful application to the rest of Canada.

Privity of contract does not alter the basic rule in *Donoghue v. Stevenson* that a manufacturer is liable to the person who ultimately consumes a product. It only suggests that claims cannot be too remote from the injury. If A buys a new truck which has a defect causing it to crash and be totally demolished, no action could be brought by B, the uninjured truck driver, on the grounds that the destruction of A's truck caused the loss of B's job.

Strict Liability

Strict liability in cases of product liability means that the consumer can sue the manufacturer and retailer for damages caused by defective products without having to prove negligence. Saskatchewan, Quebec, and New Brunswick now have such legislation.

Strict liability places strong demands upon manufacturers to ensure that products are free of defects when leaving the plant or store. It requires the keeping of extensive records so that the manufacturer can determine in which plant a product was made in order to prevent similar problems from happening again.

Sale of Goods Act

Most provinces have a *Sale of Goods Act* which may contain wording similar to the Ontario statute which reads in part:

Where the buyer expressly or by implication makes known to the seller the particular purpose for which the goods are required so as to show that the buyer relies on the seller's skill or judgment, and the goods are of a description that it is in the course of the seller's business to supply (whether he is the manufacturer or not), there is an implied condition that the goods will be reasonably fit for such purpose, but in the case of a contract for the sale of a specific article under its patent or other trade name there is no implied condition as to its fitness for any particular purpose.

The primary purpose of this section is to place an implied condition upon the sale that the goods *recommended by the seller* will be reasonably fit for the purpose which the buyer has explained to the seller. It is important to note that in such a case the buyer is revealing personal lack of knowledge and relying strongly upon the advice and direction of the seller. If the seller gives wrong advice and the buyer suffers injury, the basis for liability may be laid. If the buyer relies upon personal judgment or just buys a product by its brand name, the seller is not liable. Recent decisions tend to suggest that the courts have almost completely eliminated the practical effect of the latter part of this provision in the Act. Retailers have been held liable even though they did not specifically recommend a product. The modern view is that there is a warranty that runs with the goods and retailers must take responsibility for what they sell.

Hart v. Dominion Stores et al. Ontario, 1968

Hart was shopping in a Dominion store with his wife. As he was pushing a cart along an aisle, he approached the area where some Coca-Cola bottles were kept on shelves. There were also three bottles on the floor. Hart heard a noise and felt a pain in his right eye. He looked at the bottles and saw that one of them was shattered. He had been struck in the eye by a piece of glass from this bottle and suffered permanent partial loss of vision in the right eye. He sued Dominion Stores and Coca-Cola. Evidence showed that the bottles were purchased from the Coca-Cola plant in Niagara Falls, Ontario once a week. They were not placed on the floor by store employees, but customers sometimes took partially filled cartons and set extra bottles on the floor. When store employees found them there, they returned them to the shelves. There was no evidence that anyone had knocked over the bottle that exploded. A technical witness for Coca-Cola testified that in his opinion, the bottle broke because of an external force upon it, not because of an internal force. He used drawings of pieces of glass to support his opinion. He said that it was a sound bottle that had been dropped or damaged by someone. Other studies showed that internal force would cause the cap to blow off, but would not break the bottle. The court noted, however, that bottles are refilled many times and that the inspection process is perfunctory. Since glass weakens with use, a small crack could weaken a bottle enough to blow it apart. The court found Coca-Cola liable but not Dominion Stores. There was no evidence that Dominion knew or ought to have known of the potential danger in the bottle. The court also noted that as Hart had not yet purchased a bottle, the *Sale of Goods Act* did not apply.

Children's Torts

Liability of the Child

A principle of our common law is that children are liable for their torts. The criminal law holds that a child under the age of seven cannot be charged with a crime, and criminal proceedings are seldom taken against children under the age of fourteen. Why the difference between a crime and a tort? The difference lies in the fact that one of the necessary elements of a crime is mens rea. This means that the person must have a certain mental capacity to intend the nature and consequences of personal actions. Children cannot reason well enough to foresee what damage their actions will cause and have not developed enough mentally to understand why some things are considered wrong by other people. In tort law, malicious intention is not necessarily an ingredient of the tort; thus a child or even an insane person can commit some torts and be liable for them. Since many torts occur as a result of careless behaviour, it is no defence to say, "I did not intend that to happen."

A parent may be liable for the tort committed by his or her child if the parent failed to exercise reasonable control.

Nevertheless, very young children cannot be liable for torts because they cannot understand what they have done and what proceedings are being taken against them. The child must have achieved some age of reason. Thus, where a very young child accomplished the remarkable feat of putting in motion a parked car which ran into a store, the court held that the child was not liable because it was nearly impossible for one so young to have put the car in motion.

Some torts require a malicious motive as an element of proof. Libel often indicates an intent to harm a person's reputation. Assault and battery have the intended purpose of physical injury. If children committed torts such as these, it is doubtful they would be liable in tort, because the court would have to take the view that children are incapable of the malicious intent in such events. If children committed simple torts such as trespass, the court might find them liable, holding that the primary point is damage to the property owner, not the malicious intention of the trespasser. When a person causes damage because of negligence, the normal question that a tort case would raise is, "Were the consequences foreseeable and did the wrongdoer behave as a reasonable person would have behaved?" But, since children are not adult persons, can this rule be applied to them? They do not have the mental capacity of an adult to think ahead, and do not have the experience to understand that something they think is fun might go wrong and cause injury to someone. Should the court then adopt a rule called the rule of the "reasonable child"? It would not be very successful, for the rule of the reasonable person is difficult enough to apply without making a more complicated rule involving children. The courts hold that the behaviour of a child cannot be compared with the desired behaviour of an adult. A child is expected to conform to the intelligence and experience of other children of the same age. If unable to understand the nature of the action, negligence cannot be attributed to the child at all; but, given some understanding of the risk, the child must display the judgment and behaviour normal for a child with the same characteristics.

 ### McHale v. Watson
Australia, 1966

The plaintiff, a girl age nine, was hit in the eye by a piece of steel welding rod. The rod was thrown by a boy, age twelve, the defendant in the case. The defendant was playing a game of throwing the rod at a fence post. One end of the rod was sharp, and he was trying to get it to stick in the post. One unsuccessful throw caused the rod to bounce off the post with great speed and strike out the eye of the plaintiff who was watching the game. The plaintiff sued the boy for damages, the action being brought by her parents as next friend. The court recognized that had the defendant been an adult, there would be no question of his liability for negligence since any adult could foresee the danger to someone standing too close to the fence post. The court did not try to treat the defendant as an adult, but examined the actions in the light of the fact that the defendant was only twelve years old. Should a boy of twelve have reasonable foresight and prudence to appreciate the risk to the plaintiff from what he was doing? The court held:

66Sympathy with the injured girl is inevitable. One might also wish there was a rule that saved all children from harm. But, there is not. Children, like everyone else, must accept as they go about in society the risks from which ordinary care on the part of others will not suffice to save them. One such risk is that boys of twelve will behave as boys of twelve, and that is a risk indeed. The case against the defendant must be dismissed.99

The case, with its refusal to apply the rule of the reasonable person to a child deserves considerable recognition. It holds that, while there is a standard of care which is due from everyone, that standard is not the same for children as for adults. However, if a child is performing an adult act, such as driving a car or operating an industrial or farm machine, the same standard of care is expected from that child as from an adult. If the child is incapable of operating that machine safely, the person who permitted him or her to do it is liable.

Parental Liability for Children's Torts

Many people assume that parents must pay for damage done by their children. This is not true. If children are liable for their own torts, then their parents cannot also be liable just because they are related by blood. The parents may become liable if they in some way brought about a tort, or failed to control their children when they should have been exercising parental control. Children that are destructive may place a greater burden of control upon parents than would be required for ordinary children.

In some cases parents want to be responsible for their children's torts because such responsibility will preserve a good relationship with neighbours and because they feel a moral obligation, if not a legal one. If a suit is brought against a child, a parent may defend it as *guardian ad litem* —a term meaning a person appointed to defend an action on behalf of an infant or person under a disability. However, in this case the parent acts in a purely representative capacity and does not incur personal liability.

The behaviour of children cannot be controlled by their parents all of the time. Children must have freedom to move about as all human beings do. If parents have totally lost control, they may ask the judge to place the child in a foster home, industrial school, or some other location. This relieves the parents of the responsibility of parental control. A parent can make this request to the court even before a child has become delinquent.

School Division of Assiniboine South v. Hoffer, Hoffer and Greater Winnipeg Gas Co. Ltd. Manitoba, 1971

A fourteen-year-old boy was having trouble starting the family snowmobile because he did not have sufficient strength to pull the starting cord with one hand. His father taught him to start the snowmobile by (1) putting the machine on its kickstand; (2) tying the throttle open with a cord; and (3) pulling the cord with two hands. One day the boy forgot to put the machine on the kickstand. When he started it, it raced off with the throttle wide open. The machine went across a parking lot and into a school yard where it hit a natural gas riser pipe beside a school building. The pipe was broken by the impact and natural gas began seeping into the school building. Finally, enough gas accumulated and was ignited by a pilot light. There was an explosion which caused extensive damage to the school. An action was brought against the father, the son, and the gas company. The improper installation of the riser pipe resulted in the gas company's being 50 per cent liable. The court held that the company did not have to take extravagant precautions against the unlikely possibility of the pipe being hit by a snowmobile, but improper installation meant that the potential risk of any damage to the pipe was very great. Protective pipes should have been installed. Liability of the son and father was assessed at 25 per cent each. The court agreed that it was unlikely that either could have foreseen this particular type of accident occurring, but permitting a snowmobile to run wild was like firing a rifle blindly down a city street. The ambit of possible damage was very broad.

Civil Court Procedures

Civil cases are generally referred to a particular court depending on the amount of money involved. Each province establishes its own civil courts, and the names vary somewhat from province to province.

A special procedure is necessary in the case of an infant. An infant cannot sue personally except in a few special cases such as a suit for unpaid wages. Persons are legally classed as infants until they reach a certain age, upon which they are said to have attained their majority. The legal age is set by the provinces as follows:

Age	Province
18	Alberta, Manitoba, Ontario, Prince Edward Island, Quebec, Saskatchewan
19	British Columbia, New Brunswick, Newfoundland, Nova Scotia

A suit must be brought on behalf of the infant by a "next friend" who is the parent or guardian or any responsible adult. The purpose of requiring the suit from a next friend is to make certain that there is someone to answer to the court for the propriety of the suit and possibly to pay the costs and judgment. It is not practical to allow children to launch civil suits knowing full well that they cannot be held liable should the case be decided against them. If an adult is suing an infant, the Writ is served on the infant.

The court issues a Writ of Summons on the defendant. This Writ is usually served upon the defendant by a bailiff, but it may be served by anyone. The Writ of Summons informs the defendant of the action and gives a time limit in which to file a notice to defend the action. If a defendant does not file a defence (sometimes called a dispute or an appearance), a judgment will be entered against the defendant by default. A Writ of Summons is usually served personally on the defendant, but in some cases substitute service, such as registered mail, may be used. However, there must be some indication that the defendant knew of the action.

If the defendant wants to contest the case, he or she files a dispute, entering it in the same court where the Writ of Summons was issued. The clerk of the court sends a copy of it to the plaintiff along with a notice of trial. The notice of trial is also sent to the defendant. The plaintiff files with the court a Statement of Claim in which are outlined the demands being made on the defendant. A copy is sent to the defendant.

If the action is to be tried before a superior court, because of the amount involved, it is possible that a civil jury will be called to hear the case. In certain types of cases, including libel, false arrest, or false imprisonment, a jury is nearly always called. If one party wishes a jury trial, a jury notice is sent to the other party. If the other party does not want a jury trial, he or she petitions the judge to strike the notice out. The judge makes the final decision. Where a case involves a great deal of technical evidence which a jury might not be able to understand, a judge may refuse to grant a jury trial on the grounds that a jury could not reach a proper verdict. In Ontario, a civil jury consists of six persons, five of whom must agree in order to reach a verdict. If a juror is later discharged for some reason, the case may continue with five jurors and all five remaining jurors must agree. If more than one issue must be decided, it is not necessary that the same five jurors agree on each issue.

Alberta and Manitoba also have six jurors. In British Columbia there are eight and Nova Scotia has five. Prince Edward Island and New Brunswick require seven while Saskatchewan has twelve. Newfoundland has nine jurors. In Newfoundland, if after deliberating for three hours the jurors are not unanimous, a majority of seven jurors may return a verdict.

Each party is entitled to examine all documents which the other side intends to introduce at the trial. Some provinces permit either party to request a pretrial meeting called an *Examination for Discovery*. An Examination for Discovery is not a hearing, but an attempt to put the other party's case on the record and get the other party to admit certain facts. The two litigants (plaintiff and defendant) and all witnesses may be examined and a formal transcript is made of their testimony. This testimony can be used as evidence during the trial. Quite often after the Examination for Discovery, the two parties are able to settle out of court.

If the two parties do not settle, a trial date is set. If, when the case is called for trial, either party does not appear, the other party is entitled to judgment by default. The court's decision is called the *judgment*. The loser can expect to pay the damages asked in a default judgment. In a judgment on the merits, the loser can expect to pay the proven damages. The loser will also pay court costs. Costs include some of the lawyer's fees for the other side, but not everything that the other party has had to pay. That is, there is a distinct difference between court costs and solicitor-client costs. Suppose the plaintiff won the case. The plaintiff might pay his or her lawyer $500 in legal fees, but this does not mean the defendant owes the plaintiff $500. The court follows a schedule of fees under what is called "Rules of Practice" and, depending upon the type

Civil Court Procedure (Ontario)

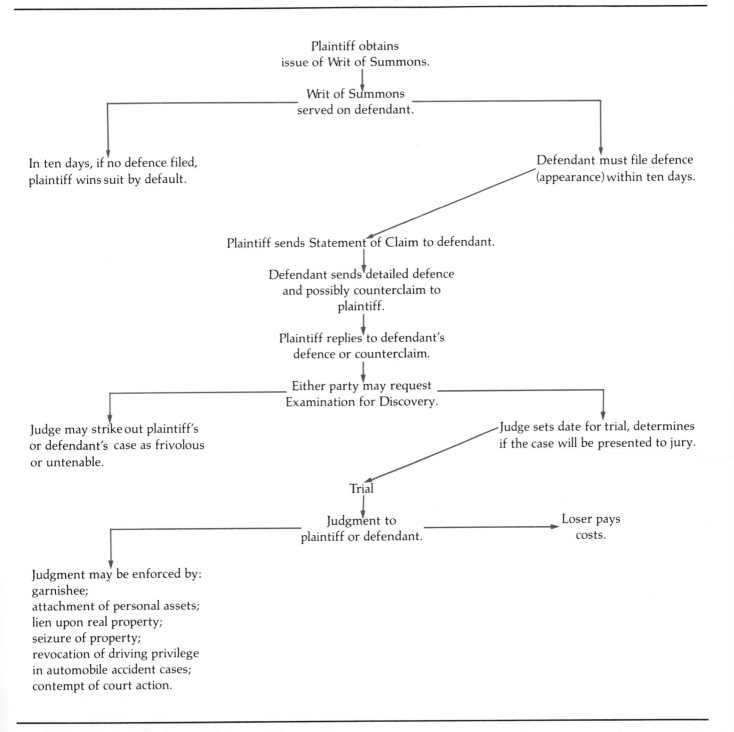

Plaintiff obtains
issue of Writ of Summons.

Writ of Summons
served on defendant.

In ten days, if no defence filed,
plaintiff wins suit by default.

Defendant must file defence
(appearance) within ten days.

Plaintiff sends Statement of Claim to defendant.

Defendant sends detailed defence
and possibly counterclaim to
plaintiff.

Plaintiff replies to defendant's
defence or counterclaim.

Either party may request
Examination for Discovery.

Judge may strike out plaintiff's
or defendant's case as frivolous
or untenable.

Judge sets date for trial, determines
if the case will be presented to jury.

Trial

Judgment to
plaintiff or defendant.

Loser pays
costs.

Judgment may be enforced by:
garnishee;
attachment of personal assets;
lien upon real property;
seizure of property;
revocation of driving privilege
in automobile accident cases;
contempt of court action.

of case, allows the winner to recover the amount shown in the schedule. Court costs also include fees paid for filing documents, making transcripts, and other expenses. No one should assume that by winning a lawsuit, he or she will have all expenses repaid. At best, one-half to two-thirds will be recovered. Any person who believes that he or she has been overcharged by a lawyer may refer the matter to the court Taxing Officer and request that the bill be reduced. This procedure is known as "taxing" and it means that the court will study the lawyer's bill against the schedule in the Rules of Practice and determine whether a client has been charged too much for the service rendered. The same rule applies to the court costs which the winner demands from the loser. If the amount demanded as costs appears too high, the loser may have the matter decided by the Taxing Officer.

If the plaintiff succeeds, the court must award some damages. Damages means money to compensate the plaintiff for loss or injury. The first type is *special damages* which is an itemized list including medical expenses, property damage, loss of employment, loss of future earnings, rehabilitation, and many other possible items for which a fairly accurate cost can be assessed. There is no limit upon the amount of special damages. The second type is *general damages* which is a lump sum for such things as pain, suffering, loss of social amenities, and other things upon which it is difficult to place a specific value. The Supreme Court of Canada has indicated that $100 000 is the limit that should be awarded in this category. *Punitive damages* are awarded when the behaviour of the defendant has been very obnoxious and his or her attitude has been offensive. *Nominal damages* represent a small amount of money awarded just to establish that the plaintiff was legally right, but suffered only a small loss. *Contemptuous damages* are awarded if the plaintiff's case is legally right but trivial, or the loss somewhat doubtful. The award could be as low as one cent.

A civil case that has been decided against either party in what he or she feels is a wrong decision may be appealed to a higher court, usually the provincial Court of Appeal. A civil case could eventually be appealed to the Supreme Court of Canada.

The question is sometimes asked, "Once a judgment has been won, how do you make the other party pay up?" The judgment may be collected in various ways including the seizure of property which is then sold at auction (called an *execution*), putting a lien against real property, attaching bank accounts or other assets, or garnishment of wages. If a debtor refuses to pay a judgment even though he or she has the money, the debtor can be brought back to court and ordered to "show cause" why the judgment has not been paid. It is possible for the judge to fine or jail the debtor for not paying the judgment. A judgment won against a person with no money has little value, since obviously nothing can be collected when the debtor has no money to give.

A person wishing to bring a civil action should consult a lawyer immediately. In each province, statutes have set time limits during which a civil action can be brought. Some give the injured person as little as ten days to take some form of legal action. If parties "sleep on their rights" too long, the right to sue may be lost.

Pure Economic Loss

Pure economic loss is a term which implies that while a plaintiff in an action was not directly injured by the defendant, the plaintiff did suffer a loss indirectly. He or she may have lost employment or money out of pocket.

The provision of remedies for economic loss is a later development of tort law since the courts traditionally held that the defendant could not have foreseen such an injury. A good illustrative case is *Weller v. Foot and Mouth Disease Institute* (England, 1966). The defendant brought a virus to England from Africa to study. It was negligently allowed to escape and it infected many cattle in the area which then had to be destroyed. This incident put the plaintiff, a cattle auctioneer, out of business for a long time. The plaintiff sued for lost income. The court denied the plaintiff damages because the defendant had a duty of care only towards cattle owners. To accept the plaintiff's claim could have led to many more claims being brought, including claims from consumers who would object to the rise in beef prices.

Yet, to the plaintiff the loss was quite real. The plaintiff would have liked the court to have utilized the "but for" rule, which basically means that the plaintiff would not have lost money but for the actions of the defendant.

The willingness of the courts to recognize economic loss is gaining, however, as the following case demonstrates:

Seaway Hotels Ltd. v. Gragg Ltd. and Consumers Gas Co.
Ontario, 1969

A gas company negligently cut a feeder line of the electric company, thereby cutting off electricity to the plaintiff's hotel. The plaintiff sued for lost restaurant and bar income, spoiled food, and loss of room rentals. The defendant accepted liability only for the damage done to the electric line. It repaired the line, but accepted no liability for the loss to the hotel. The defendant denied any duty of care to the plaintiff since the loss was not foreseeable and was too remote from the negligence of cutting the line. The court disagreed and awarded damages to the plaintiff holding that, since the gas company knew of the location of the hydro line, it could have foreseen that damage to the line would cause an economic loss to the hotel which depended upon the electricity to run its business.

In this case, also, the validity of a claim for economic loss was recognized by the court:

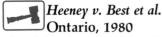

Heeney v. Best et al.
Ontario, 1980

The defendant negligently drove into some overhead power lines, thereby cutting off the electrical power to the plaintiff's farm. This interruption cut off ventilation fans in the barns where baby chicks were being raised. The power failure was not discovered for several hours, by which time the chicks were dead. The plaintiff had a battery-powered, power failure detector in his bedroom; however, for some reason the detector was not in operation that night. It was admitted that if the detector had been plugged in the chicks would have been saved.

The defendant denied liability to the plaintiff and raised a number of defences, including duty of care, foreseeability, and contributory negligence. The court awarded the plaintiff 75 per cent of his loss. The failure to plug in the alarm was contributory negligence, but by far the greater fault was that of the defendant. The sole cause of the interruption of power was the negligence of the defendant driver. The plaintiff was entitled to the uninterrupted flow of electricity to his property.

Reviewing Important Points

1. An employer is liable for torts committed by an employee if these torts are committed within the scope of employment.
2. The manufacturer or retailer of a product is liable in tort for injury caused by that product if there was a failure to exercise reasonable care in the manufacture, labelling, or inspection of the product.
3. A child can be liable for a tort once the child has reached the age of reason.
4. The standard of care expected of a child is not equal to that required of adults but rather to that required of children of similar age and experience.
5. Parents may be liable for a child's tort if the parents did not exercise control where called for or did something to encourage or instigate the tort.
6. If a lawsuit is brought against a child, the parents are served with the papers as guardian ad litem of the child. This does not mean that the parents will have to pay a judgment against their child.
7. If a plaintiff suffers economic loss because of the actions of the defendant, the plaintiff may collect damages if the loss was direct and not too remote from the negligent act of the defendant.

Checking Your Understanding

1. What is vicarious liability? How does it apply in the relationship of employer to employee and parent to child?
2. If a person purchases a product which injures a member of the family, that person may have trouble suing the seller. The problem arises under privity of contract. What is privity of contract and what problem does it present to the plaintiff?
3. Product liability may some day become "strict liability." Explain how this would alter the present law.
4. If a child performs an adult act, what standard of care is expected from that child?
5. Under what circumstances would a parent be liable for the torts of a child?
6. How is a civil lawsuit initiated?
7. What is an Examination for Discovery? What role does it play in the civil court process?
8. What type of civil lawsuit would not be suitable for a jury trial?
9. What methods are available to enforce a civil court judgment?

Legal Briefs

1. W buys a food processor as a gift for his wife. The first time she uses it, she receives a bad electrical shock because of faulty wiring. Liability of the manufacturer?
2. P uses a cosmetic and suffers serious skin problems and scarring. Tests show that P has a rare allergy to one of the ingredients in the cosmetic. Nothing on the label warns that some people may be allergic to the product. Estimates are that only one person in 50 000 may have such an allergy. Liability of the manufacturer?
3. Y uses a certain birth control pill for several years and follows directions carefully. She becomes pregnant and has a very difficult pregnancy. Laboratory examination shows that several batches of pills were improperly made and ineffective. Y gives birth to a child with a serious heart condition. Discuss the liabil-

ity of the manufacturer to Y for the unwanted and difficult pregnancy and the child's problems.
4. K drives his car negligently into a bridge support. The bridge is so weakened it must be closed for two months. During that time regular customers to B's tavern cannot reach the tavern without taking a long detour. Many decide to take their business elsewhere and B loses income. Is K liable to B?
5. G drives negligently and strikes a fire hydrant. Water floods the basement of H's shop. Liability of G to H? The water department shuts off the water while making repairs. This cuts off water to W's factory who has to shut down production for the day. Can W sue G for the day's lost production?
6. F buys fresh pork from a butcher, eats the pork uncooked and contracts trichinosis. The butcher did not know F would eat the meat uncooked (like cured sausage). Liability?
7. A three-year-old girl, seeing a baby in a carriage and thinking it is a doll, takes the baby from the baby carriage and drags it one hundred metres. The girl's parents are unaware that she has any such interest in the baby. Liability of the girl? The parents?
8. C teaches his son, H, basic marksmanship with a .22 calibre rifle. Safety is stressed at all times. One day while C is not home, H gets the rifle out and starts shooting at tin cans despite his father's orders never to shoot alone. Several friends of H come along and join in. One of them, T, is reckless and silly with the gun and negligently shoots another boy, V, causing partial paralysis. Discuss the liability of C.
9. A merchant, B, sells a pellet gun to a small boy. The boy's mother is furious and calls the merchant on the phone and demands that he take the gun back and refund the boy's money. B agrees and the mother sends the boy back towards the store with the gun. He stops enroute and takes a few shots at some birds, but hits another child. What is the liability of B? The mother?
10. A veterinarian purchased a vaccine from a retailer and injected it into cattle. The cattle died because the vaccine was contaminated. The owner of the cattle sued the vet. Who should be liable — the vet, the retailer, the manufacturer, or all three?

Applying the Law

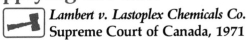

Lambert v. Lastoplex Chemicals Co.
Supreme Court of Canada, 1971

The plaintiff was using lacquer sealer manufactured by the defendant when the sealer already applied caught fire and exploded. It was determined that the cause of the fire which preceded the explosion was the contact of lacquer fumes with the pilot light in the furnace room. The labels on the cans contained warnings that the product was inflammable and should be kept away from "fire, heat and open-flame lights" and used with adequate ventilation. The plaintiff had taken steps to ensure ventilation of the work area, but had not realized that the pilot light in an adjoining room, behind a closed door, would be a hazard. He alleged that the defendant was negligent in failing to give adequate warning of the product's volatility. The court heard evidence that a competitor's product gave specific and obvious warning that "furnaces, all pilot lights, spark-producing switches, etc. must be eliminated in or near working area." The Supreme Court of Canada unanimously found the defendant liable.

66Where manufactured products are put on the market for ultimate purchase and use by the general public and carry danger . . . , although put to the use for which they are intended, the manufacturer, knowing of their hazardous nature, has a duty to specify the attendant dangers which it must be taken to appreciate in a detail not known to the ordinary consumer.99

Questions

1. Since the instructions said to keep away from "open-flame lights" was this not sufficient warning? Why or why not?
2. Since a can has only a limited space for instructions, which must be in French and English, how can a manufacturer get all the possible hazards identified on the product?
3. Was it significant that the pilot light was in another room behind a closed door? Why or why not?
4. If you were advising this company, what suggestions would you make to avoid liability in the future?

Floyd v. Bowers
Ontario, 1978

An Ontario couple were ordered to pay $81 000 in damages in trust to a seventeen-year-old youth shot in the eye with an air rifle pellet by their son.

The Ontario Supreme Court held that the parents failed to prevent easy access to the gun and ammunition and did not instruct their son, Stephen in the proper use of the gun. The son and Michael Floyd were both thirteen years old when the incident took place. They began arguing while at the defendants' cottage. Stephen went for the gun and fired two shots, the second hitting Michael in the right eye. The trial judge held that the shooting was particularly unfortunate because Michael already had very poor vision in his left eye to begin with. As the injury would reduce Michael's ability to hold a job, the award was higher than it might otherwise have been.

Questions

1. Why were the parents liable for the tort of their son?
2. What significance was put upon the fact that the plaintiff already had a vision problem? (Review the thin-skull rule.)
3. Should the court not have placed more emphasis upon the extreme youth of Stephen? Should his actions be judged as the actions of an adult or of a thirteen-year-old?

Strehlke et al. v. Camenzind et al. and Janor Contracting Ltd.
Alberta, 1980

Two boys, one almost seven years old, the other eight, while playing with matches, destroyed the plaintiff's partly built home. If the boys had been adults, their actions would have constituted actionable negligence. Both boys had been taught by their parents not to play with matches and said they had never done so before. They entered the building through an open doorway since no door had been installed. They set fire to some wood shavings left by carpenters, and then put out the fire with wet cement. They went to the basement for a while and when they came back upstairs they saw that the first floor was in flames. They reported the fire to their parents but the house could not be saved.

In a negligence case involving an infant defendant, the court applied three tests:

(1) An objective test to decide whether the infant exercised the care to be expected from a child of like age, intelligence and experience.

(2) A subjective test, where it was necessary to decide whether the child, having regard to his or her age, intelligence, experience, general knowledge, and alertness, was capable of being found negligent at law in the circumstances under investigation.

(3) A test of the actual experience of the infant concerned. It was necessary to consider the particular child—all the qualities and defects of that particular child and all of the opportunities or lack of them which he or she might have had to become aware of any particular peril or duty of care.

Applying these tests to the present case, the trial judge found that both boys knew it was wrong to play with fire but that they had little understanding of why it was wrong and the possible consequences. Neither child had sufficient experience in the handling of fire to have reasonably foreseen that playing with matches might result in a serious fire. The plaintiff's claim against the adult defendants and the third party was dismissed following the application for non-suit by their solicitors. The claim against the infant defendants was dismissed by the trial judge for the reasons stated.

Questions

1. If no one was liable for the fire, how would the plaintiff obtain justice for the loss of his house which was the deliberate act of the infant defendants?
2. Why were the parents not liable?
3. Why were the infant defendants not liable?
4. Do children who play with matches not realize the possibility of a fire? Can you draw upon your own experience to answer this question?
5. The court placed no importance upon where the infant defendants got the matches. Do you think this could have had some bearing upon the case? Why or why not?

You Be the Judge

1. The defendant carelessly drove her truck into the rear of the truck in front of her. The accident disabled both vehicles. The defendant accepted liability for the damage to the other truck; however, the plaintiff also claimed damages for the spoiled contents of the truck. The truck had been carrying lettuce which wilted and browned because of the very hot temperature on the day of the accident. Who would succeed?

2. The plaintiff suffered injury from glass particles in a loaf of bread. He sued the bakery. The bakery brought forth evidence to show that it had the most modern equipment and a very thorough inspection system. None of the equipment used in the manufacture of bread contained glass parts. There was no report of any broken glass anywhere in the bakery. It was the position of the defendant that the glass must have somehow entered their product after the bread had left the bakery. The plaintiff testified that the wrapper on the bread was unbroken when he purchased it. Who would succeed?

3. Children riding sleds down a hill were using a fence at the bottom of the hill to stop them from going onto the road. There were holes in the fence and at times a sled went through the holes and across the road. A passing delivery vehicle had to swerve to avoid a child shooting across the road. The vehicle hit a pole, injuring the driver who sued the parents of the child. Who would succeed?

4. The owner of an apartment building had a contract with another company to perform inspection, service, and maintenance on the building's elevator. One month, a mechanic performed maintenance and lubricated parts of the elevator, but did not report to the

building owner that the elevator had a very badly worn part that should be replaced. The elevator collapsed down the shaft and injured a building tenant who sued the building owner and the service company. Who would be liable?

5. The plaintiff purchased ground meat from the defendant food store. He became very ill after finding a human finger in the meat. He could not eat meat of any kind for months and suffered chronic digestive problems. The food store defended the action by demonstrating that no employees were missing any fingers. Who would succeed?

6. A woman parked her car in front of a dry cleaning shop and left the motor running. The transmission was in "Park" and the hand brake was not applied. In the front seat was a small child in a car seat. The child crawled out of the seat and either bumped or pulled on the gear shift lever. The car went into gear and rolled forward. It crossed an intersection and struck a pedestrian. The pedestrian brought an action against the woman for negligence. The action alleged that the tort had been committed by the child but that the parent had failed to demonstrate reasonable control of the child in a potentially dangerous situation. The defendant stated that the child often rode in the car seat and had never crawled out of it. She said she left the motor running only so that the windshield defroster would keep operating on the very cold winter day when the accident happened. Who would succeed?

Unit
Six

Contract
Law

Consensus facit legem ("Consent makes law")
Parties are legally bound to do what they
have contracted to do.

Chapter 14

Rules Governing Contracts

Usually, the mere mention of the word *contract* fills average citizens with dismay. They picture long documents with tiny print in a strange language. To some extent these suspicions are correct. Contracts can be long, and they contain what seems to be unnecessary wording which often repeats itself over and over again. This is not to say that average citizens cannot understand contracts. They can, if they will take the time to read them. It is generally the length of contracts that discourages people from reading them. They are so often in a hurry to sign.

What the average citizen may not realize is that many contracts are entered into each day without any formal process at all. The person who makes a purchase at a store has completed a contract. There exists a contract of employment between the employer and the employee, whether it is in writing or not. There are different types of contracts for different purposes.

First, what is a contract? A contract can be defined as an agreement voluntarily entered into, which the parties intend to be enforceable at law. The phrase "enforceable at law" implies that either of the parties would be able to sue if necessary to require the other to keep the obligation. A contract must be distinguished, then, from a mere *social agreement*. If two persons made an agreement to engage in some social activity, one could not sue the other if the agreement was not kept.

Contracts are generally divided into two categories, simple contracts and specialty contracts. *Simple contracts* may be in written, spoken, or implied form, but are not under seal and require no special form to be enforceable. *Specialty contracts* are those contracts which pertain to a special formal event and as such must be in writing and under seal.

Specialty Contracts

In early England, nearly every contract was in writing except for the ordinary business transactions such as buying and selling small amounts of goods. It was common practice to *seal* a written contract by dropping melted wax on the corner and them impressing some letter or design into the wax to indicate the genuineness of the signer. Today, wax is seldom used for contracts. Instead, a red sticker is pasted on the paper and often a machine presses an insignia through the seal and the paper. However, a red sticker need not be used as long as there is some wording used to denote the seal. On many contracts the word "Seal" is printed next to where the parties sign, or in other contracts the letters "L.S." meaning *locus sigilli* (the place for the seal).

The specialty contract, because it is in written form, signed, and under seal is the more secure form of contract. It can be used for any transaction which the parties feel is of sufficient importance to require a formal contract. There are some legal transactions, including mortgages, long-term leases, and deeds, that require a specialty contract. Some of the contracts requiring formal preparation are included under the *Statute of Frauds*.

The Statute of Frauds

The *Statute of Frauds* of England is one of the oldest known statutes. It was originally passed in 1677 to meet a rising problem of fraud and perjury pertaining to contracts. Too many contracts which were made orally were later challenged by one of the parties who claimed the other had violated the terms. Without a written contract, the matter fell to the courts to try to determine which party was telling the truth. The *Statute of Frauds* was enacted to solve the problem. Certain important contracts were to be made in writing. Failure to do this meant that the contract could not be enforced in court. The statute did not specifically require seals, but since seals were commonly placed on important contracts anyway, the practice generally continued. Each province in Canada has enacted a *Statute of Frauds* similar to the original English version. Quebec covers the matter under the Quebec *Civil Code*. The Ontario *Statute of Frauds* contains provisions requiring certain significant contracts to be in writing. If they are not in writing the court cannot enforce the contract. The types of contracts include:

(1) Long-term leases, applying to leases for a period of longer than three years.

(2) Contracts for the sale of land or an interest in land, to apply to royalties, rights, mortgages. This would include such things as mineral rights, oil production royalties, etc.

(3) A promise by one person to pay the debt, miscarriage, or default of another person—generally referred to as "guarantee."

(4) A contract that will not be completed within one year of the making. If no specific time period is mentioned, the court will consider whether or not the contract could have been completed within one year of the making.

(5) A promise by an executor of an estate to pay the debts of the estate out of his or her own pocket. Such a promise must be in writing and the executor must receive some form of consideration for the promise.

The Ontario *Statute of Frauds* originally contained a similar provision for the sale of goods of a value of $40 and upwards. This provision is now covered in the *Sale of Goods Act*.

A formal contract does not necessarily have to be in a particular form. The law will accept any written document or collection of documents which taken together form what is called a "written memorandum," proving the existence of the agreement. Letters, telegrams, even notes have been accepted as proof of the existence of a written contract.

Johnson v. Nova Scotia Trust Company
Nova Scotia, 1974

The appellant, Laura Johnson, claimed possession of a house belonging to a deceased woman. The woman had persuaded Johnson to come and live with her in 1967 as a companion and had promised that if she was still with her at the time of her death she would receive the house and furnishings. Several letters and the testimony of a number of witnesses were adduced to prove the existence of the agreement between the two women. The deceased had made out a will in her own handwriting and had given it to the appellant along with a copy of the deed, saying, "Now there, Laura, is your security." Later, the deceased changed her will without telling Johnson. The trial judge refused to award the property to Johnson. The Court of Appeal held that the letters and the handing over of a copy of the deed formed sufficient "written memorandum" within the meaning of the *Statute of Frauds* to form a binding contract. It was not an agreement that the deceased woman was free to change later on by changing her will. Johnson received the house and furnishings.

The effect of the *Statute of Frauds* is quite easy to understand. If certain types of contracts are to be made enforceable, then they must be made in writing.

Doctrine of Part Performance

The doctrine of part performance is normally applied to contracts for the sale or purchase of land, but it can be applied to other types of cases.

Part performance is a rule that where a contract has been partly carried out by one of the parties, the other cannot use the absence of a written contract as an excuse not to pay for work done. The defendant cannot stand by and allow the plaintiff to perform part of the contract and then refuse to fulfill his or her part by merely saying, "Ha! We don't have a formal, written contract so you can't do anything to me." In such a situation it would really amount to fraud to permit the defendant to use the *Statute of Frauds* in this way.

However, this does not mean the courts will waive the normal requirement to have certain contracts in writing when they are the type stated in the *Statute of Frauds*. The intent is only not to let one party misuse the statute to take unfair advantage of another person who may be unaware of the legal requirement.

Unjust Enrichment

If a person has expressly requested another person to perform a service without specifying any remuneration, but with an understanding that the service is to be paid for, there is an implied promise to pay *quantum meruit* which means "whatever amount the person deserves." A claim under this rule requires that the work has been done and that the person doing the work believed he or she was entitled to be paid. In such a case, the absence of a formal contract will not prevent the person from being paid what has been earned.

A more difficult situation may arise if the plaintiff did something which had the side effect of giving the defendant a benefit. Does the plaintiff have a right to demand payment in such a case? In a very unusual case, *Ulmer v. Farnsworth* (Maine, 1888), both men had quarries filled with water. When Ulmer pumped the water out of his quarry, he unintentionally pumped the water out of Farnsworth's quarry as well, as the

two were connected by a channel. Ulmer sued Farnsworth for half the pumping cost but the court would not require Farnsworth to pay. There was no contract between the two men and if Farnsworth got a "free" job out of the situation, that was his good fortune. The leading Canadian case is the following one:

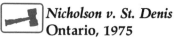

Nicholson v. St. Denis
Ontario, 1975

St. Denis entered into an agreement of purchase and sale with Labelle. Labelle took possession of the land and house, then contracted with Nicholson to install siding on the house. Labelle had no lawful authority to enter into such a contract but Nicholson did not check on who owned the house. The siding was installed but Labelle did not pay. He did not pay St. Denis, either, and St. Denis evicted him. It was only then that St. Denis learned that Labelle had contracted to have the siding put on. St. Denis refused to pay Nicholson because he did not want the siding. Nicholson sued on the basis that St. Denis would obtain "unjust enrichment" in the form of a remodelled house at no cost to him. The Ontario Court of Appeal held that St. Denis did not have to pay.

&&St. Denis neither sought nor desired the work to be carried out on the property and was given no opportunity to express his position until long after the work was completed. He has been guilty of no wrongdoing, nor of encouraging the plaintiff in his work. I can see no grounds, under the circumstances of this case, for extending the doctrine of unjust enrichment or of restitution to the circumstances of the case.&&

Simple Contracts

A simple contract is sometimes referred to in law as a *parol contract*. Parol in the strictest sense means oral, but the word is often used to mean any simple contract. Simple contracts include any contract not made under seal. They can be in writing, made orally, or made by the implied actions of the parties. Implied actions can include shaking hands, raising one's hand at an auction, or any physical behaviour that leads the other party to assume a contract has been made. The primary danger of a simple contract that is not in writing is that later the two parties may disagree about what the terms were, and unless there are witnesses, it becomes a matter of one person's word against another's.

Simple contracts are enforceable if they meet certain requirements regarding the manner in which they came into existence. One of the requirements is that there must be a proper offer and acceptance.

Offer and Acceptance

A contract comes into existence when one person, called the *offeror*, proposes a contract which is accepted by another person, called the *offeree*. An offer must be made within certain general rules or it is not an offer at all. Quite often parties have a major disagreement about whether something that was said was an offer or not. The essential elements of a proper offer are as follows:

- The offer must be communicated to the person or a class of persons for whom it was intended. If the offer never arrives, and the offeree hears about it later, he or she cannot act upon it. If an offer is delivered to the wrong person, it is not properly communicated to the person who received it by mistake. This person cannot act upon it because it was not intended for him or her.
- The offer must be definite. If an offer is not precise as to what it contains, it cannot be acted upon by the offeree. If a party said to another party, "I am thinking about selling my car," this is not an offer to sell.
- An offer must be seriously intended. Offers made in anger, as a joke, or hastily thrown out in retort to an insult are not valid offers.
- An offer must be distinguished from an advertisement. Advertisements such as newspaper ads are not offers in the true sense. The law regards them as invitations to the public to come in and inspect merchandise and then offer to buy. However, some advertisements can be worded in such a way that

they become offers. For example, offers of rewards published in the newspaper are enforceable if a person meets the requirements of the offer. If an offer is made to "Any person finding a gold watch lost on Manitoba Street," then the finder of the watch may rightfully demand the reward as a condition of returning the watch.

Once the offer has been made to the offeree, there are certain rules which apply if the offeree wishes to accept the offer and form the contract:

- The acceptance must be made in the manner and time stipulated in the offer. If no manner is stipulated, acceptance may be made in any customary manner. If no time is stipulated, acceptance must be made within a reasonable time.

- The acceptance must be communicated to the offeror. An offer cannot be worded in such a way that if the offeree says nothing, he or she accepts. For example, if an offer is worded: "If you do not reply to my offer within ten days, I shall assume you accept," the offer is not valid. It is a rule of law that "silence does not make consent." Once it was common practice to send unsolicited goods to people and then bill them. To discourage this, most provinces put no obligation on the person receiving unsolicited goods. Ontario and Saskatchewan have enacted laws allowing the offeree to treat the goods as gifts.

- An acceptance must be unconditional. The offeree cannot try to accept and change the terms of the offer at the same time. If the offeree does so, he or she is deemed in law to have done two things: (1) refused the offer; and (2) made his or her own offer, called a *counter offer*. Once an offer has been refused it is dead and cannot be accepted later. If one of the parties wants to discuss the offer in more detail, this may be done without actually refusing the offer. If Jones offers to sell a car to Smith and Smith asks, "Does that include the spare tire?" or "Would you consider taking less?" Smith is not turning down the offer, just asking for more information about it.

Revoking an Offer

After an offer has been made, it can be taken back or *revoked* by the offeror who may revoke it by notifying the offeree that the offer no longer stands. An offer is automatically revoked if (1) the offeror dies before acceptance; (2) a counter offer is made; or (3) acceptance is not made within the time stipulated.

The time question can be important when trying to revoke an offer, since the rule regarding acceptance differs from the rule regarding revocation. An acceptance becomes effective when mailed, deposited with a telegraph office, or telephoned to the offeror. An acceptance by mail is effective when posted, meaning accepted by the post office for delivery. It is wise to use registered mail as proof of the exact time the letter was posted. If a letter is lost in the mail, acceptance could still be enforced in court because the letter became effective when posted, even if it was not delivered. By contrast, a revocation becomes effective when received by the offeree. In the case of a mailed revocation, it would become effective when delivered to the offeree by the post office. Unlike an acceptance, a revocation lost in the mail could not be enforced in court because it was never delivered.

The post office assumes no liability for mail lost or delayed. The same rule applies to telegraphs either misprinted or lost. In one case, the offeror offered the offeree a special price for fifty items and sent a sample for examination. The offeree wired back saying, "Send *three* items as per sample." The telegraph office mistakenly changed the wording to "Send *the* items as per sample." The offeror sent fifty items, which the offeree refused to accept. The court ruled there was no contract as the two parties had never agreed to the terms because of the mistake. There had been no "meeting of the minds." The telegraph company was not held liable, either.

When Is a Contract Binding?

Once any contract is made, specialty or simple, problems may arise, from many sources, as to whether or not the contract has been properly made and whether it can be enforced at law. To describe the correctness of a contract, three terms are generally used:

- *Valid:* A contract is valid if it meets all the legal requirements and can be enforced by either party against the other. It is a contract without major defects.
- *Void:* A contract is void if it fails to meet the essential requirements of a contract. Neither party could enforce such a contract, and in most cases the court would hold that the contract never existed, since it was defective from the start.
- *Voidable:* A contract is voidable if one party could escape the terms at his or her option. In other words, there is a defect which one party may use to declare the contract not binding. If this party does not so choose, the contract remains valid and enforceable.

Parol Evidence Rule

It would be wise to consider at this point a very important rule regarding contracts. Sometimes referred to as the *Parol Evidence Rule,* it generally means this: Where there is a dispute concerning a written contract, the court will consider only the terms of that contract. Evidence cannot be introduced to alter or contradict the clear, unambiguous terms of a written contract unless there is an attempt to show that the entire contract is a fraud. This means that no matter what has been said between the two parties, the court will only enforce what is put down in written form. This should make it clear to everyone that verbal promises have no legal effect unless included as part of the written contract. No formal wording is needed. It is sufficient to just write out the additional terms anywhere on the contract and have both parties initial the wording. The reverse situation also applies. The parties may strike out terms of a written contract and initial the omission. It is unwise to accept oral promises from the other party such as, "Oh, don't worry about that. We never enforce that."

Coderre (Wright) v. Coderre
Alberta, 1975

The defendant husband, after twenty-seven years of marriage, left the matrimonial home registered in his name to live with another woman. The wife and the couple's three children remained in the home. The wife petitioned for divorce and a decree *nisi* (interim divorce) was granted on the grounds of adultery. On the way home from the court, the husband was alleged to have agreed orally to let the wife have a one-half interest in the house. This claim was not included in the agreement worked out by the lawyers and the wife later sued for a rectification claiming this was a clerical error. Her suit was dismissed. The court would not alter a written agreement unless the applicant could prove beyond a reasonable doubt that the written agreement was not the complete agreement and that there was a term which both had intended to include. The plaintiff was unable to prove to the satisfaction of the court that the husband had made the promise she claimed.

The court can also accept oral evidence to show that the written contract is not the entire contract. If the conversation leading up to the signing of the written contract contained some specific terms of agreement that are understood by the parties to be part of the contract, then this oral evidence may be heard by the court to determine what else there is to the contract.

Under the Ontario *Business Practices Act,* which is discussed in a later unit, the court may ignore the parol evidence rule if "the consumer is not reasonably able to protect his [or her] interests because of . . . physical infirmity, ignorance, illiteracy, inability to understand the language of an agreement, or similar factors." Alberta and Saskatchewan have similar legislation.

The best rule remains: Get it in writing.

The Small Print

If people don't read the contracts they sign, are they bound by them? As a general rule, we must conclude that people are bound by the printed terms on documents whether they read them or not. They may try to escape the provisions of the printed wording by saying that (1) the print was so small they could not read it; (2) the print was hidden or obscured so they would not know it was there; or (3) they were totally unaware that there was any printing involved or that the document contained contract conditions.

In recent years, a trend has developed in our courts not to hold someone liable upon a contract containing important wording which was not read, if the other party knew the person did not read the contract and failed to bring the important wording to the person's attention. The courts have come to accept that some contracts are so long that few people have time to read them entirely; they have taken the position that the person who has prepared these "standard forms" has a duty to point out the important parts. This was emphasized in the following case.

Tilden Rent-a-Car Co. v. Clendenning
Ontario, 1978

While in Vancouver, Clendenning rented a car from the plaintiff company. The clerk asked Clendenning if he wanted "additional coverage" (insurance) and he said "Yes." The contract was presented and signed, without being read, in the presence of the clerk. A provision in the contract was that the customer would not operate the vehicle after consuming any alcohol whatsoever. Clendenning thought he was fully insured for every possibility.

He was involved in an accident while driving the car. He had consumed a moderate amount of alcohol, but was not impaired and was not charged by the police. Relying upon the terms of the contract, Tilden sued Clendenning for the damages to the car. The court held that the contract was very long and that most people renting cars have no time to read such a document. The clerk knew Clendenning did not read the contract. Since the company was aware that the contract was being signed without being read, the company was under an obligation to take reasonable measures to draw attention to the wording which stated that any consumption of alcohol would invalidate the insurance. If the company failed to do so, such terms were not enforceable against a party who did not know that such words were in the contract.

The *Clendenning* case should not be misunderstood to mean that a person may sign all contracts without reading them and rely upon the court for protection. The case illustrates that if a contract contains important wording which could have a great effect upon the signer's rights, there is a duty upon the other party to ensure that the signer knows about such wording.

Reviewing Important Points

1. While most contracts may be either written, oral, or implied, certain special contracts must be in writing in order to be enforceable.
2. A formal contract does not necessarily have to be in a particular form, since the law will accept any written document or collection of documents which prove the existence of the agreement.
3. In order for an offer to be valid, it must be clear, communicated to the other person, and seriously intended.
4. The acceptance of an offer must be made in the manner stipulated in the offer and within the time given or within a reasonable time.
5. If a contract has been partly carried out, it may be binding even if it should have been in writing.
6. An offer may be revoked any time before it has been accepted. The notice of revocation must reach the offeree before acceptance has been made.
7. A person who has performed labour must be paid a fair compensation even if the contract should have been in writing.

Checking Your Understanding

1. What is the general effect of the *Statute of Frauds* with regard to contracts? Name three types of contracts that are covered by the statute.
2. What is the basic rule of law regarding a person who signs a contract without reading it?
3. What is unjust enrichment?
4. What is the parol evidence rule? State two possible exceptions to the rule.
5. Can a newspaper advertisement be an offer? Give an example of an advertisement that would be an offer. Give an example of an advertisement that would not be an offer.

Legal Briefs

1. R viewed a house for sale by T. T wanted $80 000 but they finally agreed upon $75 000. The two of them shook hands. Binding agreement?
2. K, a fifteen-year-old, stole and wrecked B's automobile. K's parents telephoned B and said "If you don't report this to the police, we will purchase a new automobile for you." B was aware that K's parents were wealthy and didn't report the accident. K's parents never replaced B's automobile as promised. Enforceable agreement?
3. C looked at a boat which S had for sale and wanted to buy it. S refused to take a cheque so C gave S $25 in cash "to hold the boat." A week lapsed and C did not return so S sold the boat to someone else. The next day C returned with the rest of the money. S refused to return the deposit saying, "We had no agreement and I held the boat for a week." Advise C what to do.
4. The CS Co. advertised a reward for anyone who took its flu pills for three weeks and caught the flu. C took the pills for three weeks and promptly caught the flu. C demanded the money. Must CS pay?
5. H embezzled $4000 from G, her employer. She told her parents about it and expressed the opinion that she would soon be detected and arrested. The parents and H went to G together and admitted the theft. The parents then signed a contract, not under seal, to

repay the money in installments of $200 per month. They made three monthly payments; then H left home and went to live in another province. The parents made no further payments and G sued. Must the parents pay?

6. Y proposed marriage to K but K did not like the fact that she would have to leave her elderly parents and move to another province where Y had his business. Y promised that he would later buy a home for the parents near their marital home and would move them as well. The marriage took place but the promise was never kept. The parents knew about the promise. Could they sue Y?

7. B entered into an oral agreement with L to build a house. B had completed the foundation when L told him he had been transferred to another province and did not want the house. Can B sue L in the absence of a written contract?

8. P purchased a used automobile but told the salesperson he insisted that new tires be put on the car. The salesperson orally agreed to this condition. When P arrived to take possession, the new tires had not been put on the car; the salesperson had quit; and the sales manager said P must take the car "as is" because he had signed the contract. P refused and the manager said his $500 down payment would be forfeit. Advise P.

9. When F's father died, the house was willed to F, but F's mother would have possession of the house as long as she lived; then F would take over. F's mother spent $10 000 in needed repairs and renovations and demanded that F pay half the bill. "You'll get the benefit of all this some day," she told F. "Why should I pay all of it?" Must F contribute?

Applying the Law

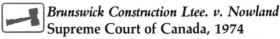

Ruabon Steamship Co. v. London Assurance
England, 1900

The plaintiff company owned a ship that was scheduled to be brought into dry dock so that the insurance company, Lloyds of London, could examine the hull and rate the ship for insurance premiums. Just prior to this, the ship was rammed by another ship and had to come into dry dock for repairs, the cost to be paid by the other ship's insurance company, London Assurance. There was no disagreement about the liability of the insurance company to pay for repairs. The ship's owners saw an excellent chance to kill two birds with one dry dock and quickly summoned their insurance agent to do the inspection while the ship was being repaired. This neatly eliminated the need to bring the ship into dry dock a second time. The owners also saved the entire cost of bringing it in. When London Assurance found out what had happened, they felt that the steamship company had obtained a benefit to which they were not fully entitled and sued to recover half the cost of the dry dock rental. The House of Lords denied the claim, holding that the cost to London Assurance had not been increased one cent by what happened. They were obliged to pay for the ship's repair and that is what they paid — nothing more. The fact that the shipowners obtained some secondary benefit or advantage did not compel the shipowners to reimburse the insurance company. The judges disputed the idea that there exists some general principle of justice, that a person should not get an advantage unless that person pays for it.

Questions
1. Why did the House of Lords not require the steamship company to reimburse the insurance company for some of the costs of the dry dock?
2. Is there in law such a thing as a "lucky break"? How might this case illustrate that?
3. Why did the insurance company feel that it should be reimbursed? Do you agree or disagree with their position? Give a reason for your decision.

Brunswick Construction Ltee. v. Nowland
Supreme Court of Canada, 1974

This case was appealed to the Supreme Court of Canada from the Supreme Court of New Brunswick. The respondents hired an architect to design a house. The appellant, a contractor, assumed full responsibility for the building of the house. Due to leaking, the wood in the house began to rot and the house became uninhabitable. The respondents sued the contractor for damages. The trial judge held the contractor not liable for the damages resulting from the implementation of defective plans; this damage was calculated to be $36 000. The judge found the contractor responsible only for poor workmanship, but held that a dollar value could not be given to this item of damages because it was not possible to determine which damages had resulted from poor design and which had resulted from poor workmanship. In other words, the judge could not separate the fault of the contractor from the fault of the architect. On appeal, the Court of Appeal found the contractor and the architect jointly and severally liable for the damages. From this decision, the contractor appealed to the Supreme Court of Canada. The court held against the contractor and dismissed the appeal. The contractor ought to have known of the defects in the plans and was under a duty to warn the respondents of these defects. Therefore the contractor was in breach of the contract and liable for the failure of the work. The contractor was familiar with the construction of the houses in that region and could readily see that the plans presented were seriously defective, and that the result would be damage to the building. A contractor cannot proceed with plans, knowing they are defective.

Questions

1. As the contractor was hired to follow the plans of the architect and did so, why was the contractor liable?
2. What responsibility does this case appear to place upon persons who contract to do a specific task and are of the opinion that some other person has erred?
3. Is the contractor expected to have the same knowledge and skill as the architect?

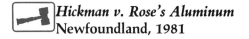

Hickman v. Rose's Aluminum
Newfoundland, 1981

The defendant filed for non-suit on the basis that the action brought against him was contrary to the parol evidence rule. The Rose's Aluminum Co. was indebted to the Hickman Co. for more than $16 000. The credit manager had a talk with Harry Rose about this debt and mentioned that a lawsuit was possible. Rose asked the credit manager to "hold off" on any lawsuit because he was in the process of selling his trailer and would have $6000 to pay towards the debt of the company. He said he would personally guarantee the entire debt of his company. The credit manager wanted this in writing and typed a statement which Rose signed. It read: "Sirs: This letter is to personally guarantee payment in full plus accumulated interest charges at one and one-half percent per month to cover the account of Rose's Aluminum, all charges up to and including February 1979 to be paid in full by May 31, 1979. (Harry Rose)"

When the $6000 was not paid, the credit manager called the Rose home and Rose's wife said that the trailer had been sold but that she was keeping the money because it was her trailer. The Hickman Co. then sued. Counsel for Rose wanted the suit dismissed because the evidence of the credit manager should not be admissible to add to, vary, or contradict the terms of the written contract. He further argued that Rose received no consideration for his written statement and, since it was not under seal, it was not binding. The Hickman Co. wanted the credit manager to be permitted to testify that Rose said, "Hold off." If a person holds off on a lawsuit upon promise to pay a debt, that is valid consideration. (Consideration is discussed in more detail later in this unit.) The court held that the parol evidence rule did not prevent the credit manager from testifying about what Rose said just prior to signing the agreement. The court held that it is permissible to hear oral evidence to show that the written contract is not the complete contract. The credit manager was permitted to testify and the court refused to dismiss the lawsuit.

Questions

1. What is the parol evidence rule and how does it normally operate?
2. Why was it important that the court take notice of the fact that Rose said "Hold off" before the agreement was signed?
3. How might this problem have been avoided? How should the statement have been worded? What form should it have taken?

You Be the Judge

1. The plaintiff cared for her father from 1966 until 1972 when he died. Since she received very little from her father's will, she sued his estate for the value of six years of service for which she had not been paid. The executor of the estate defended the action on the grounds that there was no contract between the two parties specifying that any payment should be made. The plaintiff replied that her father had admitted he could not pay her cash but had suggested that she would be able to get just compensation after he died. Her father had made this statement on two occasions in front of independent witnesses. Who would succeed?

2. A contractor gave a homeowner an oral estimate that renovations would cost "about $4000." There was no written contract, plans, or specifications. The job was completed and the homeowner was given a final bill, much higher than $4000, which she refused to pay. The contractor sued and presented a detailed list of all materials purchased and the number of hours of work done. The homeowner said that if she had known what the true, final bill would be, she would not have had the work done at all. She claimed that the contractor had deliberately made the oral estimate too low, in order to lure her into going ahead with the project. Who would succeed?

3. The plaintiffs sought a court order to require the defendants to sell them a certain lakefront property. At a time when the two parties were great friends, the plaintiffs purchased a lot near the defendants. They could not afford to buy the adjoining lot at the time; however, they wanted both properties since the lot they had bought was small. The defendants told them that they would keep the property for them until the plaintiffs could afford to buy it. The parties had a quarrel and did not talk to each other thereafter. The plaintiffs saved their money and sought, through their lawyer, to buy the lot; however, the defendants refused to sell it to them. The plaintiffs then asked the court to order the sale to be completed as promised. Who would succeed?

4. The plaintiff's car was mechanically sound, but the exterior was in very poor appearance. The paint was so faded that it was nearly invisible and there were numerous spot-paint jobs on the car. The defendant negligently drove into the plaintiff's car and crushed a fender. The repair estimate included a new fender and a complete paint job for the entire car. "You can't paint just one fender," was the plaintiff's position. "You should not get a free paint job out of this," was the reply of the defendant's insurance company. Who would succeed?

5. The plaintiff bought a ticket and entered an arena where a rock concert was to be performed. He did not look at the ticket; he just stuck it into his pocket. The rock group failed to appear and some inebriated people in attendance started a disturbance. Bottles were thrown and people were injured as they crowded towards the exits to escape the danger. The plaintiff was hit by a bottle and suffered injury. He sued the arena owner and the concert promoter for failing to provide adequate security. The defendants relied upon the wording on the back of the ticket which read in part: "The holder of this ticket agrees to exempt the company from liability for all injury to any person, including death, or for damage or loss of any property belonging to the holder." The plaintiff testified that he had never read the words on the back of the ticket and did not know there were any words there. Who would succeed?

Chapter 15

Legal Capacity To Make Contracts

The law starts off with the basic assumption that everyone can make contracts and thereby is deemed to be a *competent party*. A competent party is anyone capable of understanding the nature of the contract entered into, who thus makes the contract enforceable against him or her. But not everyone can enter into a contract. Some persons are protected by law because of their inability to make contracts wisely. Their legal capacity is generally restricted because their mental capacity is restricted. Other persons are prevented by law from making contracts because of some special status. Those having some special status are:

- Minors, that is persons under legal age;
- Intoxicated persons, or those under the influence of drugs;
- Mentally impaired persons;
- Indians on reservations;
- Limited companies.

Minors

Persons are legally classed as minors (or infants) until they reach a certain age upon which they are said to "attain their majority." When persons attain their majority, they legally become adults. The legal age is determined by each province and differs across Canada.

Age of Majority	Provinces
18	Alberta, Manitoba, Ontario, P.E.I., Quebec, Saskatchewan
19	B.C., New Brunswick, Newfoundland, Nova Scotia, Northwest Territories, Yukon Territory

Minors' Liability for Contracts

To protect minors (also called infants or children) from their lack of knowledge and experience, the common law has generally held that contracts entered into by minors are voidable by the minors. The mechanism of

A minor may be liable on any contract which provides the minor with "necessaries of life."

voidability permits minors to contract with adults, but permits the minors to cancel their contracts without penalty in most cases. The adults, however, are usually bound on their contracts with minors to the same extent that they would be with other adults.

When the court examines a minor-adult contract it is relevant to determine how the contract has affected the minor. There are some basic rules that apply:

- A contract clearly detrimental to the minor's interest is void from the outset and neither party can sue the other on the terms of the contract. The parties could recover any money paid.
- If a minor has performed work under a contract which is void because it is detrimental to the minor's interests, the minor should be paid a fair value for the labour and materials provided.
- Those contracts which are for necessaries of life are looked upon as valid and binding upon the minor if the contract is for the minor's benefit.

Contracts for Necessaries

Under the common law, necessaries have been stated to include those things the minor requires for basic living. These include whatever is necessary to obtain those basic things. Food, clothing, shelter, medical care, tools to earn a living, transportation to work, and other basic items have been held to be necessaries.

To be a true necessary, the item must be within the minor's *station in life*. In other words, the minor must live within his or her accustomed style. While it might seem surprising that the law would make a distinction between "rich kids and poor kids" it has been recognized that the normal life style for one minor might be totally out of place for another. In any action against a minor the burden is upon the plaintiff to show that the goods supplied were suitable to the station in life of the minor and also that the minor did not have the necessaries at the time of sale and delivery.

If the contract is for employment, the court will look at the terms of the contract, comparing them with the terms normally extended by other employers in the same field or trade. The court will also take into con-

sideration the lack of bargaining skill a minor has when entering into a contract.

A minor can cancel any contract, including a contract for necessaries, if the minor has never received any benefit under the contract. For example, if a minor signed a contract to take a training course, the minor could cancel the contract before beginning the course since no benefit had yet been received under the contract. If the minor took the course, then tried not to pay for it, the situation would be different.

Toronto Marlboro Major Junior "A" Hockey Club v. Tonelli
Ontario, 1977

John Tonelli signed a two-year contract to play with the Toronto Marlboros. He was sixteen years of age at the time. The following year, this contract was superceded by a new three-year contract with a fourth year at the club's option. The contract provided that if Tonelli obtained a contract with a professional hockey club, he would pay the Marlboros 20 per cent of his gross earnings for each year of his first three years with that club. In return, Tonelli would receive a salary, coaching, and the chance to play in the Junior A League. The contract was assignable by the Marlboro's and could be terminated at the club's discretion.

When he turned eighteen, Tonelli repudiated his contract and signed a contract with the Houston Aeros. His contract would pay him $320 000 over the next three years. The Marlboros brought an action against Tonelli for breach of contract.

The Ontario Court of Appeal held that the contract was too heavily weighted in favour of the Marlboros. It was not freely negotiated between the parties but was really offered to the player on a "take it or leave it" basis. In effect, the club had its players over a barrel which is known as an unequal bargaining position. From Tonelli's point of view, the requirement to pay 20 per cent of his first three years' earnings was excessive. Although the court recognized that Tonelli received some benefit under the contract, careful examination must be made of one-sided contracts, particularly when signed by infants:

> **66**The question is whether this contract at the time it was made was beneficial to this player having regard to its terms and the circumstances surrounding its execution.**99**

The court held that the contract could not be enforced against Tonelli.

Contracts for Non-Necessaries

In the case of non-necessaries, the status of minors is less clear. If minors purchase items but never use them, they should be able to get full refunds if they return the goods in new condition. If they used the items, the minors are entitled only to a partial refund depending upon how much wear they put upon the goods. If the minors bought the items on instalment contracts, they can refuse to make any more payments if they return the goods, but they will be unlikely to get back any money already paid.

If minors lie about their age when entering into contracts for non-necessaries, they are still protected by the law and the contracts cannot be enforced against them. However, they can be sued in tort for making fraudulent misstatements about their age. They can also be prosecuted under the criminal laws for obtaining credit by false pretences. Therefore, it is wise to remember the saying, "Infancy is a shield, not a sword." Minors who set out to play games with merchants, using their infancy to protect them, will end up in trouble.

Minors' Contracts after Becoming Adults

It sometimes happens that minors enter into contracts and continue in those contracts until after they become adults. Can they later avoid the contracts? The law tries to distinguish here between two types of contracts.

- *Contracts affording one-time benefits:* The contract may have afforded the minor a benefit on one occasion only, such as purchase of property, in which case the law requires that the minor specifically *ratify* the contract in writing after becoming an adult. If the minor does not do this, he or she could still repudiate the contract years later.
- *Contracts affording continuous benefits:* The contract may have afforded the minor a continuous benefit, such as the use of a car bought on the instalment basis, in which case the law requires that the minor specifically *repudiate* the contract immediately after becoming an adult. If the minor says nothing, or continues to use the item and make payments, the law then interprets the minor's actions as having *ratified* the contract as an adult. He or she cannot avoid it later.

Parental Liability for Minors' Contracts

The years sixteen to eighteen (or nineteen) are awkward years in the legal sense. In most provinces parents may legally stop supporting a child at age sixteen if the child has withdrawn from parental control. However, the child cannot fully contract until age eighteen or nineteen. In this interim period, there are some grey areas over the obligation of the parent to support the child. The rules also tend to vary depending upon where the child lives.

A parent is liable for necessaries which a child, living at home, charged to the parent's credit because the parent was not providing the necessaries. The parent would also have to pay for necessaries for a child under age sixteen not living with the parent. In many cases, an order for support may be issued by a family court.

A parent is not liable for a child's debts for non-necessaries unless the parent has guaranteed them in writing or has somehow indicated to the creditor that the parent will pay the debts on a continuing basis. The creditor may continue to look to the parent for future debts of the child until the parent clearly indicates that he or she will no longer pay. Thus, a parent who gives a child access to a credit account or guarantees a credit card may have to make payments for merchandise which he or she did not specifically allow the child to purchase.

Other Special Status Persons

Intoxicated Persons

Persons who enter into contracts while intoxicated can later repudiate the contracts if they can prove three things: (1) that they were truly impaired to the point where their mental processes were not operating properly; (2) that the other parties to the contracts knew or ought to have known of their condition; and (3) that they sought to repudiate the contracts within a reasonable (usually very short) period of time. If a person does not act promptly after recovering from impairment, it will be assumed that that person is content with the contract. The person must also return as many benefits obtained under the contract as possible in an attempt to return the parties to their original position.

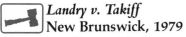

Landry v. Takiff
New Brunswick, 1979

The plaintiff, an elderly man, conveyed a half-interest in a wood lot to the defendant. A few months later the old man conveyed the other half to the defendant. The plaintiff was in a state of drunkenness at the time and received no consideration (value) for the second conveyance. He permitted a number of months to go by before trying to rescind the deed.

The court held that the plaintiff could not have the second conveyance set aside because he failed to act promptly when he became aware of the circumstances entitling him to have the deed set aside. The plaintiff was taken to have affirmed the second conveyance.

Mentally Impaired Persons

A person's mental impairment may be caused by a variety of factors including disease of the mind, senility, strokes, and even hypnosis. Someone suffering from mental impairment is still liable for contracts made for necessaries which have been received. Such a person is not liable for any other contracts entered into.

The consumer protection laws of many provinces have also extended special protection to persons who are physically or mentally infirm, illiterate, or ignorant of the subject matter of the contract. This is discussed further in Unit Nine   Consumer Protection.

Indians on Reservations

Indians on reservations are wards of the Crown and occupy a status similar to infants. They cannot enter into contracts, except for necessaries, and Indian lands and property cannot be pledged as collateral or seized for non-payment of any debt.

Limited Companies

A limited company or a corporation may be considered as an "artificial person" that may sue or be sued in its own name. It may also contract and own property in its own name. A company may only enter into contracts that pertain to the business identified in its charter. All other contracts are ultra vires.

Genuine Consent to a Contract

A contract may be void or voidable if the parties did not give their *genuine consent* to it. If the parties lack legal capacity to contract, there can be no genuine consent. In addition, there are situations that may challenge whether or not there was genuine consent. These include mistake, duress, undue influence, and misrepresentation.

Mistake

A contract may be set aside if there is a significant mistake in the terms. By mistake, we do not mean a bad decision on the part of one party. A mistake refers to a misunderstanding about the subject matter of the contract. If the two parties both make the same mistake as to the existence of the subject matter of the contract, this is called a *common mistake*. For example, if two parties sign a contract for the sale of a building — not knowing in the meantime the building burned down — they are both making the same mistake and the contract is void from the start.

A contract is also void if the two parties are making two different mistakes, but neither is aware of misunderstanding the other. This is called a *mutual mistake*. For example, if Jones and Smith reach an agreement for the sale of Smith's horse, and they are discussing two different horses but don't know it, a mutual mistake is made and the contract is void.

One cannot claim that a bad bargain was a mistake. Clearly, if you paid five times what something was really worth, your friends will tell you what a mistake you made. This is not mistake in the legal sense and you are stuck with the deal.

With regard to clerical errors, the law holds that one party cannot be allowed to profit from an obvious clerical error on the part of the other. If a party received an offer containing an obvious clerical error, sometimes called a *palpable error*, that party cannot accept it and thereby bind the other party to a disastrous contract. If the error is small, and the receiving party had no reason to believe there was an error involved, he or she may accept it, and the offeror will then be bound. This is provided that the error was actually made by the offeror. If the error was made by someone such as the telegraph company, the contract will probably be declared void as there was no meeting of the minds.

Ontario Water Resources Commission v. Ron Engineering
Supreme Court of Canada, 1980

In July 1972, Ron Engineering submitted the low bid on an Ontario Water Resources Commission contract, and as a requirement of the tender submitted a cheque for $150 000 as a deposit of good faith. The money would have been returned after completion of the contract or if Ron Engineering did not get the contract. The company's bid was $2 748 000 which was the lowest of eight bids. It was $632 000 less than the closest bid. When the company employee, present at the bid-opening, learned that Ron Engineering's bid was so low, she contacted the firm's president and suggested that a mistake must have been made. About an hour after the bids were opened, the company sent a Telex message to the commission stating that the bid was $750 000 less than it should have been because of an error caused by the rush in compiling the final figures. The company sought to show how the error had been made and to withdraw its erroneous bid. The commission would not accept the withdrawal and Ron Engineering sued to recover its deposit. The company argued that because the firm's bid was a mistake, no contract existed.

The Supreme Court of Canada, hearing an appeal from the Supreme Court of Ontario, held that the deposit would not be refunded. The defence of mistake must be such that the mistake is apparent at the time the tender is submitted and not at some later date after a demonstration of a calculation error. There was no "mistake" in the sense that the contractor did not intend to submit the tender as in form and substance it was.

Duress

If persons enter contracts because of actual or threatened violence against themselves or members of their families, the contracts can later be avoided. Compelling a person to enter a contract by threats of harm, criminal prosecution, or libel is called *duress*. As soon as the person works free of the duress, that person must seek to declare the contract void. If the person says nothing after escaping the duress, the contract becomes binding. Ordinary business pressure is not duress. If a person is driven to a certain contract because of financial pressures, the person cannot claim duress, as long as the business pressure applied was lawful.

Undue Influence

The contract may be voidable because the consent of one of the parties was obtained under circumstances that rendered that party "morally unable" to resist the will of the other. This is called *undue influence*. The law recognizes that some people exert tremendous influence over other people because of a family or business connection. A trusted adviser can generally tell a person what decisions to make. Undue influence lies in having the person make contracts that are not to his or her betterment, but to the betterment of the adviser.

Contracts involving undue influence are voidable at the option of the person so influenced. While the burden of proving undue influence is upon the person who alleges it, there are some situations where the relationship is so close that the court will presume that some degree of influence most likely exists. The plaintiff must then establish that the influence was undue. Such relationships include: husband and wife, parent and child, guardian and ward, lawyer and client, doctor and patient, minister and parishioner.

Charges of undue influence are often made when wills are probated and the relatives find that an unusual settlement has been made in favour of one person —particularly a person who spent much time with the deceased during the last few years of the deceased's life.

Tannock v. Bromley
British Columbia, 1979

The defendant, who was a practising hypnotherapist not belonging to any professional association and not having any special educational qualifications, treated the plaintiff for arthritis and an emotional problem. The hypnotic treatment lasted two and a half years and during the course of it the plaintiff transferred about $100 000 worth of real and personal property to the defendant. The plaintiff sought the return of the real property and judgment for the value of the personal property transferred. He also sought a refund of fees paid to the defendant for treatments. The plaintiff succeeded in recovering most of what he asked. Where it was shown that one party had dominated over the other, the law presumes that gifts by the latter to the former were the result of undue influence. In

this case, the defendant controlled the plaintiff and a money relationship existed between the parties. The defendant abused her position of trust. There was no evidence to rebut the presumption of undue influence. Accordingly, it was ordered that the defendant transfer back the real property and that she account for the benefit received from other transfers. However, the plaintiff's claim for a refund of fees paid to the defendant for treatment was denied. The plaintiff's claim was denied because of the illegality of his own contract with the defendant. The evidence did not show misrepresentation or fraud. The plaintiff knew that the treatment was illegal because the defendant was not a registered medical doctor.

Misrepresentation

Misrepresentation can render a contract voidable, if it can be proven, which is often difficult to do. Misrepresentation is a false statement of material facts, which induced the offeree to sign the contract. It is generally assumed to have been made accidentally, without intention to deceive. A person cannot avoid a contract because some petty detail was not looked after. Furthermore, material facts must be separated from opinion. A salesperson is expected to be enthusiastic about a product, and will naturally describe it in glowing terms. Such expressions as "durable, best-quality, sturdy, versatile, attractive, etc." which form part of any sales talk, are not material facts, they are opinions. However, if the salesperson makes false statements about such things as what the product is made of, where it was made, what condition it is in, and does so sufficiently that the offeree is persuaded to enter into the contract, the contract is voidable on the grounds of misrepresentation.

Misrepresentation applies to all contracts, not just sales of goods. It is an interesting aspect of law that also comes under tort law. It gives the injured party two possible ways to attack the contract and the wrongdoer.

A severe form of misrepresentation is *fraud*. Fraud is also an offence under criminal law and a tort. Fraud differs from misrepresentation in that it is an intentional, deliberate misstatement of facts, while misrepresentation can be accidental. Fraud renders a contract void, and the injured party may sue for the return of money paid and additional damages as well. Misrepresentation only renders a contract voidable, and the injured party can sue to get his or her money back, but not for damages.

It has also been held to be fraud where one person makes a reckless misstatement of facts, having no real knowledge as to the truthfulness of what is being said, in order to induce another person to enter into an agreement to that person's detriment.

Non Est Factum

If a person has entered into a contract in ignorance of its true character, that person may raise the common law defence of *non est factum* which means "it is not his or her deed." To be successful the defendant must show (1) an absence of intention; (2) an absence of carelessness; and (3) an instrument (document) which is fundamentally different from that which the party believed he or she was signing.

In this day and age when illiteracy is uncommon, the defence is not used as it was in earlier times when people could not read what they signed. Non est factum is not a valid defence for a person who simply did not read a document.

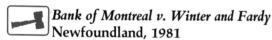

Bank of Montreal v. Winter and Fardy
Newfoundland, 1981

The bank instituted an action against the co-signers of an overdue loan to a company. Judgment had been entered against one co-signer but he died so the action was brought against the other co-signer, an employee. The employee alleged undue influence, lack of independent legal advice, and non est factum. The employee was told by the owner of the company that he would be promoted to secretary-treasurer of the company. He was later approached by the owner to sign some papers, which he believed were related to his new capacity as secretary-treasurer. The employee did not read the papers; he had been an employee for twenty years, and trusted his employer. He also maintained that the bank should have insisted that he have independent legal advice from someone other than the company's lawyer before signing the papers and guaranteeing a very large loan.

The Newfoundland Supreme Court dismissed all the defendant's arguments and held that his negligence in not reading what he signed was no defence. The bank had no duty to ensure that the defendant had independent legal advice. The court found no evidence of duress or undue influence. The defendant was an educated man who took no steps to safeguard his interests. He could not expect others to do so for him. The defendant was held liable to the bank.

Consideration

Since, for the most part, a contract is a business venture, the law assumes that the purpose for entering into the contract was to exchange values in some manner. The value which each party exchanges in the contract is called *consideration*, and a contract generally cannot be enforced without some consideration being shown to both parties. The court would hold that a contract without consideration is really a promise to do something for free, and is thus a gift which is not legally enforceable. This rule does not apply to contracts under seal, which require no consideration. With contracts under seal, the court presumes that even if the two parties do not mention consideration they must have seriously intended to make the contract, otherwise they would not have made it formally. Simple contracts, then, require consideration to prove that the two parties were serious.

As a rule, people cannot enforce promises to pay them to do things they were already required to do. A police officer cannot charge a citizen a protection fee — the police officer is already bound to protect the citizen.

In an unreported case, a ship's captain promised the crew that if they would help to work the disabled ship back to port rather than abandon ship, the captain would see that they were paid a large bonus. The crew stayed aboard the ship, but the ship's owners refused to pay them any bonus. The court held that it was the crew's duty to remain with the ship as long as it was seaworthy, and therefore there was no added consideration on their part for the promise of the bonus. The crew could not demand payment for doing something they were already obligated to do.

Consideration may take many forms, such as cash, property, labour, forbearance, and so on. The important thing is that consideration must be something that can be expressed in terms of dollars; it cannot consist of intangible things such as affection, loyalty, etc. *Forbearance* is a form of consideration which means to give up a legal right in return for payment. For example, if a person agrees to give up the right to sue a second person, that person is entitled to some monetary payment for doing so.

Adequacy of Consideration

A person may use poor judgment in entering a contract and realize later that the consideration received is very small in comparison to what has been given the other party. Unless fraud or misrepresentation can be proved, or the contract can be set aside on some other grounds, the court will uphold the contract. All the law requires is that there is some mutual exchange of consideration. The law does not require that each party receive equal consideration. Since it is assumed that in business transactions each party will try to strike the best bargain possible, and that quite often one party will come away with a better deal, there is no legal procedure for one party to ask the court to increase the consideration received. The position of the court is summed up in a rule of law which states, "The court will not make bargains." An important exception to the rule pertains to minors. The court can intervene on behalf of a minor who was charged too much for necessaries and require the minor to pay only a fair market price.

Promises of Gifts

A promise by one person to make a gift to another is generally treated as a *gratuitous promise,* lacking consideration, and therefore not legally enforceable. Thus, if someone promised you a gift of great value and did not fulfill that promise, you have a moral complaint to register, but no cause for legal action since you promised no consideration in return.

Circumstances can arise, however, where a promise to make a gift becomes legally enforceable. If the intended recipient made personal legal commitments on the basis of the promise of a gift, that person could require the donor to hand over the gift. The best example of such cases is the promise to donate money to a charity. Whenever a person makes a subscription to a hospital, church, college, or united fund he or she may think a gift is being promised. But, there are legal grounds to enforce this promise:

- Since a charity performs good services for the entire community, all donors benefit and thereby receive consideration indirectly.
- The charity may have ordered building materials, hired contractors, and made other legal commitments on the basis of that pledge. Since the charity has become legally liable on the contracts it signed, the charity may in turn require the donors to actually pay the money promised.
- Since others have also pledged money, each donor must oblige the other donors by honouring his or her own pledge. If all donors don't fulfill their obligation, the entire campaign may fail.

When very large sums of money are involved, the charity usually requests that the donor make the pledge in writing, under seal. If a donor is elderly, the charity usually requests that the donor make a codicil to his or her will to provide for the payment to the charity should the donor die before the pledge is honoured.

Charitable donations are enforceable only if the money is used for the purpose for which it was solicited in the first place. If a church raised money to rebuild the bell tower, but later decided it would be better to buy a new organ, donors who pledged money to the bell tower campaign could back out since their money was not going to be used for the original purpose.

Past and Future Consideration

A promise to do something in return for benefits already received is in effect a gift and not enforceable. The making of the promise is voluntary and not contingent upon the other party's doing something in return. For example, if you see that your neighbour's driveway is plugged with snow, and you bring your snowblower over and clean it out—without being asked to do so—it is a gift from you to the neighbour. Your neighbour may be pleased by your actions and say, "Next summer I am going to cut your grass all summer long in return." This promise cannot be enforced against the neighbour whose promise was made after you did your good deed. This is *past consideration* which will not support a contract. On the other hand, you might have said to your neighbour before beginning, "I will clean the snow out of your driveway this winter, if you will cut my grass next summer." If the neighbour accepted your offer, this would be a binding contract. You obtained the promise before you carried out your work. You and your neighbour have exchanged consideration and have a binding agreement.

A promise to do something in the future in return for benefits to be immediately received or to be received in the future results in *future consideration*. This type of contract is valid and enforceable. For example, if a merchant orders goods to be delivered next week but ordinarily pays at the end of thirty days, the contract is valid as the promise to provide the consideration is extracted now even though it will not be forthcoming until later.

Legal Purpose

There are numerous statutes that forbid certain acts, most of which provide a penalty for violation. If a contract is entered into that violates the law, the contract

is void *ab initio* ("from the beginning"). The court cannot enforce a contract that is contrary to law, or the court itself would break the law. Generally, the court must throw out the entire contract and not just parts of it.

The contract could have been legal when it was signed, but a change in the law could later make it illegal. If this happens, the contract is rendered void and the parties must stop carrying it out. They may try to seek a settlement from each other under the *Frustrated Contracts Act* which prevails in most provinces.

Gaming Contracts

The law permits two private persons to make a friendly, personal bet. This is not illegal, but neither is it enforceable in court. If Jones and Smith want to make a bet on the outcome of a sporting event, they

While private wagers are not illegal, debts incurred as part of organized gambling are unlawful and uncollectible.

may do so. However, if Jones refuses to pay up after losing the bet, Smith can do nothing about it. Betting and gaming are still considered immoral and the court is not going to be party to collecting the money from the loser.

Organized, unlicensed gaming is illegal under the *Criminal Code*. Charities and governments are now operating numerous lotteries and other games which are legal if licensed. A person who wins a licensed game can legally sue for the prize.

Illegal Interest

When a person borrows money or buys something on credit, the person is charged an additional sum of money, called *interest*. Charging a rate of interest that is too high is called *usury*. Usury can render a contract voidable and if interest is charged in excess of 60 per cent per year it is also a criminal offence.

If the method of calculating the interest is so vaguely worded that the debtor doesn't realize how high the interest will be, the contract may be set aside as *unconscionable* under most provincial laws. As well, the federal *Interest Act* contains provisions concerning unconscionable interest. If a contract states that interest is to be paid, but does not state the rate of interest, the *Interest Act* requires that it shall be the current bank lending rate. The cost of borrowing must be clearly explained to the debtor. This requirement is discussed in more detail in Unit Nine   Consumer Protection.

Illegal Restraint of Trade

Attempts to restrict the free flow of trade are generally illegal, although some restraints are imposed upon trade by government in order to ensure an orderly market system. Where individuals or companies combine their efforts, not to improve business but to form a monopoly to limit free trade, the law intervenes. The *Combines Investigation Act* is a federal statute which contains various provisions that attempt to prevent "combines" or monopolies from forming to limit competition or fix prices. There may, however, be legitimate reasons for limiting competition between com-

panies in certain geographical areas. Contracts between companies have been held as legal where their purpose was to prevent price wars or excessive competition which the market could not support.

The *Combines Investigation Act* is discussed in more detail in Unit Nine   Consumer Protection.

When people join companies as employees, they may be required to sign contracts that if they quit their jobs with their present employers they will not go to work for their employers' competitors, or set up their own competing businesses within a certain period of time or distance. The reason for such contracts is to prevent competitors from "raiding" each other's personnel in order to obtain trade secrets known only to employees. It also prevents employees from using inside information in order to set up their own businesses and undercut their previous employers.

The restraint must be reasonable to both the employees and to the public. The public cannot be denied a needed service because of a private agreement.

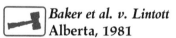

Baker et al. v. Lintott
Alberta, 1981

A physician contracted with partners not to compete within twenty-five miles of the City of Medicine Hat for two years after voluntarily leaving the partnership. Evidence showed that the partnership constituted almost 60 per cent of the medical practice in the area. In an action for an injunction to enforce the agreement, the plaintiffs argued that the restriction was a reasonable one when considering the training, experience, and exposure to the public that a new doctor received by being a partner for the clinic. It was also stressed that the prohibition was for just two years, not permanent.

The Court of Queen's Bench held that while the contract might be reasonable between the parties, it was contrary to the public interest in that it was unduly restricting the access of the public to the defendant doctor's medical services. Those patients not satisfied with the treatment provided by the clinic should be afforded an alternative. The court noted that there are two tests to be applied to such a contract. The first is the test of reasonableness between the parties. The second, and more important test, is that the contract must not seriously deprive the public of a choice of service.

Contracts Made on Sunday

The *Lord's Day Act,* a federal statute, prohibits the making of ordinary contracts on Sunday. Any such contract is void. There are, however, exceptions to this general rule. Firstly, the Act does not prohibit anyone from performing acts of mercy. Thus, if a person had an operation in hospital on a Sunday, the bill would have to be paid. Secondly, the Act does not prohibit contracts for essential services such as those provided by gasoline stations, drug stores, restaurants, etc. These operations may remain open on Sunday, particularly where they service interprovincial travellers.

The *Lord's Day Act* does not prohibit the writing of a cheque on Sunday. However, if the cheque is written as part of a contract also written on Sunday, the contract and the cheque could be declared void as being part of the same thing.

The federal statute has allowed each province to establish its own version of the *Lord's Day Act* and to make exceptions to the federal law. Many provinces now permit Sunday movies, sporting events, and other activities which are ordinary business transactions. Most provincial laws require these events to begin after 1:30 p.m.

Newfoundland does not have a *Lord's Day Act*, so the federal act and the common law prevail.

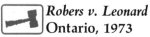
Robers v. Leonard
Ontario, 1973
The case arose out of an agreement to sell real property. The defendants and plaintiffs reached an agreement of purchase and sale of real property for the sum of $15 000. The agreement was made on Sunday, August 8, and a memorandum to the effect that the agreement was made was signed.

Subsequently, the defendant vendor (seller) refused to complete the transaction. The plaintiffs brought an action for specific performance, meaning the enforcement of the sale as agreed, or if the court would not order specific performance, the plaintiffs sought monetary damages for breach of contract. The action was dismissed since the contract was void under the *Lord's Day Act.*

Contracts in Restraint of Marriage

A contract that has as its basis the prohibition of a certain marriage taking place is void. This applies to wills which contain provisions that money is to go to a certain person, provided that person does not marry a particular person or does not marry someone of a certain religion. Some restrictions are not void if they do not put undue restraint upon freedom to marry. Thus, where a woman provided money in her will for her granddaughter with the condition that she "complete her education before marrying," the court held that this was not an undue restraint upon the granddaughter and was a valid condition of the will. One peculiar exception to this rule is that a man may make a provision in his will that if his widow remarries, she is cut off from any benefits of his estate. The law will generally uphold such a provision despite its restrictions upon the widow.

Contracts Contrary to Public Policy

A contract made with the purpose of defeating public justice and public policy is illegal and void. The meaning of public policy is generally expressed as "that which is in the best interests of the public." For example, a contract to commit a crime would be void. A contract to use the powers of a political office for personal gain would also be void. Government officials who have private business interests on the side must be very careful not to do business with themselves. If they use their official position to obtain a contract for a private company in which they have an interest, this creates a conflict of interest that would jeopardize the legality of the contract.

Discharge of Contract

A contract does not remain in force forever. It has some determinable ending point, usually when both parties have carried out their obligations. Alternatively, a contract may be interrupted before completion by the wrongful actions of one party or by intervention from outside.

Discharge by Performance

If both parties to a contract have carried out their obligations, the contract is said to be performed and the parties discharged. When one party offers to perform (tenders) and the other party refuses to allow this, the first party is excused from any further obligation. A proper tender must be made exactly as the contract calls for. If the contract calls for the payment of money, the recipient may insist upon the payment in "legal tender of Canada" as follows:

- Bank of Canada notes (dollar bills)
- Canadian silver coins up to $10
- Canadian copper coins up to 25 cents

Creditors do not have to make change if they don't want to. Many commercial operations are now insisting upon "exact change" because they can reduce the risk of robbery by not carrying excessive amounts of money in order to make change. Although many businesses accept cheques, cheques are not legal tender and there is no obligation on the part of any person to accept them.

If a dispute arises over how much is due, and the debtor wants to offer a partial settlement which he or she thinks is fair, the debtor should mark the payment and accompanying letter with the words "Without Prejudice," which means without prejudice to the debtor's legal rights. The importance of these words is that the debtor indicates he or she owes the creditor something, but is not making a commitment to full liability by offering this payment. This rule extends to other matters as well. If a person wants to discuss a possible settlement of a legal dispute by letter, he or she should mark the letter "Without Prejudice."

Discharge by Mutual Agreement

If the two parties decide to cancel their contract, they may do so. Ordinarily a written statement to this effect will be drawn up and signed by both.

Discharge by Impossibility of Performance

The fact that a person finds a contract very difficult to carry out does not necessarily excuse the person from it. Each party must anticipate possible problems, such as late deliveries, strikes, etc, and provide for them in the contract. But, there are certain situations which are generally held to be beyond anyone's control and render a contract impossible to perform. Some examples would be:

- The subject matter has been destroyed. A contract to buy a building would be declared void if the building burned down.
- Illness makes the performance of a *personal service* impossible.
- A change in the law makes the contract illegal and therefore impossible.

Where personal services are involved, if a person has contracted to do a job based on personal skill, that person cannot send someone else to do the job. Suppose Green hired Rembrandt van Swipe to paint Green's portrait. If van Swipe suddenly became ill and sent a student, Peter Muffitt, to paint the portrait, Green could refuse to accept this change. Green was paying for talent, not paint, but Green could not sue van Swipe for not performing the contract. However, the defence of impossibility cannot involve the predicament of someone else. Thus, when a singing star missed a performance because a member of the family was ill, the singer was not excused from the contract on the grounds of impossibility of performance. This was so despite testimony that the singer's worried state would have made a good performance impossible.

Vancouver Milling and Grain Co. v.
C.C. Ranch Co.
Supreme Court of Canada, 1924
The defendants, C.C. Ranch Co., sold to the plain-

tiffs, the Vancouver Milling and Grain Co., a large order of wheat to be delivered to Vancouver during September and October. The contract did not say anything about the method of shipment, but it was common knowledge that the only possible method of shipment was by Canadian Pacific Railway. The defendant tried to ship the grain, but because of a shortage of grain cars, only part of the grain was delivered and the grain company sued for breach of contract. The defendant pleaded impossibility of performance. The court ruled in favour of the defendant, saying:

> **66**The principle of *lex non cogit ad impossibilia* (the law does not compel the impossible) must be applied to the case as follows: Was the defendant's obligation absolute, or was it conditional upon rail cars being available? It is common ground that the CPR is the only railway available and was the carrier contemplated by the contract. The defendant had wheat ready and the shortage of cars is not attributable to any fault of the defendant.**99**

The court dismissed the lawsuit.

Discharge by Breach of Contract

Where one party to a contract fails to carry out his or her obligation, this party is said to be in *breach of contract*. This breach frees the other party from his or her obligation. There is no requirement on one party to continue the contract when the other party is clearly not going to fulfill the obligation. The contract having been ended by breach, the two parties may then proceed to court to argue the matter of settlement of damages arising out of the breach of contract. This can involve a lot of money, for if one party had legal commitments based upon the existing contract, the breach of contract may have caused that person to fail to carry out numerous other contracts.

It is sometimes important to determine whether or not a contract was *substantially performed*, before the breach occurred. Substantial performance means that most of the contract was carried out, and the breach is a small one. In such a case, the injured party might be

allowed some damages, but would not be allowed to declare the entire contract void because of a small failing.

Keks v. Esquire Pleasure Tours Ltd. and Pleasure Tours Canada
Manitoba, 1974

Relying on representations contained in a travel brochure received from the defendant, a travel agency, the plaintiff booked a two-week vacation to Hawaii for his family and housekeeper-cook. The contract provided for accommodation with kitchen facilities. Upon arrival, the party found that no kitchen facilities were available. The plaintiff sued for damages due to breach of contract. The action was allowed, and the defendant was held liable to pay $1936 in damages for the cost of additional meals, extra gratuities, cost of airfare for the housekeeper-cook (who wasn't needed), tranquillizers, and general damages.

In some cases, the injured party may ask the court for *specific performance*. This means that the defaulting party would be ordered to carry out the obligation. Specific performance is allowed only where monetary damages will not suffice. As an example, if Hodges agrees to sell a rare painting to Yorty, and later refuses to do so, Yorty may sue Hodges and ask for specific performance. Since the painting is rare, it is of no use to Yorty to get money from Hodges; Yorty wants the painting. A contract for personal services will not be enforced by an order for specific performance. The court will not order one person to work for another, as this would amount to servitude. This rule does not apply to labour unions. A court may order an entire union back to work.

Another possible remedy for breach of contract is an *injunction*, which is a court order requiring a person either to perform an act or to stop doing an illegal act. An injunction has many possible uses, but as it pertains to contract law it is generally used to prevent a person from entering into a contract of employment with one employer while that person still has a valid contract with another employer. Professional athletes who break their contracts with one club may find that they cannot play for another club because their legitimate employer has obtained an injunction prohibiting this.

Discharge by Bankruptcy

The *Bankruptcy Act* allows a debtor who has no hope of paying debts to be relieved of most of the debts by filing an *Assignment in Bankruptcy*. A Trustee takes over all the property of the bankrupt company or individual and tries to liquidate the assets to pay the liabilities.

A person must owe creditors at least $1000 and must be unable to meet current obligations. A person thinking of bankruptcy should discuss the matter with a chartered accountant. The accountant will handle the required paperwork and will eventually prepare a report for the creditors indicating how much, if anything, they might hope to receive. Eventually the court is asked to accept the report and declare that all debts of the bankrupt person are extinguished. Some debts are not eliminated by bankruptcy, including debts incurred for the necessaries of life. Not all the personal assets of the bankrupt are liquidated. Certain household goods and tools of the trade are exempt.

Bankruptcy is a serious step to take and will have an adverse impact upon future credit ratings. It should be taken only upon the advice of a lawyer and accountant.

A person or business with no hope of paying its debts may be legally relieved of those debts by filing for bankruptcy.

Reviewing Important Points

1. Minors may contract for necessaries. If minors contract for non-necessaries, the contracts become binding upon them as adults unless they repudiate the contracts.

2. A limited corporation is an artificial person that may sue or be sued in its own name.

3. To be enforceable, a contract not under seal requires that consideration has been afforded to both parties.

4. A promise to make a gift is generally not enforceable because no consideration is received by the promisor.

5. Private bets, while not illegal, are not enforceable in court.

6. Contracts made on a Sunday are void except where acts of mercy, necessaries, or essential services are involved.

7. Where a person has contracted to do a job based on personal skill, that person cannot have someone else do the job on his or her behalf.

8. A party to a contract is excused from any further obligation if the other party refuses to carry out his or her part of the contract.

Checking Your Understanding

1. What is the position of a minor who wishes to cancel a contract for non-necessaries which have been used, but which are still in good condition?

2. Under what circumstances might parents be liable for their child's debts for (a) necessaries? (b) non-necessaries?

3. Under what circumstances may a palpable error permit a contract to be avoided?

4. Under what circumstances can undue influence be presumed to exist?

5. How much interest must be paid on a contract that calls for the payment of interest but does not specify the rate?

6. Under what circumstances might a promise or pledge to pay money to a charity be enforceable?

7. What is impossibility of performance? How does it apply to a contract for personal services?

Legal Briefs

1. R, a minor, charges clothing at a store on her father's credit account. R's father pays the bill and says nothing to the store manager, but angrily tells R not to do it again. Two months later, R charges additional purchases. Liability of R's father to the store?

2. K agrees to purchase some machinery from M. When M adds up the prices of all the items, he makes a $1000 addition error. K pays M $4200, obtains a receipt, and takes the machinery. Later, K notes the error but says nothing (considering it his lucky day). The next day M also finds the error and demands the $1000. Will K have to pay?

3. Z asks for bids to pave a parking lot. The C Co. makes the lowest bid and signs a written contract. Z is curious about how C can do the job for so little and is worried they will try to do a poor-quality job. Before the job is started, C's accountant calls to advise that there was an error in the bid. Z demands that the work be done or he will sue. Liability of C?

4. J books vacation passage aboard the cruise ship, Rustbottom II. When J arrives at dockside, she is told that the government has commandeered the ship to carry soldiers to an urgent U.N. assignment. J's vacation is ruined. Can she sue the ship's owners?

5. N knowingly gives money to S as part of an investment in an illegal gambling operation. Suspecting that S is stealing some of the profits, N sues to recover her investment. Can she recover it? Can she demand an "accounting" of what happened to the profits?

6. D and K enter into a contract on Sunday, March 3. D says, "Let's date the contract Monday, March 4." They do so. Is this an enforceable agreement?

7. The G Hotel hires the "Dream-Makers" for their New Year's Eve Ball. On New Year's Eve eight musicians appear, but only one of them is actually a

member of the D-M band. The other seven have just been hired from the local musicians' union hall. The "genuine" D-M says that this is a common practice. The band plays at four or five clubs on the same night and uses substitute musicians. "It's all the same music," the singer adds. Must the G Hotel accept this arrangement?

8. B is annoyed by a traffic ticket he feels should not have been issued. He collects $25 in pennies, nickles, and dimes and takes the money to the city clerk to pay his ticket. The coins are all in a metal pail which he dumps on the counter saying, "It's all good, Canadian money." Must the clerk accept this form of payment?

9. B's grandfather promised B that he would pay for her college education on two conditions. The first was that she not marry while in school, and the second was that she marry a person of the same religious faith. Payment was to be made each year on B's birthday. Two payments were made, but when B's grandfather learned that she had a boyfriend who was not of the same religious faith, he withheld the payment that should have been made on her twenty-first birthday. She sued for the money claiming that she had not broken the terms of the promise. Counsel for the grandfather raised the defence that the entire contract was void as being contrary to the sanctity of marriage. Will B get the money?

10. W, a wealthy woman, has a drinking problem known to all her friends and business associates. Most people believe that after 2:00 p.m. she is incapable of coherent thought or action. At 3:30 p.m. she telephones her stockbroker and orders the purchase of a very large block of shares of dubious quality. The broker makes the purchase but W refuses to pay raising intoxication as a defence. The broker testifies that on that particular day W's voice was steady and she discussed the stock very intelligently. Must W pay for the stock?

Applying the Law

Gabriel v. Hamilton Tiger-Cat Football Club Ltd.
Ontario, 1976

Tony Gabriel signed a contract in 1973 with the Hamilton Tiger-Cat Football Club. In so signing he undertook to play football for the respondent in "all its Conference's scheduled and play-off games" in the 1974 season. He would be paid a salary of $18 000. Although the fact had received wide public comment, the applicant had apparently been unaware, at the time he signed the contract, that the 1974 schedule of games had been increased from fourteen to sixteen games. Had this fact been known to him it may be safely assumed that Gabriel would have required greater compensation than that agreed upon in the contract. A representative of the club, present upon the signing of the contract, had not informed the applicant of this development.

A judge of the High Court of Justice determined that the number of games designated by the phrase "Conference's scheduled games" in the contract was sixteen. This was a contract for personal service and as such did not fall within that class of contracts requiring full disclosure of all material facts in order to maintain their validity. The representative of the club had been justified in his belief that Gabriel must already have known of the increased schedule. His silence on the matter had not constituted a misrepresentation to Gabriel nor could Gabriel be said to have been misled in any way. There had been no mistake, either mutual or unilateral, that affected the contract. The terms used in the contract were quite clear and the court would not imply a term to the effect that the parties to the contract must have meant the schedule to be limited to fourteen games.

Questions

1. As Gabriel was most likely represented by an agent, would it not be the agent's negligence that brought about this disagreement?

2. Why did Gabriel feel he was entitled to more money

when the contract he signed said he would play all season games and play-off games?

3. If a different player had signed a three-year agreement the year before the schedule was lengthened, do you think that player could insist upon a raise?

Tiller v. McCarthy and Community Life General Insurance Company
Newfoundland, 1982

The plaintiff brought an action against the defendant for damages arising out of a motor vehicle accident. The liability of the defendant was admitted. The issue to be resolved was whether the insurance company was obliged to indemnify the defendant. The defendant had received notice that her insurance premium was due on Sunday, the day on which the accident occurred.

The renewal premium was marked "Final Notice" and was to expire August 12, 1979 at 12:01 a.m. The accident occurred forty-nine minutes after the expiration.

The defendant telephoned the office of the insurance company on Saturday, but they were not open for business that day nor the following day, which was Sunday. On Monday morning, August 13, 1979, the defendant telephoned the insurance company and told them she had been in an accident. She was told she was covered, but when she went to the office to pay her premium and discuss the accident she was told she was not covered. Newfoundland does not have a *Lord's Day Act* so the common law rule that Sunday is a non-juridical day applies:

66The defendant was entitled to accept the third party's offer any time on that date, but the fact that August 12, 1979 fell on a Sunday extended that right to August 13, 1979. The defendant was precluded from carrying out her fixed intention of renewing her policy by one reason only, namely, that August 12, 1979 was a Sunday and the third party's office was not open for business.99

Questions

1. Why did the court conclude that the defendant's insurance policy was still in effect even though the expiration date had passed?

2. Is there any way the defendant could have paid her premium on time? What would have been the effect of writing a cheque and dropping it into a mail box on either Saturday or Sunday?

3. Do you think it was an error on the part of the insurance company to have the expiration date on a Sunday?

You Be the Judge

1. Boyd Construction was hired by the West Wind Race Track to build a new grandstand. A formal contract was signed and Boyd had materials delivered to the construction site. Shortly after some holes were dug for concrete supports, the holes filled with water. It was concluded that there was an underground stream just below the surface where the grandstand was to be put up and that it would not be safe to proceed. The project was abandoned but Boyd sued for the money lost in all the labour expended thus far. The race track company refused to pay, alleging it was an Act of God. Boyd's lawyer based the action upon the failure of the race track company to have proper soil tests done before hiring the construction company. Who would succeed?

2. Hardy and Edwards were business associates who took a trip to the United States and did some gambling where gambling was legal. Hardy lost too much money and owed a debt to the casino. Edwards loaned her the money so that they could leave the casino without any embarrassment. They also feared that the casino might have some rough methods of collecting from deadbeats. Upon their return to Canada, Edwards asked for the repayment of the loan but Hardy would not pay. Edwards sued, suggesting that the debt was no different from any other debt. Where they had gambled it was legal to do so. Hardy defended the action on the grounds that gambling is

an immoral act and that no court action could be based upon the collection of such a debt, whether or not gambling was lawful in the foreign country. Hardy also testified that Edwards kept urging her to keep gambling by saying, "Stay with it. I have a feeling your luck will change." Who would succeed?

3. The plaintiff was struck and injured by a vehicle belonging to the defendant. The plaintiff was a minor at the time. The defendant's lawyer presented a cheque and a release form to the plaintiff's parents. They signed the release and accepted the cheque. The plaintiff received none of the money but was given basic medical care until she appeared to recover. Three years later, after reaching the age of eighteen, the plaintiff was advised by her doctor that she had a medical problem that related to the previous injury, and that it would cause her serious trouble all her life. She brought a separate action against the defendant. The defendant relied upon the payment to the parents and upon the signed release form. Who would succeed?

4. Maybee hired the Pottersville Chemical Co. to spray his fields with a herbicide. Partly because of poor directions and partly because of limited visibility, the company's airplane pilot sprayed one field belonging to Maybee and two fields belonging to Young. Young was pleased to have the spraying done because he was negotiating with the company to have his fields sprayed as well. Maybee refused to pay the company for the work done, so the company brought an action against Young. He refused to pay. Who would succeed?

5. Peter Darling and some friends formed a rock band. Peter purchased an electric organ and other sound equipment on a conditional sales contract. He was to make monthly payments of $75 per month for sixty months. He made most of his payments, but missed several. When he missed a payment, his father gave him the money. Peter was seventeen when he signed the contract but he lied about his age. In a two-year period, Peter's father made five payments and Peter made nineteen. At no time did his father communicate directly with the music store and all payments were made by Peter. The band broke up when Peter was nineteen. He made no further payments and tried to avoid the contract using his infancy as a defence. The store sued Peter and his father for the remaining payments. Who would succeed?

Chapter 16

Assignments, Bailments, and Time Limitations

Assignment of Contract

It is possible for the parties to tranfer their rights under the contract to someone else. This is referred to as an *assignment of contract.* The most common form of assignment deals with the right to collect money. If a store sells goods on credit, it usually assigns the right to the monthly payments to a financial institution such as a finance company. The finance company pays off the store and then collects from the debtor. An assignment must be in writing, and must be given for valid consideration. The debtor must be notified that the assignment has been made, but there is no requirement to obtain his or her permission to make the assignment. The assignment cannot in any way increase the burden upon the debtor by the addition of such things as administration fees, etc.

While it is easy to assign a right under a contract, it is quite the reverse with regard to obligations under a contract. A person cannot assign certain obligations at all, unless the contract allows it or the other party agrees to it. These obligations include:

- *The payment of a debt:* The creditor may be willing to trust the original debtor for payment, but is not necessarily going to trust someone else. If Jones lends $5000 to Thomas, because Thomas is a good risk, Jones is not going to let Thomas assign the debt to Harvey, who is a deadbeat.
- *The performance of a personal skill:* If a person has been contracted because of a special skill, that person cannot assign the performance of the contract to someone else who does not have the same skill.

If a contract is signed where no special skill is involved, the performance may be assigned to someone else. However, the original party still remains liable on the contract. It is a common practice to hire a contractor to build a house. This does not mean the contractor will personally do all the work. The contractor will "sub-contract" such specialized work as plumbing, electrical wiring, brick work, etc. The contractor is responsible to pay the sub-contractors, and the contractor remains liable to the buyer if any of the work is done poorly. If the wiring is bad, the contractor cannot say to the buyer, "Call up that electrician and say the wiring has to be fixed." This remains the contractor's responsibility.

Special Contracts: The Law of Bailments

People often have reason to leave personal property in the care or custody of some other person. A common example is taking the family car for a tune-up.

Transactions of this kind are called *bailments.* The person who owns and delivers the property is the *bailor* and the person to whom the property is delivered is the *bailee.*

A bailment consists of the delivery of personal property to another person on the understanding that the property is to be returned at a specified time or when a certain purpose has been fulfilled, such as repair. It is clear that the parties do not intend that title to the property should change hands. Thus, a bailment is very distinct from a sale.

A person entrusted with the property of another person is expected to take care of it. However, the extent of care and the extent of liability differs depending upon whether the person was paid to take charge of the property or is doing it for nothing. Bailments are then classed as either gratuitous bailments or bailments for reward.

Gratuitous Bailments

A bailment is gratuitous if one of the parties gets some benefit or service for free. Depending upon who gets the free benefit, the bailment is either exclusively for the benefit of the bailor or for the bailee.

For example, before going away on a holiday, Green might ask a neighbour, Brown, to safeguard Green's valuable stamp collection. If Brown agrees to do so and is to be paid no fee for doing so, this is a gratuitous bailment exclusively for the benefit of Green, since Brown gets nothing out of it.

As an opposite example, let us assume that Brown's television set malfunctions. Brown borrows a set from Green while Brown's own set is in the repair shop. Brown will not pay Green for the temporary use of the set. This is a gratuitous bailment exclusively for the benefit of the bailee.

From this we must determine what responsibility a person has under a gratuitous bailment. Apart from a separate contract, if a bailment is for the benefit of the bailor only, then the bailee is required only to take such a degree of care of the property as an ordinary, prudent person would take of his or her own property. If the property is lost, stolen, or damaged while in the bailee's hands, the bailee is not liable unless the loss occurred through the serious negligence of the bailee or because the bailee ignored the instructions given by the bailor. Referring to our first example, if a thief broke into Brown's house and stole the stamp collection, Brown would not be liable to Green for the loss. If, however, for some reason, Brown took the stamp collection somewhere by car and left the car unlocked, Brown would be liable to Green if the collection were

stolen. This would constitute negligent handling of a valuable item.

If the bailment is for the exclusive benefit of the bailee, the rules differ somewhat. The obligations of a borrower of property are fairly strict. The bailee must use the article only for the purpose for which it was loaned. The bailee must take the utmost degree of care of the article and is liable for any damage caused by carelessness. The bailee is not liable for ordinary wear and tear just from using the property. In the example of the borrowed television set, if a circuit burned out just from age, this would not be Brown's fault. This could have occurred at any time and is not related to the fact that Brown was watching the set when it happened. However, if Brown took the set to a cottage and it was stolen there, Brown would be liable for its loss because the cottage was not a secure place to leave the set. Moreover, Green intended that the set should only be used in Brown's home.

Bailments for Reward

Most bailments involve the exchange of consideration between the two parties. This is called a bailment for reward. If the two parties enter into a specific contract then the terms of that contract will apply. In the absence of a separate contract, there are some general rules that apply. The rules differ somewhat depending upon what the bailee is to do with the goods. Generally, there are four types of agreements involved: (1) renting personal property; (2) repairing personal property; (3) storing personal property; and (4) transporting personal property.

Renting Personal Property

When personal property is rented, the owner of the goods is the bailor and the person renting the goods is the bailee. An example would be a person who rents an automobile from a leasing company. Each party has duties and obligations.

The bailor's responsibilities include making certain that the goods which are being rented out are fit and safe for the work for which they are rented. There is an implied warranty on the part of the bailor to be liable for damages or injuries that result from defects of which the bailor ought to have been aware. Therefore, if the automobile rented is mechanically unsafe, the bailor will be liable for any injuries that result. This is provided that the defects were such that they could have been found by inspection. If a defect is so hidden that the bailor could not find it, then there is no liability upon the bailor. The bailor is not liable to the bailee if the bailee misuses the article rented. For example, suppose that Green rents a trailer from Brown's Rent-All. The trailer has a weight limit which Green ignores. Green overloads the trailer and has an accident while pulling it. Brown is not liable for Green's misuse and the accident which results. In fact, Green would be liable to Brown for damage to the trailer.

The bailee also has obligations. The bailee must take reasonable care of the rented property and will be liable for any abuse or damage caused by neglect. Unless the agreement allows otherwise, the bailee must pay the full rental value agreed upon even though the property is returned sooner than expected. The bailee is not obligated to repair the rented property if it breaks down from ordinary wear. If the bailee does make repairs, without the consent of the bailor, the bailor does not have to repay the bailee.

Hadley v. Droitwich Construction
England, 1967

The owners of a large crane rented it to a person who employed the plaintiff. At the time the crane was rented, it needed some repairs; this fact was known to the defendant, but the defects were not considered serious or dangerous. Hadley was not an experienced crane operator. The defects in the crane became worse as Hadley used it and eventually there was an accident injuring him. The court found the defendant liable as a bailor who rented a machine which needed repair without warning the plaintiff of the defect. However, the court also held that Hadley's employer failed to service the crane properly and allowed it to be operated by an inexperienced employee. The court assessed damages equally between the plaintiff's employer and the defendant.

Repairing Personal Property

If a person takes property to another person for repair, a bailment exists. The bailor has two obligations: (1) to pay the price agreed upon, or a reasonable price; (2) to pay for the extent of work agreed upon. If the bailee does more than the contract calls for, the bailor does not have to pay the extra cost unless he or she has consented to having the extra work done.

This second point requires some clarification. When the bailor takes an item for repair, the bailor must be specific as to what is to be done. If the item is just left for repair, then the bailee will assume that the bailor wants all necessary repairs done. If the bailor signs a blank work order authorizing repairs, then the bailor must pay for everything done. If the bailor wants to limit either the amount of work done or the cost, then the bailor must specifically instruct the bailee that the work is to be so limited. The simplest way is to limit the dollar cost. Words such as "Repair authorized to a limit of $100," written on the work order, will serve as a protection against a larger repair bill. If the bailor places no limits upon repair, then the bailee is justified in doing all the necessary repairs. It is a good practice to ask for a specific estimate of repair. For major items, a written estimate is a good idea.

The bailee has the duty of doing the repairs agreed upon in a skillful and diligent manner, and taking ordinary care of the property. In the event of damage, the onus of proving absence of negligence is upon the bailee. Many repair shops have posted signs and contract terms with words such as these: "Items left at owner's risk." What do these words really mean? They are advising the bailor that the bailee is not an insurer of the goods. Thus, if the building burned down and the bailor's goods were destroyed by a fire not caused by the negligence of the bailee, the bailee would not be required to compensate the bailor for the loss. However, the courts have held that if the bailor did not see the sign or did not read the words in the contract, he or she is not bound by them.

Unless there is an agreement otherwise, the bailor must pay the bailee before the bailee returns the goods. This is because the law gives an unpaid worker a lien on the goods. Ultimately, the bailee has the right to sell the goods to satisfy the claim. Once the bailee releases the goods the right of lien is lost and cannot be recovered. For example, if Brown's Garage worked on Green's car, the garage does not have to release the car to Green until the repair bill is paid. If the garage released the car without being paid, the garage could not legally go out and repossess the car later. The garage would have to sue for payment. In British Columbia, Alberta, Saskatchewan and Manitoba, a lien may be placed upon a vehicle after it has been released if the garage has the owner's acknowledgement of the indebtedness.

Storing Personal Property

A bailee who stores goods for a fee is in the business of running a warehouse and such persons are subject to the following general rules: (1) They must use reasonable diligence and care in looking after the goods stored. The onus is upon them to prove that loss or destruction was not due to their negligence. (2) If they accept items for storage that require special facilities, such as cold storage, they are obliged to provide those facilities or accept liability for loss.

Evans Products Ltd. v. Crest Warehousing Ltd.
British Columbia, 1976

The plaintiff claimed damages for loss suffered by it when 230 crates of plywood were damaged by fire while stored by the defendant in its warehouse. The cause of the fire was admittedly that the wood had been left in too close a proximity to some electric heaters which had been left on unintentionally. The defendant admitted liability but argued that it was entitled to limit its liability to $50 per crate pursuant to a clause to that effect on the back of each warehouse receipt received by the plaintiff.

The court allowed the plaintiff's action. In the absence of an agreement to the contrary, such a clause in a storage contract was invalid. It arbitrar-

A sign of this type reminds the vehicle owner (the bailor) that the parking lot owner (the bailee) is not an insurer of the vehicle.

ily limited the liability of the warehouse to a sum that, although not nominal, was well below the actual value of the stored goods. Also, it absolved the defendant of the obligation to exercise the degree of care and diligence required in relation to these goods. In addition, the limitation clause was of no avail since the defendant was guilty of a fundamental breach of the bailment contract in storing the goods near the heaters and thus could not rely upon the clause.

Transporting Personal Property

Persons who transport goods are generally called *carriers*. There are two classes of carriers, private and common.

A *private carrier* is one who occasionally transports goods for other persons and gets paid for the service, but does not make it a regular business in a public way. This gives the private carrier the right to accept or reject either the customer or the type of goods to be carried. A private carrier is liable for any loss caused by personal negligence or negligence of employees.

Companies or persons who hold themselves out to the public as being in the business of transporting goods are called *common carriers*. A common carrier does not have the right to pick and choose either its customers or the type of goods to be carried unless the goods require special facilities which the carrier does not have. A common carrier is an insurer of the goods during their transportation and is liable for loss or damage occurring in the course of shipment, even though not guilty of any personal negligence. However, a common carrier is not liable if the goods were destroyed by an act of God, by the Queen's enemies (e.g., during a war), or by inherent defects in the goods themselves.

Carriers issue tickets when goods are shipped and the terms of the shipping agreement are printed on the tickets. In some cases the carrier's liability is limited in some manner, usually by weight or number of items. For example, items lost by an air carrier may be limited by the terms of the Warsaw Convention which is an international treaty covering air travel to many of the countries of the world.

Turgel Fur Co. v. Northumberland Ferries Nova Scotia, 1966

The defendant operated a ferry across the Northumberland Strait, which separates Prince Edward Island from Nova Scotia. A ferry was making the crossing when it was struck, unexpectedly, by a giant wave, of a sort totally unknown to those waters. A truck belonging to the plaintiff was on the ferry at the time and both the truck and its contents suffered damages. The plaintiff sued for damages, but the court held that it was an act of God which could not have been foreseen or prevented by the defendant.

Innkeepers and Hotel Keepers

Persons who operate hotels and motels are bailees for value. Hotel keepers are persons who hold themselves out to the public as being ready to provide lodging and accommodation to travellers and to accept the travellers' luggage as well. Hotel keepers must accept any fit and orderly person as a guest provided there is a vacancy. They do not have to accept pets or other animals and can limit the number of persons in a room.

As a bailee, the hotel keeper's liability is similar to that of a common carrier; thus the hotel keeper is an insurer of the goods which guests bring into the hotel. However, the hotel keeper may avoid liability by showing that the loss or damage was due to the guest's own negligence. Liability may extend to insuring the guest's car if parked on hotel property. It does not extend to the contents of the car.

The liability of the hotel keeper has been limited by provincial statute. Ontario law holds that no hotel keeper is liable to make good to a guest a sum more than $40 *except* where the goods or property have been stolen, lost, or injured either through the wilful act, default or neglect of the hotel keeper personally or of employees; or where the goods had been deposited with the hotel keeper for safekeeping. To be protected, the hotel keeper must post a copy of this section of the statute in each room. In Newfoundland the amount of liability is $150. In Alberta the room must be locked and the key left at the office; otherwise the hotel keeper is not liable.

Time Limitations

If a contract is not properly carried out, the injured party may sue the other party for damages or specific performance; but it must be kept in mind that there are time limitations involved in the right to sue. Each province has a period of limitations for bringing a lawsuit, and depending on the complaint of the injured party, the time limit can be very short or it can run for years. For example, a building contractor who has not been paid must file a lien within a specific length of time, such as the forty-five days required under the *Ontario Mechanic's Lien Act*.

The law holds that claims cannot be allowed to exist forever, since records are lost and memories fade. If a creditor could bring an action fifty years after a debt arose, the creditor could make claims which no one could refute since the people concerned would either be deceased or would quite simply have forgotten. Note that the time period refers to initiating the lawsuit, not settling it. Therefore, it is sufficient to file the action within the time period.

Simple Contract Debts

In most provinces a creditor has six years in which to initiate a lawsuit for a debt arising from a simple contract, although in some special areas a statute may require that the action begin much sooner. In Ontario an action for unpaid wages must be brought within six months of the last payment. The six-year period begins when the plaintiff is first entitled to bring the legal action. If the creditor fails to do so, the right to sue is *barred* and the debt is said to be *outlawed*. This does not mean the debt is no longer owing, but only that at the present time the creditor cannot collect it through court action. It is possible that something may occur

later which will again free the creditor to take action. The following situations could arise which would allow the creditor to take legal action again:

- The debtor may do something that *revives* the outlawed debt and starts the period of limitations running again. This would be the case if the debtor makes a part payment on the debt, or writes the creditor promising to still pay the debt. In Alberta a written acknowledgement of the debt or part payment renews the period of limitation even if the debtor also states an inability or unwillingness to pay more.
- If the debtor is running a trade balance with the creditor, the creditor may treat every item on that account as a separate debt. The six-year term begins on the date that the item was purchased. If the debtor sends a payment to the creditor and does not specify the item for which payment is being made, the creditor could apply the payment to the oldest debt in the account and thereby revive it.
- If the debtor has disappeared on the date when the creditor was first entitled to bring a lawsuit on the debt, the creditor is said to be under a *disability*, and the period of limitations does not start running until the debtor returns to the area within the local court's jurisdiction. Also, if the creditor was suffering a personal disability at the time he or she was first entitled to sue, the creditor is allowed to extend the limitations period. If the creditor was an infant when the right to sue arose, and could not sue because it was not possible to find a person to act as next friend, then the period of limitations is suspended until the creditor reaches the age of majority. There is no disability because the debtor is a minor. Under numerous circumstances the adult creditor could sue the infant debtor.

Specialty Contract Debts

Contracts under seal have a longer period of limitations than simple contracts. The availability of the formal contract as evidence makes it less important that an action be brought immediately. In most provinces, the right to sue is extended to twenty years, with the exception of the right to sue upon an unpaid mortgage, which has a limitation period of ten years. In most provinces the action must commence within one year of the date of maturity of the mortgage. In Alberta, specialty contract claims are outlawed (expired) in six years.

Laches

Laches is a common law principle which permits the defendant to show that the plaintiff has been negligent or unreasonable in delaying the assertion or enforcement of a right. "Delay defeats equity." The court may refuse to aid a plaintiff with a "stale demand" where the plaintiff has slept on his or her rights for a long time, thus compounding the problems for the defendant and making the case more difficult for the court. The claim may be denied even though the period of limitations has not run out.

Enforcement of Judgments

Once a case has been decided, the court judgment (order) can be carried out against the losing party for a period up to twenty years in most provinces. This means that if the debtor did not have any money or property which the creditor could seize at the time, the creditor would still have a period of twenty years in which to lay claim to any money or property acquired by the debtor. Also, most provinces have legislated the statutory right to renew a judgment and thereby extend its effect beyond the prescribed period. If a person won a judgment against an infant, he or she could try to collect from the infant any time during the next twenty years, long after the infant had become an adult. Rather than have judgment orders hanging over their heads for such a long time, some persons elect to go through personal bankruptcy. If bankruptcy is declared, the judgment order is treated the same as any other debt owed by the debtor and could be wiped out.

Reviewing Important Points

1. A party to a contract may assign the obligations under the contract only if the contract allows it or the other party agrees.
2. Certain time limitations apply where a creditor wishes to sue for an unpaid debt. The courts will not assist a plaintiff who sleeps on his or her rights.
3. A bailment is a contract which places the property of one person in the care of another.
4. If a bailment is for the exclusive benefit of the person receiving the goods, that person must take the utmost care of the goods.
5. If a person signs a blank work order, then he or she must pay for the work done. The bailor can place a limit on the work to be done.
6. Someone who repairs goods may hold the goods until the repair bill is paid. If the bill is not paid the person may eventually sell the goods.
7. A hotel keeper is liable for the property of the hotel's guests. This liability may be limited by posting copies of the provincial law in each room and in the office.

Checking Your Understanding

1. What rules must be observed in assigning the rights under a contract to a third party?
2. Describe two situations which would allow a creditor to take action again on an outlawed debt.
3. If a general contractor assigns part of a project to a sub-contractor, who is liable if the work is poorly done?
4. If a judgment cannot be enforced against an infant defendant, what is the purpose of obtaining the judgment?
5. State two methods by which a bailor may limit the extent of repairs he or she will authorize.
6. What duty rests upon a company that rents out equipment?
7. If the bailee releases the goods without being paid, what right does the bailee still have over the goods?

Legal Briefs

1. F sold tools to P when P was a minor. F was only paid half the money. He did not sue because he (wrongly) believed it was not possible to sue a minor. Two years later, P became an adult but F forgot about the debt. Five years later, F died. His executor demanded payment from P to the estate. Must P pay?

2. B contracted with G to build a house. G subcontracted the brick work to H, who had a reputation for shoddy work. B refused to accept this arrangement and told G that she would cancel the entire contract if H began work. Is B on safe ground here?

3. V borrowed money from R, a loan company. V was owed money by W. V wrote R that his loan would be taken over by W. Must R accept this?

4. T purchased goods on credit from D, a department store. She later received a letter from S, a finance company, stating that they now had her account and that she should make payments to them. T refused, saying she never dealt with finance companies because it would hurt her reputation. Must T make payments to S?

5. Assume in Question 4 that the letter from S also stated that there would be an added $5 per month "administration fee" to handle her account. Must T consent to that?

6. J owed money to G for three years. After receiving many bills from G, J wrote him a letter saying that he knew he owed the money but could not pay because he was close to bankruptcy. Four years later J inherited an estate and G sued. Is the debt outlawed?

7. B leaves his car at the ABC garage for repairs. An employee takes B's car to run a personal errand and wrecks the car. The garage owner relies upon a sign over the door: "Vehicles left at owner's risk." Liability of the garage?

8. Assume in Question 7 that B saw the sign. Does that change the decision in the case?

9. R rents a room at the Y Motel. She leaves valuable goods in her room while she goes to a restaurant. She is certain she has locked the door. She keeps the key in her pocket. When she returns, the valuables are gone. On the back of the door is a small card with a statement, extracted from the *Innkeepers' Act*, that the management is not liable for items of special value left in rooms. R never read the card although she saw it. Liability of the motel?

10. Assume in Question 9 that R read the card because she wanted to know when the checkout time was. She read only the top part of the card where the time was stated. The terms regarding liability were in the bottom half of the card, which R did not read. Liability of the motel?

Applying the Law

 Smith & Sons v. Silverman
Ontario, 1961

Smith parked his car on a parking lot owned by Silverman. While the car was parked there it was damaged. At the time the car was parked, a ticket was issued that stated in large letters, "We are not responsible for theft or damage of car or contents however caused." In addition, there were four large signs at different places in the parking lot with the same words. The Ontario Court of Appeal held that in this case the words on the ticket and the signs were a clear indication that Silverman was limiting his liability. Silverman had done what was reasonably necessary to bring these terms to the attention of customers and Smith could hardly have failed to see the wording at some time. Smith's claim for damages was dismissed.

Questions

1. What general duty of care does the owner of a parking lot have towards cars left there?

2. Did the sign alter the basic contractual agreement between the two parties or did the sign just remind people who parked there about what that agreement was?

3. If someone backed their car into Smith's, why would Smith feel that he should be compensated by Silverman?

Kalmer v. Greyhound Lines of Canada Ltd.
Alberta, 1981

The plaintiff arrived in Calgary by air and went to the bus depot. He spoke with a ticket agent and found that he could not get a bus to Lethbridge until 6:00 the next morning. He purchased a ticket and asked about checking his luggage. The agent behind the counter took the defendant's luggage and assured him it would be put on the bus. The plaintiff paid a fee of $1 for checking his luggage and was given a tag. He put this tag into his pocket without reading it. His luggage did not arrive the next day in Lethbridge and it took a special trace to find it. When he finally received it he had to pay an additional $5.85. The plaintiff immediately noticed a lock broken on one piece of luggage. He complained about the state of the luggage but was advised that if he did not pay the additional fee of $5.85 the luggage would be returned to Calgary.

The plaintiff went home and checked the contents and found two watches missing. They had a value of $900. He wrote a letter to the defendants who relied upon the wording on the tag:

CONDITIONS

The company shall not be liable for more than $25 in respect of loss or damage to any one package including the contents or any article not contained in a package whether such loss or damage be occasioned through negligence of the company, its agents, or employees, or otherwise, and further, there shall be no liability upon the company in respect of any such loss or damage howsoever caused unless application for delivery of such package be made within six months after date of deposit unless written notice is given to the company within twenty-four hours after delivery.

Counsel for the defendant company noted that the plaintiff had not given notice of loss within twenty-four hours. It was the position of the company that it owed the plaintiff $25 or nothing. The plaintiff testified that the transactions took place at the ticket counter and that he did not see a sign posted at the checkroom counter. He also said that he never read the wording on the tag.

The court held that the defendant was liable for the entire $900. Even though the ticket had words on the front saying, "See Notice on Back" there was nothing particularly distinctive about that print. As the defendant had not done all that could be reasonably required to bring the conditions to the plaintiff's notice, the plaintiff was not bound by those conditions and was entitled to judgment in the amount of $900.

Questions

1. Why did the court hold that the plaintiff could recover his full loss?
2. Is there any way the defendant could have acted to limit its liability? Why were the printed words not effective?
3. Do you think the plaintiff should have had to prove that he actually had two watches in that piece of luggage?

You Be the Judge

1. The plaintiff rented a riding horse from the defendant stable. An employee of the defendant adjusted the stirrup strap for the plaintiff. The strap later broke and the plaintiff fell from the horse suffering injury. The defendant argued that the defect was not one that could be seen easily and required the closest inspection. Counsel for the plaintiff argued that the defendant must be responsible for all defects preventable through an exercise of skill and diligence in checking equipment. Who would succeed?

2. The plaintiff took her watch to the defendant for repair. She returned for it ten times but it was never ready because the defendant had carelessly lost certain parts. During this time the defendant kept the watch in a safe. Later, the watch was on the workbench when a fire destroyed the building. The plaintiff sued for the value of the watch. The defendant demon-

strated that the fire was not caused by personal negligence. Who would succeed?

3. The defendant had a revolving charge account with the plaintiff store. The oldest debt on record was nine years old; the most recent was two years old. The defendant had a peculiar habit of not paying debts for long periods of time, and then suddenly paying them. This was how he managed to owe businesses so much money for so long. He sent a cheque to the store for the amount of $356.99 which just happened to be exactly the amount charged on the most recent debt. The defendant included no payment instructions with the cheque so the store applied the sum to the oldest debt. It did not cover the full amount so the store brought an action to recover the rest saying the debt was now "revived." Who would succeed?

GOLD-PLATED
10-SPEED
$4 000

Unit
Seven

Sale of Goods

Caveat emptor
("Let the buyer beware")

Chapter 17
The Nature of a Sale

What Is a Sale?

At one time, buying goods was a relatively simple matter. The buyer and seller stood across from each other and bargained. The buyer could examine the goods he or she was interested in buying, and comment upon their quality or lack of it. There could be no substitutions. That is, the buyer bought the item that had been examined. The seller could not show the buyer one item and then later substitute another identical, but damaged, item in its place. There were no guarantees other than the buyer's own judgment. There were no catalogues or show rooms, and the goods were not wrapped in cardboard and plastic. Once you bought something, it was yours and if you had made a bad bargain, it was a good lesson for you to remember in the future. The law had only one rule, and that was *caveat emptor* (buyer beware). It was assumed that the seller was trying to get the better of the buyer and vice versa. Thus, the seller tried to blow up the good points about the goods and the buyer tried to emphasize the bad points to talk the price down. The seller would say nothing about defects in the goods—just hope the buyer wouldn't see them!

This is not the law of sale today. There are now implied conditions as to quality and fitness of goods and there is no duty on a buyer to examine goods in order for the conditions to be effective. The seller does not have to point out defects if they can be easily seen, but the seller cannot hide the defects.

A *sale* can be defined as the transfer of ownership of property upon payment of a price. This differs from a barter or trade which is merely exchanging goods for other goods. If both goods and money are involved, it becomes difficult to decide if the agreement is a barter or a sale. In such cases, one must ask whether the major part of the contract involves money or not. If only a small amount of money is involved in comparison to the value of the goods being exchanged, the agreement is a barter not a sale. None of the specific statutes pertaining to the sale of goods apply to barters.

There are several different types of sales. An *absolute sale* is a sale that is final upon the completion of the sale, with ownership or title passing immediately from the seller to the buyer. If the terms of the sale agreement call for payment to be made at a later date, this does not affect title. In an absolute sale, title passes when the contract is made.

A *conditional sale* does not give immediate ownership to the buyer although he or she immediately acquires the use of the goods. Title does not pass until the buyer fulfills some condition in the contract, usually the making of full payment.

A *bill of sale* is a document used to protect the buyer who has bought goods but left them temporarily with the seller. The bill of sale is proof of the transfer of title to the buyer.

A *chattel mortgage* is not a true sale, but a mortgage against personal property. The borrower transfers title to the property over to the lender in return for a loan of money. The borrower still retains use of the property. If the borrower repays the loan, the mortgage is discharged and title reverts back to the borrower.

The Sale of Goods Act

Each province, except Quebec, has a statute similar to the British statute known as the *Sale of Goods Act*. The Quebec *Civil Code* contains some provisions regarding the sale of goods. Some provinces also have consumer protection laws that have sections dealing with the sale of goods, and more will be said about that in Unit Nine Consumer Protection.

Each province has a monetary limit above which a sale of goods requires a written contract. The amount differs from province to province, ranging from $30 to $50. In Alberta and Newfoundland it is $50; $40 in Ontario. These provincial laws hold that an unwritten contract for the sale of goods with a value above the prescribed limit is not enforceable by court action except under the following conditions: (1) The buyer accepts part of the goods and actually receives them. (2) The buyer gives something in earnest to bind the bargain. (3) The buyer makes a partial payment. (4) Some note or memorandum of the contract is made in writing and signed by the buyer or an agent.

To analyse these requirements briefly, the basic requirement is that a contract for the sale of goods over the prescribed sum must be in writing. That is the basic rule. Then, there are exceptions to the rule. The first exception is if the buyer receives and accepts any part of the goods. The second exception is if the buyer gives the seller something *in earnest;* that is, gives the seller something of value to hold until payment is made. It is a way of proving good faith. The third exception is if the buyer makes part payment (in which case it would be wise to get a receipt as proof of this part payment). The fourth exception is if there is some written memorandum signed by the buyer, to show that he or she entered into the sale. A written memorandum can be any paper or collection of papers, notes, letters, etc., that prove a contract of sale was made. The written memorandum need not be in any special form. All that is necessary is that a written document or series of documents clearly indicate the parties' intention to enter into a contract and explain the terms agreed upon.

Delivery

Generally, the *Sale of Goods Act* requires the seller to put the goods into a deliverable condition, but it does not require the seller to deliver. The buyer must collect the goods unless otherwise agreed to. When completing the sale, the buyer should make sure that the price includes delivery. The buyer may encounter such terms as *F.O.B.* (meaning "free on board"), *C.O.D.* ("cash on delivery"), and *C.I.F.* ("cost, insurance and freight"). Free on board indicates at what point the title to the goods passes to the buyer and how far the goods are being transported at the seller's own cost. If the seller says, "F.O.B. our factory," the buyer must pick up the goods or pay for delivery, and it is at the factory that title is transferred. If the contract says, "F.O.B. at destination," the seller is transporting the goods at his or her risk, and title will pass when the goods are delivered to the buyer. C.O.D. means that the buyer will pay for the goods when they are physically presented. If the buyer cannot pay, the delivery person will usually refuse to leave the goods. Title passes when payment is made. C.I.F. advises that the seller will purchase the insurance and freight and arrange all the details of transportation; the seller will charge the buyer the cost of all these services. The risk belongs to the buyer while the goods are being transported.

Payment

Unless there is some other agreement, it is assumed that the buyer will pay when the goods are picked up or delivered. If no price was agreed to, it is assumed that the buyer will pay the current catalogue price or a fair market price for the goods. There is nothing to prevent the two parties from arranging a plan for a delayed payment, such as thirty days after the sale was made. This does not affect any of the other terms of the contract.

Risk of Loss

Unless otherwise agreed, the goods remain at the seller's risk until the property is transferred to the buyer, at which point the goods are at the buyer's risk. Therefore, it is important to know when title passes from the seller to the buyer so that the parties know at all times who is taking the risk of loss. This is especially important when goods are being transported over great distances. If delivery of the goods is delayed because of the fault of either the buyer or seller, then risk passes to (or remains with) whichever party was at fault, regardless of who would ordinarily bear the risk of loss.

Ascertained Goods

Ascertained goods, sometimes called specific goods, are those goods which are specifically set aside and prepared for the buyer, and which are in a deliverable state. Under Ontario law, which is similar to legislation in most other provinces, goods are deemed to be in a deliverable state when they are in such a state that the buyer would, under the contract, be bound to take delivery of them. Title is not transferred to the buyer until the goods become ascertained and the buyer is notified of this. If the seller must do something to the goods for the purpose of putting them into a deliverable state, the title does not pass to the buyer until that thing is done and the buyer notified.

Example: A company ordered several models of a machine, but wanted three modifications made before accepting them. The seller set three machines aside, but had not made the modifications when the machines were destroyed in a fire. As the machines had not yet become ascertained, the loss was the seller's not the buyer's. Had the modifications been made, and the buyer notified, the loss would have been the buyer's.

If the seller must weigh, measure, test or do some other act for the purpose of determining what the price will be, the goods do not become ascertained until the seller has completed the weighing or testing and has notified the buyer.

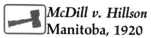
McDill v. Hillson
Manitoba, 1920
McDill agreed to buy some furniture from Hillson.

The furniture was scratched and required polishing before it could be delivered. This could not be done immediately as the plant that would do the polishing had a labour dispute. McDill paid the full purchase price and Hillson agreed to deliver the furniture as soon as possible. Before the work was done, the furniture was destroyed in a fire. McDill sued for the return of the purchase money but Hillson refused and claimed that title and risk had passed to McDill when payment was made. The Manitoba Court of Appeal found that the furniture was not in a deliverable state when the contract was made and that the agreement was that title would pass when they were in a deliverable state and McDill notified. McDill was entitled to the return of the money.

Conditions

If a contract contains a condition, the condition must be fulfilled or the entire contract can be repudiated. A *condition* is an essential part of a contract and failure to complete a condition is considered a major breach of contract. If Jones agrees to buy a machine from Smith Company, Ltd., on the condition that the machine be equipped with special safety features, this condition is an integral part of the contract. If the machine arrives without the safety equipment, Jones can refuse to accept it. Failure to meet the condition can thus mean failure of the entire contract.

Warranties

A *warranty* is not an essential part of a contract. In most cases, the warranty is a separate document and not part of the sale contract at all. The Ontario *Sale of Goods Act* defines a warranty as follows:

> **Warranty means an agreement with reference to goods that are the subject of a contract of sale but collateral to the main purpose of such contract, the breach of which gives rise to a claim for damages, but not to a right to reject the goods and treat the contract as repudiated.**

Failure to live up to a warranty does not allow the buyer to repudiate the contract, for the warranty is not the purpose of the basic sale agreement, but only runs along with the sale agreement. The buyer may bring an action to try to force the seller to live up to the warranty, but this is often difficult since many warranties are vague. (One automobile manufacturer once published a booklet entitled, "How to Read Your Warranty.") Most warranties leave the final decision to the manufacturer as to whether or not any defect is covered by the warranty. For example, the warranty for a brand-name appliance contained this provision:

> This warranty shall apply within the boundaries of Canada, and will not apply *if in the judgment of the company,* damage or failure has resulted from accident, alteration, misuse, abuse, or operation on an incorrect power supply. (Emphasis added.)

Probably the best rule in regards to warranties is this: They are worth as much as the person giving them. If the seller does not want to honour the warranty, he or she will probably find a way not to do so.

The word *guarantee* does not have much legal recognition, but it must be assumed to mean basically the same thing as a warranty.

It is important to keep in mind just who is offering the warranty. If it is a manufacturer's warranty, the retailer who sold the product is not necessarily liable if the product does not function well, although there is a growing tendency in our legal system to tie the retailer in as jointly liable.

New automobiles often have separate warranties for the tires. If the purchaser finds that the tires will not hold pressure, the car dealer will normally refer the purchaser to the local tire company outlet. Multiple warranties represent a problem and a nuisance for purchasers who find that they must deal with a collection of sellers rather than just one. There is a growing trend in Canada and the United States to impose strict liability for defective goods upon the retailers and suppliers of products. Saskatchewan, New Brunswick, and Quebec have enacted such legislation.

Implied Conditions and Warranties

Whether or not a seller gives a specific or express condition or warranty with the goods, the law holds that all goods come to the buyer with some *implied conditions or warranties*. That is, they are present whether the seller says so or not. These implied conditions and warranties are as follows:

Seller's Title

When a person sells goods, an implied warranty is given that the person owns the goods and has a lawful right to sell them. If this turns out to be incorrect, the buyer can rescind the contract and sue for damages.

For example, the buyer may have been sold stolen goods. Should the police recover the stolen property, the buyer may recover what was paid to the seller (provided the seller can be found). This rule does not apply to stolen money. A person who innocently receives stolen money as part of an honest business transaction, does not have to give back the money.

Goods purchased on the instalment plan do not belong to the person who bought them until the final payment is made. Therefore this person cannot sell the goods to a third person without the consent of the original seller; also, the third person must be willing to take over the remaining payments.

Sale by Description

Where goods are sold by sample or catalogue description, such goods must match the sample or description when delivered. If they do not, the buyer may refuse to accept them and cancel the contract. On the other hand, if the buyer receives and uses the goods, the contract cannot later be cancelled on the grounds that the goods did not match the description. However, if the buyer was unaware that the goods did not match the description, the right to sue is not affected, as the next case shows:

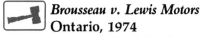

Brousseau v. Lewis Motors
Ontario, 1974

Brousseau sued the defendants for misrepresenting the sale of a 1971 Cortina. Her bill of sale and order agreement stated the car would be a 1971 model, but she received instead an unsold 1970 model. Lewis Motors relied upon instructions from the Ford Motor Company that all unsold Cortinas were to be redesignated as 1971 models as of October 15, 1970 as the model would no longer be made. Brousseau found out about the switch when she needed parts for the car and 1970 parts were ordered. She was awarded $400, the most allowable in Small Claims Court.

This principle is further illustrated by the following case:

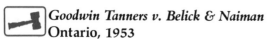 ***Goodwin Tanners v. Belick & Naiman*** **Ontario, 1953**

B & N agreed to purchase from Goodwin Tanners a number of hides described as being of No. 1 and No. 2 grades. Delivery was to be made to the premises of Canada Packers where the hides were stored. The buyers did not go and inspect the hides at Canada Packers because they did not know if they would be permitted to inspect them there. The hides were moved to the property of the buyers who checked them immediately upon delivery. They were very defective and the buyers telephoned the seller to say that they were not acceptable. The seller did not come to pick up the hides so the buyers took them to the seller's place of business, where they were refused. The seller sued for the purchase price of the hides and alleged that acceptance had taken place at Canada Packers. The seller argued that the buyers could have inspected the hides at Canada Packers if they wanted to do so; their failure to do so was at their own risk. The buyers argued that they did not have reasonable opportunity to check the hides until they were moved to their own premises. The Ontario Court of Appeal held that the contract of sale implied a condition that the hides would correspond with the description given, which they did not do, and that this breach of condition gave the buyers the right to refuse them. The buyers were justified in taking

the hides to their own place of business for inspection and until the inspection was made the buyers had not accepted them.

Fitness of Goods

Often the buyer does not know the product and must rely upon the skill and judgment of the seller. Where the buyer expressly, or by implication, makes known to the seller the particular purpose for which the goods are required and the goods are of a description or type that it is in the course of the seller's business to supply, there is an implied condition that the goods will be reasonably fit for such purpose. Thus, if the buyer says to the seller, "I don't know anything about this, but here is what I want to do—what do you recommend?" the seller must provide the buyer with the proper article for the task.

Complaints and Remedies

Disclaimer Clauses in Contracts

A sale of goods contract is frequently entered into by means of a printed contract form. These forms often contain wording that is vague and confusing to the buyer who sometimes doesn't bother to read the forms at all. Failure to do so is at the buyer's own peril! There is a duty on the purchaser to read and understand the contract. The purchaser is bound to the contract as long as he or she knows its general nature—that it pertains to a sale. The purchaser does not have to have read or understood each and every word. Terms printed on the back of a contract are usually binding if the front contains a notation mentioning that there are additional terms on the back.

One of the biggest problems arises over the quality of goods sold. The buyer complains that the goods are sub-standard, and the seller pulls out the contract and says, "I never made any promises about the quality of the goods." The buyer contends that the seller did make such statements, so the seller points to an interesting phrase in the contract which reads: "There are no conditions, express or implied, statutory or otherwise, other than those contained in this written agreement." (This is a typical disclaimer clause.)

When goods are sold, the contract sometimes includes a "disclaimer" which tries to protect the seller if the goods do not live up to the buyer's expectations.

Now, if the buyer wants to argue that the seller did make promises outside the terms printed in the contract, he or she has a problem. The *parol evidence rule* prevents a buyer from adding to, varying, or contradicting the clear, unambiguous terms of a written or printed contract. So, what has happened to the buyer is this: (1) The salesperson made verbal representations above and beyond what is contained in the contract; but (2) the buyer signed a contract agreeing that the salesperson did no such thing and acknowledging that there are no such representations in existence.

Does the disclaimer clause work every time? That is, does it succeed in destroying the buyer's argument that something was promised that was not received? Sometimes the disclaimer clause is very effective against the buyer. In other cases, it fails to stop the buyer from asserting his or her rights. What makes the difference? There is one factor that will work in favour of the buyer. The court may hold that the goods delivered were so inferior that they constituted non-completion of the entire contract on the part of the seller. A contract calls for an exchange of consideration; the buyer gives the seller money in return for goods. If the seller gives the buyer "junk," the seller does not fulfill the contract at all, since there is no proper exchange of consideration.

Marshall v. Ryan Motors, Ltd.
Saskatchewan, 1922

A car kept breaking down after the thirty-month warranty had expired. The warranty said, "No other warranty, guarantee, or representation whatsoever has been made." The court ruled that the implied condition that the goods be fit for a particular purpose was not excluded by these words and awarded damages to the plaintiff.

In subsequent cases involving disclaimer clauses, many courts accepted the legal arguments put forward in a British case by Lord Justice Denning, who said:

    "A disclaimer clause purporting to deprive a buyer of the protection and reliance of the *Sale of Goods Act* can have

no validity if it is asserted unilaterally by the seller. The seller must show that the consideration promised has actually been received by the purchaser. If the disclaimer clause insists that there was no promise it could be argued that the purchaser had not received any consideration and no binding obligation exists. **"**

Thus, where a disclaimer clause tried to limit the extent of the warranty given, it might be enforceable. However, if a disclaimer clause tries to absolve the seller of all responsibility, the court may then take the view there was no contract at all since the seller was giving the buyer no consideration. In any contract, disclaimer clauses should be carefully watched.

Brown v. Woywada
Manitoba, 1974

The plaintiff bought a nineteen-year-old tractor from the defendant for $450. The contract contained a clause saying that no warranties whatsoever were given with the machine. It turned out that the tractor used an enormous amount of oil, so the purchaser stopped payment on his cheque. The Court of Appeal eventually decided that the contract form was the total substance of the agreement and it clearly stated that there were no warranties given as to fitness. The plaintiff knew the machine was very old and very low-priced. The plaintiff was familiar with machinery and knew he was buying a machine in poor condition. Furthermore, the seller made no attempt to hide this fact. The court concluded that where an article is used or extremely old, there is nothing to prohibit the seller from making the sale without any warranty as to fitness, provided there was no misrepresentation involved.

Concern about disclaimer clauses caused British Columbia, Ontario, Manitoba, and Nova Scotia to pass legislation declaring void any term of a contract that seeks to avoid the implied conditions and warranties under provincial law. Saskatchewan, New Brunswick, and Quebec go further and also make the manufacturer and retailer jointly liable for any breach of an implied condition or warranty.

The *Sale of Goods Act* provides only a minimal warranty upon goods sold "as is." Used or damaged goods are often sold with the understanding that the buyer must take the risk and disclaimer clauses to that effect have often been upheld.

Some provincial laws afford protection for the purchaser by way of consumer protection laws which permit the courts to ignore disclaimer clauses if there has been an unfair trade practice. Other provincial laws prohibit the seller from trying to contract out of responsibilities by writing excessively broad disclaimer clauses into contracts. As an example, the Alberta *Farm Implement Act* declares void any clause in a contract under which the seller of farm equipment tries to deny liability for any consequential damages arising from the malfunction of the equipment.

Remedies of the Unpaid Seller

If a seller isn't paid for goods sold to the buyer, the seller is given certain remedies under the *Sale of Goods Act*.

- *Refuse to deliver:* If the goods were sold, but not paid for, the seller may refuse to turn them over to the buyer until paid. In doing this, the seller is essentially exercising a "right of lien" over the goods.

- *Stoppage in transit:* If the goods were shipped, but not paid for, the seller may re-route the goods to another destination or stop the goods from being delivered to the buyer. The seller must be careful in doing this, for if the goods are stopped wrongly, the seller may be guilty of breach of contract.

- *Resell the goods:* The seller may notify the buyer that unless he or she takes possession of the goods, they will be sold elsewhere. This is of particular importance if the goods are perishable, as they must be sold before they perish. The law requires the unpaid seller to take action to minimize the loss.

- *Sue for breach of contract:* A sale of goods contract is enforceable just like any other contract. Neither party can avoid the contract at will. The seller may sue the buyer either for specific performance or for damages. Specific performance is one of the remedies open to both parties under a sale of goods contract.

Remedies of the Buyer

If the buyer feels the seller is guilty of breach of contract in some manner, there are various remedies available. Generally, the buyer tries to enforce the contract against the seller by demanding specific performance. If that fails, the buyer can sue for damages.

- *Sue for specific performance:* If the buyer definitely wants the terms of the contract carried out, he or she may sue for specific performance. The buyer asks the court that, as a remedy, the seller be required to deliver the goods as agreed, and at the price agreed.

- *Sue for damages:* As an alternative to specific performance, the seller can be sued for damages. If the buyer suffered financial loss because the seller failed to deliver as agreed, damages can be sought. Where the buyer had to go out and buy the same goods elsewhere at a higher price, he or she may seek to recover from the seller the difference between their agreed price and what the buyer had to pay elsewhere.

- *Rescind the contract:* If the buyer has not received the goods, and it appears the seller is not going to be able to deliver on time or within the conditions agreed to, the buyer may notify the seller that their entire contract is being cancelled and that the buyer is going to look elsewhere for the goods.

- *Seek an adjustment of the price:* If the seller substantially performed the contract, but did not fulfill it completely, the buyer may seek an adjustment to the purchase price to compensate for the seller's failure to deliver the total amount of goods as agreed.

- *Sue for injuries:* If the buyer was physically injured by a defective product, he or she may sue for damages for those injuries.

Reviewing Important Points

1. In each province, a sale above a prescribed sum must be in writing in order to be enforceable.
2. Generally, the *Sale of Goods Act* requires a seller to put the goods into a deliverable condition, but does not require the seller to deliver them.
3. Unless otherwise agreed, the goods remain at the seller's risk until the title is transferred to the buyer.
4. Once the goods have been ascertained, meaning specifically set aside for the buyer, they become the buyer's risk in case of loss.
5. A condition is an essential part of a contract. Failure to fulfill the condition can mean the failure of the entire contract. A warranty is not an essential part of a contract.
6. Even if no specific warranties come with the goods, there are certain implied warranties such as fitness for the intended use, matching the sample or description given by the seller, and the seller's ownership of and right to sell the goods.
7. The buyer is bound to the contract if he or she knows the general nature of the contract, i.e., that it relates to a sale.
8. A disclaimer clause cannot be a defence to a fundamental breach of contract.

Checking Your Understanding

1. What is a sale?
2. Under what conditions may a sale be oral even if the amount is quite large?
3. What are ascertained goods? Why is it sometimes important to know exactly when goods become ascertained?
4. State three implied conditions or warranties contained within provincial *Sale of Goods Acts*.
5. What is a disclaimer clause? Under what circumstances might a court refuse to recognize such a clause?
6. If a seller isn't paid, what actions may be taken?

Legal Briefs

1. F buys a travel trailer from D, paying the full amount by cheque at the time. F asks that it be delivered to her home the next morning. G's employee, while towing the trailer to F's home, encounters a sudden, powerful wind which tips the trailer over. Neither party had thought to insure the vehicle. Who bears the loss?

2. V buys a used snowmobile at an auction. He does not have enough cash to pay for the machine, so he gives the auctioneer $100 and a valuable watch to be held until he returns the next day with the rest of the money. The machine is stolen that night. V demands his money and watch back. Must the auctioneer comply?

3. H offers to purchase a used motorcycle from K for $900, provided K makes some repairs. K agrees and H gives K $50 down payment; the balance is to be paid when the machine is satisfactorily repaired. K makes the repairs and calls H to tell her to pick up the machine; but H is not home. That night the garage burns down and the machine is destroyed. K demands the rest of the money. Must H pay?

4. P orders some spare tractor parts from J. When they are delivered, he notes that they look different from the ones he took out, but assumes that with the various model changes the parts are suitable. He installs them but they do not work properly. He returns them to J who advises him that they were the wrong parts but that P must now pay for them because he damaged them. Must P pay?

5. H imports a herbicide from the United States. The instructions for use are rewritten, changing imperial measurements to metric. An employee of H miscalculates the conversion and writes instructions telling farmers to apply the chemical a hundred times stronger than it should be. The farmers' crops die. Liability of H?

6. L purchased some plastic pipe from S but the pipe delivered was smaller in diameter than that ordered. S offers to take it back but L says it will do the job and only requests a partial refund of the payment. The pipe cracks when exposed to cold because it is undersized to do the job. Liability of S?

7. W sells goods to V and ships them by rail. W hears that V is going into bankruptcy and reroutes the shipment elsewhere. It turns out that the information is incorrect and that V is not going into bankruptcy. Because the goods are not delivered, V loses a contract and suffers financial loss. Liability of W?

8. U buys a used truck from D. The truck is sold without any guarantee or warranty. There is no licence plate on it or certificate of mechanical fitness. The vehicle is sold for parts only and U tows it away. D has told U that the vehicle is "basically sound" and with "a little bit of work" would run well. D knows that U intends to try to overhaul the truck and get it on the road again. In fact, U soon learns that the truck is totally shot. U sues for a refund of the purchase money. Liability of D?

9. M purchases crates of vegetables from W. She examines the vegetables at the top of each crate and finds them excellent. After taking them to the store she represents, M learns that the vegetables at the bottoms of the crates are of inferior quality and that they seem to have been packed that way. Can M return them?

10. S goes into a hardware store and explains to the clerk that he wants to seal a concrete floor and apply a certain type of tile. The clerk specifically picks and recommends a sealer. S uses it and it does not work properly. The floor is a mess and the tile is ruined. Liability of the store?

Applying the Law

Murray v. Sperry Rand Corporation
Ontario, 1980

Murray, a farmer, wanted to purchase a new forage harvester, a machine which simultaneously cuts and chops hay. He obtained a brochure from a representative of the defendant which stated in part: "You will fine chop forage to 3/16 of an inch (1.4 cm) ... season after season! ... You will harvest over 45 tons (40.5 t) per hour with ease."

Representatives from the defendant also visited the plaintiff's farm and gave him assurances that the harvester would perform as described in the brochure and that it was ideally suited for his kind of farming. Murray bought the machine but it never performed well. The defendant and local dealer made adjustments, replaced parts, and did everything possible but the machine could not do what was described in the brochure. As a result, Murray suffered financial loss and eventually had to give up farming completely. Murray sued the manufacturer and dealer for a refund of his money and damages for his financial losses. The court held that the dealer and manufacturer were liable and that the disclaimer clause was ineffective.

The dealer was liable because it was partly a result of the dealer's oral statements that Murray bought the machine. Murray relied upon the skill and judgment of the dealer and was protected by the *Sale of Goods Act*. The dealer could not rely upon the disclaimer clause in the contract as the machine's effectiveness was fundamental to the contract. The court held:

> **"**Exemption clauses have been held ineffective when a product did not operate as it should have.**"**

The court held further that the manufacturer who published the sales brochure in an obvious attempt to induce sales should not be shielded from liability just because it had not dealt directly with the buyer:

> **"**It is the law that a person may be liable for breach of warranty notwithstanding that he has no contractual relationship with the person to whom the warranty is given.... I can see no difference whether the affirmations are made orally or in writing.**"**

Questions

1. Why was the dealer liable for the plaintiff's financial loss?
2. Why was the manufacturer liable?
3. How much importance was placed upon the fact that the plaintiff was not an expert in farm machinery and relied upon what he was told by the defendants?
4. Was the sales brochure poorly worded? What care should a manufacturer take in preparing sales brochures?

 ## *Keefe v. Fort*
Nova Scotia, 1978

The plaintiff read a local newspaper advertisement offering for sale a used Alpha Romeo car. The plaintiff answered the ad and saw the car at the home of the defendant. He test-drove the car, noted several small defects, but was given accurate answers by the defendant about the car. The plaintiff returned two days later with an Alpha Romeo mechanic and the two men spent two hours in the garage looking at the car. The defendant offered to let the men take the car to the Alpha Romeo garage and make a thorough study of it, but they did not take him up on the offer. The plaintiff bought the car but found that it burned oil. He took the car to have the oil changed and the mechanic also took off the oil pan. He found a bolt out of the motor in the oil pan which indicated that new bearings were needed. After driving a total of 450 km, the plaintiff took the car to a dealership. The final estimate of needed repairs was $2216.80. The plaintiff sued the defendant alleging fundamental breach of the contract. The trial judge held for the defendant and the case went to the Court of Appeal which upheld the trial judge and dismissed the action against the defendant:

> **"**The contract was a verbal agreement and there were no exclusion clauses. The contract was that the buyer was purchasing a used car and the seller was selling a used car, and there was no fundamental breach of that. The doctrine of buyer beware applies and the burden is on the plaintiff to prove on a balance of probabilities his case. It has not been done. The doctrine of fundamental breach was never intended to be applied to situations where the parties have received substantially what they had bargained for. In recent history, the term 'fundamental breach' appears to have taken on a meaning all its own, which in its application tends to mystify rather than clarify the true meaning of the concept. In my opinion, it means nothing more or less than the type of breach which entitles the innocent party to treat it as repudiation and to rescind the contract.**"**

Questions

1. What is a fundamental breach of contract?

2. In this case, why did the court not order the plaintiff to be compensated when he had to immediately pay for repairs of more than $2000?

3. Did the defendant misrepresent in any way what he was selling?

You Be the Judge

1. The plaintiff agreed to purchase all the lumber produced by the defendant during the sawing season. Delivery was to be made to one of the plaintiff's storage areas. The first lumber arrived and the plaintiff did not inspect it, although there was every opportunity to do so. The first shipment was resold to customers of the plaintiff and the plaintiff made full payment to the defendant. Shortly after, the customers complained to the plaintiff about the poor quality of the lumber and began returning it. The plaintiff demanded that the defendant take back the lumber and refund the payment. The defendant refused, saying there had been "acceptance." Who would succeed?

2. The plaintiff purchased a mobile home and received a warranty card which was not effective unless properly filled in and returned to the manufacturer. The plaintiff never did this. The plaintiff later had problems with the vehicle and sued the manufacturer. The warranty period of one year had not yet expired but the defendant manufacturer denied liability on the basis that the "offer of warranty" had not been accepted by the plaintiff. Who would succeed?

3. The plaintiff purchased a motor vehicle from the defendant car dealer under a buyer's agreement in which there was a clause stating that there was no warranty upon the vehicle except the manufacturer's new vehicle warranty. Shortly after purchase, the paint blistered. The manufacturer's representative denied liability saying that the problem must have occurred when the plaintiff took the car through a car wash. Not content with this response, the plain-

tiff sued the car dealer. The provincial Act provided that, if goods were bought by "sample," the goods delivered would be "free from any defect rendering them unmerchantable that would not be apparent on reasonable examination." The plaintiff had purchased the car after looking at and test-driving a similar one in the dealer's showroom. It was the plaintiff's position that the disclaimer clause in the contract was ineffective because the provincial Act held the dealer liable. Who would succeed?

4. The plaintiff entered into a contract with the defendant corporation to purchase electric light bulbs. The defendant knew that the plaintiff wanted the bulbs to resell through its retail stores. The first shipment was received and paid for and distributed to stores. The plaintiff was then informed by a provincial inspector that it was selling bulbs not approved by the Canadian Standards Association. Sale of such bulbs was illegal and they were withdrawn from the stores. The plaintiff sued for the return of its money and for cancellation of the rest of the contract, relying upon the provincial law that stated that there is an implied condition that the seller has the right to sell the goods. The defendant argued that the plaintiff had accepted the bulbs and had had ample opportunity to examine them and determine if they had CSA approval. Who would succeed?

5. The plaintiff went to a car auction at which more than fifty used automobiles were sold. Each had a provincial certificate of mechanical fitness as the law required but were sold "as is" without any further guarantee or warranty. The plaintiff bought a car without any opportunity to inspect it closely or drive it. When she took possession of the car, she found that there were serious defects that required repair. She also doubted that a certificate of mechanical fitness could properly have been issued in view of the extent of the defects. She sued for return of her money. The car dealer relied upon the basic nature of the contract that the car had been sold "as is" without any warranty. Who would succeed?

Chapter 18

Conditional Sales, Chattel Mortgages, and Bills of Sale

The Conditional Sale Contract

Thus far we have dealt with absolute sales. Under an absolute sale, title passes immediately to the buyer upon the conclusion of the agreement. A conditional sale is one where title does not pass to the buyer until certain conditions are met, the most important being payment of the total price which includes an interest charge. Entering into a conditional sale contract is also known as paying on the instalment plan. The conditional sale agreement is a lengthy document and we shall not attempt to examine all its terms in detail. The most important information to be included in the contract falls into these general categories:

- Identification of the goods and acknowledgment by the buyer that they have been received.
- The total price and all other items including interest, instalment payments, etc. The interest rate must be expressed as a true annual percentage (in most provinces).
- A statement that the seller remains the owner until the buyer makes the last payment.
- Authority for the seller to repossess if the buyer does not make the payments.
- The right of the seller to resell the goods if the buyer does not redeem them within a certain time period. In most provinces the buyer must redeem the goods by making up missed payments within twenty days. Some contracts have "acceleration" or "balloon" clauses which require the buyer to pay the remaining balance if one payment is missed.

- The obligation of the buyer to make good any deficiency still remaining after re-sale. *Example:* Brenda Wilson bought a car on the instalment basis. She was laid off from her job and fell behind in her payments, which led to the car's being repossessed. Later, she received a statement showing that the car had been re-sold at auction for $2100. Since Wilson still owed $2400 on the car, she owed the finance company another $300. She was also charged for repossession, storage, insurance, and the cost of the auction. These were all legitimate charges which Wilson had to pay.
- A promise by the buyer not to remove, resell, or dispose of the goods in any way without the written consent of the seller. In some contracts the buyer promises to insure the goods as well.

Registration of a Conditional Sales Contract

The person who buys goods under a conditional sales contract obtains use of the goods but not title to them. The seller has a concern that the buyer will turn around and re-sell the goods to an unsuspecting person who does not know that the goods belong to the seller. To protect the rights of the seller, provincial law permits the registration of a conditional sales contract at the local registry office. The seller must register the contract within a set time period, normally twenty to thirty days, varying from province to province. The registration must be renewed from time to time, or it will expire. Most provinces require re-registration every three years.

The purpose of registration is to give public notice to any potential buyer of the goods that the goods really belong to the original seller and not to the person who presently has them. Any person who is thinking about buying goods from someone who is not in the business of selling such goods may go to the Registry Office and check to see who really owns the goods. If a person buys used goods by private sale, and does not make this check, then the person must surrender the goods to the true owner or pay the outstanding balance.

Not all goods have to be registered to protect the original seller. Each province has a number of exclusions to the requirement of registration. In Alberta, if the seller has an office in Alberta where inquiries can be made, and the goods have the original seller's name attached with a plate or decal, then the goods do not have to be registered.

In Saskatchewan, New Brunswick, and Newfoundland, there is no registration required if the goods are sold directly by the manufacturer and the goods have the name of the manufacturer inscribed on them. If the manufacturer has an office in the province where inquiries can be made, it is assumed that any possible purchaser would be able to contact that office to learn who owns the goods. A problem may arise if the name plate or decal was removed before resale. Generally, it has been held that the original seller retains title even if the seller's name was removed before subsequent resale. Thus, there is always a danger in purchasing goods privately.

In most provinces, goods that are sold to a dealer for resale pass to the subsequent buyer with good title even if a contract was registered. Thus, if B purchases a new car from Dealer H, B gets a clear title even if H has not yet paid the manufacturer. Most provinces have similar laws dealing with farm implements purchased in good faith from dealers.

Personal Property Security Registration System

Ontario and Manitoba have developed a computerized registration system that makes it quicker and easier to determine who owns goods being resold. When the original sale is made, the seller registers the contract by completing a financing statement which is fed into a computer. The information is available to all Registry Offices in the province. The information is filed under two headings; the name of the debtor, and the description of the goods. For the payment of a small fee, a potential purchaser can learn if any "perfected interest" exists against the goods anywhere in the province. For the payment of a slightly higher fee, the Registry Office will provide a certificate guaranteeing that, as of the date and time of inquiry, the goods were free from any interest. If it later turns out that the Registry Office made a mistake, there is an insurance fund to reimburse the purchaser for any loss incurred as a result of trusting the accuracy of the check made.

Assignment of Contract

It is a common practice for sellers to assign conditional sales contracts to finance companies. The sellers cannot afford to personally carry a large number of such unpaid accounts and sell the contracts for immediate cash, but at a discount. The finance companies must then register the contracts.

The seller does not require the consent of the buyer to assign the contract. The buyer will be notified of the assignment and given directions as to where to make payment. The debt of the buyer cannot be increased by the assignment. Normally, a promissory note is also signed that can be transferred with the contract. This is discussed further in Unit Eight   Bills of Exchange.

Repossession

The seller has the right to repossess (take back) the goods if the buyer doesn't carry out the condition of making the payments. Keep in mind that the seller owns the goods and is only recovering his or her own property, not taking something that belongs to the buyer.

A conditional sales contract authorizes the seller to repossess the goods if instalment payments are not made. However, force cannot be used to effect repossession.

In some provinces, the seller must notify the buyer that repossession is going to take place. A few provinces do not permit any repossession without a court order. In Ontario, New Brunswick, and Nova Scotia, the seller may not repossess if the buyer had paid two-thirds of the purchase price or more, except by permission of a judge of a county or district court. Manitoba places the same restriction if 75 per cent of the price has been paid.

When the seller decides to repossess, the seller may attempt to do so using personal employees or perhaps hiring off-duty bailiffs who earn extra income doing such work. Quite often the contract which the buyer signed permits the seller to enter the buyer's premises, break locks, and do all sorts of things to recover the goods. The Ontario statute permits the seller to enter the buyer's premises and "render the goods unusable" which would suggest such actions as removing essential parts from a vehicle. The legal question then becomes, "Can the seller use force to repossess the goods?" Generally, the answer is no. If the buyer gives every indication that the repossession will be resisted and the persons trying to repossess have no court order, the repossession cannot be carried out forcibly.

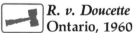 ### R. v. Doucette
Ontario, 1960

Doucette was one of three men who were repossessing a television set. The men were bailiffs, but were acting privately and not in their legal capacity as bailiffs at the time. It was a common practice for bailiffs to hire out their services to private companies for this kind of work. When the buyer vigorously protested the repossession, Doucette struck him. Doucette claimed that he thought the buyer was going to assault him, so he struck him first. The judge convicted Doucette of assault, saying:

66Even though a person enters property lawfully for the purpose of repossession, if he assaults someone he becomes a trespasser. Once it was made clear that the television set would not be removed without resistance, they grossly exceeded their authority and abused the buyer's rights and became trespassers.99

The judge doubted that they had in fact entered the property lawfully, but did not elaborate on that point.

The Buyer's Right To Redeem

Once the seller has repossessed the goods, the seller must give the buyer an opportunity to redeem (get back) the goods. The seller must keep the goods for the time period stated in the provincial law, ranging from fourteen to twenty-one days in most provinces; one month in Newfoundland.

Most conditional sales contracts contain a "balloon" or "acceleration" clause which requires the buyer to pay the entire unpaid balance to recover the goods. To this may be added the cost of repossessing, insuring, and keeping the goods.

In Saskatchewan, Newfoundland, and New Brunswick the buyer may redeem by paying the amount due on the contract price, rather than the entire unpaid balance. Upon request, the seller must give the buyer a statement showing all pertinent details including original price, amount paid, added charges, and the amount owing.

The Seller's Right of Resale

If the buyer does not redeem the goods, the seller has the right to dispose of them by resale. The resale may be by private sale or by auction. It is a rule of law that the seller cannot "sacrifice" the goods, which means sell them for any low price possible just to get rid of them. Nor can the seller purchase the goods personally.

If the amount obtained upon resale is less than that still owed by the buyer, does the buyer have to make good this amount? This is called the *deficiency* upon resale, and nearly every conditional sales contract contains wording requiring the buyer to make good any such deficiency.

In Saskatchewan, the seller cannot sue the buyer for any unpaid amount before or after repossession. The seller has only one course of action which is to repossess and resell, and take whatever amount this provides.

In Alberta, British Columbia, Manitoba, and Newfoundland, the seller has a choice. The seller can sue on the contract and not repossess, or repossess and resell and take what the resale provides as full payment. The seller cannot sue for any remaining deficiency. Thus, the seller may "seize or sue," but not both.

In all other provinces, the seller may repossess, resell, and sue for any deficiency.

Before attempting to hold the buyer liable for any deficiency, the seller must hold the goods for the required time period and give the buyer a chance to redeem. The seller must sell the goods for a fair price and not sacrifice them. The seller must give the buyer a complete statement of all transactions and clearly show the balance still owing. If all steps in the procedure are not carefully followed, the buyer will not be liable for the deficiency.

The Chattel Mortgage

A chattel mortgage is a contract under which the owner of goods assigns title to the goods to another person in consideration of a debt. For example, if H wants to borrow money from the G bank, the bank will want some sort of collateral. If H signs a chattel mortgage using a car as collateral, H transfers title of the car to the bank. This does not mean the provincial registration will be changed to the bank. The car is still registered to H. However, H cannot legally sell the car to someone else because H no longer has title to it.

The contract permits the borrower to continue to use the goods as long as payments are made. Upon completion of all payments, the mortgage becomes void.

A chattel mortgage can be registered the same as a conditional sales contract.

If payments are not made, the mortgagee may take possession of the goods and sell them.

Bill of Sale

A *bill of sale* is a document representing the sale of goods of any type. In some situations, the seller will retain possession of the goods for a period of time after selling them and the buyer would like some proof that the goods have been bought. It is for the buyer's protection, then, that a bill of sale is signed. It may be registered also since, if the bill of sale is not registered, the seller could sell the goods to another person. Such a person would acquire good title if the goods had been purchased for valuable consideration, in good faith, and without notice that the seller was contravening the rights of the earlier buyer.

Reviewing Important Points

1. Under a conditional sale agreement, the seller remains the owner until the buyer makes the last payment.

2. A seller may not use force to repossess the goods that have not been paid for under a conditional sale contract. A court order for repossession must be issued by a judge.

3. A purchaser of goods cannot get any better title than the seller had. Thus, if a person buys goods from someone who does not have title to them, that person cannot get good title.

4. Before purchasing used goods by private sale, check at the local registry office to determine if any liens or interests have been registered against the goods.

5. A person who defaults on a conditional sale contract will still be liable for the full purchase price, plus some costs for resale, except in those provinces that do not require the buyer to make good the deficiency.

Checking Your Understanding

1. Name three remedies available to the unpaid seller.
2. For what purpose is a chattel mortgage usually signed?
3. What is the purpose of a bill of sale? Whom does it protect?
4. What is the law regarding repossession by force of goods not paid for?
5. If the seller repossesses goods, what must the buyer do to redeem them?

Legal Briefs

1. R purchases a used refrigerator from B, who is moving to another city. R checks for any liens or interests registered against the appliance but finds none. Later, he is contacted by the manager of the Y Appliance Store demanding payment of $150. Must R pay?
2. H looks at a used automobile and is shown the provincial registration card and insurance card by M, who claims to be the owner. H assumes that if M has these documents, there is no possible problem with title. Is H correct?
3. When C misses two payments on his car, he decides to avoid possible repossession by parking the car in his girl friend's garage. "They can't touch it while it's on your property," he tells her. Is his belief correct?
4. S purchases a musical instrument from the G Music Store. She becomes bored with it and takes it back to the store, announcing that she will make no further payments on the conditional sales contract. The store refuses to take it back and threatens to sue under the contract terms. "You have to take it back," S argues, "because it's your instrument." Must the store take the instrument?
5. T wants to purchase a used piano from C. The piano has the manufacturer's name on it. There is only one authorized dealer in town who sells that piano. T telephones to ask if C bought the piano from them and if it is paid for. The store states that it does not give out such information over the phone. T purchases the piano and finds out later that C still owes the

dealer $2000 on it. T refuses to pay the dealer on the grounds that they would not divulge their interest. Is T correct?

6. When J bought her new automobile from the dealer, she paid cash. She did not know, nor did she try to find out, whether the dealer still owed money to the manufacturer on the car. The dealer went into bankruptcy shortly afterwards and the unpaid manufacturer claimed that J owed them for the car since the dealer had not paid them. Must J pay?

Applying the Law

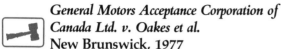

General Motors Acceptance Corporation of Canada Ltd. v. Oakes et al.
New Brunswick, 1977

This was an appeal against the decision of the trial court allowing the plaintiff's action against the second defendant after repossession and sale of a truck under a conditional sales contract. The finance company took possession of the truck but did not advertise it for sale in New Brunswick. Instead it took the truck to Ontario where prices were lower at the time. The truck was worth approximately $22 000 but the plaintiff sold it to its sister company, GMC for $12 100, after obtaining bids from two dealers, the higher of which was $12 010.

The appeal was allowed. The plaintiff failed to approach the market where the best price might be expected to be obtained and failed to deal with the truck, after repossession, in compliance with the responsibilities imposed on it by law. In departing from its obligation to sell for the benefit of the purchaser and in accord with the terms of the conditional sales contract, the plaintiff had, in effect, appropriated the truck for its own use. It had exercised its option to sell not under the conditional sales contract but under its contract with GMC. The plaintiff forfeited its right to recover any deficiency on the sale.

Questions

1. If the seller repossesses the goods and later resells them, what rules apply?

2. Why did the court not allow GMAC to recover the deficiency upon resale?

3. GMAC obtained two other competing bids for the truck, both lower than what GMC actually paid for it. Why did the court not hold this to be a valid sale?

Canadian Imperial Bank of Commerce v. Curtis
Newfoundland, 1978

The defendant's son purchased a new car under a conditional sales contract. The son purchased the car with a loan from the plaintiff bank. The son gave the bank a chattel mortgage and a promissory note as security for the loan. The defendant signed the note as guarantor. The son defaulted in his payments and the bank demanded the unpaid balance from the defendant under his guarantee. The defendant got the car away from his son and turned it over to the bank. It was resold under the chattel mortgage. The bank did not recover all that it was owed so it brought an action against the son and against the father as guarantor on the promissory note. The matter was defended by the administratrix of the estate of the father who had since died. The defence was based upon the argument that the bank's claim was paid and satisfied when it took possession of and sold the car in question. The bank could not also bring a separate action upon the promissory note.

The court held that under the *Bills of Sale Act*, in force at the date of sale of the car, the bank's claim against the son was fully paid and satisfied when it took possession of and sold the car, any agreement to the contrary notwithstanding. The defendant guaranteed the indebtedness of the borrower under the promissory note and his liability ceased when the debt was paid in full. In this case, this took place when the bank chose to seize and sell the car. The bank could have chosen to sue upon the note instead of selling the car, but it could not take both courses of action as a means to recover its money.

Questions

1. Why was the bank not able to sue upon the note?

2. Under a chattel mortgage, title had already been assigned to the bank. Why did the bank's action of selling the car affect its rights?

3. Might the case have been decided differently if the father had signed the chattel mortgage *and* the note?

You Be the Judge

1. The plaintiff corporation sold goods to J Enterprises under an unregistered conditional sales contract. J Enterprises fell behind in its commercial rent to its landlord who then seized everything within the premises. The landlord was exercising its right of "distress" which was lawful under provincial law dealing with commercial leases. The landlord eventually sold the goods and the plaintiff demanded part of the proceeds saying that it was the owner of the goods. Who would succeed?

2. The plaintiff leased cars to the defendant. The contract gave the defendant the right to buy the vehicles. It also stated that upon default the plaintiff could resell the vehicles without notice. The plaintiff did repossess and sell the cars without any opportunity being given to the defendant to redeem. The defendant refused to make good the deficiency still owing on the cars because it was not given notice as required by provincial law. The plaintiff took the position that it had acted within its rights under the contract. Who would succeed?

3. The plaintiff brought an action to require that a conditional sales contract be de-registered. The plaintiff had purchased an automobile under the contract and had defaulted. The seller decided not to repossess the car but to sue. It did so and obtained a judgment. The plaintiff still had the car and wanted to sell it but could not do so while the contract was registered against it. The plaintiff's argument was that since the defendant could not repossess the car and had a judgment, the defendant no longer had any interest or rights in the vehicle. The defendant argued that until it was paid it could leave the conditional sales contract registered. Who would succeed?

These notes and tokens were once used as currency in the fur trade of the

Hudson's Bay Company.

INCORPORATED 2ND MAY 1670.

Set of 1854 "Made Beaver" Brass Tokens 1, ½, ¼ and ⅛ denominations. Die shows E M (for East Main, district on East Mainland of Hudson Bay) and N B (meant to be M B for "Made Beaver" but misinterpreted by die-cutter.)

Unit Eight

Bills of Exchange

When the Governor of New France found himself unable to pay his soldiers because the supply ship had not arrived from France, he issued playing cards with his signature on them as "negotiable instruments."

Chapter 19

Substitutes for Money

The Bills of Exchange Act

Modern society has devised numerous methods of making financial payments without using cash (paper money or coins). The objections to using cash are the bulkiness of large payments and the fear of theft. It is particularly risky to send large amounts of cash through the mail.

The problem of how to make payments safely and conveniently is not a recent one. Merchants saw the need for "substitutes for money" several centuries ago. Over a period of time, they developed the practice of using paper documents upon which instructions were recorded that represented an exchange of value. These documents are of many types, but are generally known as *bills of exchange.* The first detailed laws regarding the use of bills were drawn up in England under what was called the Law Merchant. The British Parliament later incorporated bills of exchange into a separate statute. Canada's statute on the same subject is called the *Bills of Exchange Act* and was passed in 1890.

The first cheque known to have been drawn on a British bank was for the sum of £400 made payable to a Mr. Delboe by Nicholas Vanacker and dated London, 16 February 1659. It was made out in almost exactly the style of a modern cheque, the amount being written out first in words and then in figures.
T The *Bills of Exchange Act* of Canada defines a bill of exchange as follows:

> **17. (1) A bill of exchange is an unconditional order in writing addressed by one person to another, signed by the person giving it, requiring the person to whom it is addressed to pay on demand or at a fixed or determinable time, a sum certain in money to or to the order of a specific person or to bearer.**

This definition sets down certain necessary requirements that a bill of exchange must meet in order to be valid. Broken down into parts, they are:

- *Unconditional:* The drawer or preparer of the bill is not making payment on the condition that something be done in return.
- *In writing:* The bill must be written or printed. It cannot be oral. No particular form need be used, although custom has developed standard printed forms for everyday use.
- *Signed by the person giving it:* Without a signature, the bill is incomplete. The signature can be handwritten or printed on the bill.
- *Pay on demand:* The person who holds the bill may present it to the bank upon which it was drawn and demand payment at any time.
- *Fixed or determinable time:* The bill is either dated, after which date it is valid, or a future time is set that is determinable, i.e., " thirty days after date." An example of an indeterminable time would be "thirty days after I win first prize in a lottery."
- *A sum certain:* The amount must be expressed in exact dollars and cents. It cannot read, for example, "half of what I own."
- *To a person or bearer:* The bill of exchange must indicate who is authorized to receive payment. A specific person may be named, or just "bearer," meaning anyone having possession.

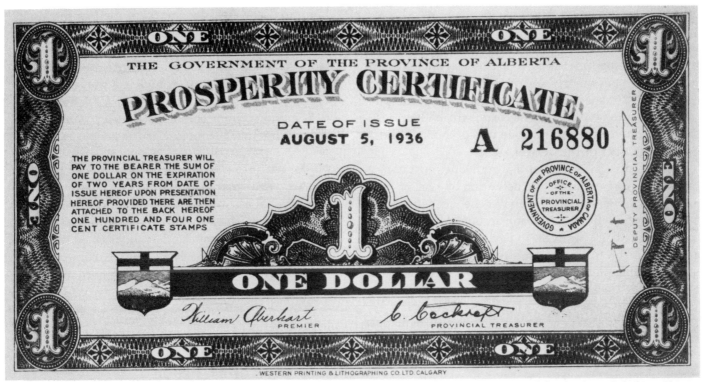

In 1936, the Government of Alberta began circulating "Prosperity Certificates" and denied they were either money or bills of exchange (which would come under federal jurisdiction). The plan was eventually declared to be unconstitutional.

These requirements may seem very technical, but they clearly indicate that bills of exchange must be properly drawn to be valid. There is considerable room for error, and this is the primary reason that printed forms are used. If the drawer fills in all the spaces provided, then, in all probability, the bill of exchange will be completed correctly.

Bills of exchange generally fall into three classes: cheques, promissory notes, and drafts. The use of drafts has declined considerably, so our discussion will centre on cheques and promissory notes. It is important to distinguish bills of exchange from legal tender. Legal tender consists of bank notes, and coins in limited amounts (copper coins up to 25 cents and silver coins up to $10). Bills of exchange are *not* legal tender and there is no obligation on any party to accept them. Any creditor may insist upon payment in legal tender if that form of payment is preferred over a bill of exchange.

Cheques

The *Bills of Exchange Act* defines a cheque as a bill of exchange drawn on a bank, payable on demand. It is important to note that a cheque must be drawn on a *bank,* not another financial institution such as a credit union. Trust companies are able to permit chequing accounts because trust companies clear their cheques through the Canadian Payments Association.

A cheque has three phases in its life cycle: (1) issue, (2) negotiation, and (3) payment.

Issue of a Cheque

A cheque is issued when it is written out and delivered to the intended recipient. Writing may include printing or other methods of reproduction. The signature can be written or printed. One person may sign a cheque for another person if he or she has the authority to do so. A cheque does not have to take a particular form and may be written on anything, including wood, stone, animal hides — anything that can be transported to the bank. Blank cheque forms are provided by banks for the convenience of their customers, enabling them to write cheques quickly and properly. The processing of cheques is made faster by the presence of a computer code printed on the cheque form, which identifies the bank upon which the cheque was drawn and the account number of the drawer.

The essential information that a cheque must contain was discussed under the definition of a bill of exchange. Generally, we say that a cheque is prepared by the person who owns a bank account (drawer), ordering the bank (drawee) to pay a sum of money to another person (payee) on or after the date shown. The following illustration points out the essential parts of a cheque.

Sequential number of cheque

Sum certain expressed in words and figures

Date

Payee   Drawee

Computer code identifying bank

Code identifying account number of drawer

Drawer

Bank of Nova Scotia v. Sanborn
British Columbia, 1975

Sanborn drew a cheque upon his credit union account, payable to a construction company. The construction company deposited the cheque in the plaintiff bank and then issued cheques to the full amount of the deposit. These cheques were honoured and paid by the bank. Before the first cheque drawn by Sanborn was presented to the credit union, Sanborn instructed the credit union to stop payment on the cheque because the construction company had not completed the work for which they were paid. The bank could not recover the money from the construction company's account because the money had all been paid out to others. The bank then sued Sanborn as the drawer of the cheque, claiming that as a holder in due course, the bank was entitled to recover from Sanborn. The court held that the document was not a cheque. The Act defines a cheque as a bill of exchange drawn on a *bank*. The judge ruled that the credit union was not a bank, the instrument was not a cheque, and the defendant, Sanborn, was not liable as the drawer of it.

Negotiation of a Cheque

Since many bills of exchange are transferred to other parties, they are also called *negotiable instruments*. The legal process of transferring (or negotiating) a cheque to someone else will vary, depending upon how the cheque was drawn. If the cheque says, "Pay to Bearer," then whoever has the cheque has the right to payment. In order to transfer a bearer cheque to someone else, all that is required is to hand it over to that person. For this reason, bearer cheques are risky. If lost, they can be cashed by whoever happens to find them.

If the cheque is drawn, "Pay to J. Smith" or "Pay to the Order of J. Smith" it must be transferred to another person by *endorsement*. An endorsement is a signature, usually with words of explanation, transferring the cheque to someone else. There are many types of endorsements, but only a few are commonly used. Endorsements are usually written on the back of the cheque so as not to obstruct the writing on the face. If further space is needed, a separate sheet of paper may be attached to the cheque. The most commonly used endorsements are discussed below.

Blank Endorsement

A blank endorsement requires only that the payee sign on the back. The legal effect of a blank endorsement is to change the cheque into a bearer cheque. A blank endorsement is normally used when the payee presents the cheque at either his or her own bank or the drawee bank for payment.

Special Endorsement

A special endorsement negotiates the cheque to a specific person, not just to anyone. That person becomes a holder and must further endorse the cheque in some manner. A special endorsement would appear as follows:

> Pay to Robert E. Lee
> Joseph Green

Restrictive Endorsement

A restrictive endorsement limits future endorsements in some manner. Where special endorsements are used, a cheque could be negotiated through dozens of persons. It might not be cashed for several months. This can be a considerable disadvantage to the drawer. In the first place, the drawer will not want specimens of his or her cheques (and signature) to get into the hands of possible forgers. Secondly, the drawer may forget all about the cheque and find that it is suddenly presented for payment at a time when he or she can hardly afford to honour it. To prevent this, the drawer can use a restrictive endorsement:

> Pay to Robert E. Lee only
> Joseph Green

In this example, the cheque can be presented for payment only by Robert E. Lee. The use of restrictive endorsements is not confined to the drawer. Any holder who wishes to limit future endorsements of the cheque may use this form of endorsement. If the holder wants to deposit the cheque, and particularly if it is going to be deposited by mail, the holder can be protected by using a restrictive endorsement such as this:

> For deposit to my
> account only
> Joseph Green

There can be no further endorsement of the cheque once a restrictive endorsement is used; therefore, a person finding a cheque with such an endorsement could not legally cash it.

If the payee's name is misspelled, the payee may endorse the cheque by writing the name correctly on the back, or may sign it twice—first with the name as it appears on the cheque and then a second time spelling the name correctly. Either method is acceptable under the *Bills of Exchange Act.*

Qualified Endorsement

An endorser may sign a cheque in a manner excusing that endorser from any later liability. This is called a qualified endorsement, and any person accepting such a bill of exchange should question why the endorser has sought this protection. Should there be a subsequent problem with the cheque, the endorser who used a qualified endorsement is free from any obligation to make good upon the cheque. An example of a qualified endorsement is as follows:

> Pay to Robert E. Lee
> without recourse to me
> Joseph Green

Payment of a Cheque

Assuming that there is nothing defective about the cheque, it must eventually be presented to the bank (drawee) for payment. If the bank finds nothing amiss, it stamps the cheque "PAID" and pays the money to the person presenting it. The bank is under a legal obligation to make payment provided:

- The cheque is in proper form and has not been altered.
- The person presenting it can present identification and is entitled to payment.
- The drawer has sufficient funds in his or her account to cover the cheque. If the account does not have enough funds, the cheque is stamped NSF (Not Sufficient Funds).
- The cheque is not stale-dated. A cheque becomes stale-dated if it is not presented for payment within six months of the date on it.
- The account has not been frozen by a court order.
- Payment has not been stopped by the drawer.

Most people deposit cheques made payable to them at their own bank rather than at the drawee bank. This is not really payment of the cheque. Although the holder's account will be credited with the amount of the deposit, the holder's bank must in turn present the cheque to the drawee bank to get the money. If the cheque is refused, the holder's bank will immediately deduct from the holder's account the amount allowed as a deposit.

Generally, the holder of a cheque has no claim against the bank on which the cheque was drawn. If there are any problems, the holder will have to take the matter up with the drawer or with the previous endorsers. One exception to the rule arises in the case of a *certified* cheque. A cheque is certified by having the drawee bank debit the drawer's account immediately by the amount of the cheque; the cheque is then stamped "certified." A cheque that has been certified carries the bank's guarantee that the funds are sufficient and will be paid. In this case, the holder has a claim against the bank for payment. A cheque is usually certified at the request of the drawer who wants to assure the payee that the cheque will be honoured by the bank and that the drawer will not later try to stop payment on it for some reason. A stop-payment order can be issued for a certified cheque under extraordinary circumstances, such as a declaration by the drawer that the payee has defrauded him or her. Banks are very reluctant to accept such orders, however, and they will be accepted only in extreme cases.

A bank will not pay a cheque against a depositor's account if it knows that the depositor has died. The holder of the cheque or promissory note should present it to the executor of the deceased's estate for payment. If the payee of a cheque dies before he or she can cash it, the general practice is for the executor of the estate to return the cheque to the drawer with a request that a new cheque be issued to the executor "in trust" to the estate.

A cheque can be dated on a Sunday or holiday. However, as we learned in a previous unit, contracts cannot be signed on a Sunday. If a cheque is part of a contractual agreement, it may be challenged if the entire agreement was made and signed on a Sunday and the cheque issued to conclude that agreement.

Dishonoured Cheques and the Holder in Due Course

A cheque that the drawee bank refuses to pay is said to be dishonoured. The question then arises: Who suffers the loss, and what rights has the person who holds the cheque? This person is known in law as a *holder in due course* and his or her legal position can be very complicated. Generally, the holder in due course should be able to collect the money if he or she acts *promptly.* Therefore, it is important to understand the position of the holder in due course as follows:

56 (1) A holder in due course is a holder who has taken a bill, complete and regular on the face of it, under the following conditions, namely:
  (a) that he became the holder of it before it was overdue and without notice that it had been previously dishonoured, if such was the fact;
  (b) that he took the bill in good faith and for value,

and that at the time the bill was negotiated to him he had no notice of any defect in the title of the person who negotiated it.

This definition indicates that the holder in due course is a person who accepted a bill of exchange on its "face," that is, just on its appearance. The person obtained the bill for value, which means it was not given for nothing, but in return for something the person gave the previous holder. Every holder in due course has the same rights as the previous holder. This trusting position of the holder has sometimes led to this person being referred to as the "innocent" holder in due course.

The holder in due course must act quickly when he or she learns the cheque has been dishonoured. The immediate action should be to give Notice of Dishonour *within one business day* to the drawer and all previous holders whom he or she intends to hold responsible for the amount. Any previous holder not notified cannot be held liable on the cheque. Notice can be given orally or in writing, as long as it clearly indicates the bill which was dishonoured. With regard to written notice, as long as the notice is mailed within one business day, this is sufficient. It is not important how long it takes for mail delivery of the notice, but it is wise to use registered mail as proof of when the notice was sent. Another form of protest is to have a formal written protest drawn. In most provinces a lawyer or notary can prepare one. A bill must be formally protested at the place where it was dishonoured. If the bill was returned dishonoured by mail, it may be formally protested at the place at which it was received.

The importance of protesting the dishonour of the bill is this: the holder may sue upon the bill itself, and not have to discuss the reasons (usually a contract) for which it was given. If the bill is not protested, this does not necessarily mean the holder will never get the money, but it means he or she will have a more difficult time getting it. It will be necessary to sue upon the contract for which it was given, claiming non-performance by the other party.

If the holder in due course has given proper notice of dishonour, the value of the cheque can be recovered from any of the previous endorsers, or from the drawer.

The writing of a bad, or "rubber" cheque is also a criminal offence. Whether or not a criminal charge should be laid should be discussed first with a lawyer so as not to leave the holder open to a later lawsuit for tort. It could be suggested to the drawer that if he or she immediately presents cash in return for the cheque, the matter will be forgotten. However, it is illegal to threaten criminal charges to force payment of a civil obligation. Therefore the holder must confine the statement to a suggestion that this would be a good way to avoid trouble; no threats must be made.

Defences

The fact that the holder was alert enough to protest the dishonour of the bill to the drawer and all previous holders does not guarantee that he or she will recover the money. There are defences that can be raised against a holder in due course. The topic of defences can be confusing, and it has complications that can be worked effectively against someone who doesn't fully understand the position.

First, we should distinguish between immediate parties and remote parties.

Jones signs a contract with Smith and gives Smith a cheque as part payment. Jones and Smith are *immediate* parties.

Smith negotiates the cheque and assigns rights to further payment to the Easy Terms Finance Company. The finance company pays Smith the remaining value of the contract less interest.

The Easy Terms Finance Company is a holder in due course and can enforce payment of the cheque on its face. The finance company and Jones are *remote* parties.

Secondly, there are two types of defences. Some defences relate to the appearance of the bill itself; these are called *real defences*. Others relate to the reasons for which the bill was given; these are called *personal defences*. Generally, real defences are successful against any subsequent holder in due course. Personal defences are usually valid only against immediate parties.

Real Defences

After the drawer has written a cheque, something may happen to the cheque which causes the drawer to stop payment. Real defences are good against all subsequent holders, because they are basic to the cheque itself, not to the parties involved. Real defences include:

- *Forgery:* Where a cheque is forged, the person whose name was forged is not liable. However, an endorser of a forged cheque can be held liable by a subsequent holder. Each party to a bill of exchange gives a guarantee to the next person of its genuineness. Forgery is also a criminal offence. The holder in due course must notify all previous endorsers about the forgery. The holder can then select any endorser to claim from. Usually, the holder collects from the nearest endorser—the person from whom he or she obtained the cheque. That endorser would in turn probably collect from the next previous endorser. Eventually, the bill would retrace its steps until the forger was identified, usually because he or she was unable to be found. Clearly, in most cases, the first person to take the cheque from the forger will be the ultimate loser.
- *Material alteration:* Once a cheque is drawn, any attempt to change the information written upon its face, or to change any of the endorsements on the back, will result in dishonour, and the drawer will remain liable only for the original amount as ordered paid to the original payee.
- *Lack of delivery of an incomplete instrument:* A partially completed cheque that is taken without the drawer's consent, and then filled in at a later date, would be subject to a real defence. It is, of course, a bad practice to leave cheques lying around partly completed.

However, if an incomplete cheque is delivered (on the understanding that the recipient will complete it, or even without this understanding), then the cheque remains valid. Thus, if you write someone a "blank" cheque, you have no defence if a larger amount than you had intended is filled in.

- *Incapacity of an infant:* An infant can write cheques and if there are sufficient funds in the account the bank will pay the sum. However, the infant is not bound on a cheque as a negotiable instrument to a subsequent holder in due course. Also, an infant cannot be liable as an endorser. It is risky to accept a cheque from an infant since he or she can easily stop payment on the cheque and repudiate the contract under which it was given.

Personal Defences

We have noted that real defences are valid against all subsequent holders. Personal defences are valid only against the person to whom the cheque was given, that is, the immediate party. Personal defences would apply if:

- No consideration was given to the drawer.
- The holder was guilty of fraud, misrepresentation, undue influence, duress, or some other act which would render the contract for which the cheque was given voidable.
- The drawer has a counterclaim against the payee. If the person who received the cheque failed to carry out his or her responsibilities fully, the drawer could stop payment on the cheque. In the event of the payee suing for payment on the cheque, the drawer could use as a defence the counterclaim that the payee did not carry out the obligations fully.
- The drawer did not have the legal capacity to draw the cheque or enter into the contract. An example would be a minor who wrote a cheque for non-necessaries. Another example would be a person whose assets were frozen under a bankruptcy proceeding and who wrote a cheque on his or her account.

Obviously, it would be tempting to an immediate party to negotiate the cheque to a third party who, as a holder in due course, could enforce it against the drawee. But this does not always work, for by our definition of a holder in due course, the person must be completely unaware of the circumstances under which the cheque was given and must have given consideration for the cheque. If someone is just co-operating with the immediate party to help collect upon the cheque, that person is not a true holder in due course and cannot succeed.

Promissory Notes

So far we have devoted most of our discussion to cheques. Let us now consider another form of negotiable instrument, the promissory note. Where a cheque is an *order* to pay, a promissory note is an unconditional *promise* to pay. Apart from this essential difference, promissory notes are subject to the same requirements of a bill of exchange as are cheques. A promissory note

is normally given as a promise to pay a debt such as a bank loan; it also commonly forms part of a conditional sale agreement. It does not have to follow any particular form but it generally looks something like the illustration shown here. Note, however, that the following illustration shows the words "CONSUMER PURCHASE" only because this promissory note was part of a contract. Money borrowed from a bank would not require these words on the contract.

An "IOU" is not a valid promissory note for several reasons. Firstly, it merely acknowledges some sort of indebtedness, but does not promise to pay it. Secondly, an IOU has no determinable time on it and does not indicate any value received for it. At best, an IOU can be considered a friendly reminder not a legally binding document.

Unlike cheques, promissory notes may contain a requirement to pay interest as well as the principal amount stated. If a note says "pay on demand" it must

---

Howard C. Ames		Barbara Knight	

SCHEDULE OF PAYMENTS		CONSUMER PURCHASE	
$ ...20.00.....	1 month after date.		
$ ...20.00....	2 months after date.	$ 200.00	Kingston, Ontario December 12 19--
$ ...20.00....	3 months after date.		Place and Province
$ ...20.00....	4 months after date.	For value received I promise to pay to the order of	
$ ...20.00....	5 months after date.		
$ ...20.00....	6 months after date.	—Ames Appliances— THE VENDOR,	
$ ...20.00....	7 months after date.		
$ ...20.00....	8 months after date.	Two hundred and 00/100———————Dollars	
$ ...20.00....	9 months after date.		
$ ..20.00....	10 months after date.	at the time or times stated in schedule of instalments hereon,	
$	11 months after date.		
$	12 months after date.	and in case default is made in payment of any of the instalments the whole amount remaining unpaid shall become due and payable forthwith. Interest after maturity upon all sums due until paid to be at the rate of **22%** per annum.	
$			
$			
$		Barbara Knight	
$		Purchaser	
$ 200.00 TOTAL		CONSUMER PURCHASE	

be paid whenever the holder so demands. If a note is payable at a future time, the debtor is permitted three business days after the given time to make payment. These are called "days of grace."

A promissory note can be endorsed to someone else who may enforce payment as a holder in due course. If the note is not paid, the holder may sue upon it in much the same way as the holder of a cheque, except that in this case there is no time limit involved. The defences mentioned earlier, personal and real, generally apply to notes in the same manner as to cheques. Notes are treated by the court as serious promises to pay, and are normally enforceable against the maker unless a very good defence is raised.

The signature of an infant on a promissory note as either the maker or an endorser is not binding, even if the note was given for necessaries.

MacMillan v. MacMillan
Saskatchewan, 1975

A father loaned his son $18 000 and the son gave in exchange a document reading: "This is to certify that I borrowed $18 000 from my father, John M. MacMillan. I have already paid back $8057 and will pay back the remainder of $9943 or at least $1000 per year starting with payment from the 1969 crop." The father stated clearly in the presence of others that he wanted to be paid no more than $3000 of the debt but he did not deliver up the document nor was his statement in writing. The widow and executor of the father brought an action against the son. At trial, it was held that the document was a promissory note. Since the note had not been delivered up and the renunciation was not in writing, the son was liable on the note. On appeal by the son, it was held that the appeal should be dismissed. The document in question was not payable at a fixed or determinable future time nor was it made for a sum certain in money. Since it was not a promissory note, it did not come under the *Bills of Exchange Act*. However, the son's argument that the document proved an agreement of indebtedness of

which there was subsequent "forgiveness" was not accepted. A debt could not be released except where there was consideration or by deed. The deceased may have intended to renounce most of the debt, but he did not do so in writing. The son was ordered to pay the full amount.

The Innocent Holder in Due Course

A genuine holder in due course is believed to be unaware of any defects and has no knowledge of the circumstances regarding the issue of the note. Such a person is "innocent" and protected by the court because he or she accepted the note in good faith. This privileged status must be maintained in order for business to function—otherwise no one would dare trust any promissory note. The question of prior knowledge can cause the holder in due course to lose his or her protected status as the next case will illustrate:

Federal Discount Corporation Ltd. v. St. Pierre
Ontario, 1962

St. Pierre agreed to purchase a home knitting machine from Fair Isle Knitting Ltd. for $365. She paid $35 in cash and signed a promissory note to make twelve monthly payments of $27.50 each. One clause of the confusing contract said that Fair Isle Knitting would buy her finished work, thus guaranteeing that she would earn enough money to pay off the machine. She paid two instalments of $27.50 and shipped what she believed to be $150 worth of knitted goods to Fair Isle, for which she was not paid. Fair Isle later notified St. Pierre that they were "suspending operations." St. Pierre then received a letter from Federal Discount Corporation Ltd. that they held her note and requested payment. The letter they sent her was stamped with the words, "Note payments must be made when due regardless of amount earned from knitting." The trial judge ruled that Federal Discount was not a valid holder in due course. The Court of Appeal of Ontario upheld the trial judge's ruling saying:

"The plaintiff was fully aware of the general course of operation employed by Fair Isle, as indicated by the notation stamped on their letter. The course of dealings between Federal Discount and Fair Isle indicates a relationship much more intimate than in a normal commercial transaction. To pretend that they were so separate that the transfer of the note constituted an independent commercial transaction ignores the true substance of their pre-existing arrangements."

The abuse of promissory notes led to a change in the *Bills of Exchange Act* in 1970 to curb the ease with which the buyer was outflanked by the "innocent" third party. Present law requires that all promissory notes attached to conditional sales contracts or given as security for an instalment purchase be marked with the words, "Consumer Purchase." Although the note can still be negotiated to a third party, the law now permits the maker to refuse to pay a third party if there is a valid complaint against the original seller. Thus, with regard to consumer purchases, the holder in due course has lost his or her traditionally safe position. It should be emphasized that a note signed in conjunction with a *business* purchase does not have this protection. For example, if A purchases a truck for business and signs a note, it would *not* be marked with the words Consumer Purchase. If A also purchases a car for personal use and signs a note, it would be marked with the words.

Joint Notes

Where two persons sign a note which reads, "We promise to pay," then the two persons are signing a joint note. This means that in default of payment, the holder must sue them both as one defendant and can only hope to obtain one judgment. If the note reads, "I promise to pay" and is signed by two persons, the note is a joint and several note. In a joint and several note, the makers sign both *together* and *individually*. They promise to pay the note together, but each signer also promises separately to make good the entire note personally, if the other signer does not fulfill his or her obligation. Therefore, the holder is not limited to one

judgment, but could if necessary sue the two signers in two separate actions to recover the full amount. If one signer of the note is required to pay the full amount, that signer may, in turn, sue the other signer for half that amount. This assumes the other signer can be found and has the money.

Guaranteeing a Note

If a borrower has a poor credit rating or is very young with no proven credit record, the lender may require that another person guarantee the note as follows:

I hereby guarantee payment of this note

Robert J. Jonas

The legal effect of such a guarantee is that the guarantor accepts liability for the note if the maker defaults. Some people regard such guarantees as mere formalities, or just a way of saying that you think the maker is a good risk. This is quite untrue. Should the maker default, disappear, suffer bankruptcy, die, or otherwise fail to pay, the guarantor will have to pay the note.

The problem of one person's guaranteeing another person's loan has received mixed treatment from the courts. It has often been held that a wife could not guarantee a husband's loan unless she received "independent legal advice." This concept presumes that the wife is not astute in business matters and that she would be influenced by the husband, the husband's banker, or the husband's lawyer. This was affirmed in a British Columbia case, *E. & R. Distributors v. Atlas Drywall Ltd.* (1981). The court held that the holder must show that the wife received a proper explanation of the note before she was asked to sign it. However, the Supreme Court of Ontario took a different point of view in the following case:

Royal Bank of Canada v. Poisson
Ontario, 1977

In this action the Royal Bank sued Marilyn Poisson for $10 000 plus interest based upon a guarantee signed on the usual bank form. She signed the guarantee at her husband's request. He was negotiating a line of credit with the bank and needed a guarantor. He was loaned more than $10 000 but no further guarantee was requested. It was learned that the original loan was reduced below $10 000 at one point and the original note given was retired and a new note executed by the husband. Counsel for the defendant argued that this relieved her of any liability as her guarantee was only for the original note. However, the bank form stated otherwise. It stated that her guarantee was not related to one specific note but continued all the time the loan was in effect. The husband's business failed and the bank wanted its money from the defendant. She claimed that she did not know she was entering into a *continuing* obligation. She had not received independent legal advice.

The trial judge concluded that Poisson was an intelligent person who understood why she was signing a note. She might not have been wholly familiar with the banking documents but she understood the general importance of what she signed:

66It is clear ... from that case [reference to an earlier case] that there is no magic to independent legal advice and in each case the question must be considered on the facts. There is no suggestion that there was any undue influence exercised on the wife or that she was misled. She knew the nature and purport of the document even though she did not appreciate its continuing effect. ... I have no alternative but to find the defendant liable to the bank under the terms of the guarantee.99

Perhaps the legal position can best be summarized by saying that when a person is asked to guarantee a note, the bank or person asking for the guarantee must disclose all the facts about the nature of the loan and explain the risk involved. It is not necessary to discuss the forms in great detail as long as the person appreciates the nature and purport of what is being done.

The best rule is simply don't guarantee someone's note. That person might be very reliable, but illness, accident, business pressures, or even death could leave the guarantor with a debt he or she could not afford.

Reviewing Important Points

1. A cheque is not legal tender. It requires no special form and may be written on anything that can be carried to a bank and cashed—provided the required information is present.
2. Once a cheque is in bearer form, it can be cashed by anyone having possession of it.
3. Every endorser of a negotiable instrument is liable to each and every subsequent holder, unless a qualified endorsement is used.
4. A promissory note may call for the payment of interest while a cheque does not.
5. Guaranteeing a promissory note makes the guarantor liable should the maker default.

Checking Your Understanding

1. What are the seven essential elements of a bill of exchange?
2. Is a bill of exchange legal tender? Is a certified cheque legal tender?
3. Y wants to deposit a cheque by mail. How should Y endorse the cheque?
4. R obtains a cheque from W. The bank returns it marked with the words "Not Sufficient Funds." What should R do?
5. What is the importance of marking a promissory note with the words "Consumer Purchase"?
6. Explain the difference between an immediate party and a remote party.
7. What is a real defence? Give two examples.
8. Can an infant have a chequing account? Explain why or why not.

Legal Briefs

1. P calls his bank with a stop-payment order. He gives all the correct information except the amount which he misstates. The bank later pays the cheque. Liability of the bank?

2. S and R co-sign a promissory note. S is a minor but lies about her age. She later refuses to pay on the note. The bank tries to collect the entire loan from R. Must R pay it all?

3. K lost a cheque payable to her. She did not tell her bank about it for five days although she had ample time to do so. The person who found the cheque was able to cash it by forging K's signature. Must the bank reimburse K?

4. F draws a cheque payable to W. When W presents the cheque for payment, he is told that a stop-payment order was issued by F. W then concocts a scheme with Y to try to get the money. W endorses the cheque to Y who tries to cash it and is also turned away by the bank. Y then "protests" the dishonour and sues F alleging that he is an innocent holder in due course. Will F have to pay Y?

5. Angered by high taxes, W writes a cheque payable to the Department of Revenue on the side of a cow. W takes the cow to the tax office to make payment. The manager tells W that a cheque must be written on a cheque form. Is this correct?

6. S mails a cheque to his insurance company for his annual life insurance premium. The cheque is received by the company but not processed immediately. Two weeks later, S dies. The bank freezes S's account. Unable to cash the premium cheque, the insurance company then argues that S did not pay his premium and that they will not pay his life insurance to S's widow. She sues. Should the insurance company pay?

7. R and H sign a promissory note which reads, "I promise to pay upon demand the sum of $5000." One month later, R is killed in an accident. H offers to pay the bank $2500 which she argues is "her half" of the loan. Is H correct?

8. B drew a cheque payable to Z. For various reasons, B was not really pleased with the transaction, so she deliberately misspelled her own name on the cheque. However, the cheque was her personal cheque, with her name and account number printed on it. Her bank paid Z. B tried to recover the money from her bank saying they should not have cashed the cheque because of the misspelling of her name. Is B correct?

9. On January 2, 19-2, H concluded a major business transaction. He was a bit nervous and dated his cheque January 2, 19-1. Should the bank cash it?

10. N borrowed money from L and gave L a document reading: "Received from L, $1000 to be repaid in ten monthly payments of $100 each, starting July, 19--." What is this document? If N does not pay, can L enforce payment using this document?

Applying the Law

Buchannan v. Imperial Bank of Commerce
British Columbia, 1979

A bank manager, concerned about the security of a loan made to a business, called in the owner and suggested that it would be advisable to get someone to guarantee the loan. The two discussed increasing the amount of the loan in order to get the business in a better cash position. The owner returned with his parents-in-law. The bank manager prepared documents which placed a mortgage on the elderly couple's home to guarantee the business debts of their son-in-law. The manager made statements to the couple about the bright prospects of their son-in-law's business and mentioned that he would be expanding the business on the basis of this guarantee. In fact, the manager had formed the opposite opinion—that the son-in-law had little hope of making his business succeed and would most certainly fail to pay his loan. The court refused to enforce the mortgage against the couple, holding that they were taken advantage of by the bank manager. In this case, the absence of legal advice, independent or otherwise, was held to be of the utmost importance.

Questions

1. If a person is asked to guarantee a loan, what must the person be told?
2. In this particular case, how important would independent legal advice have been? If the couple had obtained independent advice and still guaranteed the loan, would that have changed the court's decision?

 Bank of Nova Scotia v. Cheng Newfoundland, 1981

Cheng sold a boat to Cox on Saturday. Cox gave Cheng a cheque for $2500 which was the full price of the boat. Cox later testified that it was not the full price but just a down payment to hold the boat. The trial judge did not believe this statement. On Sunday, Cox returned with his father-in-law who was knowledgeable about boats. The father-in-law advised against buying the boat. Cox wanted his cheque back but Cheng refused, saying the sale was final. On Monday at 9:30 a.m. Cox's wife phoned the bank and told them to stop payment on the cheque. The bank clerk took down the information but did not process the stop-payment order immediately. At 10:00 a.m., Cheng entered the bank and successfully cashed the cheque. It was later in the day that the bank realized it should not have paid the money and demanded it back from Cheng. The bank stated that Cheng knew the cheque should not have been paid because Cox had told Cheng he was going to stop payment. The court referred to the case of *Royal Bank v. The King* (1931) in which the following rules were established: (1) The mistake must be an honest mistake; (2) both payer and payee must in some way be party to the mistake; (3) the facts believed to exist must impose an obligation — legal, equitable or moral to make the payment; (4) the payee must have no legal, equitable or moral right to the money.

The plaintiff bank's case was dismissed. The court concluded that Cheng believed that he had a right to the money because he considered the sale final.

Questions

1. If a person makes a purchase with a cheque, but tries to change his or her mind, is there any obligation on the part of the seller to return the cheque? Explain your answer.
2. Why did the court conclude that Cheng did not have to return the money? Cheng obviously went to the bank as soon as it opened. Did he not have some concern that he would not be able to cash that cheque?
3. If the bank could not recover the money from Cheng, would it have to return the money to Cox's account?
4. What would become of the boat?

You Be the Judge

1. Tess, while a minor, borrowed some money from a bank. She signed a promissory note which was then co-signed by her mother who guaranteed the loan. Tess repaid the entire loan. Two months later, while still a minor, she went back to the same bank and took out another loan for more money. She again signed a promissory note which was not co-signed by her mother, although Tess later told her mother that she had taken out the loan. The mother expressed surprise that the bank had insisted upon her signature for the first loan and did not make the same requirement for the second loan. She concluded that it was their concern, not hers. Later, Tess became an adult and upon her eighteenth birthday, advised the bank that she would not repay the loan. She left the province to work in another province. The bank brought an action against the mother for the unpaid amount of the loan. She denied liability. Who would succeed?

2. Workers at a large industrial plant were in the habit of cashing their pay cheques every two weeks at a bar across the street from the entrance to the plant. The volume of such cheque cashing was very large and the bar kept extra cash on hand to handle it. A forger obtained a cheque by offering to cash it for a worker; then the forger set about to copy the cheque. Using stiff paper of the same colour along with a portable

cheque-writing machine, the forger made a very good reproduction of the company's payroll cheque. When the plant closed one Friday, the forger mixed with the workers and cashed a forged pay cheque. The next day the forger cashed another. When the cheques were dishonoured, the bar owner sued the company, basing the action upon the alleged negligence of the company in not periodically altering the appearance of its pay cheques to prevent this type of fraud. The company raised forgery as a real defence. Who would succeed?

3. The defendant, Serpico, was a farmer. He ordered a pre-fabricated steel building from the C Steel Company. He paid $100 down and signed a promissory note for $5412. He thought the contract included construction but was told that assembly would cost him another $1000. He then signed a second note, which was blank. The amount later filled in was $6523. The building was then assembled by the steel company. However, it was assembled poorly and was nearly useless. During the time it was being assembled, a representative of the I Credit Company called Serpico. He asked how the work was going and whether Serpico was happy with the building. The defendant replied that he could not tell until it was finished. Estimates were that at least $3000 would be required to take the building down and re-construct it.

He then learned that the credit company had purchased his note the day after their talk on the phone. The credit company brought suit for non-payment on the note. The note was not marked "Consumer Purchase" since this was a business transaction. Who would succeed?

4. A finance company issued a cheque to a person who was impersonating another person. The impersonator cashed the cheque. Before the cheque was presented for payment the finance company learned what had happened and stopped payment. The cheque had been cashed in a store and the store owner sued the finance company. Who would succeed?

5. Gloria purchased a used car from Gwen, but wanted a few days to make certain the car was sound. She gave Gwen a postdated cheque. Gwen cashed the cheque immediately because the bank teller did not notice the date on the cheque. Gloria decided she did not want the car and tried to return it to Gwen who refused to take it back. When Gloria went to stop payment on the cheque, she learned that her bank had cashed it. The bank refused to refund the money to Gloria who sued the bank. The bank added Gwen as a defendant on the grounds that Gwen knew the cheque was postdated and knew she should not have been cashing it on the day she did. Who would succeed?

Unit
Nine

Consumer
Protection

*Consumer demand thus comes to depend
more and more on the ability and
willingness of consumers to incur debt.*

J.K. Galbraith
The Affluent Society

Chapter 20

Federal Laws To Protect Consumers

The Purpose of Consumer Protection

Reason for New Legislation

Without a doubt, no field of law has witnessed the enactment of more legislation in the last twenty years than has that of consumer protection. The complexity of these statutes indicates that the general common law rules pertaining to such matters as the sale of goods have been found inadequate to regulate current consumer practices.

One purpose of consumer protection laws is to protect Canadians from false or exaggerated claims.

The rules of the traditional market place, having worked well for many centuries, now appear outmoded. What has happened in the last few decades suddenly to render them obsolete? There are many possible answers to this question, but generally four things have contributed greatly towards the need for modernized legislation:

- *Packaged goods:* Traditionally, buyers carefully examined the goods they bought before they accepted them. This is not always possible today, since many goods are packaged in cardboard and plastic, or sealed in metal containers, and often cannot be opened. In the case of perishable food, to open the package would result in contamination of the food. Therefore, the consumer tends to rely upon the description of the goods as to their quality rather than examining the goods themselves. The old common law rule of "If you don't like it, don't buy it" hardly works when the buyer cannot see the goods until after they are purchased.

- *Distant manufacturers:* In earlier times, goods were generally sold within close proximity to their place of manufacture. Granted, certain items were traded around the world, but these items were the exception rather than the rule. If buyers did not like the quality of the things they bought, they could usually go directly to the manufacturer and complain of the poor quality. Today, international trade has expanded to the extent that many products available to the consumer are of foreign manufacture. The unhappy consumer cannot return a television set to

Japan to complain about its poor quality. Consumers often find that the agent of a foreign manufacturer plays a "cagey game" of passing all blame for a defective product onto the distant manufacturer, knowing that the consumer cannot communicate directly with that manufacturer.

- *Obscured manufacturers:* At one time producers proudly put their trademark on their goods as an indication to the public that it could expect good quality. Today, many goods are marketed without any clue as to the name of the manufacturer. This is commonplace in the food industry, where many items are labelled simply: "Produced *for* the XYZ Stores." This clearly indicates that the store is only the marketing agent, not the producer. Our labelling laws still do not require that the actual producer be identified on the label. There are various possible reasons why the identity of the manufacturer is withheld. One likely reason is that a one single producer will often manufacture identical products for a number of different stores; each store puts its own label on the product and sells it at a different price. As a result of this arrangement, the consumer often finds that price is not neccessarily a true indication of quality. There is also a lack of consistent standards, since the retailer may change from one producer to another without any identifying change in the label. Thus, consumers could find that products they liked have suddenly undergone a quality change for no apparent reason.

- *Complexity of products:* With the advances of modern technology, products of increasing complexity have been put on the market, and the likelihood of the consumer's having detailed knowledge of their workings has rapidly diminished. Today, some electrical appliances are so complicated that consumers can only rely upon the brand names or hope that the various reports they read or hear are accurate. When appliances malfunction, consumers must rely on the judgment of repair persons as to what needs to be done, and have no way of knowing whether the repairs have been properly carried out — except by bitter experience.

Definition of a Consumer

Although there are numerous statutes which use the word "consumer," very few statutes offer a definition of the term. For example, the federal *Bills of Exchange Act* does not define a consumer, but defines a "consumer purchase" as follows:

> **188. In this Part, "consumer purchase" means a purchase, other than a cash purchase, of goods or services or an agreement to purchase goods or services**
> **(a) by an individual other than for resale or for use in the course of his business, profession or calling, and**
> **(b) from a person who is engaged in the business of selling or providing those goods or services.**

Looking ahead for a moment to provincial legislation, we see that the Ontario *Consumer Protection Act* does not offer any definition of a consumer. Consequently, it is difficult to ascertain just who the Act is intended to protect. The Act does, however, define a "consumer sale" as follows:

> **A consumer sale means a contract for the sale of goods made in the ordinary course of business to a purchaser for his consumption or use, but does not include a sale,**
> **(a) to a purchaser for resale;**
> **(b) to a purchaser whose purchase is in the course of carrying on business;**
> **(c) to an association of individuals, a partnership or corporation;**
> **(d) by a trustee in bankruptcy, a receiver, a liquidator or a person acting under the order of a court.**

The Ontario *Comsumer Protection Act* thus attempts to clarify itself by defining the transaction rather than the individual. The Ontario *Business Practices Act* defines a consumer as "a natural person but does not include a natural person, business partnership, or association of individuals acting in the course of carrying on business." It is very difficult, on the basis of these various statutes, to come up with an acceptable definition of a consumer. The only thing that appears to be uniformly accepted is that a consumer is a natural person rather than a company or corporation. It is generally viewed that consumers are acting in their own personal regard rather than engaging in some form of business transaction either for their own business or their employer's. While there is nothing particularly wrong with this lack of specific definition, it should be questioned why all business transactions are outside the protection of the law. Does a business person purchasing a vehicle for use in business have fewer rights than a person purchasing a vehicle for personal use? If the meaning of consumer is taken to be "one who consumes or uses" then businesses should not be excluded, for they consume or use goods just as individuals do.

The Ontario Law Reform Commission recommended that the term "consumer" be defined as "an individual acquiring a consumer product (that is, goods that are regularly, though not necessarily exclusively bought for personal use or consumption) for his [or her] own use or consumption or for the use or consumption of another individual." This is a rather cumbersome definition and is not necessarily a good definition, but the attempt is made to identify the consumer rather than deal solely with the transactions that might be entered into. Thus far, few provinces have made any attempt to define "consumer." The argument put forward is that it is easier to try to classify a transaction than an individual.

Not only is there no clear-cut definition of a consumer, there is also no clear distinction, under the *Constitution Act, 1867,* as to which level of government should protect the consumer. However, as far as the federal government is concerned, the Act grants several powers which effectively authorize that government to legislate in the consumer protection field. These powers include weights and measures, the post office, bills of exchange, and others. In this section, we shall not attempt to deal with every such statute, but only with those most directly affecting consumer protection.

Selected Federal Statutes

The *Bills of Exchange Act*

This statute, modelled after a similar Act passed in England, defines what are considered to be bills of exchange or negotiable instruments. The primary negotiable instrument used in consumer transactions is the promissory note. Promissory notes are commonly signed when a person finances the purchase of an expensive item—that is, buys it on the instalment plan. Basically, the note is a promise to pay which is enforceable solely on the face of the note. No other conditions or provisions need to be proven to enforce collection. Notes can be transferred to another party, often a finance company, and can be collected by that party, as a holder in due course, without regard as to why the note was originally given. For example, a person bought an appliance in a store and signed a conditional sale contract and a promissory note to pay for it over a period of fifteen months. The store assigned the note to a finance company which began collecting the monthly payments. The appliance stopped working and the store would not honour the guarantee. The buyer refused to make any more payments until the appliance was repaired. Would the buyer have a right to stop making payments? Traditionally, no. The finance company had every right to receive payments, and had no obligation or interest in what took place between the store and the consumer. As an innocent holder in due course, the finance company could collect the payments solely on the face of the note, and any quarrel between the original two parties was none of its concern. The consumer had, in fact, very few defences against paying a promissory note to a holder in due course.

This is not the case today. On June 26, 1970, royal assent was given to a bill amending the *Bills of Exchange Act* which changed in an important way the character of promissory notes given in connection with consumer purchases. The amendment provided that such notes must be prominently and legibly marked on their face with the words "Consumer Purchase." Where a promissory note is so marked, the purchaser has the same defences or rights of set-off against claims of a holder in due course as he or she would have had in a claim by the seller. Finance companies will no longer be able to rely on the status of holder in due course and insulate themselves from disputes between the purchaser and the seller over delivery, performance, service, quality, warranties, and other aspects of the sale contract. This will make it more difficult for unscrupulous vendors to operate, because they will have trouble getting finance companies to take notes off their hands. Today, a dissatisfied consumer has the same rights against any holder of a note if the item purchased is defective or sold under a dishonest scheme.

Canadian Imperial Bank of Commerce v. Lively et al.
Nova Scotia, 1974

The defendant Roberts had sold some chinchillas and related equipment to the defendant Lively. The purchase was financed by a bank loan secured by a promissory note. Roberts arranged the loan through a contact at the bank; the money was paid by the bank directly to Roberts and the bank took the promissory note from Lively. The defendant Lively did not make any money on the business of raising chinchillas and stopped payment on the note. The bank then brought an action against both Lively and Roberts. It was argued for Lively that the note had been given on a consumer purchase and since it was not marked "Consumer Purchase," it was void. The court held that the plaintiff bank could collect upon the note. The purchase of chinchillas and equipment was not a consumer purchase under s. 188 of the *Bills of Exchange Act*. The chinchillas and equipment were bought for use in a business.

The *Lively* case emphasizes that the nature of the transaction is the key point, not the identity of the purchaser. Lively was setting up a business, and the note given to finance that business did not qualify as a consumer note.

The *Combines Investigation Act*

The *Combines Investigation Act* is a fairly comprehensive piece of legislation prohibiting certain unfair practices designed to prevent fair trade and competition in Canada. The Act created the Restrictive Trade Practices Commission to oversee the enforcement of its provisions. As well, there is a Director of Investigation and Research who has the responsibility of looking into any alleged violations.

The main thrust of the Act is to provide penalties for every one who conspires, combines, agrees, or arranges with another person for one of the following purposes:

- To limit facilities for transporting, producing, manufacturing, supplying, storing, or dealing in any product.
- To limit or lessen the production of a product.
- To prevent or lessen competition or injure competition unduly, or to fix prices.

The maximum possible penalty for any of the above actions is imprisonment for five years or a fine of one million dollars, or both.

Atlantic Sugar Refineries Co. Ltd. et al., v. The Attorney General of Canada
Supreme Court of Canada, 1980

Four sugar companies were charged with conspiring to enhance unreasonably the price of sugar in eastern Canada and to prevent, or lessen unduly, competition in the production, sale, and supply of sugar contrary to the *Combines Investigation Act*.

The companies imported sugar, refined it and marketed it in eastern Canada. During World War II, their markets were allocated by the government. After the war, the companies seemed to keep the same percentage of the total market. At various times companies tried to increase their market share by price cutting, but it always failed and each company settled down to a policy of maintaining its market share. The Supreme Court of Canada held that a company does not have to actively try to take business from its competitors. A company may also follow the price changes of its competitors up or down. Such price moves do not establish a conspiracy. The court held that the offence is one that requires mens rea and that the

Crown must show that the accused were trying to lessen competition *unduly,* or at least that there was an agreement the effect of which was to lessen competition unduly. As the Crown could not provide such evidence, all the accused companies were acquitted.

The Act also prohibits misleading advertising, directly or indirectly. Misleading advertising includes giving false claims or warranties about a product or misrepresenting the price at which a product has been sold or is ordinarily sold. False mark-downs, specials, or discounts are illegal and may result in a fine of twenty-five thousand dollars or imprisonment for one year, or both.

 ### R. v. Hoffman-La Roche Ltd. of Canada
Ontario, 1980

The accused corporation was convicted of price fixing contrary to the *Combines Investigation Act.* The accused was the Canadian subsidiary of a large multi-national drug company and over a one-year period had engaged in a policy of giving Valium to hospitals, free of charge, in order to prevent competitors from entering the diazepam market, or to keep them from succeeding in that market. The accused ultimately gave away $2 600 000 of the drug at an actual cost to itself of $900 000. The accused's actions were primarily directed at one other large drug manufacturer. Even though the policy was a financial disaster and was abandoned, the accused was fined $50 000.

Some special provisions of the Act are as follows:

- *Professional sports:* It is unlawful to unfairly restrict the opportunity of a person to play for the team of his or her choice.
- *Testimonials:* It is unlawful for a person to give a false testimonial about the quality of a product.
- *Double ticketing:* If a product has two prices marked on it, it must be sold at the lower of the two prices.
- *Pyramid selling:* Pyramid selling is prohibited unless authorized by provincial legislation. A pyramid scheme is one whereby a person is induced to purchase large quantities of goods on the premise that he or she may establish a selling group of other persons and induce them to make similar bulk purchases.
- *Referral selling:* Referral selling is prohibited unless authorized by provincial legislation. Referral selling is a scheme to enter a sale agreement under the representation that the buyer will receive a discount or commission on sales to other persons whose names are passed on to the seller.
- *Bait and switch selling:* It is unlawful for a person to advertise, at a bargain price, a product he or she does not supply in reasonable quantities having regard for the normal market. (The seller usually tries to switch the consumer to another, higher-priced product.)
- *Sale above advertised price:* No person may sell an item at a price above that advertised.
- *False contests:* It is unlawful to offer promotional contests and prizes without an adequate and fair disclosure of the actual number and value of the prizes that will be awarded.
- *Credit cards:* No credit card company may prohibit retailers from giving discounts to customers who pay cash.
- *Price control:* No manufacturer or supplier can require a retailer to sell a product at a set price. Neither can the manufacturer or supplier cut off supplies of a product because the retailer sells the product at a price below the recommended sale price.

The Act allows any six persons resident in Canada who are not less than eighteen years of age to make written complaint to the Director, and the Director is required to carry out an investigation. As well, if one person makes a written complaint, an investigation may be carried out on the Director's own authority if it is felt that the complaint has merit.

In the case of *R. v. K.C. Irving* (1976), it was held that in order for the accused to be convicted of a merger or monopoly charge, it was necessary to prove "public detriment."

The *Food and Drugs Act*

The origins of the *Food and Drugs Act* can be traced back to England where it was once commonplace for merchants to try to hide deterioration in food by the use of spices and other ingredients. In 1861, the British Parliament passed a law known as the *Act for the Prevention of Adulteration of Articles of Food and Drink.* Prior to the passage of this law, several people had died from eating peppermint that was adulterated with arsenic. A laboratory study of food regularly sold in the market place found arrowroot mixed with starches, chicory mixed with coffee, and plaster of Paris used to hide

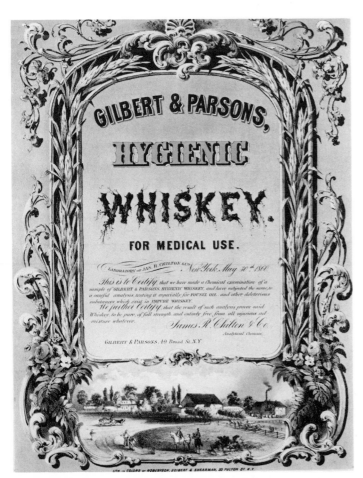

To escape public disapproval of alcohol, some brands of whiskey were sold as medicine. Eventually, all such products were covered by the Food and Drugs Act *or the* Patent Medicine Act.

defects in the pigmentation of numerous foods. Many of the additives were commonly used to disguise tainted meat. Some of the additives were poisonous.

In 1874, the Canadian Parliament passed the *Adulteration Act.* It required that food be clean and safe to eat and that no poisonous additives be used. This law was eventually replaced by the *Food and Drugs Act* of 1920, which remains in effect today.

The *Food and Drugs Act* is largely concerned with the use of drugs which are considered sufficiently dangerous to require restricted use. These drugs are controlled and can only be obtained by prescription. Drugs can only be sold without prescription if they are registered under the *Proprietary and Patent Medicine Act.*

The *Food and Drugs Act* also covers food, household chemicals, cosmetics, medicines and vitamins, and prohibits the advertisement of "cures" for certain diseases including alcoholism, cancer, venereal disease, diabetes, leukemia, and many others. The Act provides that no drugs shall be sold that were prepared in unsanitary conditions. All drugs must be properly labelled under regulations prescribed by the Governor in Council.

Labatt Breweries v. A.G. of Canada
Supreme Court of Canada, 1979

The plaintiff marketed a product called "Labatt's Special Lite" beer. The beer did not qualify as a "light beer" under a grade standard defined in a regulation passed under the *Food and Drugs Act.* Among other things the regulation required that "light beer" have a maximum alcoholic content of 2.5 per cent alcohol. Labatt Special Lite contained 4 per cent alcohol. Although s. 91 (2) of the *B.N.A. Act* [now the *Constitution Act, 1867*] makes the federal government responsible for trade and commerce and s. 91(27) makes the federal government responsible for criminal law, the Supreme Court of Canada held that the compositional standard for beer could not be justified as an exercise of either the trade and commerce power or the criminal law power. The court thus invalidated an important feature of the *Food and Drugs Act* — the power of the

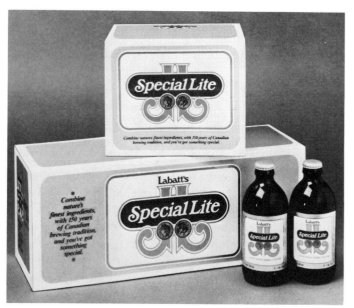

In Labatt Breweries v. A.G. of Canada *the Supreme Court of Canada limited the power of the federal government to establish specific recipes for products.*

federal government to set standards for what may be contained within food.

The decision in the *Labatt* case may bring successful challenges to the powers of the federal government in other areas of legislation including the *Consumer Packaging and Labelling Act* and the *Hazardous Products Act.*

The *Weights and Measures Act*

Section 91 of the *Constitution Act, 1867* specifically grants the Parliament of Canada the power to legislate in the field of weights and measures. This ensures a uniformity of standards all across Canada. The Act permits the inspection of all weighing and measuring devices. It permits inspectors to examine any device used for measurement including coin-operated machines which dispense liquids or measure time, such as parking meters and automatic washers and dryers in laundromats. The Act also prohibits tampering with odometers on used cars in order to show that they have been driven less than is in fact the case.

The Act has been amended to allow for conversion to the metric system in Canada.

The *Hazardous Products Act*

This Act provides standards for the manufacture and labelling of hazardous products in Canada and prohibits the sale of goods brought into Canada which do not meet the required safety standards. Toys have specific standards regarding the use of flammable materials and toxic paints, and must be made in such a way as to prevent a child from choking on or swallowing small detachable parts. Clothing and bedding must meet rigid flammability tests, particularly baby clothing and blankets.

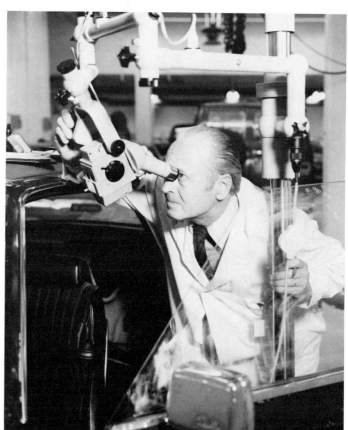

Products manufactured or imported into Canada may be banned if they are hazardous to consumers. Products are regularly checked in government laboratories.

The Act requires that products be marked with a symbol or warning sign indicating that the product is explosive, flammable, corrosive, or poisonous, etc. If special instructions are needed for the safe use of a product, these instructions must be clearly printed on the product.

The *Consumer Packaging and Labelling Act*

The Act protects consumers from misleading packaging, either in size or shape. The package must state the quantity of the product by count, mass, or capacity. If the product makes a claim that it will provide a certain number of servings, it must indicate the mass of each serving.

The *Textile Labelling Act*

Textile manufacturers have developed some extraordinary fabrics in recent years, many of which are termed "miracle fabrics." It has been estimated that over six hundred names have been invented to describe the approximately thirty basic chemical contents. To eliminate some of the confusion and to prevent exaggerated claims being made about fabrics, the *Textile Labelling Act* requires the labelling of clothing, rolls of cloth, and household textiles such as drapes to be made in the generic name of the fibres used. Therefore, nylon must be marked nylon, not Krinklon or some other fictional name. Labels must also indicate, by the use of symbols, how the fabric is to be cleaned and any special treatment required.

The *Post Office Act*

The *Post Office Act* prohibits the sending of unsolicited goods C.O.D. (cash on delivery) to any person resident in Canada. This prohibition was enacted when it was discovered that dishonest sellers had developed a scheme of mailing unsolicited goods C.O.D. to the residence of persons recently deceased. The goods were often vastly overpriced. Relatives of the deceased often paid for the goods believing that the deceased had requested them.

The *Criminal Code of Canada* makes it an offence to use the mail for the purpose of transmitting or delivering letters or circulars concerning schemes devised or intended to deceive or defraud the public.

Reviewing Important Points

1. It is generally recognized that a "consumer" is an individual person rather than a company and that the person is acting in his or her own personal regard rather than engaging in some form of business activity.
2. The *Bills of Exchange Act*, a federal law, requires any promissory note given as part of a consumer purchase to be marked with the words "Consumer Purchase." The buyer has the same rights and remedies against any holder of such a note as he or she had against the original seller.
3. The *Combines Investigation Act* makes such practices as false advertising and price fixing illegal.
4. Under the *Food and Drugs Act*, the federal government may restrict the sale of drugs.
5. Federal law prohibits sending unsolicited goods C.O.D. by mail.

Checking Your Understanding

1. Identify three reasons why there has been an increased need for consumer protection legislation.
2. What is a "consumer sale" or "consumer purchase"?
3. What unfair practice was the 1970 amendment to the *Bills of Exchange Act* (regarding promissory notes) intended to eliminate?
4. What does it mean to say that a violation of the *Combines Investigation Act* (conspiring to lessen competition) is a mens rea offence?
5. What is bait and switch selling? What is referral selling?

Legal Briefs

1. The R Company offers a contest saying all who make a purchase are eligible to win a free trip to Europe. No winner is chosen. The company states that an insufficient number of people entered. Has R committed an offence?

2. K, a retailer, advertises a *camera* at a very low price. The price does not include a lens which must be purchased extra at a very high price. False advertising?

3. L, a retailer, displayed a new shotgun beneath a sign reading, "Sale — $179   Regular Price — $299." The store was told by the manufacturer that similar shotguns of comparable value, made by other companies, have sold for $299. False advertising?

4. S is a very large grocery chain. In certain communities it lowers all prices severely every time a competing store is opened in that community and keeps its prices low until the other store goes out of business. Prices are then raised again. Legal activity?

5. P, an actor, does a television commercial stating that his daughters use a certain cosmetic for skin problems. In actuality, they have rarely used it because they seldom have skin problems and when they do they use several different products. Has P committed an offence?

6. C, a food company, prepares a television commercial for a vegetable soup, called "Chunky." Feeling that the camera does not do justice to the soup, the director puts clear, glass marbles in the soup bowl. When the soup is ladled into the bowl, the chunks stay at the top while the broth goes to the bottom making the soup appear less watery. However, nothing is added to the soup. False advertising?

7. F advertises that its product, a fabric softener used in the washing machine, softens "three times more than any dryer product." F has never conducted any specific tests to prove its claim but has hired an independent test firm who reported that F was "superior by a wide margin." False advertising?

8. G purchases a truck which she uses on her farm and also for personal use. She estimates that the vehicle is used about 50 per cent of the time for farming and 50 per cent of the time for personal use. G signs a promissory note when she buys the truck. Should it be marked "Consumer Purchase"?

9. B sells a device to be added to the carburetor of automobiles and claims it will improve fuel efficiency. B has no personal knowledge that the device works but has a booklet from the manufacturer claiming that field and laboratory tests show that greater efficiency was achieved by using the device. False advertising?

10. H and T signed a promissory note for the purchase of a new car. The note was marked "Consumer Purchase." T disappeared with the car leaving H liable on the note. H found the terms of payment too difficult so she negotiated smaller payments over a longer period of time. A new note was drawn up to replace the old note but was not marked "Consumer Purchase." Later, H sought to avoid liability under the note. Can she do so?

Applying the Law

R. v. Colgate Palmolive Ltd.
Ontario, 1969

Colgate Palmolive was charged with unlawfully making a materially misleading representation by advertising a bottle of Halo Shampoo as "Special $1.49" contrary to the *Combines Investigation Act*. A magistrate dismissed the charge and the Crown appealed. The bottle in question was 13 $\frac{1}{8}$ ounces (365 mL). The label contained no mention of any regular price. Prices for the same bottle ranged from $0.99 to $1.49 in various stores but nowhere was it sold for more than $1.49. Thus, in the Crown's argument, there was nothing special about the price at all.

The company defended the action on a different line. The company already marketed three smaller sizes of the same shampoo. The 13 $\frac{1}{8}$ ounce bottle (365 mL) bottle was the largest bottle now made and in comparison with the other bottles should have sold for much more. However, because they wanted the product to be well-received by the public, the company was selling it for less than they really should have — hence the "special" price label. A judge of the Court of Appeal said:

> **1.** Would a reasonable shopper draw the conclusion from the diagonal red band with the words and numbers 'Special $1.49' that he was being offered Economy Size Halo Shampoo at a price below that which that size bottle is ordinarily sold?
>
> 2. If the answer is 'Yes' would such a representation be true?
>
> Upon a review of all the evidence before me, I have no difficulty in answering the two questions posed. My answers are:
>
> 1. A reasonable shopper upon reading the words and numbers 'Special $1.49' might very well conclude that he was being offered Economy Size Halo Shampoo at a price below which it is ordinarily sold.
>
> 2. Such a representation would not be true.
>
> I must accordingly allow the appeal and convict the respondent of the offence charged.**

Questions

1. Did the label imply that the product was "regularly sold" at a higher price?
2. Why did the company believe that its label was not misleading even though the product had never been sold for more than $1.49 by anyone? Was it significant that the advertisement did not state that there was a "regular price"?
3. As a consumer, what meaning would you put upon the word "special" when referring to a price?
4. Was the case rightly decided? Why or why not?

 ### R. v. World Book Childcraft of Canada, Ltd.
Newfoundland, 1981

The Crown appealed the acquittal of the accused encyclopedia company on a charge of participating in a referral selling scheme contrary to s. 36.4 (2) of the *Combines Investigation Act*. A representative of the company told a school principal that if letters were sent home to the parents of the pupils, the company would give the school a free encyclopedia. In addition, the company would credit the school with a $3 certificate for each parent who agreed to a sales visit and $15 for every purchase made by a parent acting upon the letter. The District Court dismissed the appeal. The court held that there was not proof beyond a reasonable doubt that there had been a "sale" of an encyclopedia to the school.

Questions

1. Why was the company not guilty of the offence?
2. What is referral selling?
3. If a salesperson offers to make a "free" gift to person A if A recommends other persons to the salesperson, is this not referral selling?
4. Do you think the case was rightly decided? Why or why not?

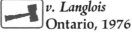 ### Canadian Imperial Bank of Commerce
v. Langlois
Ontario, 1976

The defendants agreed to purchase from a company a mobile home in which they intended to live. A sales employee of the company took them to the plaintiff bank with a view to their obtaining a loan with which to pay the greater portion of the purchase price of the home. The bank's loan officer was made aware of the purpose for which the loan was required and approved the defendant's application for the loan. A cheque for $13 000 was made payable to the company. One defendant signed a promissory note in that amount and the other defendant signed as guarantor. The cheque was handed to the company sales employee. The cheque was negotiated at once. However, before the defendants could complete the purchase, the company went out of business and the defendants did not get the mobile home. The promissory note was not marked with the words "Consumer Purchase" on the face as required by the *Bills of Exchange Act*. The bank brought an action against the defendants for the amount of the loan together with interest, but the claim was dismissed. The court held that the omission of the words "Consumer Purchase" on the note rendered it void. The note was issued in respect of a consumer purchase and accordingly it was void since it was a consumer note as defined by the Act. The fact that the bank did not negotiate the note to a third party did not affect its validity.

Questions

1. What is the purpose of marking a note with the words "Consumer Purchase"?
2. Is a mobile home something that would fit into the definition of a *consumer* purchase?
3. Why did the court not require the defendants to pay the note?
4. Did the bank handle this transaction in the best way possible? Can you suggest a better way?

You Be the Judge

1. Two corporations each operated a newspaper in two different cities. Each closed up one of its newspapers, and thereby each obtained a monopoly in one city. This eliminated any competition between the two newspaper corporations for such things as advertising rates and subscriptions. The corporations explained this action as cost cutting and stated that the cities involved could not support two daily newspapers. They were charged with a violation of the *Combines Act* for conspiring to lessen trade. Who would succeed?

2. A manufacturer of a snack food packaged its product by mass and correctly labelled the box with the mass contained. However, the box was 25 per cent larger than it needed to be to hold the mass it contained. This produced an air space at the top of the box. The company argued that it did not change box sizes when converting to metric and that much of the air space was caused by "settling." The government charged the company with false packaging on the grounds that the consumer would think there was more in the box because of its size. Who would succeed?

3. A corporation sold a container of toothpaste. The package displayed the words, "Free — Three Felt Pens." Details inside the container stated that the consumer must purchase two tubes of toothpaste and mail the box ends to obtain the pens. When charged with false advertising, the corporation argued that the words on the container did not comprise the total offer which was accurately stated inside. The government argued that the words suggested that by the purchase of one container the consumer would obtain three pens. Who would succeed?

4. The accused store was charged with violation of the *Consumer Packaging and Labelling Act.* It sold packages labelled "beef sirloin" and "sirloin tip" which did not contain these cuts. The accused claimed that the false labelling was the result of an honest mistake of the labeller who was a new employee. The company demonstrated that it had a good employee training program and used due diligence in attempting to avoid such mistakes. The Crown argued that any violation was grounds for conviction and that the defence of "due diligence" did not apply. Who would succeed?

5. The accused corporation was charged with having made a misleading and deceptive advertisement as to the price of multiple vitamins. The advertisement in the catalogue read in part: "1¢ SALE. 1¢ buys you a second bottle of the same product." It also read: "1 bottle, $3.89, 2/$3.90" followed by "100-tablet bottle, $3.89, 2/$3.90." There was evidence that the accused offered for sale the same tablets in one of its current catalogues at a price of $3.79 for 250 tablets. The store contended that it was in the process of changing bottle sizes and that its ad was not misleading. The consumer could purchase exactly what the ad offered or the consumer could purchase the larger bottle if preferred. The fact that the larger bottle might provide more value did not make the ad false. Who would succeed?

Chapter 21

Provincial Laws To Protect Consumers

Consumer Protection Legislation

The provincial governments have been very active in the field of consumer legislation. The first area of legislation involved the charging of unfairly high interest rates on loans. Almost all the provinces passed statutes entitled the *Unconscionable Transactions Relief Act* which permitted a court to set aside a contract where the debtor was charged a rate of interest that was harsh and unconscionable.

The second area of provincial activity came in the form of laws aimed at stopping dishonest sales methods and misleading advertising. The extent of this legislation is too broad to be explained in total. For complete information, the reader would have to obtain information from the various provincial government agencies responsible for supervising consumer legislation.

Disclosure of Terms and Conditions

One of the concerns to which the provincial legislatures responded was the failure on the part of the seller or creditor to tell the buyer or debtor all the facts. There was a need for more "Truth in Lending" and "Truth in Selling." Most provinces now require a minimal amount of information to be clearly explained in writing. Typical is Ontario's *Consumer Protection Act* which requires every executory contract to be in writing and to state:

(1) The name and address of the seller and the buyer;
(2) A description of the goods or services sufficient to identify them with certainty;

(3) The itemized price of the goods or services and a detailed statement of the terms of payment;
(4) Where credit is extended, a statement disclosing the true cost of borrowing;
(5) Any warranty or guarantee applying to the goods, and where there is no warranty or guarantee, a statement to this effect.

The Ontario Act requires a full disclosure of how costs and interest are calculated. The Act specifies that every lender must furnish to the borrower, before giving the credit, a clear statement in writing showing:

- The sum, (1) expressed as one sum in dollars and cents, actually received in cash by the borrower, plus insurance and/or official fees, if any, actually paid by the lender, or (2) where the lender is a seller, being the amount of the cash price of the goods or services, including any insurance or official fees;
- Where the lender is a seller, the sums, if any, actually paid as a down payment or credited in respect of a trade-in, or paid or credited for any reason;
- The cost of borrowing expressed as one sum in dollars and cents;
- The percentage that the cost of borrowing bears to the sum borrowed;
- The amount, if any, charged for insurance;
- The amount, if any, charged for official fees;
- The basis upon which additional charges are to be made in the event of default.

An executory contract is not binding on the buyer unless the contract is signed by the parties and a duplicate original copy is in the possession of each of the parties.

The Ontario Act requires a contract to be complete and to state all the terms and conditions. Previous records show that a buyer was often given a contract only partially completed and that the seller later filled in certain terms, such as interest, which the buyer knew nothing about. Often the seller didn't give a copy of the contract to the buyer, but now it is obligatory to do so.

The *Consumer Protection Act* of Newfoundland is very similar to the Ontario statute. In addition the Newfoundland Act requires that a lender offering variable credit must give the borrower a statement every five weeks. Any lender who places an advertisement for credit must disclose in the advertisement the true annual interest rate.

Schofield Manuel Ltd. v. Rose et al.
Ontario, 1975

The defendant contracted with the plaintiff for the supply of interior decorating services. The contract did not comply with the *Consumer Protection Act* in that it was not signed by the plaintiff and did not contain a warranty or a statement that no warranty was given. The goods were delivered and the services performed. The defendant had made several payments on account, then defaulted. The plaintiff sued for the balance owing. The defendant claimed that since the contract did not comply with the Act, there was no obligation to complete payment. The plaintiff was successful. Although the original contract was not in compliance with the Act, the performance of the contract by the plaintiff acted to execute it and removed it from the requirements of the statute as it was no longer an "executory" contract. The contract was then binding on both parties.

Exempt Transactions

Consumer protection laws do not apply to all contracts. Real estate transactions are exempt as are business-to-business transactions. Manitoba, New Brunswick, Newfoundland, and Saskatchewan generally exclude any transaction relating to farm implements and services to agriculture. Some provinces exclude motor vehicles. There may be a monetary limit as well. For example, Ontario sets a minimum of $50; Alberta, $25.

Right To Rescind

The popularity of door-to-door selling has caused the provinces to effect "cooling-off" periods. The buyer may rescind a contract not signed in the seller's permanent place of business by delivering a notice of rescission in writing to the seller.

The cooling-off period varies from province to province. Ontario and Manitoba have the shortest period—only two days. Alberta and Saskatchewan permit four days. In British Columbia and Prince Edward Island it is seven days. New Brunswick allows five days, while Nova Scotia, Quebec, and Newfoundland have the longest time period—ten days.

Some provinces also allow the consumer to rescind the contract if it is not completed within a certain time period. Alberta law, for example, permits cancellation "not later than one year after the date on which the copy of the sales contract was received by him [or her] if all the goods and services are not provided within one hundred and twenty days after the date the sales contract was signed by the buyer and no date for delivery or performance was set."

Several provinces require that the right to rescind be clearly explained on the contract form itself. This requirement is presently found in British Columbia, Alberta, Manitoba, New Brunswick, Nova Scotia, and Saskatchewan.

The *Consumer Products Warranties Act* of Saskatchewan

Saskatchewan has enacted new and tougher standards for the sale of manufactured goods. The law allows consumers to have goods repaired without cost, or even returned for a refund, if either the seller or the manufacturer is found to have breached the warranty standards set out in the Act. It does not matter whether the complaint is excluded from the merchant's guarantee or other sales agreement, or whether the guarantee has expired.

The Act establishes a contract at the point of sale between the consumer and the manufacturer as well as with the vendor/retailer. Consumers may take action if a product or any of its parts are not "durable for a reasonable period of time."

Similar legislation has been passed in New Brunswick and Quebec.

The Ontario *Business Practices Act*

One of the most extensive pieces of consumer legislation was passed in Ontario in 1975. The *Business Practices Act* has basically two functions: (1) It identifies business practices that are deemed unfair and are thereby prohibited; and (2) it establishes special defences for consumers who enter into contracts unwisely because of their own physical or mental inabilities or lack of understanding of the contract. There are more than twenty unfair practices identified, including (to name just a few):

- To misrepresent that goods have characteristics, ingredients, or capabilities they do not have;
- To misrepresent that used goods are new when they are not;
- To misrepresent that service and parts are available when they are not;
- To misrepresent by exaggeration, innuendo, or ambiguity as to a material fact or failing to state a material fact if such tends to deceive.

The statute also affords protection to consumers who:
- Were unable to understand the contract for such reasons as ignorance, infirmity, or illiteracy;
- Were grossly overcharged;
- Did not receive a "substantial benefit" from the sub-

ject matter of the contract, or where the contract was so adverse to the consumer as to be inequitable.

Consumers who wish to assert their rights under the Act and revoke their contracts must do so within six months after the agreements are entered into. The statute further provides for a maximum fine of $2000 or imprisonment for not more than one year, or both, in the case of an individual engaging in an unfair practice. The maximum fine for a corporation is $25 000.

It would take too much time to analyse in detail every provision of the *Business Practices Act*. Yet, here is a statute that tries to strike aside nearly every defence raised to defeat a consumer's complaint, including "caveat emptor," "salesperson's puffing," "parol evidence rule," "disclaimer clauses," and others. This is a complete turnabout from centuries of law which held that a bargain is a bargain. The consumer can rescind a contract for a great many reasons, including personal ignorance. Whether the consumer needs such extensive protection will be evidenced by the cases that arise under the provisions of the statute.

The Newfoundland *Trade Practices Act,* passed in 1978, while not identical to the Ontario law, is very similar in nature and form. It also contains a list of unfair and unconscionable trade practices.

The *Unfair Trade Practices Act* of Alberta

This statute is intended to prevent unfair business practices and to aid consumers in recovering losses caused by such practices. The goods covered by the Act are those used primarily by an individual or a family, but do not include real estate.

The Act deals with four types of consumer services. Included are services provided to maintain or repair goods; services provided to an individual involving the use of social, recreational, or physical fitness facilities; moving, hauling, and storage services; and certain kinds of educational services.

Three major transactions are identified by the Act as being so objectionable that a court may declare the entire transaction unfair and award damages for loss. The first is the subjection of the consumer to undue pressure by the supplier to enter into the contract. The second is the inability of a consumer to understand the nature of the transaction and the fact that the supplier took advantage of the consumer's inability to understand. The third is the existence of a major defect in the goods, resulting in the consumer's not getting value for his or her money. If the supplier knows about this defect and also knows that the consumer does not know about it, then the transaction is unfair.

The Act contains a list of twenty-one unfair practices that may mislead or deceive the consumer. The Act permits cancellation of any contract that was signed as a result of any unfair practice being employed by the supplier.

Credit Bureaus

The popularity of credit has brought about a need for some sort of information centre that keeps track of users and abusers of credit. In order to provide a merchant or lending institution with a rating for a prospective credit customer, credit bureaus have sprung up all over Canada and the United States. These private companies keep a file on every individual in the community who has ever borrowed money in any form. Stores and lending institutions have a membership with the credit bureau for which they pay an annual fee. They also pay a small fee for each referral they make to the bureau. The credit bureau gives an interested member a credit rating for an individual. The bureau does not make the decision to grant credit, but only recommends what should be done by way of the rating it assigns to an individual.

Problems encountered by consumers with inaccurate and damaging reports compiled upon them compelled all provinces to pass some sort of legislation regulating this industry. The statutes vary from province to province, but most are very similar to the Ontario *Consumer Reporting Act* which contains the following basic provisions:

- All reporting agencies must make a reasonable effort to corroborate unfavourable personal information in their reports.
- Reporting agencies are restricted as to whom they may give access to information.
- In the case of bankruptcy, no information more than seven years older than the date of bankruptcy may be included in the report. However, if the person was bankrupt more than once, there are no restrictions upon how far back the information may go.
- No information as to race, creed, colour, sex, ancestry, ethnic origins, or political affiliation may be included.
- Any person knowingly supplying false information in the preparation of consumer reports is liable to prosecution.
- Consumer reporting agencies cannot use any information that is not stored in Canada. (At one time, most of the information about Canadian consumers was kept in a computer in Texas.)
- Every consumer has the right to see his or her own file and can insist that the file be corrected if there are any inaccuracies.

Married women are one group that have had continual problems in the area of credit reporting and they have often found it difficult to obtain credit. Often a married woman is told that she cannot obtain credit unless her husband guarantees her debts. This requirement is often put forward despite provincial laws that state that a married woman can contract in her own name. Several provinces, including Ontario and British Columbia, have developed "guidelines" for lenders which prohibit discrimination against married women. Although these guidelines do not have the force of law, most major lending institutions have entered into programs with the government to follow the guidelines. One of the important aspects of the guidelines is that a married woman is not to have her credit rating lowered because of the poor credit rating of her husband. This is particularly offensive to a woman separated or divorced from her husband.

Ontario and Nova Scotia law prohibits reporting information on criminal convictions that occurred more than seven years previously. In Saskatchewan, a job candidate is not protected from details about a personal bankruptcy being given to an employer for fourteen years.

In Ontario, British Columbia, Manitoba, and Prince Edward Island, communicating what is termed adverse information about a job applicant is a violation of the law if information goes back more than seven years. This would include such things as whether the applicant was recently divorced, had a drinking problem, or other personal matters.

There is no credit reporting legislation in Alberta. A person has no statutory right to see, obtain, or change a credit record. Credit bureaus do welcome proof that an item on file is incorrect, but are under no obligation to change any records.

Collection Agencies

Collection agencies are essentially debt collectors. They do not lend money and therefore do not obtain notes. A person who is owed money and is unable to collect it, may engage the services of an agency. Where court action is taken by a collection agency on the creditor's behalf, it is usually the debtor who pays most of the costs in the long run.

Collection agencies have various methods of collecting the money owed, usually involving a combination of letters, phone calls, and personal visits. The agency cannot take the matter to court without the creditor's consent, but if this is given the agency may file suit.

The methods used by a collection agency cannot be threatening and above all cannot suggest *criminal* action should the debtor refuse to pay. Collection agencies cannot send letters containing excerpts from the *Criminal Code* as a way of intimidating debtors. Nor can the agency use letterheads or seals to make the letter appear to be a court document.

Newfoundland, Nova Scotia, Saskatchewan, Quebec, and British Columbia have the strongest legislation regarding collection agencies. The other provinces have statutes worded very generally and rely upon government pressure to stop unacceptable collection tactics.

Some Special Features of Provincial Legislation

Substituted Actions

One of the problems a consumer often has is that the consumer does not have the money to engage a large corporation in a lawsuit.

Both Alberta and British Columbia have enacted legislation that permits the provincial government or one of its agencies to enter into the lawsuit directly and substitute itself for the consumer. This is called a *substituted action*. Thus, the power of the government can be brought into the legal battle against a powerful corporation or financial institution engaged in a legal dispute with a consumer. The government normally intervenes only when the matter is of interest to many consumers and where the government believes the corporation has not attempted to resolve the matter fairly.

Voluntary Compliance

Most provinces permit a supplier to enter into an Agreement of Voluntary Compliance. This agreement is a contract between the enforcement authority and the supplier by which the latter promises to refrain from engaging in deceptive or unfair conduct and often to reimburse some consumers. In return, the government agrees to withdraw any court proceedings that may have commenced and to let the supplier's business continue.

Some examples under the Ontario legislation include:

- A company was to stop telling trainees that graduates of a nursing school the company operated had the same qualifications as registered nurses.
- An inventor was to stop advertising that a device he sold could save consumers 25 per cent on heating bills. Lab tests found no change in furnace efficiency with the device.
- A language school agreed to stop telling students that it had the approval of the Minister of Education.
- A company was to stop advertising that it sold

vegetable seeds which produced giant vegetables such as tomatoes which weighed 20 kg.

Class Actions

The *Rules of Practice* of all provinces appear to permit class action suits, but in many provinces it is very difficult to bring a successful class action. A class action brings together the claims of a number of persons, against the same defendant, arising from a common complaint. The action can be brought by a group of people, or by one plaintiff who asks to be allowed to bring the action on behalf of all other persons having the same complaint. If the latter occurs, the other class members are not strictly parties and cannot be ordered to pay the costs.

A class action can have some advantages: (1) A class action eliminates the possibility that different courts will reach opposite decisions on the same question of fact; and (2) by joining together, the class can afford the costly process of suing the defendant.

There is a major disadvantage of a class action. If the class action is ineptly handled, it will prevent any other persons from suing on their own behalf. There is no requirement that all members of the class be notified that the action has been brought on their behalf. While they cannot be made liable for the costs, these individuals may have been prevented from carrying out their own actions. There is a danger that one class action will prejudice many class members who might have been successful in suing the defendant themselves. There is a potential danger that a defendant faced with court action might pay one potential plaintiff to start a class action and to deliberately mishandle and lose the case. This would wipe out all possible future claims from other plaintiffs. For this reason and for others, courts are very strict about whether or not they will recognize that certain individuals constitute a "class."

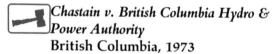

Naken v. General Motors
Ontario, 1978

The plaintiffs tried to form a class action alleging that each of them had purchased a Firenza automobile which was warranted by G.M. to be durable, reliable, and fit for use. Each alleged that the cars sold were not of merchantable quality and that the resale value was $1000 less than the resale value of comparable cars sold by other manufacturers. There were 4600 persons in the class. The Ontario Court of Appeal held that the plaintiffs were not a proper "class." Some of the purchasers had relied upon brochures printed by G.M. while others did not read the brochures. Some of the purchasers had been given oral sales talks by dealers while others had already decided that they wanted to buy a Firenza without any sales talk. Each dealer charged a different price. The cars did not have the same options. Thus, the court took the view that the purchasers all had complaints against the defendant, but they were not identical complaints, only similar:

> **"**The damages claimed on behalf of the class were personal to each purchaser, and plaintiffs could not, by simply lumping the individual claims together, transform them into a claim for damages suffered by the class as an entity distinct from its members.**"**

The British Columbia *Trade Practices Act* is unique in that it specifically allows a class action to be brought on behalf of consumers in the province. Thus, the obstacles that normally prevent a class action from being started have been mostly overcome in that province.

Chastain v. British Columbia Hydro & Power Authority
British Columbia, 1973

The plaintiff sued the Power Authority for return of a "security deposit" the Authority had collected from him when he first applied for service. The plaintiff argued that the Authority discriminated by demanding deposits only from persons who were considered poor credit risks. The plaintiff asked to be allowed to bring together as a class the 23 624 consumers who had paid security deposits. The Authority objected to this being made a class action, but the court ruled that the class was comprised of "a group having the same interest in the cause." The action was successful and the deposits were returned.

Unsolicited Goods

If a consumer receives goods in the mail or by delivery that the consumer did not order, the law often permits the consumer to keep or dispose of the goods as desired. In Ontario, if you receive goods you have not ordered you are under no legal obligation or responsibility for their use, misuse, loss, or theft unless you know that they were intended for some other party. The consumer must not withhold them from the correct party.

Similar wording is contained in the Newfoundland *Unsolicited Goods and Credit Card Act* which provides that "an action shall not be brought by which to charge any person for payment in respect of unsolicited goods, notwithstanding their use, misuse, loss, damage or theft."

In Alberta, unsolicited goods are not a gift unless circumstances clearly indicate that a gift was intended by the sender. An example would be something marked, "Free Sample." If the goods have been delivered, the consumer does not have to pay the cost of sending them back, but the goods should not be used as usage may indicate acceptance. The sender should be notified to pick up the goods.

Credit Cards

The use of a credit card comes under the general law of contracts. When a person applies for a credit card, that person fills out an application form agreeing to be liable according to the terms of the agreement which will accompany the card.

If the card is issued by the credit card company, the terms of the contract provide that the card remains the property of the company. The privilege of using the card can be withdrawn at any time. The consumer agrees not to charge more than a certain amount with the card. This is referred to as the *credit limit*. The card

company accepts no responsibility for the quality of the goods bought under the card system. The agreement is essentially an agreement by the cardholder to make payments to the credit card company rather than to each merchant. It does not cover any agreement between the cardholder and the merchant from whom the goods are purchased. The credit card company is specifically excluded from any such transaction. The sales contract between the cardholder and the merchant remains their exclusive agreement. The burden is on the consumer to make all purchases wisely, for payment cannot be withheld from the card company as a means of putting pressure on the merchant. This is true even if the credit card was obtained through the merchant in the first place. Thus, the protection provided under the *Bills of Exchange Act* for "Consumer Purchases" has no effect upon a purchase made with a credit card. There is no method of "stopping payment" as can be done with a cheque.

When the first bank credit cards were issued by a group of four Canadian chartered banks, there was considerable criticism voiced regarding the method used to issue the cards. In many cities, the cards were mailed at random to people whose names were selected from the telephone directory and business directories. Many people used the cards thinking they were not going to be liable for the debts they incurred. Other people complained that the cards had never been delivered to them, but that somehow these cards had been used by unknown persons to run up bills in their names. To prevent a recurrence of this type of distribution of credit cards, the provinces passed legislation of two varying types. Most provinces made it a law that a person accepts no liability for the issue of any credit card which was not solicited or requested. If the card is lost or misused, the card company must bear the loss. However, if the person who receives the card uses it, this is deemed to be a valid acceptance of the card and that person must pay for what is charged. This is the law in Newfoundland, Ontario, and Alberta.

It is illegal for any company to mail out an unrequested card in Quebec, Prince Edward Island, New

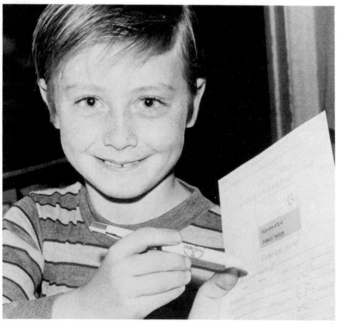

Problems with unsolicited credit cards (in this example, one mailed to a nine-year-old) have caused some provinces to prohibit the issuance of an unrequested card.

Brunswick, Manitoba, and Alberta. Perhaps the most effective law is found in British Columbia and Saskatchewan. In those two provinces, a person receiving an unsolicited credit card may use it and not have to pay for the debts charged.

Any person receiving an unsolicited card should destroy it. It would be wise to have someone witness this destruction. A letter should then be sent to the card company advising them that the card was destroyed. The card should not be mailed back since this only increases the possibility that some unauthorized person will obtain possession of it.

If a credit card is lost, most companies limit the liability of the cardholder to $50 from unauthorized use if the loss is reported promptly. The liability is stated in the contract with the card company and this should be clearly understood before accepting the card. If the loss is not reported promptly, liability may extend beyond the contractual amount. In Manitoba and Alberta, the liability of the cardholder is limited by law to $50 if loss is reported promptly.

Reviewing Important Points

1. Under the *Unconscionable Transactions Relief Act*, the court may order interest on a loan reduced if it is too high.

2. All provinces require truth in lending which means the full details of a contract for credit must be disclosed to the consumer.

3. Consumer protection laws do not apply to all contracts. Normally excluded are contracts involving real estate, and contracts for very small sums of money.

4. In Ontario, the major provisions of the *Consumer Protection Act* apply only to executory contracts and not to contracts that have been fully completed.

5. All provinces have a cooling-off period which permits the buyer to cancel a contract signed in a place other than the seller's permanent place of business.

6. Provincial legislation in many provinces identifies unfair business or trade practices and permits cancellation of a contract if such practices are used.

7. Credit reporting agencies must make a reasonable effort to verify the truthfulness of records and to allow a consumer to challenge inaccuracies.

8. A collection agency cannot use or threaten the use of criminal action to collect a debt.

9. A class action suit tries to bring together a number of plaintiffs with an identical complaint against the defendant.

10. A person who receives an unsolicited credit card should not use the card since this may imply acceptance and liability (British Columbia and Saskatchewan excepted).

Checking Your Understanding

1. If a consumer buys something on credit, what details must the contract state regarding the sum of money borrowed?

2. If a consumer buys something on credit, what details must the contract state regarding the interest rate charged?

3. In your province, how many days are provided as a cooling-off period?

4. Does a cooling-off period apply to every contract? Why or why not?

5. What does a credit bureau do? What difficulty have married women often had with credit bureaus?

6. What is a substituted action? In which provinces is a substituted action permitted?

7. What is the major difficulty encountered by persons who are considering a class action suit against one defendant?

Legal Briefs

1. A product bears a label that reads "Government Inspected." It is inspected by the government where the product is manufactured, but not by the Canadian government. False labelling?

2. A car manufacturer advertises that a new model gets 20 km/L on the highway. This claim is based on tests done in a U.S. Government test centre and not on any actual highway. False advertising?

3. A company claims its service personnel are "factory trained." The factory is in Japan. The personnel are trained in Toronto using factory assembly manuals. Are the personnel "factory trained"?

4. An oil company offers "free furnace cleaning and efficiency testing" to customers who sign a contract to buy all their oil from that company. The oil costs 2¢ more per litre than if purchased from the same company without a contract. False advertising?

5. A freezer company states that the consumer can save up to 30 per cent a month on food bills by joining a freezer club. The consumer rents a freezer from the club and must then buy $200 worth of food each month. It is shown that, if the consumer shops only the weekly specials readily available in regular stores, the freezer club food is no cheaper. False advertising?

6. A local store offers an extraordinary sale on television sets. When H arrives, the salesperson advises her that twenty sets were available and that all were sold within two hours. She then suggests that a more expensive set, of higher quality, also on sale, is a better buy. Legal sales technique?

7. K has a decorator come to her home with samples of carpets and drapes. The next day she goes to the decorator's store and signs a contract for carpet and drapes. Later, a friend advises K that she paid too much since another store will sell the same goods for less. K writes to the store saying that she is cancelling the contract. Avoidable contract?

8. When B applies for a job, she signs a form stating that the company may do a credit check. Although B is very qualified for the job, she does not get it. She suspects that the credit report contains something unfavourable concerning her husband who has a very bad credit rating. She is now separated from her husband. Advise B.

9. L purchases a stereo for $779.50. It is advertised as "40 per cent off Regular Price." L later learns that the stereo sold two months prior to her purchase at a price of $1099. L determines that this is not a 40 per cent reduction and complains to the store. The store manager counters that there is a new price list in effect, as of the day the sale started, listing the set at $1299. This price will continue in effect after the sale. Advise L.

10. M, a salesperson, demonstrates "The Watchdog" a fire and smoke detector and alarm, to K, an elderly pensioner. K already has a good system in his home but M insists that the device K has cannot detect smoke early enough. K purchases "The Watchdog" under a conditional sales contract. An independent report published in a magazine states that "The Watchdog" is only slightly superior to the system K already has. K seeks to cancel the contract. May he do so?

Applying the Law

McFarlane v. Electro-Rent, Ltd.
Newfoundland, 1975

McFarlane responded to a newspaper advertisement that offered a rental of a colour television set with the rental payments being credited to eventual purchase of the set. The set was brought to her home and she signed a statement that she received it. She also signed an agreement to pay $30 a month. One week later, she received a booklet in the mail which gave more details about the agreement. The monthly payment was $30 as advertised and it was rental only. However, the payment paid for more than just the set. A three-year service contract was included, which covered parts and labour. When she called the store, the manager confirmed that the monthly payments did include a service contract. He referred her to the newspaper ad which read: "All service, parts and labour included." The manager explained that the store had to protect the set from misuse. He also mentioned that customers liked one easy payment and if the set broke it was fixed at no extra cost. When McFarlane realized that she would pay nearly $1000 in three years for a set worth $600 she sought to cancel the contract. The store refused and she brought an action for cancellation. The store argued that the contract was a contract for *renting* the set, not buying it on time, and thus the contract did not have to disclose all the facts and figures that would be required if she was buying it. She only had the option to buy. Counsel for McFarlane argued that the contract was a credit agreement and that the consumer had the right under provincial law to be presented with all the facts and figures. The contract was also signed in McFarlane's home and she had indicated by telephone her displeasure within the cooling-off period. The court held that the contract was basically a contract of sale and that the store's failure to disclose the true cost of the set, along with all pertinent details such as an included service contract, was a failure to disclose the terms of the contract as required by provincial law. The contract was declared a nullity.

Questions

1. Do rental agreements come under most provincial laws dealing with consumer protection?
2. In this case, why did the court hold that McFarlane could cancel the contract?
3. Was it important to the case that McFarlane was renting the set but had an option to buy? Why or why not?

4. Do you agree with the decision in this case? Give a reason for your answer.

Home-Guard v. Davies
Nova Scotia, 1976

A salesperson, representing the Home-Guard Company, gave a demonstration to the Davies about their security system. The Davies were elderly, both in their late seventies, and were very concerned about a fire in their home as they feared they might not be awakened by most systems as both wore hearing aids. The saleperson showed them a complex system that combined smoke and heat detectors, alarms that involved both sound and flashing lights, and a sprinkler system that could be installed in the basement only. For reasons which were not made clear, the system also included an intercom system that would have a speaker in every room. The company later explained that intercoms were valuable in contacting other persons in a home when one person discovered a fire.

The salesperson did not accurately give the total price of the system but discussed the price of each unit separately. It was confusing as to whether the prices cited included the intercom. He filled out a form and presented it to the husband to read. Davies had poor vision and could not read small print, so he gave it to his wife. She read it for a while but did not say anything. Finally, she commented, "Well, what do you think"? Davies sort of shrugged. Both signed the contract without ever fully reading it.

The system was installed the next week. It took three days and there was some damage to the walls done by drilling to pull wires through the walls. Some wires were left visible because there was no way to get them between the walls. The wife was very unhappy about so many wires being visible, stapled to the walls and baseboards. The company presented its bill for $2800 which the Davies said was far higher than what the salesperson told them it would be. The company put a lien on their house and the Davies sought to have the lien removed. A court removed the lien as it was not properly filed. The company sued.

Evidence showed that the system was unique and not sold by any other company in the area. Therefore, the price could not be easily compared to that offered by other companies. The system worked well.

The court held that the Davies would have to pay for the system. There had been no misrepresentation as to what the system would encompass. If the couple were confused about the total price, they could have easily asked for a clarification before agreeing. They were not grossly over-charged since the unit appeared to represent reasonable value for the money. As to the problem of installation and exposed wires, it appeared that there was no choice and that the company used due diligence in its method of installation.

Questions

1. When dealing with elderly consumers, how should a company representative conduct negotiations to ensure that there will be no later disagreement?

2. Why did the court hold that the Davies must pay the full price?

3. Was it important to the case that the couple never fully read the contract that they signed? Why or why not?

4. Do you think the case was rightly decided? Give a reason for your answer.

You Be the Judge

1. A vacuum cleaner salesperson sold a machine to a consumer for $399. The consumer paid cash for the machine. It was a deluxe machine, very high quality, with numerous attachments. The price was explained to the consumer as the "factory price." The consumer later learned that stores had the same machine for $249. She brought an action to rescind. The company defended the action by stressing that stores buy machines in large quantities and obtain large discounts

enabling them to sell for lower prices. Who would succeed?

2. A funeral home sold an expensive coffin to the family of a deceased for $1000. After the funeral, the deceased was cremated but the coffin was not. Just prior to cremation the funeral home transferred the body to a plain pine box. The coffin was relined and sold again. The funeral home took the position that the expensive coffin was just for show and not for cremation. They said that if the coffin were going to be cremated it would actually cost $3500. It was "sold" for just $1000 because the home knew that it could be refitted. The family sued for a refund of $960 which was the difference between the cost of the coffin and the pine box. Who would succeed?

3. A number of consumers in a community had new cars treated with rustproofing by a local firm. All of the cars developed early rust problems. The consumers started a class action suit. They had purchased different cars from different dealers for different prices. Some were referred to the rustproofing company by a dealer while others went on their own. Some read literature about the rustproofing while others did not. They paid different prices for the rustproofing depending on the size of the car. Should a class action be permitted?

4. A food retailer published an advertisement to the effect that prices of existing shelf stock would not be increased and that there would be no increase in prices until suppliers' costs rose. Bulletins were published by the head office to this effect. Employees of the store were seen by witnesses changing some prices on the shelves. The company was charged with false advertising but defended the action by saying that the employees did not get the bulletin in time. Is the company guilty?

5. The director of the provincial consumer protection branch issued a cease and desist order against an electronics firm that was marketing an electronic television antenna. The company relied upon the fact that the device was advertised in the U.S. and that store employees had personally tried the device and found it to be very good. Who would succeed?

Unit
Ten

The Law
of Real
Property

*Whatever is attached to the land
is part of it.*

Chapter 22

Ownership of Real Property

The law of real property is very involved and is one of the most documented areas of law. Land transfer records go back in England for centuries. To a great extent, the law of real property in Canada is a restatement of the English law.

Certain aspects of the law of real property differ considerably among the provinces, but for the most part, the rules mentioned in this unit are common to all the provinces.

Title to Real Property

In the early days of English common law, property was referred to as *real property* in cases where the court ruled that the property itself must be restored to the dispossessed owner. The court would decide that the nature of the property was such that the owner could not be compensated for its loss by the payment of a sum of money. Since ownership of land was nearly always the subject of such cases, "real property" became an accepted legal term for land (and buildings on it). A person involved in a dispute over real property could bring a *real action* to recover it. Where other forms of property were concerned, only a *personal action* could be brought. For example, if a person were deprived of a wagon, he or she could not bring a real action, but only a personal action; and the person who took the wagon could either return it or pay the owner its value.

Although it is usual to talk about someone as being the "owner" of land, the basis of English law, and the law of Canada, is that all land is owned by the Crown

(government). Some land is unoccupied and is still referred to as Crown land; the rest is held by tenants who hold the land at the pleasure of the Crown. The term *estate* indicates an interest in land — that is, the land is held in tenure until disposed of in some manner. Historically, there were many types of estates, including feudal estates and special grants by the king. Today, we seldom refer to any type of estate other than *freehold*, which originally meant land given to a free person for services rendered. There are two common types of estate in freehold:

- fee simple
- life estate

Estate in Fee Simple

This is the most permanent form of estate, allowing property to pass to any named heir, not necessarily a direct descendant. Such an estate is virtually perpetual, but if there is no heir and no other person can claim to inherit, the land *escheats* (reverts) to the Crown.

Life Estate

This estate lasts for life only. During the person's lifetime the property may be enjoyed, but not disposed of or materially altered. A person might will property to a child, but allow a spouse to enjoy a life estate in the property until death. The spouse could not sell the property or will it to someone else. Even if the spouse remarried, nothing could be done to stop the property from going to the child after the spouses's death. When the spouse died, the child would assume an estate in fee simple. Life estates are usually created to avoid double taxation which would otherwise occur if a person died, leaving the estate to a spouse who, in turn, died shortly afterwards.

Right of Dower

A wife's right of dower is a right to a life estate in one-third of her deceased husband's real property which he acquired during their marriage. Dower rights exist in Quebec, New Brunswick, Nova Scotia, and Prince Edward Island.

The recent trend in most provinces has been to move away from the concept of dower towards recognition of joint and equal interest of the spouses in all real property owned. Ontario abolished dower in 1978.

Homestead Rights

The Western provinces of Alberta, Saskatchewan, and Manitoba recognize *homestead rights* which provide a married couple with the right to retain and not change the homestead, and which grant a life estate in the home to the survivor. Homestead rights protect both husband and wife, so that neither can dispose of the homestead without the other's consent.

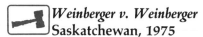

Weinberger v. Weinberger
Saskatchewan, 1975

Veronica Weinberger was separated from her husband, Karl. Karl inherited a farm from his father, with a condition that if the farm was sold the proceeds would have to be shared with Karl's mother. Karl entered into an agreement to sell the farm, and Veronica Weinberger filed an action to prohibit the sale. The court ruled in her favour. Under the *Homestead Act* of Saskatchewan, the wife can claim homestead rights if she at one time lived on the property in which the husband had a vested interest. Veronica and Karl had lived on the farm together prior to their separation. The sale of the property was not possible without Veronica's consent.

Adverse Possession

A person can become the owner of vacant land by occupying it and putting it to use. This is known as *adverse possession*. In Ontario, ten years of such possession is needed to acquire ownership. In Quebec, it requires thirty years. When a person applies for a grant of Crown land, that person must occupy and develop the land. Otherwise, another person may do so. Ownership of Crown land is obtained after sixty years which obviously suggests that occupation of the land will have to be continued by the person's descendants. Where the Land Titles System is in effect, a person cannot obtain ownership of property by adverse possession. The Land Titles System is explained later in this unit.

Maclean v. Reid
Nova Scotia, 1979

The defendant lived and worked on the family farm. In 1936, the parents conveyed the land to the defendant's brother. The brother told the defendant that he could live on the farm for the rest of his life. No agreement was ever made in writing. The brother left Canada in 1946. In 1971, the defendant, who was still occupying the land, was surprised to learn that his departed brother had sold the land to the plaintiff. The plaintiff brought an action for possession.

The Nova Scotia Court of Appeal held that the defendant could remain on the property. The defendant became a tenant at will in 1936 which tenancy ceased one year later pursuant to a statute in effect at that time. After twenty-one years from the expiry of the tenancy at will, the defendant had acquired possessory title to the land which could not be revoked by a sale of the property. In Nova Scotia, a person acquires title by adverse possession after twenty years.

Expropriation of Property

All land inherently belongs to the Crown, and the Crown may at any time assert this inherent power and take the land from the present tenant or owner. This act is called *expropriation* (or condemnation) and may be defined as action by the government to compulsorily deprive a person of a right of property belonging to that person, with or without compensation.

Some 1200 federal statutes, and several hundred provincial statutes have allowed expropriation, the majority of them being for the purpose of building railroad lines. There are statutes allowing for the expropriation of land for such things as enlarging harbours or cemeteries, building power lines, establishing national parks, or creating experimental farm stations. As an example, the federal *Expropriations Act* allows the government to expropriate "Any interest in land . . . that in the opinion of the Minister, is required by the Crown for a public work or other public purpose." Some statutes, including the *War Measures Act* and the *Atomic Energy Control Act* allow the expropriation of interests other than those in land, including such things as machinery, patents, fuel, and other personal property.

The *Railway Act* has allowed a great deal of "strip-taking" of land since the railway usually requires only a thin strip of land on which to lay tracks. This can result in great inconvenience to property owners who have their land effectively cut into two parts, with the railroad owning a strip down the middle. The construction of oil and gas pipelines has also resulted in strip-taking with the likelihood of more to come as Canada's energy needs grow.

Restrictions upon Ownership

Concern about foreign ownership and concentration of land in the hands of certain groups has caused several provinces to pass laws restricting the right to own land. Saskatchewan passed legislation forbidding anyone outside the province from owning more than 10 acres (4 ha) of land. Quebec has a similar law. Manitoba closed off purchases by non-Canadians. Prince Edward Island has limits upon ownership of land, particularly waterfront property, by non-

residents. The Supreme Court of Canada held that the Prince Edward Island legislation was intra vires the province. It is not yet certain what effect the *Charter of Rights and Freedoms* will have upon the right of Canadians living in one province to own land in another province. The protection of mobility rights and other sections of the *Charter* might make such provincial laws unconstitutional. This has yet to be tested in the courts.

Co-Ownership of Property

Property may be owned by two or more persons, each being entitled to simultaneous enjoyment of the property. This situation is generally referred to as a "tenancy," a term that indicates ownership and has nothing to do with leases. A grant of land to two or more persons in either *joint tenancy* or *tenancy in common* creates a single ownership, with the tenants having separate rights against each other and against third persons. The primary difference between the two is the right of survivorship.

Joint Tenants

Historically, a joint tenancy was preferred to a tenancy in common because it was a simple tenancy to understand. If one tenant died, there was simply one less person, but the estate remained the same. If property is to be registered as "joint," the deed must specifically state that the owners are "Joint Tenants." The property is not physically divided in any way; each owner holds an undivided interest in the property. There is no such thing as "my half" and "your half"—the joint tenants each have an equal right to enjoy all the property. Should one of the joint tenants die, the other tenants automatically assume that person's interest. Most married couples have their deeds registered as joint tenants. When one dies, the other automatically becomes the full and absolute owner. A joint tenant, with the consent of the other tenants, can sell his or her half interest in the property at which time the tenure would become a tenancy in common. All joint tenants must sign any documents pertaining to the property, including mortgages, sales, etc. If a lawsuit is brought against the owners of the property, all joint tenants must be sued together.

A joint tenancy can be severed under the laws of most provinces. It can be severed either at the request of the tenants themselves, or possibly by a creditor who seeks to recover from one of the tenants.

Sunglo Lumber Ltd. v. McKenna
British Columbia, 1975

The husband, McKenna, disappeared and his whereabouts were unknown. McKenna owed a large sum of money to a creditor, Sunglo Lumber, Ltd. The creditor sought to have the matrimonial home severed and sold by court order. The wife opposed the action as she would be forced out of the home she occupied. The court ordered the severance and sale of the property, holding that while the judge could delay the sale, it would eventually have to be sold unless the wife could work out some arrangement with Sunglo Lumber.

The significance of the *McKenna* case is that where a joint tenant defaults upon an obligation, the creditor may bring an action against that person and request the sale of real property he or she owns. If this is done, the tenancy must be severed before the property can be sold. The other joint tenants will receive a proportion of the proceeds of the sale according to their interests in the land, but they cannot block the sale merely because they occupy the property.

Tenants in Common

Co-owners who hold an undivided interest in land may also be referred to as tenants in common. The main difference is that when one of the tenants in common dies, the other does *not* automatically take over the deceased owner's interest. Tenants in common may sell their interests in the land and may will their interests to any persons, but this does not mean they can parcel or partition the land. "Partition" means to legally have the land subdivided.

When a joint tenancy has been ended by severance, it becomes in effect a tenancy in common. Severance could include partition, but it seldom does. Both joint tenants and tenants in common can make a voluntary partition of the land if all agree. Their co-ownership thus comes to an end by each of them becoming sole tenant of the land they are allotted. The partition must be done by deed and in accordance with provincial laws regulating severance and partition.

Gifts of Real Property

It is always possible for one spouse to make a gift of property to the other. This is the way in which a wife who is not employed acquires a claim to property purchased with her husband's income. If a husband buys property from his earnings, and takes the title in the joint names of himself and his wife, he is presumed to have intended to make a gift to her of one-half the value of the property. This is known as the *presumption of advancement* and applies only in one direction — from husband to wife. If a wife buys property from her own earnings or savings, and takes the title in joint names or in her husband's name alone, the presumption is that she still retains full interest in the property for herself. Her husband is deemed to be holding the property as a trustee for her. This is referred to as a *resulting trust*. Both the presumption of advancement and the presumption of a resulting trust may be rebutted if written agreements were prepared which carefully explain that the intention of the purchaser was entirely different.

Dissatisfaction with the unevenness of the law in the area of gifts of real property has caused several provinces to legislate change. The presumption of advancement has been abolished in Ontario and Newfoundland. All transfers are deemed to be resulting trusts.

Matrimonial Property

At common law, a married woman could not own real property. Her husband acquired all rights to his wife's real estate and the income resulting from it during their marriage. Her personal property also belonged to her husband and he controlled her leaseholds. She could only sell real estate with his consent. This was changed by the *Married Women's Property Act,* passed in England in 1880, which provided that a married woman could own real property and dispose of it as she wished. However, there were still inequities in actual practice. In most families, the husband earned an income and the wife stayed at home to raise the children. The matrimonial home, farm, and all other real property were in the husband's name alone. Unless the wife could show that she had contributed money to the purchase of the land, she had no legal claim to it.

The law was unjust because of its emphasis upon monetary contribution. There is no better illustration of this than the case of Irene Murdoch—a case which brought about major changes in the laws of five provinces.

Murdoch v. Murdoch
Supreme Court of Canada, 1973

Irene Murdoch sought a divorce from her husband and a half interest in their farm. They began their marriage with little or no property at all. They both worked hard and purchased more and more land, all of which was registered in the husband's name alone. During the twenty-five years they were married, the wife said she did haying, raking, mowing, driving tractors, taking cattle back and forth— in fact, everything the husband did. He was away from the farm for several months a year working elsewhere, and she had to run the farm alone for up to five months a year. The Supreme Court of Canada held that as she had not contributed *financially* to the development of the farm, she had no claim to any part of it. Her labour was held to be no different from that done by other farm wives. She could make no legal claim unless she could show that the husband was really holding part of the land in trust for her. In the absence of any formal agreement to that effect, the *Divorce Act* and provincial legislation could not be interpreted in such a

way as to permit her to receive any part of the property in the husband's name.

The Murdoch case brought home the fact that provincial laws gave scant protection to married women in the matter of property. Changes began occurring within four years.

In 1978, Alberta passed the *Matrimonial Property Act.* In brief, the Act provides that where spouses are unable to agree between themselves on how to divide their property, one of the spouses can apply to the court to divide the property for them. There are thirteen factors for the judge to consider, including the contribution made by each spouse to the marriage, whether or not that contribution was of a financial nature. Thus, the contribution by the wife of her services as homemaker and parent is considered to have an importance equal to that of a direct financial contribution. The judge has considerable discretion and need not make a 50/50 division if that is unfair to one spouse. For example, the wife could get exclusive possession of the matrimonial home. "Matrimonial home" includes any residence occupied by the spouses as their family home.

In the *Family Law Reform Act,* passed in 1978, Ontario declared that both spouses have an equal interest in the matrimonial home regardless of the name on the deed. Either spouse can seek a court order for possession of the home and contents and neither spouse can sell the home without the written consent of the other. The couple may alter this situation by written agreement. The matrimonial home and other family assets include any property the family used for household, educational, recreational, social, or aesthetic purposes. Again, the judge may award the home entirely to one spouse based upon a number of factors stated in the Act.

The *Matrimonial Property Act,* passed by the Newfoundland Legislature in 1979, is similar to the legislation in Alberta and Ontario. Each spouse has one-half interest in the matrimonial home owned by either or both spouses, and has the same right of use, possession, and management of the home as does the other spouse.

The British Columbia statute, the *Family Relations Act* of 1979, also recognizes family assets including the matrimonial home and recognizes the wife's contribution of labour as a contribution towards acquiring those family assets. The home may be awarded to one spouse alone if the court sees fit.

Clearly, the provinces are moving towards a system that treats a marriage as a true partnership and recognizes that the contribution made by both spouses towards the marriage consists not just of money but also of services.

While most provincial statutes do not fully recognize common law relationships, a decision of the Supreme Court of Canada was of some importance to people living together but not married to each other.

Pettkus v. Becker
Supreme Court of Canada, 1980

Becker stated that she supported Pettkus for five years and then worked on his farm for fourteen years. Pettkus had the benefit of nineteen years of labour while Becker received little in return. The Supreme Court of Canada held that she was entitled to an equal share of the value of property acquired and developed during those years. The fact that she was not legally married to Pettkus did not affect her claim:

"Remedy was always available in equity for property division between unmarried individuals contributing to the acquisition of assets.... The fact there is no statutory regime directing equal division of assets acquired by common law spouses is no bar to the availability of an equitable remedy in the present circumstances.**"**

There is some doubt that the *Pettkus* decision could be applied in all provinces where provincial law may specifically cover common law relationships, but it is significant that the court said that remedy was *always* available. The *Pettkus* case differs from the *Murdoch* case in two important ways: Becker did contribute some money, as well as her labour, to the farming operation.

Since the couple was not married, it could not be presumed that she was performing traditional farming tasks as a farmer's wife; rather, she was acting as an equal investor in the business.

The division of assets upon marriage breakup is discussed further in Unit Eleven   Family Law.

Bregman v. Bregman
Ontario, 1978

The husband had built a very successful private business while the wife remained at home, raised a family, and entertained the husband's business guests. The husband was asked at the divorce trial by the wife's lawyer, "Could you have become successful, as you did, if you had to stay home and raise the children and manage the household?" To this question, Bregman replied, "Certainly not." This set the stage for application of s. 4 of the Ontario *Family Law Reform Act* which allows the judge to divide all assets, including business assets, if it would be inequitable to divide just family assets. The wife had contributed her joint responsibility to the development of the husband's business and was entitled to part of it.

The court ordered the matrimonial home sold and the proceeds divided equally. Half the furnishings or the value thereof would go to each spouse. The husband was permitted to keep all of his Persian rug collection since the wife showed no interest in his rug collection during their marriage and the rugs were kept in a cabinet, not displayed in the house.

It should be noted that the 1982 Supreme Court of Canada's decision in *Leatherdale v. Leatherdale* may alter the decision reached in *Bregman* regarding non-family assets. The *Leatherdale* case is discussed in Chapter 24 and a further examination of the *Bregman* case is also included in that chapter.

Special Rights to Property

A person may acquire a special right to property without actually owning it. This claim often arises from the historic use of the property. The common law recognized a number of rights which a person could acquire over land belonging to someone else. These rights were referred to as *easements* or *profits*. Examples of easements would include such things as rights of way and water rights. Profits would include rights to cut wood, dig gravel, or hunt and fish. Today, the law tends to lump both easements and profits together under the heading of easements.

Easements

An easement is a right which a person has obtained to use land for personal benefit. A right cannot exist without conferring a benefit upon the person claiming it. The benefit must be one that can be practically and frequently utilized. Thus, a person living in Manitoba could not continue to claim a right of easement in Nova Scotia unless he or she periodically went there and exercised that right.

Easements generally arise by either *specific grant* or *prescription*. A specific grant means that a landowner (grantor) says to someone else (grantee), "You may use my property for your benefit." Generally, a grant may be withdrawn by the grantor within a reasonable period of time. If the easement continues for a long time, it may become permanent unless the original grant specifically said that it could be revoked.

The legal basis of an easement by prescription is that if long enjoyment of a right is shown, the court will uphold the right by presuming that it had a lawful origin in the first place. The court may presume that the easement was once specifically granted as a permanent right. Our common law, and some provincial statutes, generally recognize a rule of twenty years of uninterrupted use to create an easement by prescription. The possession which the claimant claims must have been *open, exclusive, notorious,* and *continuous.* The use must have been open in the sense that everyone could see it. The claimant must have used the property to the exclusion of the general public. Notorious use suggests that it was bold and well known to the true owner. Continuous requires that there was absolutely no interruption during the entire twenty-year period.

After twenty years of use by the claimant, if the owner tries to remove a right of easement by putting up a fence or barring access, the claimant must protest or the right may be lost. Protest usually involves a lawsuit, but it can include more direct methods, such as removing the obstacle, if minimum force is used.

Estey v. Withers
New Brunswick, 1975

The father of the defendants purchased a summer home in 1954, the only access to which was a road that had been used since 1924 without any objection from any owners. The road was a private, unimproved road which the defendants' father maintained at his own expense. In 1968, an owner blocked off the road. The summer home was not in use at that time. The owner later sold the property to Estey. In 1973, the defendants' father died and the defendants inherited the summer home. They decided to refurbish the home. They entered the property, filled in a ditch, and removed a barricade to reopen the road which had been blocked off since 1968. Estey objected and brought suit. The court ruled that the defendants were justified in entering upon the roadway since a right-of-way by prescription was acquired in accordance with the provisions of the *Easement Act* of New Brunswick — that is, the road had been used for a continuous period of over twenty years after 1924. The court required the defendants to pay the plaintiff $25 in trespass, because in removing the barricade more damage was done than necessary to enforce their right-of-way.

Another form of easement is an *encroachment*, which exists where a building has been situated on the wrong side of a property line for more than twenty years. After twenty years, the property owner cannot demand that the building be pulled down or compensation paid.

An easement is not confined to just the original user, but may be passed on to the next occupant or user. Once established, the right cannot be extinguished by the mere sale of the property. Therefore, a prospective buyer should find out about such rights before buying the property.

Fixtures

It is a rule of law that anything attached to the land is part of it. It also means that if something is not attached, it may be removed. This becomes important if property is sold and the previous owner removes things which the purchaser considered to be part of the land. Whether something is actually a fixture is sometimes difficult to determine. Some things are attached temporarily. Other things are very large and, while not attached, sit heavily upon the land. The status of an above-ground swimming pool might be a good case in point. In one case, the seller removed large statues from a garden. They just sat upon the ground and the seller thought they were chattels. The buyer argued that they were part of the design and beauty of the garden and belonged to the property. The court held that they were part of the land even though not specifically fastened down in any way. Problems arising over fixtures can be avoided by careful wording of the sale contract to ensure that every item which should stay with the property is included in the Offer to Purchase.

Mineral Rights

What rights does the property owner have to the minerals under his or her land? Basically, the rule of law is contained in the maxim *cujus est solum, ejus est usque ad coelum et ad inferos.* Translated into English, it means, "The owner of the soil is presumed to own everything up to the sky and down to the centre of the earth." The common law would therefore permit the owner of land to dispose of minerals under the surface and profit from them. But there are a number of exceptions. In some parts of Canada mineral rights do *not* specifically belong to the owner. In Ontario, Quebec, and Alberta the mineral and oil rights on land must be made by special grant. In those parts of Canada under federal control, mineral rights must be leased from the Crown.

Water Rights

A landowner has no property in the water which either percolates through the land or flows through it in a defined channel. However, the common law allows the landowner to make free use of water percolating through the land (such as a spring) without regard for any claims made by a neighbour. Thus, the law appears to say, "You don't own the water, but you are allowed unlimited use of it." In the case of water flowing through a defined channel, the *riparian owner* (the owner of the land through which the water flows) cannot take all the water. The owner can make use of it for personal needs, but cannot dam it, block it, or divert it from its course so that a downsteam neighbour is denied its use. Nor can the riparian owner pollute or foul the water so that a neighbour is unable to use it.

The principle of common law is that it is the duty of anyone who interferes with the course of a natural stream to see that the works which are substituted for the channel provided by nature are adequate to carry the water which may be brought around even by extraordinary rainfall.

Where a natural watercourse becomes part of an artificial drainage system it is no longer immune under the law, so the entire system must have a safe and proper outlet.

The right to use underground water for irrigation is more secure than the right to use a surface source. The owner of land containing underground water, which percolates by undefined channels and flows to the land of a neighbour, has the right, within his or her own land, to use the water for any purpose, and to divert or sell it, even if the neighbour is thereby denied use of the water.

Recording of Land Titles

There are two main systems used for recording the interest or ownership of land. The system which has been in use the longest is called the *Registry System,* and this prevails throughout most of Canada. A registry office is maintained at the county court. The purchaser must make a *title* search of the property he or she wants to acquire. If a clear title is established from the original owner to the present owner, and there are no adverse claims against the property, the purchaser can assume that a good and clear title would be acquired upon purchase. A title search requires considerable reading and should be done by a lawyer, who can interpret the various documents. In Ontario, as in most provinces, the lawyer must trace the title back forty years to establish a "good root of title."

A more recent system is the *Land Titles System*, also called the *Torrens System*. It was first devised in Australia, and is similar to a system long used to register ships. Each new transaction that takes place must be approved before registration. The government, acting through a Master of Land Titles, guarantees the accuracy of the title as shown on the record, which is brought up to date with each transaction. The essential difference between the two systems is that with the Registry System the researcher must use personal judgment and must interpret the documents. If the researcher makes an error, the purchaser may not get a valid title to the land. The Land Titles System provides the purchaser with a declaration as to the legal situation involved with the land. The legal work is done by the government and presented to the purchaser as a completed package, which is much easier to read. The chance of error is greatly reduced under the Land Titles System, yet it is still not used in most of Canada. Only British Columbia, Alberta, parts of Manitoba, Saskatchewan, and parts of Ontario presently use the Land Titles System.

Purchasing Real Property

Most people who want to buy or sell a house do so through a real estate agent. This is not strictly necessary, as private sales without the use of an agent are quite lawful. However, since most people use a real estate agent, let us create a hypothetical transaction and follow its sequence.

Listing the Property

Let's assume the Jacksons want to sell their house. They list the property with the Roberts Real Estate Company and sign a contract (listing agreement) with Roberts, making the company their agent in the sale of the house. The contract should state that Roberts will be paid a commission only when the deal closes. The Jacksons will include a minimum price below which they will not sell their house. This is important to protect both the Jacksons and Roberts, because Roberts is legally required to pass on any offer made to the Jacksons.

Roberts then advertises the house (at the realtor's expense) and shows it to prospective buyers. Roberts finds that Bowen is interested in buying a house. The Jacksons have asked $70 000, but Bowen is only willing to offer $66 000.

Offer To Purchase

At this point, Roberts draws up an *Offer to Purchase*, sometimes called an *Agreement of Purchase and Sale*, and asks Bowen for a deposit payable to the realtor "in trust." The deposit meets the requirement for consideration. If the offer is refused, the deposit is returned to Bowen. The Offer to Purchase should include:

(1) A full description of the property.
(2) The price offered and the terms of payment.
(3) What is included with the property.
(4) Closing date of the sale.
(5) Any mortgage or financing arrangements. This usually includes the mortgage to be arranged or taken over from the seller, interest rate, monthly payments, etc. The entire offer is often *conditional* upon the purchaser being able to arrange financing. If this can't be done within a stated time, the deal is off.
(6) A time period for acceptance by the seller.
(7) A time period for the purchaser to check the title to the property, at the purchaser's expense.

There are other details in the Offer to Purchase, but the important points are those given above. The realtor carries the offer to the seller (vendor) who may accept it by signing it, or refuse it. The vendor might sign it, but also change the terms of the offer, thus making a counter offer. Let's say that the Jacksons accept Bowen's offer by signing it, but change the figure $66 000 to $68 000. Bowen can refuse to accept this change, in which case there is no agreement. But, hopefully, at some point, the parties will agree on all the terms of the sale, including the price.

There is a tendency on the part of real estate agents to try to rush people into signing the Offer to Purchase. However, both parties should have a lawyer read the Offer to Purchase before they sign it. It is an important, binding document.

Checking the Title

Once the Offer to Purchase has been signed, the purchaser is allowed a period of time in which to check the title to the property. As mentioned, it is preferable to have a lawyer do this. A check should be made of the following:

- Property title, which should be registered and clear;
- Liens against the property;
- Mortgages registered against the property;
- Survey of the property correct;
- Taxes paid;
- Property in agreement with local by-laws;
- Easements;
- Oil or gas leases;
- Dower rights of previous owner's wife (not applicable in some provinces), which by this stage should be barred;
- Any other encumbrances against the property, such as builders' liens, judgments, etc.

If there are defects in the title, the purchaser will notify the vendor and give him or her a chance to clear them away. If the vendor cannot do so, the purchaser can refuse to go through with the sale. Note that the Offer to Purchase usually specifies a time within which such notice must be given to the vendor. However, let us assume that the property is clear, so that the purchaser concludes the financing. Very likely the purchaser will be taking over the vendor's mortgage,

and the mortgage company usually charges a fee for arranging the transfer. The Offer to Purchase should specify who will pay the fee to discharge the previous mortgage and register the new one.

Statement of Adjustments

The next step is for the solicitors of the two parties to reach agreement on the final payment. To do this, a *Statement of Adjustments* is worked out. For example, taxes may be unpaid at the time the vendor leaves. Therefore the vendor should pay the purchaser the amount owing since the purchaser will assume responsibility for payment. On the other hand, the vendor may be leaving oil in the furnace tank, in which case the purchaser should reimburse the vendor for it. These adjustments are worked out so that as of the closing date the two parties have made a fair agreement.

Financing the Purchase

In this transaction, Bowen has decided to arrange financing personally. Bowen elected to increase the present mortgage on the house, but will deal with the same mortgage company. The interest would be subject to negotiation with the mortgage company — Bowen is not guaranteed the same interest rate that the Jacksons were paying. The mortgage company obtains Bowen's signature on the new mortgage, then forwards to Bowen's lawyer a cheque for the amount by which the old mortgage was increased.

Bowen's lawyer holds the mortgage company's cheque pending final closing. Since the mortgage does not cover the full value of the house, Bowen also gives the lawyer a cheque to make up the difference. The lawyer then pays the correct amount to the Jackson's lawyer, who pays the Jacksons. The lawyers meet on the day of closing at the court house. The mortgage is registered, the previous mortgage discharged, and the deed is transferred to Bowen. The keys to the house are handed over to Bowen's lawyer. In some provinces, the purchaser also must pay a Land Transfer Tax.

Interests in Land: Mortgages

When the purchaser of real property cannot pay the full purchase price, a mortgage is taken out on the property. The lender of the money is called the mortgagee and the borrower is called the *mortgagor*. The mortgage is a conveyance of a legal or equitable interest in property with a provision for redemption, meaning that if the loan is repaid the conveyance will become void. The wording of a typical mortgage contract includes this wording: "The said Mortgagor (who conveys as beneficial and sole owner) doth grant and mortgage unto the said Mortgagee." This indicates that the title to the property passes to the mortgagee. A legal and equitable interest means that the mortgagee has the right to recover the property from the person holding it, if the agreed terms of repayment are not kept. In those provinces where a Land Titles System is used, a mortgage does *not* convey title to the mortgagee. It places a "charge" upon the land, similar to other forms of deeds.

Modern day mortgages are generally thought of as security for a loan. The mortgage creates a claim upon the property by the mortgagee which must be cleared away before title can pass to anyone else. Under the contract, the mortgagor gives a "personal covenant" to pay the principal and interest on the loan. Then, the mortgagor further pledges the property as security on this covenant, and is thus legally bound in two ways.

Registration of a Mortgage

The mortgagee protects his or her interest in the property by registering the mortgage at the court house (Registry System). Any subsequent purchaser of the property assumes the existing mortgage, and registration denies such a purchaser the right to claim ignorance of the mortgage. If two mortgages exist on the same property, it is the first mortgage registered that gets first claim to the property.

Once the mortgage is fully paid, the mortgagor should obtain from the mortgagee a *Discharge of Mortgage*. This should be registered at the court house as proof that the mortgage has been paid.

The Mortgagee's Rights

If a mortgagor fails to pay according to the contract, the mortgagee may proceed in several ways:

- Sue for payment on the basis of the mortgagor's personal convenant in the contract.
- Take possession of the property. If this is done, the mortgagee must pay all expenses owing such as taxes, utilities, etc. The mortgagee may then rent the property to a tenant and apply the rent to the mortgage payments. If a second mortgagee takes possession, the first mortgagee must be paid off in full. In this situation, the mortgagor still retains ownership of the property, but is denied the use of it or control over it. The mortgagee might eventually pay off the mortgage by renting the property, at which time the mortgagor could reassert title.
- Take possession and obtain a court order to sell the property. This is generally referred to as a forced sale. Any proceeds from the sale that remain, after the mortgage has been paid, must be returned to the mortgagor. If the sale does not raise enough money to pay off the mortgage, the mortgagor must pay the balance on his or her personal covenant.
- Take possession and apply to the court for a full foreclosure. If foreclosure is granted, it means that the mortgagee becomes the sole owner, with the mortgagor losing all title to the property. When faced with the possibility of foreclosure, the mortgagor may request a forced sale instead. The important difference between sale and foreclosure is that under a sale the mortgagor can recover some of the equity in the property. Under a foreclosure, the mortgagor will recover nothing.

Prepayment of the Mortgage

At some stage, the mortgagor may want to pay off the mortgage on the property all at once rather than continue to pay instalments plus interest. There is no obligation on the mortgagee to agree to this. The mortgagee receives a high rate of interest from the mortgagor under the contract, and is not required suddenly to cancel this contract to his or her own detriment. However, under the *Interest Act of Canada,* if a mortgage is not payable until more than five years after the date of the mortgage, the mortgagor may pay off the entire amount of the mortgage still owing any time after the first five years. With this prepayment, the mortgagor must pay the equivalent of three months' interest.

The Term of the Mortgage

Many property owners do not understand the mortgage on their houses. For example, they may be confused by the fact that while the payment may be calculated on a twenty, thirty or forty year period of time, the actual *term* of the mortgage may be five years or less. The term is the period of time during which the mortgagee cannot demand repayment of the entire principal. The rate of interest is fixed for the duration of the term.

When interest rates move up and down rapidly, it is not uncommon for both borrowers and lenders to become very uncertain about the future. During such periods of financial instability, mortgage terms become shortened. Thus, during the early 1980s, many mortgages carried just a one-year term and had to be renewed every year. When the term expires, the mortgage must be renegotiated. If the parties cannot agree on a new interest rate, the mortgagor must pay off the balance in full. If the mortgagor cannot do so, he or she may lose the property.

Agreement of Sale

Property may be sold under the instalment plan. Normally only a small down payment is needed for the purchaser to obtain possession, but title remains with the seller until the last payment is made. Each payment also requires interest. The danger of such an agreement is that if the contract is not carried out, the purchaser may not receive back any of the money paid out, since it is treated as rent.

Building a House

The legal procedure in building a house differs from that in purchasing a house already constructed. The contract with the builder should be read by a lawyer and should carefully stipulate:

The plans to be followed: Clearly defined house plans should be used, showing the overall design of the house and details of construction, and containing a specific list of what is included in the price and what will be extra.

The materials to be used: Although a builder assumes overall responsibility for the construction of the house, the builder will normally sub-contract specialized work such as plumbing, electrical wiring, etc. There is no contract between the buyer and the sub-contractor. The contractor remains liable to the buyer if the sub-contractor did a poor job. The sub-contractor looks to the contractor for payment. However, if the contractor does not, or cannot pay the sub-contractor, the sub-contractor may file a lien against the property.

A *lien* is the right to hold or lay claim to another person's property as security for the performance of an obligation. In the case of a building under construction, the right of lien extends to labourers, contractors, and suppliers of materials. Each province has passed a statute allowing unpaid contractors or labourers to bring their claim against the property, but requiring that this be done within a certain time. In most of the provinces the time limit is between thirty and sixty days. In Ontario, it is forty-five days — thirty-five days in Alberta.

There is a statutory requirement to hold back part of the final price until the time for filing a lien has run out. Ontario law requires that 10 per cent be held back. If no liens are filed within the time required, the buyer is relieved of any responsibility, and the contractor will be paid the final 10 per cent. It is therefore important that any person considering placing a lien on property should consult a lawyer quickly. If action is not taken within the time required, the right of lien is lost and the claimant reverts to the status of an ordinary unpaid creditor.

A specific date for completion: While a completion date should be included, most contracts allow for delays caused by unavailability of materials or by labour stoppages.

Ontario has a New Home Warranties Plan that protects the buyer for up to five years against major structural defects. All contractors must be licensed and registered with the plan. Small defects are covered up to one year. Alberta has a similar plan, but participation by builders is voluntary.

When contracting to have a house built, a property owner should always demand that clearly defined house plans be used.

In Newfoundland, under the *Building Contractors Licensing Act,* a building contractor cannot carry on business in the province without a valid licence. Thus, shoddy workmanship can be dealt with by revocation of licence.

What can be expected from a building contractor? In most provinces there are three general expectations:

(1) To do the work undertaken with care and skill.
(2) To use materials of good quality. In the case of materials described expressly this will mean good of their expressed type.
(3) To do the work and provide the materials that will be reasonably fit for the purpose for which they are required, unless the contract excludes any such obligation.

Condominiums

The popularity of condominiums has required a rapid development of law in this field. The condominium is a form of communal living, where residents own instead of rent their apartments. The residents also jointly own the overall building and grounds. Usually, they elect a committee to administer the building; this includes the passing of rules and regulations. Each resident must share the joint costs such as maintenance, taxes, insurance, etc. If a resident wishes to leave, he or she must sell the unit.

The position of a condominium owner can give rise to numerous problems under the terms of occupancy, and a person should consult a lawyer before making a purchase. For example, the joint expenses on a new condominium building will be greater than those on a building that has been in existence for some time. A new building requires extensive landscaping, and this and other initial costs must be borne by the residents who first move in. Furthermore, some units in a new building will probably not be sold immediately, and in the meantime the joint costs will have to be spread over the smaller number of residents who have already moved in.

Reviewing Important Points

1. All land belongs to the Crown. An individual may hold title at the Crown's pleasure, but the land may be expropriated (taken back) by the Crown, with or without compensation.
2. The most permanent form of land ownership is fee simple, allowing land to pass to any named heir.
3. The trend in Canada is to afford both spouses an equal interest in the matrimonial home, regardless as to whose name is on the deed.
4. Property may be owned by two or more persons, either as joint tenants or tenants in common.
5. If a person has enjoyed the right to use land for an uninterrupted period, usually twenty years, this right cannot be revoked.
6. Both the buyer and seller of real property should have every document checked by a lawyer before signing it.
7. Repayment of a mortgage may be calculated on a twenty, thirty, forty or more year basis, but the actual term of the mortgage is much shorter, often as short as one year. When the term expires, the interest rate must be renegotiated.
8. When a person is contracting to have a house built, clearly defined plans, not simple sketches, should be used.
9. A condominium purchaser owns his or her living unit but the common building and grounds are collectively owned by all occupants.
10. Under an agreement of sale, real property can be purchased under the instalment plan.

Checking Your Understanding

1. What does it mean to grant a life estate to one person and an estate in fee simple to another person for the same property?
2. Explain the major distinction(s) between joint tenants and tenants in common.
3. What circumstances must exist in order for an easement to be legally recognized?

4. What is adverse possession?

5. What does the common law say in regard to the riparian owner's rights to water which passes through the land in a clearly defined channel?

6. If the mortgagor fails to make payments, what options has the mortgagee?

7. State four things that should be stipulated in a contract with a builder of a house.

8. What is the liability of the house buyer with regard to payment of sub-contractors and suppliers?

9. Identity three precautions that should be taken before purchasing a condominium.

Legal Briefs

1. When R died, she gave her mother, B, a life estate in a house. Upon B's death, the property would pass to C, R's granddaughter. B approached her banker with a view towards putting a larger mortgage on the house because she needed some cash. Should the bank agree to her request?

2. H and D, brothers, owned a parcel of land as tenants in common. The land was in poor condition and H left the area saying he had no interest in being a "dirt farmer." D worked for two years, expended some money improving the land, and was able to put in a crop of grain. When it was harvested, H wrote to D and demanded part of the proceeds of the sale of the grain. Discuss H's claim.

3. To increase the size of a pond where her animals watered, M diverted a stream running nearby. The stream originated from a crack in some rocks on a hillside on M's property. When M did this, she reduced the water flow in the stream by 90 per cent, depriving her neighbour, R, of the water. R's rights in this matter?

4. A planted a hedge along the edge of the property line between her property and her neighbour's property. By miscalculation, the hedge was two metres from the line, on A's side. A noted that the neighbour cut the grass up to the hedge and generally accepted that the two metres were hers. Why should A be concerned about this situation? Other than moving the hedge, what might A do?

5. C started a new business and thought it wise to put his house completely in his wife's name so that potential creditors could not place a lien against it. A year later, they separated. What is C's position regarding the house?

6. When J sold a house to P, the agreement stated that all fixtures would be included. J took with her a large chandelier from the hallway, saying that it was a family heirloom. J said that she clearly told her real estate agent that the chandelier did not go with the house. However, the agent failed to tell P and it was not specifically listed in the Offer to Purchase. Who owns the chandelier?

7. When L inspected a house in April, he was shown a well full of water. He did not ask any specific questions about the flow of water, but had a test done to determine that the water was potable. After buying the house, he learned that the well went dry every summer and the seller had to truck in water. L had a new, deeper well drilled and sued the seller for the cost. Will L recover the cost?

8. G, a great television enthusiast, put a giant television antenna on his roof. When turned in a certain direction, part of the antenna protruded over the edge of B's property. What are B's rights?

9. Q purchased a house from R who claimed to be a widow and signed an affidavit to this effect when title was transferred. R then left Canada. Six months after taking possession, Q received a letter from the lawyer of R's "deceased" husband, claiming half the value of the property. In fact, R was not a widow; she was only separated from her husband. Discuss Q's position.

10. H entered into an Agreement of Sale under which she would sell a house to T. T took possession and called V, a swimming pool company, and told them to put a pool into the back yard. V did not check the title to the property. T kept referring to the house as "my house" and signed a contract as owner. The pool was put in but T did not make her payments. Nor did she pay H. The pool company put a lien on the house. H was served notice of this and confronted T who readily admitted that she had ordered the pool. T then went to live elsewhere, leaving H with the house, the

pool, and the lien. Has H acquired a free pool or must she pay the bill to clear the lien?

Applying the Law

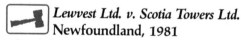

Lewvest Ltd. v. Scotia Towers Ltd.
Newfoundland, 1981

The defendant was a building contractor constructing a building on the corner of a street in St. John's. In the course of construction, the boom of a sky crane swung over the adjacent property belonging to the plaintiff. The plaintiff was concerned about this practice and sought an order stopping it. The principle of common law is *cujus est solum ejus usque ad coelum* which means, "whoever owns the land owns what is above it." The defendant could construct the building in a different manner but at a cost of nearly one-half million dollars more. No damage was being done to the plaintiff's property and little inconvenience. The court held that the defendant was trespassing:

&&Under our system of law, property rights are sacrosanct. For that reason, the rules that generally apply to injunctions do not always apply in cases such as this. The balance of convenience and other matters may have to take second place to property rights. What has happened is that the defendant, by trespassing, can save itself close to half a million dollars. If it can save the money, so be it, but the court is not going to give it a right to use the plaintiff's property. That is a right that it must negotiate with the plaintiff.... If a third party can gain economic advantage by using the property of another, then it must negotiate with that other to acquire user rights. The court cannot give it to him.&&

Questions
1. What is the basic rule of law regarding the air space above real property?
2. As the defendant did not cause any injury to the property of the plaintiff, why should this temporary situation not be allowed to exist?
3. Do you think the plaintiff is really concerned with this action or just seeking a way to extract a payment from the defendant?

Silverman v. Silverman
Ontario, 1978

When the Silvermans divorced, the wife wanted to keep the house because it was her "dream home" and she wanted to live in it for the rest of her life.

The court made it clear that this would not be possible since the law said that each spouse had an equal interest in the matrimonial home:

&&It is usually the case that upon separation both spouses must expect a lower standard of living than that enjoyed while they were together. Usually there is simply not enough money available for both to live as well separately as they did when living together.... She will have to reduce her standard of living and her expectations as her husband has had to do.&&

Questions
1. When people divorce, what reasons might cause a judge to award the matrimonial home to one spouse?
2. What did the judge mean in this case by saying that people living apart must expect a lower standard of living than that enjoyed while living together?
3. Has modern legislation changed the traditional position of spouses in regard to matrimonial property?

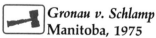

Gronau v. Schlamp
Manitoba, 1975

The defendant discovered a serious crack had developed in his apartment building. His engineer advised him that this was the result of soil erosion caused by water and that it would take an expensive construction job to underpin the building. The defendant did not want to incur such a high cost. He hired a bricklayer to patch up the brick and had some landscaping and decorating done with the objective of making the building appear to be in good condition. After this work was done the building was sold to the plaintiff. When the plaintiff discovered the defect he applied to the court to have the sale rescinded. The defendant relied upon the rule of "buyer beware" but the court did not agree. The buyer beware rule did not apply where defects were actively hidden by the vendor. It applied to defects such as were discoverable by inspection. The patching job was done solely for the purpose of concealing the defect from the purchaser. This amounted to deceit and material misrepresentation. The purchaser received something completely different from what it was represented to be.

Questions

1. What is the rule of "buyer beware"?
2. In this case, why did the court not accept that rule as a valid defence?
3. If a person selling real property knows of a serious defect in the property, must a prospective buyer be openly told about it? Must small defects be described? How could serious or small be defined?
4. Recently many homes were insulated with a compound containing formaldehyde. Strong fumes made the occupants ill. If a person sold a house with this insulation and did not tell the buyer, what could the buyer do later on, when learning about the insulation?

You Be the Judge

1. The plaintiff owned a garage which he purchased in 1944. For sixteen years, he parked vehicles on land next to the garage, although he did not own this land. He did this openly and without trying to hide the fact that he was using the land. In 1960 he sold the garage to a new owner, but the garage went broke. In 1964 he bought the building back and started up a business once more. He again parked vehicles on the adjoining land until 1977 when the land was sold. The purchaser demanded that he stop using the land but the plaintiff brought an action asking that he be declared the owner of the property because he had used it for twenty years in an open, notorious, and exclusive manner. The defendant who had just purchased the land argued that the use was not continuous. Who would succeed?
2. The plaintiffs claimed that the ground water table below their properties had been substantially lowered by the construction of a collector sewer on lands of the

National Capital Commission located nearby and that their homes and lands were seriously damaged by the resulting subsidence. They also claimed damage as a result of drilling and blasting. The plaintiffs claimed that they had a right to the *support* of water beneath their land. Who would succeed?
3. The plaintiff rented a lot from the owner of an adjoining property in 1951. Due to a mutual mistake about the boundaries of the lots, the plaintiff treated a piece of her landlord's land as hers. The landlord put up a fence which left the disputed land on the plaintiff's side. In 1966 the plaintiff purchased the land she had been renting. Before the purchase she had a survey done which clearly showed where the property line was; however, the plaintiff ignored it and built a garage and driveway that took up part of the disputed land. In 1973, the defendant bought the land previously owned by the landlord. In 1979, the defendant also had a survey done and realized that the fence and garage were on the wrong side. The defendant wrote to the plaintiff demanding removal of the fence, but not of the garage. The plaintiff initiated an action to have herself declared owner of the property by adverse possession. Who would succeed?
4. The plaintiffs bought a restaurant that had been advertised as an excellent investment and a going concern. The plaintiffs appraised the building and found it to be in poor condition. It was their stated intention to improve and enlarge the building. The defendant, the seller, said it would be an excellent idea. The plaintiffs bought the building and drew up plans for renovation. They then applied for a building permit. The building inspector came to look at the building and said no permit would be granted. The renovations would not be safe because they would place too much weight on a weak building. The building would have to be torn down and a new one built. Blocked in their plans, the plaintiffs brought an action to have their purchase rescinded. They based their action partly upon the fact that the seller had also considered renovation and expansion and had also been told by the building inspector that it could not be done. Thus, when they mentioned their idea to the seller, they should have

been told that it would not be permitted. The defendant said that they had only mentioned that they "might" want to do some renovations. They did not at any time say that they would buy the building only if a building permit could be approved. Also, they could have had the building inspector there before they bought the property. Who would succeed?

5. Two brothers owned some land as tenants in common; they had inherited the land from their father. Since the brothers never got along together, they verbally agreed to divide the land into two sections, using a road which ran down the middle as a boundary. Both men paid 50 per cent of the taxes. When one brother made some improvements in his "half" of the land, the other said nothing. When the elder brother died, he left his half to his son who then sought to sell the land. At this point the surviving brother objected; he brought an action to prevent the sale of the land. The deceased man's son argued that as twenty-three years had gone by since the two brothers had divided the land, he could dispose of it as he wished. Who would succeed?

Chapter 23

Renting Real Property

Landlord and Tenant

Historically, the term *landlord* refers to the feudal law rule which held that "all land which is held in any estate shall be of a lord." The word *tenant* comes from "one who holds (tenure) in land." Theoretically, a tenant owes fealty (service and loyalty) to the landlord—something most tenants today would not be eager to accept.

There are two areas of law to consider when discussing landlord and tenant. First, there is a large body of common law going back many centuries in British history. Second, each province has enacted specific legislation dealing with landlord and tenant matters. Where there is a contradiction between the common law and statute law, the statute takes priority.

Historically, the common law tended to favour the landlord whose powers over the land, and over the tenants upon the land, was absolute. There are many examples of this including the "Highland Clearances" when Scottish landlords, deciding that sheep were more profitable than small farmers, evicted tens of thousands of people with no place for them to go. Many emigrated to Canada.

The statutes passed by the provinces have generally tried to balance out the relationship between landlord and tenant. Some landlords would argue that matters have gone too far in the opposite direction giving tenants licence to abuse property and not pay rent.

Since the statutes in each province vary in certain details, our discussion on the subject of landlord and tenant must be general, with some specific references to a number of provincial statutes.

Essentials of a Lease

Basic Requirements

By definition, a *lease* is a document creating an interest in land for a fixed period of certain duration in consideration of the payment of rent. A lease creates a legal estate, good against the whole world. Leases first appeared in the thirteenth century. They may be granted for any length of time, although they cannot be perpetual. Leases for a period of several hundred years are not uncommon in history.

Not every document resembling a lease is necessarily a lease. There are certain requirements that must be met, either in specific words or implied actions. For example, a distinction must be made between an agreement to lease and a lease itself. An agreement to lease is a contract to enter into a lease agreement at a later date, but it does not create an estate. A person who signed a lease, but who was denied possession of the property, could sue for possession. A person who signed an agreement to lease could not sue for possession, but only for damages arising from breach of contract. All leases, whatever form they take, must contain a minimum of information.

- *Exclusive possession:* The purpose of the lease must be to grant exclusive possession. The lease will not be valid if the person granting the lease continues to occupy or have direct control over the property. Thus, a boarder or lodger does not have a lease.
- *Premises must be defined:* The agreement must clearly point out just what the tenant is obtaining. An

address, apartment number, or some other discernible area must be spelled out.

- *Intention:* An agreement may be defective in some way, but if the court accepts that the intention of the parties was to create a lease, it will be interpreted as a lease.

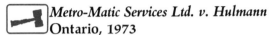

Metro-Matic Services Ltd. v. Hulmann
Ontario, 1973

The case involved whether or not the plaintiff had been granted a "lease" or a "licence" under an agreement with the defendant. The court noted that the wording of the document included such terms as "lease" and "demise" and other words usually used to create an estate or interest in land. The covenant for quiet enjoyment gave the plaintiff exclusive control over the property. There was nothing in the document to indicate any intention by the parties except to enter into a lease, and it was so interpreted.

Agreement to Lease

An agreement to lease is a document which promises the renting of property at some future time. In other words, the document states that the landlord will rent the property to the tenant some time in the future. In most provinces the agreement to lease must be in writing. The document itself is not a lease and does not create a leasehold by the tenant. However, if the tenant manages to actually take possession of the property, it is understood that a lease has been granted. If the landlord refuses to make the property available as promised, the prospective tenant can sue for breach of contract but cannot sue to get the property itself.

Formal Leases

At common law, a lease could be granted orally and today many leases are still entered into on the basis of an oral agreement. The original *Statute of Frauds,* passed in England in 1677, required all leases to be in writing.

The situation today is generally that a lease of more than three years' duration must be in writing. In some provinces, particularly the Western provinces, the lease must also be under seal.

A valid lease should contain certain essential information including:

- The names of the parties (landlord and tenant);
- A clear description of the property;
- The date the lease begins;
- The duration of the term;
- The amount of rent and how it is to be paid;
- The specific terms of the contract including who pays for utilities;
- Limitations upon the use of the property.

In all provinces the tenant must be given a copy of the lease or he or she may refuse to pay rent. In Ontario and Alberta this copy must be provided within twenty-one days. In Newfoundland the tenant must also be given a copy of the statute, the *Residential Tenancies Act.*

Informal Leases

In most provinces, leases for a term of three years or less may be informal. This means they may be written, oral, or implied and do not have to be under seal. However, the absence of a written lease may make it difficult for the tenant to prove there is a lease if the landlord subsequently refuses to allow occupancy of the premises. For protection of rights, the tenant should make every effort to occupy the premises immediately or even move one article of personal belongings into the premises. The reason for this is that the tenant wants to demonstrate "part performance" of the contract, which makes it binding. The law may then be summarized as follows: No formality is needed for a lease which is for less than three years and takes effect in possession, for the doctrine of part performance ensures that a tenant who has gone into possession has a valid lease.

An oral lease may have the advantage that the parties do not feel legally bound to the extent that parties to a written lease are bound. If an informal lease is preferred, there is nothing wrong with that. However, both parties should realize that if a difference of opinion arises, there is little or no protection in an oral lease.

Standardized Leases

Reform of landlord and tenant law has led in some provinces to concern about the wording of leases that are complex and sometimes one-sided. In response to these problems, several provinces have taken steps to make the form of leases used more uniform.

The provinces of Newfoundland, Nova Scotia, and Saskatchewan have prepared certain conditions which must be contained in every tenancy agreement. The landlord or tenant may agree to additional terms, but cannot delete any of the minimum terms. The terms added may not contravene the provincial statute.

The provinces of Manitoba and New Brunswick have provided a standard lease form which is to be used for all residential tenancies. Some additions are permitted but no deletions are permitted.

Ontario developed a standard form in 1980 as part of a major revision to its provincial law, but the Supreme Court of Ontario declared that much of the entire statute was ultra vires and the standard lease form was not adopted.

Type and Duration of Tenancy

Before discussing the various types of tenancy, two new terms should be introduced. Lease forms do not refer to the two parties as the landlord and the tenant. The landlord is the person leasing the property and is called the *lessor*. The tenant is the person accepting the offer to lease and is called the *lessee*. The terms may be used interchangeably with "landlord" and "tenant."

The period of time for which the tenancy will run is sometimes a confused matter. Often the two parties are unclear in their intentions as to the term of the lease, or the wording is ambiguous. There are many types of leases based upon time period, of which the following are the most common.

Leases for a Fixed Period

This type of lease may run for any certain duration. The length of the lease is not important in this respect; it may be as little as a few days or as long as a hundred years. What is essential is that both the time the lease begins and the time it ends must be determinable. For example, a lease for five years to commence August 1, 1984 is determinable. However, a lease to run "until the war is over" does not state a determinable time for the lease to end and is not valid. The two parties obviously could not know in advance how long the war would last.

When the fixed period ends, the tenancy ends. Neither party need specifically remind the other that the tenancy has been concluded. However, under the common law, if the tenant remains in possession and continues to pay rent which the landlord accepts, a periodic tenancy is created. The court often presumes that the terms of the original lease have been renewed. If the original lease was for one year, and the tenant holds over, a year to year tenancy will be presumed. Ontario law states that an agreement is considered to be *automatically* renewed on a month to month basis if it comes to an end before a new agreement is made.

Periodic Tenancies

A periodic tenancy is one that is renewed from week to week, month to month, etc. This type of tenancy can be created by express agreement or by implied behaviour such as payment of rent on a regular basis. Where no other agreement exists, the court may use the period of rental payment to determine the nature of the periodic tenancy. For example, where no specific period was agreed to, but the landlord stated, "The rent is $200 a month," it was presumed that the parties entered into a tenancy from month to month. However, payment of rent on a monthly basis can also be interpreted as paying by instalment on a yearly tenancy. A yearly tenancy is one which begins with a period of at least one year and continues from year to year until ended by proper notice. The lease normally uses the phrase, "for one year and so thereafter from year to year."

Tenancy at Sufferance

A tenancy at sufferance exists when a tenant occupies property without the owner's consent and the owner has not taken any action to remove the tenant. The owner may eject the tenant at any time, and the fact of having allowed the tenant to remain thus far does not indicate acceptance of the tenant's presence.

Tenancy at Will

A tenancy at will arises when the tenant occupies property with the owner's consent, but without any lease agreement or the payment of rent. Either party may terminate such a tenancy at any time.

A tenancy at will might arise where a person moves onto land with the owner's consent, but on the understanding that the stay is only to last a short while. If the person does not move on, the owner may evict him or her.

Assignment of a Lease

A tenant who signs a lease for a fixed period is normally bound to pay rent for the full term of the lease. What happens if for some reason the tenant is obliged to move? In such a case, the tenant would be advised to try to cancel the lease agreement, but if this is not possible, the lease may be assigned to another person. This person, called the *assignee,* effectively becomes the new tenant, with the same rights and obligations as the previous occupier. However, the original tenant is still liable to pay the rent should the assignee fail to do so. An assignment seldom occurs without the consent of the landlord, who may oppose the assignment for various reasons.

There are other circumstances in which a tenant may wish to *sublet* the premises. Subletting differs from assignment in two major ways. First, the tenant does not give up all interest in the property. He or she may sublet for a period of time and then reoccupy the premises; or the tenant may sublet part of the premises and continue to occupy the remainder personally. Secondly, the tenant remains completely liable to the landlord for rent and damage. That is, the tenant cannot ask the landlord to accept rent from the subtenant, and if the subtenant damages the premises the landlord may look to the tenant for the cost of repair. Whereas an assignee has the same rights as the original tenant, the subtenant is legally in a much weaker position. The subtenant must pay the rent to the tenant, who is expected to pay it to the landlord. But, if the tenant fails to pay the landlord, the subtenant will be evicted. The subtenant seldom leases the property from the tenant on anything other than a month-to-month basis, and may be suddenly ordered to vacate because the tenant wants to move back in. If the subtenant causes damage for which the tenant must pay the landlord, the tenant may in turn sue the subtenant for the amount paid.

A problem may arise for the subtenant if the tenant gives notice to the landlord that the tenant is vacating the premises. If this happens, does the subtenant have any right to retain the premises? The law generally says no. This has allowed some unscrupulous landlords to operate a nasty trick upon tenants. The landlord rents all the units to a company, which in turn sublets the units to tenants. The tenants are unaware that they are not dealing with the landlord and are also unaware that they are actually subtenants, not tenants. If the landlord wants to get rid of an occupant of one of the units, he or she advises the tenant company to give notice. The landlord then orders the occupant to surrender the premises, saying that since the tenant has terminated the lease the subtenant has no further rights to the property. To prevent this kind of chicanery, the Ontario *Landlord and Tenant Act* requires that the name of the true landlord be posted in the rented building.

A landlord can transfer rights under a lease to a third party. He or she could, for example, sign over the right to receive rent to a third party. This is not particularly important to the tenant unless it turns out that the assignee is not as co-operative as the landlord about such things as repair, etc.

The tenant must normally request permission from the landlord before subletting. However, the landlord cannot "unreasonably" withhold permission to sublet. The law in Newfoundland, Ontario, Alberta, and British Columbia specifically state so, which means that unless the tenant is planning to sublet to a very undesirable person the landlord cannot withhold permission. Most provinces generally permit the landlord to charge a small administrative fee for subletting and the landlord may hold onto any security deposit.

Rent, Rent Increases, Rent Controls

The tenant must pay the rent on the dates stated in the lease. Rent is not payable in advance unless so stated. The tenant cannot withhold the rent because of a dispute with the landlord. The payment of rent is not conditional upon being totally satisfied with the landlord or the building.

There are some specific exceptions to the normal rule. If the tenant does not receive a copy of the lease, rent may be withheld. If the building is in poor condition, the tenant may apply to the court for permission to spend some of the rent money upon repairs. If the landlord is not living up to the contract (by not providing heat, for example), the tenant may apply to the court to have the rent reduced.

There has been a growth in the number of boards and tribunals to deal with landlord and tenant matters. This has been carried farthest in British Columbia where the Office of the Rentalsman was established in 1974. This office mediates disputes and acts as an informal court. Newfoundland and Nova Scotia have residential tenancy boards, with jurisdiction to deal with some aspects of landlord and tenant matters.

The most common point of disagreement has been over the payment of rent. Every province has experimented with rent controls and they still exist in over half the provinces. These controls normally limit rent increases to one per year and limit the increases to a set percentage. Landlords may apply for special exemption where they can show financial need.

Each province establishes the time period for giving notice to the tenant that the rent will be increased. In Newfoundland, a year-to-year tenancy requires three months' written notice. A month-to-month tenancy requires three months' notice as well. Alberta requires ninety days' written notice. In Ontario, a monthly or year-to-year tenancy requires ninety days' notice before the last day of the tenancy. The landlord must also give some justification of the necessity for the increase.

Termination of a Tenancy: Giving Notice

A periodic tenancy is usually terminated at the end of a rental period by either party giving *notice to quit*. Most provinces now require written notice and the notice must be served in a proper manner. Ontario requires the notice to be hand delivered to the tenant or to another adult living in the premises. If the tenant avoids service by staying away from the property, substitute service may be used including posting the notice in a prominent place or by mailing it by registered mail. The notice must be given sixty days in advance and must contain a reason if the landlord is directing the tenant to quit. The tenant does not have to give the landlord a reason if he or she is vacating.

In Alberta the landlord must give the tenant three months' written notice. The tenant must give notice of one month if the tenancy is monthly or sixty days if the tenancy is yearly. Notice can be served personally or by registered mail.

In Newfoundland either party must give three months' written notice to terminate a yearly lease. To terminate a monthly lease, the landlord must give three months' notice but the tenant need give only one month's notice. The landlord must hand deliver the notice but the tenant may hand deliver or use registered mail.

Rights and Duties of the Parties

Both the lessor and the lessee have certain rights and duties under their lease agreement. Some of these rights and duties arise under common law, and others may be prescribed by provincial statute.

Maintenance

In most provinces, the landlord is responsible for maintaining residential premises in a good state of repair and "fit for habitation." Some provinces apply the fit for habitation rule only to furnished premises. Ontario requires it for all residential premises. The landlord must comply with municipal health and safety standards.

 Pajelle Investments Ltd. v. Herbold
Supreme Court of Canada, 1976
The Supreme Court of Canada held that "rented premises" includes much more than just the tenants' living space. Where the landlord had induced the tenants into a rental agreement by offering a number of luxury features of the building, such as a swimming pool, the landlord had a duty to keep all such facilities in good working order. Short periods of breakdown and repair were tolerable, but where they existed for very long periods of time, the tenants were denied something they paid for and were entitled to an "abatement" (reduction) in their rent.

The tenant is responsible for ordinary cleanliness of the rented premises and for the repair of damage caused by wilful or negligent conduct or that of persons whom the tenant permits on the premises. The tenant is not responsible for damage caused by fire (provided the tenant did not start it), flood, tempest, or for normal wear and tear—unless he or she agreed in the lease to be responsible for these things. This means the tenant does not have to repair something that simply wears out through normal use, nor does he or she have to repair something damaged by a storm, flood, etc. The tenant is responsible for damage done by members of the family and their guests. The tenant would be liable to the landlord if he or she negligently started a fire, caused a sink to overflow and

flood the premises, or committed any negligent act which seriously damaged the premises or (in an apartment house) the surrounding premises.

The tenant can be liable to other tenants if he or she causes damage to their property. A tenant who permits a sink to overflow is liable to the tenants below whose property is water damaged. For this reason it is advisable to consider tenants' insurance.

If a third person is injured on the property, the landlord would be liable if the injury arose from a dangerous situation which it was the landlord's obligation to repair. The tenant is liable for unsafe conditions created by the tenant, or a member of the tenant's family. Thus, the tenant would be liable for leaving an object on a flight of steps and thereby causing a person to trip and fall down those steps.

 Lewis v. Westa Holdings
Ontario, 1975
The plaintiff had rented residential premises from the defendant. Included as a term of the lease was use of an inside parking space. The plaintiff sought damages for injuries suffered in attempting to open the garage door. The plaintiff had previously notified the defendant of the condition of the door. The action was allowed. The garage formed a part of the rented premises. The defendant was in breach of the duty to maintain the rented premises in a good state of repair and safe for the tenants.

Quiet Enjoyment

The tenant has an implied right to quiet enjoyment. This does not mean the landlord must ensure there is no noise around. It means that the landlord cannot bother the tenant by such things as continually entering the premises at will. There are some situations whereby the landlord has a right to enter, including:

(1) In cases of emergency;
(2) To show the property to a prospective tenant, at reasonable hours, after notice of termination has been given;

(3) To inspect the condition of the premises where the landlord has given written notice to the tenant. In Ontario notice must be given twenty-four hours in advance;

(4) If the tenant allows the landlord to enter.

The landlord cannot abuse the right to inspect the property by making frequent inspections and becoming a nuisance.

Post-Dated Cheques

Some landlords prefer to obtain from the tenant a number of post-dated cheques as a form of security that rent will be paid on time. Alberta and Ontario prohibit this practice upon penalty of a fine.

Withholding Services

A landlord may not withhold essential services such as heat, light, water, and telephone as a means of harassing the tenant to get him or her to quit. Most provinces prohibit this practice upon penalty of a fine.

Changing Locks

Neither the tenant nor the landlord may change the locks on the doors of the premises without the consent of the other. For example, the landlord cannot change the lock on the door while the tenant is out and thereby deny him or her entrance. Nor can either party install a second lock in addition to the existing one to deny the other entrance. The tenant may install a bolt or chain lock on the inside of the door for safety, since such a lock would be open when the tenant is out.

Security Deposits

When the tenant moves in, the landlord may ask for a security deposit. This sum of money has a variety of purposes. In most provinces it can be used by the landlord as compensation if the tenant skips without paying rent or leaves the building in poor condition.

Alberta permits one month's rent to be collected as a security deposit. The tenant will be paid 6 per cent interest on this sum each year. The landlord must give

the tenant an accounting ten days after the tenant vacates. If the landlord has deducted anything from the deposit, he or she must state the nature of the deduction. The landlord cannot withhold the tenant's money for ordinary wear and tear of the building.

Newfoundland permits a deposit of one-half of one month's rent which is returnable within thirty days after the tenant vacates. It earns interest at 6 per cent. Ontario permits the landlord to collect one month's rent which can only be used as payment of the last month's rent. The landlord cannot withhold this money because of alleged damage. Rent deposits earn 6 per cent interest.

Discrimination

A landlord may not refuse to rent to a person on the basis of race, religion, creed, colour, sex, marital status, or ethnic origin. Various provinces have other specific prohibitions regarding discrimination. Ontario adds age, ancestry, receipt of public aid, handicap, and family status. Newfoundland also includes political affiliation.

Would such a rental "policy" be lawful in your province?

Generally, landlords can refuse to rent to tenants owning animals. An exception in several provinces is the seeing-eye dog of a blind person. However, in 1982, an Ontario court held that a tenant could not be evicted simply because the tenant violated her lease by purchasing a dog. The court held that there must be evidence that the presence of the dog caused a problem.

A difficult area of law involves the exclusion of children. If a landlord states a policy that no children will be permitted within the building, most provincial laws do not prevent this form of exclusion. However, if the tenants have a child after occupying the building, some provinces will not permit them to be evicted just because they now have a child. Ontario and British Columbia specifically prohibit eviction because of "family status."

Eviction

If the tenant refuses to vacate after being given notice by the landlord, the landlord may seek to evict the tenant. The manner in which this may be done lawfully differs from province to province, but generally the landlord is prohibited from using violence. Forceful eviction must be accomplished, if necessary, by the sheriff and bailiffs upon the order of a court. In Ontario, the eviction procedure must follow this sequence:

(1) The landlord must file for a writ of possession in the county court. A copy of the motion must be delivered to the tenant who may file a dispute within four days.

(2) The tenant may appear at a hearing before the clerk of the court on the date specified in the motion and make it known that he or she denies the landlord's right to possession. If the tenant does not dispute possession, the landlord will be granted the writ of possession and the sheriff ordered to obtain possession. The time of repossession may be delayed for a few days to allow the tenant to vacate quietly.

(3) If the tenant disputes possession, the final decision concerning possession will be decided at a full hearing before a county court judge. At this time the judge will either grant the landlord the writ of possession or deny it. If the tenant wishes, he or she may appeal this decision to a higher court.

In order to get possession in Alberta, the landlord must first obtain an order for possession. If the tenant still remains, the landlord may then apply for a writ of possession.

If a tenant commits a "substantial breach" of the lease, the tenant may be ordered to quit without being given the normal time period of notice. Substantial breach may include damaging the property, annoying other tenants, endangering the safety of other tenants, using the premises for illegal purposes, or having a sufficient number of persons on the premises to contravene health and safety standards.

A tenant can eventually be evicted for non-payment of rent, but this is a more difficult process. Most provinces will not permit a landlord to immediately evict a tenant for a late or missed rent payment. The landlord may sue for the payment but a writ of possession is normally granted only where there is no likelihood that the tenant will ever pay the rent.

Non-payment of rent may eventually lead to eviction, although in some provinces it requires a court order.

Distress

If a tenant failed to pay the rent, the early common law permitted the landlord to exercise a right of distress. This meant that the landlord had the right to enter the premises and seize the tenant's personal property in order to distrain for unpaid rent. The tenant had to pay the rent to get his or her belongings back.

The provinces have abolished distress as far as it applies to residential properties. The unpaid landlord can no longer seize the property of the tenant (in a residential lease) for unpaid rent. The landlord must sue in civil court like any other creditor.

Removal of Fixtures

It is a common law rule that all fixtures (with some exceptions) are the landlord's fixtures. When tenants vacate, they have the right to remove their chattels. They can remove their property which is attached to the premises if they can do so without damage, but they cannot tear out built-in cabinets, or remove tiles or wall coverings. Tenants may not uproot or take away plants or shrubs they have planted. Any buildings erected by tenants must remain, and tenants would be advised to bear this in mind before starting any construction work on property. The rule is, *superficus solo credit* ("whatever is attached to the land is part of it"). Actual physical attachment is not essential — for example, a stone wall is part of the land even if it just sits on the land. Statues, figures, and stone seats have been held to be part of the land because they were part of the design of the property, even though they were merely standing by their own weight.

Tenants have no inherent right to alter materially the appearance of the premises. If a tenant embarks upon a home decorating binge, the irate landlord may require the tenant to restore the premises to exactly their original appearance when rented. In one instance, the tenant cut a door through a wall, thinking it would be convenient. The landlord rightly insisted that the wall be restored.

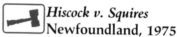 *Hiscock v. Squires*
Newfoundland, 1975

The tenant leased some business premises on a monthly basis and undertook some renovations at a cost in excess of $8000. Two months later, the landlord gave him a notice to quit which he refused to do. The landlord sued and the tenant counterclaimed for the cost of the renovations. The court held that the landlord did not have to renew the lease even though the tenant had invested so much on the assumption that he would have use of the premises for a long period of time. Nor did the landlord have to compensate the tenant for the renovations.

It was established that certain exterior alterations were carried out in distinct contradiction of the landlord's wishes. One of the compelling reasons for which the landlord gave notice to quit was the concern that the tenant was going to make more renovations which would change the nature and appearance of the building permanently. The tenant's unwillingness to heed the landlord's orders to stop changing the building was a valid reason to be required to give up possession.

Subsequent Foreclosure or Sale

Although the tenant is granted the right of possession of the property leased, the landlord still remains the owner of the property and may sell it at any time. Normally, if this happens, the lease is not affected. The purchaser of the property accepts the presence and rights of the tenant in possession when buying the property, and the tenant simply pays the rent to the new owner. The tenant would be doubly protected if he or she took the time to register the lease.

Where the property is mortgaged, the position of the tenant is less secure. If the landlord fails to pay the mortgage, and the mortgagee forecloses and takes possession, the tenant could be required to vacate. This is a vague area of law, but it usually depends on whether it was the mortgage or the lease that was signed and registered first. If, as is usually the case, the mortgage was arranged prior to the lease, the tenant must give way to the claim of the mortgagee.

Reviewing Important Points

1. A lease must meet certain minimum requirements, including (a) exclusive possession, (b) defined premises, and (c) an intention to grant a lease.
2. A lease for a fixed period must start and end at a determinable time.
3. A periodic tenancy can be created by express agreement or by implied behaviour such as payment of rent on a regular basis.
4. A tenant who sublets remains completely liable to the landlord for rent and damage to the property.
5. Where a lease for a fixed term is held over, it is presumed that the original term has been renewed.
6. In most provinces, the landlord is responsible for maintaining residential premises in a good state of repair and "fit for habitation."
7. Rent is not a conditional payment. The tenant cannot withhold the rent every time he or she has a dispute with the landlord. Rent is not payable in advance unless the lease requires it.
8. A tenant has no inherent right to alter materially the appearance of the premises.

Checking Your Understanding

1. Under what conditions can an oral lease be binding?
2. What is the difference between a lease and an agreement to lease?
3. Explain the major distinction between assigning a lease and subletting.
4. If a tenant does not pay the rent, what action can the landlord take?
5. Explain briefly the tenant's right of quiet enjoyment.
6. What is a tenancy at will?
7. What is the landlord's responsibility in regard to maintaining the premises?

8. If a tenant is dissatisfied with the landlord, can the tenant withhold the rent to force some change in performance?
9. Under what circumstances may the landlord enter the premises?

Legal Briefs

1. V, a tenant, tells P, the landlord, that the steps leading to the rented house are rotten. The landlord takes no action and G, a guest of V, is injured when the steps collapse. V did not give G any verbal warning about the steps. Liability of V and P?
2. T lives in an apartment owned by L. The lease calls for heat to be provided from October 1 to April 30 each year. One spring the winter does not seem to recede and the weather remains cold into May.
T demands that the heat be left on since the apartment is not "fit for habitation" when it is so cold. Must L comply?
3. S is a tenant of R. On July 1, she receives a notice by ordinary mail stating that her rent will increase effective August 1. Her tenancy is month to month. Must she pay the increase? (Answer may vary by province.)
4. B is a tenant of W, renting half a duplex. W advises B that the property will be inspected on Christmas Eve. Must B accept this arrangement?
5. H, a tenant, calls upon N, the landlord, to have a burned-out hot water tank element replaced. N sends an electrician who does the work. Later the electrician tells N that there was a smell of marijuana in the house. N gives H notice to vacate immediately because of "certain illegal activities on the premises." Must H vacate?
6. When B and L, a married couple, rented their apartment from K, only B, the husband, signed the lease. Later they separated and L remained in the apartment. She paid the rent for four months and K accepted the payments. Then, L acquired a new boyfriend who moved in with her. K gave her a notice to quit stating that she had no right to be in the apart-

ment because she had not signed the lease. Must L vacate?

7. When R, a landlord, decided to increase her tenants' rent, she went through the building and shoved notices under all the doors. Valid notice?

8. Y was two months behind in the rent. When Y was out one day, the landlord removed Y's stereo and television set and left a note saying they would be returned when the rent was paid. Lawful action by the landlord?

9. C rents an apartment from F. Unhappy with the poor appearance of tile floors, C installs wall-to-wall carpet in the living and dining rooms. She later decides to vacate and plans to take the carpet. F warns her not to take the carpet because it is a fixture. When the carpet was installed carpet nails were driven into the floor around the walls of the rooms. Is the carpet a fixture?

10. When the J's applied to rent an apartment, the rental agent asked them how many children they had. They replied "one." After they had moved into a two-bedroom apartment, the rental agent learned that the couple really had three children. They received a notice to quit with the stated reason being "misrepresentation and overcrowding." The J's contended that they could only afford a two-bedroom apartment. Must they vacate?

Applying the Law

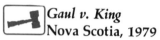

Gaul v. King
Nova Scotia, 1979

A tenant was injured when her foot went through a wooden board on the back veranda. Neither the landlord nor the tenant was aware of the danger. On appeal from dismissal of the tenant's action, the appeal was dismissed. The provincial statute created an implied covenant whereby the landlord was obligated to keep the rented premises in a good state of repair, fit for habitation, and in a condition that conformed to the standards set out in the statute. These enactments included city ordinan-

ces. The landlord could not be held strictly liable but could be held liable for negligence if there was a failure to repair. A breach of this duty could not be considered prima facie evidence of negligence and the duty was upon the plaintiff to prove negligence. While it was not a requirement of liability that the tenant give the landlord notice of a defect, the landlord could not be held liable for defects of which the landlord had no knowledge and which were not discoverable by the exercise of reasonable care and skill.

Questions

1. Why was the landlord held not to be liable?
2. Is ignorance a defence in a situation such as this? Could the landlord always escape liability by never inspecting the property?
3. Is a rotten board not something that can be detected? If you were conducting an inspection, how would you inspect a wooden veranda?

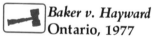

Baker v. Hayward
Ontario, 1977

The appellant was the subtenant in a rooming house which the tenant leased from the owners. The tenant defaulted under the lease and the owners obtained a writ of possession ordering the sheriff to restore possession of the premises to the owners. The appellant applied to a county court judge for an order staying execution of the writ. The basis of the action was that the subtenant had never been given notice that the writ was being sought and had not been granted a hearing as the Act required. The Court of Appeal held that a subtenant was entitled to notice of the application for a writ of possession and had a right to be heard. A subtenant may also apply for relief against forfeiture either on a personal application or in the landlord's application.

Questions

1. What did the Court of Appeal conclude regarding the rights of a subtenant?

2. If the landlord did not know of the existence of the subtenant, would this make any difference in the decision?

3. Could the subtenant bring an action against the tenant for defaulting on the lease and causing the problem in the first place?

You Be the Judge

1. The plaintiff, the widow of a man electrocuted by a pump motor, sued the defendant, her landlord, alleging negligence causing her husband's death. The landlord had purchased and installed a sump pump in the basement of the rented house. The basement was very small with an earth floor. One day the pump started making a great deal of noise and then stopped running. Water began to accumulate in the basement so the husband went down to check the pump. He was not a qualified electrician nor an expert in pumps but had a basic knowledge of how they worked. When he touched the pump, an electrical short circuit gave him a fatal shock. It was determined that he was standing in water at the time which increased the severity of the shock. The pump was later examined and was found to have been hooked up incorrectly by the landlord. The landlord defended the action by saying the deceased man should not have attempted to deal with something about which he had little knowledge. An expert would have disconnected the pump before ever touching it. Who would succeed?

2. The plaintiff landlord sued the defendant tenant for breach of contract. The two had a discussion about a one-year lease for an apartment and the tenant obtained the key, paid two months' rent, and moved some personal items into the apartment. The landlord said that a written lease would be available as soon as her lawyer returned from vacation in three weeks. At the end of the first month the lease was still not available and the tenant moved out saying that the building was too noisy and that there were fumes from an underground garage constantly in the apartment. The tenant had not yet signed the lease and asked for the return of the second month's rent. The landlord sued for breach of contract, saying they had a one-year lease. Who would succeed?

3. The defendant couple signed a lease with the plaintiff landlord and stated that they had two children. Four months later the brother and sister-in-law of the husband moved in with them, along with their two children. The landlord objected to this arrangement and gave them a notice to quit. The defendants argued that the situation was only temporary as the brother had lost his job and they had no place to stay until he found another. They were not making excessive noise and there was no violation of any health code. The lease did not specifically limit the number of persons who could live in the premises. Who would succeed?

4. When the defendant looked for an apartment, she had no success. Landlords rejected her because she was unmarried, had two children, and was living on welfare. She then had a friend rent an apartment in his name, but she moved in. The friend signed a document subletting the apartment to her but did not tell the landlord. When the landlord learned of this fact, the woman was ordered to leave because it was stated she had no legal right to be in the building at all. The rent had been paid each month by the defendant's friend, but she gave the money to him. When she refused to leave, the landlord sought a writ of possession. Who would succeed?

5. The plaintiff landlord sought to recover a house from the defendant tenant. Shortly after moving in, the tenant began taking in boarders, sometimes as many as five persons at one time. The lease did not specifically prohibit boarders but did require that subletting could not be done without the permission of the landlord and payment of a fee. The tenant argued that she was not subletting. The landlord noted that there were only three bedrooms in the house and that having so many people living there increased the wear and tear on the building substantially. Who would succeed?

Unit
Eleven

Family Law

Cruelty is hard to define but easy to recognize.

Chapter 24

Marriage, Annulment, Separation, and Divorce

The topic of family law is a very expansive one, much affected by the surge of law reform during the last decade. Thus, it is not possible to cover all the laws of all the provinces in our discussion here.

Marriage: Some Historical Notes

In order to understand the present-day legal status of marriage, it is helpful to look at the historic origins of that form of marriage sometimes referred to as "common law" marriage. For many years, the Roman Catholic Church in England had authority over marriage and, surprisingly, canon law permitted marriage without any formal ceremony. All that was required was that the couple exchange consents, meaning that they would take each other as husband and wife. The marriage was completed once sexual intercourse took place. This was referred to as "consummation."

Informal marriages continued to be recognized in England until the passage of *Lord Hardwicke's Act* in 1753. This Act required a public church ceremony, two witnesses, and a record of all marriages. It was repealed in 1823 and replaced with a less rigid *Marriage Act*. *Lord Hardwicke's Act* did not apply to Scotland, Ireland, or any lands across the sea. English people crossed the border and had informal marriages performed in Scotland for many years. Particularly popular were marriages performed by the blacksmith in Gretna Green, Scotland.

It is unclear whether *Lord Hardwicke's Act* ever applied to Canada, but the provinces have all enacted statutes requiring some type of formal marriage. Only certain vestiges of common law marriages are still recognized.

Marriage and Constitutional Law

Under the *Constitution Act, 1867* the federal government has the power to enact laws concerning "Marriage and Divorce." The provincial governments have the power to enact statutes in relation to "Solemnization of Marriage."

This division basically means that the federal government may establish the essential requirements of what constitutes a valid marriage. This would include freely consenting to the marriage, being of sound mind, and not being already married.

The provinces control the formal requirements of marriage, such as issuing licences, and stipulating residency requirements. Failure to meet a formal requirement does not necessarily render a marriage void as long as the essential requirements have been met.

Sometimes it is unclear whether the government creating certain requirements really has the legal power to do so. For example, it would be within the power of the federal government to decide who may not marry because they are too closely related. However, because the federal government has not enacted such a list, the provinces have moved into the void and created their own lists. An example of such a list is shown a little later in this unit. The constitutionality of such lists has been successfully challenged on more than one occasion, as the following case indicates:

Christians v. Hill
Alberta, 1981

The issuer of marriage licences for Alberta refused to issue a licence to the applicant for her intended marriage to the brother of her divorced husband, who was still living. In the Alberta regulation there is a list of twenty persons a man may not marry and a list of twenty persons a woman may not marry and these lists are intended to be bars to the lawful solemnization of marriage. The twentieth person on the list that a man may not marry is his brother's wife and the twentieth person on the list that a woman may not marry is her husband's brother. If the divorced husband had died, the marriage could be permitted, but as he was alive the marriage fell within the group of banned marriages. The Court of Queen's Bench held that the province did not have the constitutional power to determine eligibility to marry since that power belonged to the Parliament of Canada. The court further noted that Parliament, by giving the parties to a marriage the unrestricted right to remarry after a decree absolute (final decree) of divorce has been granted, has demonstrated that there is no prohibition against a woman's marrying the brother of her divorced husband.

Qualifications To Marry

There are few legal requirements for marriage. The basic requirements are that the person is not already married, is of sound mind, has a sexual capacity, and is free from duress or threats. Sexual capacity means that the person is capable of performing the act of intercourse with another. A marriage would be void if the person married knowing that he or she was incapable of performing the sex act. While provincial statutes do not specifically prohibit persons of the same sex from marrying, the common law does require that the couple be of opposite sex. In *North v. Matheson* (1976), the Manitoba Court of Appeal held that a marriage ceremony uniting two males was a nullity even

though the provincial statute refers only to the marriage of "two persons."

The various provinces have enacted residency and licensing requirements. Information should be obtained from the nearest licensing office. In some provinces it is permissible to marry without a licence. The couple must arrange for the publication of church banns for three consecutive Sundays. Persons who have been divorced must obtain a licence.

Each province establishes minimum age requirements. Some require a blood test. The following chart summarizes these requirements:

MARRIAGEABLE AGE

Province	Without Parental Consent	With Parental Consent	Blood Test Required
Alberta	18	Under 18	yes
B.C.	19	16-18*	no
Manitoba	18	16*	yes
New Brunswick	18	Under 18	no
Newfoundland	19**	Under 19	no
Nova Scotia	19 or over	16	no
Ontario	18	16	no
P.E.I.	18	Under 18	yes
Quebec	18	Male 14 Female 12	no
Saskatchewan	18	16-18	yes

*Under 16 requires court order
**Except expectant mothers or mothers of illegitimate children

The question sometimes arises as to which parent may give consent to the marriage of a minor. If the parents are living together, the consent is normally given by the father. If they are separated, the parent with custody should give consent. For example, Newfoundland law requires the consent of the father, if he is living, unless the mother or another person has custody of the child; or the father is mentally incompetent; or the father is not supporting the child. Ontario law requires the consent of both parents if they are living together. If one is deceased, or they are separated, consent must be given by the parent with custody of the child.

If consent is unreasonably withheld, application may be made to the court to have the requirement of parental consent dispensed with and permission given to marry.

Disqualifications from Marriage

Some persons are legally disqualified from marriage. In addition to not meeting the qualifications already discussed, the following conditions would bar legal marriage.

Close Relationship

A person cannot marry anyone with a blood relationship that is too close. The relationship by blood or descent is call *consanguinity*. The prohibition is a recognition of the relationship between physical and mental disorders and intermarriages. As well, if a relationship is created by marriage, it is one of *affinity* and there are prohibitions within that category as well.

The prohibited degrees of consanguinity and affinity are stated in the *Marriage Act* of each province. The list in each province is very similar to the following list taken from the Ontario statute:

FORM 1
(Section 19)
Degrees of affinity and consanguinity which, under the statutes in that behalf, bar the lawful solemnization of marriage.

A man may not marry his	A woman may not marry her
1. Grandmother	1. Grandfather
2. Grandfather's wife	2. Grandmother's husband
3. Wife's grandmother	3. Husband's grandfather
4. Aunt	4. Uncle
5. Wife's aunt	5. Husband's uncle
6. Mother	6. Father
7. Step mother	7. Step father
8. Wife's mother	8. Husband's father
9. Daughter	9. Son
10. Wife's daughter	10. Husband's son
11. Son's wife	11. Daughter's husband
12. Sister	12. Brother
13. Granddaughter	13. Grandson
14. Grandson's wife	14. Granddaughter's husband
15. Wife's granddaughter	15. Husband's grandson
16. Niece	16. Nephew
17. Nephew's wife	17. Niece's husband

The relationships set forth in this table include all such relationships, whether by the whole or half blood.

Mistake

A marriage is not legal if either party was unaware of the nature of the ceremony being performed. An example would be a person of foreign birth, speaking no English, who went through a marriage ceremony believing it to be only an engagement ceremony.

It should be noted that marriage is considered to be a voluntary agreement, unless proved otherwise. This means that the two parties are obligated to learn all the facts about each other before the wedding. Neither an annulment nor a divorce will be granted on the grounds of "deception" by one party. Therefore, if a person did not disclose some personal characteristic fault to the other, there is no remedy once married. Thus, a person could not seek an annulment or divorce on such grounds as, "I didn't know he or she had been married before," or "I didn't know he or she drank." Also, promises made but not kept are not grounds for annulment or divorce. For example, if one spouse promised never to smoke, to build a cottage, and to move the other spouse's parents in with them — and then broke all these promises — there is no remedy at law for these failings.

The Traditional Marriage Relationship

At common law, marriage altered the legal status of the two persons who married and created one legal personality. This was called *conjugal unity.* The marriage had the greatest legal impact upon the wife. She was deprived of the legal capacity to own property in her own right. In exchange, she acquired the right to be supported by her husband and had a claim upon his property in the form of her right of dower. If the wife separated from her husband for any reason other than his gross misconduct, she lost all right to support. However, the common law placed no duty upon the wife to ever support her husband. If the couple separated because of the husband's wrongdoing, the courts would require him to support the wife for the rest of her life, as long as she remained married to him or did not marry again following a divorce. The wife had to remain chaste and not live with another man to continue to receive this support. When the husband died, he did not have to leave anything in his will to his wife and children. He could disinherit his family without reason. If the wife took a job outside the home, this could be interpreted as desertion. All important decisions regarding the children were made by the father and he alone could sign contracts.

Marriage Contracts

The common law did not permit any such device as a contract between married spouses for two main reasons. The first was the fact that marriage created one legal person and a minimum of two persons are required to enter into a contract. The second was the absence of any legal standing in the wife to enter into any contract.

All provinces now permit marriage contracts of some type. The legislation in Alberta, Saskatchewan, Manitoba, and Nova Scotia permits contracts between married spouses only, while in the other provinces it extends to unmarried couples as well. In British Columbia, it extends only to unmarried couples. Marriage contracts can cover an almost unlimited variety of topics, but most concentrate upon the rights of the spouses under the marriage, upon separation, or upon death, including:

- Ownership in or division of property;
- Support obligations;
- The right to direct the education and moral training of children.

In Ontario and Newfoundland it is not permissible for the marriage contract to provide for custody or access rights to children. These matters can only be dealt with in a separation agreement and even then only the court can make the final decision as to what is in the best interests of the child. The Ontario statute also states that any provision in a contract that requires a spouse to give up an interest in the matrimonial home is void.

Most provinces provide that the parties may make provision in a marriage contract regarding the death of either spouse. This may lead to a conflict with other provincial laws pertaining to wills. Only the Newfoundland statute states that the court may enforce the contract notwithstanding the provisions of the *Wills Act.*

Thus, a potential problem could arise where a person might make one commitment in a marriage contract and then prepare a last will and testament with completely different terms. Which takes priority? There is no immediate answer to this problem, but the case of *Phillips v. Spooner* (Saskatchewan, 1975) may be of assistance. In that case, the plaintiff sued the estate of her deceased husband because his will did not provide for her as promised in a separation agreement. The court held that she had a valid claim against his estate. It was held that a person may contract to dispose of his or her assets by will.

Marriage contracts should not be cluttered with trivial matters, such as who will wash the dishes, since the courts do not enforce contracts for personal services and have no way of enforcing personal matters within the matrimonial home.

The Newfoundland and Ontario statutes state that the court may disregard anything in a contract that does not provide for the best interests of a child.

The Ontario law provides that the court may ignore a provision for financial support in any contract where the terms are unconscionable, or a spouse would have to go on welfare if the contract was enforced. The court may set the amount of financial support at any level it sees proper.

Another problem that could arise might be the existence of more than one domestic contract. Let us assume that a woman lives with her husband with whom she has a marriage contract. She leaves her husband and lives with a second man with whom she signs a cohabitation agreement. The promise to share assets is the same in both contracts. Would the current cohabitation agreement take priority or would the previous marriage contract have more validity? We have no settled case to use as a guide.

Cohabitees

Persons who are not married, but who live together, are not fully protected by provincial laws. They need a *cohabitation agreement* more than married couples need a marriage contract. Unfortunately, not all provinces will permit cohabitation agreements. The agreement should be formally executed with competent witnesses and seals. It should cover all matters relating to property, support, and children. It is important to remember that unmarried cohabitation is voluntary and that neither person is affected by the obligations and rights normally found in a legal marriage. Our discussion will be limited to two key areas: support and property.

Support

At common law there is no obligation of support as far as cohabitees are concerned. In all provinces, the provincial laws do not include cohabitees in the rules of inheritance. Therefore, one cohabitee may receive nothing if the other cohabitee dies without leaving a will. Ontario law includes as a "spouse," *for purposes of support only,* a man or a woman who have lived together

continuously for a period of not less than five years; or who have lived together in a relationship of some permanence which has resulted in their becoming the natural parents of a child. Ontario requires the longest period of cohabitation—B.C. requires two years, while Nova Scotia, Newfoundland, and Manitoba require only one year.

Property

Persons who live together have no claim upon each other's property unless it can be shown that one person contributed money to the acquisition of the other's property; or that one person was just holding the property in a "constructive trust" for the other. Once again, the importance of a cohabitation agreement should be emphasized in relation to property.

In the case of *Pettkus v. Becker,* discussed in Unit Ten, the Supreme Court of Canada awarded Becker an equal share of the property on the basis that a constructive trust existed and that it would be unjust enrichment for Pettkus to get everything. The decision reads in part:

> 66 The compelling inference from the facts is that she believed she had some interest in the farm and that the expectation was reasonable in the circumstances.... There is no evidence to indicate that he ever informed her that all her work performed over the nineteen years was being performed on a gratuitous basis. He freely accepted the benefits conferred upon him through her financial support and her labour. 99

 Slemko v. Yarmak
Alberta, 1982

The plaintiff and the defendant each contributed money to the purchase price of land and a house; however, the property was registered in the name of the defendant alone. The evidence was that the defendant and her mother wanted to buy a house and that the plaintiff, a friend of the defendant, found a house for her and contributed some of the money. The transfer papers originally showed the house in the names of both the plaintiff and the defendant, but the defendant became very angry about this and refused to complete the purchase. The plaintiff then told the lawyer to put the house in the name of the defendant alone. They lived together in the house for a short time before the plaintiff moved out. He brought an action to have a declaration that he was entitled to an interest in the property. The defendant argued that the money paid by the plaintiff was a loan to her and that he had no interest in the property. The court noted that for the plaintiff to prove an interest in the property the two things that had to be considered were the nature of the conveyance and the common intention of the parties. The court held that there was no resulting trust and that the plaintiff had no interest in the property. The defendant clearly indicated that she intended that the house would be her house, for the use of herself and her mother. The money paid by the plaintiff was to be regarded as a personal loan to the defendant.

In a few areas, legislative recognition of cohabitees or common law spouses has occurred. The *Workmen's Compensation Act* of most provinces permits the payment of benefits to the common law spouse of a person accidentally killed on the job. The *Canada Pension Plan* recognizes the common law spouse for pension purposes.

Matrimonial Property

Family Assets

In Unit Ten the disposition of the matrimonial home was discussed. In this unit, we shall take a further look at assets other than the home.

The case of *Murdoch v. Murdoch* brought home the weakness in the previous law — the value of a woman's labour in the home was given no recognition. The Supreme Court of Canada found that, in the absence of legislative recognition, a wife did not obtain ownership rights to property in a husband's name merely because she worked hard to assist him in acquiring and developing that property. Much of the recent law

reform has been aimed at altering that situation. Perhaps most striking are the words of the Ontario *Family Law Reform Act* which read:

4. (5) The purpose of this section is to recognize that child care, household management and financial provision are the joint responsibilities of the spouses and that inherent in the marital relationship there is joint contribution, whether financial or otherwise, by the spouses to the assumption of these responsibilities, entitling each spouse to an equal division of the family assets, subject to the equitable considerations set out in subsections 4 and 6.

These words should perhaps be printed in giant letters, for it has finally been established, in law, what has been known, in fact, for centuries—that marriage is a partnership to which the contribution of labour is

When Irene Murdoch was told by the Supreme Court of Canada that she had no legal claim to her husband's farm, the case aroused such concern that nearly all provinces changed their laws regarding matrimonial property.

of equal value to the contribution of money. The statutes of Alberta, British Columbia, and Newfoundland are very similar. For example, s. 17 of the Newfoundland *Matrimonial Property Act* is almost identical to the Ontario statute. For more specific information, the appropriate provincial statute should be consulted.

The courts may now divide equally all family assets, including personal property and bank accounts. Different provinces have different definitions of what constitutes family or matrimonial assets. Some exclude property acquired before marriage. Property given to one spouse as a gift, or an inheritance, may be exempt from any claim by the other spouse. It is possible for a spouse to claim part ownership in business assets built up by the other spouse if (1) the spouse worked without pay for that business; or (2) the work of one spouse in taking care of the home and children freed the other spouse to devote full time to building a successful business. The concept here is that if one spouse shouldered all the domestic tasks while the other concentrated upon a business, they have both contributed equally to acquiring the family assets.

Bregman v. Bregman
Ontario, 1978

In considering the financial arrangements applicable to the spouses since their marriage in 1948, the court found:

1. The wife was the wage earner during the early years of the marriage; her wage contributions went to household expenses and to savings.
2. Upon the birth of the first child in 1951, the wife ceased employment and devoted herself to the management of the household and the care of the child. The husband acted as the financial mainstay of the family.
3. To provide financial security for the family, the husband created one company, wholly owned by the wife, and another company (with his partner), in which the wives held 50 per cent of the shares. A trust had also been created by the husband, valued at $150 000 of which the children were the beneficiaries.

4. The husband's income, in part, was paid into a joint account out of which household expenses were paid. After 1975, in lieu of the wife's use of this joint account, the husband paid the wife $2500 per month.

In discussing how family assets should be identified, the court held:

1. The onus is upon the person who is claiming division of family assets to establish what property is so included under the heading of family assets.

2. The fundamental test for the determination of a family asset is that it be ordinarily used or enjoyed by the other spouse, or a child, during the period of cohabitation.

The court made the following decisions regarding family assets:

1. The husband's collection of Oriental rugs, kept in a separate receptacle and not generally used or displayed in the home, were considered to be his private collection and not family assets.
2. A sailboat purchased for $160 000 by a private company, of which the husband was the sole shareholder, was not a family asset since it was used by only one spouse. This was so notwithstanding the fact that the other spouse alleged that the sailboat had been purchased in lieu of a summer home.
3. A painting, valued at $24 000, which had been transferred from the husband's office to the home, was a family asset even though it belonged to the husband's company.

In further dividing the assets, the court held:

1. The fact that the wife was the wage earner until the birth of the first child—contributing to household expenses, and, through her parents, providing lodging for the spouses—brought her under the section of the Act which recognized the traditional role of a wife and mother in the financial success achieved by a husband.
2. Some distribution of non-family assets was necessary to recognize the wife's contribution to their acquisition by the performance of a domestic role. The wife's assumption of these domestic

responsibilities had left the husband free, physically and mentally, to work at his profession and to manage his considerable personal assets.

3. The court allocated to the wife non-family assets of $300 000, in addition to those assets, worth $130 000, already provided to her by the husband. This brought her total assets to $774 000 with a net annual income, after taxes, of $31 000.

4. The husband's net worth was assessed at $2.5 million with an annual net income of $200 000.

5. The wife should not, at the age of fifty-six years, be forced by the court to go to work to supplement her income. Therefore, for her protection in case circumstances should change, the husband was ordered to pay her maintenance. The maintenance was initially set at the nominal sum of one dollar per year; however, if circumstances required it, the wife could return to the court to ask that the order be varied and the amount increased.

6. The matrimonial home was to be sold and the proceeds divided equally.

When dividing the property, the court should take into account the duration of the marriage, the date the property was acquired, and the estimated living costs of the spouses. However, couples must realize that, when they separate, they cannot both expect to live at the same standard as when they were married. Both must expect some reduction in the standard of living to which they have become accustomed.

Badcock v. Badcock
Newfoundland, 1981

The parties, both aged sixty-eight, separated in 1978. The husband was a sailor and the wife assumed the major responsibility for child and home care. The wife oversaw the building of a new house, but refused to live in it. The husband turned his wages over to the wife, and this money went into the home. The husband had also acquired land before the marriage. The wife brought an action for disposition of the matrimonial assets under the *Matrimonial Property Act.* It was held that the property

should be divided equally. The new house was a matrimonial asset and would be divided equally. The land acquired by the husband before the marriage was not a matrimonial asset. In the circumstances it was not desirable to dispose of the house immediately. The husband was to be given time to purchase the wife's interest in the house.

Non-Family Assets

In Manitoba, Saskatchewan, Alberta, and Quebec, the law starts with the principle that everything acquired during marriage is to be equally shared. The court may modify that 50-50 split of assets to achieve fairness.

In the other provinces, the law takes the view that a spouse may claim an interest in non-family assets but must prove that it would be unfair not to be given an equal share. The Ontario statute states that "The court shall make a division of any property that is not a family asset where the result of a division of the family assets would be inequitable in all the circumstances." The section then gives recognition to the contribution of one spouse in managing the responsibilities at home while the other spouse is free to pursue an income outside the home. However, in *Leatherdale v. Leatherdale* (1982), the Supreme Court of Canada concluded that the Ontario law afforded a wife only a share of non-family assets *in accordance with her contribution as a wage earner.* In the *Leatherdale* case, the wife had worked outside the home for nine years and had worked at home for ten years of the marriage. The Ontario court had awarded her 50 per cent of the non-family assets, consisting mostly of stocks and a retirement plan in the husband's name. The Supreme Court of Canada reduced this to 25 per cent saying that she was only entitled to that portion which represented the years she worked outside the home. It is likely that this decision will necessitate a change in the Ontario statute.

Financial Support

At long last we have a statute which tells us precisely the facts to be taken into account when support or maintenance of a dependant is assessed.... The key words are the words, *"in relation to need."* I suggest that these words be framed and never forgotten. Douglas Lissaman, Q.C.

The common law had a very inflexible concept of spousal support. Only the wife was entitled to support and the husband had to provide the wife with support for life unless she was guilty of some misconduct.

Law reform is moving away from this concept. The courts will now consider the financial situation of *both* spouses and will award support to the wife on the basis of her need rather than just as a matter of right. Most dramatic is the wording of the Ontario statute which states that each spouse has an obligation to support himself or herself to the extent the spouse is capable of doing so. If the spouses separate, each spouse will be expected to fend for himself or herself as soon as reasonably possible. The court will take into consideration the age and health of the spouses and the desirability of one spouse's remaining at home to care for children. The court must also avoid tagging one spouse with a lifetime of support payments, since there is a possibility that that spouse might wish to remarry and might not be able to support two families. Thus, to the extent possible, the first spouse and family should become self-supporting at the earliest reasonable date.

The concept of "in relation to need" is not absolutely clear or final. Consequently, there is a great deal of uncertainty when a court makes an order for financial support and courts often vary earlier orders for financial support. Moreover, in orders for financial support, courts have begun to include a built-in provision that the amount will increase in accordance with the cost of living index.

One important aspect of the Ontario law, as well as that of some other provinces, is that financial support can be claimed by either the husband or the wife. The common law only recognized the right of the wife to seek support.

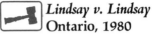 *Lindsay v. Lindsay*
Ontario, 1980

The petitioner wife sought a divorce from the respondent husband and included in her petition a request for financial support. A very unusual part of her request was her contention that the husband should recompense her for the loss of a pension she had enjoyed from a previous marriage. The wife was a widow whose first husband had been killed in World War II. She had been paid a widow's pension for a number of years before she decided to marry the respondent. Her remarriage meant that she would forfeit her pension. In her petition she claimed that she had expected to be able to maintain a much higher standard of living than the present husband had afforded her. The court held that the petitioner had much larger financial assets than the respondent and that her voluntary surrender of a pension, in order to marry him, did not entitle her to later claim reimbursement for the loss of this income. The petition for divorce was granted but no order was made for support.

Annulment of Marriage

Annulment does not dissolve an existing marriage, but declares that the marriage was not lawfully performed or that the marriage union was never completed. The grounds for annulment include:

(1) *Lack of legal capacity:* That is, if either party was under age, intoxicated, mentally defective, etc., or if the parties were closely related.

(2) *Lack of genuine consent by either party:* Existence of mistake or duress.

(3) *Grave defects in the ceremony:* A service performed by a person not legally qualified to do so would not be legal. Two persons "married" on a motorcycle by a mechanic reading from a repair manual were not lawfully married.

(4) *Lack of consummation:* If either party is unable or unwilling to engage in sexual intercourse, either party may file for annulment. Later impotence dur-

ing the marriage is not grounds for annulment, but it may be grounds for divorce.

Heilen v. Andersson
Alberta, 1978

A husband, domiciled in Alberta, applied for a declaration of nullity of marriage. The applicant, while temporarily living in California, was tricked by the respondent wife and another man into taking narcotics, which it was not his custom to do. For the next few weeks, the applicant was kept under the influence of narcotics. He then went through a ceremony of marriage. He lived with the respondent for twenty-eight days after the ceremony, but throughout that period was kept by the respondent and her friend in a condition of helplessness by being given narcotics.

A declaration of nullity was granted. The marriage was void *ab initio* ("from the beginning"). When the applicant went through the marriage ceremony he was so affected by the narcotics that he could not give consent. The conspiracy between the respondent and her friend to give him narcotics resulted in a disability which made any consent given a nullity.

Legal Separation

Some provinces have a system whereby a married couple may appear in court and obtain a *judicial separation*. Others permit an out-of-court settlement called a *legal separation*. A separation agreement should be drawn by two different lawyers, each acting for a different spouse. It is a binding agreement and may later be incorporated into a divorce decree, although the divorce court does not have to accept any of its terms. The agreement should cover division of assets, support obligations, custody and access to children, and any other matter in the settlement of the couple's affairs. The support agreement should be carefully worded so that it leaves open the possibility of later renegotiation. For example, if one spouse accepts a fixed amount, inflation or later illness may cause financial difficulties.

Separation agreements sometimes place unfair restrictions upon the wife. These restrictions are usually of two types:

- *Dum casta:* The wife is entitled to financial payments only while she remains chaste.
- *Dum sole:* The wife is entitled to financial payments only if she refrains from living with another man.

Ontario law has abolished both types of clauses. The agreement can allow termination of support if the spouses divorce and remarry since the divorce decree takes precedence over the separation agreement.

Divorce

Divorce in Canada is governed by a federal law, the *Divorce Act*. Originally, it was extremely difficult to obtain a divorce in Canada; the grounds most likely to be accepted were adultery or desertion. As a result, it became common practice for couples to fake adultery just to obtain a divorce. To liberalize the divorce law, the then Justice Minister, Pierre Trudeau, introduced a bill, for the reform of divorce, which was passed in 1968. It was a welcome change to an estimated 500 000 persons, living in common law relationships, who were unable to obtain a divorce.

Grounds for Divorce

All of the grounds for divorce are listed in the Act and generally fall into two categories: (1) the "fault" category, and (2) the "marriage breakdown" category. The most common grounds in the fault category are adultery and cruelty. The marriage breakdown category proposes as grounds for divorce the fact that the marriage is simply not working. The court is asked to allow the spouses to go their separate ways and to remarry if they wish.

Adultery

Adultery strikes at the very core of marriage, and is grounds for divorce if committed even once. By definition, adultery is "voluntary sexual intercourse with a person of the opposite sex, other than one's spouse." By definition, adultery can only be committed by a married person. Note that acts of homosexuality are, by definition, not adultery. The proof of adultery can be obtained in numerous ways. The general test is that there must be "a preponderance of credible evidence" of the act. This does not mean that the wrongdoer must be caught in the act. The court may also accept evidence that:

(1) The wrongdoer acted overly affectionately towards another person.
(2) The wrongdoer was found in a state of undress, or in bed with another person.
(3) The wrongdoer and another person spent a night together or lived or travelled together.
(4) The wrongdoer visited a brothel.
(5) The wrongdoer contacted V.D. (not from his or her spouse).
(6) The wife had a child when the husband could not have been the father because he was physically absent at the time of conception.

The fact that the respondent does not appear in court does not relieve the petitioner from proving adultery. Even if the case is not contested, adultery must be proved.

Despite the more liberalized law, some adultery cases are still not genuine. If the court finds that the evidence is not authentic, it will take a very stern attitude towards the parties involved, and possibly towards their lawyer, for bringing a trumped-up case into court. There are certain "bars to relief" that will prevent a divorce from being granted on the grounds of adultery:

• *Collusion:* Collusion means that the spouses concocted a divorce scheme by faking adultery.
• *Condonation:* If it can be shown that the petitioner condoned the behaviour in any way, or has in any way forgiven the act, or has again cohabitated with the respondent, divorce is barred.

Cruelty

Either physical or mental cruelty is grounds for divorce. The wording of the Act is that the respondent "has treated the petitioner with physical or mental cruelty of such a kind as to render *intolerable* the continued cohabitation of the spouses." Physical cruelty is

easier to recognize than mental cruelty. In *Gollins v. Gollins* (1964), the House of Lords held that intent to be cruel does not have to be proven when the cruelty results from intentional acts. Mental cruelty exists when there is a refusal to put a stop to the known suffering of the other person. This does not mean that a spouse must give in to the wishes of the other spouse on every point or be labelled "cruel."

M. v. M.
New Brunswick, 1974

The parties were married in 1962, when the petitioner was only seventeen years old. The couple now had three children. The wife's petition for divorce and custody of the children was based on the grounds of physical and mental cruelty. The husband, who had once attempted suicide, threatened to maim or kill the petitioner. She had been forced throughout their marriage to participate in unnatural sex acts which she did not enjoy. The divorce was granted. While the husband's drinking, suicide attempt, and threats to the wife would not by themselves constitute cruelty to establish the basis for divorce, when considered in conjunction with his abnormal sex habits they did amount to cruelty rendering continued cohabitation intolerable.

We may find it difficult to believe that in the preceding case the judge did not find that a wife had been subjected to cruelty because she had to live with a husband who attempted suicide and constantly threatened his family. But the fact is that there is simply no hard and fast rule as to what constitutes cruelty. It may be useful to note that the following grounds have been accepted by a Canadian court at some time: severe physical mistreatment; mental abuse that threatens the spouse's very sanity; coitus interruptus; transvestism and other deviate behaviour; enormous change of life style; unreasonable sexual demands; and undergoing a sex-change operation.

Matrimonial Offences

There are other acts which are considered so detrimental to the marriage that a divorce will be granted. They include sodomy, bestiality, rape, and homosexual acts.

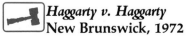 *Gaveronski v. Gaveronski*
Saskatchewan, 1974

The husband petitioned for divorce on the grounds that the wife had engaged in homosexual acts with her friend. The two women had been very close over a long period and this had led to the breakdown of the marriage. There was much hugging and kissing between them and an exchange of passionate love letters, beyond ordinary letters between friends. The issue turned on the proof of a homosexual act as required by the statute:

> **3. Subject to section 5, a petition for divorce may be presented to a court by a husband or wife, on the ground that the respondent, since the celebration of the marriage**
> **(a) has committed adultery;**
> **(b) has been guilty of sodomy, bestiality or rape, or has engaged in a homosexual act;**

The court found that for an act to be a homosexual act, evidence of vaginal contact was not required. In the present case the homosexual act was found to be the caressing of the bosom of one female by another; this went beyond a friendly caress.

Separation

If the married couple have been living apart for a period of not less than three years, either may petition for divorce. The exception to this waiting period is where one spouse deserted the other (discussed below). Separation does not necessarily mean living in separate houses. In numerous cases, where the two parties remained in the same house but had separate bedrooms and generally avoided each other, they were deemed to have been separated for all purposes.

Haggarty v. Haggarty
New Brunswick, 1972

The husband petitioned for a divorce on the ground of permanent breakdown of the marriage by reason of the parties having lived separate and apart for more than three years. The husband and wife were living under one roof but they slept in separate rooms and they did not eat meals together. The husband ate most of his meals in restaurants. The divorce was granted. The parties were "living separate and apart" within the meaning of the Act.

There is one exception to this rule. The spouses may live together again, for a period not longer than ninety days, for the purpose of attempting a reconciliation without the three-year waiting period being affected. That is, the spouses have one opportunity to attempt reconciliation without jeopardizing their chance of getting a divorce at the end of three years. One attempt only is allowed.

Goodland v. Goodland
Ontario, 1974

This was a petition for divorce on the ground of permanent breakdown of marriage due to separation of more than three years. About a year after the separation the petitioner husband returned to the respondent wife's residence and remained there for one week; during this time he had sexual relations with her. The following year there was a similar occurrence. The husband indicated that he went to the wife's residence because he was down on his luck and "had no other place to go." The petition was dismissed since there was not a separation for three years. The *Divorce Act* permits only one single occasion of resumed cohabitation.

Desertion

It is necessary to distinguish between desertion and separation. If B walks out on C, without the consent and approval of C, then B has deserted C. Assuming they do not reunite, then if C wishes a divorce, the waiting time is three years because C is "separated" from B. If B wants a divorce, the waiting time is five years, because B has "deserted" C. The person doing the deserting is penalized by having to wait an additional two years.

The deserting party is not necessarily the person leaving the home. Where the unbearable behaviour of one spouse forces the other to leave, the departing spouse is not the deserting one. The law would hold that the spouse who drove the other from the home is guilty of *constructive desertion*.

Addiction

A divorce can be granted where the respondent has been addicted to alcohol or drugs for a period of not less than the preceding three years, with no hope of rehabilitation.

Disappearance

Where a spouse has not been seen, and his or her location is unknown for three years, a divorce may be granted. As part of the evidence it must be shown that the petitioner has made a reasonable effort to find the respondent.

Non-Consummation

Just as a marriage could be annulled for non-consummation, so may a divorce be granted on the same ground. If the marriage has never been consummated within one year after the marriage ceremony, either spouse may petition for divorce.

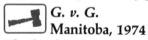
G. v. G.
Manitoba, 1974

The husband sought a divorce on the ground that the wife had refused to consummate their marriage. The parties had lived together for about two months; then the wife moved out. They had known one another for about one year prior to marriage and had had sexual intercourse on a number of occasions. Immediately after the marriage the wife's attitude changed and she rebuffed all the husband's overtures. A psychiatrist's report stated that the wife's attitude had come about because, around the time of the wedding, she had suddenly developed negative feelings about the husband and now felt that she did not love him. The divorce was granted. The fact that the parties had engaged in sexual intercourse prior to marriage was irrelevant. Consummation required sexual intercourse after the marriage and one act was enough to bind the parties as husband and wife. The wife had no right to refuse to engage in intercourse after the marriage.

Bigamy

Where a person enters into a marriage while already legally married to someone else, such an action is called bigamy and both marriages can be terminated. The second marriage would be annulled because it did not legally exist. The first marriage could be dissolved by divorce on the grounds of the bigamy committed. Bigamy is also a criminal offence.

Imprisonment

A divorce may be granted:

(1) Where the respondent has been imprisoned for one or more offences for a total period of not less than three years during the five years immediately preceding the presentation of the petition;
(2) Where the respondent, immediately preceding the presentation of the petition, has been imprisoned for a period of not less than two years for an offence for which he or she was sentenced to death, or to imprisonment for a term of ten years or more, provided that all rights of appeal have been exhausted.

Thus, where a spouse has suffered having the other party in and out of jail for a total period of three out of the last five years, a divorce may be granted. Or, if the spouse has gone to jail on a long stretch, and appeals are exhausted, the other spouse may file for divorce after two years of separation.

Residency Requirements for Divorce

Before a person petitions for a divorce in Canada, that person must be living in Canada and must intend to continue living there. One spouse can petition for divorce in the place where he or she lives, no matter where the other spouse may be. In order for a province to grant a divorce, at least one of the parties must live in that province. This is normally understood to mean residence in the province for at least ten months of the year preceding the petition.

Foreign Divorces

The divorce laws of other countries can be very lax compared with those of Canada. A Canadian who goes to another country for the purpose of obtaining an easy divorce will find that Canada does not recognize such divorces. A person who emigrated to Canada after obtaining a divorce in the country of origin would probably have the divorce recognized by the Provincial Secretary. What is not acceptable is a divorce obtained in another country merely for convenience.

Divorce Proceedings

In a divorce action, the person seeking the divorce is called the *petitioner.* His or her spouse is called the *respondent,* and if a third person is involved he or she is called the *co-respondent.* The petition for divorce must give the names and addresses of all parties, the nature of the remedy sought (divorce), the grounds, the request for maintenance, custody of the children, and a request that the other party pay the costs. If adultery is charged, the petitioner must try to name the co-respondent. The respondent may choose not to defend the action, or may defend only against custody of the children and the maintenance. A co-respondent may defend to deny allegations made. The court may refuse to grant the divorce, but if it does grant the divorce it awards a "decree nisi" (meaning literally a decree "unless"). After three months, if no facts have come before the court to cause doubt that the divorce should go through, the court awards a "decree absolute" which is the final decree. After the decree absolute, the parties are free to remarry.

Financial Support

Section 11 of the *Divorce Act* permits the court to make an order requiring the husband to pay such lump sum or periodic sums as the court thinks reasonable for the maintenance of the wife and children. The same power

applies to having the wife support the husband. The Act also permits that the order be varied from time to time. Thus, the door is never fully closed.

Since the *Divorce Act* takes priority over any provincial legislation, the judge does not have to pay any attention to the law reform found in provincial laws. What has developed is a tacit recognition that the provincial laws provide an excellent rationale for making an award under the *Divorce Act.* Therefore, most judges follow the provincial law when making the support order.

People often confuse the terms *alimony* and *maintenance.* Alimony is financial support paid to a wife who is separated and awaiting a divorce. Maintenance is support paid to a spouse who has received a divorce. Ontario has abolished alimony but a spouse can apply for interim maintenance while seeking the divorce.

Enforcement of Orders

If an ex-spouse does not make the payments ordered, the other spouse can enforce the order in court by having the defaulting spouse brought into court to "show cause" why the payment has not been made. If the ex-spouse goes to another province, the decree and order can be registered and enforced in that province, since the provinces have reciprocal agreements to enforce orders from other provinces. However, if the ex-spouse has no money, there is little that can be done about it. The court cannot make a person pay money which that person does not have.

Some Additional Points Regarding Divorce

Any rights a spouse has under the other spouse's insurance policy expire after a divorce, whether or not the spouse was specifically referred to as "my wife" or "my husband." An ex-spouse will lose any rights under a pension plan held by the other. An important exception is the Canada Pension Plan. A divorced spouse is entitled to half the contributions his or her spouse made to the C.P.P. if the couple lived together during their marriage for thirty-six consecutive months. It works both ways, so whichever spouse made the largest contribution will lose credits to the other.

A divorced woman may continue to use her married name or she can revert to her maiden name. If she was previously married, she can use her name by that marriage.

Reviewing Important Points

1. The requirements of a valid marriage are very basic. The parties must be of lawful age, free to marry each other, and in possession of a proper marriage licence.

2. Marriage is a voluntary agreement. It is not a contract bound upon any condition.

3. An annulment is a declaration that the marriage never existed ab initio (from the beginning).

4. In most provinces, married persons may separate without a court order. Generally, a contractual agreement is drawn up under which the parties agree as to the division of property and financial support.

5. Since 1968, divorce has become much more accessible for Canadians. Before 1968, adultery was practically the only ground for divorce.

6. The general test of whether adultery occurred is that there must be a preponderance of credible evidence of the act.

7. Canadians, who go to another country to obtain an easy, convenient foreign divorce, will find that such divorces are seldom recognized in Canada.

8. All provinces now permit marriage contracts under which the spouses may agree about division of property, support obligations, and children's education.

9. Persons who live together without being married to each other (cohabitees) should have an agreement in the eventuality that they separate.

10. Persons who live together have no claim to each other's property unless one person contributed money to acquiring property in the name of the other, or can show that the other is holding the property in trust on his or her behalf.

Checking Your Understanding

1. Name three reasons why persons could be disqualified from marriage.

2. What are the "bars to relief" as regards divorce on the ground of adultery?

3. Under what circumstances could a person petition for divorce on the ground of (a) separation, or (b) desertion?

4. Give an example of how a marriage might be declared void on the ground of "mistake"?

5. Under the common law, what rights and responsibilities did the wife have? What rights and responsibilities did the husband have?

6. What is one matter that may not be made part of a marriage contract?

7. Who has more need of a domestic contract—a married couple, or an unmarried couple? Why?

8. What is the primary criterion upon which financial support should be ordered?

9. What is the meaning of "cruelty" as defined in the *Divorce Act?*

10. If a divorce is uncontested, will it always be granted? Why or why not?

Legal Briefs

1. C lives with D and with E, D's son by a previous marriage. After D is killed in an accident, C and E apply for a marriage licence. Valid application?

2. When F and R are engaged, they sign a marriage contract that states that during their marriage they will have no children. After the marriage, R becomes pregnant and F insists that under the terms of the contract R must have an abortion. Enforceable agreement?

3. K marries G, who has two children by a previous marriage. G insists that she and K sign a marriage contract. As G is very protective of her two children, she insists that a clause be inserted giving her exclusive rights over the rearing of the children and absolute custody of the children should G and K separate. Valid agreement?

4. R lives with L in a house which is registered in her name only. He gives her money each month to run the household and once in a while extra money to help her make mortgage payments. R does all the repairs around the house and has built a sun deck, at his expense, on the back of the house. Does R have any legal interest in the house?

5. During twenty years of marriage, J, the husband, practised medicine while C, the wife, raised a family and looked after the house. When they divorced, C realized that everything was in J's name because he had always looked after the money. Advise C.

6. During thirty years of marriage, the wife, B, had one main hobby; she collected china dolls from around the world. The husband, D, had no interest in this hobby. When they separated, D argued that the doll collection was a family asset and that any division of property should include half the value of the collection. Is D correct?

7. When W and Y separated, W agreed to pay Y support of $2000 per month. This support provision later became part of the divorce decree, with the amount left open for possible variance. Four years later, Y inherited a large estate. W asked for an order relieving him of making any further support payments. Y countered that only she was entitled to bring the issue back to court for possible variance. Who is correct here?

8. The husband, C, is impotent and has sought medical help to no avail. The wife, E, petitions for divorce on the ground of mental cruelty. E argues that an intention to be cruel need not be shown and that unintentional cruelty is a valid ground to support the petition. Valid petition?

9. Z and T are married, live in the same house, and have not spoken to each other for three years. They use separate facilities and entrances. The one thing Z does for T is purchase food. T still gives Z a monthly household allowance. Are they separated?

10. The husband, R, started a business which went badly into debt. The wife, M, worked at a job to try to repay the debts. Over her protests, R started another business which had no chance of success. Not wanting to have any connection with these new debts, M ordered R to pack up and move; R did so. Who deserted whom?

Applying the Law

Bruce v. Reynett
Federal Court of Canada, 1979

The applicant, a prisoner named Bruce, applied for a court order to ascertain whether the respondent, Reynett, was acting in excess of his authority in denying Bruce permission to marry. Bruce then sought an injunction restraining Reynett from exceeding his authority by transferring Bruce to another prison. Reynett was the warden of the prison in which Bruce was held and had denied a request from the inmate to be allowed to marry the woman to whom he was engaged. The marriage was not allowed to take place, either inside or outside the prison. Bruce and the woman alleged that this was contrary to the *Bill of Rights* and that marriage was a basic right which was not revoked just because a person was sent to prison.

The application was dismissed. Reynett was acting within an administrative capacity and it was not open to the court to review the merits of his decision, but only to determine whether he acted fairly. Bruce had not been the object of discrimination, nor had he been denied equality before the law. Very few inmates had ever been granted permission to marry while in prison. When a person committed an offence resulting in a prison sentence, that person lost many of the enjoyments possessed by other members of society. Marriage, or the freedom to marry, was one of these. As Bruce would not have the opportunity to live with his intended wife, and since he was in a prison that did not permit conjugal visits, the marriage could not be consummated and would be a nullity.

Questions

1. Is marriage a right of every person? Why or why not?

2. Why was the decision of the warden not subject to review by the court?

3. Why did the court conclude that Bruce's rights had not been violated?

4. Should inmates ever be allowed to marry? Under what circumstances do you think such permission might be granted?

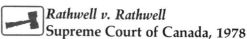

MacIntosh v. MacIntosh and Wright
Prince Edward Island, 1976

The wife's petition for divorce was on the ground of adultery. It was not defended. The husband was present at the hearing and testified as a witness for the wife. He was living with a woman in Halifax. The wife was living with, and being supported by, a former husband whom she planned to remarry. The alleged adultery upon which the petition was based was committed after the wife informed the husband that their marriage was at an end. The husband admitted his adultery during a telephone conversation with the wife.

The petition was dismissed. The *Divorce Act* imposes a duty upon the court (a) to satisfy itself that there has been no collusion; (b) to dismiss the petition if it found that there was collusion. The court doubted that there had been full disclosure from the witnesses. On the basis of the evidence before the court and the inferences which could be drawn from that evidence, the court was not only far from satisfied that there was no collusion but also had a strong belief that there was.

Questions

1. If two parties separate, each living with another person, each admitting adultery, why would this not meet the requirements of adultery under the Act?

2. The court seemed to be suspicious because of the cooperative nature of the parties. Would the parties have a greater likelihood of success if they had been hostile towards each other?

3. If one party leaves home and is living with the co-respondent, and the petitioner doesn't seem to care,

does this affect the petitioner's chances of obtaining a divorce?

Rathwell v. Rathwell
Supreme Court of Canada, 1978

The Rathwells were married in 1944; the husband was in the armed forces at the time. At the end of the war, they decided to make farming their occupation. They opened a joint bank account with their combined savings of $700. In 1946, the money was used as a down payment on a farm in Saskatchewan. Income from the farm was deposited in this joint account and from time to time more land was purchased. Title for all the land was taken in the name of the husband only. One reason for this was that the government loans to veterans generally required that the land be purchased in the name of the veteran exclusively. The wife did the chores when the husband was busy on the land. She also looked after the garden; canned produce; milked cows; drove machinery; and kept all the books and records. In 1967, the couple separated and the wife claimed one-half of the farm. The case reached the Supreme Court of Canada which held that she should get half the farm. The court held that this case was different from the *Murdoch* case because the money initially used to purchase the farm came from a joint bank account in both spouses' names. Three of the Justices also stated that they thought the years of work should also be taken into consideration when deciding if a farm wife was entitled to any of a farm. The wife should succeed whether one applied the theory of resulting trust or the equitable doctrine of constructive trust. In this case, there could be no distinction between matrimonial property and business property because in every sense they were one.

Questions

1. Why did the wife succeed in the *Rathwell* case but fail in the *Murdoch* case?

2. What is a constructive trust? A resulting trust?

3. Is a farm different from other types of businesses in ways that would prevent this decision from being applied to other cases where the couples were not engaged in farming?

You Be the Judge

1. The petitioner wife brought an uncontested action for divorce on the ground of adultery by the respondent. The couple were married in 1973 and the marriage was unhappy from the start. The wife complained that the husband ran around and drank. She stated that she first knew of the co-respondent woman in the winter of 1974 and that she had seen the husband in this woman's company from time to time around town. The wife further stated that the husband and the co-respondent had lived together at a certain address, although the wife offered no proof of this fact. She also stated that she "knew" that a child was born to the respondent and the co-respondent. The petitioner's mother testified to seeing the husband and the co-respondent in various public places. One further witness testified that he had talked with the respondent husband who told him he was having financial problems because he had fathered a baby whom he could not afford to support. Is there sufficient basis to grant a divorce?

2. The wife petitioned for divorce on the ground of separation for three years. In her petition she stated that she had two children, ages six and two. When asked by the judge who was the father of the two-year-old child, the wife stated that the husband was. She gave further information that the husband was a truck driver and that, while he kept most of his personal articles in an apartment, he did leave some items of clothing and sporting equipment in the house for lack of space elsewhere. The wife and the husband were not on "bad terms" with each other. When he was in town he came to the house and questioned the wife about the welfare of the older child and gave the wife money. During one of these visits the couple discussed a possible reconciliation and the husband remained in the house for three days before leaving on a trip. During this time, the wife had become pregnant with the younger child. The couple later decided against reuniting. Is there sufficient basis to grant a divorce?

3. The husband petitioned for divorce on the ground of non-consummation. Prior to the marriage, the husband had had strong fears that he might be impotent. The wife had been very supportive and had said that she was certain that with medical assistance his problem would not persist. After the marriage ceremony, the problem continued and he remained totally impotent. The couple lived together for fourteen months without once having sexual intercourse. Feeling very inadequate, the husband filed for divorce. The wife defended against the action saying that she was prepared to live with the husband despite the absence of sexual relations. She said that sex was not important in her life and that the personal interaction with the husband, whom she admired for other qualities, was adequate. Should the divorce be granted?

4. The petitioner husband sought a divorce from the respondent wife on the grounds of cruelty. The husband had married the wife on the false belief that he was the father of a child she carried while they were dating. When the child was three years old, a medical problem required blood typing. The child's blood type was very unusual and the petitioner did some research which showed that he could not be the father. The wife contested the divorce saying that she had always believed the petitioner was the father of the child and that during the marriage she had been a suitable mate and loving spouse. She admitted that another man could have been the father of the child but that she had never had any real affection for that man. Should the divorce be granted?

5. The wife petitioned for divorce on the grounds of cruelty. When the spouses had married, the husband had promised to adopt the religion of the wife who was very strong in her religious beliefs. The husband did not convert as promised and began to ridicule the wife's religious beliefs as "voo-doo" and "rubbish." This not only upset the wife but she was afraid that their two children would also abandon the religion which

she very much wanted them to embrace. The husband defended the action by saying that he had never brought up the subject until the wife had badgered him about not going to church. Then, he had given as his reason for not going the fact that he thought the religion was "rubbish." He had a tacit understanding with the wife that he would say nothing if she would drop the subject. He would not deter the children from going to church, but he wanted them to have alternate religions and philosophies explained to them so that they would not just be "brainwashed." Should the divorce be granted?

6. The wife brought a petition for divorce on the ground that her husband treated her with physical and mental cruelty. After they married, the wife discovered heroin and needles among the husband's effects. The husband then admitted that he was an addict but said that he was trying to break the habit. At times he seemed to be succeeding; then he would steal money from the wife and disappear for days at a time. His health was generally deteriorating and he refused to consider professional care. The wife said she was a nervous wreck for fear that her family would learn the truth or that the husband would be arrested and jailed for a long time. She wanted to have children but not by the respondent because she believed that any child he fathered would be unhealthy. Should the divorce be granted?

Chapter 25

Children and Estates

Children and the Law

Parentage

Every child must have a name. In Ontario, the birth of a child must be registered within thirty days according to the *Vital Statistics Act*. The child is registered on a form that shows the mother's name. If the mother is married, the child must take the surname (last name) of the mother's husband. If the mother is not married, the child's surname is the same as the mother's. If the mother and father marry after the birth, a new registration can be obtained and the name changed.

Seldom is there doubt about the true identity of the mother, although it has been known for a married family member to claim to be the mother of a child born to an unmarried family member. More often, there are legal disputes about the identity of a child's father. Blood tests provide one of the simplest ways to prove that a man is *not* the father of a child. Blood tests cannot prove who is the father. To be meaningful, blood samples must be taken from the man, the woman, and the child; however under Ontario and Alberta law, a blood test requires the consent of the person. The court cannot order a person to take a test, but the court may draw such inferences from a refusal as it thinks appropriate. In short, refusal to take a blood test will greatly hurt the person's case. Under Newfoundland law, the alleged father can be required to post bond to assure that he will appear in court to reply to a paternity suit. If he does not post bond, he can be jailed pending the hearing.

The burden of proof varies from province to province. In Alberta, the alleged father must give evidence to show why he should not be declared the father. However, the court will not declare a man to be the father solely on the claims of the mother. There must be some other evidence, such as evidence that the two persons were living together when the woman became pregnant. Newfoundland law requires that "an affiliation order shall not be made upon the evidence of the mother ... unless her evidence ... is corroborated by some other material evidence." The Ontario statute contains "presumptions of paternity" including the fact that the alleged father:

(1) Was married to the mother of the child when the child was born;
(2) Was married to the mother within three hundred days before the child was born;
(3) Was married to the mother after the child was born and acknowledged himself to be the father;
(4) Was living with the mother in a common law relationship of some permanence either when the child was born or within three hundred days prior to the birth;
(5) Was registered as the father under the *Vital Statistics Act*;
(6) Was found to have been the father by previous court proceedings.

Evidence of physical resemblance may be admissible but the value of such evidence differs with the circumstances. If the man and the woman are of a different race such evidence would be helpful to the court; but if they are not very far removed from each other in their heritage such evidence is of little value.

A judge who believes a man to be the father, will issue an *affiliation order* declaring the man to be the father and ordering him to pay support for the child. The man is referred to as the *putative father*. He remains the father of the child permanently unless very unusual circumstances cause the court to declare some other man to be the father at some later date. A difficult situation arises when more than one man might readily be the child's father. In Newfoundland, the court may issue an affiliation order against *two or more* possible fathers. This possibility discourages an alleged father from trying to avoid an order by having other males testify that they, too, had sexual relations with the mother.

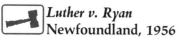

Luther v. Ryan
Newfoundland, 1956

When the pregnant woman told the alleged father that he was the father of the child she carried, he neither admitted it nor denied it. His silence continued after the child was born. The court held that, in some circumstances, silence can prove acceptance or an admission, especially where a serious allegation has been made and a denial would normally be expected. The man was held to be the father of the child.

Legitimacy and Illegitimacy

At common law, a child born outside a marriage was regarded as *filius nullius*, which means "child of no one." He or she was deemed to be *illegitimate*—a status which made the child a person without rights or obligations to his or her parents. Most seriously, the child could not inherit or demand support from either parent and neither parent had a right to the custody of such a child. This harshness in the law was later softened somewhat by the passage of statutes recognizing a child as legitimate if the parents subsequently married after the child was born.

Ontario and New Brunswick have abolished the concept of illegitimacy entirely. In those provinces, every child is a legitimate child with equal rights. The Ontario *Children's Law Reform Act* reads:

> **1. (1) Subject to subsection (2), for all purposes of the law of Ontario, a person is the child of his or her natural parents and his or her status as their child is independent of whether the child is born within or outside marriage.**

In the other provinces, an illegitimate child takes the name of the mother and she is the only legal guardian. The father is a person with no automatic right of custody or access to the child, even when the father must provide support. The father must apply to the court for custody or access. An illegitimate child can inherit from the mother's estate just as if the child were legitimate. He or she cannot make a claim upon the father's estate, but the father can specifically include the child in his will.

Support

The right of a child to support is enhanced by both the federal criminal law and provincial civil law.

Under s. 197 of the *Criminal Code*, a parent, foster parent, or guardian can be convicted of a criminal offence for not providing a child with the necessaries of life. It is also a criminal offence to abandon a child under the age of ten years, or to cause the child's life or health to be endangered.

Provincial laws also place a burden upon parents to support their children. For example, the Ontario *Family Law Reform Act* requires *both* parents to provide support and education for their child until the child either reaches the age of eighteen or marries. However, if the child is sixteen years of age or older and withdraws from parental control, the parents are not obliged to support that child.

Under the *Divorce Act,* a court is empowered to order support for children over the age of eighteen if such children are unable to provide for themselves.

Some provincial laws permit a court to order a person to support a child even if the person is not the natural parent of the child. The Ontario statute defines "parent" to include a person "who has demonstrated a settled intention to treat a child as a child of his or her family." For example, if B lives with C and C's children in a common law relationship, B could later be required to support C's children if B had treated the children like family.

Riopelle v. Daniel
Ontario, 1982

The applicant, J, applied for an order granting her custody of her two children, A and T. She also requested that the court order the respondent, N, to pay support for both children on the grounds that he was the natural father of T and that he had demonstrated a settled intention to treat A (who was fathered by the applicant's legal husband) as a child of his family. Blood tests revealed that the respondent was not the natural father of T. The applicant, who elected not to proceed with the claim for support of A, nevertheless argued that the respondent was obligated to support T since he had demonstrated a settled intention to treat her as a child of his family. The respondent argued that he should not be found to be a parent of T because he had treated her as his child under the mistaken belief that she was his child. The court held that the respondent was obligated to support T. The respondent had clearly demonstrated a settled intention to treat the child as his. The law did not require that he be aware of the fact that he was not the natural father of the child. To conclude otherwise would be to make the child's interests dependent on the knowledge of the respondent. If the legislature had intended such a result, it would have so stated in the Act. The respondent was the only father T had ever known.

Interestingly, Ontario law may also require a child to support needy parents.

Alberta law also extends the requirement of support beyond the natural parents. The definition of "children of the marriage" may include children of either the husband or the wife (by a previous marriage, for example), children adopted by either or both spouses, and children cared for by the spouses on a permanent basis. The two main tests are that the spouse has supported the child and has indicated an intention to continue supporting the child. The requirement to support generally ends at age sixteen. The requirement can be extended beyond sixteen if the child is infirm or in school.

The Newfoundland *Child Welfare Act* defines a "child" as an "unmarried boy or girl actually or apparently under the age of sixteen years." The obligation to support generally ends at age sixteen. Under the Newfoundland *Matrimonial Property Act* the definition of "child" includes a "child born within or outside the marriage" and includes a child whom the parent has demonstrated a settled intention to treat as a child of his or her family. However, the Act does not encompass support provisions, but affects children in the areas of matrimonial assets and domestic contracts.

In those provinces that still classify some children as illegitimate, the primary responsibility to support a child belongs to the mother. The father can be ordered to make an additional contribution.

Custody and Access

During the marriage, each parent has an equal right to determine the care, control, and upbringing of the children of the marriage. This right remains with each parent when the couple separates, but the situation is complicated by the fact that the children usually live with one parent of the marriage.

The couple may agree in a separation agreement that one parent will have custody. If they cannot agree, the court will make an order giving one parent custody. However, a number of courts are experimenting with the idea of giving both parents joint custody. The parent who has custody is responsible for the care, control, and upbringing of the child.

If the couple divorce, the *Divorce Act* permits the court to investigate "the conduct of the parties and the condition, means and other circumstances of each of them" in order to decide who should have custody. In

every case, the overriding principle is the "best interests of the child," not the wishes of the parents. The
court tries to give custody to the most suitable parent
and may take many things under consideration in trying to reach that decision. Important considerations
are the mental and physical fitness of the parents,
conduct of the parents, and their future plans. Also
important is the age of the child, the health of the
child, and the preference of the child.

Traditionally, very young children were placed in the
custody of the mother since it was believed that young
children needed maternal care more than they needed
fatherly affection and guidance. Older girls often went
to the mother and boys to the father. These guidelines
have generally been abandoned and the court makes
no such presumptions when hearing a custody matter.

A custody order is not permanent. If future events
make it difficult for a child to live with a parent, the
court may review and change its previous custody
order.

Re: Barkley and Barkley
Ontario, 1980

When the Barkleys separated, the two male children went to live with the father, the female child
with the mother. The father sought custody of the
female child on the ground that the mother had
developed a homosexual relationship with another
woman with whom she lived. The relationship was
not hidden in the least since the two women slept in
the same bed. The father believed that the daughter
would eventually become aware of the sexual rami-
fications of this arrangement and that this was not
a suitable environment for her. The court held that
homosexuality was not a bar to a mother's having
custody. Where the evidence indicates that any risk
in the area of the child's adjustment is speculative,
and where the mother is neither militant nor
flaunting in her sexual activity, an award of custody
in favour of the mother is appropriate.

Parental Child Abduction

When parents separate and one parent is awarded custody of a child, the other parent often takes the child
out of the jurisdiction of the court and refuses to
return the child. The parent having lawful custody
must then do one of several things. The parent may
register the custody order in the jurisdiction to which
the child was taken and ask the local court to order
return of the child. Such an action can be opposed by
the other parent who may try to obtain custody in the
local jurisdiction by alleging some "changed circumstances." Another possible action is for the parent to
try to steal the child back. Obviously, this is not a
healthy situation for the child.

If the child has been removed from Canada, the
problems are increased. Just locating the child can be
extremely difficult and foreign courts often give no
recognition to custody orders obtained in a Canadian
court.

The criminal law contains measures to discourage
the taking of a child. Under s. 250.1 of the *Criminal
Code*, it is an offence to take, entice away, or detain
a child from the person having lawful care with intent
to deprive that person of the child. The section does
not apply to a person who obtains possession of the
child believing in good faith that he or she has a right
to possession of the child. The latter part has made it
difficult to convict a parent who believes he or she has
a right to possession, but would rule out a parent who
has not been given custody by a court. Defiance of an
interim child custody order may subject the parent to
prosecution. However, where provincial legislation
gives joint custody of the child to the father and
mother, in the absence of a court order giving sole custody to one parent, the other parent may not be convicted of this offence.

The problem of child abduction is not unique to
Canada but is a world problem. There is hope that the
problem will be reduced by the adoption of the *Convention on the Civil Aspects of International Child Abduction* signed
in den Hague, Netherlands. The signatory states will
cooperate in locating and returning children removed
from one country to another. In Canada, the conven-

tion is being considered by the various provincial governments. Ontario and Alberta have adopted it.

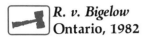

R. v. Bigelow
Ontario, 1982

The father was to have the child for one weekend; however, he took the child to Calgary and refused to return the child to the mother. The mother had custody under an Ontario court order. The father was charged with *detaining* the child, but not with taking the child. There was a legal problem since the offence of detaining took place entirely in Alberta; therefore, the jurisdiction of the Ontario court was in doubt. However, under s. 432(b) of the *Criminal Code,* if an offence is commenced within one territorial division and completed within another, the offence shall be deemed to have been committed in any of the divisions. Since the accused father obtained possession of the child in Ontario and then flew to Alberta, his actions formed one single plan covering both provinces and were not simply an illegal act taking place in Alberta. The accused had formed his intention before boarding the plane.

Adoption

Legal adoption is a process by which a person or persons ask the court to declare the person or persons as the lawful parent(s) of a child. Adoption may be sought by a couple who have obtained custody of a child voluntarily given up for adoption, or adoption may be sought by a step-father or step-mother who wish a child from a previous marriage to be declared a child of the present marriage. Such an adoption involves, in many cases, the divorced parent who may oppose the adoption on a number of grounds. One very important reason why a parent might oppose the adoption of his or her child is that access rights could be terminated by the adoption order. That is, once it has been declared that the divorced parent is no longer the parent of the child, access may be terminated by provincial law. A divorced parent may also oppose

adoption on the grounds of not wanting to have the child's last name changed.

When a child has been placed for adoption by a provincial agency, the true name of the natural parents is treated as confidential information. However, the desire of parent and child to later locate each other has caused some provinces, including Ontario, to accept a policy of informing either party that the other is trying to locate him or her. If both parties indicate a willingness to be reunited, the responsible agency will notify them where to find each other.

Artificial Insemination

Medical science is finding numerous ways to enable childless couples to have children. The growing use of "surrogate mothers" is just one more controversy about the status of children who are the offspring of two natural parents but carried in the womb of a third person. Artificial insemination may use the sperm of the father or the sperm of a donor male if the father is sterile. No serious legal problems arise if the husband's sperm is used in artificial insemination. If another male's sperm is used, there are legal complications. Some courts have declared that such children are illegitimate. This would have no application in Ontario, which holds that all children are legitimate. There are many other questions such as the name of the father on the birth certificate, the legal responsibilities of the father to support the child, and so on. If a surrogate mother is used, the issue is whether the surrogate mother can just give (or sell) the baby to the mother who will raise it.

Provincial laws have little or no content which deals with these issues. It is likely that the technology of making babies will eventually compel the provincial legislatures to enact such laws.

Defining Death

There are various statutes, including the *Criminal Code,* which contain provisions for determining the moment when a person becomes a human being. That is, the moment life begins has been defined in the legal sense. There is no federal statute that defines death — when life ends.

This may seem surprising in view of the fact that the moment of death can be very important in both the criminal and civil law. The determination of the moment of death and the cause of death is a fundamental element of crimes for which persons have been hanged or sent to prison for life. While s. 210 of the *Criminal Code* states that, for culpable homicide to exist, the victim must die within a year and one day of the last event connected with the death, there is no definition of death in the *Code.* Therefore, if the victim is kept connected to a machine that appears to be keeping the victim alive, although there is no real brain function, is the victim dead?

Determination of death is very important for the purposes of organ transplant. The longer the surgeon waits to remove the donated organs from the donor, the more deterioration takes place. However, surgeons must be sure that the donors are dead before removing any organs or they could face both criminal and civil actions.

There have been actual cases that centred around this absence of death. In 1968, surgeons who did a heart transplant were sued by the donor's brother who contended that the donor was not dead before the transplant was done. In 1970, a husband and wife were injured in an automobile accident, leaving the husband dead at the scene and the wife in the hospital on a respirator. She never responded at all and the respirator was eventually shut off. Relatives argued that the couple actually died simultaneously, but the court held that the husband died first.

The Law Reform Commission of Canada has studied the problem and notes that there is no single moment when all doctors agree that a person is dead. While there appears to be great interest in what is called "brain death" not all doctors agree as to what that means. The Commission has developed what it believes is a workable definition of death and has urged that the federal and provincial governments adopt it. The proposed definition reads as follows:

A person is dead when an irreversible cessation of all that person's brain functions has occurred. The cessation of brain functions can be determined by the prolonged absence of spontaneous cardiac and respiratory functions. When the determination of the absence of cardiac and respiratory functions is made impossible by the use of artificial means of support, the cessation of the brain functions may be determined by any means recognized by the ordinary standards of current medical practice.

To date, this recommendation has not been incorporated into legislation by any government.

Wills

It is an extraordinary thing that many supposedly knowledgeable, educated Canadians do not prepare their wills. Probate courts can verify that perhaps 40 per cent or more heads of families die without having made provision for their dependants. Yet, many persons who are so indifferent about the welfare of their families after death, were very good providers while they were alive.

The person who dies without having prepared a will places the family in a state of legal limbo. The estate will be frozen, casting the spouse into possible destitution which may require an appeal to the courts for financial assistance. If both parents are killed, the absence of a will means that no guardian for the children has been named. The surviving children may end up as wards of some person of whom neither parent would have approved.

A great deal has been written on the subject of wills. For this reason, our discussion here will be limited to some essential facts that hopefully will persuade all readers of the importance of a will.

Definition of Terms

A male person who prepares a will is referred to as a testator; a female person preparing a will is known as a testatrix. In any will, a person must be named to carry out the wishes of the testator or testatrix regarding the disposition of the estate. If this person is male, he is called an executor; if female, she is called an executrix.

For the sake of clarity and simplicity, in the general discussion of wills throughout the next several pages, the person making the will will always be referred to as the testator; the person carrying out the provisions of the will will always be referred to as the executrix. Nevertheless, all such references should be understood to apply equally to a testatrix and an executor. In specific cases, any person making or administering a will will be designated by the term applicable to the actual gender of that person.

Legal Capacity

The person who prepares a will must have the legal capacity to do so. Thus, in order to make a will, the testator must be:

- *Of legal age:* The testator must be an adult. An exception is that if the testator is a member of the armed forces or a sailor on active duty at sea, he may make a will at any age. Ontario law also permits a person under legal age to execute a will if the person is married or executes the will in contemplation of marriage. The legal age is eighteen years in Ontario and Alberta, but only seventeen years in Newfoundland.

- *Of sound and disposing mind:* The testator must have sufficient mental capacity to understand what he is doing, and cannot be under the influence of alcohol or drugs. Nor can he suffer from senility or any disease of the mind that affects his thinking.

- *Free from undue influence:* The testator must have sufficient mental capacity to be making his will of his own free will, not because someone (usually a relative or close adviser) is exercising undue influence over him. Undue influence is often alleged by relatives who find that the disposition of the estate favours one person, usually a person who was close to the deceased before death.

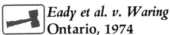

Eady et al. v. Waring
Ontario, 1974

The testator, by a will dated May 3, 1969, revoked his former will in which he provided for a bequest to his niece of shares worth $11 000 and the rest of his estate worth more than $100 000 to be divided among his two brothers and one sister. He was seventy-seven years of age and lived with his unmarried brother and widowed sister. As a result of a quarrel with his sister, he then went to live with his other married brother and his wife. After living with them a year, he made a new will cutting off his sister, bachelor brother, and niece. They contested the will, and the trial judge agreed with their claim that the new will was prepared under "suspicious circumstances." The married brother appealed to the Supreme Court of Ontario which agreed with the trial judge. While the circumstances fell short of undue influence, nonetheless the cumulative effect of the evidence of failing health, faulty memory, lack of control, coupled with a drastic change in personal habits raised suspicions about the testator's mind and memory. Further, the court said that the doctrine of "suspicious circumstances" was not limited to situations in which a beneficiary was instrumental in the preparation of the will.

The above case illustrates that the court does not necessarily require absolute proof of undue influence. Rather, it may apply a rule generally referred to as "suspicious circumstances" under which the preparation of a new will to the detriment of persons who were beneficiaries under a previous will, is sufficient for the court to refuse to accept the validity of a new will.

Preparation of a Will

All provinces have statutes prescribing the elements of a valid will. Some requirements are part of our common law as well, and some can be traced back to Roman law. The signing of the will is properly called the *execution* of the will. Traditionally, a will had to be properly witnessed, but there is a growing trend towards *holograph* wills. A holograph will is a will written entirely in the handwriting of the person making it. For this reason, printed forms, available in stationery stores, must *not* be used as holograph wills because such forms combine printed wording with the words inserted by the person making the will. A proper holograph will must be completely handwritten. Alberta, Ontario, and Newfoundland all recognize holograph wills. Generally, however, holograph wills should be avoided. The preparation of a will should be done by a lawyer who will ensure it covers all the important points and is clearly worded. It is said that every year in London, England, the annual convention of barristers (lawyers) begins with a toast to those who prepare their own wills and thus provide the legal profession with an excellent source of revenue from court battles over such improperly drawn documents.

In most provinces, a soldier on active duty, or a sailor at sea, needs no witnesses for a will. This custom can be traced back to Roman law when every soldier was allowed to make a *Testamentum Militaire* before going into battle. The soldier could even make it orally.

Proper witnessing of a will requires two witnesses who (1) watch the testator sign his will, then (2) sign in the presence of the testator and each other. Thus, all three people must be present at the same time. The witnesses are not entitled, nor are they required for any reason, to read the will. Their only function is to guarantee the signature of the testator. Neither a witness nor his or her spouse should be a beneficiary under the will. If a witness benefits under the will, this does not invalidate the entire will, but the witness will not receive the benefit promised. The executrix named in the will can be a witness provided she is not also a beneficiary. The original copy of the will should be placed with the family lawyer or with the executrix of the estate. Carbon copies are seldom acceptable unless there is strong evidence that the copy is genuine.

Changing a Will

If a small change is required, the testator may make the change with a pen in the presence of two witnesses, then initial the change and sign in the left margin next to the change. The witnesses do the same. A better way to make a change is to prepare a *codicil,* which is a separate sheet of paper with the stated change. The codicil must be witnessed in the same manner as the will. For major changes, a new will should be executed, declaring all previous wills void.

Revocation of a Will

A will is not irrevocable. The testator can revoke it entirely and become will-less again. The testator can revoke his will by burning, tearing, or otherwise obliterating it. He can also direct another person to destroy it. However, accidental destruction of the will does not constitute revocation because there is no intent to destroy the will. The execution of a new will which expressly states that the prior will is revoked is effectively a declaration that the prior will no longer exists, even if it is not physically destroyed.

Settling the Estate

Once the deceased is pronounced legally dead, the estate becomes a trust under the direction of the executrix. The executrix must establish the validity of the will and act under the scrutiny of the Probate Court. The entire process is referred to as "probating the will." If the will is ambiguous, the executrix must apply to the Probate Court for a ruling as to its meaning.

Re Fairfoull
British Columbia, 1974

The executor applied for instructions regarding the interpretation of the will and a codicil. In his original will prepared in 1951 the deceased made provision for his son and two daughters. In the codicil, prepared in 1954, he made the bequest to his son conditional upon his divorcing his present wife. The court ruled that the condition placed upon the son was void, being against public policy in that it encouraged him to divorce his wife. As such it was *malum prohibitum* (a bad act prohibited by law). The income which should have been paid to the son, who was now deceased, was ordered paid to his personal representatives.

In the *Fairfoull* case, the executor recognized a provision in the will that was either unclear or possibly contrary to law. The executor then applied to the court for instructions as to what should be done. It was not possible to merely ignore the will's provisions; the court's instructions were required.

The executrix is a person with great power and important duties to perform. She may take possession of all assets and possessions of the deceased person, and may examine all personal papers of the deceased. Generally, her duties are as follows:

- Arrange the funeral of the deceased according to the instructions given in the will. Note that the wife or husband of the deceased cannot change this request. The body belongs to the executrix at this point.

- Collect all claims owing to the deceased, which are now owing to the estate.

- Advertise for any creditors of the estate to make a claim with the executrix.

- Pay the debts of the estate in the following order:
  1. Funeral expenses.
  2. Administration expenses.
  3. All other debts. If there is not enough money to pay them, no one is liable to pay them. Debts cannot be inherited and the executrix is not personally liable.
  4. Pay any estate taxes and income taxes due.
  5. Obtain a release from the government that no further taxes are due and then distribute the rest of the estate according to the will.

Since the executrix fills such a vital position, it is wise to name a responsible person for this position. Trust company representatives and family lawyers are superior choices over "chums."

Preparing Your Own Will

Blank will forms can be purchased from stationery stores. Supposedly, if the testator fills out this form and has it witnessed, he has a valid will. Considering the importance of this document, it is unwise to prepare it yourself, whether a printed form is used or just plain paper. Legally, however, there is nothing to stop a person from personally preparing a will as long as it is properly executed. Some of the major things the will must contain include:

- A statement that it is a "Last Will and Testament" and that the testator was of sound mind when he declared it to be his will.

- A statement declaring all previous wills void.

- Instructions for the appointment of an executrix. It is wise to name a nominee-executrix should the first choice be unable or unwilling to serve.

- Instructions for the payment of debts.

- Instructions for the disposition of the estate.

- Appointment of a guardian for infant children should the spouse predecease the testator or die with him.

Overall, the essential thing is to make the will clear. Far too many wills have to be referred to the courts for interpretation as to the meaning of a phrase or even a single word. Some examples of unclear wording referred to the courts include:

- *Issue:* Where a woman bequeathed her estate to her issue, did she mean her children or children and grandchildren?

- *Child:* Where a deceased bequeathed her estate to her natural children, did she intend to exclude a foster child?

• *Bank balance to nearest relative in Ontario:* The deceased used this expression which raised confusion on two points: (1) what was included in "bank balance"? (2) what was meant by "nearest relative"? Nearest in distance, or nearest in relationship?

These examples point out that what might have been clear to the testator is not necessarily clear to his executrix. Therefore, wills sometimes appear exceedingly wordy—full of legal phrasing—but in most cases the intent is to avoid later confusion.

Intestate Succession

If a person dies without a will, the person is said to have died *intestate.* If this occurs, the province names an administrator for the estate. The estate is distributed according to a provincial statute providing for such instances. There are hundreds of possible family situations that could arise; far too many to explain here. The objective of the law is to determine who "stands closest" to the deceased and distribute the estate according to a formula.

If a person died intestate in Ontario and was survived by a spouse and more than one child, the estate would be divided as follows:

• First $75 000 to surviving spouse;

• One-third of the remainder to surviving spouse;

• Two-thirds of the remainder to children, to be shared equally.

In Alberta the division would be the same except that the spouse's preferential share is only $40 000. An illegitimate child cannot inherit from the father, but only from the mother. A common law spouse inherits nothing by intestate succession. A spouse who has deserted the other and is living in an adulterous relationship at the time the other spouse died, loses all estate rights.

The formula in Newfoundland is more complex, but using the basic example of a deceased leaving a spouse and children, the surviving spouse takes one-third and the children equally share the other two-thirds. There is no preferential share in this particular situation. Illegitimate children cannot inherit from their father and a spouse who has deserted the deceased and was living common law at the time of death does not inherit.

Registrar of Supreme Court v. Mullins and Murphy
Newfoundland, 1981

The husband died intestate on October 13, 1976. The deceased and his wife had separated in 1934 after only two years of marriage. The wife had left at the husband's request. In 1954, the wife commenced living with another man. In 1975, she ended this common law relationship and lived alone. The registrar, as administrator of the estate of the deceased, applied for an interpretation of the Newfoundland *Intestate Succession Act* which provided that where a wife had left her husband and was living in adultery at the time of his death, she took no part in his estate. The court held that the wife was entitled to inherit. The word "left" used in s. 18 (1) of the Act meant that she had deserted him, i.e., left him of her own volition. The wife had not done so. The wife had terminated the common law relationship more than one year before the husband's death. There was no indication that she had done so just in the expectation that the husband would die and that she would inherit. She had discontinued the adulterous relationship before the husband died and the Act clearly required that she would inherit unless she was living in an adulterous relationship at the time of the husband's death.

The most important thing to stress in a discussion about intestate succession is that the entire problem could have been avoided by preparing a will! It should be remembered that when the surviving spouse is left with small children, that part of the estate which goes to the children will be placed in the hands of a public trustee. The widow or widower would have to apply to the trustee for money for the care of the children.

Re Spears
Nova Scotia, 1974

The widow of an intestate claimed her share of the inheritance, but the court found that her marriage to the deceased was invalid since she had never been legally divorced from her former husband. She had married the deceased in 1947 upon the assurance of her lawyer that she was free to do so. The court found that she was not the deceased's wife and would not allow her to recover compensation claimed for her work as a housekeeper. The court did allow her payment of $24 600 for her work as the deceased's bookkeeper at a rate of $50 per week for fourteen years (for which she had never been paid). It also allowed recovery of a loan of $2200 she made to the deceased.

The *Spears* case illustrates the difficulty in which a woman found herself because a man, whom she believed was her husband, died intestate. Had he prepared a will, she could have inherited whatever he specifically bequeathed to her because the will would not have required that she prove she was his lawful wife.

If a person dies intestate, leaving no known next-of-kin in the province where he or she is domiciled, or where the only next-of-kin are infants and there is no near relative willing and competent to administer the estate, the Crown will apply for Letters of Administration. In most provinces, an official known as the Public Trustee performs this function. Where an inheritance is left to an infant with no appointed guardian, the Crown will administer the estate until the infant reaches the age of majority. This function is performed in Ontario and British Columbia by an official known as the Official Guardian.

Dependants' Relief

A will cannot cut dependant persons off from financial support and make them a burden upon the govern-

ment. Such a will can be successfully contested and the court may order such support as it considers adequate to be paid out of the estate of the deceased for the proper support of the dependants.

The issue then becomes, who is a dependant? There are substantial differences province to province. The most general and widespread usage is in Ontario which brings into the web the spouse, common law spouse, children, grandchildren, parents, grandparents, brothers, sisters, and children of the common law spouse towards whom the deceased demonstrated a settled intention to be viewed as a parent. All of these categories are subject to some further definition and it should not be assumed the law imposes an automatic responsibility towards all such persons.

Alberta law confines "dependant" to mean a husband or wife, or a child under eighteen or a child over eighteen who, because of illness or infirmity, is unable to earn a living. The law does not include a common law spouse or a child of a common law spouse. Newfoundland law is similar to the Alberta statute.

Adams v. Broughton and Yorke
Alberta, 1982

The parties were married in 1977 when the deceased husband was fifty-seven and the wife was forty-three. Although the husband petitioned for divorce in 1979, the action was not proceeded with. There were three separations during the marriage, lasting approximately one month each, but the parties resumed cohabitation after each separation. Shortly before his death in 1980, the husband executed a will in which he left his entire estate to his seven children of a previous marriage. He specifically provided that he did not wish the wife to benefit from his estate, which included property valued at $50 000 and a $25 000 life insurance policy. The wife applied for support and maintenance under the *Family Relations Act*. The court held that the wife was entitled to maintenance. The wife had not disentitled herself to maintenance under the Act merely because the husband's children believed she was greedy, had used his credit card for substantial purchases, and did not really care for him. The husband had always resumed cohabitation with the wife in spite of any differences. The wife had no one else to turn to for support and her income from pensions was inadequate. The fact that the parties had lived just above the poverty line was not a valid reason for limiting her maintenance to the same level when assets were available to provide proper maintenance.

Survivorship

Each province has a statute that provides rules of survivorship. At times it is important to know who died first, husband or wife, mother or daughter, etc. They may have died together, and the question of who died first can have important consequences when it comes to settling the estates. The rules laid down generally hold that where two or more persons die at the same time, or in circumstances rendering it uncertain which of them survived the other, the younger shall be deemed to have survived the elder; if one is the beneficiary of a life insurance policy of the other, the beneficiary shall be deemed to have died first. Under Ontario law, where two or more persons die at the same time, or in circumstances rendering it uncertain which of them survived the other(s), the property of each person shall be disposed of as if that person had survived the other(s).

Representation

Representation applies only in situations involving complete or partial intestacy. A properly prepared will should eliminate any necessary reference to representation. Children are said to be *lineal descendants* of their parents, grandparents, and so on. This means that they are a product of the direct line of family heritage. As such, children may "represent" their parent should the parent be deceased. At one time, only a male child had any right of representation. Today, there is no dis-

tinction by sex or by the fact that a child is the natural offspring of the parent or an adopted child. All children must share equally. If a person dies intestate after his or her child has died, any surviving grandchildren may represent their deceased parent. For example, Adam Jones dies intestate. He had two children, Jane and Sandra. If they were both alive, they would share their father's estate equally. However, assume that Jane is already deceased, and is survived by her widower and their two children. Jane's two children may represent their mother and share equally the inheritance she would have received if she were alive. Jane's widower cannot represent his wife since he is not a lineal descendant of Adam Jones.

Brothers, sisters, spouses, cousins, etc. are not lineal descendants. They are referred to as *collateral relatives* and do not represent a deceased person. If there are no lineal descendants of a deceased person, then the inheritance may go to collateral relatives. It is often hard to determine which collateral relatives should inherit, but the court attempts to locate the person(s) who stands closest to the deceased.

When a person prepares a will, he or she should make provision for the possibility that an heir may die first. It should be indicated that if an heir has died, then another person should receive the inheritance. A will should be reviewed periodically to determine if changes are necessary because of the death of an heir.

Domicile

The place where a person is born is the person's *domicile of origin;* where the person lives is the *domicile of choice.* A wife acquires a husband's domicile. If a person changes his or her domicile of choice, it may be necessary to change the will. The rule is that the will must provide for the disposition of real property according to the law where the real property is situated. Personal property is disposed of according to the law of the testator's place of domicile at the time of his death.

Some Important Additional Points about Wills

If the testator anticipates that someone may contest a will because that person is not mentioned in it, it is a good idea to mention that person by name and either make a small bequest or state that there is no bequest and why.

The testator may include a clause providing that if any beneficiary contests the will and loses, that he or she will lose the benefit given in the will as a penalty for contesting it. If a will libels someone, the estate may be sued. It is preferable to name a guardian in a codicil which is read out only if both parents die.

A will should contain wording that provides for an orderly distribution of the estate in the event that husband and wife die together in a mutual accident. If this is not done, confusion may arise as to whether one spouse's assets must first go to the other, whose will will then further distribute these assets. The law generally holds that in the absence of any wording, and if it is believed that both spouses died at the same time, then the estate will assume that the elder person died first.

A will cannot contain provisions which are contrary to public policy. For example, a will could not contain wording that directed a person to commit a crime in order to receive a bequest. A will cannot contain requirements of any person which are cruel, immoral or so severe that it would be unreasonable for the person to meet such requirements. For example, a will which required a daughter to divorce her husband in order to inherit would not be valid.

In most provinces, if a will was prepared while the testator was single, the will is automatically revoked if the testator marries. An exception to the rule is if the testator stated in his will that the will was prepared "in contemplation of marriage." This means that the testator knew at the time that he would soon marry but he wanted the terms of the will to remain the same.

Living Wills

Some Canadians are so concerned about the ability of medical science to keep them alive by the use of respirators that they have prepared what are called "living wills." These documents have no legal validity, but are an expression of the patient's attitude that might affect the attending physician's decision to continue using a respirator. A sample living will might read as follows:

> I wish to live a full and long life, but not at all costs. If my death is near and cannot be avoided; if I have lost the ability to interrelate with others and have no reasonable chance of regaining this ability; if my suffering is intense and irreversible, then I do no want to have my life prolonged. In this event, I would ask not to be subjected to surgery or resuscitation. Nor would I wish to have life support from mechanical ventilators, intensive care services, or other life-prolonging procedures, including the administration of antibiotics and blood products. I would wish, rather, to have care which gives comfort and support, which facilitates my interaction with others to the extent that this is possible, and which brings peace.

Living Trusts

Elderly persons should consider setting up *inter vivos trusts* to look after them should they become incompetent. If an elderly person had a stroke, for example, a trustee could care for the person without any court action. Otherwise, the person's property could end up in the control of the Public Trustee. Alternatively, a power of attorney may be given to someone to act during a period when a doctor declares a person to be incompetent. An inter vivos trust is revocable should the person become competent and wish to revoke it. A trust company is a suitable trustee.

Reviewing Important Points

1. If the court believes that a man is the father of a child, the court may issue an affiliation order declaring the man to be the father and ordering payment of child support.

2. An illegitimate child has no claim upon the father's estate, except in Ontario and New Brunswick which declare all children to be legitimate.

3. The overriding consideration, when determining who shall have custody of a child, is the best interests of the child.

4. There is no accepted, legal definition of death.

5. The preparation of a will can prevent problems from arising. A will requires no particular form as long as its meaning is clear and it is properly executed.

6. A holograph will is a will completely written in the handwriting of the testator. Some provinces will not recognize holograph wills.

7. Neither a witness nor his or her spouse may be a beneficiary under the will.

8. A will is not irrevocable. A testator can revoke it entirely and make a completely new will; or the will can be amended.

9. A will cannot cut dependants off from financial support. Such a will can be contested by the dependants no matter how it is worded.

Checking Your Understanding

1. What can a blood test prove regarding parentage?

2. What last name does an illegitimate child take?

3. In most provinces, at what age does the requirement of a parent to support a child end?

4. What is the legal definition of death?

5. Explain the rule of "suspicious circumstances" with regard to the preparation of a will.

6. Explain what is meant by the proper witnessing of a will.

7. List and explain three ways a will may be changed.

8. What generally are the duties of the executrix of an estate?

9. When two people die simultaneously, what does the law generally say regarding survivorship?

10. Name five major things that a will should contain.

Legal Briefs

1. J is very dark-skinned with black hair. G has light skin, brown hair, and a very protruding nose which runs in his family. They lived together for four months, then separated when G thought J was seeing another man. When J had a child, the child had a very small nose and brown hair. Would this description refute any claim that G was the father?

2. R lived with B, but maintained a very personal relationship with C, her former husband. She spent numerous weekends with him but continued to live with B. When R had a child, both men declined to take a blood test. What decision should be reached regarding parenthood?

3. W, a resident of Ontario, lived with S and her two small children by a previous marriage. The children called W, "Uncle" and he supported them; however, he told numerous people that they were not his children. After two years, W and S separated and S sought support from W for the children. Must W pay?

4. M was divorced from R, who was remarried to T. T sought to adopt the children of M and R. M did not object to this and after it was accomplished, T advised M that he had no further right of access to the children since he was no longer their father. Advise M.

5. D executed a will in which a bequest was made to her daughter, C. The bequest stated that C would inherit only if she was unmarried when D died. When D executed the will, C was married to B, whom D disliked very much. Valid bequest?

6. When C died, he left an estate valued at $3 000 000. His will contained this provision: "Upon my death, I hereby give all of my money and all of my property to my three daughters and their children." The eldest daughter had five children, the middle daughter had three children, and the youngest daugh-

ter had two children. They quarreled over the meaning of the will. The eldest daughter said the estate was to be divided into thirteen equal parts. The youngest daughter said each family was to receive $1 000 000 to share among the family members. How should the estate be divided?

7. R, having no living spouse, left all her estate to a foundation, leaving nothing to her four adult children who were self-supporting. They brought an action to have the will declared void on the grounds that, as their mother's "living issue," they had to inherit the estate. Are they correct?

8. When Y died, most of his estate went to a church. His daughter contested the will on the grounds that the church had exercised undue influence over her father by planting in his mind the idea that by leaving money to the church he would increase his chances of going to heaven. The daughter argued that heaven did not exist. She further contended that if the church could not prove that heaven exists, the bequest should be declared void. Would she succeed in her attempt to contest the will?

9. L purchased a blank will form at a book store and wrote in some terms in her own handwriting. The will was signed but not witnessed. She put this will into a Bible where it was found after her death. Valid will?

10. In 1958, P entered the military and executed a will upon the advice of military authorities who said P would be sent overseas on a U.N. Peacekeeping Mission. P left his estate to his mother and gave the will to her. He forgot all about it and never executed another will. He married E in 1965 and they had three children. P died in 1981. Who would inherit?

Applying the Law

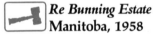

Re Bunning Estate
Manitoba, 1958

Bunning was in his eighties and suffered a stroke which affected his thinking. At times he was quite alert and could converse well, but at other times he could hardly speak and remembered very little. He had a housekeeper who lived in the same house, and a daughter who lived nearby and came to check on him daily.

One day as the daughter was entering the house, the housekeeper ran to her in great concern, saying that Bunning was burning papers in a fireplace. The daughter went into the study and found her father throwing paper into the fire. He muttered that he did not want old papers around. Some of the things he was burning were valuable, including stock and bond certificates and his will. Parts of the will were recovered from the fire, but much of it could not be read.

Since Bunning was no longer mentally competent, he could not make a new will; however, the family lawyer had a carbon copy of the will which had been burned. When Bunning died, this carbon copy was put forward to be accepted as a valid will. It was argued that Bunning had not wanted to destroy his will and had not known what he was doing. The will left most of the estate to the housekeeper and to the daughter. About 5 per cent was left to Bunning's son, whom he seldom saw and did not like. The son argued that the father had died intestate and that the son and daughter should divide the estate equally.

The court accepted the carbon copy as a true will on the guarantee of the family lawyer that it truly represented the contents of the original. In looking at the circumstances, the court concluded that there was no intention on the part of the testator to revoke his will. The destroying of a will without intention to revoke is not "destruction" as required when it is argued that a person has died intestate. While the act might not have been completely accidental, neither was it part of an intent to revoke a will.

Questions

1. Why was the will not revoked when burned?

2. If no carbon copy had been found, what would have happened to the estate?

3. As Bunning was sometimes mentally alert, should the court have assumed on this particular date that he wasn't? Why or why not?

4. In your opinion, was the case rightly decided? Why or why not?

5. Might the case have been decided differently if someone else had accidentally destroyed the will? Why or why not?

Re Morris
Ontario, 1949

Morris lived all his life in Ontario. He had three children with whom he was on excellent terms most of his life. He was also fond of his grandchildren. In 1945, his wife died. Starting in 1947, Morris' health declined and he spent most of his remaining years in a hospital. When his family visited him, he spoke about the excellent care he received in the hospital.

During the last year of his life, he became somewhat difficult to get along with. His children visited him less because he was prone to emotional outbursts and the hospital staff warned that these outbursts might cause a fatal heart attack. Out of concern, the family stayed away from him which caused him to accuse them of faithlessness and unkind behaviour. He often said that the only persons in the world who cared about him were the staff at the hospital.

Two months prior to his death, he called his lawyer and asked that the lawyer come to the hospital. In his room, Morris dictated a new will, revoking his previous will that had been prepared in 1938. In the new will, he left his entire estate to the staff of the hospital and to the hospital itself. The lawyer stated that Morris was "lucid, alert, and mentally keen" at the time. The children attacked the validity of this will on the grounds of undue influence and lack of mental competence. The hospital argued for the validity of the will. At no time had any member of the hospital staff discussed money or bequests with Morris.

The court declared the will to be invalid. While there had been no deliberate attempt to affect Morris' mind to get money from him, the circumstances in which he found himself caused him to be unduly influenced by the presence of the staff. His judgment was affected and altered in favour of the hospital. While it might have appeared to the lawyer that Morris was mentally competent, Morris was acting under a set of circumstances that were very inaccurate. He wrongly believed his family had deserted him and his final act of changing his will was part of that misconception.

Questions

1. Why did the court conclude that Morris was not totally of sound mind?
2. Why did the court conclude that there had been undue influence?
3. What is inadvertent influence?
4. In your opinion, was the case rightly decided? Give reasons for your answer.

You Be the Judge

1. Although the deceased had referred to her will on several occasions during her life, no will was found following her death. Several documents in the deceased's handwriting were found. Two of these documents, which acknowledged debts owed by her, were signed by her and made reference to her will stating that the debts were to be repaid "notwithstanding any provision in her will." The other documents were found in an envelope upon which the deceased had written her name and the nature of the contents described inside as being supplemental notes to her will. The documents themselves listed various articles and the names of persons to whom they were bequeathed. Although none of these documents was signed, the deceased had written her name on the top of one of them. The administrator of the estate applied for advice and direction as to whether the documents constituted valid holograph testaments. Should the documents be regarded as a will?

2. A father made out a cheque to his daughter and kept it in his wallet, saying it would be hers if anything happened to him. He suffered from emphysema and cancer of the lung. He was admitted to a hospital on

several occasions and each time gave his wallet to his daughter. Each time he was released, she returned it. On the father's final admission to the hospital, the daughter was informed that her father would not survive the night. She deposited the cheque into her bank account. The cheque was honoured on the date of the father's death, several days before the bank had notice of his death. In an action by other beneficiaries of the estate against the daughter, it was argued that the cheque should not have been honoured because she knew of his impending death. Should the daughter have to return the money?

3. When William Shales died, his will was found in his safe deposit box. The will had been prepared five years earlier by the family lawyer and was properly executed. However, there were changes made on the face of the will with a pen. Some of the bequests had a line drawn straight through them. Some of the amounts of the bequests had been changed with a pen. Lastly, below the signatures of the parties, there was something of a "postscript" believed to be in Shales' personal handwriting. There was a statement that the bequest of $20 000 to Shales' youngest son was to be eliminated since Shales was displeased with the personal behaviour of this son. The executor applied to the court for direction as to how to read the will. Was the original wording valid or were the revisions to be taken into account?

4. Unmarried and pregnant, the petitioner asked her doctor to arrange for an adoption. After the baby was born, she completed all the legal formalities. Months later, she decided that she had made a mistake. She sought to have the adoption declared void on the grounds that she had signed the papers under duress. She contended that she was weak and depressed at the time she signed the papers. Should the adoption be voided?

5. The petitioner had given a child up for adoption three years prior to the matter being brought before the court. While she did not seek to have the adoption cancelled, she sought visiting rights and access to the child. She asked that the province be required to tell her where the child was and that she be permitted to establish a normal relationship with the child. It was her contention that the blood relationship of mother and child is never terminated by adoption. Rather, a legal relationship with the new family is formed which can coexist with the blood relationship. Should the natural mother be granted visiting rights?

CATCH UP KEEP UP

B.C. GOVERNMENT EMPLOYEES' UNION

ON STRIKE FOR JOB SECURITY

Unit
Twelve

Labour
Law

"I find it difficult to take seriously any concern that entrenching in our Constitution the right of people to work anywhere in Canada could frustrate legitimate provincial objectives."

**William Davis,
Premier of Ontario**

Chapter 26

Law and the Workplace

Labour Law under the Common Law

The subject of labour law must be divided into two general areas: common law and statute law. Labour is a field of law that comes generally under provincial jurisdiction as laid down by the *Constitution Act, 1867*. Some federal laws have been enacted in the labour field as well, but primarily labour remains within the provincial jurisdiction. This naturally creates a wide difference of laws across Canada from province to province. This unit will therefore not try to be too specific for the obvious reason that there are so many statutes among the provinces—and they are constantly changing—that it would not be feasible to cover them all.

The common law did not develop sufficient rules that protected the rights of workers. Courts repeatedly refused to interfere in such matters as wages and working conditons, holding that it was for Parliament to regulate such things, not the courts. In the view of the judges, these were private contractual matters. The absence of any comprehensive legal protection helped speed the progress of the labour union movement. However, it would be incorrect to say that the common law had nothing to say about labour relations, for it did and still does. The purpose of special statutes is to fill in gaps that the common law does not cover. Statutes have also altered the common law in the area of freedom to contract between master and servant.

Master and Servant

The traditional term used to describe a person who works for another person is *servant*. A more common term today is employee, but the law still favours servant—some provinces have a statute called the *Master and Servant Act*. The term "servant" is not meant to be derogatory, but is meant to clarify the fact that a person is in the direct employment of another person who is referred to in law as the person's *master*.

An independent contractor is a person not under the direct control of the person doing the hiring. Generally, a person who employs a contractor to do a particular job does not supervise or control the details of the work or the manner in which it is done. The person who hires a contractor only checks to see that the terms of the contract are fulfilled. Ordinarily, the contractor provides the equipment and materials and any workers on the job are employed directly by the contractor. Any attempt by the person who hired the contractor to give direct orders to those workers would be viewed as unlawful interference.

An independent contractor may be a company or a single individual, sometimes called a "jobber" in lay terms. Generally speaking, a person engaging an independent contractor is not liable to third parties for damage due to the contractor's negligence; neither is the person liable to the contractor for injuries suffered by the contractor or any of the contractor's workers. The person who engages an independent contractor is also not obliged to make deductions for Unemployment Insurance, Canada Pension Plan, and federal income tax on the contractor's behalf.

At times, it is difficult to determine whether the relationship is that of master and servant or independent contractor. Nevertheless, it can be important at times to determine the exact status of the parties. Therefore, the courts look to see what the worker is required to do and the control exercised over the worker's method of doing the job. If it can be shown that the employer has substantial control over the method of work, then the relationship is usually held to be that of master and servant.

Ontario law is typical of the law in most provinces which defines an "employee" as a person who "performs any work for or supplies any services to an employer for wages; does homework for an employer; or receives any instruction or training in the activity, business, work, trade, occupation, or profession of the employer."

"Employer" includes "any person who as the owner, proprietor, manager, superintendent, or overseer of any activity, business, work, trade, occupation, profession, has control or direction of, or is directly or indirectly responsible for, the employment of a person therein."

The following case was centred around these definitions and the common law interpretation of master and servant.

 Re Becker Milk Company Ltd.
Ontario, 1973
Several store managers of the Becker Milk Company complained to the Employment Standards Branch that they were required by the nature of their jobs to work in excess of the forty-eight hour week prescribed in the Act as the maximum work week, and that they were not receiving overtime pay, vacation or holiday pay as the Act required. The company argued that the Act did not apply to the store managers as they were independent contractors, not employees. The Labour Arbitration Board concluded that the store managers were employees and entitled to the benefits of the Act. The managers' situation satisfied a four-fold test for employment: (1) They had very little chance of profit; and (2) little risk of loss since Becker's

insured and owned all the merchandise in each store and restricted what managers could order. (3) Becker's owned the stores, fixtures, and merchandise; and (4) although there was a small amount of discretion about hours, there was a company policy that the stores had to be open from 9:00 a.m. to 11:00 p.m., seven days a week. The manager's duties, prescribed by the company, required the manager to be in the store most of these hours:

❝The detailed examinaton of the control component clearly indicated that *control* must be a relevant consideration when determining the applicability of the *Employment Standards Act*. It appears reasonable that minimum employment standards should only be imposed where a person does in fact control the work situation of another.❞

Prior to the enactment of any special statutes, common law rules developed regarding this relationship of master and servant. These rules generally gave very limited protection to the servant, and dealt primarily with the contractual matter of hiring and firing. The common law rules could be summarized as follows:

The Contract of Hire
The relationship between the master and servant is a contract for services. It is therefore subject to all the rules pertaining to contracts. Such topics as hours of work, duties to be performed, and pay should be included in the contract. A contract of hire may be oral or in writing. It could be said that most Canadians are employed on the basis of an oral contract.

Terminating the Contract
A contract of employment may have a fixed term. If a person is hired for two years, the contract ends at that time and there is no obligation on either party to renew it. If the contract of hire is indefinite, and has no fixed ending date, it is assumed that the two parties may continue in the contract as long as they are satisfied with the relationship. Should either party want to end the contract, the common law would require that the party desiring to end the contract of hire give the

other party "reasonable notice." What constitutes reasonable notice depends upon a variety of things, including the availability of a replacement, the frequency of pay periods, etc. This requirement of reasonable notice applies to both the master and the servant. If a master fires the servant without just cause and without reasonable notice, the servant could sue for financial loss while unemployed. There are exceptions to the reasonable notice rule on both sides. For example, the master may fire the servant without notice for any one or more of the following reasons:

- Absence from the job without permission;
- Dishonesty;
- Incompetence;
- Insubordination or refusal to carry out instructions.

The servant also has grounds to quit the job without giving the master any notice. Such reasons include:

- Not being paid;
- Unsafe working conditions;
- Incompetent fellow workers who are a hazard;
- Being assigned duties that are not within the contract of employment or are degrading;
- Being assigned duties which are contrary to law.

Provincial laws and the common law support the concept that an employee must be given either reasonable notice of dismissal or salary in its stead. The courts have also held that a resignation that has been forced is the equivalent of a firing. Employees who resign because they have been demoted, harassed or ridiculed, or transferred to very undesirable assignments may also demand compensation from their employers.

Every employment contract, whether written or verbal, has a built-in understanding that the employee will not be fired without reasonable notice unless it is for just cause. An employer who fires without cause will be held liable for the "inevitable economic consequences" suffered by the employee. As well, the employer could be liable for side effects which the trauma of dismissal may cause.

In 1976, the Alberta courts decided in favour of a salesperson in a suit against a former employer. The salesperson was transferred, with a raise, but given little more information about the new position. When the salesperson wanted more information, the employer demanded acceptance of the position or resignation. The salesperson resigned and sued and was awarded six months' salary. Today, a similar case might bring an award of twenty-four months' salary.

 ### Pilon v. Peugeot Canada Ltd.
Ontario, 1980

The plaintiff, a mechanic by trade, had worked for the defendant as a service manager for seventeen years. The defendant gave its employees an assurance of life-long security, and the plaintiff had rendered continuous loyal service. The plaintiff was wrongfully dismissed. In an action for damages, he sought further damages for mental distress, anxiety, vexation and frustration caused by the defendant's breach of contract. The court held that if there had been a breach of contract, and if the employee was wrongfully dismissed, that it was recognized that the mental distress which followed was actionable against the employer:

&&On all of the evidence, I am satisfied that the plaintiff did, in fact, suffer serious mental distress, or to use the words of Judge Borins, 'vexation, frustration and distress' as a result of his discharge, which was a breach of the contract of employment.&&

The plaintiff was awarded $7500 for mental distress. He also received one year's wages but no compensation for "loss of job opportunity" based on his age. Pilon argued that because Peugeot fired him so late in life (he was over fifty) that his chances of developing a career with another company were nil. The court did not accept this argument.

Liability of Master to Servant

The common law generally did very little in the way of allowing a servant to sue a master for an injury received at work. Every job was assumed to have some risks, and if those risks resulted in a foreseeable injury, there was no liability on the part of the master. This area of law generally comes under tort law. In two areas only did the common law recognize that the master could be liable for the injuries suffered by a servant. These were:

(1) If the master was personally negligent in not providing the servant with a safe place to work;
(2) If the master was personally negligent in not providing competent fellow workers.

The immediate problem that a servant faced was in trying to prove that the master was *personally* negligent in these matters, since most servants worked for a manager, supervisor, or some other representative of a company. Also, the servant had little money to use for lawsuits.

 Paris v. Stepney Borough Council
England, 1951

The plaintiff was a mechanic in a garage owned by the defendant. The plaintiff was blind in one eye, a fact well known by his employer. While working on a truck, he used a hammer to loosen a rusted bolt. The hammer knocked away a piece of metal which blinded the plaintiff's other eye rendering him 100 per cent sightless. He sued his employer on the grounds that his employer failed to provide him with goggles to protect his eye. The defence argued that the accident was freakish; that none of their mechanics wore goggles; and that the employer owed no greater duty of care towards an employee with one eye than towards employees with two eyes. The trial court held in favour of the defendant, saying:

> **❝**A one-eyed man is no more likely to get a splinter in his eye than a two-eyed man.**❞**

However, this decision was overturned by the Court of Appeal which held that the gravity of harm was so severe that a reasonable employer would have shown greater concern for a one-eyed employee and required him to wear goggles even if the other employees did not. The plaintiff had a special need of protection which was known to the employer.

Liability of the Master to Third Parties

If a servant committed a tort while acting in the course of employment for a master, the master was liable in tort to the third party who was injured. The master could, in turn, sue the servant and recover any money paid out because of the servant's negligent actions. This is discussed further in Unit Five   The Law of Torts.

Principal and Agent

A different type of relationship from master and servant is that of principal and agent. An *agent* is a person employed to act on the behalf of another person, called the *principal*. The relationship is such that an act of an agent, done within the scope of that agent's authority, binds the principal. Agents are:

- *Universal:* Appointed to act for the principal in all matters;
- *General:* Appointed to act in transactions of a class, e.g., employment agent;
- *Special:* Appointed for one particular purpose.

Creation of Agency

The relationship of an agency may be created in numerous ways, including the following:

- *Express appointment:* The express appointment of an agent means that the principal directed the agent to act on his or her behalf and gave the agent explicit powers and instructions. Often the principal makes the appointment in writing and signs what is called a *Power of Attorney,* a document outlining in great detail the extent of the agent's powers to act on behalf of the principal. Any contracts signed by the agent within the scope of this authority are binding upon the principal just as much as if the principal had signed them personally. For this reason, it is prudent to select an agent very carefully.
- *Agent by estoppel:* Anyone who allows another person to act as his or her agent, even though never appointing that person for this purpose, is *estopped* (prevented) from later denying the agency. If a principal knows that someone is acting as his or her

agent, but remains silent about it, the principal will be legally obligated to fulfill the contract the (self-appointed) agent has signed. Whenever a person learns of such a thing being done, that person should immediately deny the existence of any agency and inform all interested persons that he or she has no intention of honouring such contracts.

- *Agent by necessity:* Anyone who has to act out of necessity on behalf of another person is said to be doing so as an *agent by necessity.* For example, if someone found an unconscious person who had suffered a heart attack, an ambulance could be summoned on behalf of the unconscious person—as that person's agent by necessity. The importance of this point is that the unconscious person would have to pay the costs of the ambulance which the agent by necessity summoned. It must be kept in mind that necessity has to be interpreted in a very strict sense. Necessity does not include doing things because someone might appreciate it. Where a person entered into certain contracts on behalf of a neighbour and bought certain goods for the neighbour, that person was not acting as an agent by necessity. If the neighbour did not immediately protest such an action, the neighbour could be estopped.

- *Agent by ratification:* If a person enters into a contract on behalf of someone else, without any authority to do so, the unwilling principal must repudiate the contract completely immediately upon learning of it. If the principal remains silent, he or she may be bound upon the contract by the principle of estoppel, as was previously discussed. The principal cannot ratify part of the contract that favours him or her and repudiate the rest. The act of giving approval to the agency after the contract has been signed makes the contract just as binding upon the principal as if he or she had expressly appointed the agent. It is very unwise to do such a thing, for the person who acted as agent is free to continue doing so, and the principal will continue to be bound by this person's actions.

- *Agent by apparent authority:* When a principal puts a person into a position which carries certain powers, it is apparent to third parties that the person is an agent. The principal will be bound by any contract which falls within that "apparent" authority even if the agent exceeds his or her real authority. *For example:* J was a buyer for a lumber company. She had authority from her company to buy up to $100 000 of lumber under any one contract. She entered into a contract with the M Company to buy $150 000 of lumber because she obtained such an excellent price. Her employer sought to cancel the contract because J had exceeded her true authority. The employer could not cancel the contract because, despite the fact that J had exceeded her true authority, she had acted within her apparent authority as far as the M Company could tell.

Comparing Agent and Servant

A primary difference between an agent and a servant is that a servant cannot enter into contracts in the master's name; however, an agent can enter into contracts in the principal's name. While an agent can be given definite guidelines under which to operate, the principal does not direct the work of the agent closely.

Agents' Responsibilities to their Principals

Primarily, agents are responsible to their principals for carrying out the instructions they were given. They are bound to do this with reasonable skill, for if they obtained their positions by telling their principals that they had special skills, then they must demonstrate them.

Agents by their nature must be loyal to their principals, for they are really acting in the name of their principals. Agents cannot make secret commissions on the side, or sell their own goods to their principals and claim that they bought them from third parties. If agents are given money by their principals, they must account for that money.

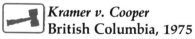

Kramer v. Cooper
British Columbia, 1975

The defendant, Cooper, listed lots for sale with a real estate agent. The plaintiff, Kramer, was an employee of the real estate agent. He himself had a licence to deal in real estate. Kramer told his employer he was interested in buying the lots himself, but at a price less than that wanted by the defendant. Kramer signed an interim agreement which only said that he "held a licence in real estate and is purchasing for rental purposes or for resale." At no time was Cooper aware that Kramer worked for the real estate agent Cooper had employed. After the sale, Kramer received half the real estate agent's commission from his employer.

Cooper subsequently learned who Kramer worked for and then refused to proceed with the sale. Kramer sued for specific enforcement of the sale. The court dismissed the plaintiff's case. Specific performance should not be ordered when an agent's employee allows personal interest to conflict with the principal's interest. Here, the conflict was apparent. The plaintiff wanted to buy the property at a cheap price. The defendant wanted to sell at a high price. The failure to disclose to the defendant that the plaintiff was the buyer, and that he was employed by the defendant's agent, were material facts and the suppression of these facts justified denial of specific performance.

Rights of Agents
Agents have the right to be paid for their services, provided they carried out their duties properly, and to be paid for any extra expenses they incurred in doing so. Agents have a right not to be fired in order to beat them out of commissions.

Liability of Principal to Third Parties
The principal is liable on any contract as long as the agent was acting within his or her apparent, implied or express authority. The principal cannot revoke the contract on the grounds that the agent exceeded the instructions and authority given, provided that third parties did not know the agent was exceeding this authority. If a third party knew the agent was exceeding the authority given, the contract is not binding upon the principal.

A principal is also liable for torts committed by the agent, if committed in the course of employment. This might include such torts as fraud or theft.

Proving the Agent's Authority
Often persons deliberately give the impression that they represent a company when they do not. A salesperson may be selling a particular line of products and give the impression of being an agent of that company. The person may make promises or offer guarantees that are alleged to be backed by the company. These representations may be false.

The third party has a responsibility to require the agent to prove his or her authority, particularly where the terms of an agreement seem too good to be true. The third party should request that the agent produce evidence of authority from the principal.

Termination of Agency
Just as any contract may have a predetermined date upon which it ends, so may a contract for an agency have a predetermined ending date. The agency contract can also be ended by either party terminating it by giving notice to the other. A principal should notify interested third parties that a particular agent is no longer in the principal's employ.

If the principal dies, is disabled, goes bankrupt, or is declared mentally unfit, the agency ends. Since the principal is no longer able to contract personally, the agent cannot contract on the principal's behalf.

Who May Be an Agent?
Any person capable of contracting may be a principal. Since the agent acts for the principal, the agent need not be someone capable of contracting. Thus, a minor can be an agent and can make contracts that will be binding on the principal.

A wife is a husband's agent for necessaries for herself and her family. She may pledge the husband's credit for the purpose of providing those necessaries. A wife is not a husband's agent in matters such as his business affairs unless he agrees to this and she has been appointed as his agent. If a husband and wife separate, the wife can continue to pledge the husband's credit for necessaries, but he is not responsible for any other debts she incurs. If there is a separation agreement, the wife must accept the funds provided under that agreement and stop using the husband's credit.

How an Agent Signs

An agent should sign all documents to indicate clearly that it is the principal who is being committed, not the agent. The agent should sign the principal's name first, then sign his or her own name and indicate the capacity in which he or she acts—for example: R.E. Ames Company, Ltd., per Terry Hawkins, General Manager.

If the agent does not carefully identify the principal, the agent may be personally liable on the contract. The same thing would apply to cheques signed by the agent.

Federal Labour Legislation

The federal government has jurisdiction over navigation, shipping, interprovincial railways, canals, telegraphs, steamship lines, airports, ferries, air transport, and radio stations. The *Canada Labour Code* covers fair employment practices, equal pay for women, and the minimum wage for all persons employed in those occupations. The Code extends to the employees of the federal civil service.

There are also federal laws, such as the *Canada Pension Plan*, which apply to all Canadians.

The Unemployment Insurance Act

This Act is a federal statute and applies to all parts of Canada. It includes all general industrial jobs but some occupations are excluded because of their nature. The Act provides benefits in the areas of unemployment insurance, maternity benefits, and retirement. Complete details should be obtained from your local office of the Unemployment Insurance Commission.

Canada Pension Plan

This plan, which started in 1966, is a contributory social insurance plan designed to help people have a more secure retirement and to afford financial assistance in case of disability or death. The plan operates in all parts of Canada except Quebec, which has its own similar pension program.

To have coverage, a person must be between the ages of eighteen and seventy and must have earnings above a minimum level called the Basic Exemption.

Workers contribute on employment income only, which is salaries, wages, or tips. Self-employed persons must contribute to their own plan. Benefits under the plan include:

- *Retirement pension:* A monthly pension payable as early as age sixty-five.
- *Disability benefits:* A monthly pension for contributors who become disabled, within the meaning of the Act, before age sixty-five.
- *Survivors' benefits:* A death benefit payable to the estate, a monthly pension for the surviving spouse and dependent children are provided for through the Plan. Benefits to dependent children under the age of eighteen are payable to the person having custody of them. Benefits to children aged eighteen to twenty-five are payable directly to them provided they are considered to be in full-time attendance at school or university.

The *Human Rights Act*

The Canadian *Human Rights Act* became law in 1978. The Act prohibits discrimination in employment and covers those employed within the constitutional jurisdiction of the federal government.

> **3. For all purposes of this Act, race, national or ethnic origin, colour, religion, age, sex, marital status, conviction for which a pardon has been granted, and, in matters related to employment, physical handicap, are prohibited grounds of discrimination.**

The Act further discusses practices of employment which are specifically prohibited. They include:

- Employment or employment advertisements or applications showing preference. The application may require that the applicant indicate basic matters such as age, sex, place of birth, etc.

- Denial of membership in an employee organization. The exception is where the person is past retirement age or below the legal age to obtain employment.

- Discriminatory promotion, training, apprenticeship, or job transfer.

- Discriminatory payment scales based on sex. Males and females are to be paid the same wages if they are performing *work of equal value.*

Re British American Bank Note Co.
Canada, 1978

This case involved the complaint by twenty-five women inspectors at British American Bank Note Co. that their wages were lower than those of unskilled male workers at the same plant. The arbitrator settled the case by comparing the women's wages with those paid to inspectors at the Canadian Bank Note Co. The arbitrator did not deal directly with the issue of whether the inspectors' work was of equal value to that of the male workers.

The concept of "work of equal value" is a difficult one to assess. All provincial legislation uses a different phrase — "equal pay for equal work." This means that if males and females both do the same work, they must be paid the same. The federal law has a different wording and could mean that a company would have to pay a truck driver and a secretary the same wages if it was held that they both did work that provided the employer with equal value. The problem of putting "value" upon work will be very difficult in many situations. More than one million Canadians are employed by the federal government or companies under federal jurisdiction. The criterion stated in the Act are the "skill, effort and responsibility required in the performance of the work and the conditions under which the work is performed."

The *Charter of Rights and Freedoms*

One of the provisions of the new *Charter of Rights and Freedoms* is "mobility rights." It states:

> **6. (1) Every citizen of Canada has the right to enter, remain in and leave Canada.**
> **(2) Every citizen of Canada and every person who has the status of a permanent resident of Canada has the right**
> **(a) to move to and take up residence in any province; and**
> **(b) to pursue the gaining of a livelihood in any province.**

Although general restrictions may not be placed on a worker moving from one part of the country to another, the ordinary rules of employment in the province will apply to newcomers the same as to long-term residents. These could include qualifications, union membership, experience, and so on. Further, a province in which the employment rate is below the national average will have the right to undertake "affirmative action programs" for socially and economically disadvantaged individuals.

One area of interest is the Quebec *Language Bill* which requires persons in certain occupations to pass a written and oral test in French. A test of this law in the courts is very likely to determine whether it violates the *Charter* by denying persons not fluent in French the right to work in the Province of Quebec.

Provincial Labour Legislation

The provincial governments have legislative authority over many aspects of the work force. There is a considerable body of statutes that apply to safety, health, and job discrimination. Provincial governments also have power over employers and employees through licensing powers which can be used to require adherence to certain practices under threat of withdrawal of a necessary licence.

Collective Bargaining and Labour Relations Acts

The formation of unions for the purpose of collective bargaining was at first viewed as a conspiracy to restrain free trade. Laws were passed against unions in many countries, and England deported union organizers to Australia, calling the unions "secret conspiratorial societies." Gradually, however, the governments of the industrialized nations began to realize that the union movement was based on real causes for complaint. After long, and sometimes violent strikes in the coal mines, textile plants, and other general manufacturing centres, governments became increasingly aware that the industrial revolution had not brought benefits to everyone. Conditions in factories and mines were so bad that workers had to form unions since this was the only way they could bargain for better conditions. In 1872 the Canadian Parliament passed the *Trade Unions Act* and amended the *Criminal Code* to bring protection to organized labour. Prior to 1872, any attempt to picket an employer's business was an offence under the *Criminal Code* known as "watching and besetting" a place.

The Provincial legislatures generally have the responsibility of recognizing unions and granting them legal status. Most provinces have labour legislation similar to the *Labour Relations Act* of Ontario which provides rules for the recognition of a union as a collective bargaining agent for a particular group of persons and lays the groundwork for collective bargaining and legal strikes. The main points of such legislation are as follows:

- Every employee is free to join a trade union and participate in its lawful activities.

- No employer can discriminate against an employee because of union membership. Such discrimination would include: refusing to employ or continue to employ a person because of union membership; imposing any condition to restrain an employee from joining a union; and/or using the threat of dismissal or any other means to compel an employee to leave the union or to refrain from becoming a union member.

- An employer cannot participate in or interfere with the formation or administration of a union, or contribute financial support to it.

- Where a union has been accepted (or certified) as the bargaining agent by the employees, the employer must deal only with that union when negotiating a collective agreement.

- Collective agreements must contain a provision stat-

For many years, unions were illegal because they were considered conspiracies to limit free trade.

ing that there will be no strikes or lockouts while the agreement remains in force.

- Collective agreements must contain a provision for settlement by arbitration, without stoppage of work, of all differences between employer and employees arising from the interpretation, application, or alleged violation of the agreement.
- Members of a union cannot be expelled or penalized because they refuse to take part in an illegal strike.
- Where an employee is wrongfully dismissed, the employer may be compelled to reinstate the employee and/or pay compensation for loss of earnings.
- Both employers and unions are liable to penalties for refusing or failing to comply with the provisions of the Act. The most usual form of penalty is a fine, but a union may also be ordered back to work.

Legality of Strikes

In some cases, the legality of a strike is difficult to ascertain. Generally, a strike is legal when a union has no current labour contract with the employer (the previous contract may have expired), and when the union has attempted to bargain in good faith and has served notice on the employer of its intention to strike.

Amoco Canada Petroleum Co. Ltd. v. Hubert et al. Ontario, 1974

The case concerned a motion for an interim injunction to restrain the defendants from picketing the plaintiff's premises and from continuing an illegal strike. The defendants and other members of their union had a valid collective agreement with the plaintiff. The defendants went on strike, preventing anyone from entering or leaving the premises, and doing harm to the plaintiff's business. The defendants admitted that an injunction should be issued enjoining all but peaceful picketing, but argued that neither the picketing nor the strike itself should be enjoined. The court ruled the strike illegal since it contravened s. 63(1) of the *Labour*

Relations Act which prohibited a strike when a collective agreement was in operation. Where the strike was illegal, activities such as picketing should be prohibited if the plaintiff was being harmed.

If a strike is called illegally, an injunction can be obtained for the purpose of prohibiting further picketing. An injunction can also be issued if the purpose of the picketing is to induce breach of contract, or the furtherance of a conspiracy. Mass picketing or blockade picketing is illegal.

Specific performance is a remedy against a union engaged in an unlawful strike. That is, a court may order a union to go back to work. Specific performance is not a remedy against one individual—the court will not order one person to go back to work. To do so, in the view of most jurists, would amount to involuntary servitude. Therefore, an individual who wrongfully stays away from work may be sued, but the court will not order that person to go back to work.

Re Windsor School Board Ontario, 1975

Windsor, Ontario secondary school teachers refused to continue working in the fall of 1974 after failing to reach a salary settlement with the Board of Education. The teachers also began picketing the schools. The Board of Education sought an injunction ordering the teachers to stop picketing and return to their classrooms. The Ontario Supreme Court refused to grant the injunction, holding that:

66There is neither a collective agreement nor a statute imposing a particular code of labour relations upon these parties. Teachers who are governed by the *Teaching Profession Act* are excluded from the *Labour Relations Act*. This court will not depart from the principle that individuals will not be compelled to perform contracts of personal service.99

The court did agree that the teachers were in violation of their personal contracts and could be sued for breach of contract.

The contract which a union signs is binding upon all its members. Employees cannot be compelled to join a union, but if they do not, the contract with the union may not extend to them—they may have to make their own bargain with the employer. Some companies have signed union agreements under what is called the Rand Formula. This agreement stipulates that employees do not have to join a union, but that the employer must deduct union dues from their pay. Any benefits acquired by the union for its members also apply to non-members who have been paying dues. In 1980, Ontario made the Rand Formula part of the *Labour Relations Act*.

If a union conducts an illegal strike, the union can be held liable for the financial loss of the company struck and also losses suffered by other companies that normally do business with the company against whom the strike was brought. After a sixteen-day illegal strike by CUPW (Canadian Union of Postal Workers) in 1974, a Quebec court awarded Santana, Inc., a shoe manufacturer, damages for loss of sales and the cost of courier services. A number of major lawsuits are before the courts against Local 785 of the International Fireman's Association of Montreal and forty firemen. The plaintiffs claim damages resulting from an illegal strike in 1974 when fire destroyed their homes.

Workers' Compensation

Every province has enacted some form of compensation for workers seriously injured on the job. For

Strikers may lawfully picket their employer only if they do so in a peaceful manner and do not prevent persons from entering and leaving the premises.

example, the *Workmen's Compensation Act* of Ontario provides compensation where there is personal injury by accident arising out of and in the course of employment, and in some cases illness caused by an industrial disease such as black lung disease. Compensation includes payment of wages, medical expenses, surviving spouse's benefits, and funeral expenses. The cost of the program is financed primarily by payments by employers. No deduction may be made from any employee to pay the costs of the plan.

In order to qualify for compensation, the injury must have occurred on the job or in some act related to the job. The two major exceptions which will prevent a person from receiving benefits are:

- Where the injury does not disable the worker beyond the date of accident from earning full wages at the work at which the worker was employed.

- Where the accident is attributable solely to the serious and wilful misconduct of the worker and does not result in serious injury or death.

Workers' compensation generally does not attempt to put the blame on any particular person for the injury, although a negligent employer can be fined for a poor safety record. The question of negligence on the part of the worker does not affect the payment of compensation. Only by the serious and wilful disregard of safety regulations does an employee jeopardize the receiving of benefits.

If the Workmen's Compensation Board must pay out compensation, the Board has the right to recover the cost from any third person who caused the injury to the employee. A worker injured on the job must report the injury to the employer immediately. Failure to do so may jeopardize the worker's claim to have been injured on the job. There have been false claims submitted by persons injured at home who later claimed the injury occurred at work.

Some occupations are not covered by the plan, including the employees of banks, trust companies, and barber shops, domestic servants, and casual or occasional employees.

Employment Standards

Every province has a statute, or series of statutes providing for hours of work, minimum wages, vacation with pay, and numerous other matters of importance to the employee. Each province also has a series of statutes and accompanying regulations dealing with safety. Hence, there are construction safety regulations, logging regulations, mining regulations, and many others. Ontario has at least six such statutes and several hundred regulations stemming from them. The provinces also have laws or regulations pertaining to the employment of women and children, and relating to discrimination by way of age, sex, nationality, colour, etc.

Human Rights

All the provinces have legislation prohibiting forms of discrimination by employers or trade unions. The basis for discrimination differs from province to province.

Newfoundland prohibits discrimination on the basis of a person's race, religion, religious creed, sex, marital status, political opinion, colour, or ethnic, national or social origin, or on the basis of age for persons between the ages of nineteen years and sixty-five years, subject to bona fide occupational requirements. There are restrictions upon job application forms and advertisements concerning employment.

The Alberta *Individual's Rights Protection Act* prohibits discrimination on the basis of race, religion, colour, sex, marital status, age, ancestry or place of origin. It requires equal pay for similar or substantially similar work.

The Ontario *Human Rights Code* prohibits discrimination on the basis of race, colour, ancestry, place of origin, citizenship, ethnic origin, creed, family status, sex, marital status, age, handicap, and record of offences. The *Code* also provides penalties for employers who subject employees to sexual harassment or sexual solicitation. Handicapped persons cannot be denied work unless it can be clearly shown that their handicap prevents them from performing the duties of the job.

Reviewing Important Points

1. When a contract of hire is terminated, the law generally requires that an employee be given reasonable notice.

2. A servant may quit a job without notice if he or she has not been paid, if conditions are unsafe, or if the servant is assigned to duties which are demeaning in nature.

3. A master can direct the manner in which a servant must perform tasks. An independent contractor is free from direction as to how a task is to be done.

4. An agent is a person who may enter into contracts on behalf of a principal and bind the principal just as if the principal had signed the contract personally.

5. A servant cannot contract in his or her master's name.

6. Federal and provincial law prohibits discrimination in employment on such grounds as race, religion, sex, creed, and place of origin.

7. While specific performance cannot be ordered against an individual, a union may be ordered back to work.

Checking Your Understanding

1. For what reasons may an employer dismiss an employee without notice?

2. What is wrongful dismissal? What liability might an employer have for wrongful dismissal?

3. What two things are considered unethical on the part of an agent with regard to the principal?

4. It is important that an agent sign a contract or cheque carefully. How should an agent sign?

5. For what reasons might an employee be denied workers' compensation benefits?

6. What is "equal pay for equal work"? What is "equal pay for work of equal value"? Do they have the same meaning? Why or why not?

7. How can the court determine if a worker is a servant or an independent contractor?

Legal Briefs

1. The following advertisement is placed in the local newspaper. How many things in this advertisement would be unlawful?

> **HELP WANTED:** Male employees to work in northern logging town. Must be able to do heavy manual work. Minimum education, grade ten. At least two years of Canadian experience necessary. Only persons born in Canada may apply. Proof of age must be supported by birth certificate. Applicants must also provide proof of legal entitlement to work in Canada. All applicants must be in good physical condition and be able to pass a physical examination given by the company doctor. Base pay, $12.50 per hour. Send application letters, along with a recent photograph, to Box 374.

2. Tracy Robinson, Purchasing Agent for the Sensational Products Corporation, signs a contract for the company in the following manner:

> "Tracy Robinson, Purchasing Agent
> Sensational Products Corporation"

Advise Robinson whether or not this is the best manner in which to sign contracts.

3. B finds a window broken by a storm in a neighbour's cottage. Knowing that the neighbour will not return for two weeks, and realizing that rain will cause damage if it blows through the window, B purchases and installs a new window. Is B an agent?

4. G is slightly injured on the job Friday afternoon. Thinking the injury to be slight, she tells no one about it. By Monday morning, her condition is much worse. Will she receive workers' compensation benefits if unable to work?

5. While making deliveries for a major oil company, the driver overfills a tank causing damage to the contents of the lower level of a home. The oil company denies responsibility by stating that the driver does not work for the oil company. The truck driver is an independent contractor who owns the truck and makes deliveries for the oil company on a contractual basis. Liability of the oil company?

6. If, in Question 5, the truck driver delivers exclusively for the oil company, has the name of the oil

company painted on the truck, and the homeowner has a contract for oil with the oil company, would the final decision in the case be the same?

7. M, a female, applies for a job with the C Mining Co. She is refused employment because the company does not have separate showers, change room, or rest room facilities for female workers. Advise M.

8. K is from Ontario and applies for a job with the E Co. in Northern Alberta. She is told that the only positions still open are being specifically held for native people from the local community who are being trained. K believes she has more qualifications than the trainees and feels that she has a case against the E Co. for discrimination. Advise K.

Applying the Law

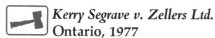
Kerry Segrave v. Zellers Ltd.
Ontario, 1977

The complainant alleged that he was refused employment and training, by Zellers Ltd., because of his sex and marital status. The applicant arranged for an interview with Zellers in response to an advertisement in a newspaper for personnel manager trainees and credit manager trainees. He was interviewed by a female management trainee who told him that only women held the position of personnel manager and that the salary would not be attractive to a male. Her district manager had told her, "We could get an executive at half price by getting rid of men." She also told him that they did not hire men because women would not go to them with their problems. The applicant then expressed an interest in the credit manager trainee position. He was given a preliminary interview for the position, but was not processed further because of his undesirable marital status. He had been divorced three months before and Zellers took this as a sign of "instability in his background which could cross over into his business life as well."

Zellers was ordered to pay Segrave a general damage award and to administer employment tests

to him. If he passed the tests, he would have to be offered a job and the company would have to pay him for the twelve weeks during which he was unemployed after applying for a job.

Questions

1. Upon what basis was Zellers ordered to make a payment to the plaintiff?
2. Why did the company not want to hire the plaintiff?
3. Since the interviewer was a woman, what *condition* existed at Zellers and was being *preserved* by the company as conveyed to Segrave?

McNulty Cartage Ltd. v. McMannus
New Brunswick, 1980

The defendant ordered sand and gravel from the plaintiff for a property he owned. Later, he retained his limited company to do work at this property and advised the plaintiff to bill him at his business address. The limited company went bankrupt and the plaintiff sued the defendant personally. The defendant acknowledged only partial liability — for the materials delivered prior to his limited company's becoming involved. The court held that the plaintiff should have judgment for the full amount from the defendant. A person who orders work to be done or materials to be furnished is liable to pay for the work or materials. The defendant had originally contracted to make himself personally liable without any limitation of that liability. He had made the initial order, had it delivered to his personal property, and paid the account himself. Subsequent delivery slips had been made out in a manner indicating that the plaintiff looked to the defendant personally to pay the account. The essence of the subsequent dealings between the parties indicated only that the address to which invoices were to be sent had changed. The customer appeared to be the same. None of the subsequent dealings were inconsistent with the original intention that the defendant was personally liable.

Questions

1. If a person commences business dealings on a business-to-person basis, then wishes to change those dealings to a business-to-business basis, what steps should the person take to make this clearly understood?
2. Why did the court hold the defendant fully liable?
3. Was it important to the case that the work and materials were sent to property personally belonging to the defendant? Give a reason for your answer.

You Be the Judge

1. A law clerk appealed her dismissal without notice by her employer. The clerk was advised by her employer that before issuing a writ, she must always obtain approval from one of the lawyers. On one occasion it appeared that a writ had been issued without such approval and a discussion ensued between the clerk and the senior lawyer. During the discussion, the clerk admittedly said: "What the (deleted) do you think I am? I've been taking (deleted) from everybody around here for so long I'm fed up. So, what are you going to do about it?" The action alleged wrongful dismissal since she was only expressing an opinion. If she was to be discharged for poor performance, she was entitled to notice and severance pay. The law firm argued that it had grounds to dismiss without notice. Should the clerk receive notice and severance pay?

2. The defendant real estate agent informed a purchaser that the owner had accepted her offer. Based on this information, the purchaser then concluded the sale of her present house. In fact, the owner had not accepted the offer and the plaintiff found herself with no place to live. She sued the agent for the cost of temporary lodging and storage of furniture. The agent argued against accepting liability for such unforeseen results since the agent did not know that the purchaser was trying to sell her previous house. Who would succeed?

3. The defendant attempted suicide. He was brought to the plaintiff hospital and cared for by the plaintiff physician. Upon his recovery, the defendant refused to pay either the hospital or the physician because he had not wanted their services. The plaintiffs argued that lifesaving was a public duty and that it was also a criminal offence not to apply the means to save a life where the means were available. Who would succeed?

4. The plaintiff owned an apartment house and employed her son to do many of the small jobs required around the building. In fact, the tenants never saw the plaintiff, but only saw the son and grew accustomed to going to him for everything they wanted done. Unknown to the plaintiff, the son began accepting rent payments from the tenants. When she found out about this, the plaintiff had a major argument with her son and told him never again to take any rent money since that was her responsibility. However, the plaintiff did not advise the tenants not to give the money to her son and continued to employ him as overseer of the building. The son again collected rent money and left the city. The plaintiff sued the tenants for the (unpaid) rent. They refused to pay saying that they had properly paid their rent. Who would succeed?

Glossary of Legal Terms and Principles of Law

abet   To aid in the commission of an offence.

abortion   Procuring the miscarriage of a female person.

absolute discharge   After the charge has been proven or the accused has pleaded Guilty, the court may discharge rather than convict the accused. No punishment or restrictions are placed upon the accused.

absolute liability   A type of offence which holds that the mere doing of the act imports criminal intent.

acceptance   The act of assenting to an offer.

accessory   Any person involved in a crime other than the principal offenders who commit the crime.

accomplice   Any person who has been associated with another person in the commission of an offence.

acquittal   Discharge of an accused person by a verdict of Not Guilty.

act of God   An act caused by natural forces beyond human control.

action   A civil proceeding commenced by writ or statement of claim.

actus non facit reum, nisi mens sit rea   The act itself does not constitute guilt unless done with a guilty intent. One of the elements of a crime, usually expressed in its shortened form, *actus reus.*

adjournment   The suspension of the sitting of the court.

administrative law   The body of rules and regulations which govern the exercise of executive functions by the officers or public authorities to whom such powers have been granted by the legislative branch of government.

adultery   Voluntary sexual intercourse with a person of the opposite sex who is not the person's spouse.

adverse possession   Occupation of land which a person does not own but over which that person claims a right because of possession.

adverse witness   A witness who proves unexpectedly hostile to the party that called him or her.

agent   A person empowered to act on the behalf of another.

alimony   An allowance ordered by a court to be made to a wife for her support while separated from her husband.

appellant   One who appeals the decision of a court to a higher court.

arraignment   The first step in a criminal trial. The accused hears the charges read by the court clerk and is asked to enter a plea.

arrest   To deprive a person of liberty upon the making of a lawful charge.

assault   To threaten harm to a person with the ability to carry out that threat.

attempt   Any act done with intent to commit an offence.

audi alteram partem   Hear the other side. A principle of law that affords both parties a chance to tell their version of the facts.

automatism   A defence alleging that the accused was not in control of physical actions and was acting without mind-directed purpose. Automatism can be insane or non-insane automatism.

autrefois acquit   Formerly acquitted. A special plea

that the accused has already been tried for the offence and found Not Guilty.

autrefois convict   Formerly convicted. A special plea that the accused has already been convicted of the offence.

bail   The practice of releasing an accused person prior to trial. Bail may be granted either upon the person's own recognizance (promise to attend at trial) or upon the payment of a sum of money to guarantee the person's presence at trial.

bailee   A person to whom the possession of goods is entrusted by the owner for a purpose other than a sale.

bailment   The delivery of goods to a person for a purpose other than a sale, e.g., a repair, loan, etc.

bailor   One who entrusts property to another for a purpose other than a sale.

banns   A proclamation in a church of the intended marriage of two persons.

battery   A tort; namely, the unauthorized touching of another person.

bearer   The person in possession of a bill of exchange.

bill of exchange   An unconditional order in writing, addressed by one person to another, signed by the person giving it, ordering the person to whom it is addressed to pay on demand, or at a fixed or determinable future time, a sum certain in money to the order of a specified person or bearer.

bill of indictment   See indictment.

bill of sale   Any document representing the sale of goods.

breach of contract   A breaking of the obligation which a person had accepted under the terms of a contract.

C.I.F.   Cost, insurance, and freight.

canon law   Rules developed by the Christian Church, often having the force of law.

capital punishment   Punishment by death for certain offences (now abolished in Canada).

case stated   A procedure in criminal matters whereby one party may direct the judge to submit a question of law to an appeal court for a decision. Sometimes called *stated case*.

caveat emptor   Let the buyer beware. A rule of law holding that the seller does not have to disclose to the buyer facts about the goods which would be detrimental to the seller's interest if known. The seller may remain silent and let the buyer use his or her own judgment.

challenge of jurors   An objection to persons being considered as jurors in a case. Some objections may be for specific reasons *(for cause)* and others are allowed without reason *(peremptory)*.

chattels   Any property other than real property.

circumstantial evidence   A series of circumstances leading to the inescapable conclusion of guilt of the accused, even though direct evidence is not available.

codicil   A document executed by the testator (maker) of a will which makes a change to the original will.

codification   The orderly arrangement of laws into understandable, compact volumes.

collusion   In a divorce, collusion means that the spouses have arranged or faked evidence allowing one spouse to file for divorce, usually on the grounds of adultery.

common law   The law of England that developed through centuries of court decisions. Sometimes referred to as the unwritten law.

condition   A provision which is an integral part of a contract.

conditional discharge   After the charge has been proven or the accused has pleaded Guilty, the court may discharge rather than convict the accused. The accused is released with the requirement of meeting certain conditions of behaviour. If the accused violates those conditions, he or she may be brought back to the court, convicted and sentenced for the original offence.

condonation   The forgiveness by the injured party of the actions of the wrongdoer. Usually found in matrimonial cases where one spouse has forgiven the wrongdoing of the other and the right to seek a divorce is barred.

consideration   Those things of value which parties

to a contract exchange in order to indicate their serious intention to be bound by the contract.

conspiracy The agreement by two or more persons to commit an offence.

consummation The completion of marriage by the act of intercourse.

contract An agreement intended to be enforceable at law.

contributory negligence The defence in an action for negligence that the injured party was partly responsible for the injuries.

conversion A tort which is committed by a person who deals with chattels not belonging to him or her in a manner which is inconsistent with the rights of the owner, thereby denying the owner the use and possession of them.

conveyance The transfer of property or an interest in property, such as a deed.

corroboration Additional evidence which implicates a person materially and does not rest solely upon the testimony of a witness.

count Paragraphs of an indictment, each containing a separate charge of an offence.

counterclaim A claim made by the defendant in a civil action against the claim made by the plaintiff.

covenant A solemn personal promise which creates an obligation, usually given under seal.

cruelty Physical or mental mistreatment, often cited as grounds for divorce.

cujus est solum ejus est usque ad coelum Whoever owns the soil also owns what is above it.

damages Compensation for loss suffered owing to breach of contract or tort.

decree absolute A final divorce decree.

decree nisi An interim divorce decree.

deed A written instrument conveying title to property.

defamation The tort of publishing false statements harmful to a person's reputation. Generally of two types: slander, which is oral defamation, and libel, which is written or printed defamation.

defendant The person against whom the plaintiff has brought a civil action or who has been charged with a criminal offence.

desertion A matrimonial offence whereby one party leaves the other without the agreement of the other and without reasonable cause.

disability Legal incapacity, as in the case of a person mentally infirm or under legal age.

disclaimer A clause in a contract denying that any promises, guarantees, or warranties have been given about the quality of goods. Generally, a denial of liability or responsibility.

distress The taking of chattel property from someone who is considered a wrongdoer for some reason, e.g., for non-payment of rent.

dower The right of a wife to a life estate in one-third of her deceased husband's real property acquired during their marriage.

drawee The person to whom a bill of exchange is addressed.

drawer The person who makes a bill of exchange.

due process The adherence to proper procedure in legal matters as a safeguard of individual rights.

duress Constraint or threats of injury or imprisonment. A defence against a contract entered into involuntarily.

easement A right to land enjoyed by a person other than the owner.

encroachment The unauthorized extension of the boundaries of land, e.g., erecting a building that goes across a boundary line.

endorsement The signing of a bill of exchange, usually on the back, as a method of transferring it to another person.

entrapment A defence alleging that the accused committed the unlawful act only at the instigation of police officers or other persons acting in a law enforcement capacity. A defence not officially recognized in Canada.

equity A body of rules, founded upon the principle of fairness. At one time, equity was a separate branch of the law, but is now a general characteristic of our common law.

estate   An interest in land.

executor   A male person to whom the duty of carrying out the provisions of a will have been entrusted by the person who made the will.

executory   That which remains to be done. A contract is executory if its terms have not been carried out.

executrix   A female person to whom the duty of carrying out the provisions of a will have been entrusted by the person who made the will.

expropriation   Action of the government in compulsorily depriving a person of a right of property belonging to that person.

F.O.B.   Free on board.

fee simple   An estate of freehold, giving the most extensive interest a private citizen can hold in land.

fixtures   Anything attached to property.

foreclosure   The taking of property by a person who has loaned money on the condition that the loan be repaid or the property forfeited.

fraud   Intentional deceit or misrepresentation of material facts.

garnishee   A debtor whose wages or savings have been attached by court order. A garnishee order directs a person having funds belonging to the debtor to pay them to a creditor.

habeas corpus   A principle of law requiring that an accused person be told the charge and that he or she be brought to trial without undue delay.

habitual criminal   A person leading a continuous life of crime. A person declared an habitual criminal may be sentenced to prison for an indeterminate period of time.

hearsay   What someone has been heard to say, as contrasted with the direct evidence of the witness personally. Hearsay is generally excluded as evidence.

holder in due course   One who takes a bill of exchange, regular and complete on its face, in good faith before it is overdue and without notice of dishonour, for value.

holograph   A document or will written in the handwriting of the drawer.

homicide   The killing of a human being.

hybrid offence   An offence that can be prosecuted as summary conviction or indictable at the choice of the Crown Attorney.

ignorantia facti excusat; ignoranti a juris non excusat   Ignorance of the facts excuses; ignorance of the law does not excuse.

indictable offences   Offences of a serious nature often tried by judge and jury.

indictment   A written or printed accusation of a crime.

infant   A person under legal age. Sometimes referred to as a *child.*

infanticide   The killing of a newborn child.

information   A written complaint or charge that a criminal offence has been committed; must be sworn before a justice of the peace.

injunction   A court order telling a person to cease committing an act he or she has no lawful right to do.

inquest   A hearing to discover facts. Previously called an inquisition.

inter vivos trust   A legal agreement whereby a living person places personal and business matters into the hands of another person, the trustee. Such a trust is normally created when the living person is infirm and no longer able to look after such matters.

intestate   A person who has died without leaving a will.

invitee   A person who enters property on business in which the person entering and the occupier have a mutual interest.

judgment   The decision or sentence of a court.

laches   Negligence or unreasonable delay in asserting or enforcing a right. The court will not assist a person who has slept on his or her rights or acquiesced for a long time.

leading question   A question which tends to indicate the answer wanted. Allowed only during cross-examination.

lease   A grant of the possession of property to last for a term of years or other fixed period, usually with the requirement to pay rent.

liability   A legal obligation arising from contract or tort, or from a statute imposing such an obligation.

libel   Defamation in written or printed form.

licencee   A person who enters property as the guest of the occupier and has licence to move freely about that property.

lien   The right to hold property as security until an obligation involving that property has been paid.

manslaughter   A form of homicide; the lesser included offence of murder; where death is caused by culpable negligence or an act done in the heat of passion caused by provocation.

mens rea   Guilty mind. The mental capacity to commit the offence charged. One of the essential elements of most crimes.

mistake   A misunderstanding about the existence of the subject matter of the contract. It may render the contract void since there was no "meeting of the minds."

mortgage   The transfer of a legal estate or interest in land for the purpose of securing the repayment of a debt.

murder   A form of homicide; causing death by an unlawful act done with the intent to cause death or bodily harm likely to cause death.

necessaries   Those things which are required for sustaining life.

negligence   A tort, arising from the defendant's failure to take care not to injure someone where it was foreseeable that he or she might do so.

negotiable instrument   An instrument which may be transferred from one party to another as a form of payment. The most common type is a bill of exchange.

next friend   An adult who initiates a lawsuit on behalf of an infant.

novus actus interveniens   The intervention of human activity between the defendant's act and its consequences, thus breaking the chain of causation begun by the defendant.

nuisance   Interfering with the rights of other persons to enjoy the comforts of their property. A nuisance may be public, causing annoyance to the public in general, or private, causing annoyance to one person or class of persons.

obscene matter   Matter which contains an undue exploitation of sex, or of sex coupled with crime, cruelty, horror, or violence.

parol   Verbal or oral, not in writing or under seal.

plaintiff   The person who initiates a civil action.

plea   The reply to a charge.

plea bargaining   An unofficial process involving the prosecutor and defence counsel, normally resulting in the accused's pleading guilty to a lesser offence than originally charged.

precedent   A judgment or decision of a court cited as an authority for deciding a similar set of facts.

principal offender   The person having the most active part in the commission of an offence.

privilege   An exceptional or extraordinary right, immunity, or exemption of a person in virtue of his or her office or status.

probate   The process of determining the validity of a will.

procurer   A person who solicits the aid of others to take part in a crime.

provocation   Acts or words which would cause a reasonable person to lose self-control.

remand   To adjourn a hearing to a future date.

remedy   The means by which a violation of a right is prevented or compensated.

res ipsa loquitur   The act speaks for itself. A rule of law in tort cases which states that whenever it is so improbable that an accident would have occurred without negligence on the part of the defendant, the defendant should be found negligent even in the absence of other evidence.

respondent   A person against whom a petition is presented or an appeal filed.

right of way   The right to pass over the land of another.

robbery   Theft, coupled with threat or violence.

sale   Transfer of a right of property in return for payment of a sum of money.

slander   Defamation by spoken words or gestures.

statute   A written law; an Act of Parliament or a provincial legislature.

strict liability   Similar to absolute liability except that the accused may use as a defence evidence that he or she used reasonable care or due diligence in trying to comply with the law.

subpoena   A document commanding the appearance of a person in court, usually as a witness.

subsidiary legislation   Regulations, enacted under the power of a statute, having the force of law.

summary conviction offences   Offences of a less-serious nature which are tried by a judge alone without the presence of a jury.

tenant   One who holds land.

tender   An offer by one party to perform an obligation.

testator   A male person who makes a will.

testatrix   A female person who makes a will.

theft   Taking, without a claim of right, the property of another with the intent to deny the owner of the property the use and enjoyment of the goods, temporarily or permanently.

tort   A civil wrong committed by one person against another, not arising from a contract obligation.

tortfeasor   One who commits a tort.

trespass   A general term, meaning to pass beyond without right; to interfere with a person, or with that person's property or rights.

ultra vires   Beyond the power. An act in excess of authority and therefore invalid.

undue influence   To exercise control over a person's decision-making powers because of a close, personal and trusted relationship.

unjust enrichment   An action alleging that the defendant has received money which, in equity, belongs to the plaintiff under circumstances which have permitted the defendant to acquire some benefit for which nothing has been paid.

vendor   A seller of goods or property

void   Of no legal effect and unenforceable against either party.

voidable   An agreement or contract which one party may seek not to carry out if he or she wishes.

voir dire   A hearing of a witness by a judge in which the witness is required to "speak the truth" so the judge may determine if the witness is of sound mind and has evidence that may be heard by the jury.

volenti non fit injuria   Whoever consents to the risk cannot complain of the injury. A rule of law that in negligence cases it is a defence to show that the injured person knew of the hazard and voluntarily accepted it.

will   A document made by a person stating how personal property is to be disposed of after that person's death.

Index

4 5 011802 88 87 86